FOURTH EDITION MENTAL RETARDATION

A LIFE CYCLE APPROACH

CLIFFORD J. DREW, Ph.D.
Professor, Department of Special Education
Professor, Department of Educational Psychology
University of Utah, Salt Lake City, Utah

DONALD R. LOGAN, D.Ed.
Professor, Department of Special Education
University of Utah, Salt Lake City, Utah

MICHAEL L. HARDMAN, Ph.D.
Associate Professor and Chair
Department of Special Education
University of Utah, Salt Lake City, Utah

Merrill Publishing Company
A Bell & Howell Information Company
Columbus   Toronto   London   Melbourne

To
Herbert J. Prehm
From three of us who are his professional progeny.
Yes Herb, once there was a Camelot.

Photo credits (all photographs are copyrighted by individuals or companies listed): 2, 148, 202, Merrill Publishing/Kevin Fitzsimons; 52, 291, Merrill Publishing/Tom Hutchinson; 74, 278, 334, 343, Merrill Publishing/Lloyd Lemmerman; 100, John Telford; 174, 240, 454, Merrill Publishing/Bruce Johnson; 253, Marjorie McEachron; 282, 284, 320, 330, Merrill Publishing/Andy Brunk; 288, 294, Randall Williams; 298, Merrill Publishing/Celia Drake; 301, Cuyahoga County Board of Mental Retardation; 326, Franklin County Board of M.R.D.D./Michael Davis; 356, Merrill Publishing/ Egan; 378, Edgar Bernstein; 414, Merrill Publishing/Jo Hall.

Cover Art: Aaron Rogers, Junior Level, Southeast School.

Published by Merrill Publishing Company
A Bell & Howell Information Company
Columbus, Ohio 43216

This book was set in Trump Medieval and Helvetica.

Administrative Editor: Vicki Knight
Production Coordinator: Sally Serafim
Art Coordinator: Jim Hubbard
Cover Designer: Cathy Watterson

Library of Congress Catalog Card Number: 87–72033
International Standard Book Number: 0–675–20831–9
Printed in the United States of America
1 2 3 4 5 6 7 8 9–92 91 90 89 88

PREFACE WITHDRAWN

As you begin your reading in *Mental Retardation: A Life Cycle Approach*, we would like to give some perspective regarding what you will encounter. Our intent is to provide an introduction to the field of mental retardation that is both readable and comprehensive. As suggested by the title, the foundation concept of this volume is strongly based in human development. One of our reviewers for this edition termed it "womb to tomb." You will follow the development of mentally retarded individuals from conception through birth, infancy and early childhood, then through the elementary, adolescent, and adult years. You will view these people as they become elderly. Mental retardation is a field in which this complete cycle of human life is important for a full understanding of the problems and issues involved.

Our intent is also to discuss the field of mental retardation from the prospective of many disciplines. A diagnosis of mental retardation and subsequent intervention may come from any of several disciplines and often requires their collaboration. Consequently, it is important to examine such interdisciplinary effort and how it impacts the retarded individual, to see how society and its various agencies respond to, interact with, and assist these people and their families.

This text is designed primarily for students in the social and behavioral sciences (broadly defined) who are at the upper division undergraduate or beginning graduate level. Students in psychology, educational psychology, special education, sociology, education, rehabilitation, and social work will find this volume particularly relevant to their preparation. However, pre-med students and individuals anticipating professional work in nursing, law, and administration will find much that facilitates their careers.

Changes in This Edition

Our purpose for this version is largely the same as it was with the release of the first edition 13 years ago. As authors, we hope that we have refined our skills and come closer to achieving the general dream that was present from the outset. Additionally, the field has changed; new topics emerged as knowledge accumulated and societal emphases fluctuated. We have tried to reflect those changes while also retaining essential foundation information.

Viewing this book purely from the standpoint of volume of material, certain areas are clearly more harmonious with that dream. For example, the text is, and always has been, focused on the full life cycle of human development. Consequently, the gentle chiding of an early reviewer regarding the limited volume of material on older retarded citizens was especially meaningful and has been seriously heeded. This comment, in particular, emphasized the need for development of a knowledge base in the area at the time, a need to which the field is responding. Other matters, in addition to retarded adults and the elderly, have also received increased attention.

The changes in this edition were made based on suggestions from many sources and our own observations of growth within the field. For example, the transition concept has now blossomed; where readers of the third edition found this topic beginning to emerge, those using this volume will encounter substantially more attention. Important new material has also been added on the subjects of assessment, early causation, infancy and early childhood, adolescence, aging, the family, social and ethical issues, and legislation.

In addition to the basic information presented in the text, we have added a number of pedagogical features to actively engage the reader, facilitate a more complete understanding of the material, and provide instructors with a wider variety of teaching options. Each chapter begins with essential core concepts to be found in the text. Each core concept is replicated within the narrative at the point where it is discussed and, finally, is related to core questions at the end of each chapter designed to promote student comprehension. At the end of each chapter there is a "round table discussion" section which presents an issue or topic of interest in a challenging format aimed at stimulating dialogue. All of these features have been incorporated to encourage active participation and interaction with the material, a posture sought by most instructors and students and widely accepted as facilitating learning.

Supplements

We have expanded the instructor's manual. Summaries, suggested instructional activities, and a large pool of test items are provided for each chapter. With the help of Dr. William Callahan, University of Nebraska at Omaha, we have also incorporated a greater variety of instructional options to meet differing teaching styles. Most instructors will find questions and material that are suited to their teaching approach. Certainly no instructor's manual can provide everything that will totally meet the needs and wishes of all faculty. However, this manual will provide considerable assistance in course planning and implementation and also a significant head start on the development of examination preparation, which should be a great deal of help for all of those with frantically busy schedules.

Acknowledgments

A complete inventory of those who have helped us in preparation of this volume would require more space than our publishers have allowed, and even then there is the risk of omitting someone. As before we owe a great debt of gratitude to our students who have provided continual feedback. We are also appreciative to our colleagues around the country who have taken time to write or call and give us suggestions. To those of you that gave so generously of your time reviewing earlier versions of this manuscript, we thank you. In particular we appreciate the assistance of Teresa Mehring, Emporia State Teachers College; Peter Matthews, Lock Haven University; Vern H. McGriff, Jersey City State College; and Martin Zlotowski, West Chester University. Their meticulous review of the manuscript and cogent comments helped greatly.

Finally, for the extra help in reading the manuscript when we couldn't find time, for accepting our frequent claims of fatigue, for providing encouragement, support, and generally putting up with us, we once again thank our families. The type of suffering they put up with may probably be found somewhere in our chapter on ethical concerns.

Clifford J. Drew
Donald R. Logan
Michael L. Hardman

CONTENTS

ONE

INTRODUCTION

1

Concepts, Definitions, and Classifications

1. The concept of mental retardation is made more complex because of the varying disciplines involved, which represent widely divergent viewpoints.

2. Definitions of mental retardation have changed over the years as behavioral science has grown, become more complex, and included attention to broader aspects of the environment.

3. It is important to distinguish between incidence and prevalence when determining how frequently mental retardation occurs as well as when considering other factors such as SES, severity, and age.

4. Definitions and classifications of mental retardation have varied greatly over the years with respect to those factors receiving attention and the ages of primary concern.

5. Parameters or bases of classification for mental retardation have differed a great deal over time.

6. Parameters of classification are fluid and, in some cases, implicit rather than explicit and thoughtfully conceived.

7. The purposes and uses of definition and classification schemes must be considered and related to the assessment procedures employed as well as the impact of labels used.

8. Viewing mental retardation across different countries suggests that there are various similarities and distinctions in both definitions and classifications.

We are all aware that people vary a great deal with regard to many factors. For the most part, however, there is a range of variability that is considered to be "normal." Behaviors and other characteristics of this sort are not so extreme that they attract great attention. In other cases the differences are sufficiently extreme that they do attract attention. These abilities, behaviors, or characteristics exceed what we typically view as normal variability. Individuals with such physical, mental, and behavior differences have been of interest since the beginning of human existence. Many perspectives have been prominent throughout history, including those of religion, psychology, education, and various branches of medicine. Perceptions of abnormality have varied greatly over time and among disciplines (Mahendra, 1985). Definitions and concepts of abnormality still differ and will likely continue to change as our knowledge base expands and societal values shift. The history of mental retardation has followed the variable path of other disorders, as will be seen throughout this volume.

The concepts and definitions of mental retardation require attention at the very outset of this discussion. What is mental retardation? Such a question would seem rather simple to answer, yet it has plagued educators, psychologists, and other professionals for many years. Like questions in many areas of behavioral science, it is deceiving in its simplicity, but an answer that is at all complete is exceedingly complex. In reviewing the literature related to mental retardation, one finds that the response to this question has received a great deal of attention, particularly during the past 35 years. The current chapter examines mental retardation from the standpoint of concepts, definitions, and classification systems used historically and currently employed. Review of this material and that found in the following chapters will provide the reader with an overview of mental retardation. It will become evident that the phenomenon is multifaceted. Mental retardation presents a challenge to education, medicine, psychology, law, and society in general, and always to the family involved. What we have attempted in this volume is to place mental retardation in its broadest perspective, squarely in the center of human existence, because above all, mental retardation is a human problem. If one wishes to obtain an accurate and comprehensive perspective, it cannot be viewed from a narrow focus.

MENTAL RETARDATION AS A CONCEPT

Core Concept 1   The concept of mental retardation is made more complex because of the varying disciplines involved, which represent widely divergent viewpoints.

Mental retardation literature suggests strongly that the conceptual issues involved are complex and still unclear (Barnett, 1986). Professionals often begin to define mental retardation by discussing what it is not and describing causes. Refinement of the concept of mental retardation has become increasingly complex as many factors that were previously unknown are taken into account.

The study of or interest in mental retardation began earlier than the study of other areas that are considered handicapping conditions. Hippocrates and Confucius provided descriptions of mental retardation that date several hundred years B.C. Some believe that mental retardation was implicitly involved in legal codes perhaps as early as 2500 B.C. (Scheerenberger, 1983). With such a lengthy record of attention, it is of some interest why confusion and vagueness about its classification and definition remain.

Many factors contribute to this lack of precision and definition. It is commonly accepted that mental retardation is related to a reduced level of intelligence. The concept of intelligence, perhaps more than any other factor, has played a central role in the definition of mental retardation. All of the controversy concerning the nature of intelligence has a direct impact on the field of mental retardation. Consequently, part of the difficulty in defining mental retardation relates to the notion of permanence and measurement of intelligence.

The great interest and activity of many disciplines vis-à-vis mental retardation have also contributed significantly to the problems of definitional and conceptual clarity. There has never been a legitimate "science" of mental retardation, in isolation from other disciplines. The problem of mental retardation has been addressed by psychiatrists, sociologists, psychologists, educators, anthropologists, and many others, each with a somewhat separate perspective and language. The many different definitions and classification systems of these disciplines often tend to focus on the constructs of a particular profession rather than on the individual who is retarded. Thus sociologists set out to study retardation as a social problem, psychologists examine it as a psychological problem, physicians treat it as a medical problem, and so on. Even within professional areas such as clinical, developmental, and experimental psychology (see, e.g., Kopp & Krakow, 1983), wide variations are evident. The current authors do not intend to negate the value of a multidisciplinary attack on any problem; in fact, we strongly subscribe to such an approach. We wish, however, to highlight the fact that the central conceptual focus, the retarded individual, is in danger of being ignored. We intend to present mental retardation from a multidisciplinary perspective while maintaining a focus on the concept of the retarded individual.

As noted above, mental retardation has often been conceptualized from a multitude of viewpoints, depending on the purpose and discipline involved (e.g., social, administrative, medical, educational, and legal viewpoints). This is to be expected to some degree; however, the absence of a single core conceptualization that is logically and theoretically sound but still functional has seriously detracted from the preparation of professionals who work with those who are retarded. Although a high degree of sophistication has been developed in certain technical aspects of programming for children (e.g., diagnosis, behavioral control), the lack of an effective, generic concept of mental retardation has impeded the overall progress of service delivery to these people. Professional expertise is often limited by a deficiency with respect to a perspective of mentally retarded individuals in their total environment, despite a great deal of technical skill in certain areas. Consequently, efforts are now being exerted toward formulating conceptual frameworks that will facilitate more effective professional preparation. Individuals with mental retardation must be viewed as developing human beings with varying needs and characteristics who live within a contemporary society that has fluid and complex performance standards.

In our viewpoint, one conceptual cornerstone serves this exacting task, across disciplines, causes, and the full range of human life—*human development*. This conceptual cornerstone is also the source of the title of this book—A Life Cycle Approach. As you read this volume you will find that its overall structure is the life cycle, from conception through the years of life. Certain topics tend to stand somewhat alone; in most cases where those warrant a chapter, you will find a "mini-discussion" of the topic in the context of development. The perspective of human development has proved useful to each of us, and we hope that you will also find it useful as you examine the complex and fascinating study of mental retardation.

DEFINITION OF MENTAL RETARDATION

Core Concept 2   Definitions of mental retardation have changed over the years as behavioral science has grown, become more complex, and included attention to broader aspects of the environment.

Mental retardation definitions have varied considerably over the years and between disciplines. There is currently considerable agreement among the general definitions being used. The American Association on Mental Deficiency (AAMD) definition has basically been adopted by the American Psychiatric Association; it is also essentially intact in the Federal Rules and Regulations for Public Law 94-142. The AAMD definition of mental retardation involves two main dimensions—adaptive behavior and measured intelligence. According to the most recent definition of the AAMD, mental retardation is "significantly subaverage general intellectual functioning existing concurrently with deficits in adaptive behavior and manifested during the developmental period" (Grossman, 1983, p. 1). The following statements illustrate the similarities in current definitions:

> "Mentally retarded" means having significantly subaverage general intellectual functioning existing concurrently with deficits in adaptive behavior and manifested during the developmental period. (Proposed Regulations, 1982, pp. 33, 485)

> The essential features are: (1) significantly subaverage general intellectual functioning, (2) resulting in, or associated with, deficits or impairments in adaptive behavior, (3) with onset before the age of 18. (American Psychiatric Association, 1980, p. 36)

The AAMD has attempted to enhance the clarity of concepts in its definition. Important terms have been specifically defined in the published manual. For convenience, the complete articulation of these term definitions has been excerpted and is presented in the appendix to this chapter. Over the years, some professionals have viewed the inclusion of adaptive behavior in AAMD definitions as placing clarity in jeopardy (e.g., Clausen, 1972; Penrose, 1972). Despite the longevity of the idea in relation to mental retardation, *measurement* of adaptive behavior has not achieved the sophisticated precision that would be desirable, although a great deal of effort has focused on this area (Meyers, Nihira, & Zetlin, 1979). In 1972, Clausen contended that adaptive behavior was representative of an "ill-defined elusive concept, the inclusion of which results in added confusion, rather than increased clarity" (p. 52). (See Symposium No. Seven in which Clausen article appears for a detailed discussion of issues involved in this topic.) Despite such controversy, adaptive behavior has become a very important concept and point of consideration in the mental retardation field (Meyers, Nihira, & Zetlin, 1979). In fact, professionals in other areas of exceptionality (e.g., learning disabilities) have begun to follow suit and consider adaptive behavior in attempting to assess more completely the important factors contributing to differences.

Including adaptive behavior in definitions during the early 1960s represented a rather dramatic broadening of formally stated criteria for viewing mental retardation. Adaptive behavior had been largely ignored in definitions for many years. This particular criterion does, however, raise certain issues relating to the relevant attributes of mental retardation. A person who is retarded may be viewed essentially as one requiring some type of action on the part of the community for the protection or enhancement of the individual, or others, in the community. Two factors usually enter into this perception: (1) the retarded individual's deficits or level of functioning and (2) the threshold of community tolerance. When such action is taken depends on the degree to which the individual deviates from community norms—from those zones of behavior or performance that are deemed acceptable by society.

People who are mentally retarded often come to the attention of someone in the community of individuals surrounding them because their behavior deviates (or is thought likely to deviate) enough from the norm to be noticeable. This is true regardless of the degree of retardation. Identification of the more severely retarded individual may occur at birth or during the very early part of life—usually because some anomaly, either physical or behavioral, is sufficiently obvious to be observable at this stage of development. For those who are less deviant, identification of mental retardation may not occur until much later, as they begin to develop language or enter school. Initial suspicions of deviancy may then be further investigated through formal diagnostic evaluation and clinical observation by professional personnel. More details about diagnosis and evaluation are discussed later in this volume.

INCIDENCE AND PREVALENCE

Core Concept 3   It is important to distinguish between incidence and prevalence when determining how frequently mental retardation occurs as well as considering other factors such as SES, severity, and age.

Two terms have frequently been confused in the field of mental retardation—incidence and prevalence. *Incidence* refers to the number of new cases identified during a given time period (often a one year basis). Such cases would involve a count of all individuals who were newly identified as retarded during that period, whether they are newborns or youngsters so diagnosed in school. *Prevalence* includes all of the cases existing at a given point in time. Prevalence thus involves newly identified cases plus those others that are *still* labeled as retarded from some earlier diagnosis. Figure 1–1 illustrates incidence and prevalence concepts, how they differ and how they are related. Obviously these two counting procedures do not result in the same number. However, the terms have often been used rather loosely, sometimes interchangeably, in the literature. We will examine incidence and prevalence separately in those cases where it is possible, although we must often rely on earlier literature in which the terms were often used carelessly.

How frequently do individuals evidence sufficient deviancy to be considered mentally retarded? A precise answer to this question is difficult to obtain for a variety of reasons. Accurate accounting is neither easy nor economically feasible. The difficulty of obtaining consistent definition and classification schemes over the years has made determining actual frequency even more formidable, particularly from a cross-cultural perspective (Gallagher, 1985). Estimates of the prevalence of mental retardation in the United States generally range from about 1 to 3 percent of the general population, with the 3 percent figure being most consistently cited (Grossman, 1983; Mercer, 1973b; Tarjan, Wright, Eyman, & Keeran, 1973). Similar figures for *both* incidence and prevalence were found in an actual census study over a 14-year period by Rantakallio and von Wendt (1986) in northern Finland. Translating United States estimated percentages into numbers of retarded individuals is interesting although difficult, and most estimates are quite dated. Scheerenberger (1964) estimated that in 1964 there were about 5.4 million mentally retarded people in the United States. He further projected that by 1970 there would be 6.5 million retarded individuals residing in the United States. The President's Task Force on the Mentally Handicapped (1970) estimated that there were 6 million Americans who were mentally retarded. In its seventh annual report to Congress (1985), the United States

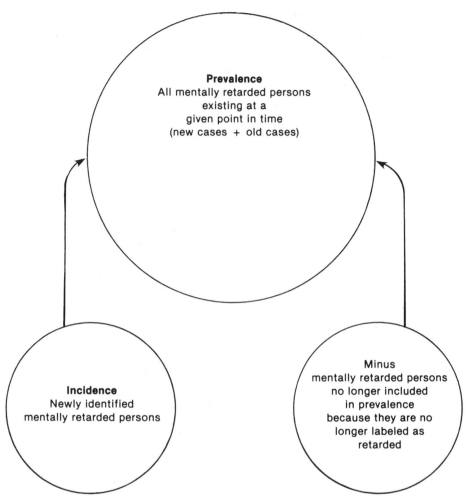

Figure 1–1. Incidence and Prevalence of Mentally Retarded Individuals

Department of Education indicated that over 750,000 mentally retarded youngsters between 3 and 21 years of age were being educated in America's public schools and that over 19,000 of these were between the ages of 3 and 5. Which figures are accurate? We simply do not know with any degree of confidence. Figures such as these defy confirmation because of the astronomical cost of a complete census of such a population.

Those in the mildly retarded range represent by far the largest portion of the retarded population. Grossman (1983) concluded that an estimated 2.5 percent of the total population was mildly retarded. The moderate level of mental retardation, on the other hand, is generally thought to involve about 0.3 percent of the total population, and the severe and profound levels combined to account for approximately 0.1 percent. These figures do not total exactly 3 percent, although they are quite close. With respect to the population of mentally retarded people per se, these figures suggest that somewhat over 86 percent of the group functions at the mild level of retardation, about 10 percent at the moderate level, and between 3 and 4 percent at the severe and profound levels.

Some researchers have questioned the 3 percent figure. A hypothetical community of 100,000 was used by Tarjan et al. (1973) to generate estimates using both 1 and 3 percent levels. These authors found their 1 percent estimate to be quite similar to actual data collected by Mercer (1973a, 1973b) in a California community of 100,000. Interestingly, Mercer's data were collected during the mid-1960s, when the upper IQ limit for being classified as mentally retarded was 85. Tarjan et al. (1973) considered an IQ of 70 as the upper limit. It should be noted that researchers have reported prevalence rates in other geographical settings that are somewhat over 3 percent; others have found less than 1 percent (e.g., Baird & Sandovnick, 1985; Cooper, Wilton, & Glynn, 1985; Lemkau & Imre, 1969). Many factors may contribute to the variations in both prevalence and incidence rates, and although estimates have been *relatively* stable recently, some controversy continues (e.g., Baird & Sandovnick, 1986; Richardson, Koller, & Katz, 1986).

Considerable variation is found in the incidence of mental retardation as one views different chronological age levels. Research has consistently indicated the highest incidence of retardation occurs during the school years, approximately 5 to 18 years, with rather dramatically reduced numbers being identified both at preschool and postschool levels. This distribution relates both to level of retardation and to the tasks that are presented to the individual at different ages. Before a child enters the formal school environment, very little is required that cannot be adequately performed by all but the more severely handicapped. Thus youngsters identified as being retarded before about age 6 are often moderately, severely, or profoundly retarded. As noted earlier, these lower levels of retardation constitute a small percentage of all retarded individuals, particularly in relation to the percentage falling into the mild range of intellectual functioning. As children enter school, they encounter a rather concentrated emphasis on abstract learning, such as the acquisition of academic skills, which places retarded children in a visible position, since abstract skills are their area of greatest difficulty. The majority of retarded youngsters identified at this stage are in the mild range of intellectual deficit. Subsequent to the years of formal schooling, the identification of mental retardation decreases dramatically. A majority of mentally retarded individuals have been identified by the time formal school years end. Further, if an individual has not been identified during the school years, when tasks emphasize abstraction, it is unlikely that he or she will be identified in a postschool environment, where such a focus is reduced.

The prevalence of mental retardation also varies a great deal as a function of age. Table 1–1 presents data based on the overall 1 percent estimates by Tarjan et al. (1973). Although representing estimates, these data are congruent with prevalence data collected by Mercer (1973a, 1973b). Inspection of Table 1–1 reveals that estimated prevalence differs considerably as a function of both age and IQ. The total figures across all IQs reveal that by far the highest prevalence occurs in the age range of 6 to 19 years (68 percent of the retarded population). The pattern of prevalence is similar for those who are retarded with IQs of 50 and above, except that there is an even higher percentage falling within the age range of 6 to 19 years (80 percent), with smaller percentages in the preschool and postschool age ranges. There are several factors that contribute to this pattern, some of which were mentioned previously in the discussion of incidence. As we noted there, the years of formal schooling are particularly taxing for those with mental retardation. The tasks require conceptual performance in areas in which they are most deficient. The drop in prevalence after school-age years is interesting and occurs for reasons that are related but somewhat different from incidence influences. On termination of the tasks of formal education, many retarded individuals (particularly in the 50 + IQ range) are placed back into an environment where the requirements are less focused on their area of greatest difficulty. They seem more able to adapt in the postschool environment than in that presented by formal education. In addition to a lower incidence during postschool years, prevalence is reduced because some individuals may no longer be functioning as retarded and are thus "declassified." This phenomenon has often been referred to as "disappearing" or "six-hour" retardation (referring to the time spent in school). Some have long suggested that this may indicate that the school curriculum is out of phase with later life and thus may not represent effective education (Drew, 1971;

Table 1–1. Estimated Prevalence of Mental Retardation in a Community of 100,000 as a Function of IQ and Age (Overall Prevalence of 1 Percent)

IQ	Age (years)				
	0 to 5	6 to 19	20 to 24	25 +	Total
0–19	8	18	4	20	50
20–49	36	70	20	74	200
50 +	25	600	25	100	750
TOTAL	69	688	49	194	1000

Adapted from Tarjan, G., Wright, S.W., Eyman, R.K., and Keeran, C.V. *The American Journal of Mental Deficiency*, Vol. 77, p. 370, 1973. Copyright, 1973, the American Association on Mental Deficiency. Reprinted by permission.

Spicker & Bartel, 1968). This notion is explored more fully in later chapters relating to education of retarded youngsters.

Prevalence patterns also differ as a function of age for the lower IQ ranges in Table 1–1, with a much lower rate occurring during the ages of 6 to 19. This pattern is influenced by a higher incidence during the early years of life and a higher mortality among more severely retarded individuals when they are young. As one views the data in Table 1–1, it should also be kept in mind that the age-range categories do not include the same intervals. This affects the percentage figures noted, but the general pattern of prevalence remains reflected in these data.

Finally, mental retardation prevalence also varies across different levels of socioeconomic status (SES). Various estimates have suggested considerable prevalence differences as a function of SES and degree of impairment. Table 1–2 summarizes approximate prevalence rates of retardation per 1,000 school-age children by educational classification and community SES level. As indicated in Table 1–2, there is no evident difference in prevalence as a function of SES level in the dependent and trainable levels of impairment. The educable and slow-learner levels, however, indicate an increasing prevalence as SES decreases. These figures suggest that in the lower levels of retardation, where greater central nervous system damage pervades, different SES levels are somewhat equally vulnerable. The milder impairments, however, seem more sensitive to environment influences with respect to prevalence. The fact that the majority of retarded individuals are mildly impaired highlights the social dimensions of mental retardation.

Table 1–2. Retardation Prevalence per 1,000 School-Age Children by Education Classification and Community SES Level*

	Socioeconomic status		
Degree of impairment	**High**	**Middle**	**Low**
Totally dependent (IQ below 20)	1	1	1
Trainable (IQ 20 to 50)	4	4	4
Educable (IQ 50 to 75 or 80)	10	25	50
Slow learner (IQ 75 or 80 to 90)	50	170	300

*IQ ranges are given for the convenience of the reader. They represent approximate ranges that vary to some degree depending on the source of data.

DEFINITION AND CLASSIFICATION BACKGROUND

Core Concept 4   Definitions and classifications of mental retardation have varied greatly over the years with respect to those factors receiving attention and the ages of primary concern.

Both definitions and classification systems concerning mental retardation have changed considerably over the years. Definitions of mental retardation have been problematic from at least two general standpoints. First, an historical examination of definitions reveals that early views focused on adults to the relative exclusion of other age groups. The second area of difficulty involves which factors to include in a definition of mental retardation. This latter problem has provided a very visible arena of professional disagreement and also relates to classification. When we classify any phenomenon, we must have some basis or bases for placing one individual in a certain category and another in a different category. These bases for identifying or grouping individuals have been termed *parameters* of definition and classification (Hardman, Drew, & Egan, 1984). Different parameters (bases) for viewing a person's behavior as being retarded have been employed over the years and have emerged in both definition and classification schemes.

Definitions

At least two factors have been prominent historically in definitions of mental retardation. These are (1) the ages involved and (2) the definitional parameters to include.

For What Ages. Early definitions of mental retardation varied to some degree with respect to age focus. Tredgold (1937) defined the mentally retarded adult in the following manner: "A state of incomplete mental development of such a kind and degree that the individual is incapable of adapting himself to the normal environment of his fellows in such a way as to maintain existence independently of supervision, control or external support" (p. 4). Nearly twenty years later, Benda (1954) gave the following definition of the mentally retarded adult: "A mentally defective person is a person who is incapable of managing himself and his affairs, or being taught to do so, and who requires supervision, control, and care for his own welfare and the welfare of the community" (p. 1115).

Neither approach provided adequate latitude for the full range of attentions that were surfacing in mental retardation. The emphasis on adult behavior was particularly troublesome for professionals, who were primarily inclined to work with children. Doll's (1941) perspective, in obvious contrast, highlighted the appearance of the handicap as a developmental phenomenon. Although other controversies revolved around Doll's work, it was an important forerunner for what was to follow with respect to the chronological age dimension. As noted, Doll addressed the issue of mental retardation in childhood. However, he also provided broad latitude by including in his definition the retarded adult in addition to the youth. Doll (1941) was specific in stating that retardation represented mental subnormality "which has been developmentally arrested" that "obtains at maturity." This full range of chronological ages is essential in order to address the necessary breadth of the retardation problem, a factor that is becoming increasingly important today.

In 1957 a project was begun under commission from the AAMD. The purpose of this activity (part of a larger project on technical planning in mental retardation) was to develop a manual of definition and classification terminology concerned with retardation. The resulting product was adopted as a formal definition statement by the AAMD (Heber, 1961). This definition has undergone refinement over the years (Grossman, 1973, 1977, 1983), and its most current form was presented previously (p. 7). The AAMD statement (1961 and more current revisions) represented several significant changes in the areas of definition and classification of mental retardation. It addresses the problem of latitude in chronological age very specifically. It approaches mental retardation from a developmental framework but also attends to the adult who is retarded within the concept of adaptive behavior. Although similar to Doll's definition in ranging from infancy to adult, the terminology is substantially different to avoid other definitional problems, such as incurability.

What to Include. As mentioned above, a second problem area has been the inclusion or exclusion of particular definitional parameters. A number of these factors have changed over the years (either appearing or disappearing). Current literature still reflects strong differences of opinion regarding what should be included in the definition of mental retardation (e.g, Barnett, 1986; Hodapp & Zigler, 1986; Zigler, Balla, & Hodapp, 1984).

Social Adaptation. Many definitional efforts in mental retardation have, in one fashion or another, involved concepts of social adaptation or adjustment through the years. These have reflected considerable professional consensus that important factors beyond measured intelligence are involved in mental retardation. It is of some interest that, despite this apparent conceptual agreement, a thrust toward formal functional measurement of social adaptation has been evident only in about the last 25 years. Although sporadic attempts were made to assess other behavioral dimensions, measured intelligence previously served as the primary criterion of mental retardation.

Even after its inclusion in formal definitions, adaptive behavior emerged rather slowly as an actual measured criterion for diagnosis. It should also be noted that, in some quarters, measured intelligence is still employed as the preeminent, if not the sole, criterion in practice. Questions regarding the relative roles of intelligence and social adaptation are of continuing interest (Barnett, 1986; Hodapp & Zigler, 1986, Zigler, Balla, & Hodapp, 1984).

Constitutional Origin. A number of definitional problems were caused by two factors that appeared periodically and repeatedly during the historical evolvement of mental retardation definitions. These are best exemplified by Doll's (1941) definition, which specifically stated that mental subnormality "is of constitutional origin" and "is essentially incurable." These two criteria generated considerable debate and became problematic on various fronts. Although not clearly defined, Doll's discussion of constitutional origin centered around the idea of biological pathology as the cause of mental deficiency. He specified that this may involve inherited biological problems or developmental alterations that biologically generate mental retardation.

A constitutional origin requirement posed particular difficulties with respect to that segment of the retarded population that does not present identifiable etiology. Primarily with the group that is termed "cultural-familial," adherence to a constitutional origin criterion required one of two decisions. Either this group, for which constitutional origin could not be identified, should not be considered retarded, or one must operate on the basis of an assumed but unidentifiable constitutional origin. Both of these alternatives present problems. The former tends to ignore the greatest portion of the population that functions at a retarded level. If taken literally, this approach could deter delivery of much needed services to these persons. The latter alternative sets a basic premise of the definition on extremely weak and vulnerable grounds. More recent thinking has virtually achieved consensus that the constitutional origin criterion is too restrictive and cannot serve well in a functional conceptualization of mental retardation.

Incurability. Incurability, as a definitional requirement for mental retardation, has now met a similar fate. However, this concept enjoyed considerable endorsement in past years with resultant problems. One of the difficulties to which incurability contributed was a pessimistic attitude toward expenditure of effort and resources for work with the retarded population. Although a more optimistic attitude is becoming increasingly prevalent, some would still relegate the allocation of resources for the mentally retarded population to the lowest priority level.

Incurability also presented logical difficulties in situations in which an individual was diagnosed as mentally retarded at point A, but later, at point B, evaluation did not reveal retardation. This situation may exist because of a number of specific factors but generally involves two broad possibilities. Obviously an error could have been committed such that either of the measurements indicated a false diagnosis. Second, it is possible that indeed the individual was mentally retarded at point A but that, because of factors intervening between the measurements (e.g., specific instruction or maturational change), retardation no longer exists at point B.

Regardless of the cause, individuals did seem to surface as mentally retarded at one point but not another. If the second general possibility were true, strict adherence to the concept of incurability would not be possible. By definition, such a situation could not occur. Consequently a complementary concept of pseudo-retardation evolved (sometimes termed *pseudo-feeblemindedness* in early literature). The term *pseudo-retardation* is an example of the need to explain or strengthen weak logic by the development of compensatory concepts. Often, as with the case of pseudo-retardation, these compensatory concepts were equally weak and lacking in sound logic. Benton (1956) discussed the concept of pseudo-feeblemindedness from two frameworks, errors in diagnosis and the difference between an existing condition and some "true" mental retardation. He stated emphatically that the situation of diagnostic error ought not "be given the status of a clinical entity," which is the case if pseudo-feeblemindedness is used in this way. When Benton stated that pseudo-feeblemindedness is not a relevant concept for use in cases of error in diagnosis, he essentially denied the first general explanation made necessary by incurability. An error in measurement is just that—an error in measurement. It is much sounder logic to recognize it as such, rather than to search for a clinical entity as an excuse.

Benton described pseudo- feeblemindedness from a second framework as "a condition of behavioral retardation or deficiency which is ascribable to factors other than those customarily held to be the essential antecedent conditions of 'true' mental defect." This framework somewhat combines the concepts of constitutional origin and incurability. The idea that there exists "true" mental retardation (and thus "false" or pseudo-retardation) was cumbersome, to say the least. First, it implied that there were agreed-upon causes that were identifiable. Such an implication relates to the criterion of constitutional origin, which has previously been discussed with respect to its weakness. Second, the situation of retardation at point A but not at a later point B defies the incurability concept in that the individual must not have been retarded at the first measurement or retardation would have also been present at the second.

The complexity of these interrelated concepts was magnified by a controversy that was occurring simultaneously in the field of measured intelligence. The question was a long-standing one and involved whether intelligence tests assess functioning or potential capacity. More recently, the consensus among professionals favors functioning, although the issue is not completely dead. Interpretation of intelligence scores as measures of functioning dramatically clarifies the issues involved with incurability, pseudo-retardation, and, more generally, the definition of mental retardation.

If intelligence is viewed as behavioral functioning, it is quite reasonable to expect situations in which an individual functions as mentally retarded at one time and not at another. Intervening experiences may have altered the level of functioning on the second measure to such a degree that the person does not exhibit a behavioral deficit. Such a viewpoint denies the incurability criterion and certainly makes the concept of pseudo-retardation unnecessary and nonfunctional.

It was noted previously that the AAMD definitions (Grossman, 1973, 1977, 1983) represented several substantial departures from the general trend of early definitional efforts. One of these important changes was the formalization of a position concerning the framework from which intelligence measures are viewed. The AAMD definition specifically rejects the principle of potential intelligence and views mental status as representative of behavioral functioning level at the time of assessment. These conceptual changes in definitional position should not be interpreted as suggesting that professionals now uniformly view all mental retardation as curable. Such a position would be totally unrealistic. It is the case, however, that the requirement of incurability has been largely discarded from definitions because as a framework from which to view the broad problem of mental retardation it is nonfunctional. Two major advances have been evident in the evolution of definition and philosophy. Mental retardation is on much firmer conceptual ground than it was previously. Additionally, changes in the AAMD definition legitimatize the conceptual framework by bringing it more in harmony with the realities of mental retardation as viewed by the community.

Comments. Despite the advances just discussed, definitions of mental retardation still face some philosophical problems that affect decisions regarding services. Perhaps the most serious problem is simple and obvious. It does not seem efficacious to spend time and effort defining mental retardation without asking, "What is the purpose or objective of this definition?" The purpose or objective of definition, of course, has not been completely ignored. Obviously, each of the early workers who presented definitional statements was progressing in a given interest area, probably with objectives clearly in mind. Their purposes were, however, most likely in line with the particular segment of effort involved and were not necessarily attentive to the broader problems of mental retardation. It is our contention that the confusion evident in the historical evolvement of an encompassing definition of mental retardation is characteristic of an effort proceeding without overall purpose or direction. Absence of an overall purpose is perhaps most obvious in the area of educational programming. A definition should be useful, or there is little reason to have it. Yet we often find the definition of mental retardation being of questionable use for educational programming, a facet of services that touches a major proportion of the retarded population. This issue surfaces again as we consider classification schemes, and it is discussed more fully in chapters 8 and 9.

Classification

Core Concept 5   Parameters or bases of classification for mental retardation have differed a great deal over time.

The historical evolution of classification schemes for mental retardation has evidenced confusion in concept and direction nearly parallel to that apparent in definition efforts. Perhaps the most serious difficulty with all classification schemes relates to the choice of parameters for classification. This problem has been particularly troublesome in the mental retardation field, again partially because of the wide variety of disciplines interested in the phenomenon. Other difficulties related to the range of disciplines involved have been generated by the purpose or objective underlying the classification process. For example, a given difference in purpose held by school administrators and physicians does not necessarily mean that the classification schemes are mutually exclusive or in conflict. However, compatibility or joint focus has seldom been evident.

Problems also arise when the parameters of classification are unclear or incompletely described in a given classification system. It has not been unusual for categorization to emphasize one parameter and simultaneously employ one or two others that seem to be added in a rather informal and imprecise fashion. The difficulty does not emerge from using multiple parameters for classification—mental retardation is a multifaceted problem. However, in using a given scheme it is important to be explicit and precise regarding the parameters that are employed and to determine which are primary, secondary, and of decreasing importance (if that is the case). As Hardman et al. (1984) noted:

> A given classification . . . represents a single photograph of a condition. What is recorded only represents a given behavior at a particular time and in a particular set of circumstances. Parameters of classification provide us with a powerful tool for analyzing various category systems. Some parameters are present in one or two systems, whereas others are used to a certain degree in several. The parameters are important because they allow us to view exceptionality *across* differing classification perspectives. (p. 72, emphasis added)

| **Core Concept 6** | Parameters of classification are fluid and, in some cases, implicit rather than explicit and thoughtfully conceived. |

Parameters for Classification. The literature reveals that a wide variety of parameters has been used in different classification schemes, both historically and currently. Parameters represent the *basis or bases* for classifying a condition or behavior. Although used with varying frequency, six general parameters seem evident: (1) symptom severity, (2) symptom etiology, (3) syndrome description, (4) adaptive behavior, (5) educability expectations, and (6) behavioral manifestations. These parameters are not necessarily mutually exclusive—they often intersect in some fashion. For example, symptom severity is frequently associated with intelligence in the area of mental retardation. However, adaptive behavior and behavioral manifestations may also be viewed in terms of the severity of functional deficits. Parameters may also intersect as one is diagnosed as being mentally retarded. The AAMD requires such an intersection between symptom severity (in terms of measured intelligence) and adaptive behavior. (AAMD also employs a symptom etiology parameter that will be discussed in a following section.) Figure 1–2 presents parameters of classification and illustrates how they may converge in a particular case of mental retardation. This conceptualization represents a flexible model wherein different parameters may be used in varying types of parameter intersections illustrated, depending on the case and the system employed.

Symptom Severity. The most common criterion used in relation to the symptom severity parameter has been measured intelligence. Classification on this basis, of course, necessitates grouping individuals by IQ in some fashion and identifying these groups with a designative term or label. For example, several early classifications used terms like borderline retardate, moron, imbecile, and idiot. Terman (1916) used these labels with IQ unit groups of 70 to 79 for borderline, 50 to 69 for moron, 25 to 49 for imbecile, and 25 or below for idiot. Wechsler (1958) used the same terminology but with slightly different IQ units of 30 to 49 for imbecile and 29 or below for idiot. Use of the terms moron, imbecile, and idiot has been discontinued in the United States because of negative connotations. However, these terms are still found in some literature from other countries. Grouping by measured IQ remains in heavy use, as exemplified by the AAMD classification. Using the terminology of mild, moderate, severe, and profound retardation, the AAMD IQ units are based on standard deviation of the test used (a statistical concept relating to variability). For example, on the revised Stanford-Binet test these ranges are IQ 52 to 67, 36 to 51, 20 to 35, and below 20 for the respective categories noted before. Table 1–3 summarizes

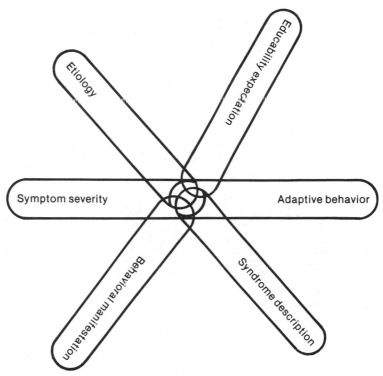

Figure 1–2. Parameters of Classification

From Hardman, M.L., Drew, C.J., and Egan, M.W. *Human exceptionality: Society, school, and family.* Boston: Allyn & Bacon, Inc., 1984. Copyright 1984 by Allyn & Bacon, Inc. Reprinted, by permission.

selected symptom severity classifications based on measured IQ for comparison purposes.

Symptom Etiology. Etiology of the symptoms represents a second general parameter for classification. Etiology has primarily involved the biomedical aspects of mental retardation. As such, this parameter is most often viewed in a medical context and has often been called the medical classification. Three major systems have been instrumental in the current view of etiological classification in mental retardation. The World Health Organization published its *International Classification on Diseases* (ICD-9, 1978); the American Psychiatric Association developed the *Diagnostic and Statistical Manual* (DSM-III, 1980); and the AAMD refined its manual, *Classification in Mental Retardation* (Grossman, 1983). Although not identical, these systems are compatible with respect to etiology classification. AAMD included the following 10 categories in its etiological classification:

1. Following infection and intoxication (e.g., congenital rubella, syphilis)
2. Following trauma or physical agent (e.g., mechanical injury at birth)

Table 1–3. Selected Symptom Severity Classifications

Measured intelligence*

Source	Classifications (high to low IQ)
Terman (1916)	Borderline—IQ 70 to 79; Moron—IQ 50 to 69; Imbecile—IQ 25 to 49; Idiot—IQ 24 or below
Wechsler (1958)	Borderline—IQ 70 to 79; Moron—IQ 50 to 69; Imbecile—IQ 30 to 49; Idiot—IQ 29 or below
American Association on Mental Deficiency (1961)	Borderline intelligence— −1 S.D., IQ 68 to 83; Mildly mentally retarded— −2 S.D., IQ 52 to 67; Moderately mentally retarded— −3 S.D., IQ 36 to 51; Severely mentally retarded— −4 S.D., IQ 20 to 35; Profoundly mentally retarded— −5 S.D., IQ 19 or below
American Association on Mental Deficiency (1973, 1977, 1983)†	Mildly mentally retarded— −2 S.D., IQ 52 to 67; Moderately mentally retarded— −3 S.D., IQ 36 to 51; Severely mentally retarded— −4 S.D., IQ 20 to 35; Profoundly mentally retarded— −5 S.D., IQ 19 or below
American Psychiatric Association (1980)	Mildly mentally retarded—IQ 50 to 70; Moderately mentally retarded—IQ 35 to 49; Severely mentally retarded—IQ 20 to 34; Profoundly mentally retarded—IQ below 20

IQ scale reference points: 90 80 70 60 50 40 30 20 10

*IQ ranges from Stanford-Binet standard deviations (S.D.).
†The 1983 AAMD classifications placed a narrow band of IQ scores at each end of each level but are essentially the same as those in the table.

3. With disorders of metabolism or nutrition (e.g., phenylketonuria or PKU, galactosemia)
4. Associated with gross brain disease, postnatal (e.g., neurofibromatosis, intracranial neoplasm)
5. Associated with diseases and conditions resulting from unknown prenatal influence (e.g., hydrocephalus, microcephaly)
6. Associated with chromosomal abnormality (e.g., Down syndrome)
7. Associated with other perinatal (gestational) conditions (e.g., prematurity)
8. Following psychiatric disorder (e.g., autism)
9. Associated with environmental influences (e.g., cultural-familial retardation)
10. Associated with other conditions

Approximately 75 to 85 percent of the total population of retarded persons fall into categories 9 and 10, with the remaining 15 to 25 percent distributed among categories 1 through 8. Categories 9 and 10, on closer scrutiny, are somewhat miscellaneous categories that essentially specify the absence of verifiable structural characteristics. From this it is evident that the other categories often involve retardation associated with observable or at least verifiable existing characteristics. As noted, these eight etiological classifications account for a relatively small portion of all mental retardation (this point emphasizes why earlier definition approaches encountered difficulty).

Syndrome Description. Another approach to classification involves the description of syndromes by symptom grouping. Like etiology, the syndrome description scheme has been used with greater frequency by medical workers than by others. Syndromes are usually identified by observation of a pattern of physical and behavioral characteristics, although physical descriptions have predominated. Of course, in any given case a syndrome may involve such characteristics in varying degrees and patterns.

The syndromes (such as Down syndrome, or mongolism; microcephaly; and hydrocephaly) seem to portray the stereotype of mental retardation often held by people not working in the field. It is not uncommon for the visual image of a Down person to be thought of when mental retardation is mentioned in a lay context. This may be because the defining characteristics for syndromes are often visible, or because the syndrome approach to classification has a rather long history. Syndrome names usually include either the name of the pioneering worker discovering the syndrome or, in many cases, the technical clinical terminology involved in diagnosis (as in neurofibromatosis). Carter's (1978, 1979) volumes on medical aspects of mental retardation and the syndrome atlas by Gellis and Feingold (1968) contain detailed treatment or reference to particular syndromes.

Adaptive Behavior. Adaptive behavior or related concepts have been involved in definition and classification for a major portion of the history of effort in mental retardation. Only in about the past 35 years, however, have conceptualizations progressed to a point that adaptive behavior is viewed by many as a parameter of classification. Even today there are a number of difficulties in using adaptive behavior as a parameter to categorize individuals.

Considerable impetus for the current view of adaptive behavior came from the work of Sloan and Birch (1955). Their material was adapted for the AAMD *Manual on Terminology and Classification* in 1961 (Heber, 1961) and further developed by later revisions of this manual (Grossman, 1973, 1977, 1983). One of the important factors in adaptive behavior as a classification parameter is that it attends to human development. The appendix to this chapter provides the definitional framework for adaptive behavior as articulated by the AAMD manual. Table 1–4 summarizes the illustrations of adaptive behavior levels by ages presented in the manual.

Adaptive behavior presents certain difficulties as a parameter of classification even today. Table 1–4 indicates that adaptive behavior intersects with the parameter of symptom severity (mild, moderate, severe, and profound notations). This intersection led many to assume that deficits in adaptive behavior similar to those of measured intelligence should be similarly classified (i.e., based on standard deviation deficits). Such an assumption was furthered because discussion of both parameters employed the same label terminology and both appeared in the same document (the AAMD manual). Unfortunately, there were at least two problems with this reasoning: (1) adaptive behavior is only imperfectly correlated with intelligence (and evidence regarding the strength of such a correlation is currently inconclusive) and (2) the measurement of adaptive behavior is still under study in terms of reliability, validity, standardization, cultural fairness, and scientifically established links to classification labels (e.g., Coulter & Morrow, 1978; Iowa Task Force on Adaptive Behavior, 1981; Meyers, Nihira, & Zetlin, 1979). The importance of this dimension in mental retardation does not seem to be in question. What has been and remains in question is the establishment of an empirical base for assessment, so that it can become a more functional classification parameter. It is clear that adaptive behavior must relate to various ages, environments, cultural milieus, and previous opportunities to learn. Thus even within this one parameter of classification, we find multiple elements for consideration.

Educability Expectations. Educability expectation was viewed as a parameter of classification by Scheerenberger (1964). Predominant in the field of education for many years, this approach to classification is also known as the educational classification. Preference for including the term expectation is based on the essential characteristic of this approach, which is a

Table 1–4. Example Adaptive Behavior Levels by Age

Age and level indicated	Illustrations of highest level of adaptive behavior
Age 3 years and above: *profound* (NOTE: All behaviors at greater degree of impairment would also indicate *profound* deficit in adaptive behavior for persons 3 years of age or above.)	*Independent functioning*: Drinks from a cup with help; "cooperates" by opening mouth for feeding *Physical*: Sits unsupported or pulls self upright momentarily; reaches for objects; has good thumb-finger grasp; manipulates objects (plays with shoes or feet) *Communication*: Imitates sounds, laughs or smiles back (says "Da-da," "buh-buh" responsively); no effective speech; may communicate in sounds, gestures, or signs *Social*: Indicates knowing familiar persons and interacts nonverbally with them
Age 3 years: *severe* Age 6 years and above: *profound*	*Independent functioning*: Attempts finger feeding; "cooperates" with dressing, bathing, and toilet training; may remove clothing (socks) but not as an act of undressing as for bath or bed. *Physical*: Stands alone or may walk unsteadily or with help; coordinates eye-hand movements *Communication*: One or two words (Mama, ball), but predominantly vocalization *Social*: May respond to others in predictable fashion; communicates needs by gestures and noises or pointing; plays "patty-cake"; plays imitatively with little interaction; occupies self alone with "toys" for a few minutes
Age 3 years: *moderate* Age 6 years: *severe* Age 9 years and above: *profound*	*Independent functioning*: Tries to feed self with a spoon with considerable spilling; removes socks, pants; "cooperates" in bathing, may indicate wet pants; "cooperates" at toilet *Physical*: Walks alone steadily; can pass ball or objects to others; may run and climb steps with help *Communication*: May use four to six words; may communicate many needs with gestures (pointing) *Social*: Plays with others for short periods, often as parallel play or under direction; recognizes others and may show preference for some persons over others
3 years: *mild* 6 years: *moderate* 9 years: *severe* 12 years and above: *profound*	*Independent functioning*: Feeds self with spoon (cereals, soft foods) with considerable spilling or messiness; drinks unassisted; can pull off clothing and put on some (socks, underclothes, boxer pants, dress); tries to help with bath or hand washing but still needs considerable help; indicates toilet accident and may indicate toilet need *Physical*: May climb up and down stairs but not alternating feet; may run and jump; may balance briefly on one foot; can pass a ball to others; transfers objects; may do simple form-board puzzles without aid *Communication*: May speak in two or three word sentences (Daddy go work); names simple common objects (boy, car, ice cream, hat); understands simple directions (put the shoe on your foot, sit here, get your coat); knows people by name, if nonverbal, may use many gestures to convey needs or other information

Adapted from Grossman, H.J. (Ed.) *Manual on terminology and classification in mental retardation.* Washington, D.C.: American Association on Mental Deficiency, 1977. Copyright 1977 by the American Association on Mental Deficiency. Adapted by permission.

Table 1–4. Example Adaptive Behavior Levels by Age—Cont'd.

Age and level indicated	Illustrations of highest level of adaptive behavior
	Social: May interact with others in simple play activities, usually with only one or two others unless guided into group activity; has preference for some persons over others.
6 years: *mild* 9 years: *moderate* 12 years and above: *severe* 15 years and above: *profound*	*Independent functioning*: Feeds self with spoon or fork, may spill some; puts on clothing but needs help with small buttons and jacket zippers; tries to bathe self but needs help; can wash and dry hands but not very efficiently; partially toilet trained but may have accidents *Physical*: May hop or skip; may climb steps with alternating feet; rides tricycle (or bicycle over 8 years); may climb trees or jungle gym; plays dance games, may throw ball and hit target *Communication*: May have speaking vocabulary of over 300 words and use grammatically correct sentences. If nonverbal, may use many gestures to communicate needs. Understands simple verbal communications including directions and questions ("Put it on the shelf." "Where do you live?") (Speech may be indistinct sometimes.); may recognize advertising words and signs (ice cream, stop, exit, men, ladies); relates experiences in simple language *Social*: Participates in group activities and simple group games; interacts with others in simple play ("store," "house") and expressive activities (art and dance)
9 years: *mild* 12 years: *moderate* 15 years and older: *severe*	*Independent functioning*: Feeds self adequately with spoon and fork; can butter bread; needs help with cutting meat; can put on clothes and can button and zipper clothes; may tie shoes; bathes self with supervision; is toilet trained; washes face and hands without help *Physical*: Can run, skip, hop, dance; uses skates, sled, and jump rope; can go up and down stairs alternating feet; can throw ball to hit target *Communication*: May communicate in complex sentences; speech is generally clear and distinct; understands complex verbal communication, including words such as "because" and "but." Recognizes signs, and words, but does not read prose material with comprehension. *Social*: May participate in group activities spontaneously; may engage in simple competitive exercise games (dodge ball, tag, races). May have friendship choices that are maintained over weeks or months *Economic activity*: May be sent on simple errands and make simple purchases with notes; realizes money has value but does not know how to use it (except for coin machines) *Occupation*: May prepare simple foods (sandwiches); can help with simple household tasks (bedmaking, sweeping, vacuuming); can set and clear table *Self direction*: May ask if there is "work" for him to do; may pay attention to task for 10 minutes or more; makes efforts to be dependable and carry out responsibility
12 years: *mild* 15 years and over: *moderate*	*Independent functioning*: Feeds, bathes, dresses self, may select daily clothing; may prepare easy foods (sandwiches) for self or others; combs and brushes hair; may shampoo and curl hair; may wash, iron, and store own clothes *Physical*: Good body control; good gross and fine motor coordination *Communication*: May carry on simple conversation; uses complex sentences. Recognizes words, may read sentences, ads, signs, and simple prose material with some comprehension

Table 1–4. Example Adaptive Behavior Levels by Age—Cont'd.

Age and level indicated	Illustrations of highest level of adaptive behavior
	Social: May interact cooperatively and competitively with others *Economic Activity*: May be sent on shopping errands for several items without notes; makes minor purchases; adds coins to dollar with fair accuracy *Occupation*: May do simple routine household chores (dusting, garbage removal, dishwashing; preparing simple foods that require mixing) *Self direction*: May initiate most of own activities; attends to task 15 to 20 minutes (or more); may be conscientious in assuming much responsibility
15 years and adult: *mild* (NOTE: Individuals who routinely perform at higher levels of competence in adaptive behavior than illustrated in this pattern should NOT be considered as deficient in adaptive behavior. Since by definition an individual is not retarded unless he shows significant deficit in *both* measured intelligence and in adapetive behavior, those individuals who function at higher levels than illustrated here cannot be considered to be retarded.)	*Independent functioning*: Exercises care for personal grooming, feeding, bathing, toilet; may need health or personal care reminders; may need help in selection and purchase of clothing *Physical*: Goes about home town (local neighborhood in city, campus at institution) with ease, but cannot go to other towns alone without aid; can use bicycle, skis, ice skates, trampoline, or other equipment requiring good coordination *Communication*: Communicates complex verbal concepts and understands them; carries on everyday conversation, but cannot discuss abstract or philosophical concepts; uses telephone and communicates in writing for simple letter writing or orders but does not write about abstractions or important current events. *Social*: Interacts cooperatively or competitively with others and initiates some group activities, primarily for social or recreational purposes; may belong to a local recreation group or church group, but not to civic organizations or groups of skilled persons (photography club, great books club, or kennel club); enjoys recreation (bowling, dancing, TV, checkers, but either does not enjoy or is not competent at such activities as tennis, sailing, bridge, piano playing, or other hobbies requiring rapid, involved or complex planning and implementation) *Economic activity*: Can be sent or can go to several shops to make purchases of several items without a note to shopkeepers; can make change correctly, but does not use banking facilities; may earn living but has difficulty handling money without guidance *Occupation*: Can cook simple foods, prepare simple meals; and perform everyday household tasks (cleaning, dusting, dishes, laundry); as adult can engage in semiskilled or simple skilled job *Self direction*: Initiates most of own activity; will pay attention to task for at least 15 to 20 minutes; conscientious about work and assumes much responsibility but needs guidance for tasks with responsibility for major tasks health care, care of others, complicated occupational activity)

statement or prediction of expected achievement. Generally there are three categories—educable, trainable, and custodial or severely multiply handicapped (SMH)—although some professionals have included a fourth classification known as dull normal, which ranges just above the educable in terms of measured IQ (approximately 75 or 80 to 90). Measured IQ ranges associated with the other categories are 50 to 75 or 80 for the educable, 20 to 49 for the trainable, and below 20 for the SMH or custodial. Table 1–5 summarizes classifications by educational expectations.

Weaknesses are evident in most classification schemes. However, the educability expectation approach is particularly vulnerable from a variety of standpoints. To permit adequate treatment of these limitations, they will be scrutinized and specifically addressed in later portions of this chapter.

Behavioral Manifestation. The final classification parameter mentioned before was, for our purposes, termed behavioral manifestations. This approach has enjoyed considerable popularity in a number of areas of psychology as well as in several educational applications. It is derived from applied behavior analysis and evaluates an individual in terms of behavioral observation of task performance. The behavioral description perspective differs conceptually from previously discussed classification schemes. Essentially this framework is not primarily concerned with grouping but focuses on the skills a person has or does not have (more precisely, to what degree a task can be performed). The most prominent focus, then, is on determining the individual skill level rather than placing a person in a category. This difference in approach deemphasizes norm-referenced or interindividual comparisons (a child's performance compared with others) and places assessment more in the context of an intraindividual or criterion-referenced framework (a child's performance compared with no others but him or herself).

Table 1–5. Classification by Educational Expectation

Terminology	Approximate IQ range*	Educational expectation
Dull normal	IQ 75 or 80 to 90	Capable of competing in school in most areas, except in the strictly academic areas, in which performance is below average
		Social adjustment that is not noticeably different from the larger population, although in the lower segment of adequate adjustment
		Occupational performance satisfactory in nontechnical areas, with total self-support highly probable
Educable	IQ 50 to 75 or 80	Second- to fifth-grade achievement in school academic areas
		Social adjustment that will permit some degree of independence in the community
		Occupational sufficiency that will permit partial or total self-support
Trainable	IQ 20 to 49	Learning primarily in the areas of self-help skills, very limited achievement in areas considered academic
		Social adjustment usually limited to home and closely surrounding area
		Occupational performance primarily in sheltered workshop or an institutional setting
Custodial (SMH)	IQ below 20	Usually unable to achieve even sufficient skills to care for basic needs
		Will usually require nearly total care and supervision for duration of lifetime

*IQ ranges represent approximate ranges, which vary to some degree, depending on the source of data.

For professionals who are devoted proponents of behavioral analysis, it is the only evaluation parameter used. Employed in this fashion, the behavioral manifestation parameter does not intersect with other classification parameters. Traditional categories and labels are deemed unimportant relative to a precise description of behavioral status that is used for specific treatment intervention (i.e., instruction or behavior shaping efforts aimed at enhancing skills). Obviously, behavioral descriptions of some type are used in many classification systems. However, in such a context the behavioral description is typically a means by which one can determine a category and is therefore secondary to the basic purpose of classification. As a single parameter, behavioral manifestation is a primary means of evaluation that is aimed at treatment rather than categorical grouping.

The behavioral approach has considerable relevance for educational programming, an area in which other frameworks have been particularly weak. It does not necessarily serve all purposes well, however. There are reasons for grouping and labeling, such as administrative needs or determination and allocation of funds for programs.

PURPOSES AND USES OF DEFINITIONS AND CLASSIFICATIONS

Core Concept 7	The purposes and uses of definition and classification schemes must be considered and related to the assessment procedures employed as well as the impact of labels used.

Definition and classification statements are developed for a wide variety of reasons. At times these schemes provide a conceptual picture of what is being defined or classified. In serving the conceptual function, such postulates often contribute to communication in a professional shorthand fashion. Beyond these roles, however, remains possibly the most vital function of definition and classification systems—the translation of statements into action or operational terms.

The adequacy with which a classification scheme translates into practice is perhaps the acid test of the system itself. A number of factors influence the ease with which this translation can occur. Two factors seem to be particularly evident from our previous discussion of definitions and classification. The first concerns the degree to which a scheme is in harmony with reality; the second relates to how well the purposes or objectives of the group using a definition or classification are served.

If a classification or definition system does not relate to the configuration of actual circumstances, it is of questionable value and will likely fall into disuse. Perhaps the best example of such a situation in mental retardation involves the concepts of constitutional origin and incurability. Constitutional origin is out of phase with reality because it cannot be verified in many individuals who are functioning as retarded. This situation requires that either constitutional origin must be assumed or, if strict adherence to the definition is maintained, services cannot legitimately be rendered. The idea of incurability is similarly out of harmony with reality, as exemplified by the necessity of a compensatory concept of pseudo-feeblemindedness.

One must also consider the second influence, that is, of how well the purposes or objectives of the group using a scheme are served. Purposes and objectives concerned with mental retardation have been nearly as numerous and diverse as the disciplines involved. Heber noted that mental retardation has historically been treated as "a social, administrative, and legal concept, rather than a scientific one" (1969, p. 69). A synthesis of the current literature reveals little reason for disagreement with this statement; furthermore, it highlights the absence of discussions of mental retardation with clearly stated intervention purposes in focus.

Many current and past attempts at defining and classifying mentally retarded individuals have approached this process from a "grouping" standpoint. Grouping, or placing like individuals together on some dimension, serves certain types of purposes well, yet other objectives are met only minimally or not at all by such an approach. For example, a grouping framework may serve administrative convenience quite efficiently. Individuals may be easily counted, funds distributed by type of individual, and justifications of service rendered to legislatures. Similarly, a grouping process serves legal purposes well. If a given individual is placed in a particular category, decisions can be made concerning legal responsibility for action or guardianship can be determined with relative ease. It is important for the reader to be cognizant that this discussion is couched in the perspective of a service professional or agency whose purpose is involved. In both of these examples a certain degree of impersonality is involved in decision making. Administrative personnel, legislators, and legal agencies often work with numbers and names rather than with individuals, even though the numbers and names represent individuals. We are not addressing the question of how well the individual is served by such decisions. From the individual's standpoint, service or justice may be marginal or absent.

We do not intend to detract from or negate the extreme value that has been accrued and the progress that has been made in the field of mental retardation because of classification by grouping. In fact, impetus provided by legislation and administration of funds at local, state, and federal levels has permitted dramatic service improvements over the years. The issue is that one classification framework may be used effectively in one disciplinary segment but not serve well for another segment whose purposes are different.

For the most part, educational classifications of retardation have employed the grouping approach, which has been used effectively in other contexts. Unfortunately, such an approach may not be effective for the purposes of instruction, particularly with problem learners. Evidence rather consistently indicates this, and educators of retarded youngsters recognize the problems of group classification for instructional purposes.

The earlier discussion of educational classification indicated two approaches involved in categorization. The first, termed educability expectation, was illustrated by Kirk's (1962) statements of expectation for educable and trainable retarded individuals. However, symptom severity with respect to IQ was also used with ranges of approximately 75 to 80 or 90 for the dull normal, 50 to 75 or 80 for the educable, 20 to 49 for the trainable, and below 20 for custodial (SMH). The IQ range approach essentially serves a grouping function, whereas the statements of expectation would seem to provide guidelines for prognosis. As noted before, various administrative purposes are served by grouping, such as convenient allocation of fiscal resources. Problems arise, however, when educational programs adopt these purposes rather than purposes, objectives, and resulting classificatory schemes more in harmony with the instructional process itself. This issue has long been mentioned in the literature, and concern has been expressed when review seems to indicate that the curriculum for the retarded population reflects convenience in administrative arrangement as much as consideration of the needs of the student being taught (Drew, 1971; Spicker & Bartel, 1968).

An interesting phenomenon begins to emerge from a review of a number of sources discussing mental retardation. Since the topics of classification and definition are related to diagnosis and evaluation, one rather serious deficit seems evident with respect to both assessment and conceptualization. The conceptual weakness revolves around the relationship among evaluative assessment, classification, and ultimately, programming. We have evaluated; this is the classification; now what? Early approaches (e.g., Benton, 1956, p. 382) to this topic often suggested allowing nature to take its course, that we can "predict a typical course and outcome with a fair degree of confidence." This reflects quite closely the early educability approach taken by Kirk (1962). The diagnostic purposes seem to be served adequately here if the only inclination is a passive response—passive in the respect that no active educational or instructional intervention is implied. Current trends in instructional philosophy and technique would not support a passive predictive approach but instead would dictate active intervention with specific behavioral objectives.

Criterion-Referenced versus Norm-Referenced Measurement

Definitions per se are not always precise, and definitions of mental retardation have had difficulties compounded by the fact that measurement *is* specified. Thus this facet of the AAMD definition, which has been justifiably viewed as an important strength, has also been instrumental in promoting some difficulties. Because of the absence of stated purpose for educational programming, there is an apparent lack of purpose underlying a combination of definition, classification, and assessment techniques. The grouping approach promoted both in the definition and classification schemes and in the measurement technique involving evaluation has long been known as norm-referenced assessment. Norm-referenced evaluation has not historically been of much value for educational programming. Thus, more conceptually sound and pragmatically oriented evaluation approaches have been developed in areas other than mental retardation. Regardless of origin, these concepts need to be explored with regard to the instruction of retarded persons if such educational programming efforts are to become more effective.

Norm-referenced evaluation involves the type of psychological testing with which most people are well acquainted. Probably the best-known assessment of this nature is the intelligence test. Essentially, norm-referenced evaluation provides a measure of an individual's functioning in comparison with some standard or group norm. From this framework, a score provides an indication of whether the person stands above or below another student or some hypothetical average student. This type of evaluation is of value for purposes of grouping; beyond that, it has relevance for certain educational decisions. As suggested by earlier discussions, however, the purposes served by such an evaluation approach have several limitations in the overall arena of instructional programming. It therefore cannot be expected to provide all the information necessary for the actual teaching process. Such a global acceptance of the norm measure in the past has led to a diminished educational effectiveness for those with mental retardation and a great deal of frustration focused on psychometric information in general.

A counterpart evaluation concept has come into focus during the past 15 years to meet a variety of needs not being addressed by norm-referenced assessment. Criterion-referenced evaluation does not place the individual's performance in a relative or comparative context with either other students or a normative standard. Often focusing on more specific skills, criterion-referenced assessment is viewed more as an absolute level of performance. It focuses on the actual level of mastery that an individual exhibits or, from a different perspective, the level at which a student becomes unable to perform a given task. This type of information is useful to a teacher, in that it indicates the level at which to begin instruction. Criterion-referenced evaluation has enjoyed considerable popularity in recent years. Despite the obvious use for certain aspects of instruction, criterion-referenced evaluation in isolation does not provide all of the information needed for a well-reasoned total educational effort. Concerted energy has been focused on the development of more effective total evaluation models related to learning over the years (Bloom, 1982; Bloom, Hastings, & Madaus, 1971; Bloom & Madaus, 1981; Drew, Freston, & Logan, 1972; Hammill, 1971;). These efforts are discussed in detail in chapter 4.

Labeling

In examining classification it is important to also consider labeling. Labeling in relation to classification systems has been a source of controversy and concern for many years. For example, Maslow (1948) examined the potential problems of labeling, and his work has been followed by a continuing interest regarding possible difficulties associated with such designations, (e.g., Bromfield, Weisz, & Messer, 1986; Chassin, Stager, & Young, 1985; Hobbs, 1975a, 1975b, 1975c; Johnson, Sigelman, & Falkenberg, 1986; MacMillan, 1982; MacMillan, Jones, & Aloia, 1974). Classification and labeling are not necessarily synonymous. Hobbs (1975a) noted that "by *classifying* we mean the act of assigning a child or a condition to a general category or to a particular position in a classification system. . . . By *labeling* we mean to imply more than the assignment of a child to a category. We intend to include the notion of public communication of the way the child is categorized" (p. 43). This distinction is logical and important as we continue research on labeling. However, under current classification schemes it may have limited practical significance for those working as care providers. It is difficult to imagine a case in which an individual would be referred, evaluated, and classified without having some label attached. The nature of our human communication involves giving names to phenomena we observe. To speak about something will cause us to label it, whether with a given name, a type name, or an impression that the phenomenon gives to the speaker (and we typically have names or labels for such impressions). Labeling occurs more commonly than most of us consciously realize as laypeople. There are many labels, types of labels, and sources of labeling (e.g., societal, official, and unofficial labeling). Furthermore, what a label is intended to signify may differ from the associated meanings of the term. It is clear that terms evoke a variety of responses from different individuals (Bromfield, Weisz, & Messer, 1986; Chassin, Stager, & Young, 1985) and result in many types of services for those labeled. This is certainly the case for labels of deviance (Cromwell, Blashfield, & Strauss, 1975; MacMillan & Borthwick, 1980; MacMillan et al., 1974; MacMillan, Meyers, & Morrison, 1980). This illustrates the complexity of the relationship between labeling and other factors related to categorization and treatment. It also illustrates part of the difficulty encountered in determining the effects of labeling per se (MacMillan et al., 1974).

Many have denounced labels and labeling as detrimental or not useful. Many have advocated eliminating labels, believing that labeling has a negative impact on those so designated. This perspective has great appeal from an emotional view. However, empirical evidence isolating the effects of labeling has been difficult to obtain because of the complex interrelationship between labeling and other factors as mentioned earlier. Herein lies the importance of Hobbs's (1975a) previously quoted statement. If we are to continue and progress in research on the effects of labeling, we must be able either to isolate the effects or to study the problem within the context of its complexities.

The idea of self-fulfilling prophecy has played a prominent role in controversy related to the impact of labeling. This notion is essentially based on an assumption that one's behavior is largely determined by expectations and resulting treatment by those associated with the labeled individual. Such expectations are assumed to be substantially influenced by the label. This perspective was popularized largely because of the widely cited work by Rosenthal and Jacobsen (1966, 1968) although the idea was presented before (e.g., Dexter, 1956, 1958, 1960, 1964). Despite its intuitive appeal, solid, empirical evidence supporting the self-fulfilling prophecy notion has been limited. The Rosenthal and Jacobsen (1966, 1968) work has been severely criticized for serious methodological flaws (Elashoff & Snow, 1971; Snow, 1969; Thorndike, 1968). For example, Thorndike (1968) reviewed this work and described it in the following manner:

> In spite of anything I can say, I am sure it will become a classic—widely referred to and rarely examined critically. Alas, it is so defective technically that one can only regret that it ever got beyond the eyes of the original investigators! Though the volume may be an effective addition to education propagandizing, it does nothing to raise the standards of educational research. (p. 708)

Thorndike (1968) summarized by noting the following: "The indications are that the basic data upon which this structure has been raised are so untrustworthy that any conclusions based upon them must be suspect. The conclusions may be correct, but if so it must be considered a fortunate coincidence" (p. 711).

Thorndike was certainly correct regarding the attention focused on Rosenthal and Jacobson's work. He also appears to have been correct with respect to methodological flaws. Numerous studies have been unable to replicate their findings (e.g., Claiborn, 1969; Dusek & O'Connell, 1973; Fleming & Anttonen, 1971a, 1971b; Jose & Cody, 1971; Kester & Letchworth, 1972; Meichenbaum, Bowers, & Ross, 1969; Mendels & Flanders, 1973; Sorotzkin, Fleming, & Anttonen, 1974). Such evidence seems devastating to the self-fulfilling prophecy notion. However, it is important to emphasize that these studies were only unable to replicate the findings of Rosenthal and Jacobsen; even Thorndike noted that "the conclusions may be correct" (1968, p. 711). It is most unfortunate that such an important problem was studied with such flawed research methodology (particularly when it drew so much attention). There is little question that people such as teachers *do* form expectations. Evidence has accumulated over the years that strongly supports this contention (Brophy & Good, 1970; Dusek & O'Connell, 1973; Foster, Ysseldyke, & Reese, 1975; O'Connell, Dusek, &

Wheeler, 1974; Rist, 1970; Ysseldyke & Foster, 1978). However, it is unclear what information teachers use in forming such expectations (Dusek, 1975), and the precise effect of expectations (and labels) remains inconclusive. Attention to this topic continues (Brophy, 1983) and is important in the field of mental retardation.

INTERNATIONAL DEFINITIONS AND CLASSIFICATIONS

Core Concept 8   Viewing mental retardation across different countries suggests that there are various similarities and distinctions in both definitions and classifications.

Material on definition and classification presented thus far has pertained largely to the area within the geographical boundaries of the United States. It is useful for students of mental retardation to be aware of other approaches to this phenomenon and to have an idea of how they compare. This section provides a brief overview of perspectives used in other countries and a comparative picture of how they relate to approaches being used in the United States. At the outset readers should be aware that in many cases limited information is available from other nations. The countries discussed here were selected because of their divergent perspectives from those of the United States or the availability of information.

Soviet Union

Descriptions of scientific philosophies and methods used in one country by scientists of another country are often subject to misinterpretation. Whether because of inadequate information, bias, or some other factor, inaccuracies do occur and often serve to deter communication as well as to promote discord. It is our opinion that this type of difficulty may have been operative as some have interpreted the approach to mental retardation taken by the Soviet Union.

Most generic descriptions of the approach to mental retardation in the USSR have suggested that the only mental subnormality acknowledged is that accompanied by central nervous system damage. Indicative of this interpretation is Scheerenberger's (1964) discussion, which stated that in the Soviet Union, "mental retardation is dependent upon the occurrence, or suspected occurrence, of brain injury." Although providing more latitude than many interpretations, Scheerenberger's treatment is somewhat out of harmony with the impression conveyed by the Soviet scientist Luria (1963) in his description of research in the USSR. Interpretations by scientists in the United States and elsewhere seem to be subject to an error of incompleteness rather than direct bias, if we are reading Luria accurately.

Luria's description of the Soviet Union's approach does strongly emphasize the concept of nervous system impairment. In this respect the interpretations noted before are harmonious. The difference seems to emerge in terms of the way in which the emphasis is stated. As described by Luria (1963), the Soviet viewpoint is that failure to attempt identification of nervous system impairment, either central or peripheral, precludes "genuinely scientific analysis of the symptoms." One could certainly take issue with the potential profit of such a philosophical base, but the scientist is ideally more responsible for the soundness of method than for the philosophical framework. The emphasis conveyed by Luria, however, is somewhat different from that generally given in the interpretations of others.

The Soviet approach also emphasizes mental retardation as a developmental phenomenon. Luria indicates three ways in which retardation can occur. The first is that "a definite link indispensable to the normal development of mental activity becomes deranged owing to an early (more often intrauterine) disease and sometimes to an inborn defect." Luria emphasizes that USSR scientists do not believe all retardation to be inborn or hereditary. The second manner in which retardation can occur, according to Luria, involves the link

> hindering the further mental development of the child, formed by a certain defect in a particular mental function [such as visual or auditory signal analysis]. Finally, in still other cases a retardation of the development of cognitive processes and of the higher psychological systems may be caused by defects in the intercourse of the child with adults, as well as by defects in training (p. 357).

This latter statement is one that is particularly uncommon in interpretations of the Soviet approach to mental retardation. Although maintaining the stand of inferred nervous system impairment, Luria essentially said that retardation may occur by influences of deprivation either in training or in early childhood interaction with adults. The case being suggested is that actual changes in the nervous system may occur because of these influences in the environment. Such speculation is not without support even by research efforts in the United States in which autopsies of animals and humans subjected to extreme environmental influences have revealed a variety of changes in nervous system material (e.g., John, 1967).

Holowinsky (1982) reviewed selected literature on mental retardation in the Soviet Union between 1970 and 1980. He noted the following: "Mentally retarded individuals are described in the Soviet Union either as *umstvenno otstaly* . . ., a generic concept that could be translated as intellectually backward, or as oligophrenics (mentally deficient) who show definite evidence of neurological insult" (p. 369). The *umstvenno otstaly* seems to be similar to what is called in the United States mild mental retardation for which etiology is often unknown or speculative. Oligophrenia, on the other hand, would more often refer to more severe deficits for which etiology of neurological damage can be confirmed. Russian literature suggests that oligophrenia is studied in terms of heredity (e.g., Portnov, Marincheva, & Gorbachevskaya, 1985). Although the terminology and conceptual approach are different from what most of us are accustomed to, the outcomes are similar to some classification literature that has emerged in the United States (e.g., Hardman et al., 1984, 1987). Pevzner (1973) suggested that oligophrenia could be viewed in terms of five types, including those associated with (1) frontal lobe maldevelopment, (2) psychopathological behavior, (3) a variety of visual-motor and auditory defects, (4) perceptual impairments and cortical defects, and (5) diffuse maldevelopment of cortical hemispheres but without substantial neurological implications. Although these specific classifications are somewhat different from many categorization approaches, they are generically similar to the *types* of classification involved in parts of the AAMD medical categories (Grossman, 1983). Clearly the parameters of classification differ, however.

Argentina

The concept of mental retardation generally used in Argentina involves central nervous system impairment with biological etiology. Environmental influences are usually not thought to be involved in causing mental retardation. The primary classification scheme is a symptom severity model with measured intelligence as the criterion measure. The term "mentally weak" has been commonly used to make generic reference to mental retardation. This term is also used in combination with the category labeled "teachables," which is characterized by an IQ range of 50 to 70. Measured IQs ranging from 25 to 50 are associated with a category termed "imbeciles" or "trainables" and IQs of 0 to 25 fall into the lowest category which is designated as "idiot" or "custodial." This approach employs multiple classification parameters in an interactive fashion. Clearly a symptom severity parameter is evident regarding measured intelligence. In terms of labels there seems to be a mixture of parameters. The labels of teachable, trainable, and custodial seem similar to those used with an educability expectation parameter. Corresponding terms such as imbecile and idiot appear in early literature on mental retardation, but their use has been discontinued for the most part. These labels were just that, *labels*. They did not serve as adjectives on any symptom severity continuum (such as mild, moderate, and severe). These labels also did not describe syndromes or etiology in any specific sense. The use of such terms in Argentina likely represents a classification scheme in transition.

Australia

Symptom severity has also been the general approach to classification of mental retardation in Australia with an emphasis on a clinical/medical model rather than a social systems or "normalization" approach (Cocks, 1985). Primarily employing the AAMD classification scheme, both measured intelligence and social adaptability serve as criteria. In line with the AAMD approach, Australians carefully consider developmental history in diagnosis. Categories in terms of IQ ranges are usually from 55 to 79 for mildly handicapped or slow learners; approximately 30 to 50 for moderately handicapped, intellectually limited, or trainable, and below 30 for severely retarded people. This approach basically uses two classification parameters, symptom severity and educability expectation.

France

Interest in mental retardation problems in France has been evident since as early as the 13th century although, as in other countries, viewpoints have varied over the years (Mahendra, 1985). France essentially defines mental retardation with the intelligence test. In one way this is not surprising, since it was Binet's task to identify children with learning problems when he developed his intelligence assessment instrument. Lafon and Chabanier (1966) suggested considerable diversity of approach within the French professional community working in the area of mental retardation. From a research framework they noted two primary philosophical camps: (1) the psychological (psychometrics, social psychology, and sociology as techniques) and (2) the organic (focusing on a search for organic etiology).

Lafon and Chabanier (1966) outlined a classification scheme that seems to represent a synthesis of several frameworks, including clinical, educational, and measurement concerns:

1. A threshold or marginal category, important but particularly difficult to define, including children who are not defective but are unable to attain the average level of their classmates. These are children with a limited intelligence representing, so to speak, the lowest level of normal intelligence. They are characterized by a certain slowness in performing their school work and they have serious difficulties in conceptualization. As a rule they are at the bottom of their class. Their IQ lies between 80 and 100. They are only unadapted within

the academic framework, which distorts the current educational structure.

2. Persons with a mild mental deficiency (IQ 65 or above), capable of an independent life and adjustment to a working community.
3. Persons in whom a mild mental deficiency is complicated by associated disorders. These children are not, strictly speaking, intellectually inferior to those of group 2, but the "extra burden" they carry makes their social adjustment more difficult.
4. Moderate mental deficiency (minimum IQ 50). Comparative independence and adaptation to simple work is possible after rehabilitation, but these cases usually require special care throughout their lifetime.
5. Severe mental deficiency (IQ 30 to 50). This "semieducable" group is capable of some social adjustment in a sheltered environment.
6. Profound mental deficiency, "profoundly retarded" group (IQ less than 30). These cases are educable only very slightly or not at all, and their adaptation to group life is doubtful and risky. (p. 225)

Germany

There is no German word that translates directly into our label of "mental retardation." The term most commonly used in German is *Schwachsinn*, which most closely translates into feeblemindedness and mental deficiency. *Schwachsinn* implies both descriptive and etiological concepts. From a descriptive classification standpoint, the symptom severity parameter is employed using IQ for the most part. (Three classification levels have often been found in the literature—moronity, imbecility, and idiocy.) Schmidt and Baltes (1971) noted that "there is a strong trend, however, primarily with respect to research efforts, to get away from a global IQ measure to a multivariate consideration of the pattern of intelligence" (p. 351). The German research literature has typically viewed etiology in terms of three categories of mental retardation: (1) psychogenic-reactive, (2) exogenous, and (3) endogenous. Psychogenic-reactive mental retardation includes such causation as psychological disorders (e.g., neurosis) and sociocultural deprivation. Exogenous mental retardation represents a category in which there is demonstrated brain damage of an organic nature but not resulting from heredity. The endogenous category involves no evidence of brain injury or other neurological pathology and also searches for a familial history of retardation.

Great Britain

From a legal framework there have been two main categories generally used in Great Britain, "subnormality" and "severe subnormality" (Simon, 1978).

This terminology was a result of the Mental Health Act of 1959 and is legislatively defined in social and developmental terms. Subnormality was defined as the following (Stevens & Heber, 1968): "A state of arrested or incomplete development of mind (not amounting to severe subnormality) which includes subnormality of intelligence and is of a nature or degree which requires or is susceptible to medical treatment or other special care or training" (p. 6). Severe subnormality was defined as the following: "A state of arrested or incomplete development of mind which includes subnormality of intelligence and is of such a nature or degree that the patient is incapable of living an independent life or of guarding himself against serious exploitation, or will be incapable when of age to do so" (p. 6). The term mental subnormality is employed generically, irrespective of severity. The upper limit is not specifically delineated, but usage seems to focus on an upper measured IQ boundary of 70.

British scientists working in mental retardation occasionally use terminology that predates the 1959 Mental Health Act. Terms such as mentally defective and mentally deficient as well as feebleminded, imbecile, and idiot can be found in the post-1959 British literature and were defined for research and clinical purposes aside from those involved in legislative definitions. Tizard (1965) stated:

> Interesting as the United States classification is, however, the traditional, and for many purposes still the most useful, way of classifying the mentally subnormal behaviourally is according to the severity of *grade* of the defect. Three main grades have been distinguished, namely (1) idiots, (2) imbeciles, and (3) feeble-minded persons (British terminology) or morons (United States usage). (p. 8)

(Idiot and imbecile groups were frequently termed as "low-grade" defectives whereas the feebleminded or moron individuals were referred to as "high-grade" defectives.) Tizard was apparently combining the United States terminology at that time with other of a much earlier vintage, since symptom severity was being employed and the moron terminology had been discontinued for some time. The British terminology was linked to IQ level with general ranges of 50 to 70 for the feebleminded, 20 to 50 for imbecile, and below 20 for the idiot classification.

Scandinavia

Work with mentally retarded individuals in Scandinavian countries has had a tremendous impact on efforts in the United States during the past two decades. This influence has emerged more in terms of philosophy than of definition or classification. Definition and classification issues in Scandinavia are considered much less important than issues related to treatment of mentally retarded people. One of the most important current concepts related to mental retardation is that of *normalization*, which refers to an existence that is as close to mainstream society as possible. The principle of normalization came from Scandinavia and was articulated in print by both Danish and Swedish professionals (Bank-Mikkelsen, 1969; Nirje, 1969). This notion has been an important contribution in mental retardation internationally although little research on the principle has been conducted outside of Scandinavia and it has been subject to frequent misconceptions and resistance in some areas (Anstey & Gaskin, 1985; Nirje, 1985; Perrin & Nirje, 1985). Wolfensberger (1972) stated that "until about 1969, the term 'normalization' had never been heard by most workers in human service areas. Today, it is a captivating watchword standing for a whole new ideology of human management" (p. 27).

Comments

As discussed earlier, several classification frameworks are used in the United States. The AAMD manual of terminology includes three parameters in an attempt to meet the diverse needs of professionals working in the field of mental retardation. The etiological classification scheme has been used by medical personnel and others primarily involved in diagnosis and treatment of clinical forms of retardation. The adaptive behavior and measured intelligence parameters are ostensibly used in combination for a variety of service purposes. Measured intelligence in the AAMD scheme is essentially a symptom severity approach, similar to the educational classification of educable, trainable, and custodial (SMH) mental retardation. Although the educational approach involves statements of expected achievement, the primary classificatory technique is measured intelligence.

The variety of international approaches to mental retardation is apparent even from the cursory overview given here. Certain countries are rather firmly settled into a particular philosophical framework and are pushing forward in efforts aimed at progress from that framework. Others evidence much more variation, and occasionally confusion, with respect to both definition and classification. Certain factors seem to thread through all. A developmental emphasis is present in the definition and classification systems of several countries, even those with highly divergent philosophical positions (e.g., the USSR, Great Britain, France). Similarly, the social adaptation factor is present as at least a partial international concern (e.g., in the United States, Great Britain, France). Perhaps the most common factor cutting across international borders is that of symptom severity in terms of measured intelligence.

Core Questions

1. How has the concept of mental retardation differed among disciplines, and how might this affect an individual retarded person?
2. How has consideration of adaptive behavior complicated the view of mental retardation, and how has it been a positive influence?
3. What is the difference between incidence and prevalence?
4. When considering the question of how frequently mental retardation occurs, how do SES, age, and severity affect the answer?
5. In what ways did the "constitutional origin" and "incurability" factors found in early definitions of mental retardation cause problems? How have they been addressed in more current definitions?
6. What ages were primarily addressed in early definitions of mental retardation? Why and how have definitions changed with respect to age?
7. How has the presence of many disciplines working in mental retardation been both an advantage and presented problems?
8. In what ways are definitions and classifications similar between the United States and other countries? How are they different?
9. How do differences in the parameters of classification employed influence statistical comparisons of incidence and prevalence of mental retardation between countries?
10. What is a parameter of classification?
11. How are parameters of classification employed in an interactive fashion to identify a mentally retarded individual?
12. How do variations in classification specificity influence incidence and prevalence?
13. How might the use of unspecified parameters of classification cause difficulties in obtaining funding for service to mentally retarded individuals?
14. How can definition and classification systems serve some purposes well and yet be inappropriate for others?
15. Why is it important for there to be a relationship between definitions, classifications, assessment, and programming?
16. What might be some of the difficulties encountered in using a grouping-oriented classification system and criterion-referenced assessment?
17. What might be some of the difficulties encountered in using norm-referenced assessment in conjunction with a definition that did not focus on grouping but instead emphasized functional skill levels?

ROUND TABLE
DISCUSSION

When discussing or otherwise considering any phenomenon, the definition of what is being addressed is the vital foundation upon which that discussion is based. Communication between you and your student colleagues would be difficult indeed if some of you were talking about automobile transportation and others were considering airplanes, but you all were using the same term, say "Mustifig." You would encounter difficulty agreeing on cost per mile, miles easily traveled in an hour, and many other factors. This illustration is exaggerated, but in some ways it is not all that different than mental retardation, defined, categorized, counted, and served.

In your study group or on your own, examine mental retardation from the perspective of (for example) sociology, medicine, psychology, education, and politics. Characterize the phenomenon, discuss service, and address various aspects of how it should be conceptualized. Examine parameters of classification, labeling, assessment, and also consider worldwide input as though you were receiving scientific information from all parts of the globe. After completing this exercise, determine how you will conceptualize the phenomenon of mental retardation in order to best learn all that must be known about it and how those so affected can best be served. Reflect back on the information provided in this chapter and consider the task of early professionals working in mental retardation. They did (and do) not have a simple assignment; it is hoped you will do better.

REFERENCES

American Psychiatric Association. (1980). *Diagnostic and statistical manual of mental disorders* (3rd ed.). Washington, DC.

Anstey, T. J., & Gaskin, M. (1985). Service providers' understanding of the concept of normalization. *Australia and New Zealand Journal of Developmental Disabilities, 11*, 91–95.

Baird, P. A., & Sandovnick, A. D. (1985). Mental retardation in over half-a-million consecutive livebirths: An epidemiological study. *American Journal of Mental Deficiency, 89*, 323–330.

Baird, P. A., & Sandovnick, A. D. (1986). Reply to Richardson, Koller, and Katz. *American Journal of Mental Deficiency, 90*, 451–452.

Bank-Mikkelsen, N. E. (1969). A metropolitan area in Denmark: Copenhagen. In R. Kugel, & W. Wolfensberger (Eds.), *Changing patterns in residential services for the mentally retarded* (pp. 227–254). Washington, DC: President's Committee on Mental Retardation.

Barnett, W. S. (1986). Definition and classification of mental retardation: A reply to Zigler, Balla, and Hodapp. *American Journal of Mental Deficiency, 91*, 111–116.

Benda, C. E. (1954). Psychopathology of childhood. In P. Mussen (Ed.), *Manual of child psychology* (2nd ed., pp. 1115–1116). New York: John Wiley.

Benton, A. L. (1956). The concept of pseudofeeblemindedness. *Archives of Neurology, 75*, 379–388.

Bloom, B. S. (1982). *Human characteristics and school learning.* New York: McGraw-Hill.

Bloom, B. S., Hastings, J. T., & Madaus, G. F. (1971). *Handbook of formative and summative evaluation of student learning.* New York: McGraw-Hill.

Bloom, B. S., & Madaus, G. F. (1981). *Evaluation to improve learning.* New York: McGraw-Hill.

Bromfield, R., Weisz, J. R., & Messer, T. (1986). Children's judgments and attributions in response to the "mentally retarded" label: A developmental approach. *Journal of Abnormal Psychology, 95*, 81–87.

Brophy, J. E. (1983). Research on the self-fulfilling prophecy and teacher expectations. *Journal of Educational Psychology, 75,* 631–661.

Brophy, J. E., & Good, T. L. (1970). Teachers' communication of differential expectations for childrens' classroom performance: Some behavioral data. *Journal of Educational Psychology, 61,* 365–374.

Carter, C. H. (1978). *Medical aspects of mental retardation* (2nd ed.), Springfield, IL: Charles C. Thomas.

Carter, C. H. (1979). *Handbook of mental retardation syndromes* (3rd rev ed.). Springfield, IL: Charles C. Thomas.

Chassin, L., Stager, S., & Young, R. D. (1985). Self- labeling by EMR high school students in their mainstream and special education classes. *American Journal of Community Psychology, 13,* 449–465.

Claiborn, W. L. (1969). Expectancy effects in the classroom: A failure to replicate. *Journal of Educational Psychology, 60,* 377–383.

Clausen, J. (1972). Quo vadis, AAMD? *Journal of Special Education, 6,* 51–60.

Cocks, E. (1985). Roadblocks to appropriate services for persons with an intellectual disability in Australia. *Australia and New Zealand Journal of Developmental Disabilities, 11,* 75–82.

Cooper, T., Wilton, K., & Glynn, T. (1985). Prevalence, school progress and referral of mildly retarded children in regular classes. *Exceptional Child, 32,* 5–11.

Coulter, W. A., & Morrow, H. W. (Eds.). (1978). *Adaptive behavior: Concepts and measurements.* New York: Grune & Stratton.

Cromwell, R. L., Blashfield, R. K., & Strauss, J. S. (1975). Criteria for classification systems. In N. Hobbs (Ed.), *Issues in the classification of children* (Vol. 1, 4–25). San Francisco: Jossey-Bass.

Dexter, L. A. (1956). Towards a sociology of the mentally defective. *American Journal of Mental Deficiency, 61,* 10–16.

Dexter, L. A. (1958). A social theory of mental deficiency. *American Journal of Mental Deficiency, 62,* 920–928.

Dexter, L. A. (1960). Research on problems of mental subnormality. *American Journal of Mental Deficiency, 64,* 835–838.

Dexter, L. A. (1964). *The tyranny of schooling: An inquiry into the problem of "stupidity."* New York: Basic Books.

Doll, E. A. (1941). The essentials of an inclusive concept of mental deficiency. *American Journal of Mental Deficiency, 46,* 214–219.

Drew, C. J. (1971). Research on social adjustment and the mentally retarded: Functioning and training. *Mental Retardation, 9,* 26–29.

Drew, C. J., Freston, C. W., & Logan, D. R. (1972). Criteria and reference in evaluation. *Focus on Exceptional Children, 4,* 1–10.

Dusek, J. B. (1975). Do teachers bias children's learning? *Review of Educational Research, 45,* 661–684.

Dusek, J. B., & O'Connell, E. J. (1973). Teacher expectancy effects on the achievement test performance of elementary school children. *Journal of Educational Psychology, 65,* 371–377.

Elashoff, J. D., & Snow, R. E. (1971). *Pygmalion reconsidered.* Worthington, OH: Charles A. Jones.

Fleming, E. S., & Anttonen, R. G. (1971a). Teacher expectancy or my fair lady. *American Educational Research Journal, 8,* 241–252.

Fleming, E. S., & Anttonen, R. G. (1971b). Teacher expectancy as related to the academic and personal growth of primary-age children. *Monographs of the Society for Research in Child Development, 36,* 5.

Foster, G. G., Ysseldyke, J. E., & Reese, J. H. (1975). I wouldn't have seen it if I hadn't believed it. *Exceptional Children, 41,* 469–473.

Gallagher, J. J. (1985). The prevalence of mental retardation: Cross-cultural considerations from Sweden and the United States. *Intelligence, 9,* 97–108.

Gellis, S. S., & Feingold, M. (1968). *Atlas of mental retardation syndromes.* Washington, DC: U.S. Government Printing Office.

Grossman, H. J. (Ed.). (1973). *Manual on terminology and classification in mental retardation.* Washington, DC: American Association on Mental Deficiency.

Grossman, H. J. (Ed.). (1977). *Manual on terminology and classification in mental retardation.* Washington, DC: American Association on Mental Deficiency.

Grossman, H. J. (Ed.). (1983). *Classification in mental retardation.* Washington, DC: American Association on Mental Deficiency.

Hammill, D. D. (1971). Evaluating children for instructional purposes. *Academic Therapy, 6,* 341–353.

Hardman, M. L., Drew, C. J., & Egan, M. W. (1984). *Human exceptionality: Society, school, and family.* Newton, MA: Allyn & Bacon.

Hardman, M. L., Drew, C. J., & Egan, M. W. (1987). *Human exceptionality: Society, school, and family.* Newton, MA: Allyn & Bacon.

Heber, R. (1961). A manual on terminology and classification in mental retardation (2nd ed.). *American Journal of Mental Deficiency, Monograph Supplement.*

Heber, R. (1962). Mental retardation: Concept and classification. In E. P. Trapp & P. Himelstein (Eds.), *Readings on the exceptional child: Research and theory* (pp. 69–81). New York: Appleton-Century-Crofts.

Hobbs, N. (1975a). *The futures of children.* San Francisco: Jossey-Bass.

Hobbs, N. (Ed.). (1975b). *Issues in the classification of children* (Vol. 1). San Francisco: Jossey-Bass.

Hobbs, N. (Ed.). (1975c). *Issues in the classification of children* (Vol. 2). San Francisco: Jossey-Bass.

Hodapp, R. M., & Zigler, E. (1986). Reply to Barnett's comments on the definition and classification of mental retardation. *American Journal of Mental Deficiency, 91,* 117–119.

Holowinsky, I. Z. (1982). Current mental retardation research in the Soviet Union. *Journal of Special Education, 16,* 269–378.

Iowa Task Force on Adaptive Behavior. (1981). *Assessment, documentation and programming for adaptive behavior: An Iowa task force report.* Des Moines: Department of Public Instruction.

John, E. R. (1967). *Mechanisms of memory.* New York: Academic Press.

Johnson, C. G., Sigelman, C. K., & Falkenberg, V. F. (1986). Impacts of labeling and competence on peers' perceptions: Mentally retarded versus nonretarded perceivers. *American Journal of Mental Deficiency, 90,* 663–668.

Jose, J., & Cody, J. J. (1971). Teacher-pupil interaction as it related to attempted changes in teacher expectancy of academic ability and achievement. *American Educational Research Journal, 8,* 39–49.

Kester, S. W., & Letchworth, G. A. (1972). Communication of teacher expectations and their effects on achievement and attitudes of secondary school students. *Journal of Educational Research, 66,* 51–55.

Kirk, S. A. (1962). *Educating exceptional children.* Boston: Houghton-Mifflin.

Kopp, C. B., & Krakow, J. B. (1983). The developmentalist and the study of biological risk: A view of the past with an eye toward the future. *Child Development, 54,* 1086–1108.

Lafon, R., & Chabanier, J. (1966). Research on mental deficiency during the last decade in France. In N. R. Ellis (Ed.), *International review of research in mental retardation* (Vol. 2, pp. 253–277). New York: Academic Press.

Lemkau, P. V., & Imre, P. D. (1969). Results of a field epidemiologic study. *American Journal of Mental Deficiency, 73,* 858–863.

Luria, A. R. (1963). Psychological studies of mental deficiency in the Soviet Union. In N. R. Ellis (Ed.), *Handbook of mental deficiency: Psychological theory and research* (pp. 353–387). New York: McGraw-Hill.

MacMillan, D. L. (1982). *Mental retardation in school and society* (2nd ed.). Boston: Little, Brown.

MacMillan, D. L., & Borthwick, S. (1980). The new educable mentally retarded population: Can they be mainstreamed? *Mental Retardation, 18,* 155–185.

MacMillan, D. L., Jones, R. L., & Aloia, G. F. (1974). The mentally retarded label: A theoretical analysis and review of research. *American Journal of Mental Deficiency, 79,* 241–261.

MacMillan, D. L., Meyers, C. E., & Morrison, G. M. (1980). System-identification of mildly mentally retarded children: Implications for interpreting and conducting research. *American Journal of Mental Deficiency, 85,* 108–115.

Mahendra, B. (1985). Subnormality revisited in early 19th century France. *Journal of Mental Deficiency Research, 29,* 391–401.

Maslow, A. (1948). Cognition of the particular and of the generic. *Psychological Review, 55,* 22–40.

Meichenbaum, D. H., Bowers, K. S., & Ross, R. R. (1969). A behavioral analysis of teacher expectancy effect. *Journal of Personality and Social Psychology, 13,* 306–316.

Mendels, G. E., & Flanders, J. P. (1973). Teacher expectations and pupil performance. *American Educational Research Journal, 10,* 203–212.

Mercer, J. R. (1973a). *Labeling the mentally retarded.* Berkeley: University of California Press.

Mercer, J. R. (1973b). The myth of 3% prevalence. In R. K. Eyman, C. E. Meyers, & G. Tarjan (Eds.), Sociobehavioral studies in mental retardation. *Monographs of the American Association on Mental Deficiency,* No. 1.

Meyers, C. E., Nihira, K., & Zetlin, A. (1979). The measurement of adaptive behavior. In N. R. Ellis (Ed.), *Handbook of mental deficiency, psychological theory and research* (2nd ed., pp. 431–481). Hillsdale, NJ: Lawrence Erlbaum Associates.

Nirje, B. (1969). The normalization principle and its human management implications. In R. Kugel & W. Wolfensberger (Eds.), *Changing patterns in residential services for the mentally retarded* (pp. 179–195). Washington, DC: President's Committee on Mental Retardation.

Nirje, B. (1985). The basis and logic of the normalization principle. *Australia and New Zealand Journal of Developmental Disabilities, 11,* 65–68.

O'Connell, E. J., Dusek, J. B., & Wheeler, R. (1974). A follow-up study of teacher expectancy effects. *Journal of Educational Psychology, 66,* 325–328.

Penrose, L. S. (1972). Mental deficiency. *Journal of Special Education, 6,* 56–66.

Perrin, B., & Nirje, B. (1985). Setting the record straight: A critique of some frequent misconceptions of the normalization principle. *Australia and New Zealand Journal of Developmental Disabilities, 11,* 69–74.

Pevzner, M. S. (Ed.). (1973). *Clinical-genetic research of oligophrenia.* Moscow: Pedagogika.

Portnov, V. A., Marincheva, G. S., & Gorbachevskaya, N. L. (1985). Familial craniometaphyseal dysplasia in combination with oligophrenia. *Zhurnal Nevropatologii i Psikhiatrii, 85,* 404–409.

President's Task Force on the Mentally Handicapped. (1970). *Action against mental disability.* Washington, DC: U.S. Government Printing Office.

Proposed Regulations. (1982). *Federal Register, 33,* 845.

Rantakallio, P., & von Wendt, L. (1986). Mental retardation and subnormality in a birth cohort of 12,000 children in Northern Finland. *American Journal of Mental Deficiency, 90,* 380–387.

Richardson, S. A., Koller, H., & Katz, M. (1986). Comments on Baird and Sandovnick's "Mental retardation in over half-a-million consecutive livebirths: An epidemiological study." *American Journal of Mental Deficiency, 90,* 449–450.

Rist, R. G. (1970). Student social class and teacher expectations: The self-fulfilling prophecy in ghetto education. *Harvard Educational Review, 40,* 411–451.

Rosenthal, R., & Jacobson, L. (1966). Teacher expectancies: Determinants of pupils' IQ gains. *Psychological Reports, 19,* 115–118.

Rosenthal, R., & Jacobson, L. (1968). *Pygmalion in the classroom.* New York: Holt, Rinehart & Winston.

Scheerenberger, R. C. (1964). Mental retardation: Definition, classification, and prevalence. *Mental Retardation Abstracts, 1,* 432–441.

Scheerenberger, R. C. (1983). *A history of mental retardation.* Baltimore: Brookes.

Schmidt, L. R., & Baltes, P. B. (1971). German theory and research on mental retardation: Emphasis on structure. In N. R. Ellis (Ed.), *International review of research in mental retardation* (Vol. 5, pp. 349–392). New York: Academic Press.

Simon, G. B. (1978). Services in the United Kingdom. In J. Wortis (Ed.), *Mental retardation and developmental disabilities* (Vol. 10, pp. 242–258). New York: Brunner/Mazel.

Sloan, W., & Birch, J. (1955). A rationale for degrees of retardation. *American Journal of Mental Deficiency, 60,* 258–264.

Snow, R. (1969). Unfinished Pygmalion. *Journal of Contemporary Psychology, 14,* 197–199.

Sorotzkin, F., Fleming, E. S., & Anttonen, R. G. (1974). Teacher knowledge of standardized test information and its effect on pupil IQ and achievement. *Journal of Experimental Education, 43,* 79–85.

Spicker, H. H., & Bartel, N. R. (1968). The mentally retarded. In G. O. Johnson & H. D. Blank (Eds.), *Exceptional children research review* (pp. 38–109). Washington, DC: Council for Exceptional Children.

Stevens, H. A., & Heber, R. (1968). An international review of developments in mental retardation. *Mental Retardation, 6,* 4–23.

Tarjan, G., Wright, S. W., Eyman, R. K., & Keeran, C. V. (1973). Natural history of mental retardation: Some aspects of epidemiology. *American Journal of Mental Deficiency, 77,* 369–379.

Terman, L. (1916). *The measurement of intelligence.* Boston: Houghton-Mifflin.

Thorndike, R. L. (1968). Review of *Pygmalion in the classroom* by R. Rosenthal and L. Jacobsen. *American Educational Research Journal, 5,* 707–711.

Tizard, J. (1965). Introduction. In A. M. Clarke & A. D. B. Clarke (Eds.), *Mental deficiency: The changing outlook* (Rev. ed., pp. 3–22). New York: Free Press.

Tredgold, A. F. (1937). *A textbook of mental deficiency* (6th ed.). Baltimore: William Wood.

U.S. Department of Education. (1985). *To assure the free appropriate public education of all handicapped children.* Seventh Annual Report to Congress on the Implementation of the Education of the Handicapped Act.

Wechsler, D. (1958). *The measurement and appraisal of adult intelligence* (4th ed.). Baltimore: Williams & Wilkins.

Wolfensberger, W. (1972). *The principle of normalization in human services.* Toronto: National Institute on Mental Retardation.

World Health Organization, (1978). *International classification of diseases.* (Vol. 1, 9th rev. ed.). Geneva.

Ysseldyke, J. E., & Foster, G. G. (1978). Bias in teachers' observations of emotionally disturbed and learning disabled children. *Exceptional Children, 44,* 613–615.

Zigler, E., Balla, D., & Hodapp, R. (1984). On the definition and classification of mental retardation. *American Journal of Mental Deficiency, 89,* 215–230.

APPENDIX

This definition information is excerpted in adapted form from *Classification in Mental Retardation,* ed. H. S. Grossman, pp. 11–15, copyright 1983 by the American Association on Mental Deficiency. Reprinted by permission.

Definitions

Mental retardation refers to significantly subaverage general intellectual functioning resulting in or associated with concurrent impairments in adaptive behavior and manifested during the developmental period.

General intellectual functioning is operationally defined as the results obtained by assessment with one or more of the individually administered standardized general intelligence tests developed for that purpose.

Significantly subaverage is defined as IQ of 70 or below on standardized measures of intelligence. This upper limit is intended as a guideline; it could be extended upward through IQ 75 or more, depending on the reliability of the intelligence test used. This particularly applies in schools and similar settings if behavior is impaired and clinically determined to be due to deficits in reasoning and judgment.

Impairments in adaptive behavior are defined as significant limitations in an individual's effectiveness in meeting the standards of maturation, learning, personal independence, and/or social responsibility that are expected for his or her age level and cultural group, as determined by clinical assessment and, usually, standardized scales.

Developmental period is defined as the period of time between conception and the 18th birthday. Developmental deficits may be manifested by slow, arrested, or incomplete development resulting from brain damage, degenerative processes in the central nervous system, or regression from previously normal states due to psychosocial factors.

Figure 1–3 illustrates possible combinations of measured intellectual functioning and adaptive behavior. Retardation may occur through physical trauma or central nervous system deterioration at any age beyond the developmental period. When manifestations occur later, the condition is more properly classified as *dementia* (see DSM-III—Organic Mental Disorders).

The term *mental retardation*, as commonly used today, embraces a heterogeneous population, ranging from totally dependent to nearly independent people. Although all individuals so designated share the common attributes of low intelligence and inadequacies in adaptive behavior, there are marked variations in the degree of deficit manifested and the presence or absence of associated physical handicaps, stigmata, and psychologically disordered states. These variations greatly affect the needs of retarded individuals, the nature of the problems and services required by their families, and the burdens posed to community agencies and supportive systems. The differences are highly related to etiological factors, setting biologically damaged persons apart from psychosocially disadvantaged individuals on a number of significant dimensions: performance, problems, potentials, and prognosis.

Conceptually, the identifiable mentally retarded population can be divided into two distinct, albeit overlapping, groups. One group, approximately 25 percent of the total population, constitutes the "clinical types." Individ-

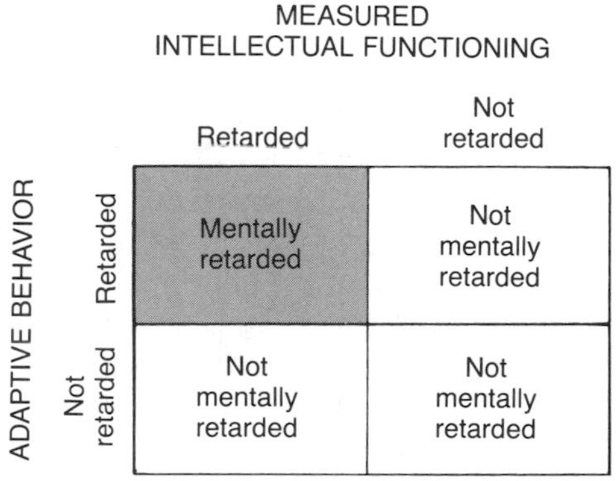

Figure 1–3. Possible Combinations of Measured Intellectual Functioning and Adaptive Behavior

uals of this group generally demonstrate some central nervous system pathology, usually have IQs in the moderate range or below, have associated handicaps or stigmata, and can often be diagnosed from birth or early childhood. Individuals of the second group, comprising the majority of the retarded population in the United States and elsewhere in the world, appear to be neurologically intact, have no readily detectable physical signs or clinical laboratory evidence related to retardation, function in the mildly retarded range of intelligence, and are heavily concentrated in the lowest socioeconomic segments of society. Often, they are identified as retarded only during the school years.

Neither of these groups represents "pure" entities. Children with central nervous system abnormalities can and do function within the mild range of intelligence, and many children from seriously disadvantaged homes are further handicapped by biological deficiencies. Nevertheless, the association of IQ and physical signs is very high, and the differentiation of the two groups by primary etiological agents of biological versus social-environmental origin has meaningful implications for prevention, planning, and treatment.

The complex of symptoms subsumed under the term *mental retardation* overlaps considerably with the legislative definition of *developmental disabilities* as contained in P. L. 94–103 and amended in P. L. 95–602, Title V. In the Developmental Disabilities Assistance and Bill of Rights Act, the term *developmental disabilities* refers to a severe, chronic disability that "is attributable to a mental or physical impairment or combination of mental and physical impairments" that are (a) manifested before age 22, (b) likely to continue indefinitely, and (c) result in substantial functional limitations in three or more areas of major life activity.

The areas of limitation clearly apply to the more severe forms of mental retardation and to some mildly retarded individuals during certain periods of their lives. For severely retarded people, nearly all of the defined areas of limitation are substantial and applicable: self-care, receptive and expressive language, learning, mobility, self-direction, capacity for independent living, and economic self-sufficiency. For mildly retarded individuals, many of whom achieve self-sufficiency in adulthood, the disability may be confined to impairments primarily in the areas of learning and possibly self-direction.

Other conditions embraced in the definitions of developmental disability that share some characteristics in common with mental retardation are cerebral palsy, epilepsy, and autism. Significant proportions of these populations function intellectually at retarded levels.

Developmental disabilities are therefore distinguishable from the milder forms of mental retardation and less severe conditions of cerebral palsy, epilepsy, and autism by the nature of the functional limitations described. In order to satisfy the definition, individuals must demonstrate *substantial* functional limitations that are age-specific. Although the term *substantial* is not explicitly defined, the requirement that these limitations reflect a need for services that are of life-long or extended duration and are individually planned and coordinated clearly delimits the target population.

The concepts of mental retardation and developmental disabilities, although parallel in many respects, reflect some marked differences. Both are developmental in origin and stress impairment in adaptive behavior. Most clinical types of retardation involving central nervous system pathology and IQs below approximately 55 fulfill both the physical and mental criteria of developmental disability. For this subgroup in retardation, the handicap is permanent and "substantial." The differences between the two categories occur primarily at the upper end of the retarded intellectual range. *The AAMD definition carries no connotation of chronicity or irreversibility and, on the contrary, applies only to levels of functioning.* "Significantly subaverage" is precisely defined, if not precisely measured, and imposes as a guideline a ceiling for performance that is clearly higher than inferred under the newly defined term *substantial handicap.* The fact that psychosocially disadvantaged mildly retarded children often are functionally impaired in the school years only, have no demonstrable neurological disorders, and achieve some level of adult independence indicates that they fall outside the definition of developmental disabilities.

Children with autism, in particular, share many attributes with severely and profoundly mentally retarded children. Although there is considerable variation in the behavior patterns of the latter, many of them, like autistic children, fail to develop interpersonal relationships, have serious communication and receptive language deficits, and engage in repetitive and compulsive behavior. Approximately 70 percent of autistic children have IQs within the retarded range, and all have behavioral impairments that are manifested before 30 months of age.

2

A Multidisciplinary Viewpoint

Mental retardation is a conceptual abstraction that only assumes meaning in personal, social, and behavioral contexts. The various approaches discussed in chapter 1 regarding classification and definitions emphasize the changing concepts that have influenced our perceptions of mental retardation. As an entity, mental retardation changes, sometimes quite dramatically, depending on a variety of social perceptions and influences. In this chapter we will discuss aspects of services and programs that are needed to facilitate research and service provisions for the mentally retarded in our society.

HISTORICAL PERSPECTIVES

A historical review is necessary for several reasons. Perhaps foremost is the need to provide a background for the person who wishes to be more knowledgeable about the events that have influenced our thinking about mental retardation. Although history does not provide a blueprint for the future, the past does provide a framework for future considerations. An understanding of historical events should also provide us with a sense of perspective. Present advances have been built on the courage of a few insightful and caring persons who felt the pain of the mentally retarded and had a compassionate desire to improve the conditions of their fellow humans. We are both the end of the past and beginning of the future. Without an understanding of the past we are isolated in a cognitive sense.

It should be noted that many of the disciplines referred to in following sections in this chapter were either nonexistent or in their infancy during the 1800s. Consequently, their contributions were not manifested until recently. This brief historical review is therefore included to trace some of the more important developmental roots of programs for the mentally retarded.

Core Concept 1	Mental retardation is a fluid concept which is influenced by economic, societal and situational factors.

Mental retardation has existed in one form or another in all societies throughout time. This in no way means that the classifications for retarded persons have remained unchanged. The mentally retarded have been described in different terms, involving many diverse conceptualizations and varying characteristics, depending on societal and situational influences at the time. In fact, as one looks at the history of mental retardation, the picture is chameleon-like, with its appearance changing according to the attitudes and convictions of the time. Mental retardation has been an elusive concept for a variety of reasons, not the least of which have been the temporal factors associated with economic, social, and political climates of the various cultures existing throughout history.

The following historical synopsis is intended to provide a succinct accounting of *(a)* the attitudinal changes based on the needs, ideas, and temporal conditions until the nineteenth century and *(b)* the developing interest and concern about mental retardation experienced since 1800. For more complete information and understanding of historical events see Scheerenberger (1982).

Before 1800, with a few notable exceptions, the mentally retarded were not considered to be an overriding social problem in any society. This is because the more severely retarded either were killed or died of natural causes at an early age. Those who today we would term mildly retarded were usually sufficiently able to contribute meaningfully to an agrarian society.

Although the earliest written reference to mental retardation is the Therapeutic Papyrus of Thebes dated 1552 B.C. (Doll, 1962), anthropological studies have generated evidence of mental retardation substantially predating this time. Severe head injuries were probably not uncommon during prehistoric existence and most certainly resulted in mental aberrations. Additionally, human skulls dating to the Stone Age have been discovered that indicate that crude surgical operations had been performed. Such surgical procedures were apparently intended to cure what was perceived as abnormal behavior. The methods used may have been based on the assumption that abnormal behavior was caused by evil spirits and that opening a hole in the skull permitted imprisoned demons to escape. Certainly not all such "operations" were performed on mentally retarded persons. Regardless of the reason, however, the treatment at times may have produced retarded-like behavior.

Through the ages, human understanding and treatment of mental retardation have been influenced considerably by the socioeconomic conditions of the times. Mental and physical defects were naturally viewed by primitive nomadic tribes with fear and disgrace, largely because of the stigma attached to such conditions by superstitions and myths. Other influences on the way the handicapped were viewed resulted from the economic drain on the tribe by these individuals. Nomadic tribes in particular could ill afford to be burdened by nonproductive members who consumed their limited food and water supplies but did not tangibly contribute to the group's common welfare. Even as tribal civilization progressed and a less nomadic existence prevailed, the retarded were frequently viewed harshly. Farming and maintaining herds had become a way of life, but the threat of famine remained constantly on the horizon. The economic picture for the handicapped was, therefore, similar to that which it had been during more nomadic times. Neither the religious nor the economic perspective was conducive to the care and maintenance of the retarded—nonproductive citizens were expendable.

Political authority also has represented a potent power base throughout history in terms of determining the lot of the mentally retarded. At times such authority provided harsh circumstances for handicapped individuals, whereas at other times a much more humane approach prevailed. During the latter part of the sixth century, Pope Gregory I issued a decree that instructed the faithful to assist those who were crippled. This period saw various types and degrees of care provided for the handicapped, including the retarded, who were commonly referred to at that time as idiots. In a similar vein, the English under the rule of King Henry II during the twelfth century enacted legislation known as *de praerogative regis*. This statute made individuals who were "natural fools" wards of the King and for the first time distinguished those whom we would now view as mentally retarded from those we would call mentally ill. These are merely isolated examples of efforts on behalf of the retarded. History is replete with other situations that were in diametric opposition and that generated extremely discriminatory and repressive practices. The retarded, as well as those with other handicapping conditions, have long been at the mercy of the more able majority.

This discussion has been focused on historical references to mental retardation. However, issues concerning the lives of the mentally retarded remain among our most pressing problems today. Many times we look at the postures of earlier societies as being extremely primitive and uninformed, but a serious examination of current thinking and practices results in a much more balanced perspective. The fight of numerous advocacy groups in the courts and other arenas is public testimony to the fact that many issues remain to be settled. It is quite likely that future professionals will view our present efforts as being nearly as primitive as we now consider those of the past.

A historical discussion of mental retardation, regardless of how brief it might be, cannot ignore the specter of reproductive sterilization, which has come to the fore periodically. The sterilization issue has always been deeply embroiled in numerous other questions such as nature versus nurture dispute, political and economic issues, and moral and social debates. However, at times publicity has been so extensive and emotionally charged that the issue of sterilization became a prominent dispute in and of itself.

Some early genealogical studies were very influential in generating the sterilization controversy in the United States. One such study reported by Goddard (1913) received particularly widespread attention. Goddard traced the descendants of a revolutionary war soldier whom he named Martin Kallikak. At one time in his life, Kallikak had sexual relations with a barmaid and fathered an illegitimate child. The descendants of this union were reported to be primarily thieves, prostitutes, and other social-moral undesirables. Kallikak later married a "normal woman" and their descendants were purportedly normal and, in some cases, superior. The resulting conclusion was that because of genetics, one group was doomed to a life of degeneracy, whereas the other was almost certainly destined to be successful. As a result of such reports, a sterilization movement was begun in the early part of this century. Support for controlling methods, such as sterilization and incarceration, became relatively widespread because of the fear of mental retardation. The result was an almost immediate and virtual destruction of special schools in some states. The purpose of the schools then became custodial in order to protect society and prevent reproduction. This represented a considerable philosophical shift, since there had previously been at least guarded optimism that institutions would be able to provide education and training for their retarded residents. Societal fears therefore have influenced the nature, role, and function of such institutions in society.

With the shift in purpose, the institutionalized retarded were viewed as permanent residents. They were in no way trained for an eventual return to society. Such actions represented simplistic solutions in terms of preventing "problem" members of society from having children (who might in turn also become problem citizens). This approach also provided a means of denying responsibility for undesirable social conditions for at least some proponents of institutionalization and sterilization.

Although sterilization remains an issue (15 states still have legal provision for compulsory sterilization), there has been a fortunate reevaluation of the situation. This has been the result of considerable expansion of knowledge concerning heredity as well as advances in the training of the mentally retarded. With increased sophistication in research methodology, serious questions began to be asked about previous studies such as Goddard's. For example, professionals are much less inclined to discount the effect of environmental influences on human development than was once the case. It is quite probable that the descendants of Kallikak and the barmaid were victims of their social situation as well as their heredity. On the other hand, the descendants of the second union received more favorable educational, social, and genetic influences. A rational perspective requires consideration of both dimensions to avoid decisions and practices based on inadequate evidence.

RETARDATION AND THE DISCIPLINES

Disciplinary Perspectives and Contributions

Reference has been made in both this and the preceding chapter to the variety of disciplines concerned with mental retardation. After a brief discussion of historical factors, we now turn our attention to the various dimensions of interdisciplinary collaboration related to the complex problem of mental retardation.

Core Concept 2   Persons with mental retardation often require a greater involvement by many disciplines/professions than those not considered retarded.

In a very real sense, persons with mental retardation are no different from the rest of the population. Their need for love, independence, support, and respect is the same as for everyone else. The necessary services for those with normal intelligence include medicine, education, psychology, sociology, anthropology, social work, and religion to name only a few areas. The mentally retarded may require attention from all of these disciplines also, but perhaps to an even greater degree. Here the previous notation concerning "no different" becomes an obvious overstatement. During the lifetime of retarded citizens, they will probably interact with a broader range of disciplines than their more able counterparts. This even more dramatically highlights a need to consider the multiple professions dealing with the retarded.

Core Concept 3   No single discipline has the necessary breadth and depth
of expertise and resources to provide for persons con-
sidered mentally retarded.

The understanding and delivery of services for individuals with mental retardation are far beyond the scope of any single discipline. As a social phenomenon, mental retardation is within the purview of a number of academic
areas. This has at times caused us to be unduly influenced about the nature
of the condition. For example, most people are surprised to find that approximately 15 to 20 percent of known cases of mental retardation can be
directly related to a biomedical cause; 80 to 85 percent is due to other and
unknown influences, of which environmental conditions are often suspected
(Bruininks and Warfield, 1978; Zigler, 1978).

The various disciplines are organized naturally around a circumscribed
body of knowledge. However, the intellectual parameters are somewhat
arbitrary (Campbell, 1969), and tend to overlap other disciplines and experience paradigmatic shifts over time (Kuhn, 1970). Still, the academic model
of establishing a disciplinary focus has been an effective method for directing
intellectual efforts in particular areas. However, societal problems do not
tend to align themselves according to disciplinary organizations. Before addressing the problem of better disciplinary cooperation, let us briefly examine some linguistic considerations and then explore contributions of some
disciplinary areas.

Terminology

Core Concept 4   The term *mental retardation* encompasses a wide range
of behavior; it is both a label of "fact" and a label of
"conjecture."

Mental retardation has a ring of precision to many persons. That is, one is
either mentally retarded or one is not. This is in part due to the scientific
orientation of the West in which constancy, regularity, and predictability
are assumed. As has been seen in past definitions of mental retardation, the
perceptions of the phenomenon have changed over time from being a genetically determined and incurable condition (e.g., Doll, 1941) toward a more
fluid conceptualization that not only includes biomedical causes but also
incorporates social factors in determining whether someone is retarded at

a given time (e.g., Grossman, 1973, 1977, 1983; Heber, 1961; Mercer, 1973). The change is the result of a number of factors, including advances in the natural and social sciences, economics, and the use of less temporally pejorative terms (i.e., mild, moderate, and severe/profound rather than moron, idiot and imbecile).

As a concept, mental retardation shares with other phenomena the distinction of being linguistically influenced. "Since language meaning develops in a social context it is not surprising there have been many definitions of mental retardation; time and conditions have had an important impact on determining its nature, scope, and importance within a society" (Logan, 1981, p. 3). As with other labels, that of mental retardation is an encompassing labeling term that includes a wide range of behavior depending on the social milieu in which it is invoked. It shares with other such "people-labeling terms" the attribute of being a convenient, generalized expression about persons or groups of persons.

As Cromwell, Blashfield, and Strauss (1975) have indicated, mental retardation is both a "label of fact" and a "label of conjecture." This linguistic separation is necessary to prevent the confusions of the past. A label of fact reflects the logical positivist tenets of being quantifiable and verifiable, whereas a label of conjecture is related to phenomenological concepts which are hypothesized and often ephemeral.

As a label of fact, mental retardation must demonstrate observed characteristics that are verifiable and quantifiable, usually ascertained by biomedical diagnosis. Classifications such as Down syndrome, Tay-Sachs disease, and anencephaly are examples of conditions that can be verified through observation and medical techniques, although only approximate intelligence levels can be quantified with extant tests. Only about 20 percent of mental retardation is caused by biomedical factors however. For the remaining approximately 80 percent of mentally retarded people, the actual cause is uncertain. Therefore, mental retardation is also a label of conjecture. Environmental influences have been a major area of speculation, as the incidence of milder forms of mental retardation appears to correlate with lower socioeconomic classes.

The framework within which a discipline views mental retardation influences societal perception of the nature and extent of the problem. The technologically oriented society of the United States responds to "breakthroughs," "cures," and "innovations" more than it does to the social complexity and ambiguous nature of cultural problems. The so-called natural sciences tend to be more favored by the population because the results seem more tangible and dramatic. The social sciences, on the other hand, are more suspect because their domains involve more directly the values, perceptions, and beliefs of the society.

The orientational framework of a discipline affects its view of the mentally retarded. Differences in orientation result from factors that led persons into their particular discipline and from the training philosophy inherent in each discipline. It is not surprising therefore that physicians look for medical causes, psychologists seek psychological factors, and sociologists are involved with group influences on the behavior of individuals. Obviously, each discipline, at least initially, sees a mentally retarded person from its own perspective and legitimately so. This should not preclude, however, the various professions from at least tangentially being aware of and appreciative of the contributions of their colleagues in related areas.

Contributions of Biological and Medical Sciences

Mental retardation as a label of fact is best exemplified in the areas involving an identifiable condition. These conditions are most frequently caused by a biomedical reason that results in structural damage to some degree. However, even in this area the cause of retardation is not always clear. Some chromosomal abnormalities are not always inherited (e.g., Down syndrome and microcephaly), and environmental factors can play a part in causing structural damage (e.g., lead poisoning and infections).

Core Concept 5   The medical profession has had a long history of involvement in the field of mental retardation.

The medical profession has long been involved in mental retardation in a number of ways. The physician is very frequently the first professional who is active in identification, diagnosis, and parent counseling. When the retardation is evident at birth (e.g., the more severely handicapped either by birth trauma or by congenital condition), the physician is usually the first professional to come in contact with the child. When retardation is not evident at birth but development is slower than usual, the physician is also frequently the first professional consulted. This is because most parents have a family physician or pediatrician with whom they have had previous contact. At this point, if something appears to be amiss, the parents will most likely turn to the professional they are accustomed to consulting.

In most cases the physician views retardation as a physiological problem. Although progressive changes are evident in the medical field, physicians frequently have not had the background to understand the nonmedical ramifications of mental retardation. This substantially limits the effectiveness with which they can approach the total impact that retardation has on a family. It certainly deters them from providing maximally effective parent counseling, which, as noted previously, has often been one of their tasks.

Changes in medical training promise considerable improvement in the physician's overall impact on the field of mental retardation.

One other important area of the medical field certainly warrants mention—that of medical research. Advances in medical research have had a dramatic impact on certain types of mental retardation. Because of intense efforts in investigating some of the clinical syndromes, such as phenylketonuria (PKU) and hypoparathyroidism, it has become possible and even common practice to implement procedures that will prevent some forms of mental retardation. To reach this point, however, collaboration across disciplinary lines was required. Once the causal factor was identified through medical research, it became necessary to turn to those skilled in chemistry and nutrition to implement actual preventive measures. Thus, even in what appears to be a very limited area—preventing a few selected types of mental retardation—the importance of interdisciplinary effort is evident.

The first major breakthrough was discovering the cause of cretinism to be iodine deficiency, which often resulted in retardation to some degree. However, not until the discovery of the cause of PKU in 1934 was there a surge of interest by biomedical researchers. Since that time, medical research has made significant contributions to the prevention of some types of mental retardation. In particular, research at the cellular level has spurred biomedical research.

Advances in the field of genetics have opened avenues that allow us to prevent some forms of mental retardation. Present research in genetic engineering gives the promise of the future elimination of many of the more extreme deviations. As with many advances, both positive and negative aspects must be considered. At present some forms of mental retardation are preventable before conception. Prospective parents who may be carriers of defective genes can undergo genetic screening and receive counseling regarding the likelihood of their having defective offspring. Parents at risk are then faced with the decision whether to have children. Similar options are currently available to parents who have conceived but face the probability of giving birth to a defective infant. The many moral and social issues surrounding these decisions can well be imagined.

The discipline of psychiatry has a very lengthy history in dealing with mental retardation. Potter (1971) noted that, when the American Association on Mental Deficiency was organized in 1876, it began with eight charter members, all of whom were psychiatrists.

Psychiatrists, when they have dealt with the mentally retarded, have primarily focused on the more severely handicapped. This has resulted in a rather inaccurate perspective with regard to the broad spectrum of mental retardation. In addition, past approaches have tended to operate from a curative, traditional medical model. In view of such a posture it is little wonder that the profession in general has become somewhat discouraged and uninterested in mental retardation. However, leaders and thinkers in psychiatry have advocated a rather dramatic shift in viewpoint from the microscopic approaches of the past. Menolascino (1970) has suggested that the psychiatrist should begin to function more as a generalist than in the past. Such an approach would be more commensurate with the many facets associated with mental retardation, particularly the community mental health viewpoint, which includes persons who are mildly retarded. Potter (1971) similarly sees the role of the psychiatrist shifting. He notes that the modern psychiatrist, at least in the United States, is more a behavioral scientist than a medical scientist. With such forces at work within the discipline of psychiatry there is considerable hope that disciplinary territories will become less distinct, which would be a potentially positive shift for more adequate delivery of services to the retarded.

Contributions of the Behavioral Sciences

Core Concept 6   Many behavioral sciences, particularly psychology, have been concerned with mental retardation.

Since mental retardation is in part a social phenomenon, it would be expected that the academic areas concerned with behavior would have expressed interest in the condition. Although there have been many important contributions, most behavioral science disciplines have been only tangentially involved with mental retardation. They have generally operated independently and within the confines of their own terminology and parameters. The consequent reduction in effective contributions to the education of the mentally retarded has been previously documented (Drew, Freston, & Logan, 1972) and perhaps exemplifies the importance of interdisciplinary collaborations. Still the contribution of each of these disciplines has added to the store of knowledge about mental retardation.

Psychology has been the most directly involved in studying mental retardation of all the behavioral science disciplines. Perhaps the three most important areas to which psychology has contributed are intelligence theory and testing, learning theory research, and social aspects. Since each of these will be further discussed in succeeding chapters, only a brief review will be presented. Although intelligence testing was initially developed by a physician (Alfred Binet) at the behest of educators, psychologists such as Lewis Terman, Maud Merrill, and David Wechsler refined and expanded the earlier tests. Learning theory has had direct implications for the mentally retarded. The work of such learning theorists as J. B. Watson, B. F. Skinner, D. O. Hebb, Albert Bandura, Julian Rotter, and Jean Piaget (an ethnologist) among many others, has made significant contributions in developing theories that help explain human learning behavior. Few of these theorists, however, have directly addressed mental retardation, but their ideas have prompted others to extend their work to persons with subaverage mental functioning (e.g., Rue Cromwell's application of Rotter's social learning theory, Sidney Bijou's and Ogden Lindsley's applications of Skinnerian behaviorist models, and Mary Woodward's extension of Piaget's work to the mentally retarded).

Anthropology as a discipline has focused very little attention on mental retardation, and yet it might offer some extremely important insights into the broader perspective of the problem. Edgerton (1968) described the anthropological study of mental retardation as essentially nonexistent and makes a plea for drastically expanded efforts in this regard. An earlier work by Edgerton (1967) represents the most visible contribution by an anthropologist and has resulted in significant information concerning the adaptation of the retarded to their environments. Although the data provided by Edgerton (1967) and Edgerton and Bercovici (1976) were important in and of themselves, this research approach makes contributions that appear to have far-reaching implications in other ways.

From the standpoint of research methodology, anthropology offers some intriguing possibilities. The anthropological approach to research is basically one of observing and recording information about people in their natural environment. This is a substantially different approach from that usually used in the study of mental retardation. More often than not, mental retardation researchers have adopted an experimental psychology research method, whereby the mentally retarded person is studied in terms of performance or reaction to some artificially imposed treatment or situation. Consequently, we know little about the performance or adaptation of the retarded in a variety of environments. The anthropological method of investigation may provide useful information that will complement the knowledge base that presently exists. In fact, it has been suggested that educational planning might profit substantially from knowledge about how the retarded individual operates in a natural setting (Drew, 1971). At any rate, anthropology represents a discipline that has not been heavily involved in mental retardation to date, but one that may contribute meaningfully in an interdisciplinary effort.

Sociology is an area that has been involved in mental retardation, at least tangentially, for a number of years (Farber, 1968, 1986; Mercer, 1973). A recent series of articles (Carrier, 1986a, 1986b; Milofsky, 1986) has addressed the use of sociological models in placing special education in a historical framework. The articles discuss the need to view disabilities from a sociological perspective rather than from the traditional clinical model (e.g., categories, severity levels, syndromes, etc.). Such issues should become increasingly important in the years to come as the United States and other countries continue to be faced with "competing equities." The work of Mercer and Lewis (1977) in developing a pluralistic model for assessment is but one example of a multidisciplinary approach to diagnosis. Their system of multicultural pluralistic assessment (SOMPA) is derived from a multidisciplinary conceptualization of the problem with a definite sociological base. However, the potential contribution of sociology toward our understanding of the retarded in a larger societal framework has been largely untapped. For example, Wolfensberger's (1972) work relating to normalization is an area that would appear to be particularly fruitful from a sociological perspective.

The preceding discussion of selected disciplines is intended to exemplify disciplinary perspectives as well as to stress the absence of essential interaction between them. Other areas could easily have been selected for inclusion because of their attention (or lack of it) to mental retardation. Certainly psychology has contributed from many standpoints; knowledge about mental retardation would not have progressed as far as it has without the data and knowledge generated from experimental psychology. Likewise, the testing and evaluation provided by psychometric researchers and school psychologists have long been a part of the overall picture in providing programs for the mentally retarded. This discipline, as with others, has frequently operated independently, within the confines of its own terminology and perspective.

The law has periodically been an important force in the area of mental retardation. Unfortunately, the legal profession, as opposed to other disciplines, has often found it necessary to operate in an adversary role. Such a situation is exemplified by the case of *Covarrubias v. San Diego United School District*, in which special class placements were challenged. An injunction negated further placements until procedural changes were made. Only recently have collaborative alliances been formed between the legal and other professions (Turnbull and Turnbull, 1975).

Many other disciplines and sub-areas within disciplines have interacted with problems associated with mental retardation in one fashion or another. A full discussion of each and a detailed examination of the respective frameworks are far beyond the scope of this text; entire textbooks have been written that attend to only a single area as it relates to mental retardation (e.g., on psychiatry, Menolascino, 1970; on social work, Schreiber, 1970).

Contributions of Education

Core Concept 7   Education has probably been more centrally concerned
with problems associated with mental retardation than
any other discipline or profession.

Many other areas have contact with individuals with mental retardation as the need or interest arises; however, education—specifically special education—is comprehensively involved by its nature and delegated role in our society. Educators do not have the luxury of viewing the world from a restricted framework or retreating behind disciplinary fences when faced with the multidisciplinary needs of the mentally retarded. The role of education in mental retardation has been primarily one of instruction. However, in a service delivery model, instruction is an oversimplification because people do not exist in isolation nor learn in a vacuum. The real contribution of education in aiding the understanding of mental retardation has been one of *(a)* identifying needs, *(b)* stimulating research and theory, and *(c)* coordinating a host of disciplinary services.

A litany of the direct and indirect influences of education in furthering the knowledge and service provisions for the retarded is perhaps not necessary. However, to specify a few events would perhaps aid in placing the contribution of education in perspective. The first intelligence test worthy of the name was developed by Alfred Binet at the behest of the French Minister of Public Education. The task was to develop a way of identifying children who would probably fail in the regular programs and would need special help. The measurement of intelligence has therefore been largely influenced by educational needs rather than disciplinary concern, per se. Intelligence testing forced the realization that people differ in *degree* rather than in *kind* and that a single test was inadequate in determining mental retardation. Over the years it was recognized initially by educators and then by theorists and test makers that personality factors were also important in determining both present and future performance levels of a child. We have since been introduced to the concepts of "adaptive behavior" and "social intelligence." It is submitted that these and other constructs were greatly facilitated by the involvement of education with the mentally retarded. In other areas the great strides in differential diagnosis, individualization of instruction, task analysis, and contingency management techniques were all enhanced by educators and their interest in providing better services for the retarded. For example, the need to understand mild mental retardation has influenced research efforts in increasing our understanding of the importance of environmental influences on intelligence. The development of secondary school programs has created a need for appropriate curriculum and has prompted research in sociological factors that relate to community placement for adolescent and young adult mentally retarded persons.

It is believed that, without the proactive recognition by education of the needs of the mentally retarded, we would be nowhere near where we are today in either understanding or providing service for this group of people. This is not to disparage the academic disciplines and their contributions but only to place the relative contributions of each into proper perspective. Education often has been a central core from which disciplinary contributions have been stimulated and used for the betterment of society.

Disciplinary Factionalism

Core Concept 8	There is a continuing need to overcome disciplinary friction in order to better serve and provide for individuals with mental retardation.

The foregoing discussion has outlined various disciplinary perspectives. As one reviews their contributions, it becomes evident that efforts within a profession, in isolation of meaningful interdisciplinary collaboration, often result in less effective delivery of services to the retarded. This discussion should not be taken to mean that a totally pessimistic outlook prevails. Although change has been slow, there are indications that considerable progress is being made toward bridging gaps between disciplinary perspectives as well as diminishing disciplinary friction. The latter will be examined shortly.

At least two influences have prompted such progress. First of all, experience has shown that the mentally retarded persons being served are the ultimate victims of inadequate cooperation. This has provided considerable impetus toward rectifying the situation. The second influence that has promoted change involves the realization that something can actually be done to promote interdisciplinary collaboration and that it may not be so terribly difficult to accomplish. Differences in perspective as well as disciplinary friction are generated at least partially by knowledge that is limited to professional boundaries. In most situations in which progress has been evident, there have been persons in an area who have accumulated at least some knowledge about the cooperating discipline. This has not meant that a professional in one discipline has had to acquire advanced expertise in the other area, but it has involved the acquisition of at least enough information that an understanding of the other perspective is possible. Occasionally the broadened knowledge base may also indicate that what appeared to be differences in perspective were actually not as divergent as they were first thought to be.

Friction between disciplines is frequently not discussed openly but remains operative at a sub rosa level. It is a fact of life, regardless of how undesirable or irrational it may be. The present examination is sequenced, following the note on improvement in interdisciplinary cooperation, to remind the reader that progress is being made, a point that might be overlooked if the sequence were reversed.

Beyond the problems resulting from different perspectives per se, professional jealousy and perceived territorial rights often serve to generate additional differences to a point where open antagonistic factionalism sometimes exists between persons in different disciplines. Such factionalism operates at numerous levels ranging from published criticism to the daily interaction by practitioners working in the field of mental retardation. To some degree the examination of roles and issues in the public forum, such as published articles, is more healthy than other approaches and may often be constructive. Obviously the most positive outcomes may be expected when such an article represents a rational examination of issues (Roos, 1971) rather than an emotionally charged attack that generates a defensive response instead of positive dialogue.

Dissonance is frequently evident among various disciplines within an organization. Although this phenomenon may be observed in a variety of settings, some of the most visible examples are within professional organizations that deal with mental retardation. One has only to attend regional or national conventions to hear derogatory comments about "the medical contingent," "those educators," "this division," or "that psychology group." Such an atmosphere results more in political conflict than in constructive improvement and tends to deter substantially from interdisciplinary collaboration. These comments have been essentially unchanged in all editions of this text. It is fortunate that collaborative advances have been made, but the problem still remains.

Beyond the professional organization level, similar factionalism exists openly in state service and political arenas. Because agencies frequently compete for limited funds with which to carry on their programs, and lobbying techniques may involve divisive interdisciplinary competition aimed at improving the lot of one group by making another appear inadequate. Although such tactics are obviously valuable in terms of agency or disciplinary self-preservation, they often cause people to lose sight of the real reason for cooperation: to serve the mentally retarded.

With the previously noted factionalism existing at various levels, it is of little surprise that some friction also occurs at the practitioner level, the contact point between the service delivery system and the client. The same professional jealousies and perceived territorial rights are operative in daily interactions between the various professionals who are in actual contact with the retarded. The teacher may become angry because the school psychologist does not provide information that is helpful in terms of instruction. The psychologist may derogate the teacher for being unable to understand the psychological report and make the intuitive leap to instructional activities. Examples could be endless, but the point is made. Beyond the differences in the way the retarded individual is viewed—whether from the standpoint of instruction or that of test performance—an overlay of professional antagonism magnifies the problem of inadequate cooperation.

Disciplinary factionalism becomes most blatantly unpalatable when it is discussed in the context of the practitioner. It is here that it becomes most obvious who suffers as a result of an inability to cooperate, but it is also the level at which improvement appears to be most evident. The practitioner has greater opportunity to view the unfortunate results of inadequate service than those professionals more removed and serving in other capacities. It is therefore much more difficult to ignore or remain unaware of the crucial necessity of interdisciplinary cooperation and mutual effort.

Overcoming Factionalism

There are two broad aspects that must be differentiated relative to cooperative relations between disciplines. One is the knowledge base, and the other is the service base.

The accumulation of data from which knowledge is developed is perhaps best approached through both multidisciplinary and interdisciplinary models. Multidisciplinary efforts are those in which the various disciplines approach a particular problem from their own disciplinary focus (e.g., psychological aspects of mental retardation, medical aspects of mental retardation, etc.). The data base of each discipline is thereby enhanced, but frequently little information is generated relative to overcoming disciplinary boundaries in terminology and concepts. The interdisciplinary model, on the other hand, exemplifies attempts to develop "knowledge bridges" between disciplines. As a consequence, we have subdisciplinary areas such as social psychology, sociolinguistics, and neuropsychology.

There has recently been a serious movement in special education to terminate the labeling of handicapping conditions. Terms such as mental retardation, behavior disorders, and learning disabilities, although convenient for communication, frequently tell extremely little about the individual child's characteristics or skill level. Likewise, the terms evolved in social contexts tend to assume an entity status that may be inappropriate and thus result in imprecise application and inaccurate generalizations. Tradition has also designated disciplines by labels, such as psychology, education, and psychiatry, which are extremely convenient for communication and a variety of other purposes. Contemporary society could not operate without terminology that indicates labels or that designates or classifies events and phenomena. Disciplinary labels generate certain difficulties, however. They communicate in restricted settings or areas, but they also generate a myriad of connotations concerning what each discipline represents. They also frequently serve to delineate territorial boundaries of operation—territorial rights. Such territorial rights have been noted earlier as a deterrent to effective interdisciplinary collaboration.

It has previously been suggested that a broadened knowledge base appears to facilitate interdisciplinary collaboration. In retrospect this seems only logical and perhaps even simplistic. Without at least some information about another person's profession it is extremely difficult to even communicate, much less effectively collaborate on a task.

Knowledge may be acquired in a variety of fashions. Naturally, we are quite experienced at obtaining information by reading such materials as journals and books. In many cases, however, this approach alone does not provide an adequate foundation to break down interdisciplinary barriers. An additional means of broadening knowledge and perspective is necessary. Personal and open contact with individuals from other professions serves this purpose well. In fact, some would maintain that such contact is not only helpful but a prerequisite to facilitating interdisciplinary efforts.

When the topic of interdisciplinary collaboration is raised, people often indicate that a change in attitude is necessary for it to occur. Although most would agree with such a statement, few would be able to specify how this might be accomplished. Attitude is an extremely elusive concept and rather difficult to define. Consequently, it is not at all easy to determine how one knows when an attitude has changed. It is somewhat easier, however, to speak in terms of certain behaviors that need to be altered.

One behavioral change that appears important for interdisciplinary collaboration involves reaction to terminology differences. Frequently there are rather dramatic differences in terminology between professions. Such terminology differences often seem to generate negative reactions, sometimes even openly derogatory remarks, from individuals with different disciplinary perspectives. It is easy to see how such reaction lends itself to friction and antagonism rather than to cooperation. Consequently, the individuals involved in an interdisciplinary task must overlook or control reactions to differences in terms. This does not mean that one must adopt another's terms, concepts, and approaches, but it does imply that value judgments about the appropriateness of the approach of the individual from the other discipline should be minimal. For example, I may not choose to incorporate "ego strength" into my vocabulary or conceptualization, but if that is an important term in your disciplinary perspective, I can understand its meaning and judge it as different but not inappropriate terminology. Certainly, the acceptance of "differentness" is a goal of persons working for the benefit of the mentally retarded. Such improvements in interactions among professions can result in far less friction and ultimately promote greater effectiveness in terms of interdisciplinary collaboration.

The second major aspect to be considered is the delivery of services to the mentally retarded. As with the generation of knowledge, the same terms (multidisciplinary and interdisciplinary) have been used and in much the same way. We have seen the various disciplines operating through their applied branches (e.g., educational psychology, social work, etc.) working independently of one another. The educator has often been left with a series of tests and reports that are for the most part meaningless relative to educational planning for a given child. In an interdisciplinary service approach model, although assessments are independently derived, the program parameters are collaboratively decided. There have been some drawbacks to this approach, however. Hardman, Drew, and Egan (1984) have pointed out that too often professional cooperation has diminished after the initial program development, and efforts at coordinating services are often limited.

A third method called the transdisciplinary approach has emerged as an effort to overcome concerns associated with the other two models. The approach emphasizes a role of primary therapist, who acts as the contact person for service provisions, so that the number of professionals having direct child contact is minimal. Hart (1977) has indicated that in this plan no discipline is dominant, but all have the purpose of supporting each other and making their unique contributions. This approach is most evident in specific situations and requires a professional and mature attitude that recognizes and allows for relevant disciplinary contributions. The emphasis is on the mentally retarded person and his or her needs rather than on the disciplines working independently or without coordination.

One of the most crucial points to be made in a chapter on disciplinary collaboration involves the purpose of the professional effort to begin with. Often workers in the various disciplines that attend the mentally retarded lose sight of the appropriate focus for their effort—the retarded citizen. Far too much time and attention are devoted to professional self-preservation, sometimes to the detriment of the individuals being served. We frequently focus more on our professional image than on the needs of the retarded. Whether the perspective is primarily one of medicine, education, psychology, or any of the other disciplines involved, it is essential that we maintain our focus on serving the total individual.

Core Questions

1. How did political, economic and basic life-styles affect the lives of persons with mental retardation before 1900?
2. What were some of the factors that influenced the development of institutions for persons with mental retardation in the United States?
3. Why is the term "mental retardation" considered to be linguistically influenced?
4. Why is mental retardation both a label of "fact" and a label of "conjecture"?
5. What is the difference between the "medical field" and "medical research"?
6. What are three areas in which psychology has contributed to our understanding of those with mental retardation?
7. What are the primary contributions of education in helping to understand the phenomenon of mental retardation?
8. What are some of the reasons that disciplinary factionalism has arisen and continues to exist?
9. What can be done to reduce frictions between disciplines and professions involved with persons with mental retardation?

ROUND TABLE
DISCUSSION

As a concept, mental retardation has been with us throughout recorded history. Our perception of what is and what is not deemed "mentally retarded" has continually changed through time. With the development of scientific approaches to the study of human behavior, many disciplines and professions emerged and began to identify areas of primary investigation, concern, and service.

In a discussion group consider the societal influences on mental retardation and how they may or may not be reflected in present-day attitudes toward persons with mental retardation. What would be some realistic approaches to overcoming disciplinary/professions friction?

REFERENCES

Bruininks, R. H., & Warfield, G. (1978). The mentally retarded. In E. L. Meyen (Ed.), *Exceptional children and youth: An introduction*. Denver: Love.

Campbell, D. G. (1969). Ethnocentrism of disciplines and the risk-scale model of omniscience. In M. Sherif and C.W. Sherif (Eds.), *Interdisciplinary relations in the social sciences*. Chicago: Aldine.

Carrier, J. G. (1986a). Sociology and special education: Differentiation and allocation in mass education. *American Journal of Education, 94*, 281–312.

Carrier, J. G. (1986b). Reply to Milofsky's comments on "sociology and special education." *American Journal of Education, 94*, 322–327.

Cromwell, R. L., Blashfield, R. K., & Strauss, T. S. (1975). Criteria for classification systems. In N. Hobbs (Ed.), *Issues in the classification of children*, (Vol. 1, pp. 4–25). San Francisco: Jossey-Bass.

Doll, E. A. (1941). The essentials of an inclusive concept of mental deficiency. *American Journal of Mental Deficiency, 46*, 214–219.

Drew, C. J. (1971). Research on social adjustment and the mentally retarded: Functioning and training. *Mental Retardation, 9*, 26–29.

Drew, C. J., Freston, C. W., and Logan, D. R. (1972). Criteria and reference in evaluation. *Focus on Exceptional Children, 4*, 1–10.

Edgerton, R. B. (1967). *The cloak of competence: Stigma in the lives of the mentally retarded*. Berkeley: University of California.

Edgerton, R. B. (1968). Anthropology and mental retardation: A plea for the comparative study of incompetence. In H. J. Prehm, L. A. Hamerlynck, and J. E. Crosson (Eds.), *Behavioral research in mental retardation* (pp. 75–87). Eugene, OR: Rehabilitation Research and Training Center in Mental Retardation.

Edgerton, R. B., & Bercovici, S. M. (1976). The cloak of competence: Years later. *American Journal of Mental Deficiency, 80*, 485–497.

Farber, B. (1968). Sociological research in mental retardation. In H. J. Prehm, L. A. Hamerlynck, & J. E. Crosson (Eds.), *Behavioral research in mental retardation* (pp. 97–109). Eugene, OR: Rehabilitation Research and Training Center in Mental Retardation.

Farber, B. (1986). Families with mentally retarded members: An agenda for research 1985–2000. In J. J. Gallagher & B. B. Weiner (Eds.), *Alternative Futures in Special Education* (pp. 25–41). Reston, VA: The Council for Exceptional Children.

Goddard, H. H. (1913). *The Kallikak family.* New York: Macmillan.

Grossman, H. J. (Ed.). (1973). *Manual on terminology and classification in mental retardation.* Washington, DC: American Association on Mental Deficiency.

Grossman, H. J. (Ed.). (1977). *Manual on terminology and classification in mental retardation.* Washington, DC: American Association on Mental Deficiency.

Grossman, H. J. (1983). *Classification in mental retardation.* Washington, DC: American Association on Mental Deficiency.

Hardman, M. L., Drew, C. J., & Egan, M. W. (1984). *Human exceptionality: Society, school and family.* Boston: Allyn & Bacon.

Hart, V. (1977). The use of many disciplines with the severely and profoundly handicapped. In E. Sontag (Ed.), *Educational programming for the severely and profoundly handicapped* (pp. 391–396). Reston, VA: Council for Exceptional Children.

Heber, R. L. (1961). A manual on terminology and classification in mental retardation (2nd ed.). *American Journal of Mental Deficiency, Monograph Supplement.*

Kuhn, T. S. (1970). *The structure of scientific revolutions.* Chicago: University of Chicago.

Logan, D. R. (1981). *Mental retardation and public policy.* Paper given at the Third Linguistic Institute on Language and Public Policy, Cancun, Mexico.

Menolascino, F. J. (1970). Psychiatry's past, current and future role in mental retardation. In F.J. Menolascino (Ed.), *Psychiatric approaches to mental retardation* (pp. 709–744). New York: Basic Books.

Mercer, J. (1973). *Labelling the mentally retarded: Clinical and social perspective on mental retardation.* Berkeley: University of California.

Mercer, J. R., and Lewis, J. F. (1977). *System of multicultural pluralistic assessment.* New York: The Psychological Corp.

Milofsky, C. (1986). Is the growth of special education evolutionary or cyclic? A response to Carrier. *American Journal of Education, 94,* 313–321.

Potter, H. W. (1971). Mental retardation: The Cinderella of psychiatry. In F. J. Menolascino (Ed.), *Psychiatric aspects of the diagnosis and treatment of mental retardation* (pp. 14–27). Seattle: Special Child Publications.

Roos, P. (1971). Misinterpreting criticisms of the medical model. *Mental Retardation, 9,* 22–24.

Scheerenberger, R. C. (1982). *A history of mental retardation.* Baltimore: Paul H. Brookes.

Schreiber, M. (Ed.). (1970). *Social work and mental retardation.* New York: John Day.

Turnbull, H. R., III, & Turnbull, A. P. (1975). Deinstitutionalization and the law. *Mental Retardation, 13,* 14–20.

Wolfensberger, W., with Nirje, B., Olshansky, S., Perske, R., & Roos, P. (1972). *The principle of normalization in human service systems.* Ontario, Canada: National Institute on Mental Retardation.

Zigler, E. (1978). National crisis in mental retardation research. *American Journal of Mental Deficiency, 83,* 1–8.

3

Theories of Intelligence

Early Speculations About Intelligence
Toward a Scientific Approach
   The Concept of Intelligence
Development of Intelligence
   Factors Influencing Intelligence
Measurement of Intelligence
Contemporary Trends
Core Questions
Round Table Discussion
References

Core Concepts 1. Of all of the ways people differ, none has generated as much continuing interest and speculation as has the concept of intelligence.

2. As people have moved from primarily hunting-gathering and/or agrarian societies an interest in the development of intelligence has been emphasized.

3. The relationship between intelligence and mental retardation was established soon after the application of the scientific approach to the study of human behavior.

4. Intelligence, due to the development of quantitative measures, has too often been thought of as linear, but due to societal influences qualitative aspects also must be considered.

5. The question of whether intelligence is primarily genetically determined or environmentally influenced was stimulated by discussion about the causes of mental retardation.

6. The influence of a person's perceptions, expectations, and motivations has stimulated research on the environmental influences on intelligence.

7. The measurement of intelligence has generated considerable controversy regarding definition.

8. Guilford and Piaget: Two different approaches to the complex task of understanding the nature of intelligence.

Core Concept 1 Of all of the ways people differ, none has generated as much interest and speculation as has the concept of intelligence.

The fact that individuals differ in a variety of ways has long been recognized. Human differences are concretely manifested by height, weight, skin and hair coloring, physical coordination, sex, and many other distinctive attributes that allow for recognizable differentiation of people. In much more subtle ways we also are able to differentiate people in regard to their creativity, personality, and intelligence, to name but a few of the more abstract human traits. All of these traits are of interest, but none has been as controversial as the concept of intelligence. Intelligence has been an intriguing subject for philosophers, psychologists, and lay people for a variety of reasons. In Western culture few concepts have been as avidly pursued as has intelligence, both from definitional and measurable dimension. Indeed, we have been so caught up in quantitative perspectives that we may have difficulty keeping the concept in focus.

Perhaps two causes of the problem are *(a)* our too-rapid development of tests that purport to reflect intelligence and *(b)* the simplistic notion that test performance is valid and reliable regardless of cultural and/or motivational influences. There certainly has not been a lack of awareness regarding these influences. Investigators in all behavioral sciences have pointed out the definitional problems engendered and the influence of behaviors that do not lend themselves to quantification in any direct sense. Our "success" in developing tests is perhaps our greatest handicap, particularly if the tests neglect other relevant aspects of intelligent behavior such as the influence of social and cultural mores, early environmental influences, physical development, and sexual role expectations.

Core Concept 2   As people have moved from primarily hunting-gathering and/or agrarian societies an interest in the development of intelligence has been emphasized.

Intelligence as a phenomenon has been of interest for centuries. At what point people became aware of differences in mental abilities is of little consequence, but it surely antedates recorded history. As the gregarious nature of humans became evident through social groupings, the need to specify skills and competencies of various group members became a priority to facilitate an efficacious division of labor. The need to effectively prepare individuals for group membership became a problem when it became grossly evident that some were more skilled in some areas than others. As societies developed and became more and more complex, the need to explain individual differences became increasingly important. The development of theories of intelligence parallels society's progress from hunting groups through agrarian communities to industrial metropolitan areas and into the atomic and space-age megalopolitan regions.

Intelligence has become an extremely important concept in some cultures. Societies that have moved away from primarily hunting-gathering and agricultural pursuits, and have instead pursued industrial and information capabilities, require people who possess greater abstract intellectual abilities. Each society emphasizes those areas that best provide for its needs and common welfare. In less technologically advanced societies, skill in hunting, fishing, farming and so on primarily calls for a sound body, capable of many hours of hard physical work. In those societies that have emphasized technology, machinery has been developed to the extent that physical ability is a declining requirement for employability. To be able to function at a minimal level in a technological society, education has become more and more a necessity.

The advent of the space age and the development of world markets emphasized the need to identify those who have high intellectual ability. Governments of industrial nations have spurred searches and provided concomitant rewards for the intellectually capable through government grants for higher education, merit scholarships, and the promise of exciting, well-paid positions in a variety of areas. Conversely, this emphasis has also brought about an increased attention to those whose intellectual capabilities are limited.Such individuals constitute a concern in technologically advanced societies because they frequently become social liabilities. In less mechanized times those individuals with limited intellectual ability could often make a contribution to the immediate social milieu. As technology has advanced and influenced the entire spectrum of society, the need for unskilled and semiskilled individuals has diminished as machines now more effectively do the work formerly done by individuals with little formal education. This has not been a great problem to those who have the requisite intellectual ability but simply lack the necessary educational training to do more skilled labor. The public school system in the United States has made an outstanding contribution in helping to provide the academic experiences required. However, for those who cannot profit educationally to the same extent as their more intellectually endowed fellow citizens, the opportunities for high status and a fulfilling life have sharply decreased. Any humane society must therefore explore ways to reduce the social and economic liability of all the less-gifted citizens, including the mentally retarded, and at the same time provide educational opportunities commensurate with those individuals' intellectual abilities. Since self-respect often depends on developing resources through education, to do less degrades and demeans both the citizens of a society and the society itself.

The need to identify and isolate particular characteristics that are associated with limited mental ability, both from biological and environmental causes, becomes a paramount consideration. As has been inferred, limited intellectual ability has been identified as the central problem. The term "intelligence," connoting relative intellectual brightness, has been a popular abstraction for centuries. Intelligence as a concept has been variously recognized by most civilized cultures as an important factor for group survival, development and progress, but as with other abstractions it has been an elusive, mercurial concept to define. The need to understand, define, and measure this phenomenon remains an important task as we attempt to provide better care for the mentally retarded in our society.

Humankind's attempts to come to grips with intelligence is manifested in an almost infinite number of theories about its nature. Theories play a vital role in assisting us as we attempt to delineate and specify the inherent nature or substance of intelligence, as they do with other presently unexplainable phenomena. Intelligence is not a directly observable phenomenon but in many respects a will-o'-the-wisp because of the influence of social values, socioeconomic conditions, and technological advances that tend to affect our perception, both individually and collectively. Because this is so, well-delineated theories can assist us in identifying its relevant attributes for further empirical investigations. Theories, as Marx (1963) observed, serve the dual purpose of being both a tool and a goal. Theories assist us in developing researchable hypotheses for empirical investigation and are goals in providing scientists with a way of integrating and ordering existing empirical laws (Marx, 1963).

The following sections attempt to trace the development of theories about intelligence from early times through the present day. The intent is to provide the reader with a historical appreciation for the problems encountered in humankind's attempts to investigate intellectual capabilities.

EARLY SPECULATIONS ABOUT INTELLIGENCE

Concern about cognitive abilities and the recognition of individual differences can be traced to the Chinese, who used testing to determine capabilities of applicants for civil service positions over 4,000 years ago (Linden and Linden, 1968). The earliest recorded mention of mental retardation is thought to be in the Therapeutic Papyrus of Thebes in 1552 B.C. (Doll, 1962). Plato in *The Republic* recognized the importance of determining individual differences in intelligence. Greek philosophers such as Anaxagoras (c. 528–500 B.C.), Diogenes (412–323 B.C.), and Aristotle (384–322 B.C.) were interested in and concerned with the mind relative to its composition and nature. The Greek physician Hippocrates (460–375 B.C.) and the Roman physician Galen (c. A.D. 139–200) attempted to provide a natural, as opposed to a supernatural, explanation of mental abilities and mental phenomena.

The use of achievement examinations in Western culture "dates back approximately to the year 1200, when the University of Bologna in Italy held the first oral examination for the Ph.D. degree" (Linden & Linden, 1968, p. 19). An early interest was the need to identify the mental ability of a person charged with a crime. Sir Anthony Fitz-Herbert (1470–1538) is credited with being the first to provide a working definition that was legally useful and that included developmental, intellectual, and social aspects— giving it a fairly modern ring:

> And he who shall be said to be a sot (i.e., simpleton) and idiot from his birth, is such a person who cannot account or number twenty pence, nor can tell who was his father or mother, nor how old he is, etc., so as it may appear that he hath no understanding, that he know and understand his letters, and so read by teaching or information of another man, then it seemeth he is not a sot nor a natural idiot. (Quoted in Doll, 1962, p. 50)

Swineburne (1560–1623) added as tests the ability to measure cloth or to repeat the names of the days of the week (Linden & Linden, 1968) to assist in determining a lawbreaker's mental ability and, consequently, that person's responsibility under the law. The seventeenth-century legal criterion for responsibility was that the person charged needed to have the understanding of a 14-year-old (Linden & Linden, 1968). In earlier times society had difficulty differentiating between retardation and mental illness. Doll (1962, p. 23) quotes John Locke, who in 1690 provided what is purported to be the first usable differentiation between "idiocy" and "insanity": "Herein seems to lie the difference between idiots and madmen, that madmen put wrong ideas together and reason from them, but idiots make very few or no propositions and reason scarce at all."

Many questioned the feasibility of attempting to quantify mental abilities, simply because of the intangible and elusive nature of the concept. Linden and Linden (1968) report that de Malenbranche (c. 1675), who believed that mental ability was not measurable, was later supported by Plouequet (c. 1763) and Kant (c. 1786). However, others felt that it was possible to measure psychic ability. "Wolff advocated a 'science of psychometry' and Eberhard (c. 1776 and c. 1786) believed that 'a mathematics of the soul' could be devised. Eschenmayer (c. 1822) recognized the possibility of 'psychical' measurements" (Linden & Linden, 1968, p. 1).

As early as the sixteenth century Juan Huarte, a Spanish physician cited in *Examen du Ingenios*, aptly identified mental abilities when he wrote:

> All the ancient philosophers have found by experience that where nature disposes not a man for knowledge, 'tis in vain for him to labor in the fules (fools) of the art. But not one of them has clearly and distinctly declared what that nature is, which renders a man fit for one, and unfit for another science, nor what differences of wit is observed among men, nor what arts and sciences are most suitable to each man in particular, nor by what marks they may be discerned, which is one of the greatest importance. (Roback, 1961, p. 25)

While Huarte was naturally influenced by the theories of his day, he did pinpoint some of the problems in attempting definitions and subsequent measurement difficulties.

TOWARD A SCIENTIFIC APPROACH

Core Concept 3   The relationship between intelligence and mental retardation was established soon after the application of a scientific approach to the study of human behavior.

For all intents and purposes, the application of the scientific approach to human behavior began with a group of researchers who in the late eighteenth and early nineteenth centuries began investigating individual differences. Their academic backgrounds represented a variety of scientific disciplines, from astronomy to philosophy. They became interested in differences in individual observations, both among observers reacting to the same phenomenon or event and within an individual over repeated observations. Since observational variations influenced the scientific approach with its demands for accuracy and reliability, many scientists became interested in being able to control and/or account for the now recognized influence of individual differences. Through the work of Ernst Weber (1795–1878), Gustav Fechner (1801–1887), and Wilhelm Wundt (1832–1920), the application of scientific principles was first utilized in a systematic manner to explore human behavior through investigations of individual differences. Weber's work in the psychological realm spurred Fechner, a contemporary, to expand and provide mathematical formulations to Weber's investigation in *difference limens* (that is, different responses to stimuli). Such investigations inspired others to devote their energies to experimentation with variations in human behavior. Wundt, who was interested in the commonalities of behavior rather than their differences, established a laboratory at the University of Leipzig in which experimentation was carried on under rigidly standardized conditions. His work attracted many of the researchers who were to assume leadership in the mental measurement area.

A contemporary of Wundt's was Sir Francis Galton (1822–1911), whose work on individual differences laid the groundwork for later advances in this area. Galton was interested in heredity, and particularly in hereditary genius, primarily because of the recurrence of genius in his family. Galton was instrumental in furthering the emerging field of statistics to assist in measuring individual differences. The principle of the statistical method of correlation was initially developed by Galton, and a colleague of his, Karl Pearson (1857–1936), worked out the necessary mathematical formulas. James McKeen Cattell (1860–1944), an American, worked for three years with Galton, pursuing their mutual interests in individual differences. Cattell had previously studied with Wundt at Leipzig. Although the Leipzig laboratory was investigating Wundt's primary interest in general laws of human behavior, Cattell requested and received permission to study individual differences. He was an early advocate of mental testing and was at the forefront of attempts to develop predictive measures concerning mental ability and academic achievement.

In France a concern for the mentally deviant prompted work in mental measurement. Jean Etienne Esquirol (1772–1840), Jean Itard (1774–1838), and Edouard Seguin (1812–1880) are almost legendary figures in work with the mentally disabled.

During the late 1700s an attempt was made to move from theory to practice in regard to intellectual development. In 1779 an 11- or 12-year-old boy was found wandering wild and naked in the woods of Aveyron in France. The boy, later named Victor, was brought to Jean Itard at the National Institute for the Deaf and Dumb in Paris. Itard, who had been forewarned that Victor might be an "imbecile," began working enthusiastically with the boy. It was not particularly uncommon at this time to find persons with apparent mental abnormalities who had wandered from their homes and were found again after a few days in the same state as Victor. There were, however, many who felt that these "wild souls" had been lost in infancy and reared by animals. Such individuals were viewed as having a lack of normal intelligence because they had been deprived of the appropriate sensory input needed for their intellectual development. Etienne Condillac (1715–1780), a French philosopher, had previously advanced a theory that lack of stimulation would produce retarded development. Itard felt that if the wild boy of Aveyron were exposed to the right kind of sensory input, his intelligence would develop. Itard's goal was to provide him with sensory and motor training and the "experience" Victor had supposedly missed. Itard worked with Victor for five years in all, keeping detailed records of all of his activities. At the end of this time Itard confessed his failure, since among other things Victor never learned to speak, although he did learn to read simple words and to dress himself.

Itard's supposed "failure" was really a victory because he had amply demonstrated that a rather seriously retarded boy could be greatly improved and brought to a higher level of functioning than anyone had previously imagined. His work gained him the recognition of the French Academy and opened a new field of education.

At about the same time Jean Etienne Esquirol, a French physician and a colleague of Itard, differentiated between mental retardation and mental illness. Esquirol further pinpointed lack of language as a primary deficit of the retarded and determined that defective persons *could* often learn unskilled tasks and do elementary reading and writing. Alfred Binet and Theophile Simon later capitalized on Esquirol's observations that the deficits of retarded people were mainly intellectual and not sensory and that language ability would be a useful diagnostic criterion in developing a standardized intelligence scale.

Edouard Seguin, who had been a student of both Esquirol and Itard, believed that the retarded could be helped. He spent his mature years demonstrating that with patience and determination mentally defective children could be educated. In 1837 Seguin began a school for the mentally retarded which attracted professional persons from all parts of the world who came to observe his methods of working with the retarded. Seguin moved to the United States in 1850, where he was instrumental in developing programs for the mentally retarded and proposed the formation of a national association for a concerted attack on the problem of mental deficiency. This work is presently carried on by the American Association on Mental Deficiency (AAMD).

In France the need for objective measures in identifying mentally subnormal persons became increasingly important not only to determine responsibility under the law, but also to place people in special classes that were becoming prevalent in the late 1800s. Subjective appraisals for placement were increasingly found to be inadequate, and searches for more objective measures to ascertain mental ability were undertaken. Although many scientists interested in human behavior were investigating and attempting such measures it was Alfred Binet (1857–1911), a Frenchman trained in law and medicine, who became interested in psychology. He and his student Theophile Simon (1873–1961) developed the first intelligence test. Primarily because of Binet's interest in intelligence—manifested through his book *The Experimental Study of Intelligence* published in 1902—the Minister of Public instruction in 1904 commissioned Binet and Simon to investigate the feasibility of developing a test to assist schools in placing mentally defective children in appropriate classes. In 1905 Binet and Simon published a 30-item scale, which was considered by the two authors to be only a perfunctory approach to the problem. In 1908 a revision was published in which 59 subtests were grouped over age levels from 3 to 13 years. Binet is credited with being "the first to identify central intelligence—as opposed to peripheral disturbances—as the essential problem of the retarded" (Doll, 1962, p. 50).

Henry Goddard, Director of Research at the Vineland Training School, was traveling in Europe in 1908 and came across the Binet-Simon scales; in 1910 he translated them into English. Although the scales were modified by several psychologists, it was Lewis Terman who, after many validity checks using American populations, published a test in 1916 based on the original 1908 Binet-Simon Scale of Intelligence. Despite bitter attacks, the Binet scales revolutionized diagnosis and treatment of the mentally retarded.

The Concept of Intelligence

Core Concept 4   Intelligence, due to the development of qualitative measures, has too often been thought of as linear, but due to societal influences qualitative aspects also must be considered.

As with many other perplexing phenomena, there are about as many ways to define intelligence as there are persons interested and motivated enough to try. Although this may be an overstatement, Abraham (1958) reported that 113 different definitions of "the gifted" were found by a student writing a term paper on the subject. Likewise, mental retardation, at the other end of the intellectual spectrum, has produced a plethora of definitions. The number of definitions for these two intellectual extremes has probably led many people to think of intelligence in a quantitative sense. Intelligence, however, cannot be considered *solely* as a linear phenomenon ranging from "more to less" or from "bright to retarded." The complexity of human intelligence dictates that qualitative aspects must also be considered. An appreciation of the many determinants affecting intelligence is necessary if we are ever to fully understand and appreciate this puzzling phenomenon. From genetic selection before and at conception through prenatal, natal, postnatal, and early development, there exists an almost infinite number of variables that can affect the intellectual abilities of the developing human organism. As scientists have grappled with the intelligence concept, two questions have continually emerged: how is intelligence developed, and how can we gain some understanding of its composition in order to make predictions about future behavior? Both of these questions are not yet completely answered. The first question has been asked from at least the early Greek and possibly Egyptian times; Plato, in *The Republic*, pursued the second question, with his interest being to identify capable leaders. As science has developed, we have found continued exploration of each question both as parallel and as intertwining aspects of intelligence.

DEVELOPMENT OF INTELLIGENCE

Core Concept 5   The question of whether intelligence is primarily genetically determined or environmentally influenced was stimulated by discussions about the causes of mental retardation.

The question of how intelligence develops has generated what is most commonly referred to as the "nature versus nurture" controversy, which was directly stimulated by the phenomenon of mental retardation. Is intelligence genetically determined with little or no contributions from later environmental conditions and influences, or is intelligence primarily dependent on environmental factors with a limited genetic contribution? Advocates of both positions have been at times exceptionally vociferous in championing their view and lamenting the naivete of their counterparts. As was indicated in chapter 2, the controversy has been almost continuous in this country since the turn of the century, with many social and economic implications affecting the way society views and provides for the mentally retarded. (To compare present discussions with the turn-of-the-century furor or with the repressive actions of Nazi Germany toward the mentally retarded is unrealistic, however.) Out of this controversy has emerged a more reasoned approach, attempting to establish the interrelatedness and interaction of both heredity and environment. It would seem to be an indication of maturity to move from extremes toward a midposition that presumes to recognize and draw from the facts established by both sides of the question. The dilemma that spurs such heated debates is not really whether hereditary factors or environmental conditions play the major role in mental retardation, but the presumed effect. That some conditions such as genetic microcephaly, neurofibromatosis, and Tay-Sachs disease are a function of hereditary factors has been well established. Similarly, that environmental conditions can affect the level of mental functioning has been repeatedly manifested both through research and observations. It is therefore not debatable whether or not genetically induced aspects affect human intelligence or whether or not environmental factors play a part in the dynamics of intelligence. Both aspects play a role in which each depends on the other for intelligence to be manifested. Dobzhansky (1955) used the phrase "range of reaction" to characterize the duality of nature *and* nurture. In this sense the contributions of heredity in setting the limits of intelligence are recognized, and the influence of environmental factors is accounted for in determining the range of intelligence. Gottesman (1963) illustrated this (Fig. 3–1), showing that the inherited genetic material (genotype) of particular individuals or groups when affected by the environmental factors produces an observable result (phenotype) that is directly proportional to the favorableness of the environment.

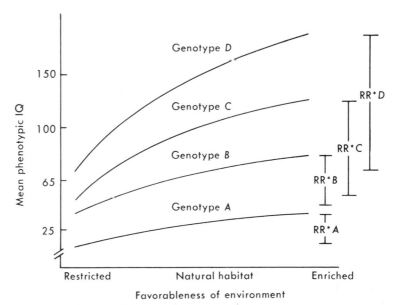

Figure 3–1. Scheme of the Reaction Range Concept for Four Hypothesized Genotypes Note: Marked deviation from the natural habitat has a low probability of occurrence. RR Signifies reaction range in phenotypic IQ.

From Genetic aspects of intelligent behavior by I. Gottesman. In *Handbook of mental deficiency*, Ellis, N. Copyright 1963, McGraw-Hill. Used with permission of McGraw-Hill Company.

Whereas the interaction between heredity and environment is acceptable to almost all scientists, there remains a controversy about the degree each contributes. It is apparent that, at present at least, we do not have the capability to partition genetic and environmental contributions into percentiles to indicate precise "amounts" that each contributes to individual performance. There continue to be attempts to ascertain the relative contributions of each, ranging from "best guesses" to research. Studies using twins have generally found that identical twins are more similar than random pairs of non-related persons, whether raised together or apart (Erlenmeyer-Kimling & Jarvik, 1963). There are problems even in this research methodology because all variables cannot be controlled and twins are often placed in similar environments when raised apart.

Probably the most controversial example of the whole nature-versus-nurture debate has been Arthur Jensen's (1969) publication in the *Harvard Educational Review*, "How Much Can We Boost IQ and Scholastic Achievement?" and his book entitled *Straight Talk About Mental Tests* (1981). These two publications have generated a number of responses, both for and against, about *(a)* the dangers inherent in proposing racial intellectual differences, *(b)* erroneous statements in the material, *(c)* the extent of academic freedom, and *(d)* the supposed "weight of evidence" reported by Jensen and others regarding black intellectual inferiority. Jensen's thesis is that there are two types of learning tasks. Type I refers to "associative learning" tasks, which are of a rote-learning nature that requires negligible transformation of the material learned; Type II is learning of a conceptual nature in which transformation of the learned material is requisite for success. Jensen concludes that whites possess Type II learning to a greater extent than blacks. Jensen's topic is not new but certainly contained the most shock value. In addition to these two learning types, Jensen implied that heredity may have more of an effect than environment; that as a group whites score higher on IQ tests than blacks; and that projects such as Head Start, which are based on environmental enrichment activities, will fail because of the effect of heredity (Rice, 1973). Jensen not only has added fuel to the controversy of nature versus nurture but also has fanned the flames with the implications relative to the intellectual capabilities of blacks and whites.

Factors Influencing Intelligence

Core Concept 6   The influence of a person's perceptions, expectations, and motivations has stimulated research on the environmental influences on intelligence.

Intelligent behavior is affected by a variety of factors that are only partially amenable to measurement techniques. In schools the initial concern about a child is caused not by a perceived lack of intelligence but by inappropriate behavior. The AAMD definition now includes a measure of adaptive behavior (see chapter 1) that attempts to address these related and, in a practical sense, more important influences on personal and social success.

Expectancies are those attitudes that prompt a person to decide whether something may or may not occur. They are related to one's previous experiences. A person with an expectancy of failure, for example, cannot be expected to enter the same or similar situations with a positive expectation of success. A major theorist in this area is Julian Rotter (1954). Several researchers (Cromwell, 1976; Gruen, Ottinger, & Ollendick, 1974; Ollendick, Balla, & Zigler, 1971) have provided evidence that those who are mildly mentally retarded tend to have lower expectancies for success than do the nonretarded, but that successful experiences raise their expectancy levels.

Motivation is related to expectancies as well as to competence and anxiety. A person who expects to fail and who does not feel competent will generally have little motivation to engage in new or different tasks. Such behavior can influence test results by preventing a maximum effort in responding.

Social Intelligence reflects a person's ability to understand and effectively engage in social situations. Adaptive behavior is a parallel of social competence. It has been recognized for some time that social behavior is one of the primary factors in determining whether a person is mentally retarded or not. We are all familiar with persons who, despite a low IQ, are socially aware to the degree that they can function adequately in society. There are a number of attributes (subcomponents) of social intelligence that have been identified. Greenspan (1979) has indicated the following as components of social intelligence: *(a)* role taking, which refers to the ability to see the world through the eyes of another; *(b)* social inference, which differs from role taking in that the focus is on determining what is happening in a given social situation; *(c)* social comprehension, which refers to a person's knowledge about social institutions and processes between people; *(d)* psychological insight, which is concerned with an understanding of individual characteristics; *(e)* moral judgment, which is a process of value clarification through discussions and introspection; *(f)* referential communication, which is oriented toward relations with others, both verbally and nonverbally, depending upon how one is thinking, feeling, and perceiving; and *(g)* social problem solving, which is the ability to persuade others to give assistance and to deal with emotionally laden situations. For a more complete description of each of these subcomponents, see Greenspan's chapter entitled "Social Intelligence in the Retarded" (1979).

MEASUREMENT OF INTELLIGENCE

Core Concept 7   The measurement of intelligence has generated considerable controversy regarding definitions.

The question regarding the measurement of intelligence similarly elicits a controversy concerning definition. The way in which intelligence is defined influences the methods used in attempting to determine relative degrees of intelligence for prediction purposes. Basically there are two extremes that comprise our theorizing about intelligence. There are those who take a factorial approach, in which the attempt is made to isolate and identify component parts of the intelligence concept. Others conceptualize intelligence as a holistic construct that is either hypothetical at best or is so intrinsically related to the total personality that it cannot be conceived of as a separate and distinct entity. With variations, most definitions fall between these two extremes.

It is one thing to theorize about the nature of intelligence and another to attempt to measure its integral parts. To measure any concept, one must make a decision regarding the components or aspects that comprise the essentials of the phenomenon under consideration. If, for example, a prospective test maker believes that intelligence cannot be understood apart from personality, then the test subsequently developed must necessarily include measures of such things as emotions, experiences, physical condition, age, and other factors involved in personality development. This would certainly provide a better measurement than we presently have, not only to predict behavior but also to foster intellectual ability and capabilities. The obvious difficulty in this approach is that it is presently impossible to construct such tests to include all of the infinite number of factors that would be required. Because of this, our present intelligence tests can only measure limited samples of behavior at a given time in a given place.

The best tests of intelligence presently available cannot and should not be considered as the right way or the only way of measuring the intelligence concept. Intelligence cannot be measured directly. As with any other concept, its primary components must be identified before any inferences can be made. As Nunnally (1967) points out, the measurable attributes of a concept (in this case, intelligence) must be isolated, evaluated, and subjected to experimental analysis. This is what Binet did, for example, in deciding that judgment was involved in intellectual functioning. The degree to which the test maker is successfully able to identify *measurable attributes* (usually referred to as subtests), standardize them, and provide validity and reliability data is the essence of test development. Our present intelligence tests are composed of attributes that the test maker believes are the best of the measurable aspects of attributes of intelligence presently available. How well a person performs on the components of a test (e.g., vocabulary, judgment, analogies, etc.) determines how much we may infer about the individual's relative intelligence.

How well a test of intelligence, or any other test for that matter, is able to adequately measure attributes of intelligence has generated considerable debate. In this regard Binet was aware of the shortcomings of his scale when he stressed "the importance of qualitative variables that affect test results, e.g., the persistence and attention of a child while taking a test have an influence upon the score obtained" (Linden & Linden, 1968, p. 17). The adequacy of a single diagnostic test, much less a single IQ score, has been harshly attacked (Garcia, 1972; Mercer, 1972; Watson, 1972), especially when minority groups are involved.

As the use of intelligence tests with many different groups has increased over the years, it has become apparent that there are many factors that mitigate against indiscriminate use of tests and quick stereotyping of a person by an IQ. We hope that a renewed call for consideration of the rights of others, as exemplified by the civil rights movement, has raised a new consciousness. Many of the early psychologists and educators in the mental testing movement in the United States warned against an indiscriminate use of intelligence and IQ tests and belief in their sanctity. Lightner Witmer was only one of the early twentieth-century psychologists who cautioned that we must recognize "the etiological importance of emotional deprivation, lack of experiential stimulation, functional nervous disease, inadequate or improper nutrition, sensory defects, physical illness and improper discipline" (Doll, 1962, p. 50).

Much of the problem can be attributed to expediency. As the use of intelligence tests gained in popularity and became more widespread, the concern for theory as a base was, if not negated, at least diminished in importance.

As we approach the end of the twentieth century we find ourselves in the position of having promised too much, of having neglected important aspects of the intelligence puzzle, such as social and motivational aspects, and of having allowed practical consideration to outdistance theoretical speculations. In order to keep this caution clearly in mind and to avoid getting ahead of ourselves, we now need to turn back and look at theory development and its relationship to the testing movement.

Most tests have emanated from the factorialists rather than from those who have taken the holistic approach discussed earlier. Charles Spearman (1863–1945), who initiated the factorial approach, believed that intelligence could best be expressed through two factors: a general or "g" factor and a specific or "s" factor. Spearman (1904) assumed that the "g" factor represented "true intelligence" in that the various tests of intelligence were consistently intercorrelated. He then hypothesized that a "g" factor was present in all valid tests of intelligence, since it appeared to be an ubiquitous entity. Since the intercorrelations were not perfect among tests, Spearman further hypothesized than an "s" factor was also present, but to a lesser degree than the "g" factor, and resulted from those activities that could be associated with particular situations.

A contemporary of Spearman, Edward L. Thorndike (1874–1949), took a somewhat expanded view in developing a multifactor theory in which he proposed that there were three kinds of intelligence: abstract, concrete, and social. In so doing, Thorndike took issue with Spearman's two-factor theory, maintaining that the intercorrelation of tests, although demonstrably high, was not necessarily attributable only to the "g" factor. The results of a study on transfer of training (Thorndike & Woodworth, 1901) indicated that a student's improvement in one subject did not always bring about a concomitant improvement in another. This study was used by Thorndike to refute Spearman's "g" factorial approach because it seemed evident that all intellectual traits did not result from one factor. Instead, Thorndike believed that intellectual functioning could be divided into three overall factors: *(a)* abstract intelligence, in which a facility for dealing with verbal and mathematical symbols is manifested, (b) mechanical or concrete intelligence, in which the ability to use objects in a meaningful way is stressed, and *(c)* social intelligence, in which the capacity to deal with other persons is paramount. Further, Thorndike believed that intelligence is influenced by neural interconnections in the brain and that the number of these interconnections is manifested in a person's performance capabilities.

A considerable debate arose as a result of the apparent disagreement between Spearman and Thorndike. However, by the late 1920s the differences between the two had abated because the researchers were in agreement that "when a number of variables are correlated, these variables always can be factored into either a general factor and specific factors or into a number of independent factors" (Linden & Linden, 1968, p. 70) and that more heat than progress had been generated as a result of the quasi-debates. But then in 1933 Louis L. Thurstone (1887–1955) put the elements of Spearman's "g" factor through multifactor analysis to develop his primary mental abilities test, in which seven factors were isolated in the belief that they could account for almost all of the correlation among intelligence tests. The seven factors that appeared to support Thorndike's multifactor theory and to oppose Spearman's "g" factor theory were spatial (S), perceptual (P), number (N), verbal (V), word fluency (W), memory (M), and reasoning (R). In 1940, however, Cyril Burt (1955) demonstrated that the supposed difference between Spearman and Thurstone was more a result of different statistical methods than of any substantive differences between the theories.

Core Concept 8   Guilford and Piaget: Two different approaches to the complex task of understanding the nature of intelligence.

Although it is evident that the factorial approach has not—perhaps because of relatively crude measuring devices—provided any conclusive data on what true intelligence is or how to measure it, there have been significant advances in testing. Even though the debate remains unsolved and proponents of the multifactor versus the single-factor theory are still at loggerheads, albeit presently in a quiescent state, the importance of the issue remains. The work of J. P. Guilford and Jean Piaget, two theorists who have approached the problem from different theoretical frameworks, will be briefly reviewed to provide an idea of the immense task of defining intelligence.

Guilford and his associates at the University of Southern California have continued Thurstone's factor analysis approach in identifying the primary elements of intelligence. Guilford has proposed a three-dimensional theoretical model that specifies parameters (operations, products, and contents), incorporates previously identified primary factors, and posits the existence of yet unidentified factors. This model (Fig. 3–2) postulates the existence of 150 possible primary intellectual abilities. Guilford (1982) has indicated that the model should not be seen as a collection of orthogonal factors, but as a model to stimulate thinking about intelligence.

Guilford and his associates believe that human thought processes involved in the *content* division can be subdivided into five major categories:

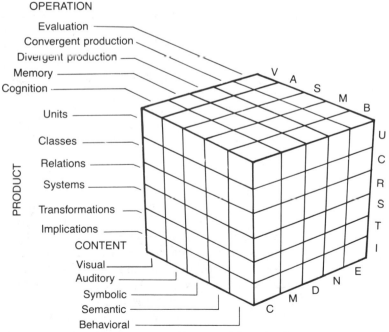

Figure 3–2. The Structure-of-Intellect Model with Three Parameters

Adapted from *The Nature of Human Intelligence* by J.P. Guilford. Copyright 1967, McGraw-Hill. Used with permission of McGraw-Hill Book Company.

(a) visual (having a visual or tactile form such as books, trees, houses, and clouds), *(b)* auditory (involving the processing of sounds into meaningful symbols), *(c)* symbolic (possessing a summarizing quality such as numbers, musical notes, and codes), *(d)* semantic (requiring meanings be attached to intangible materials, such as the association of the word "pencil" with the object pencil), and *(e)* behavioral (involving essentially nonverbal dimensions, such as perceptions, desires, and moods).

The *product* aspect is currently categorized into six major types or categories which serve to organize figural, symbolic, and semantic content dimensions. The subdivisions include *(a)* units (the processing of a single item such as a number, letter, or word), *(b)* classes (the classification of sets of items or information by common properties, such as with figure symbols or semantics), *(c)* relations (the activity of developing relationships between a product subdivision and a content subdivision or even relationships between relations), *(d)* systems (an aggregate of interacting parts, such as in sentence diagramming, numerical operations, or social situations), *(e)* transformations (the more abstract and creative activity of transforming material into results, conclusions, or physical configurations different from those anticipated), and *(f)* implications (the most abstract of the product subdivisions—one that involves anticipation and making predictions).

The third division, *intellectual operation,* includes the mental processes involved in using the information or content with which it works. Guilford defines five types of operations: *(a)* cognition (the process of comprehension, knowing, understanding, familiarity, such as the comprehension of material in a non-threatening atmosphere that tends to stimulate interest, for example, games, television, etc.), *(b)* memory (the ability to recall specific information, such as arithmetical steps, telephone numbers, and others; both short- and long-term memory are included in this subdivision), *(c)* evaluation (mental activities, such as judging, comparing, contrasting, decision making, and others), *(d)* convergent production or thinking (the process of being able to produce an acceptable response derived, it is assumed, from a large quantity of material), and *(e)* divergent production or thinking (the process of being able to generalize and produce alternatives based on information possessed or provided).

In this structure of intelligence (SI) model, the intent and attempt are to identify and provide discrete factors so that they may be distinguishable from one another to provide a conceptual understanding of all 150 hypothetical factors individually and collectively. For example, the cell memory-visual units (MVU) represent the ability to recall forms or objects, such as correctly identifying the shape B as the letter *B.* The method of factor analysis as represented in the SI model provides a way of precisely describing missing factors so that further exploratory investigation or research is in large part predetermined (to the extent that the various abilities are isolatable and the necessary instrumentation for precise measurement is available). It is expected that the SI model may change in form as research progresses. Indeed, it has been expanded from the earliest model (Guilford, 1959) in which only 90 abilities were hypothesized.

Jean Piaget (1896–1980) is unique among theorists in that he has approached the problem of intellectual functioning from an entirely different framework. In place of developing various tasks and then evaluating the correctness of the response(s), Piaget has focused on the psychological process that led to the response(s). In addition, he has approached the task developmentally, being primarily concerned with interpreting the development of behavior.

Whereas Guilford was influenced by early work in factor analysis by such psychologists as Spearman, Thorndike, and especially Thurstone, Piaget's early training was in biology and zoology. His approaches have evolved over the course of more than 50 years of investigations. During this time there have been three distinct phases to his work (Hunt, 1969). In the first phase, he investigated children's language and thought, judgment and reasoning, conception of the world, conception of physical causality, and moral judgments (Hunt, 1969). It was during this phase that Piaget questioned the view that child development resulted completely from either environmental or genetic influences. His investigations demonstrated that mental growth was influenced neither entirely by nature nor entirely by nurture, but rather by the continual and constant interaction of both aspects. In the second phase, he attempted to observe intelligence and reality development in his three children by observing their behavior in situations involving objects, persons and situations (Hunt, 1969). Piaget demonstrated a genius for observation that was continually guided by his theoretical formulations. These observations provided significant evidence for his theories on the development of cognitive structures. In the third phase, he and his associates investigated a number of aspects, all of which emanated from his early theories: concrete operations, conservation, relations, preconceptual symbolization, formal operations, sensorimotor stages, probability, perceptions, illusions, logical operations, and so on.

Piaget has postulated a series of intellectual developments in which the order of their appearance is important, not the age at which they appear. He believed that intelligence is an *adaptive* process and is only one special aspect of all biological functioning. The environment places an individual simultaneously in the position of adapting to it and modifying it. The term "accommodation" was used by Piaget to describe the adaptation of the individual to the environment; he used the term "assimilation" to describe the individual's modification of the environment to fit his or her perceptions. An organism is considered to be "adapted" when there is *equilibrium* (balance) between accommodation and assimilation. Piaget has used this biological concept in describing learning activities. For example, a child, when playing, uses assimilation (the stick becomes a fishing pole, rifle, or baton;

the shoe becomes a car or boat), but when the child is playacting accommodation becomes predominant (thus the youngster becomes the most feared gunman in the Old West, a movie star, or a champion tennis player) in an attempt to initiate the desired model through accommodating ephemeral perceptions. Assimilation and accommodation are complementary and antagonistic functions. Consequently, both aspects create alternate states of disequilibrium until they are gradually resolved into a state of equilibrium. The organism becomes adapted only when accommodation and assimilation are in equilibrium, that is, when there is harmony between the individual and her or his environment.

Piaget has hypothesized that *mental assimilation* involves the comparison and possible subsequent adjustment of sensory information with the person's present response patterns. *Mental accommodation* is the adapting of the response patterns to the sensory information. Piaget calls these response patterns *schemata*, which are collections of behavior sequences defined in behavioral terms. For example, once a schema (or strategy) has been worked out to solve an environmental problem, it tends to be repeated in similar situations. Piaget had recognized that developmentally there are various types of assimilation, such as reproductive assimilation, which is the tendency to repeat (practice) schemata so that they may be integrated and become habitual. However, this repetition brings about changes in schemata by the individual. Practiced in a larger or slightly different environmental arena which fosters a *generalization of assimilation,* these changes in turn create *recognitory assimilation* as the individual encounters and recognizes differences. Higher-order schemata are developed through *reciprocal assimilation* brought about by combining several schemata that were previously separate. Similarly, accommodation is concurrently taking place as the organism continually revises the existing schemata to better incorporate complex perceptions.

Piaget had postulated a sequence of developmental periods and substages that he believes to be generally the same for everyone. According to Piaget (1960), maturation and experience influence a child's rate of progress through the following sequences. Also, different cultural and social environments can contribute to differences in the average age of attaining different stages. The four main periods and their substages are as follows:

1. *Sensorimotor period.* This period is from birth to about 1 1/2 to 2 years of age. In this period the child is involved in a number of behavioral activities leading to a stable imagery. As Hunt (1969) explains, "These kinds of behavior include imitation of models no longer present, solving problems while looking at them and without motor grouping, and following desired objects that are out of sight in a box through a series of hidings in which only the box is visible" (p. 47).

2. *Preoperational period.* The preoperational period is divided into two substages: preconceptual and intuitive.

  a. *Preconceptual substage.* This substage occurs from about 1 1/2 to about 4 years of age. The development of symbolic thought and language are now manifested, indicating awareness of objects and realization of the child's relation to and interrelation with them. The child is now able to initiate actions and assume the future position of things.

  b. *Intuitive substage.* From about 3 to 7 years of age the child is involved in thinking that is restricted to what is directly perceived. The child enters this stage unable to understand constancy; for example, the amount of liquid is the same and not less in a bowl rather than a narrow cylinder. By the end of this stage, however, the child is able to recognize other points of view but is not able to transfer generalizations to other situations.

3. *Concrete operations period.* This period roughly relates to the ages between 7 and 11 years of age. During this stage the child moves toward the ability to understand the conservation of quantity, length, and number. The youngster now understands, for example, the constancy of the amount of liquid regardless of the size or shape of the container and is able to generalize about other situations. "Piaget interprets this development as an equilibrium between the assimilation of objects and their relations to the subject's actions and the accommodation of the subject's schemata of thinking" (Woodward, 1963, p. 309).

4. *Formal operations period.* From approximately 11 years of age onward, the child is involved in a continuous refinement of approaches to complex problems. The child engages in reasoning activities that are beyond a concrete operational approach in that now "hypothesizing," from which correct deductions are concluded, is more frequently engaged in and utilized. Verbal symbolization, providing the developing human being with increasingly abstract concepts that can be manipulated, is now a primary tool used to solve problems.

In the foreword to *Young Children's Thinking* (Almy, 1966), Piaget succinctly points out why he believes traditional learning theories have not had a great impact on education:

> This is the essential conclusion, as far as education is concerned: learning cannot explain development, but the stage of development can in part explain learning. Development follows its own laws, as all of the contemporary biology leads us to believe, and although each stage in the development is accompanied by all sorts of new learning based on experience, this learning is always relative to the developmental period during which it takes place,

and to the intellectual structures, whether completely or partially formed, which the subject has at his disposal during this period. In the last analysis, therefore, development accounts for learning much more than the other way around. (p. v)

Piaget has provided us with a developmental theory of intelligence. As the preceding discussion indicates, Piaget sees both qualitative and quantitative differences as the person develops. His orientation has been different from other theorists engaged in studying intelligence and as such has provided us with a different way of looking at children's intellectual growth. Flavell (1982, 1985) has questioned the efficacy of Piaget's developmental stages relative to the future study of intellectual development. As Mann and Sabatino (1985) have pointed out, Piaget's influence on education, particularly on special education, has not had the impact that many persons had hoped. His theories have not shown to have a direct application to educating the mentally retarded, but they are useful as a framework for understanding the behavior of children. For a thorough review of research using a Piagetian base with the mentally retarded, see Woodward (1979).

CONTEMPORARY TRENDS

Although there is and will continue to be a need to focus on intelligence as a concept, there appears to be a trend away from test development per se and toward a reconceptualization of what we know about intelligence and testing. The work of both Guilford and Piaget must be seen as monumentally contributing to our knowledge and understanding. In addition, the contributions of other researchers working from other disciplinary and conceptual frameworks (Cole, Gay, Glick, & Sharp, 1971; Cole & Scribner, 1974; Cromwell, 1976; Merrifield, 1977; and others) have provided—and continue to provide—different perspectives regarding intelligence.

An example of an approach using broadened assumptions of intelligence and testing is the work of Jane Mercer and June Lewis (1977). The importance of their work in this context is not in theory development per se, but in utilization of a measurement approach that attempts to include advances made in testing along with a recognition of sociocultural influences. Although their approach is discussed at some length in chapter 4, it seems appropriate to include their conceptual approach in here because it is one of the very few attempts to approach diagnosis from a broader intelligence framework. Although there have been many tests that purport to be "culture free" or "fair," or that were designed to measure adaptive behavior, either the efficiency has been questionable or the standardization was so limited that the predictive validity and reliability were doubtful. Mercer and Lewis (1977) have developed what they refer to as a System of Multicultural Pluralistic Assessment (SOMPA) that requires a view of a child from these different frameworks: medical, social system, and pluralistic. This system, although using extant tests, places considerable emphasis on the effects of sociocultural influences on learning ability. We believe that the SOMPA model is exemplary of the growing recognition that traditional testing of intelligence (such as learning ability) has limited uses in a pluralistic society. However, difficulties in administering the test (the training of personnel and the time required) have lessened its impact as a functional instrument in everyday school use.

A second example is the work of Feuerstein (1979) and his colleagues. Feuerstein has attempted to shift the focus from product-oriented tests (i.e., test scores) toward a process approach that emphasizes the modifiability of behavior for indicating potential. He has developed the Learning Potential Assessment Device (LPAD) to assess learning potential based on what a person *can* learn rather than on what *has* been learned. The LPAD is another example of increasing interest in nontraditional assessment techniques. At the present time there is a need for further empirical evidence of its validity, and there is a need to address reliability concerns among those administering the instrument.

Core Questions

1. How have societal changes affected our concepts of intelligence?
2. Why are theories both a tool and a goal?
3. What was the impetus for developing the first "intelligence" test?
4. Why is the work of Jean Itard important?
5. What is meant by the nature-versus-nurture controversy, and why is it important?
6. Why is social intelligence an important aspect of intelligence?
7. Why can't intelligence be measured directly?
8. What is the orientation of the "factoralists" toward understanding intelligence?
9. What approach did Piaget take in his study of intellectual development? How does it differ from the factoral approach?

ROUND TABLE DISCUSSION

Humankind's search for the critical aspects and the keys to the development of intelligence has been rigorously carried out by many scientists. We have moved from rather simplistic views of what intelligence is to rather complex theories about its characteristics. In doing so we have identified both quantitative and qualitative aspects of intelligence. For those interested in the study of mental retardation, an understanding of the past history and present formulations and future considerations about intelligence is both important and necessary.

In a study group discuss the development of our knowledge about intelligence up to the present day. As a part of the discussion members should relate both what they feel were important developments and what they were surprised to learn. To stimulate discussion, divide the group into subgroups who will present and be advocates either for the "factoralists" or for the "developmentalists." Each subgroup should present arguments for its position and be able to emphasize its strengths as opposed to the other approach. Subsequent discussion should consider what the individuals feel about the different approaches and how their perception of persons with mental retardation has been influenced taking one or another approach.

REFERENCES

Abraham, W. (1958). *Common sense about gifted children.* New York: Harper & Row.

Almy, M. with Chittenden, E., & Miller, P. (1966). *Young children's thinking: Studies of some aspects of Piaget's theory.* New York: Teachers College.

Burt, C. (1955). The meaning and assessment of intelligence. *Eugenics Review, 47,* 81–91.

Cole, M., Gay, J., Glick, J., & Sharp, D.(1971). *The cultural context of learning and thinking.* New York: Basic Books.

Cole, M., & Scribner, S. (1974). *Culture and thought: A psychological introduction.* New York: John Wiley & Sons.

Cromwell, R. (1976). Ethics, umbrage and the A B C Ds. *Minnesota Educator, 2,* 42–47.

Dobzhansky, T. (1955). *Evolution, genetics and man.* New York: John Wiley & Sons.

Doll, E. E. (1962). A historical survey of research and management of mental retardation in the United States. In E. P. Trapp & P. Himselstein (Eds.), *Readings on the exceptional child* (pp. 21–68). New York: Appleton-Century-Crofts.

Erlenmeyer-Kimling, L., & Jarvik, L. (1963). Genetics and intelligence: A review. *Science, 142,* 1477–1479.

Feuerstein, R. (1979). *The dynamic assessment of retarded performers.* Baltimore: University Park.

Fitz-Herbert, A. (1962). *New natura brevium.* Quoted in E. P. Trapp & P. Himelstein (Eds.), *Readings on the exceptional child.* New York: Appleton-Century-Crofts.

Flavell, J. H. (1982). Structures, stages, and sequences in cognitive development. In W. A. Collins (Ed.), *The concept of development: The Minnesota symposia on child psychology, XV.* Hillsdale, NJ: Erlbaum.

Flavell, J. H. (1985). *Cognitive development.* Englewood Cliffs, NJ: Prentice-Hall.

Garcia, J. (1972). IQ: The conspiracy. *Psychology Today, 6,* 40–43, 92, 94.

Gottesman, I. (1963). Genetic aspects of intelligent behavior. In N. Ellis (Ed.), *Handbook of mental deficiency.* New York: McGraw-Hill.

Greenspan, S. (1979). Social intelligence in the retarded. In N. R. Ellis (Ed.), *Handbook of mental deficiency: Psychological theory and research* (2nd ed.). Hillsdale, NJ: Lawrence Erlbaum.

Gruen, G., Ottinger, D., & Ollendick, T. (1974). Probability of learning in retarded children with differing histories of success and failure in school. *American Journal of Mental Deficiency, 79,* 417–423.

Guilford, J. P. (1959). Three faces of intellect. *American Psychologist, 14*, 469–479.

Guilford, J. P. (1982). Cognitive psychology's ambiguities: Some suggested remedies. *Psychological Review, 89*, 48–59.

Hunt, J. McV. (1969). The impact and limitations of the giant of developmental psychology. In D. A. Elkind & J. Flavell (Eds.), *Studies in cognitive development* (pp. 3–66.) New York: Oxford.

Jensen, A. (1969). How much can we boost IQ and scholastic achievement? *Harvard Educational Review, 39* 1–123.

Jensen, A. (1980). *Bias in mental testing.* New York: Free Press.

Jensen, A. (1981). *Straight talk about mental tests.* New York: Free Press.

Linden, K. W., & Linden, J. D. (1968). *Modern mental measurement: A historical perspective.* Boston: Houghton Mifflin.

Mann, L. & Sabatino, D. A. (1985). *Foundations of cognitive process in remedial and special education.* Rockville, MD: Aspen.

Marx, M. H. (1963). The general nature of theory construction. In M. H. Marx (Ed.), *Theories in contemporary psychology.* New York: Macmillan.

Mercer, J. R. (1972). The IQ: The lethal label. *Psychology Today, 6*, 40–43, 92, 94.

Mercer, J. R. & Lewis, J. F. (1977). *System of multicultural pluralistic assessment.* New York: Psychological Corp.

Merrifield, P. (1977). *Guilford and Piaguet: An attempt at synthesis.* Unpublished manuscript.

Nunnally, J. C. (1967). *Psychometric theory.* New York: McGraw-Hill.

Ollendick, T., Balla, D. & Zigler, E. (1971). Expectancy of success and the probability learning performance of retarded children. *Journal of Abnormal Psychology, 77*, 275–281.

Piaget, J. (1960). The general problems of the psychobiological development of the child. In J. M. Tanner & B. Inhelder (Eds.), *Discussions on child development* (pp. 3–27.) London: Tavistock.

Piaget, J. (1966). Foreword. In M. Almy with E. Chittenden & P. Miller, *Young children's thinking.* New York: Teachers College.

Rice, B. (1973). The cost of thinking the unthinkable. *Psychology Today, 7*, 88–93.

Roback, A. A. (1961). *A history of psychology and psychiatry.* New York: Philosophical Library.

Rotter, J. (1954). *Social learning and clinical psychology.* Englewood Cliffs, NJ: Prentice-Hall.

Spearman, C. E. (1904). General intelligence: Objectively determined and measured. *American Journal of Psychology, 15*, 201–293.

Thorndike, E. L., & Woodworth, R. S. (1901). The influence of improvement in one mental function upon the efficiency of other functions. *Psychological Review, 8*, 247–261, 384–395, 553–564.

Watson, P. (1972). IQ: The racial gap. *Psychology Today, 6*, 48–50, 97–98.

Woodward, M. (1963). The application of Piaget's theory to research in mental deficiency. In N. Ellis (Ed.), *Handbook of mental deficiency.* New York: McGraw-Hill.

Woodward M. (1979). Piaget's theory and the study of mental retardation. In N. R. Ellis (Ed.), *Handbook of mental deficiency: Psychological theory and research* (2nd ed.). Hillsdale, NJ: Erlbaum.

4

Assessment Issues and Procedures

Issues and Concepts
- *Assessment Utilization*
- *Technical Soundness*
- *Normative and Criterion Referencing*
- *Formative and Summative Evaluation*
- *Assessment Bias*
- *Commentary*
- *Mental Age and Intelligence*
- *Commentary*

Early Life
- *Screening Concepts*
- *Early Life Assessment*

Preschool Years
- *Intellectual Functioning*
- *Language Functioning*
- *Perceptual-Motor Functioning*
- *Social/Adaptive Behavior*

Elementary School Years
- *Intellectual Functioning*
- *Achievement*
- *Assessment Systems*

The Adolescent and Adult Years
- *Intellectual Functioning*
- *Vocational Functioning*

Assessment and Aging

Core Questions

Round Table Discussion

References

Core Concepts

1. Careful attention to the proper use of assessment instruments has a great impact on the outcome of measurement.

2. The technical soundness of psychoeducational assessment involves several factors, some of which have not always been carefully considered in instrument development and utilization.

3. The purpose for conducting an assessment has considerable influence on the procedure(s) employed and the manner in which data are interpreted. This has led to the development of important concepts such as norm- and criterion-referencing as well as to formative and summative evaluation.

4. Mental age and IQ have historically been central in assessment related to mental retardation although many other areas are emerging as important to full evaluation.

5. Vastly different assessment procedures become important depending upon age and performance area being evaluated.

6. Screening assessment is very important throughout the life span but is crucial in early life.

7. Prenatal evaluation can provide extremely important information regarding the status of a fetus.

8. Assessment of the newborn infant may identify problems that prompt immediate intervention to prevent mental retardation.

9. Evaluation beyond the newborn stage broadens to include many assessment areas not previously amenable to measurement.

10. Intellectual, language, perceptual-motor, and social/ adaptive behaviors are each important in evaluating the status of preschool youngsters, and proper assessment must employ procedures appropriate for this age range.

11. Multiple areas of functioning must be evaluated during the elementary years, and proper evaluation requires use of technically and conceptually sound procedures appropriate for this age range.

12. Assessment during the adolescent and adult years also involves utilization of age or functioning level-appropriate procedures as well as attention to the changing purposes for evaluation that emerge during these years.

Psychological assessment has a richer and lengthier history than do other areas of behavioral science. Intelligence measurement is the area in psychological assessment that has received the most attention. Work in the measurement of intelligence has been a major force and impetus in all of psychological assessment, which places the roots of psychological assessment squarely in the field of mental retardation.

It is commonly accepted that serious efforts aimed at measuring intelligence began with the work of Alfred Binet in 1904. Binet was commissioned by school officials in Paris to develop a means by which those children who were "truly dull" could be identified. Although there had been interest in psychological measurement before this time, Binet's assignment is generally viewed as an important milestone in the assessment field. The influence of psychological assessment long has been felt far beyond the area of mental retardation, and the methodology has become increasingly complex, sophisticated, and, some would say, elegant. In certain areas, however, the sophistication may be more superficial than elegant. The purpose of this chapter is to discuss assessment issues, frameworks, and procedures from the perspective of mental retardation. In keeping with the format of this text, assessment will be discussed in terms of the various phases of the developmental life cycle.

ISSUES AND CONCEPTS

As noted before, work in the measurement of intelligence has a very long history. Efforts to evaluate other areas of function, such as personality, language, and social development, have also been under way for a considerable length of time. Despite the longevity of such efforts, much of the work has not been undertaken as thoughtfully as might have been appropriate or desirable. A number of these problems and issues will be examined.

Assessment Utilization

Core Concept 1	Careful attention to the proper use of assessment instruments has a great impact on the outcome of measurement.

One difficulty plaguing behavioral evaluation over the years is related to the way assessment procedures are used. Instrument development has occurred at a very rapid rate—many times at the expense of careful and deliberate conceptualization concerning the purposes and uses of the tests. Assessment literature reflects many years of serious concern regarding usage (e.g., Anastasi, 1950; Fuchs & Fuchs, 1986; Gronlund, 1985; Haney, 1984; Ysseldyke & Algozzine, 1982). Drew (1973) stated that "evaluators and educators seem plagued with an *instrumentation fixation* to the near exclusion of attention to questions of 'Why are we testing' " (p. 324). He further noted that "technical precision in psychological assessment has nearly always been far in advance of conceptual precision" (p. 323). Technical precision in this context refers to instrument construction, and conceptual precision refers to considerations of the underlying purposes for assessment and the intended use of resulting information. There are some serious arguments regarding the degree of technical precision that has been generally achieved (e.g., Flynn, 1985; Ysseldyke & Algozzine, 1982). The usage problem is fundamental and may be even more serious, since logic would dictate that concepts need to be in place before an evaluation can take place. Even evidence from current practice raises serious questions in this regard. Ysseldyke, Algozzine, Richey, & Graden (1982) found minimal relationships between assessment data and decisions made by placement teams (correlations ranging from −.13 to +.29). Schenck (1980) also reported limited relationships between assessment information and the instructional prescriptions of Individualized Education Programs (IEPs) designed for 243 handicapped children. Mentally retarded subjects constituted a relatively small part of the sample (learning disabled [LD] = 186, emotionally disturbed [ED] = 28, educable mentally retarded [EMR] = 29.), but the assessment concerns remain just as serious for this population as for the other groups. Schenck concluded that "results of the investigation indicated that the long-term goals and short-term instructional objectives of the IEP *have limited foundation in the psychological assessment"* (1980, p. 341, emphasis added). She further noted that "procurement of diagnostic data solely for purposes of differential diagnosis denies the need to address the unique learning requirements of the learner" (p. 341). Perhaps a more direct question reflects the concern over purpose: Why does one test if the information is not directly used for instruction or other intervention? The *conceptual* problems related to purpose and usage may also be reflected in *practical* applications of assessment in the field.

Psychoeducational instrument development has been voluminous over the past 20 years. There is probably an instrument available that purports to measure every facet of human behavior that one would want to evaluate. Further, new instrumentation is being developed and placed on the market continually (and at what seems to be an accelerating rate).

As noted above, there are questions regarding the degree of technical precision that has been achieved in much of psychoeducational assessment. This concern is an appropriate one, as shown by data that will be presented in a following section. However, the problems related to technical precision are not the result of a lack of knowledge or theory about instrument development and measurement. Measurement theory has become a rather highly developed area in behavioral science and has been studied for many years (Cronbach, 1984; Ebel, 1972; Horst, 1966; Hopkins & Stanley, 1981). Unfortunately, many instruments are on the market that do not reflect adequate attention to sound measurement practices. The great demand from the field appears to have resulted in some instruments that are inadequate in terms of measurement theory.

Technical Soundness

Core Concept 2   The technical soundness of psychoeducational assessment involves several factors, some of which have not always been carefully considered in instrument development and utilization.

Several factors relate to the technical soundness of psychoeducational instruments. Ysseldyke and Algozzine (1982) identified three fundamental areas that need to be addressed in the development of standardized tests: norms, reliability, and validity.

Norms. Norms (or norm data, or normative data) should be collected as the test is developed and refined. This part of the standardization process provides an estimate of typical performance with which an individual's test scores may be compared. To obtain such data, an instrument is administered to a sample of subjects who are representative of the group with which the test is intended to be used. Norm data adequacy is important in standardized instrumentation. The norm group should include a representative sample, the sample must be large enough to provide confidence that an adequate sample of performance has been obtained, and data should be relatively current—revisions undertaken at least once every 15 years (American Psychological Association, American Educational Research Association, & National Council on Measurement in Education, 1974). Additionally, norm data and the data collection process used must be adequately described so users can evaluate this aspect of the test.

Reliability. Reliability, the second basic area of instrument technical soundness, refers to the degree of consistency with which an instrument measures a behavior or performance level (i.e., the degree to which similar performance under similar conditions results in similar assessment scores). Evaluation by means of a particular instrument is of little use if resulting scores fluctuate widely even when behavior is stable. Reliability is expressed in terms of reliability coefficients (e.g., .50, .85, .90), the higher coefficients indicating more reliable measurement. Different reliability levels may be acceptable depending on the type of decision for which the data are to be used. Salvia and Ysseldyke (1985) suggested that test scores being used for "administrative purposes and reported for groups" should have a minimal reliability of .60 (p. 126). They further noted that for individual student decisions such as "tracking and placement in a special class" the minimum reliability should be .90 and that individual screening instruments should have at least a .80 reliability (p. 127). Test developers should adequately describe their reliability data and how the coefficients were derived.

Several methods may be used for determining test reliability. *Test-retest reliability* represents a measure of stability over time and is obtained by administering the instrument to a large group of subjects and retesting them after a period of time has passed. Scores from the two sessions are then correlated to obtain a reliability coefficient. *Alternate-form reliability* determines the degree to which two forms of a test measure the same trait. To obtain alternate-form reliability a large group of subjects is given two forms of the test, and the scores on these alternate forms are correlated. *Internal-consistency reliability*, also known as split-half reliability, is derived by testing a single group of subjects once. The test items are split (e.g., odd-even) and scores on the two halves are correlated.

Validity. Validity generically represents the degree to which a test measures what it purports to measure. If the objective is to assess intellectual functioning, scores are of limited value if they mostly represent test anxiety, shyness, or socioeconomic status. Instrument developers should provide evidence to users regarding the validity of their test and how it was derived (American Psychological Association, American Educational Research Association, & National Council on Measurement in Education, 1974). This requirement is also part of the federal regulations for Public Law 94–142.

There are a number of methods for evaluating validity. *Content validity* is determined by examining the content of the test to judge whether the instrument adequately assesses what it is intended to. *Criterion-related validity* is an assessment of the degree to which an individual's performance on a task can be estimated by his or her test score. This may be accomplished in two fashions, *concurrently and predictively.* Concurrent criterion-related validity involves administering the test instrument and the task to be performed simultaneously (or as nearly as possible). Predictive criterion-related validity involves administering the test to predict performance on a task undertaken at some later time. In both types the test and performance scores are correlated.

Establishing the technical soundness of psychoeducational assessment is rather involved, as this brief discussion indicates. Professionals do not lack the theoretical and technical knowledge with which to accomplish this end. For a variety of reasons, however, standardized tests frequently have been developed, marketed and used that fall short in some fashion with respect to technical soundness. Salvia and Ysseldyke (1985) examined normative information on numerous standardized, norm-referenced instruments and found nearly 25% of them had inadequately constructed or described norms. Additionally, the reliability of many commonly used tests may be questionable (Ysseldyke & Algozzine, 1982) and the validity of a number of standardized instruments has been challenged (Salvia & Ysseldyke, 1985).

Instrumentation weaknesses noted above represent serious concerns for all behavioral scientists involved in assessment and treatment of disordered individuals. They are discussed because we believe that professionals should be conscious of weaknesses in the procedures so that they can be guarded against and improvements made. We do not advocate discontinuing psychoeducational assessment or using existing instruments when appropriate. These measures are not advocated even by those who have studied instrumentation and found it lacking (e.g., Ysseldyke & Algozzine, 1982). We would, however, encourage more care and thoughtfulness in instrument use and development than has often been evident in the past.

Normative and Criterion Referencing

Core Concept 3   The purpose for conducting an assessment has considerable influence on the procedure(s) employed and the manner in which data are interpreted. This has led to the development of important concepts such as norm- and criterion-referencing as well as to formative and summative evaluation.

Our earlier discussion mentioned norms and norm-referenced assessment. One important conceptual development in the field of assessment has been the distinction between norm-referenced and criterion-referenced evaluation. This distinction has become well known in educational and psychological circles.

Norm Referencing. Early assessment of intelligence focused on how an individual performed as compared with others. A child's test score is viewed in relation to his or her age-mates, or some standard norm. The norms or bases for such comparisons are usually established through research and repeated testing of individuals at various ages. Similar procedures are used in assessment of factors other than intelligence. Personality measures usually compare one's response on certain questions with the responses of others who have particular personality descriptions. Educational achievement is often measured by the amount of information a child has accumulated as demonstrated by correct responses on a variety of test questions. Such performance is then compared with those of others who are about the same age or grade level.

This type of assessment, in which the performance of an individual is compared with that of others, is known as norm-referenced evaluation. Reading the term quite literally, the idea is self-explanatory. Interpretation of an individual's performance is referenced in relation to the scores of others in the form of established norms. Mental age (MA) is a norm-referenced concept, which is what Binet and Simon (1908) had in mind in their initial definition of MA. Many other areas of assessment, particularly those using standardized tests, are also based on a norm-referenced framework.

This approach has been a predominant evaluation framework for many years. For the most part, professionals involved in all types of assessment (e.g., developmental status, intelligence, personality) have interpreted performance relative to norms. This has served some purposes well. During the development of assessment as a science, norm-referencing has been an important foundation for both researchers and practitioners working all areas related to human behavior. A number of rather serious problems have been generated, however.

As the science of human behavior progressed, measurement problems developed that obviously needed attention. Standardized tests provided information that was useful for certain purposes but not very helpful in other areas. Educators, for example, frequently found that scores from norm-referenced evaluation were not helpful for planning actual teaching. A single score was often used for decisions about educational placement, with little or no additional information provided about the child. From such an evaluation a teacher received meager guidance concerning the activities and specific areas that should be involved in the instructional process (Galagan, 1985). Where to begin in teaching specific math or reading skills, for example, was not indicated by a global score or by a psychologist's report, leaving teachers with many practical problems to solve concerning how to teach the child. There appeared to be no logical link between evaluation and actual instruction.

Working with mentally retarded and other handicapped individuals brought to light similar problems in social-vocational efforts and other aspects of the adult world (Felce, de Kock, Mansell, & Jenkins, 1984). Placement, planning, and programming were not facilitated to any great degree by norm-referenced assessment information. Professionals working in social agencies such as welfare, employment, and sheltered workshops soon found that they had to augment such information with their own more specific evaluations. Directors of sheltered workshops, for example, had to determine which specific skills were present in a retarded client and which needed to be taught for the client to perform productively.

Criterion Referencing. Criterion-referenced evaluation has become nearly synonymous with what norm-referenced evaluation is not. Individual performance is not compared with that of others or with some norm. Further, criterion-referenced evaluation assesses specific skill areas individually rather than generating a score based on a composite of several skills. Each of these notions warrants more detailed discussion to understand this important evaluation concept.

As noted, criterion-referenced evaluation does not compare the individual's performance with that of others. Tasks are usually arranged in a sequence of increasing difficulty. A person's functioning is viewed in terms of absolute performance level or the actual number of operations completed. If a child is being tested on counting skills and is able to progress successfully through counting by twos but no further, that is the way in which performance is viewed. The child can count by twos with 100% accuracy but cannot count by threes. This level of performance may be referenced in one or both of two ways. First, the evaluator and the teacher (frequently the same person) would ask, "Is this level of proficiency adequate for this child at this time?" The level of proficiency necessary for the child is the criterion, hence the term criterion-referenced evaluation. If a child needs to have the skill of counting by threes, the teacher knows exactly what instruction is necessary at this point. As the child progresses or grows older, he or she may be required to perform at a more advanced skill level depending on environmental requirements. This results in a changed criterion for this skill for the next phase of evaluation and instruction.

A second way that performance or skill level is referenced involves comparison of a given individual's performance in one area with performance in others; for example, a child performs well in letter recognition but poorly in sound blending. Performances in such various skill areas are examined, frequently a profile of the child's strengths and deficits is constructed, and instructional effort is specifically pinpointed based on this profile. In this fashion the second referent for evaluation data remains within a given individual's performance but between skill areas. Usually the measurement involves performance of specific tasks. No inference is made concerning abstract concepts (e.g., intelligence), and measurement is directly related to specific instruction. This has improved the logical relationship between evaluation and teaching, changing the way education is conceived and executed.

Past years have witnessed a theoretical difference of opinion in child assessment. Obviously norm- and criterion-referenced evaluations operate from different approaches. Proponents of each viewpoint have spent considerable time and effort defending their respective positions, often without careful examination of what the other approach has to offer. This is unfortunate because such professional conflict has had little positive result, and the effort and energy expended may have been used much more productively. While arguments continue to some degree, attention to basic measurement principles has begun to replace rhetoric (e.g., Haertel, 1985).

Scrutiny of both frameworks has led some authors to conclude that neither approach in isolation will result in a totally effective evaluation process (Drew, Freston, & Logan, 1972). Criterion-referenced evaluation is useful for specific instructional programming, while norm-referenced evaluation does not serve that need well. However, many children will ultimately be functioning in a larger world, perhaps partially in a regular educational setting, which is largely a norm-referenced world. To a great degree this broader world operates on a competitive basis, and children's performances often are viewed in relation to each other. To maximize a child's probability of success, information must be obtained that will indicate how the child's performance compares with others in the larger world. It would be disastrous to bring a child's skill level from point A to point B (criterion-reference evaluation) and find that point C was necessary for success in a regular educational setting. Those working with mentally retarded individuals cannot afford to be rigid by using only part of the tools available to them. Since they serve different purposes, both norm- and criterion-referenced evaluation must be used to work effectively with retarded children. (See Drew, Freston, & Logan [1972] for a more detailed discussion of criterion- and norm-referenced evaluation.)

Formative and Summative Evaluation

Other conceptual developments in the field of evaluation have related directly to the purposes of evaluation. Bloom, Hastings, and Madaus (1971) presented one such notion that received rather wide-spread attention. They viewed evaluation in terms of two broad categories: formative and summative. Formative evaluation in this framework is assessment that does not focus on terminal behaviors, but rather on those that represent the next step in an instructional program. In this model, formative evaluation is frequently an integrated part of the instructional program and is an ongoing assessment. Summative evaluation is quite different. It involves assessment of terminal behaviors and is seen as an evaluation of a child's performance at the end of a given program. These conceptualizations have also been combined with those of norm- and criterion-referenced evaluation in terms of functional and comprehensive views of assessment. The myopic views of evaluation and psychological assessment seem to be diminishing in favor of more thoughtful approaches to the broad field. It is promising that professionals working in the field are being more thoughtful and reasoned in their consideration of assessment.

Assessment Bias

Other issues in assessment requiring attention involve questions concerning discriminatory testing. These questions have surfaced particularly in terms of standardized, norm-referenced testing of minority-group children. Blacks, Hispanics, and American Indians, as well as others, have legitimately claimed that there is cultural bias and prejudice involved in the construction and use of evaluation instruments (Roberts & DeBlassie, 1983; Slate, 1983). Since such instruments are usually devised by individuals from the cultural majority, it is likely that test items are more representative of that group than others. Similarly, norms are usually established by groups having more individuals from the cultural majority than from minority subgroups. When minority children's scores are compared with norms established on other populations, then, they often appear at a disadvantage because of cultural differences (Wood, Johnson, & Jenkins, 1986). Efforts to construct culturally unbiased instruments have been attempted for many years with very disappointing results, which has led some to contend that conceptual foundations and uses of norm-referenced evaluation are more important issues than instrumentation (Drew, 1973). Serious attention to this problem is imperative, and professionals working with retarded people cannot afford to wait passively for others to take the lead. Minority children represent a disproportionately large segment of the identified retarded population (Prasse & Reschly, 1986). The questions must be asked: Are these children identified as retarded because of cultural bias and prejudice in testing? If so, what are the implications? Beyond asking questions, however, rapid movement toward action is crucial.

Commentary

Although the preceding discussion involves issues that have been articulated in the past, this is not an implication that the problems have evaporated with passing time. Problems involving educational uses and misuses of norm-referenced assessment have been addressed only in a limited fashion (Drew, Freston, & Logan, 1972; Hammill, 1971; Ysseldyke & Algozzine, 1982) and only by a limited segment of the educational profession, primarily those working with handicapped learners. Norm-referenced evaluation and the complex issues involved in assessment of cultural minorities have only begun to be explored (Bartel, Grill, & Bryen, 1973; Drew, 1973; Jensen, 1980, 1983; Meeker & Meeker, 1973; Newland, 1973; Oakland, 1973). Further, professional training in diagnostic assessment remains limited in scope and needs considerable attention (Elbert, 1984). Much work remains to be completed (Bennett, 1983), and considerable development regarding the underlying concepts of assessment/evaluation is yet to come.

Mental Age and Intelligence

Core Concept 4   Mental age and IQ have historically been central in assessment related to mental retardation although many other areas are emerging as important to full evaluation.

Two additional concepts require brief attention. They are not new to the field of psychological assessment; in fact, they have great historical significance and have been particularly prominent in the assessment of intelligence: mental age and intelligence quotient. Both serve as convenient summaries of an individual's performance on tasks that elicit behavior that is presumed to represent intelligence. Both, however, have been subject to similar pitfalls, generated primarily by the ways they have been used.

Mental Age. The concept of mental age (MA) was developed by Binet and Simon (1908) as a means of expressing a child's intellectual development. Based on a developmental notion, an MA score represents the average performance of children with chronological age (CA) equal to that score. For example, a child who obtains an MA of five years six months has performed on the test in a manner that is similar to the average performances of children who are five years six months old chronologically (norm-referenced concept). MA has been a useful concept, especially in mental retardation, since it is referenced to average intellectual development at various CA levels. Little sophistication about the measurement of intelligence is necessary for understanding the general idea of mental development expressed in this manner. MA provides a convenient means of communication, particularly with parents, about retarded children. Most people have had opportunities to observe children at various ages, which provides behavioral reference points that facilitate a general understanding of retarded individuals' abilities.

The MA concept has been less useful in other contexts. Since it is a summary score derived from performance on various types of test items, MA is a composite measure involving several skill areas. The single score provides little information about a specific skill level, which is why the previous discussion included qualifying statements about understanding mental development "generally." Two children may obtain the same MA and have very different patterns of skill strengths and deficits. For example, an MA of seven years might be attained by a child who is chronologically age five years and by another who is chronologically age nine years. These children might be labeled "bright," "retarded," or a number of other terms, as noted in chapter 1. Regardless of specific terminology, the same MA may have been attained from very different specific performances. The developmentally advanced child (CA five) will more frequently succeed in verbal reasoning and abstract items. The slower child (CA nine), on the other hand, will more frequently respond correctly on items of a performance nature or those for which previous learning was quite repetitive. Because equivalent MAs do not indicate similar skill capabilities, the usefulness of the concept is limited in terms of teaching, particularly when instruction is pinpointed to skill deficit areas.

Intelligence Quotient. The intelligence quotient (IQ) came into use somewhat later than MA. Originally the IQ was derived by dividing an individual's MA by the CA and multiplying the result by 100. Thus a child six years old who obtained an MA of 6 would have an IQ of 100 ($6 \div 6 = 1 \times 100 = 100$). This approach to IQ calculation was known as the ratio IQ. Certain difficulties developed in the use of the ratio IQ, which prompted its decline beginning about the mid-1940s. Since that time, the deviation IQ has been used as an alternative to the ratio calculation. This approach uses a statistical computation known as the standard deviation to derive the IQ. Several advantages are afforded by the deviation approach to determining IQ over the ratio calculation. The ratio calculation is quite unstable from age level to age level, making IQ comparison between ages difficult. The deviation approach for deriving IQ is a standard score with much more stability along the age continuum. The ratio calculation also becomes problematical as adulthood is approached. Obviously as an individual's CA increases and adulthood is approached, there is an apparent leveling or even a decline in measured intelligence, even with more items scored correctly. The ratio IQ thus becomes conceptually less applicable as individuals other than developing children are assessed. Because deviation IQ is referenced to a standard score approach, it circumvents these difficulties and is conceptually more sound at all ages.

IQ, like MA, is a composite measure derived by performance in several skill areas. The problems noted with MA in this regard are likewise presented by IQ. The global score provides an overall assessment of performance but does not indicate specific skill strengths and deficits. This problem may have been more acute with IQ than with MA. Because of the single score and apparent simplicity, users of IQ tended to forget the component performance of the score and treated it as a unitary concept. Additionally, the score began to be viewed as a somewhat sacred and permanent quantity rather than as a reflection of performance on a variety of tasks. This misconception led to considerable misuse of and disenchantment with the concept.

IQ remains in use today, and in many cases the abuses continue. However, IQ is being used with increased awareness of what is actually being assessed and is less often viewed as a permanent status resulting in labels that become entities in themselves. Modification of the IQ concept, plus expansion of evaluation concepts in general, appears to have prompted movement in the direction of more realistic use of the IQ score.

Commentary

One final point needs to be mentioned in this section. Earlier we discussed the important link between assessment and treatment. There have been situations in which it seemed that testing was being conducted without a clear notion of resulting interventions. Such assessment is illogical. However, another issue has emerged with respect to the assessment-treatment link. Some practitioners claim that the amount of testing required significantly detracts from the instructional time available. This is a serious problem, particularly when the time available is limited (such as a school year of 9 rather than 12 months). An appropriate balance is clearly needed, since assessment is only a supportive function to the primary goal of effective intervention. If such a balance is absent, the essential purpose of human service delivery is not being met.

This discussion has explored certain issues and conceptual developments in psychological assessment. The examination is by no means exhaustive; however, it does provide a backdrop for the study of assessment procedures.

EARLY LIFE

Core Concept 5	Vastly different assessment procedures become important depending upon age and performance area being evaluated.

Different assessment procedures are necessary at various stages in the life of a child. This section will examine approaches to evaluation during the early years of life. For purposes of this discussion, early life refers to the period up to about two years of age.

Evaluation during early life is conducted for at least two interrelated purposes: (a) identification of children who are already retarded in their development and (b) identification of children who have a high probability of being developmentally retarded at a later time. The President's Committee on Mental Retardation noted these purposes as essentially being the two components of what is termed "early screening assessment." Further discussion is necessary for two reasons. First, the idea of screening itself must be examined. Second, reasons for identification and potential results require additional exploration. Identification cannot stand alone, or it would merely represent identification for its own sake. Such activity without resulting action would be merely an exercise.

Screening Concepts

Core Concept 6	Screening assessment is very important throughout the life span but is crucial in early life.

Screening has been likened to a process of size sorting for items such as oranges (Meier, 1973) in which oranges are passed across a screen with holes of a certain size. These holes permit the oranges of an acceptable size or smaller to fall through. Those above the acceptable marketable size do not fall through the screen and thus are sorted out for other purposes (such as special gift packages). Those that fall through include oranges of a marketable size plus those that are much smaller. To complete the analogy, a second screening process could then be used involving a screen with holes much smaller than in the first screen. The only oranges to fall through the second screen would be those that are unmarketable because they are too small (but are suitable for frozen orange juice). This would leave only oranges in the size range that the buying public prefers. Screening for retardation is somewhat like this. Only those who are now developmentally retarded, or who exhibit behaviors that suggest that they will later be retarded, are sorted out by early screening.

It is generally agreed that early identification of handicapping conditions is highly important for a variety of reasons. First of all, in certain cases the ultimate impact of a handicapping condition can be reduced substantially if treatment or intervention is implemented early. There is the possibility that certain handicaps may even be prevented if action is taken sufficiently early. This latter assumption is particularly focused on those children who are thought to be high risk in terms of developmental retardation at a time other than infancy. Obviously there are some children for whom neither of these possibilities realistically exists. These are children who are severely retarded, frequently because of a birth defect or congenital malformation. Such conditions make identification more easily accomplished, but because of the severity of the problems, positive action is more difficult. In these situations early identification still plays a vital role in terms of future planning, both for the child and for the family.

Despite the importance of early screening assessment in mental retardation, certain problems persist in accomplishing the desired task. One of the serious difficulties in assessing young children involves the accuracy of prediction. The behavioral repertoire of the infant is much different from that of the child 6 or 10 years of age. The infant is primarily functioning in a motor skill world. Grasping, rolling over, sitting, and crawling are but a few of the behaviors that are involved in the baby's repertoire. Vocalizations are quite limited and frequently focused around physiological factors like hunger, pain, and fatigue. Yet early screening is trying to predict later behaviors that are very different. It is little wonder that prediction is not as accurate as might be desirable. The best predictor of performance on a given task is performance on a sample of that task or a similar task. For the most part this is not possible with an infant.

Although this indicates a definite problem area in the assessment of young children, the reader should not take it to mean that no prediction is possible. If this were the case, there would be little reason even to consider early screening. All that is being indicated here is that accuracy is not as great as might be desired. Fortunately for child care workers, developmental status and progress in those psychomotor areas that dominate the world of the infant do predict, even though grossly, later levels of functioning. As noted previously, accuracy of prediction is much greater with the severely impaired infant, who exhibits clearer signs of impairment earlier. The greatest difficulty is encountered with the mildly handicapped.

Another concern in early screening assessment involves the factors being evaluated during such measurement. More recent research and thinking in this area have changed to some degree which indicators are assessed in early screening. Meier (1973) reviews research that suggests valuable predictive information is available from assessing environmental factors in addition to looking at the actual developmental status of the child. Traditionally indicators such as socioeconomic status and parental education and occupation have been used to differentiate between environments. Other factors have now been shown to be more important influences on a child's development. Some of these include parents' language style, their attitudes about achievement, and their general involvement with the young child. Research is beginning to study these areas and promises important implications for the future.

Early screening has generally been discussed in terms of its positive value for the child who is suspected of having mental retardation and for that child's parents. In a broader societal context, certain ethical issues must be posed. Although social and ethical issues are the major focus of chapter 13, they warrant brief mention here. One of the negative effects that may result from early assessment is that a child acquires some sort of label. Labels and their impact on children have been a serious concern in special education for some time. We share those concerns and find the potential for detrimental influences to be even greater when and if they are attached to a youngster at infancy. Such labeling must be avoided, and child care workers must move to behavior-and skill-oriented descriptions. An additional concern has been mentioned previously but deserves repetition to emphasize its importance. Assessment, evaluation, or early screening, or whatever term is used, cannot be justified if its purpose is only for identification. During the school years, evaluation must be related to an educationally relevant purpose or action. Such a goal is even more crucial in the early years. One may imagine the negative effect of assessing a young child, stigmatizing the child with a label, and then doing nothing in the form of positive action beyond that. If categorizing or labeling is the only purpose, we cannot support evaluation during the early years or, indeed, at any time in the life of an individual.

Earlier we mentioned the problems involved in evaluation of minority groups. These same problems are of even greater concern in early assessment. Early screening is greatly involved in the societal issues of poverty, ethnicity, and environmental quality of life. As these issues are addressed with more skill, it is anticipated that not only early childhood assessment but also early childhood education will play an increasingly important role.

EARLY LIFE ASSESSMENT

Prenatal

Core Concept 7	Prenatal evaluation can provide extremely important information regarding the status of a fetus.

Advances in medical science and health care techniques over the past decade have had a significant impact on the field of mental retardation. One area in which dramatic developments have occurred involves assessment and detection of mental retardation on a prenatal basis.

During pregnancy the most common assessment involves routine monitoring of the physical condition of the mother and fetus by the obstetrician or other trained health care personnel. Part of this assessment process includes a detailed record of the mother in terms of family and medical history, and the mother's blood pressure, uterus size, urine status, and other indicators are monitored throughout the pregnancy to assure that no symptoms are present that would signal danger for the fetus or the mother. At this level of examination the mother's physical condition is the primary source of information for assessment. The obstetrician also will examine the fetus by various means, such as fetal heart rate, as the pregnancy proceeds. This ongoing monitoring is crucial to maximize the probability of a healthy baby being born. The mother's diet is frequently altered, and occasionally medication is administered to correct minor deviations from the optimum situation for fetal development. For individuals who do not have access to such health care, a much higher risk is involved in terms of the birth of a defective child. Such higher risks are more frequent among segments of the population that cannot afford adequate health care or for some other reason do not have adequate medical resources available to them.

Ongoing prenatal assessment is generally adequate as long as a healthy mother and fetus are involved. Certain danger signs, however, prompt more extensive evaluation. If the family or medical history suggests that a particular problem may occur (such as an hereditary disorder), routine monitoring of health signs is not sufficient. If the mother's physical condition or that of the fetus progresses in a highly deviant fashion, more extensive evaluation and action are in order. In such cases evaluation becomes diagnosis aimed at the prenatal assessment of fetal status. This is accomplished by evaluating certain biological and chemical characteristics of the fetus.

Medical diagnostic procedures, such as those just mentioned, have provided professionals with a vastly improved ability to effectively work with prospective parents where potential problems exist. One of the more well-known techniques, *amniocentesis*, involves sampling the amniotic fluid surrounding the fetus in utero and analyzing it for evidence of chromosomal abnormalities or other indicators of undesirable development. Another procedure, *fetoscopy*, employs a needle-like camera which is inserted into the womb to videoscan the fetus for visible abnormalities. *Ultrasonography* uses high frequency sound waves which are bounced through the mother's abdomen to record tissue densities, enabling the detection of certain central nervous system deformities and placental status. These assessment procedures, as well as others being developed as research progresses (e.g., chorion biopsy), permit a rather complete evaluation of the prenatal youngster. However, diagnostic analyses of this type are not possible with every type of retardation, and work has focused on clinical syndromes that involve genetic metabolic disorders resulting in severe mental retardation.

O'Brien (1971) discussed 27 hereditary disorders for which accurate diagnosis is possible, including galactosemia, Gaucher's disease, maple syrup urine disease, and Tay-Sachs disease. On an individual basis these disorders occur rarely. Within an entire society, however, the ability to detect and take action is a major contribution to the field of mental retardation. Even more significant is the ability to prevent the personal tragedies resulting from the birth of children with such devastating disorders. In most cases parents of these children are forced to watch what appeared to be a healthy normal baby progressively deteriorate to a passivity or premature death.

Prenatal assessment of the type discussed has not advanced to the point at which it is routinely conducted. For the most part the general obstetric monitoring mentioned previously suffices as the first level of screening, similar to the first screening in our orange-sorting analogy. In certain cases, however, metabolic or genetic disorders have a higher probability of occurrence. Current thinking suggests that *diagnostic* prenatal evaluation should be routinely conducted in such situations. Tay-Sachs disease, for example, is a disorder transmitted genetically and primarily found in individuals of Ashkenazi Jewish origin. When two individuals with this background plan to have children, it is wise to evaluate fetal status from a prenatal diagnostic standpoint. O'Brien (1971) also argued for such evaluation with all pregnant women over 40 years of age, because maternal age is an important factor in the birth of children with Down syndrome. The detection process for prenatal identification of Down syndrome is still being refined. As this work progresses, it is quite possible that such diagnostic screening will be recommended even for others younger than 40 years.

Newborn

Core Concept 8   Assessment of the newborn infant may identify problems that prompt immediate intervention to prevent mental retardation.

A variety of assessment techniques are used with the newborn. This represents a crucial period for the child, and clinical assessment at this time is vital. Immediately following completion of the birth process several factors are noted and rated using what is known as the Apgar test. This procedure is completed by delivery room staff at "1 minute and 5 minutes of age and may be repeated until the infant's condition has stabilized" (Chinn, 1979). Five factors are included in Apgar scoring: heart rate, respiratory effort, muscle tone, reflex irritability, and color. Each is rated by giving a score of 0, 1, or 2 (0 indicating low or weak, 2 indicating high or strong), and the separate scores are then totaled. Extremely low Apgar scores on the 5-minute measure suggest that there is a potential problem. Chinn (1979) noted that children with a 5-minute score of 3 or below have three times as many neurological problems at age 1 as babies of similar birth weights with Apgar scores of 7 to 10. Apgar scores of 6 or lower are viewed with concern. Infants with such scores are usually monitored more closely for the first several days, and interventions are made as necessary.

Several other assessment procedures are conducted in the medical laboratories at the time the child is born and during the very early part of life. Many of these procedures are aimed at the detection of inherited or congenitally present abnormalities (overlapping some of those that have been discussed under prenatal diagnosis). As in the prenatal evaluation process, a biological-chemical analysis is frequently the means by which newborn screening is accomplished. Citing earlier work, Meier (1973) listed 14 different inherited abnormalities that are detectable through analysis of blood specimens alone:

phenylketonuria (PKU)*
maple syrup urine disease*
tyrosinemia*
homocystinuria*
histidinemia*
valinemia*
galactosemia transferase deficiency*
argininosuccinic aciduria*
orotic aciduria*
hereditary angioneurotic edema

galactosemia transferase or kinase deficiency*
emphysema (adult)
liver disease (infant)
sickle cell anemia
*Treatable.

Ten of these disorders are treatable in a fashion that prevents or substantially diminishes the developmental problems that result if the conditions are unknown or ignored. Because treatable disorders make up a substantial proportion of the list, significantly more newborn screening may be justified. One is prompted to wonder why such assessment is not necessarily routine. Diagnosis can be accomplished, at least on these disorders, from analysis of a dried blood spot, and in each case complete or partial automated analysis is possible. This certainly streamlines the process and permits cost-effective mass screening. It is hoped that future health care services will routinely encompass such newborn evaluation.

Certain other abnormalities are detectable by clinical observation at the newborn stage. Medical examination of conditions such as Down syndrome and cranial anomalies will indicate the existence of a problem with considerable accuracy. Such effective evaluation, however, involves those conditions that are present and observable either at birth or in the first few days of the infant's life.

Beyond the Newborn Stage

Core Concept 9	Evaluation beyond the newborn stage broadens to include many assessment areas not previously amenable to measurement.

There is certainly no widespread agreement concerning when one stage of development ends and another begins. In fact, it is somewhat misleading to suggest the idea that a stage per se is an identifiable, discrete, and existing entity. Even the theoretical concepts of stages are being strongly challenged (Flavell, 1977). Broad usage of terminology such as newborn, infant, and early childhood is fluid at best. In the previous section the term newborn was used to denote the time shortly after birth. The use of this term in such a fashion was not intended to suggest any particular "stage" but was used for convenience in communication. For purposes of the remainder of this discussion, evaluation will be placed in an age context rather than using terms that connote stages.

It has already been noted that certain measurement difficulties are encountered during the period from birth through the first few years of life (Gaussen, 1984; Hanson, Smith, & Hume, 1984). This is particularly true when one is attempting to predict later intelligence (Cohen & Parmelee, 1983). Before the acquisition of language, the child must be evaluated primarily in terms of sensorimotor development. Since later intelligence measures are heavily weighted by verbal performance items, prediction difficulty is to be expected. There has, however, been progress in this area of assessment.

Intellectual. Many instruments and evaluation procedures have been developed for the assessment of intellectual functioning in young children, of which the Cattell Infant Intelligence Scale is one of the better known. Oriented toward sensorimotor assessment, the Cattell scale is used on children from 2 months to about 30 months of age. It was designed as an extension to very young ages of the revised Stanford-Binet intelligence test. Research has indicated that the Cattell scale is useful for predicting intellectual functioning of mentally retarded children who have been referred for examination by physicians. Less accurate prediction has been demonstrated, however, using broader samples of children who have not been so referred. This would seem to suggest that the Cattell Infant Intelligence Scale may be useful for screening purposes but is less helpful for general prediction in a non-high-risk population.

Similar to the Cattell scale in some respects are the revised Bayley Scales of Infant Development. The Bayley scales, although taking somewhat longer to administer, have certain strengths over the Cattell scale. The Bayley scales include test items for the first two months after birth, which may be an advantage for situations requiring assessment both of the *very* young and of older individuals functioning at a very low level (e.g., Whiteley & Krenn, 1986). Further, there are subscales for mental and motor performance, which has clinical appeal but may be misleading if they are overinterpreted. Like the Cattell scale, the Bayley scales rely heavily on the assessment of sensorimotor performance, since there are few other means of performance evaluation at this age. Also like the Cattell, Baley Scales appear predictive for certain high-risk populations such as the premature (Ross, 1985). The two instruments overlap so greatly regarding what they measure that occasionally they have been characterized as being interchangeable for diagnostic purposes.

Research on the assessment of extremely young children has also been conducted by Kagan (1972). This work, which investigates cognitive development from a considerably different framework, may provide valuable information for early evaluation of future intellectual status. Kagan concentrated on the young child's ability to focus attention on certain stimuli for a sustained period of time. The data suggest that children proceed through a series of different response patterns when they are as young as 30 to 60 days. Additionally, a variety of stimulus conditions appears to be influential at different points in time, which may well suggest what factors in the infant's environment are important in terms of cognitive development. Although highly speculative, there is the definite impression that different processes of cognitive development are being tapped than that of the sensorimotor performance area, which is the predominant focus of evaluation in the previously mentioned techniques.

Other techniques are used by many professionals for early assessment of a child's intellectual functioning. Meier, (1973) discussed several approaches in addition to those mentioned above, including the Kuhlmann-Binet Scale (birth through 30 months), the Griffiths Scale (birth though four years), and the Revised Gesell Scale (birth through five years). The absence of discussion regarding these other efforts is not an implication of their lesser worth, but in-depth examination in any single area is beyond the scope of the present text.

Language. There has been a limited amount of effort in the separate area of early language assessment, which is closely related to assessment of cognitive development. The primary work in assessment of language before age three months has involved clinical analysis of certain factors in the infant's cry. A review of research by Ostwald, Phibbs, and Fox (1968) included 24 studies spanning a period of well over 100 years. Early language assessment has not received widespread application and thus far appears to be of limited pragmatic value in terms of early evaluation.

Language assessment after the 3-month age has been addressed in the Playtest (Friedlander, 1971) and in the Early Language Assessment Scale (Honig & Caldwell, 1966). The Playtest approach (3 to 12 months) is aimed at the assessment of children's receptive language ability, which Friedlander characterized as "the effectiveness of their listening to the fine-grained aspects of natural sound and language stimuli [and] . . . their methods of using natural sound input in the integration of their sensory experiences" (1971, p. 10). This evaluation thus goes beyond the hearing aspect of sound reception, placing natural sound processing as a central issue and also focusing on the young child's receptive abilities in terms of language.

Of particular interest in this area is research comparing children who exhibited substantial impairment in speech development with similar children who did not have such disorders. In the Playtest, television story-telling sequences were shown to the two groups of children. The narration for the story was presented to both groups both in a natural, clear fashion and in a totally garbled form. The children with normal speech development exhibited a high level of interest in and attention to the story with natural narration but not in the story with the incomprehensible narration. The children with speech development problems watched both the natural and the incomprehensible narration sequences with an equally high level of interest and attention. These results suggest that those children with speech development disorders were not discriminating between the garbled narration and the clear one. Clearly there is a significant aspect of auditory reception that is operating beyond the mere sound acuity level. This line of work may be valuable for early receptive language evaluation. It is quite possible that developmental retardation, at least in the language area, may be predicted from such assessment. Future research and development in terms of clinical use of these techniques may result in important advances in the evaluation of young children, although the sophisticated instrumentation involved would preclude such assessment on a mass screening basis.

The Early Language Assessment Scale (3 to 48 months) is designed to evaluate both the receptive and expressive language abilities of young children. Operating somewhat differently than Playtest (and with simpler apparatus) this technique primarily focuses on the young child's response to certain stimuli provided by the examiner. Using this scale, the examiner presents a variety of commands, auditory stimuli of a nonlanguage nature, certain visual stimuli, and imitation items. Depending on the response required, a child's performance is scored on a rating sheet in terms of receptive and expressive language development. Very little training is necessary for administering this evaluation, and screening in this manner appears to be feasible on a rather routine basis. Although not in widespread use, this approach appears promising in terms of routine health and well-baby evaluation. Since the primary monitoring at this age is conducted by health care personnel, it would seem that such ongoing assessment might be easily conducted during early and continuing visits with the pediatrician and office staff.

Evaluation of language development remains an emerging and increasingly important area of interest in early assessment, particularly with respect to developmental mental retardation (Rocissano & Yatchmink, 1983). As previously noted, evaluation of later mental status relies quite heavily on language and verbal functioning. Specific areas of performance level undoubtedly will become more important as professionals become increasingly discrete in their skill description. Language assessment eventually may be viewed as evaluating language skill per se rather than language skill as representative of some abstract and larger concept, such as mental development. It is already clear that an area such as language will be more discretely analyzed in terms of component behaviors. As this occurs, it is quite likely that efforts in evaluation, screening, and diagnosis will take on a very different description, increase professionals' predictive ability, and certainly become more amenable to intervention and modification.

Social/Adaptive Behavior. Evaluation of social-emotional development presents a considerable challenge to those working with young children. A variety of instruments have been developed in an effort to effectively assess this area of behavior, and in each case a common problem has been encountered: the reliability of the assessment itself. Of the 10 procedures listed in the 1973 report of The President's Committee on Mental Retardation, only three are judged as having "adequate" reliability and validity (Meier, 1973). Two of these include the time shortly after birth (Vineland Social Maturity Scale, birth to 18 years, and the functional analysis approach, birth to adult). The third ranges from one to six years (Quantitative Analysis of Tasks).

The Vineland Social Maturity Scale was constructed with sequentially ordered, age-graded items that cover several content areas. These areas include self-help skills, self-direction, locomotion, occupation, communication, and social relations. This instrument was viewed by its author as designed to assess performance and ability of the child in terms of progressing toward independence. Two approaches to data collection are involved, an interview of the parent and observation of the child. When the child is not present or available, the information is gathered solely on the basis of interview data. Although this scale has been judged as adequate in terms of both reliability and validity, there have been a number of concerns about it, including cultural bias (Slate, 1983). Workers in mental retardation have long believed that better assessment is possible, which has led to efforts to design techniques that will either augment or supplant the Vineland Scales.

One such effort is a revision named the *Vineland Adaptive Behavior Scales*, (Sparrow, Balla, & Cicchetti, 1984). (Both original and revised versions are mentioned in this text because readers are likely to encounter both during the time of transition.) The revised edition involves three versions: (a) the Interview Edition-Survey Form, (b) the Interview Edition-Expanded Form, and (c) the Classroom Edition. The Classroom Edition is usually completed by a teacher, whereas the other two are completed by someone intimately acquainted with the person being evaluated (e.g., parents). The domains of assessment overlap with the earlier version to some degree and include communication, daily living, socialization, motor skills, and maladaptive behavior (the last being an optional area of evaluation). Administration procedures have been altered, and continued research will evaluate the utility of these new scales in comparison to the earlier version.

Also applicable in the very early life of a child is assessment that, for want of a better term, has been labeled a functional analysis approach (Bijou & Peterson, 1970). Although not designed as an instrument per se, this approach is founded on the basic principles of applied behavior analysis and is highly relevant to the issues of early childhood assessment. The functional analysis approach to assessment requires direct observation of the child rather than an informant's description of behavior. It is conducted for children who are referred because of behavioral or developmental problems and is accomplished in the setting in which the problem occurs. Data are typically recorded in terms of three categories: behavioral deficits, behavioral excesses, and inappropriate stimulus control. Within these general categories the behavioral description of the child's functioning is very specific, which then permits precise intervention rather than a broad-spectrum or "shotgun treatment" approach in which the professional hopes that the treatment may help an undefined problem. This level of specificity represents a definite strength of the functional analysis assessment framework but requires substantial training in applied behavior analysis. Given appropriate preparation, either professional or paraprofessional staff members can conduct the evaluation. Another strength of functional analysis assessment is the use of direct observation of the child rather than interviews with informants. Interviews have long been viewed as problematic and have added substantially to the difficulties in reliability and validity of assessment.

Direct observation is also required by the Quantitative Analysis of Tasks developed by White and Kaban (1971), but the observer takes a considerably different approach from that in functional analysis. The White and Kaban technique also involves careful observation of a child's behavior and the environmental stimulus conditions in a natural setting. In addition, the evaluator not only observes but also makes inferences about and describes the child's apparent purpose in terms of the recorded behavior. This interpretation of the child's purpose is then coded and scored in reference to several criteria. The coding of social tasks involves numerous classifications, including gaining attention, avoiding attention, gaining approval, being annoying, maintaining social contact, competing, and providing information. Although the instructions are quite specific with regard to coding, inferences made by the observer are obviously crucial. The strength and reliability of the evaluation (or conversely, the weakness and unreliability) are probably predominantly determined by this factor. This evaluation is viewed as being appropriately administered by trained paraprofessionals. The soundness, accuracy, and reliability of assessment rest heavily on the judgment and, consequently, on the training of the observer.

Multiple Domain Assessment. The discussion thus far has focused on instruments and techniques that assess a child's developmental status in a somewhat limited area. Although the boundaries of performance areas are far from distinct, an attempt has been made by many to discretely assess intellectual development, language development, and social-emotional development as well as to consider the early health status and possible presence of inheritable disorders. Assessment in a somewhat broader framework, including infant-environment interactions, has received considerable attention in recent years (Gaussen & Stratton, 1985). This has led to the design of a variety of developmental screening techniques that evaluate several factors simultaneously while still providing specific information in each area. These techniques have grown in popularity for several reasons, one of which is the efficiency of using a single instrument to assess several performance areas. The report of The President's Committee on Mental Retardation discussed six different instruments of the multifactor type (Meier, 1973): the Rapid Developmental Screening Checklist (1972), designed by the Committee on Children with Handicaps, American Academy of Pediatrics, chaired by Margaret Giannini; Guide to Normal Milestones of Development (Haynes, 1967); the Developmental Screening Inventory (Knobloch, Pasamanick, & Sherard, 1967); the CCD Developmental Progress Scale (Boyd, 1969); the Revised Denver Developmental Screening Test (Frankenburg, Dodds, Fandal, Kazuk, & Cohrs, 1975); and the Program Assessment Chart (Gunzberg, 1963). This text does not permit full examination of each of these instruments, so only selected techniques are discussed. (For more comprehensive information concerning these instruments, see either the original sources or others focusing on this area exclusively [e.g., Meier, 1973; Salvia & Ysseldyke, 1985].)

The Revised Denver Developmental Screening Test is one rather widely used multifactor instrument. It is useful from birth to six years of age and scores a child's status in four different areas of development: gross motor, fine motor, language, and person-social. It is easily administered in about 20 minutes (including scoring and interpretation), requires no special training of the examiner, and is available in Spanish. Considerable research has been conducted on the Denver scale regarding its standardization and related prescreening procedures (Prescreening Developmental Questionnaires—PDQ) (Burgess, Asher, Doucet, Reardon, & Daste, 1984). The results generally suggest adequate reliability and validity for a screening instrument, although the full Denver norms have been questioned by some (Salvia & Ysseldyke, 1985).

Similar to the Denver scale is the CCD Developmental Progress Scale. The CCD Scale, used from birth to 8 years of age, evaluates a child's developmental status in three areas: self-sufficiency skills, communication-interpersonal skills, and motor skills, which actually represents a combination of the two motor areas of the Denver scale. It has been suggested that the CCD scale is preferable to the Denver scale for older children, while the Denver is more appropriate for younger children (Meier, 1973). This judgment is based on the concentration of test items in the Denver scale at the younger ages (birth to 18 months) with a substantial decrease in the number of items for ages four to six years. The CCD scale includes an equal number of items at all levels from birth to eight years, making this instrument far stronger than the Denver scale at the age levels above four years. In viewing test item distribution, either instrument can probably be appropriately used between two and four years of age.

Both the Denver and CCD scales use parent reporting and direct observation of the child as sources for developmental status information. Parent reporting has been notoriously problematic throughout the history of measurement and evaluation. The basic difficulty in this area lies with the accuracy of the information provided and agreement between rating sources such as parents, teachers, and others (Soyster & Ehly, 1986). Recognizing the possibility of faulty recall, Meier (1973) noted that Boyd (1969) addressed yet another point that has vital importance in relation to parental reporting in general. It is Boyd's position that to obtain accurate reports of the child's typical behavior, the phrasing of the question is crucial. Questions must be posed in a manner eliciting behavioral descriptions rather than suggesting socially appropriate answers. For example, checklist interviews tend to result in inaccurately high ratings because of parents' defensive assumption that the question itself means the child should be able to perform the task. Although requiring a description of typical behavior will not solve all of the problems involved in parent reporting, it certainly appears promising in terms of reducing one source of data bias.

PRESCHOOL YEARS

Core Concept 10   Intellectual, language, perceptual-motor, and social/adaptive behaviors are each important in evaluating the status of preschool youngsters, and proper assessment must employ procedures appropriate for this age range.

There is no clear-cut boundary at which certain instruments are absolutely no longer used and others systemically become appropriate. Some assessment techniques discussed earlier are used during the preschool years, and others are not. Likewise, some evaluation procedures discussed in this section extend downward in age to a point that could easily be termed "early years." Techniques that overlap in age ranges will not be reviewed again. This section will examine selected evaluation procedures used *primarily* during the years immediately preceding a child's school enrollment.

Intellectual Functioning

Perhaps the type of assessment most frequently associated with developmental mental retardation involves the measurement of intelligence. As suggested earlier in this chapter, intelligence has frequently assumed the status of an existing entity in the minds of many. Actually, intelligence is an abstract concept representing the ability to reason and comprehend; it is inferred to exist to some greater or lesser degree according to an individual's performance on selected tasks. Because of recent developments in evaluation it is a clearer that a particular score on an intelligence test is representative of various performances and that intelligence, as a general ability, is inferred rather than observed.

Part of the concept of intelligence just discussed certainly results from the assumptions made in the development of early instrumentation. Binet's early work was based on the idea that intelligence was a general ability factor. Consequently, his approach involved a mixture of items that aimed at an assessment representing a composite measure, presumably including performances related to the idea of general intelligence. The Stanford-Binet test, a revision of Binet's earlier work, remains an instrument that generates a composite measure. However, some use of this instrument in clinical and diagnostic settings has resulted in attempts to isolate the various performances to a certain degree (Ferinden, Jacobson, & Kovalinsky, 1970). The Stanford-Binet IV, a further revision, is beginning to appear in the field. Its usefulness is not yet entirely known, but it will certainly be of interest to professionals conducting assessments of intelligence.

The Stanford-Binet test is recommended as appropriate for age 2 years through adulthood, although other instruments frequently are used for individuals over 12 years of age because of the administration time required by the Stanford-Binet when testing older people. The Stanford-Binet has frequently been viewed as the standard against which intelligence measurement is compared. However, the 1972 edition (Terman & Merrill, 1973) has been questioned, and serious reliability, validity, and normative concerns have been raised (Salvia & Ysseldyke, 1985).

Another instrument that is frequently used with preschool children to assess intelligence is the Wechsler Preschool and Primary Scale of Intelligence (WPPSI). The WPPSI is recommended for use with children from ages 4 to 6 1/2 years and has a different design than the Binet test. The WPPSI is constructed with items organized into eleven subtests by content area, which encourages the use of the instrument as a measure of more specific skill areas. (Published in 1967, the WPPSI represents a much more recently developed instrument than other Wechsler scales, although the others have been revised.) The WPPSI has been used increasingly with the preschool child for whom evaluation of intellectual performance is required. As with most instruments, the WPPSI has considerably fewer data from a clinical and diagnostic standpoint than either the Binet or other Wechsler scales, because the WPPSI has been used less. Looking to the high end of the intelligence continuum, the WPPSI presents particular difficulties with the very capable child. There appears to be a substantial ceiling on the items, which do not establish the top limits of the more able children, resulting in inaccurate assessment for them. It does, however, provide a useful instrument for preschool children who are already suspected of functioning at a low level.

The Peabody Picture Vocabulary Test—Revised (PPVT—R) and its earlier forms (PPVT) have been described in various fashions. Bush and Waugh (1976) discussed the PPVT as an instrument for assessing intelligence in preschool children. The PPVT—R is described by its authors (Dunn & Dunn, 1981) as assessing general intelligence only in terms of vocabulary. Dunn and Dunn characterized the instrument as primarily providing an index of achievement or scholastic aptitude. The PPVT—R is a quickly administered test (typically 10 to 15 minutes) that can be used with individuals from ages 2 1/2 to 40 years. The examiner presents a printed page with four numbered pictures and reads a stimulus word. Children being tested then point to the picture they believe best represents the word that was read. Salvia and Ysseldyke (1985) noted that

> data in the technical manual indicate adequate reliability for screening purposes, but there are no data on the validity of the measure. Overall, the technical characteristics of this scale far surpass those of other picture vocabulary tests. Used properly and with awareness that it samples only receptive vocabulary, the PPVT—R can serve as an extremely useful screening device. (p. 175)

Language Functioning

As the child grows older, the assessment of language development and the assessment of intellectual functioning become increasingly similar, with distinctions between the two frequently difficult to detect. Several factors account for this. For one thing, the child rapidly grows in sophistication with regard to language structure, at least in terms of normal language development. Menyuk (1972) noted that by the time normal children reach three to four years of age they have a command of the basic syntactic structure of language. This permits a very different response mode than was possible when the very young child was operating almost totally as a sensorimotor organism. Test developers who are working with this age range take advantage of the new response mode. For the assessment of intellectual status there is an increasingly heavier verbal component to be considered as the child's age increases, and language and intellectual assessment become more closely related as the child grows older.

As an example of this situation, the PPVT—R warrants mention in terms of language assessment. Although the PPVT—R is occasionally described as an intelligence test, various professionals view it as being more appropriately conceived as a receptive language measure. In fact, some characterize it primarily in terms of receptive language (Dunn & Dunn, 1981; Lerner, 1981). Because of the nature of the item presentation, such a view appears quite credible. The inference of receptive language evaluation certainly requires the use of a less abstract concept than does that of intelligence.

Another instrument that is frequently viewed as assessing language is the Illinois Test of Psycholinguistic Abilities (ITPA) (Kirk, McCarthy, & Kirk, 1968). Developed for use with children from about 2 1/2 to 10 years of age, the ITPA is a highly complicated instrument that provides a profile of the child's performance in 12 different subtest areas. Initially the ITPA was primarily used with children who were designated as having learning disabilities. However, as ideas about prescriptive education have grown in popularity, it has enjoyed broader application to other populations, including those with developmental retardation. Although the ITPA is a useful instrument, it is not without problems. It is a cumbersome instrument to use (at least in terms of some subjects), and the examiner requires considerable training to administer it. Some of the subtests are far from being pure in terms of the specific skill being measured, and depending on the setting, may or may not provide relevant instructional information. Another problem with the ITPA involves the standardization population and has particular relevance to the testing of retarded children. Only children with IQ scores between 84 and 116 were included in the normative group, which means that a large data base does not exist for many of the retarded children. This does not preclude the use of ITPA, but the existence of such data would certainly provide a clearer picture of ITPA measurement properties when used with retarded children. Salvia and Ysseldyke (1985) summarized their examination of this instrument by noting that "the ITPA seems to have inadequate norms, poor reliability, and questionable validity" (p. 261). This statement may surprise many who have used the ITPA extensively, but it emphasizes the importance of examining the assessment devices used.

The ITPA has perhaps been more useful as a conceptual framework than as a direct assessment instrument. It has generated a definite change in the way many professionals view children. Many professionals have moved toward the functional analysis of skill level as a way of thinking, which has long been the position taken by those skilled in applied behavior analysis. A gap remains; proponents of applied behavior analysis request much more precision in skill definition than is possible by actual application of the ITPA. However, the conceptual change is significant when viewed in the broader professional perspective of purposes of evaluation.

Various language assessment instruments have been developed with differing degrees of precision and standardization (e.g., Houston Test of Language Development, Mecham Verbal Language Development Scale, Utah Test of Language Development). A complete description of all such instruments is beyond the scope of an introductory text on developmental mental retardation. It is more appropriate to discuss an evaluation approach rather than a particular instrument or technique. Many professionals who are vitally concerned with practical application have viewed assessment as being important only in relation to intervention or instruction. Such a perspective places little value on scores unless they represent performance that is precisely related to specific instructional activities which will result in skill change. As implied in previous discussion, such an approach assumes the configuration of the specific skill assessment of applied behavior analysis and tends to discount issues such as cause (except in rare cases that can be rectified by surgery). Consequently, evaluation in this framework often reflects ongoing monitoring built into the instructional program or designed specifically for a given instructional program (e.g., Distar Language Program). Such assessment is in line with concepts of prescriptive education (in fact, it represents a potent force in the development of such concepts) and is precise in pinpointing instructional effort where it is most needed.

Perceptual-Motor Functioning

Assessment of perceptual-motor skills is more commonly an evaluation conducted with children suspected to have learning disabilities than with those thought to be developmentally retarded. Although there is a theoretical basis that links perceptual-motor functioning to specific learning disabilities, motor functioning is a crucial skill area in terms of instruction for retarded children. Without the various visual-motor skills the child is in a difficult position to perform the tasks required in many instructional settings. Consequently, a child who is experiencing such performance difficulty should be assessed in terms of specific level of functioning and should have instructional activities designed in relation to these skills. In this context a brief discussion of perceptual-motor skill assessment is warranted.

One of the better-known assessment techniques in the perceptual motor area is the Frostig Developmental Test of Visual Perception. This instrument is designed for use with children from about four to eight years of age. Some latitude in age range is obviously reasonable for children who exhibit developmental retardation to a significant degree. The Frostig test can be administered either individually or to groups and assesses five different areas: (1) eye-motor (hand) coordination, (2) figure-ground perception, (3) form constancy, (4) position in space, and (5) spatial relations. Frostig has designed specific remedial activities that are coordinated with the evaluation instrument. From her viewpoint, identification of perceptual deficits is crucial in terms of the early remediation (kindergarten and first grade) that would allow appropriate school progress (Frostig & Horne, 1964).

Another device used for assessment in the perceptual-motor area is the Purdue Perceptual-Motor Survey. Although the Purdue survey was not designed specifically for preschool assessment (norms are based on children between 6 and 10 years old), there is some latitude in the age range. This survey is based on a developmental theory that portrays the child as moving through a sequence of learning stages, such as those postulated by Piaget. The survey involves 22 items arranged in 11 different subtests. Essentially, the Purdue survey is designed to tap three major perceptual-motor skill areas: laterality, directionality, and perceptual-motor matching.

Perceptual-motor assessment is also facilitated by use of the Developmental Test of Visual-Motor Integration (VMI). Developed by Beery (1967), this instrument involves a paper and pencil performance by the child in which geometric forms are presented as items to be copied. Although the VMI was designed primarily for use at the preschool and early primary levels, the manual notes that it can be administered to children from 2 to 15 years of age. The VMI was devised to assess the degree to which motor behavior and visual perception are integrated. As with other perceptual-motor evaluation, the purpose is to identify fundamental skill deficits related to performance on various academic tasks. Such deficits are pinpointed for remedial instruction aimed at preparing the child for basic performance of academic tasks.

The previously discussed assessment devices focus on perceptual-motor skill within a framework of the integration of perceptual functioning and motor performance. These two crucial skill areas must operate in concert for many academic tasks to be performed. There are instances, however, in which it is desirable to evaluate the status of one component without the other influencing the assessment. With many instruments this is not possible; a severe motor problem, for example, would substantially reduce the overall performance score. Under this condition an examiner would not be able to evaluate a child's visual perception functioning because both visual and motor components are blended in the task. Colarusso and Hammill (1972) designed the Motor-Free Visual Perception Test (MVPT), an instrument that somewhat circumvents this problem. This test presents the child with a series of drawings involving various visual images. The motor response is significantly minimized because the child may only be required to respond with a head nod as the examiner points to various drawing components. Such an approach may hold promise for situations where physical disability impairs motor responses.

Social/Adaptive Behavior

A variety of approaches for assessing social skill status were discussed in the section on very young children. In many cases the upper age range extends beyond early childhood, into preschool and elementary years, and even beyond. Consequently, only a very brief examination of social skill assessment will be undertaken here. As the child is progressing through this developmental phase and into the elementary years, judgments or ratings by others such as caretakers, teachers, and parents are often part of social skill assessment. It is important to remember that such ratings present certain problems with respect to reliability and agreement (Soyster & Ehly,

1986). These information sources are very important, and continued research is needed to solve the problems that they present.

Adaptive behavior involves skills that may be generically considered within the social competence area. As mentioned in chapter 1, adaptive behavior has become a part of the formal definition for mental retardation of the AAMD. This behavior was formerly assessed with the Vineland Social Maturity Scale. However, the AAMD had developed the Adaptive Behavior Scale (ABS) particularly for the evaluation of adaptive and maladaptive behavior. It was specifically developed for individuals who are either suspected of, or who are confirmed as being, mentally retarded. It is also described as being appropriate for individuals who are emotionally maladjusted. This instrument assesses the individual's effectiveness in adapting to the natural and social demands of the environment. Several factors are evaluated, such as self-abusive behavior, destructive behavior, sexually aberrant behavior, independent functioning, and time and number concepts. Scales are available for early childhood through adulthood, although caution must be exercised in interpreting scores per se; program planning is more appropriately based on a critical analysis of specific skill level in particular areas than on adaptive behavior. This is especially true in light of the fact that many institutional subjects were used during standardization, making score interpretation for mildly handicapped even more difficult. There are concerns regarding the standardization data on both the original ABS and the Public School Version (Salvia & Ysseldyke, 1985), but revision research has been promising (e.g., MacDonald & Barton, 1986).

The Cain-Levine Social Competency Scale was specifically developed for assessing trainable mentally retarded children from 5 years to 13 years 11 months. The clinician, however, may find that its usefulness extends beyond categorical boundaries of the trainable child. This instrument, designed as a behavior rating scale, involves 44 items divided into four subscale areas: self-help, initiative, social skills, and communication. Administration of the instrument results in an overall score as well as performance scores in each of the four subscale areas. These scores are viewed as being useful for screening, for initial planning of socially oriented training, and for evaluation of training effectiveness.

ELEMENTARY SCHOOL YEARS

Core Concept 11   Multiple areas of functioning must be evaluated during the elementary years, and proper evaluation requires use of technically and conceptually sound procedures appropriate for this age range.

The purpose of this section is to briefly discuss assessment during the elementary school years. The child who is developmentally retarded may be somewhat out of phase with regard to the usual chronological age—formal education sequence. Consequently, the term elementary years is used only as a generic guideline and primarily involves ages 5 to 11 or 12 years. Additionally, the overlapping age ranges for assessment approaches have already become evident in the previous discussion. Certain instruments that were examined in terms of the preschool child extend to and occasionally beyond the age range presently being considered. Such instruments will not be discussed again. Instead, other techniques, which become age-appropriate during the elementary years, will receive primary attention.

Within this section on the elementary years, separate attention will be given to emerging systems of assessment. For example, the System of Multicultural Pluralistic Assessment (SOMPA) (Mercer & Lewis, 1977) evaluates across several attribute areas and cannot be appropriately discussed under a specific area subheading such as intellectual or achievement.

Intellectual Functioning

Several instruments were mentioned previously under intellectual assessment that extended into the age range of 5 to 12 years. Additionally, one of the best-known intelligence tests, the Wechsler Intelligence Scale for Children—Revised (WISC—R), becomes age-appropriate in this range. The WISC—R is recommended for use with children between the ages of 5 and 15 years. This instrument was designed in a somewhat similar fashion to the WPPSI, discussed earlier for younger children. The WISC—R has 12 subtests that are divided into two general areas, verbal and performance measures. Ten of these subtests are used to generate separate scores for verbal and performance dimensions (digit span and maze subtests are not included in the scoring of this revised edition). Like most standardized instruments, the WISC—R is basically a norm-referenced instrument. Used in this fashion the resulting score is a composite IQ that indicates general ability. However, the revised edition also provides for a profiling of the child's performance in individual subtest areas, which generates more specific information than the composite IQ.

The WISC—R, developed in 1974, has a considerable history and data base as its foundation. Its predecessor, the WISC, was developed in 1949 and over the years generated a vast data base with considerable research, which helped to define the measurement properties of the revised instrument. Questions have been raised regarding the comparability of the WISC and the WISC—R (Flynn, 1985) although other measurement properties, such as test-retest reliability, have appeared to be adequate (e.g., Whorton, 1985).

Although the recommended age range extends from about 5 to 15 years, the WISC—R is not always the preferred instrument in this range. For general assessment relative to mental retardation, some believe the Stanford-Binet test is the stronger instrument up to age 8, mostly because of the standardization and clinical use. As data accumulate on the WISC—R, it may be found that this belief is no longer valid. Certainly for children from about 8 to 15 years of age, the WISC—R is more appropriate.

Achievement

Many of the specific areas of assessment previously discussed for younger age levels remain appropriate during the elementary years. Determination of which areas require evaluation is based on a critical analysis of the areas in which the child is encountering difficulty. One assessment area, however, becomes more important in terms of evaluation at the elementary level than was the case during earlier years: that of achievement. A variety of procedures is used for assessing academic achievement during the elementary years, including formal standardized instruments as well as techniques for monitoring daily progress. Certain strengths and weaknesses are present in each approach, depending on the purpose of the evaluation. This section provides a brief overview of various achievement assessment procedures.

The Wide Range Achievement Test (WRAT) (Jastak & Jastak, 1978) is a general achievement test that assesses a child's performance in three areas: reading (pronunciation and word recognition), spelling, and arithmetic (computation). Constructed with two different levels, the Level I WRAT is used with children from 5 years to 11 years 11 months of age, and Level II is used from 12 years of age to adulthood. The scores are in the form of global achievement scores and are expressed as grade equivalents and percentiles. This type of score reporting provides too little detail regarding specific skills to be of much use in planning instruction. The WRAT is generally useful for screening but highly reasonable for other uses.

Another instrument used to measure achievement is the Peabody Individual Achievement Test (PIAT). The PIAT is designed for use from kindergarten through the twelfth grade. Although it is also a general achievement measure, it is more useful than the WRAT for instructional purposes. Its five subtests include mathematics, reading recognition, reading comprehension, spelling, and general information. Easily administered, the PIAT results in a profile of the child's performance in the various areas tested. The scores are presented in a variety of forms, including percentiles, age equivalents, grade equivalents, and both standard scores and raw scores. Depending on the specific evaluation purpose, the examiner may select any of these score forms as the appropriate method of reporting.

Another set of instruments that is useful for assessing academic achievement is the Metropolitan Achievement Test battery (Balow, Hogan, Farr, & Prescott, 1978; Farr, Prescott, Balow, & Hogan, 1978; Hogan, Farr, Prescott, & Balow, 1978; Prescott, Balow, Hogan, & Farr, 1978). This is a comprehensive battery made up of several instruments with an extensive normed age range. Beyond the readiness scale, which provides a global evaluation in terms of specific skill level, the primary and advanced batteries test several different areas. These include word knowledge, word analysis (for the younger levels), reading, language, spelling (older levels), math computation, math concepts, and math problem solving. The normed areas of evaluation per se are not as important as what can be done with them. When analyzed in terms of the skills required by each item, the Metropolitan test battery can provide a vast amount of information in terms of the level of a child's functioning. This information can then be quite precisely coordinated in terms of specific determination of discrete activities for the child's instructional program (Sparrow, Blachman, & Chauncy, 1983). Such an analysis requires both considerable information and teacher training in task analysis, and precision teaching. However, when such educational expertise is brought to the teaching task, considerable relevance for the education of both mentally retarded and nonretarded children is evident in instruments such as the Metropolitan test battery. More frequently, Metropolitan data are presented in score summary form, which may be used for administrative purposes but is certainly less useful from an instructional standpoint. It should be noted that this is an example of how standardized instrumentation can be used in a meaningful fashion with retarded individuals but in a manner that the test developer may not have conceived.

The achievement instruments discussed thus far have been general achievement measures, some of which provide specific skill information. Sometimes it is necessary to use an instrument that focuses specifically on one content area and provides an in-depth assessment of subskills in that area. Such an instrument is the Keymath Diagnostic Arithmetic Test. Keymath was developed for use with children as young as preschool level and ranging through grade 7. Both traditional and new math skills are assessed, with 14 subtests in three areas: content, operations, and applications. Scores are recorded on a profile of specific skills, and Keymath may also be scored on total test performance basis for use in placement or other administrative decisions.

Achievement assessment that results in only grade- or age-equivalent scores (as well as percentiles and standard scores) is providing norm-referenced information. These same tests may be used in other fashions that become criterion-referenced when a child's performance is not compared with that of other children or with some norm. The more discrete and specific an assessment is, the more potential it has for drawing specific implications for instruction. The greatest relevance for instruction comes from assessment that is built in as an integral part of the instructional program. Such an evaluation-instructional system was mentioned previously under language assessment at the preschool level (such as the Distar Language Program) but certainly warrants further mention in relation to achievement assessment. Ideally, this kind of achievement assessment provides continuous monitoring of a child's progress in specific skills. The instruction is precisely aimed at the child's level of functioning and permits a highly efficient interface between evaluation and instruction. There is much to be said for such an approach in educating those who are developmentally retarded and those who fall into the nebulous area known as regular education.

Assessment Systems

Thus far we have examined measurement procedures that primarily focus on one area. Clinicians have often found it necessary to use several instruments to obtain a complete picture of an individual's capabilities. We will briefly discuss another form of evaluation, systems that evaluate a number of different attributes.

The System of Multicultural Pluralistic Assessment (SOMPA), developed by Mercer and Lewis (1977), evaluates a variety of attribute areas. The SOMPA represents an attempt to provide for a comprehensive assessment. It is designed to be used with children from 5 to 11 years of age. Assessment of the child is extremely comprehensive and views the individual in terms of three broad perspectives: (1) the medical model, (2) the social system model, and (3) the pluralistic model. Six different areas are evaluated within the medical model portion: physical dexterity, weight by height, visual acuity, health history, and the Bender Visual-Motor Gestalt Test. The social system model assesses adaptive behavior and school functioning level (using primarily the WISC—R). The third broad area, the pluralistic model, views the child in terms of "estimated learning potential" and two sociocultural scales (one of the child's own ethnic group and a second based on the school culture). Scoring for all measures is converted to percentile form and placed in a profile format. The SOMPA is rather revolutionary in its approach and addresses child functioning in a manner that has not been undertaken previously on any widespread basis. Some professionals are skeptical about its potential use because of the massive nature of the evaluation. However, many believe that it will be useful and will circumvent some of the problems that have been raised regarding SOMPA norms, reliability, and validity. This procedure is probably best viewed as an experimental one (Salvia & Ysseldyke, 1985).

A second assessment procedure that may be viewed as an evaluation system is the Woodcock-Johnson Psychoeducational Battery (Woodcock,

1978). This system covers an unusually wide age span (3 to 80 years) and is designed to evaluate scholastic aptitude, cognitive ability, academic achievement, and interests. The Woodcock-Johnson battery is made up of 27 subtests that are organized in three parts: cognitive ability (which assesses both cognitive ability and scholastic aptitudes), academic achievement, and interests (in both academic and nonacademic areas). Administration of the entire battery requires more than two hours, although shorter periods may be involved when only a portion of the subtests are employed to assess specific areas. Salvia and Ysseldyke (1985) judge this battery of tests to be standardized in an adequate manner, although validity data are not available to support all 12 uses recommended by the author. Caution must be employed with the Woodcock-Johnson battery as with any assessment instrument.

THE ADOLESCENT AND ADULT YEARS

Core Concept 12   Assessment during the adolescent and adult years also involves utilization of age- or functioning level-appropriate procedures as well as attention to the changing purposes for evaluation that emerge during these years.

The adolescent and adult years are only a general reference; different individuals interpret them as different specific age ranges. Assessment in this section generally applies to individuals 13 years of age and older. Many of the evaluation techniques previously examined extend well into this age range and therefore will not receive repeated attention.

Intellectual Functioning

The instrument frequently used beginning in middle adolescence is the Wechsler Adult Intelligence Scale—Revised (WAIS—R) (Wechsler, 1981). This is a slightly revised version of the earlier WAIS, which is still used periodically and is the topic of some research (Coolidge, Rakoff, Schwellenbach, Bracken & Walker, 1986). Nearly 80% of the WAIS content remained unchanged or only slightly modified in the WAIS—R. The WISC—R, discussed earlier, extends into the early adolescent years (5 to 15 years). Similar in design, the WAIS—R is appropriate for assessment of intellectual functioning above the 15-year age level. The WAIS—R subscales are the same as those of the WISC—R, except that there are 11 rather than 12 subscales. Some questions have been raised regarding its comparability to the WAIS and other instruments (Flynn, 1985; Spitz, 1986). It is assumed that this instrument will receive future attention to determine its measurement properties.

Vocational Functioning

One area that becomes increasingly important as the retarded person grows older involves evaluation of skill level for vocational training and placement. During adolescence and adulthood the retarded individual usually encounters vocational training as a part of the formal educational setting. Of course, the nature of this training (as well as later placement) varies considerably depending on the degree of impairment.

Evaluation in this area, like those previously discussed, must be considered in light of the purpose of such assessment. One purpose of past research on evaluation has involved the prediction of vocational success. A second purpose is the evaluation of training and placement success once encountered in both areas. Gold (1973) presented a comprehensive review of a variety of dimensions in both vocational training and assessment. After discussing several evaluation approaches, including intelligence tests, manual dexterity tests, and work sample tasks, Gold suggested that work samples appear to show the most promise, even though the results of this approach have been less than satisfying. The work sample assessment is most analogous to an evaluation that uses applied behavior analysis techniques. Such precise analysis of skill level has provided the most practical information in other areas, and its precision in vocational assessment is not surprising. The precision is logically generated, because the evaluation is conducted in a setting that is as natural as possible. Such a close link between the evaluative procedure and its purpose or referent setting tends to provide the most useful and most accurate data. Perhaps the most serious deterrent to more widespread acceptance of this approach is lack of convenience. Work samples, as a test per se, tend to be cumbersome in terms of development and administration. Such techniques are not nearly so inconvenient, however, when they are designed as an integral part of a training program. The logistics of developing a convenient evaluation system rationally related to program activities and to job success remain the challenge of professionals who work in assessment, particularly with handicapped individuals.

ASSESSMENT AND AGING

This chapter has examined assessment of human status from before birth through adulthood. We have discussed the evaluation of biological status, intellectual functioning, social/adaptive behavior, achievement, and vocational functioning at various developmental levels where appropriate and where the literature and research evidence provides us with information. This is a tall order for any single volume, let alone a chapter; there have been volumes written on each of the topics included. Rather than exploring these matters in depth, this chapter provides readers with an overview and serves as a guiding reference in the further study of mental retardation. This final section on assessment pertaining to elderly people is written with the same intention. It represents our view of mentally retarded individuals through the perspective of a full cycle of human development and builds fundamentally on what has been covered before.

There is little difference in instrumentation for the assessment of the elderly. We previously examined the standardized evaluation of intellectual functioning and social and adaptive behavior in the context of adulthood. We have also noted the use of what some would term "informal" assessment procedures. What *is* crucial at the elderly age level is the application of all that we know about these people as individuals and the attempt to remain aware of their needs. For example, it is important to remind ourselves that elderly people in general may be more tentative and cautious in their response to any evaluation. If a timed test or assessment procedure is employed, such cautious behavior may result in exceeding the time limits. Therefore, responses that might otherwise be considered errors because of a failure to answer in a specified time limit might be evaluated with that in mind. Perhaps extending the time or administering the assessment in an untimed format should be considered. Assessment under such conditions may be different than the basic intended use of an instrument or procedure when it was originally developed. This emphasizes the fact that assessment is and should be a clinical process rather than a blind, unquestioning adherence to specified procedures.

Inherent in these statements is also a reflection of some material presented at the beginning of this chapter. It is very important that assessment at this stage, just as at others, is conducted with constant attention to the purpose of evaluation. Why are we administering an assessment to this individual? The retarded elderly are drawing on a lifetime of experiences which probably have been very different than the population in general because they are mentally retarded (see chapter 11). They may have been tested all their lives and may have spent many years in an institution or other non-family living arrangement even though partially integrated into society. All of these considerations should be sensitively brought together in the assessment of the retarded elderly.

Core Questions

1. Why are the uses of assessment procedures so important in the outcome of evaluation?

2. A number of difficulties were found with the calculation of intelligence quotient by the ratio method. What were some of them, and why was the deviation method found preferable?

3. Why is it essential to clarify the purposes involved in assessment before embarking on a testing effort?

4. Many conceptual developments have been important in the field of assessment during the past years. Among them have been the notions of formative and summative evaluation and the distinctions between norm- and criterion-referenced assessment. How do these concepts fit into the evaluation picture, and why are they important?

5. Different reliability levels are required for different intervention decisions. Why is this, and how do our instruments stand with respect to measurement precision?

6. What are the advantages and limitations of the mental age and IQ concepts? Why do these measures alone not provide adequate information for a full evaluation?

7. What are some of the difficulties encountered in predicting later functioning from infant assessment procedures?

8. Outline potential assessment instruments or procedures that you consider important during the prenatal period. Describe the conditions which would prompt such assessment.

9. Describe assessment procedures you might employ for early life (neonatal) and preschool years. Discuss conditions which would prompt such assessment.

10. How might you plan an appropriate evaluation plan for children during their elementary school years? What considerations would come into play in your assessment plan?

11. Outline assessment considerations that might be important during adolescent and adult years. How are these different than important considerations at younger ages?

12. In reviewing the life span perspective, how do purposes change and what considerations must be given to selection of an assessment approach?

ROUND TABLE DISCUSSION

Assessment is much more complex than merely picking up a test and administering it to a child. Careful consideration must be given from the outset to why one is evaluating and what is to be the result. Additionally, throughout the assessment process care must be exercised regarding what techniques are used, how the procedures are undertaken, and how the data are to be interpreted. Proper assessment must consider the age of the individual being evaluated because different domains of status become relevant at different ages, and because different assessment techniques are suitable at different ages.

In your study group or on your own, design an evaluation plan that takes into account the various considerations examined in this chapter. If you are working with others, have each person be responsible for a different age level or for a conceptual issue related to assessment. Compare your final plan with an existing plan, such as one used in a school district. You will find that full consideration of the life span extends beyond the school years to health and social service agencies.

REFERENCES

American Psychological Association, American Educational Research Association, & National Council on Measurement in Education. (1974). *Standards for educational and psychological tests.* Washington, DC: American Psychological Association.

Anastasi, A. (1950). The concept of validity in the interpretation of test scores. *Educational and Psychological Measurement, 10*, 67–78.

Balow, I. H., Hogan, T. P., Farr, R. C., & Prescott, G. A. (1978). *Metropolitan Achievement Tests: Language Instructional Battery.* New York: Psychological Corp.

Bartel, N. R., Grill, J. J., & Bryen, D. N. (1973). Language characteristics of Black children: Implications for assessment. *Journal of School Psychology, 11*, 351–364.

Beery, K. E., (1967). *Developmental test of visual-motor integration: Administration and scoring manual.* Chicago: Follett.

Bennett, R. E. (1983). Research and evaluation priorities for special education assessment. *Exceptional Children, 50*, 110–117.

Bijou, S. W., & Peterson, R. F. (1970). The psychological assessment of children: A functional analysis. In McReynolds, P. (Ed.). *Advances in psychological assessment* (Vol. 2, pp. 63–78). Palo Alto, CA: Science & Behavior.

Binet, A., & Simon, T. (1908). Le développement de l'intelligence chez les enfants. *L'Année Psychologique, 14*, 1–94.

Bloom, B. S., Hastings, J. T., & Madaus, G. F. (1971). *Handbook on formative and summative evaluation of student learning.* New York: McGraw-Hill.

Boyd, R. D. (1969). *CCD developmental progress scale.* Experimental Form, Manual and Direction. Portland: University of Oregon Medical Center, Department of Clinical Psychology.

Burgess, D. B., Asher, K. N., Doucet, H. J., Reardon, K., & Daste, M.R. (1984). Parent report as a means of administering the Prescreening Developmental Questionnaire: An evaluation study. *Journal of Developmental and Behavioral Pediatrics, 5* (4), 201–203.

Bush, W. J., & Waugh, K. W. (1976). *Diagnosing learning disabilities* (2nd ed.). Columbus, OH: Merrill.

Chinn, P. L. (1979). *Child health maintenance: Concepts in family centered care* (2nd ed.). St. Louis: Mosby.

Cohen, S. E., & Parmelee, A. H. (1983). Prediction of five-year Stanford-Binet scores in preterm infants. *Child Development, 54*, 1242–1253.

Colarusso, R. P., & Hammill, D. D. (1972). *Motor-free visual perception test.* San Rafael, CA: Academic Therapy.

Committee on Children with Handicaps. (1972). *Rapid development screening checklist.* New York: American Academy of Pediatrics.

Coolidge, F. L., Rakoff, R. A., Schwellenbach, L. D., Bracken, D. D., & Walker, S. H. (1986). WAIS profiles in mentally retarded adults. *Journal of Mental Deficiency Research, 30*, 15–17.

Cronbach, L. J. (1984). *Essentials of psychological testing* (4th ed.). New York: Harper & Row.

Drew, C. J. (1973). Criterion-referenced and norm-referenced assessment of minority group children. *Journal of School Psychology, 11,* 323–329.

Drew, C. J., Freston, C. W., & Logan, D. R. (1972). Criteria and reference in evaluation. *Focus on Exceptional Children, 4,* 1–10.

Dunn, L., & Dunn, L. (1981). *Peabody picture vocabulary test—Revised.* Circle Pines, MN: American Guidance Service.

Ebel, R. L. (1972). *Essentials of educational measurement.* Englewood Cliffs, NJ: Prentice-Hall.

Elbert, J. C. (1984). Training in child diagnostic assessment: A survey of clinical psychology graduate programs. *Journal of Clinical Child Psychology, 13,* 122–133.

Farr, R. C., Prescott, G. A., Balow, I. H., & Hogan, T. P. (1978). *Metropolitan achievement tests: Reading instructional battery.* New York: Psychological Corp.

Felce, D., de Kock, U., Mansell, J., & Jenkins, J. (1984). Assessing mentally handicapped adults. *British Journal of Mental Subnormality, 30,* 65–74.

Ferinden, W., Jacobson, S., & Kovalinsky, T. (1970). *Educational interpretation of the Stanford-Binet Intelligence Scale form LM and the Illinois Test of Psycholinguistic Abilities.* Linden, NJ: Remediation Associates.

Flavell, J. H. (1977). *Cognitive development.* Englewood Cliffs, NJ: Prentice-Hall.

Flynn, J. R. (1985). Wechsler intelligence tests: Do we really have a criterion of mental retardation? *American Journal of Mental Deficiency, 90,* 236–244.

Frankenburg, W., Dodds, J., Fandal, A., Kazuk, E., & Cohrs, M. (1975). *Developmental screening test: Reference manual—Revised 1975 edition.* Denver, CO: LA-DOCA Project and Publishing Foundation.

Friedlander, B. Z. (1971). Automated evaluation of selective listening in language-impaired and normal infants and young children. *Maternal and Child Health Exchange, 1,* 9–12.

Frostig, M., & Horne, D. (1964). *The Frostig program for the development of visual perception: Teacher's guide.* Chicago: Follett.

Fuchs, D., & Fuchs, L. S. (1986). Test procedure bias: A meta-analysis of examiner familiarity effects. *Review of Educational Research, 56,* 243–262.

Galagan, J. E. (1985). Psychoeducational testing: Turn out the lights, the party's over. *Exceptional Children, 52,* 288–299.

Gaussen, T. (1984). Developmental milestones or conceptual milestones? Some practical and theoretical limitations in infant assessment procedures. *Child Care, Health and Development, 10,* 99–115.

Gaussen, T., & Stratton, P. (1985). Beyond the milestone model: A systems framework for alternative infant assessment procedures. *Child Care, Health and Development, 11,* 131–150.

Gold, M. W. (1973). Research on the vocational habilitation of the retarded: The present, the future. In Ellis, N. R. (Ed.), *International review of research in mental retardation* (Vol. 6) (pp. 97–147). New York: Academic Press.

Gronlund, N. E. (1985). *Measurement and evaluation in teaching* (5th ed.). New York: Macmillan.

Gunzberg, H. C. (1963). *Progress assessment chart (P.A.C.) (form I, form II).* London: National Association on Mental Health.

Haertel, E. (1985). Construct validity and criterion-referenced testing. *Review of Educational Research, 55,* 23–46.

Hammill, D. D. (1971). Evaluating children for instructional purposes. *Academic Therapy, 6,* 341–353.

Haney, W. (1984). Testing reasoning and reasoning about testing. *Review of Educational Research, 54,* 597–654.

Hanson, R., Smith, J. A., & Hume, W. (1984). Some reasons for disagreement among scorers of infant intelligence test items. *Child Care, Health and Development, 10,* 17–30.

Haynes, U. (1967). *A developmental approach to case-finding with special reference to cerebral palsy, mental retardation, and related disorders.* Washington, DC: U.S. Government Printing Office.

Hogan, T. P., Farr, R. C., Prescott, G. A., & Balow, I. H. (1978). *Metropolitan achievement tests: Mathematics instructional battery.* New York: Psychological Corp.

Honig, A. S., & Caldwell, B. M. (1966). *Early language assessment scale.* Syracuse, NY: Syracuse University.

Hopkins, K. D., & Stanley, J. C. (1981). *Educational and psychological measurement and evaluation* (6th ed.). Englewood Cliffs, NJ: Prentice-Hall.

Horst, P. (1966). *Psychological measurement and prediction.* Belmont, CA: Wadsworth.

Jastak, J., & Jastak, S. (1978). *Wide range achievement test.* Wilmington, DE: Jastak.

Jensen, A. R. (1980). *Bias in mental testing.* New York: Free Press.

Jensen, A. R. (1983). *Straight talk about mental tests.* New York: Free Press.

Kagan, J. (1972). Do infants think? *Scientific American, 229,* 74–82.

Kirk, S., McCarthy, J., & Kirk, W. (1968). *Illinois test of psycholinguistic abilities (Revised ed.): Examiners manual.* Urbana, IL: University of Illinois.

Knobloch, H., Pasamanick, B., & Sherard, E. S. (1967). A developmental screening inventory. In Haynes, U. (Ed.). *A developmental approach to case-finding.* pp. 77–85. Washington, DC: U.S. Government Printing Office.

Lerner, J. W. (1981). *Children with learning disabilities* (3rd ed.). New York: Houghton Mifflin.

MacDonald, L., & Barton, L. E. (1986). Measuring severity of behavior: A revision of Part II of the Adaptive Behavior Scale. *American Journal of Mental Deficiency, 90,* 418–424.

Meeker, M., & Meeker, R. (1973). Strategies for assessing intellectual patterns in Black, Anglo- and Mexican-American boys—or any other children—and implications for education. *Journal of School Psychology, 11,* 341–350.

Meier, J. (1973). *Screening and assessment of young children at developmental risk: Report of the President's Committee on Mental Retardation.* (DHEW Publication No. [O.S.] 73–90). Washington, DC: U.S. Government Printing Office.

Menyuk, P. (1972). *The development of speech.* New York: Bobbs-Merrill.

Mercer, J. R., & Lewis, J. F. (1977). *System of multicultural pluralistic assessment.* New York: Psychological Corp. Newland, T. E. (1973). Assumptions underlying psychological testing. *Journal of School Psychology, 11,* 316–322.

Oakland, T. (1973). Assessing minority group children: Challenges for school psychologists. *Journal of School Psychology, 11,* 294–303.

O'Brien, J. S. (1971). How we detect mental retardation before birth. *Medical Times, 99,* (2) 103–108.

Ostwald, P. F., Phibbs, R., & Fox, S. (1968). Diagnostic use of infant cry. *Biology of the Neonate, 13,* 68–82.

Prasse, D. P., & Reschly, D. J. (1986). Larry P.: A case of segregation, testing, or program efficacy? *Exceptional Children, 52,* 333–346.

Prescott, G. A., Balow, I. H., Hogan, T. P., & Farr, R. C. (1978). *Metropolitan achievement tests: Survey battery.* New York: Psychological Corp.

Roberts, E., & DeBlassie, R. R. (1983). Test bias and the culturally different early adolescent. *Adolescence, 18,* 837–843.

Rocissano, L., & Yatchmink, Y. (1983). Language skill and interactive patterns in prematurely born toddlers. *Child Development, 54,* 1229–1241.

Ross, G. (1985). Use of the Baley Scales to characterize abilities of premature infants. *Child Development, 56,* 835–842.

Salvia, J., & Ysseldyke, J. E. (1985). *Assessment in special and remedial education* (3rd ed.). Boston: Houghton Mifflin. Schenck, S. J. (1980). The diagnostic/instructional link in individualized education programs. *Journal of Special Education, 14,* 337–345.

Slate, N. M. (1983). Nonbiased assessment of adaptive behavior: Comparison of three instruments. *Exceptional Children, 50,* 67–70.

Soyster, H. D., & Ehly, S. W. (1986). Parent-rated adaptive behavior and in-school ratings of students referred for EMR evaluation. *American Journal of Mental Deficiency, 90,* 460–463.

Sparrow, S. S., Balla, D. A., & Cicchetti, D. V.(1984). *Vineland Adaptive Behavior Scales.* Circle Pines, MN: American Guidance Service.

Sparrow, S. S., Blachman, B. A., & Chauncy, S. (1983). Diagnostic and prescriptive intervention in primary school education. *American Journal of Orthopsychiatry, 53,* 721–729.

Spitz, H. H. (1986). Disparities in mentally retarded persons' IQ derived from different intelligence tests. *American Journal of Mental Deficiency, 90,* 588–591.

Terman, L., & Merrill, M. (1973). *Stanford-Binet intelligence scale: 1972 norms edition.* Boston: Houghton Mifflin.

Wechsler, D. (1981). *WAIS-R manual: Wechsler adult intelligence scale—Revised.* New York: Psychological Corp.

White, B. L., & Kaban, B. (1971). *Manual for quantitative analysis of tasks of one- to six-year-old children.* Cambridge, MA: Harvard University.

Whiteley, J. H., & Krenn, M. J. (1986). Uses of the Bayley mental scale with non-ambulatory profoundly mentally retarded children. *American Journal of Mental Deficiency, 90,* 425–431.

Whorton, J. E. (1985). Test-retest Wechsler Intelligence Scale for Children—Revised scores for 310 educable mentally retarded and specific learning disabled students. *Psychological Reports, 56,* 857–858.

Wood, F. H., Johnson, J. L., & Jenkins, J. R. (1986). The *Lora* case: Nonbiased referral, assessment, and placement procedures. *Exceptional Children, 52,* 323–331.

Woodcock, R. (1978). *Woodcock-Johnson psychoeducational battery.* Boston: Teaching Resources.

Ysseldyke, J. E., & Algozzine, B. (1982). *Critical issues in special and remedial education.* Boston: Houghton Mifflin

Ysseldyke, J. E., Algozzine, B., Richey, L. S., & Graden, J. (1982). Declaring students eligible for learning disability services: Why bother with the data? *Learning Disability Quarterly, 5,* 37–44.

TWO

EARLY LIFE AND PRESCHOOL YEARS

5

Basic Principles of Early Development

Core Concepts

1. Genotype, phenotype, growth matrix, and maturation are terms that represent important concepts in human development.
2. Theories of human development have varied dramatically regarding the importance of influences ranging from prepotency of genetic material to total environmental shaping.
3. Some have characterized the human development process as one of continuous growth, whereas others have viewed it as having rather abrupt, discontinuous stages.
4. Certain periods of development are viewed as critical for growth and are considered critical regarding vulnerability to injury and developmental risk.
5. Cephalocaudal and proximodistal growth trends, which begin very early in prenatal development, can be observed during the first few years of life.
6. Prenatal fetal development during weeks 10 through 12 is particularly important because of the tissues being formed at that time.
7. The birth process represents another important event when potential risk to the child is high.
8. The period immediately after birth is characterized by many as the most dangerous during an individual's complete lifetime.

Child development holds a very prominent position in psychology and education even though it has been addressed using the scientific method only during the last century (Berger,1983). It has been a fruitful area for both research and application and has represented a field of study essential to full understanding of human behavior. However, there have been a number of trends in recent years that have served to de-emphasize the apparent focus on this most important topic.

There has been a dramatic growth recently in the technological dimensions of education and behavioral science in general. This has occurred in many different areas. There are government funding programs for service, research, and training that are aimed at the technological (popularly termed "applied") dimensions of education. These movements have mirrored what seems to be public desire for things that are practical. Those in high-level policy-making positions clearly represent a perspective that values activities that generate the most immediate product for a given expenditure.

Sophistication has increased dramatically in areas of diagnostic evaluation, instructional techniques, and materials design. Such advancements have had definite positive effects on the education of handicapped learners. In fact, the area of handicapped education may well be leading the general field of education in its application of technologically related advancements. One of the obvious rewards has been that educators never have been so well supplied with tools to facilitate their efforts. However, these massive developments and refinements of diagnostic and instructional instrumentation have also presented challenges for students in professional preparation programs. The vast amount of information that must be acquired and the number of required skill areas have increased at an astronomical rate. Two very practical problems present themselves in this regard. The preparation time allowed to master these skills has seldom been increased in proportion to the amount of material presented, and in many areas the outcome of professional training is rather narrow and limited (e.g., Elbert, 1984).

During the time that the professional is acquiring the skills necessary for a specialized sophistication, some critical areas of mastery, such as the study of the human organism itself, are frequently neglected. This results in preparation with tool skills developed to a high degree but with a lack of concomitant understanding of the individual as a total organism. This chapter, while not intended as a substitute for a basic course in human growth and development, provides an introduction to those principles of early development that have particular relationships to mental retardation. As students progress to more advanced work in various skills, they should master knowledge about the growth and development of the child for whom the tool skills are to be used.

There are other reasons for the particular importance of basic concepts of child development to the study of mental retardation. For many subgroups of the retarded population, developmental considerations are central to their intellectual, physical, and psychological status. From a basic biological standpoint, many of the clinical syndromes are integrally related to human development. The generic psychological view of the cultural-familial retarded population, which is the largest proportion of mentally retarded children, has long spotlighted child development within the nature versus nurture controversy. Thus it seems that an acquaintance with the concepts of child development is essential to the student of mental retardation.

HUMAN DEVELOPMENT: TERMINOLOGY AND CONCEPTS

Core Concept 1   Genotype, phenotype, growth matrix, and maturation are terms that represent important concepts in human development.

The discipline of human growth and development has grown in complexity along with advancement in all of its contributing sciences. Information has exploded in biology, embryology, genetics, psychology, and many other areas—all of which has been molded into a body of highly technical knowledge that has unique properties beyond those of the contributing areas. Before beginning a discussion of child development it is important to become acquainted with certain basic terminology.

Some basic genetic terminology is an important foundation to understanding child development. *Genotype* is a term used in discussions concerning developmental aspects of the organism as it relates to heredity and refers to the basic genetic makeup of an individual. Established at conception by the joining of sperm and ovum, the genotype remains constant throughout an individual's lifetime. Only rarely does this constancy fail, as when a mutation or other error in cell division occurs that alters the subsequent course of cell division. Human genetic material is not readily accessible for actual inspection, but the *phenotype,* a term that refers to observable physical traits, may be used to draw inferences about the genotype. Pertaining to both physical and behavioral dimensions of the individual, the phenotype is the observable result of an interaction between the genotype and the environment (Gottesman,1963).

Growth matrix is a common term in child development related to phenotype; it also is the result of interactions between heredity and environment. Although partially observable (because it includes the phenotype), the growth matrix also includes all of the internal aspects of a child that generate a given response in a particular situation. The growth matrix is more than a simple combination of the phenotype and genotype, however. One distinction is that the genetic constituent remains constant, whereas the growth matrix changes as interactions occur between the organism and its environment. The growth matrix is a product of that interaction and at the same time determines or regulates subsequent individual response patterns.

Child-development specialists also use the term *maturation* in a fashion that requires definition. Although some difference in use exists, they employ the term maturation to signify any instance of development, that is, any change in the status or underlying process of a behavioral trait that takes place in the demonstrable absence of specific practice experience. In the present context one additional restriction is added: the absence of specific instruction. Thus maturation is distinguishable from learning, which refers to changes associated with specific practice or instruction. In many situations it is difficult to discriminate between changes resulting from maturation and changes resulting from learning. A certain history of maturation, learning, and a combination of the two is involved in a child's developmental status at any given time. This status and its components are very much related to the notion of readiness.

A stage of readiness exists when the child is at a point in development (including previous maturation and learning) where there is an expectation of profit from a particular situation. A frequently mentioned example is "reading readiness." From the present standpoint, reading readiness would refer to the point in a child's development at which progress might be expected as a result of exposure to reading experience or instruction. Of course, if the status from either a maturation or previous learning standpoint were deficient (i.e., not adequate to establish readiness), the child would not be expected to progress as a result of a given instruction. This is not intended, however, to imply that there is a magic formula such as "X amount of maturation plus Y amount of previous learning equals readiness." Although developmental readiness includes both maturation and previous learning, widely varying amounts and types of each may exist in different children who have reached readiness status for some given experience.

A THEORETICAL OVERVIEW

Core Concept 2	Theories of human development have varied dramatically regarding the importance of influences ranging from prepotency of genetic material to total environmental shaping.

Human development and its various complexities have been topics of interest since the beginning of recorded history. Some of the most prevalent theoretical positions have an extremely lengthy history. Some prescientific explanations of human growth and development, although amusing in retrospect, have enjoyed considerable popularity in earlier times.

Preformationist Perspective

The preformationist theory of human growth and development had a substantial following in the past. Preformationism essentially assumed that the human organism is preformed before birth; it proposed that the foundation elements of human behavior are intact from the beginning and do not develop or change from a *qualitative* standpoint during life. The preformationist thus denied the importance of growth and development except in the sense of *quantity,* or growing larger. The early homuncular theory of human reproduction exemplified the preformationist position. This theory held that a tiny, completely formed person existed in the sperm. This tiny person, a homunculus, began to grow in size at conception but did not change in the sense that tissue changes occurred qualitatively, such as in the formation of various organs.

The preformationist position largely discounted the effects of environmental influences on human development. In the homuncular theory, both prenatal and postnatal environments were viewed as inconsequential with regard to significant developmental occurrences. Usually the only concessions made to environmental effects involved a mere expansion of existing abilities, drives, and behaviors. Neither new growth nor directional influence of development was thought to be significantly different from that of the preformed organism.

Predeterministic Perspective

At first glance, the perspective of the predeterministic theorists seems to be based on assumptions similar to those of preformationism. Although they had similar outcomes, there were significant differences between the two theoretical positions.

Predeterministic positions did not view human development as a simple accentuation of a preformed organism. Instead, qualitative growth and tissue differentiation played a substantial role in most predeterminism theories. An example of this is found in the doctrine of recapitulation, described in great detail by G. Stanley Hall (1904). This notion hypothesized that the development of the child from conception to maturity progressed through all of the evolutionary phases of the human race. Although quite popular around the turn of the century, this theory fell into disfavor (Gleitman, 1986) primarily because of the absence of objective or observable data to support its sweeping hypothesis.

As noted, the conclusion of predeterminism was essentially the same as preformationism; both assumed that the influence of the environment was minimal, perhaps limited to minor roles of restricting development. Primary roles of determining growth patterns were viewed as innate or internally regulated. More recently, the disciplines of biology, genetics, and embryology have provided factual knowledge supporting the idea that certain development is primarily regulated internally (e.g., prenatal growth and certain infantile behavioral development). Predeterministic contentions of innate control, however, involved broad applications that have not been supported scientifically.

"Tabula Rasa" Perspective

Tabula rasa is a term that is used in the present context to refer to approaches that emphasize the prepotency of environmental influences. The term translates to mean "blank slate" and was popularized by John Locke in the seventeenth century as a statement of the importance of learned, as opposed to innate, behaviors. For purposes of this discussion, tabula rasa is used generically to represent positions of extreme environmental impact.

Contrasting with the approaches of preformationism and predeterminism, tabula rasa positions minimized the influence of internal factors (such as heredity) on human development. Environmental influences were seen as playing a predominant role in determining most aspects of development. Tabula rasa theorists essentially viewed the human organism as totally plastic and infinitely amenable to molding by the external influences of the environment. Thus an individual's ability was dependent on what was "written" on the blank slate through experience. The weakness of this framework, as with those of preformationism and predeterminism, was the extreme to which proponents advocated their position.

Neither the tabula rasa nor the predeterministic approach to child development has been satisfactory. There is little logical or empirical support for a belief in preformed human functioning at birth. With the exception of very simple reflex responses, there seem to be few human behavioral dimensions that are not influenced in some fashion by the environment. The fundamental error of the predeterministic proponents was one of excessively discounting the impact of experience. Tabula rasa theorists, on the other hand, caught the pendulum in the opposite extreme position. The assumption that environmental impact is a significant contributor to human growth and development is reasonable, but tabula rasa theorists were inclined to emphasize the impact of this factor far beyond reasonable limits.

Interactional Perspectives

Difficulties with the preformationist, predeterministic, and tabula rasa perspectives have been discussed briefly in the preceding sections. Current positions concerning the evolution of human development generally subscribe to the notion of an interaction between heredity and environment (Ausubel, Sullivan,& Ives, 1980; Shaffer, 1985). Both genetic and environmental factors serve to set limits for growth as well as to selectively influence each other. For example, genetic material determines the actual limits even under the most favorable environment conceivable. Likewise, the environmental contingencies serve to limit the degree to which genetic potential can be fulfilled. Genetic material determines which factors in the environment have the greatest effect by rendering the organism selectively sensitive to some more than to others. Similarly, environmental aspects, such as cultural or ecological factors, serve to selectively affect genetic expression by providing selective influences on ability development.

Thus the interactional approach to human growth and development emphasizes analysis of relationships between heredity and environment. This represents a substantial difference from previous positions discussed (e.g., tabula rasa, predeterminism), in which the prepotence of one influence over the other was a central assumption. Although other approaches may be conceptually simpler, the interaction position seems to be a more reasonable representation of reality.

THE DEVELOPMENTAL PROCESS

Growing support for the interaction approach to human development generated a more intense focus on the developmental process than was previously the case. Researchers and theoreticians alike began to ask questions that were more amenable to scientific study than were the philosophical positions exemplified by former views. In this section, an examination of various dimensions of the developmental process is presented.

Continuity Versus Discontinuity of Growth

Core Concept 3 Some have characterized the human development process as one of continuous growth, whereas others have viewed it as having rather abrupt, discontinuous stages.

The nature of the developmental process itself has raised a series of interesting questions. At times these questions have become the controversial subjects of considerable debate. One area that has generated considerable discussion involves the continuity or discontinuity of human growth. Essentially the question is whether or not development proceeds in terms of gradual continuous quantitative change or in stages typified by abrupt discontinuous qualitative changes.

The discontinuity view of human development was expressed in theories emphasizing stages. Early developmental-stage theories contended that there was little or no overlap of process occurring from one stage to the other and that each developmental stage is specifically and qualitatively different from the others. The first developmental theorist to dismiss this discontinuity notion was Piaget (1926). Piaget, with a background in biology and zoology, formulated a theory of stages of cognitive development that incorporated the occurrence of immature and mature responses at all developmental levels. He conceived of intelligence as being globally categorized into three developmental periods: (a) the period of sensorimotor intelligence, (b) the period of preparation for and organization of concrete operations, and (c) the period of formal operations (see chapter 7). Sensorimotor intelligence development is thought to begin at birth and continue for about the first 2 years of life. Piaget described the second period, from about 2 to 11 years of age, as being the development of intelligence involving the essential formation of the conceptual framework that the child uses in interaction with the environment. The third period, from 11 years of age on, is the time during which, Piaget contended, an individual becomes involved with abstract thought. During this period (formal operations) a person begins to be able to think in terms of hypothetical possibilities as distinguished from the exclusive use of concrete operations, in which cognition depends on a concrete or real object basis. Piaget conceived the total development picture as one of a dynamic interaction with the organism operating on the environment as well as being molded by it. Piaget's stage theory has come under heavy fire (Flavell,1982; Shultz, 1982). Flavell (1985), for example, has suggested that he does not believe that the stage concept will play an important role in future scientific work on cognitive growth.

The continuity position contends that growth is a gradual process rather than a series of abrupt changes alternating with plateaus, or periods of less rapid change. A variety of factors can be mentioned as possibly supporting the theory of growth continuity. First, it is well known that both mature and immature responses are made by children at all levels of development. Second, theories embodying the concept of continuity emphasize, more effectively than do discontinuous stage theories, the testing of hypotheses that are generated from general behavior theories.

There have been strong proponents for both the continuity and discontinuity positions. However, growth and development specialists have largely progressed beyond the point where polarized thinking prevails. Theoretically formulated stages are no longer viewed as being precise definitions involving exact ages, behaviors, and response levels. They are more often viewed as convenient approximations, based on averages, which are useful in conceptualizing developmental processes and suggesting directions for research (Berger, 1983).

Critical Periods and Developmental Vulnerability

Core Concept 4   Certain periods of development are viewed as critical for growth and are considered critical regarding vulnerability to injury and developmental risk.

Developmental deviance is a central concern in the field of mental retardation just as it is in other disorder areas (Schwartz & Johnson, 1985). In view of this, a topic of vital importance to those studying mental retardation is the concept of developmental vulnerability. In this context the notion of vulnerability refers to how susceptible the individual is to being injured or altered by a traumatic incident. Traumatic incident is defined broadly to include such occurrences as toxic agents (poisons) and cell division mutations as well as other deviations from the usual sequence of developmental events.

Research in biology and embryology has provided a great deal of information concerning the manner in which human growth occurs (Timiras, 1972). From the time of conception, a series of complex cell divisions occurs that ultimately results in the highly complicated entity that we call a human being. During the early part of this developmental process, the two original cells divide repeatedly from a mass which at about 14 days is no larger than the end of a sharp pencil lead to a newborn child in 9 months. Obviously this is a very dramatic growth process. Cell division occurs extremely rapidly in the first few days after the ovum is fertilized by a sperm. The mass that is to become the fetus does not actually become implanted or attached to the mother's uterus until about two weeks after fertilization, and in this two weeks cell division has progressed with considerable speed, beginning a process known as tissue differentiation. Both the speed of cell division and the process of tissue differentiation are important with regard to the vulnerability to trauma.

Tissue differentiation begins very soon after fertilization. As cell division proceeds, certain chemical reactions occur that generate new cells of different types. These cells multiply, reproducing like cells that distribute themselves to form three different layers of tissue cells: the ectoderm, the mesoderm, and the endoderm (Fig. 5–1). The tissue layers are actually named

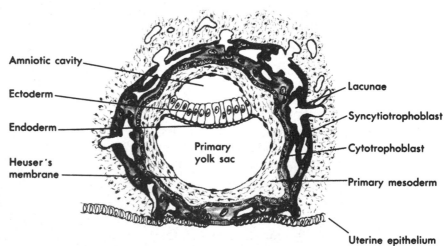

Figure 5–1. Conceptus at About 12 Days, Showing Cell Tissue Layers
From _Synopsis of Anatomy_, by L. J. A. Didio, 1972, St. Louis: Mosby, 1970.
Copyright 1970 by C.V. Mosby Company. Reprinted by permission.

by virtue of their early developmental position (ectoderm, outer layer; mesoderm, middle layer, endoderm, inner layer), but they eventually form distinctly different parts of the organism. For example, parts of the ectoderm become nervous tissue, various types of muscle come from the mesoderm, and so on. During the time that a particular organ or system is being formed, the cells that are generating that system divide very rapidly. There are specific periods when, for instance, the central nervous system is the primary part of the organism that is being developed. During that time, the cells that constitute the central nervous system are dividing more rapidly than other types of cells. It is at this time that the central nervous system is most vulnerable to trauma. If a toxic agent or infection occurs in the mother at this time, there is a high probability that the developing central nervous system (or some particular part of it) will be more affected than will other organs or systems.

Just as there are periods of high vulnerability during tissue development, there are various other critical periods during the prenatal development of a child. These periods are biologically critical for the healthy growth of the fetus. It has long been suspected by some professionals that critical periods also exist after birth. The nature of specific hypotheses has varied considerably in terms of postnatal critical periods. In some cases these critical periods of early childhood have been considered to be those times that are optimal for the child to learn or experience certain things. Others have defined the critical period in terms of irreversibility. This latter concept includes the belief that, if a child does not acquire certain skills or does not experience certain stimuli at the appropriate time, development will be altered in some fashion that is not reversible. Under some circumstances the theoretical outcome of either viewpoint is essentially the same: The child, if not taught at the appropriate critical time, may not learn given material as well as possible.

The critical period concept as applied to the growth and development of very young children has had considerable effect in both research and education. Educational programs, such as that developed by Montessori, have flourished based on the intuitive appeal of the critical period concept. It should be noted, however, that firm research evidence supporting the importance/irreversibility view has been rather fragmentary in certain areas (Ausubel, Sullivan, & Ives, 1980) and vigorously challenged by some researchers (Flavell, 1971, 1982, 1985).

PRENATAL DEVELOPMENT

The importance of the prenatal period of human development has long been recognized. As with speculation about any unknown or unexplored phenomenon, very early explanations of prenatal development tended to be more philosophical and metaphysical than scientific in orientation. This is certainly exemplified by the prescientific notion of the homunculus, which was described earlier. Contemporary advances in research methods have permitted at least limited glimpses of much of this previously unexplored region. Although much of our current information concerning prenatal development has come from studies with animals, a continually)expanding knowledge base is being generated about the human organism also. This section presents an overview of the sequence of prenatal development. Such information substantially adds to a broader understanding of developmental deviations as they relate to mental retardation.

Core Concept 5   Cephalocaudal and proximodistal growth trends, which begin very early in prenatal development, can be observed during the first few years of life.

It was noted that early cell division occurs at different rates, depending on which portion of the organism is being formed primarily at that time. Beyond these variations in developmental rates there are two important general growth trends that warrant mention. The first is known as the cephalocaudal developmental trend, or growth gradient. As the term suggests, the fetus develops more rapidly in the head area (Greek *kephale*) first, with maturation toward the lower extremities (Latin *cauda*) or "tail" following. Thus, at nearly all stages of a young child's development the upper regions (and behaviors associated with these regions) are more advanced than the lower. Dramatically evident prenatally, the cephalocaudal trend also is present after birth. A young child is skilled in a behavior involving the arms prior to a time that a similar skill is developed in the legs. The second general developmental trend is the proximodistal gradient. This term refers to the fact that the more rapid growth and development occur near the center of the organism (Latin *proximus*, near), with extremities (Latin *distans*, far) maturing later. This trend also is present both prenatally and during the first few years of infant life.

Very soon after fertilization occurs, the cell division process commences that ultimately will result in a fully formed human. As noted earlier, it takes about two weeks for the dividing cell mass to become attached to the uterus of the mother. Even before this implantation occurs, the cells begin to differentiate. As the ectoderm, mesoderm, and endoderm are initially formed, considerable flexibility remains in terms of what individual cells within those layers can become. Thus at the 14-day stage a given cell within the mesoderm could still grow into something besides that which is usually formed from the mesoderm. Determination of resulting organs at this point is more a function of layer position than the actual composition of the cell itself. Cell flexibility eventually is lost as growth proceeds. The layers themselves become increasingly differentiated, and as this occurs the individual cells become more specialized (Arey, 1974). Table 5–1 summarizes some of the organs and structures resulting from growth in the various tissue layers.

At the time of implantation the embryo is still very small. Despite all that has gone on, the mass is little more than the mark made by a sharp pencil. The actual estimated size is about that of a ball 2 mm in diameter, and the weight cannot even be estimated (Timiras, 1972). It is difficult for us even to conceive that such a tiny piece of matter is not only living but has already begun to differentiate preparatory to forming such structures as eyes, a brain, and muscles.

After implantation at about 14 days activity continues at an extremely rapid pace. By the 18- to 24-day point (from the time of fertilization, which is termed fertilization age) weight is still undeterminable; size, however, has reached the approximate proportions portrayed in Figure 5–2. Also, at this point blood cells have begun to form and are much like those that will serve in later life (Arey, 1974; Chinn, 1979).

By the time the embryo has reached the 4-week point (fertilization age) several developments have occurred. Weight is detectable at about 0.4 g. Figure 5–2 portrays the approximate size and shape of the embryo at this point. A primitive circulatory system has developed, and the heart structure has begun to pulse (Arey, 1974). The fourth week also sees initial formative stages of other systems, such as trunk muscles and those muscles necessary for respiratory and intestinal functions. Limb buds appear at this time, and the nervous system reaches a point that is crucial with respect to the development of both the sense organs and the area that will later become the spinal cord. Figure 5–2 illustrates that the tiny embryo has already assumed

Table 5–1. Cell Tissue Layers of the Embryo

Endoderm	Mesoderm	Ectoderm
Epithelium of pharynx, tongue root, auditory tube, tonsils, thyroid	Muscles (all types) Cartilage, bone Blood, bone marrow	Epidermis, including cutaneous glands, hair, nails, lens
Larynx, trachea, lungs Digestive tube Bladder Vagina Urethra	Lymphoid tissue Epithelium of blood vessels, body cavities Kidney, ureter, gonads, genital ducts Suprarenal cortex Joint cavities	Epithelium of sense organs, nasal cavity, sinuses Mouth, including oral glands, enamel Anal canal Nervous tissue

*Adapted from *Developmental Anatomy* (7th ed.) by L. B. Arey. Copyright 1974 by W. B. Saunders Co. Reprinted by permission.

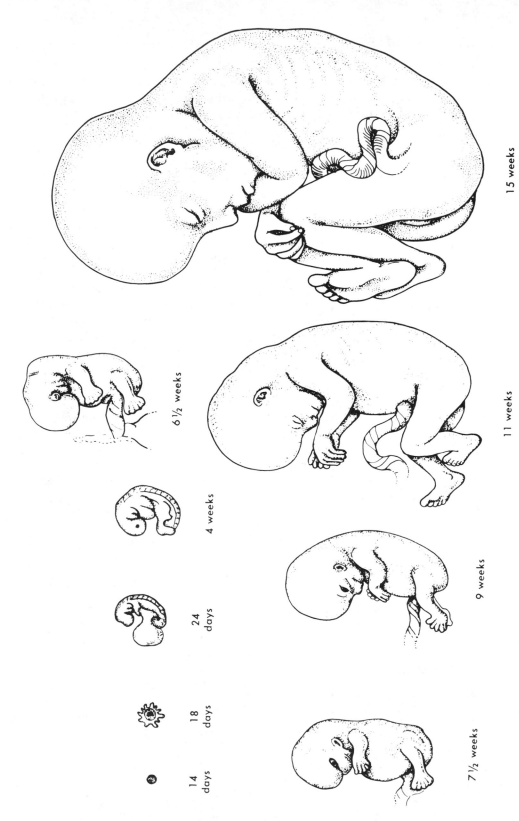

Figure 5–2. The Actual Size of Human Embryos at Early Stages of Development. Comparison of the relative stages of external development is also indicated.

From Chinn, P.L. *Child health maintenance: Concepts in family centered care* (2nd ed.). Copyright 1979 by C. V. Mosby Co. Reprinted by permission.

14 days

18 days

24 days

4 weeks

6½ weeks

7½ weeks

9 weeks

11 weeks

15 weeks

the curved shape in which unborn humans usually are portrayed. This curve is primarily generated at the 4-week period by a very rapid lengthening of the neural tube (spinal area) that is not matched by growth on the front, or ventral, side (Timiras, 1972).

At 6 ½ weeks (fertilization age) the embryo has grown and developed considerably, with the approximate size and shape indicated in Figure 5–2. The circulatory system and heart are now more nearly complete. The eyes, positioned on either side of the head area, later will assume the frontal position characteristic of the human infant. Lungs and intestinal systems become more developmentally complete, and for the first time a primitive gonad structure is observable. Differentiation of this tissue with respect to sex has not occurred yet (Arey, 1974).

Figure 5–2 portrays the embryonic growth at about 7 ½ weeks (fertilization age). At this point the embryo has begun to develop both urethral and anal openings. The circulatory system reaches a stage at which heart valves are developed, and sensory nerve tissue in the upper region progresses.

At the fertilization age of eight weeks, development has reached a stage where the embryo is essentially complete. From this point on it is commonly referred to as a fetus, although there is some difference of opinion as to when this term is applied. Most authorities use the eighth week (Arey, 1974; Chinn, 1979), but others do not consider the fetal period to begin until the twelfth week (Timiras, 1972). Figure 5–2 illustrates the size and shape of a fetus at about the ninth week. It is evident that the eyes have begun to assume the frontal position more characteristic of humans. The fetus has noticeably changed its posture. The head region at this time constitutes nearly half of the total mass, and the cerebral cortex has formed.

Core Concept 6   Prenatal fetal development during weeks 10 through 12 is particularly important because of the tissues being formed at that time.

Particularly crucial growth occurs in the head region during weeks 10 through 12. From about this time through the thirteenth week the palate completes fusion. The forehead is somewhat outsized in comparison to the rest of the head (Figure 5–2) and at this point contains a brain that is essentially complete from a configuration standpoint. The sex of the fetus may now be determined by inspection of the external organs. The skeleton begins the process of actually becoming bone matter (ossification), and the vital structures of the eyes are nearly formed (Arey, 1974).

A fetus at this point (12 weeks) has completed one of the most crucial periods in its developmental life span. By no means is the tiny fetus ready to take on the ravages of the outside world, but the primary body structures are formed. In chapter 6 reference will be made repeatedly to the first trimester (three months) of prenatal life. From our discussion of vulnerability and its relationship to tissue growth, it is very easy to see why this period is so vital. Trauma occurring during these first weeks is most likely to injure the essential body structure being formed at this time. The fetus at 12 weeks weighs about 19 g (Timiras, 1972), certainly a long way from birth weight but vastly increased since the initiation of growth when the mass was so tiny that assessment of weight was not possible.

During the second trimester of prenatal life (weeks 12 through 24), the fetus reaches a weight of approximately 600 g. From the standpoint of appearance there is no doubt at this point that the fetus is a tiny human. The second trimester is also the time when the mother first experiences fetal movement. Bodily proportions have changed somewhat, as illustrated in Figure 5–2. Several important developments occur internally during the second trimester. Various glands mature to the point that metabolic functions are begun. The lung structures become essentially complete, although they are not adequate to sustain life until the third trimester. An extremely important function called myelinization begins during the second trimester. Myelinization refers to the development of a sheath-like material that covers and protects the nervous system. During the second trimester, development of the myelin covering begins in the spinal cord area. This process continues during the third trimester, when the myelinization of higher cortical matter begins. Completion of the myelin covering of the cerebral cortex is primarily accomplished after birth (Timiras, 1972). The progression of the myelin covering also relates to the child's vulnerability to trauma, as will be discussed in chapter 6.

Development that occurs during the final trimester of prenatal life is essential for sustaining life outside the sheltered environment of the mother's body. One of the vital changes involves the final development of the lung structures. These changes continue right up to the last month of gestation. The fetus also is growing larger and stronger at a rapid rate; by the time full term is reached at about 40 weeks, the fetus will weigh about 3,200 g. Sensory organs continue to develop, reaching a functional stage at birth. The third trimester of gestation involves developments that are crucial for survival even though the basic structural components have long since been formed.

BIRTH

At the end of the pregnancy, or about 280 days after fertilization, the fetus leaves the intrauterine environment of the mother's body and begins its life in the outside world. Despite the vast improvements in delivery techniques that have occurred over the years, many facets of childbirth are still not well understood. This section presents a brief description of the more salient aspects of this dramatic event.

Core Concept 7   The birth process represents another important event
when potential risk to the child is high.

Physiological preparation for childbirth is not something that occurs at the last moment. Certain changes in the mother's anatomy have been underway since about mid-pregnancy; these changes are necessary for the birth to proceed smoothly. Figure 5–3 illustrates an advanced fetus in the uterine environment. The muscle structure of the uterus has been rearranged sub-

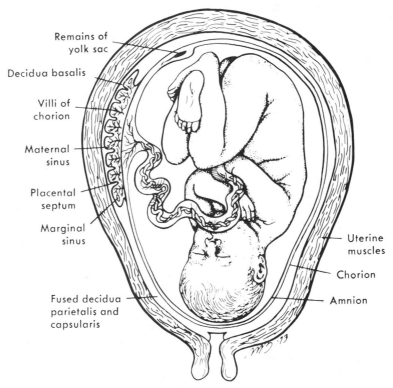

Figure 5–3. Advanced Fetus in Uterine Environment
From Chinn, P.L. *Child health maintenance: Concepts in family centered care* (2nd ed.). Copyright 1979 by C. V. Mosby Co. Reprinted by permission.

stantially in order to facilitate fetal expulsion. Another vital change has occurred in the cervix area that is essential to permit passage of the fetus through the birth canal. In the latter days of pregnancy and during the onset of labor, an expansion occurs in the upper part of the cervical area. By the time the fetus is moving down the birth canal, the cervical muscle structure has expanded to the point where the tube-like structure shown at the bottom of Figure 5–3 no longer exists. The loosening of the cervix, called effacement, is an important change in the muscle structure that must occur for the fetus to be expelled.

The exact mechanism that triggers labor is not entirely known. A variety of possibilities have been investigated, including both chemical (hormones) and mechanical (degree of uterine expansion) agents. The usual and desirable fetal position at the onset of labor is that of the head toward the cervix, as illustrated in Figure 5–3. This is the positioning that naturally occurs in over 80% of all child births. As the fetus begins to move downward into the birth canal, additional stretching takes place in the pelvic girdle area. Simultaneously, the head of the fetus is molded somewhat by pressure, which facilitates its passage through the bony structure of the pelvic girdle. This is why many newborns appear to have strangely shaped heads. Later this misshapen appearance disappears as the head returns to its natural form.

All of this movement is generated by the muscle contractions of the uterus during labor. At the same time that the fetus is moving downward, there is a counterclockwise rotation occurring. Actually the tiny body is turning to the left (this movement is generated by the uterine muscle action), much as one would unscrew a bolt. Figure 5–4 presents a series of positions that illustrate this birth process.

Once expelled, the infant is usually followed a few minutes later by the placenta, which has served to provide oxygen and nourishment and to dispose of waste. Now these functions must be accomplished by the infant. The respiratory tract is immediately cleared of remaining amniotic fluid and mucus, at which point the infant takes over the breathing function. This is the time that most new mothers and fathers remember as the first cry of their newborn. This crying serves an important function, and if it is not initiated spontaneously, the physician must provide stimulation. Through crying, the infant's lungs are expanded with air for the first time, stimulating the circulatory changes that accompany the use of the lungs and loss of the placenta.

The birth process is very complex and involves many different facets that are beyond the scope of this text. Unfortunately, the events of birth do not always proceed smoothly, and difficulties arise that ultimately may result in mental retardation. Some of the problems that can arise are discussed in chapter 6. The present overview provides a general reference with respect to most normal childbirths.

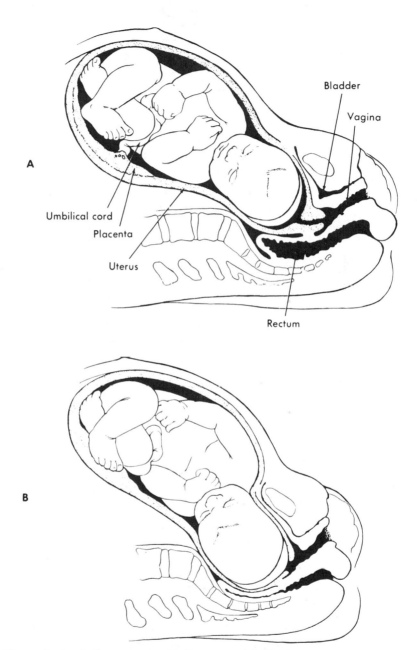

A

Bladder

Vagina

Umbilical cord

Placenta

Uterus

Rectum

B

Figure 5–4. **A**, Engagement. **B**, Descent with Flexion
A-G, From Iorio, J. *Childbirth, Family centered nursing* (3rd ed.). Copyright
1975 by C. V. Mosby Co. Reprinted by permission.

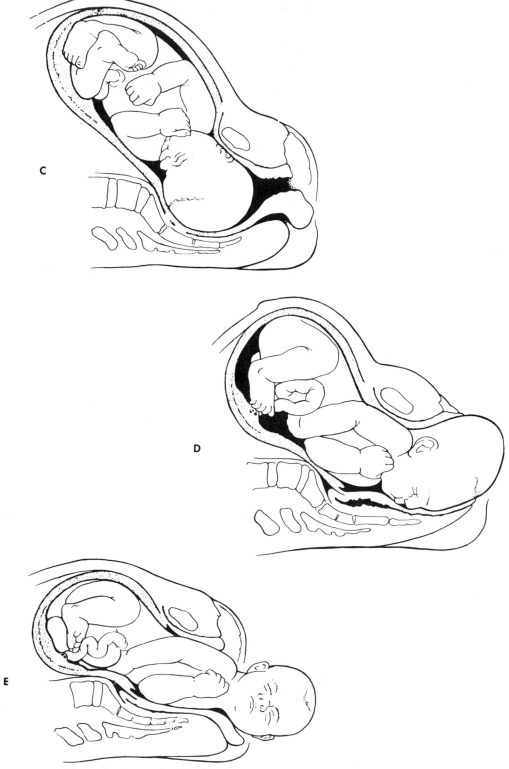

Figure 5–4, cont'd. **C,** Internal Rotation. **D,** Extension. **E,** External Rotation.

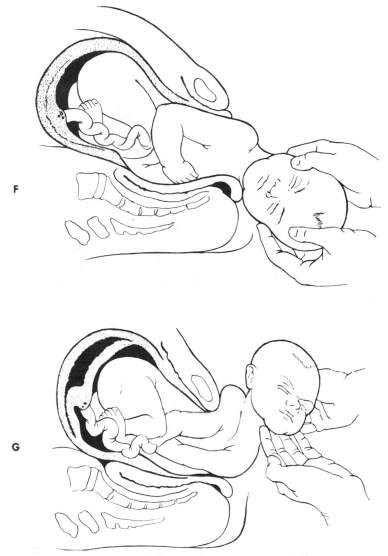

Figure 5–4, cont'd. **F**, Delivery. **G**, Lateral Flexion.

NEONATAL DEVELOPMENT

The term *neonate* is often applied to the baby during the first 2 months of life after birth. Beyond that period the terminology is varied and somewhat nonspecific. The present section examines early life, with some of the principles applicable beyond the neonatal period. Development of the infant and older child is discussed in more detail in subsequent chapters.

Core Concept 8   The period immediately after birth is characterized by many as the most dangerous during an individual's complete lifetime.

The first few weeks of extrauterine life are crucial. Most authorities have viewed the first month as being the most dangerous period in the total life span (Chinn, 1979; Timiras, 1972). Many of the developmental functions begun in utero are continuing but are without the same protective agents previously available. In addition to physiological changes, the neonate has suddenly become subject to a variety of forces that initiate a more rapid development in psychological and behavioral arenas. As development proceeds, the previous and ongoing physiological changes fuse with changes (such as learning) generated by environmental stimuli, forming that integrated complex of responsiveness known as a human being.

From a behavioral standpoint the neonate seems to be little more than a mass of reflex actions. In fact, assessment of the neonate's reflexes is the primary method evaluation of health care professionals. The movements seem primarily nonpurposeful and nonspecific and more often than not involve nearly the entire body simultaneously. This movement pattern usually involves gross motor movements often accompanied by verbal output (crying). The frequency and intensity rise between feeding periods and tend to diminish as the hungry neonate becomes satisfied. As noted previously, the cephalocaudal and proximodistal developmental trends remain operative after birth. These are perhaps most dramatically observable in the behavior patterns during the first two years of life. More mature responses tend to appear earlier in the areas closest to the brain (e.g., eye movement), and progress is downward and outward. Thus gross motor movements of the neonate precede control of more distally located movements such as of the fingers. Likewise, infants usually can reach for and grasp objects with considerable precision long before they are able to walk.

Certain physiological changes occur very rapidly during the first period of postnatal life. The central nervous system exhibits a dramatic growth during the first four years. This acceleration levels off in later childhood. For example, during this growth period the brain weight increases nearly 400 percent over that at birth. In addition to quantitative changes, the brain matter is rapidly developing convolutions or folds that are vital to later cognitive function (Timiras, 1972).

It was previously noted that a process called myelinization begins prenatally and continues after birth. The progression of this protective sheathing of nerve cells is very rapid during the first 12 months of postnatal life and declines progressively thereafter. The progression of the myelin sheath generally follows the course of the primary direction of central nervous system development. At birth the neonate is essentially governed by the lower or subcortical portion of the central nervous system (spinal cord and brain stem). This also represents the first part of the central nervous system to receive the myelin covering. Later, the higher cerebral matter is involved in myelinization and likewise begins to take charge of the child's behavior. The myelin sheath is essentially complete at age two, although fragmentary myelinization apparently continues through adolescence and perhaps even middle adult life (Timiras, 1972). In our consideration of mental retardation this myelinization process becomes important with regard to possible injury to the central nervous system, as we will see in chapter 6.

At birth the sensory organs, particularly the eyes and ears, are nearly complete from a structural standpoint. Certain parts of the retina are yet to be completed, but otherwise the basic visual mechanism exists at birth. For the first few weeks the eyes tend to operate somewhat independently rather than as a coordinated pair of organs. By about six weeks, however, eye fixation is fairly well coordinated in terms of both eyes functioning together. Visual acuity appears to be imperfect during the neonatal and infant periods. The image may be primarily one involving blurred forms, patterns, and shapes.

Auditory perception is apparently intact at birth. The neonate is responsive to a wide variety of auditory stimuli, suggesting that probably the full range of humanly detectable sound is available quite early. Additionally, the neonate seems capable of identifying the location of sounds. The development of auditory discrimination abilities has yet to be investigated in any complete sense. It is possible that a portion of the ability to discriminate various sound differences is a learned or acquired skill. Certainly if this is the case, the neonate must grow older in order to have the opportunity to accumulate a background of experience that will permit such learning.

The sense of taste is somewhat more difficult to study in a very young child than are some other sensory avenues. There is evidence to indicate that even at the neonatal stage gross taste discriminations are made. Such discrimination, however, is primarily observable in different behavioral reactions to sweetness versus other tastes, such as sourness and bitterness. This sense also appears to improve with experience. The sense of smell is even more difficult to study than that of taste. Consequently very little evidence is available with regard to it in the neonatal period. It does, however, seem that the neonate is responsive to very dramatic or intense odors and that smell sensitivity increases during the infant stage (Chinn, 1979).

It has already been noted that the behavioral repertoire of the newborn is limited. During the first few weeks of postnatal life, verbal output is primarily limited to crying. This seems to be mostly associated with discomfort of some sort, although at times the source of discomfort is not evident, as many parents well know. Hunger seem to be the standard stimulus from birth that generates the crying response. Later the young child learns to use crying as a means of communicating in a wide variety of situations that are unpleasurable. Other verbal output (for example, gurgling, cooing, and generating general noise) seems to develop considerably later, often not becoming a significant part of the behavioral repertoire until the infant is several months old.

The sucking response is an important component of neonatal behavior. In addition to its obvious value to the child in terms of feeding, it remains an important early checkpoint of well-being. A weak sucking response serves as a signal for concern. The neonate tends to exhibit the sucking response to a variety of stimuli both in terms of type of stimulus and body part that receives the stimulation (Rochat, 1983). Later the responsivity is reduced on both counts and tends to be elicited primarily in relation to the area around the mouth.

Core Questions

1. Compare the concepts of genotype and phenotype and discuss how they relate to the growth matrix.
2. The tabula rasa approach to explain human growth and development differed significantly from both the preformationist and predeterministic positions. Compare and contrast these three approaches. How do you think their proponents would differ in their explanations of mental retardation, and why might the interactional view be more helpful for a major portion of those who are retarded?
3. How are the notions of discontinuous growth and critical stages related? Discuss the views of continuous and discontinuous human growth in terms of prenatal and neonatal development.
4. In what manner does the speed of cell reproduction influence vulnerability to trauma that might cause mental retardation? How does this relate to the first trimester of pregnancy, particularly with respect to weeks 10 through 12?
5. Why would you expect a new baby's head and arm movements to be more mature than those of the legs? What other growth gradient is also typical of early development?
6. What are the important physical changes in the mother that prepare for birth? Likewise, how is the baby physically influenced during the birth?
7. Why is the neonatal period a time of risk for the baby and what important physical developments are continuing at this time?

ROUND TABLE DISCUSSION

A basic understanding of early human development is important background for the study of mental retardation. There are many prenatal influences that have a substantial impact on the status of a child. During this time many vital organs are being formed and tissue growth occurs at a phenomenal rate. This is all occurring in the womb during a relatively short period of about nine months. Biological and embryological information suggests that such processes as myelinization are taking place, central nervous system tissue is being formed, and many other tissues essential to the well being of a young child are taking shape.

In your study group or on your own, examine these processes through the eyes of a preformationist, a predeterminist, a tabula rasa theorist, and an interactionist. Using the material presented in this chapter, as well as other sources available, explain the prenatal developments mentioned (e.g., mylenization, CNS development, brain development, etc.). Also try to integrate into your arguments the concepts of continuous/discontinuous growth and critical periods from each theoretical perspective. Push your explanations and arguments to the extreme, as they were by early developmental theorists. Do you find such extremes the most difficult parts of your tasks or do you find the fundamental premises problematic? After this examination of the basic principles of development, where do you stand theoretically as you prepare to advance in your study of mental retardation?

REFERENCES

Arey, L. B. (1974). *Development anatomy; A textbook and laboratory manual of embryology* (7th ed.). Philadelphia: Saunders.

Ausubel, D. P., Sullivan, E.V., & Ives, S. W. (1980). *Theory and problems of child development* (3rd ed.). New York: Grune & Stratton.

Berger, K.S. (1983). *The developing person through the life span.* New York: Worth.

Chinn, P. L. (1979). *Child health maintenance: Concepts for family centered care* (2nd ed.). St. Louis: Mosby.

Elbert, J. C. (1984). Training in child diagnostic assessment: A survey of clinical psychology graduate programs. *Journal of Clinical Child Psychology, 13,* 122–133.

Flavell, J. H. (1971). Stage-related properties of cognitive development. *Cognitive Psychology, 2,* 421–453.

Flavell, J. H. (1982). Structures, stages, and sequences in cognitive development. In W. A. Collins (Ed.), *The concept of development: The Minnesota symposia on child psychology* (Vol.XV) (pp. 1–28). Hillsdale, NJ: Erlbaum.

Flavell, J. H. (1985). *Cognitive development.* Englewood Cliffs, NJ: Prentice-Hall.

Gleitman, H. (1986). *Psychology* (2nd ed.). New York: Norton.

Gottesman, I. I. (1963). Genetic aspects of intelligent behavior. In N. R. Ellis (Ed.), *Handbook of Mental Deficiency.* (pp. 253–296). New York: McGraw-Hill.

Hall, G. S. (1904). *Adolescence: Its psychology and its relation to physiology, anthropology, sociology, sex, crime, religion and education.* New York: Appleton-Century-Crofts.

Piaget, J. (1926). *The language and thought of the child.* New York: Harcourt Brace.

Rochat, P. (1983). Oral touch in young infants: Response to variations of nipple characteristics in the first months of life. *International Journal of Behavioral Development, 6,* 123–133.

Schwartz, S., & Johnson, J. H. (1985). *Psychopathology of childhood: A clinical-experimental approach* (2nd ed.). New York: Pergamon.

Shaffer, D. R. (1985). *Developmental psychology: Theory, research, and applications.* Monterey, CA: Brooks-Cole.

Shultz, T. R. (1982). Rules of causal attribution. *Monographs of the Society for Research on Child Development,* Serial No. 194, *47,* (1).

Timiras, P. S. (1972). *Developmental physiology and aging.* New York: Macmillan.

6

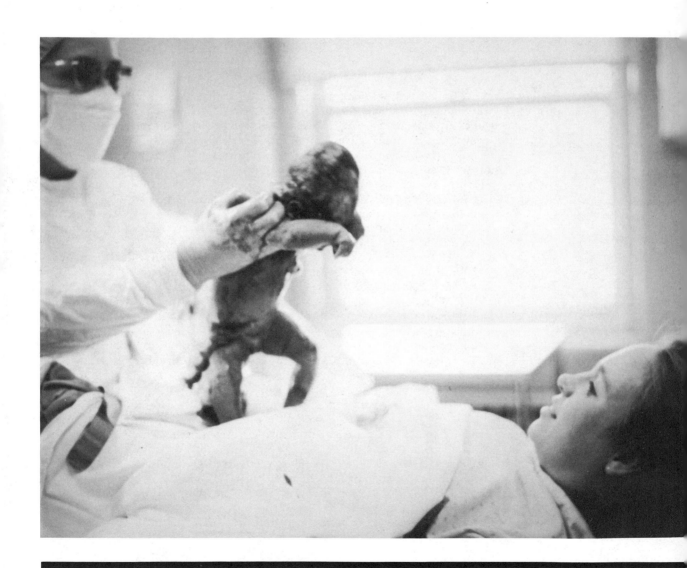

Mental Retardation: Influences and Causation During the Prenatal and Neonatal Periods

Core Concepts

1. Inadequate birth weight and incomplete gestation, both of which can be caused by a number of factors, are the most prevalent conditions that place an infant at developmental risk.
2. Chromosomal abnormalities and genetic errors cause a number of mental retardation syndromes.
3. Various interactions between the mother and fetus can cause damage resulting in mental retardation.
4. Fetal damage causing reduced mental functioning may result from such factors as maternal infection and drug ingestion.
5. Problems occurring during the delivery of a baby may cause damage that results in mental retardation.
6. Professional intervention during the prenatal and neonatal periods may prevent or minimize mental retardation.

Early life is a period of human growth and development that warrants considerable attention in the study of mental retardation since it is such a crucial part of the life cycle. The tiny human is essentially at the mercy of the environment and is vulnerable to its impact, both prenatally and after birth. Chapter 5 examined normal developmental processes during early life. This chapter examines the same period (conception through early infancy) in a consideration of influences and causes of mental retardation.

Discussion of influences and causation of mental retardation during the prenatal and neonatal periods requires attention to certain abnormal physiological conditions and the treatment, when possible, of these conditions. It is primarily the medical profession that is interacting with a child at risk for mental retardation during this early period. We will not present an in-depth examination of the medical aspects of mental retardation, but will provide a description of some influences on mental development during early life. We will examine the more common conditions of retardation beginning during this period as well as those for which intervention can prevent or minimize retardation. Reduced intellectual functioning can result from the disruption of a variety of developmental and ongoing life processes during early life. The beginning student may wonder how children can progress through this period at all without deviation or abnormality. The vast majority of children, however, do develop to a level of functioning that is considered normal or average.

Maternal and fetal conditions play a central role in the development of a fetus. It follows that a variety of maternal and fetal conditions occurring during the early life period may also be involved in causing mental retardation varying from profound or severe levels to only mild deviations from normal. Several years ago a group of researchers, working primarily at the Johns Hopkins University, suggested an interesting conceptual framework for considering the range of disability severity during early life (Lilienfeld & Pasamanick, 1956). Termed the *continuum of reproductive casualty*, this notion views the mildly handicapped child at the less extreme end of the casualty continuum and the more severely retarded individuals and the stillborn are at the harsher end of the continuum. Spontaneous abortion occurring early in pregnancy may represent one extreme of the continuum; mild retardation or slight disabilities in basically normal children represent the other extreme. Lilienfeld and his associates contended that this concept is useful in identifying areas needing investigation because of handicapping conditions during early life.

EARLY CAUSATION

We have already seen the extreme importance of the first portion of the life cycle. Development during the prenatal period and the time immediately after birth is viewed by many as the most critical in the entire life span. Fortunately, most infants enter extrauterine life after a full and successful gestational period, with an uncomplicated labor and delivery and no factors during the first month of life that lead to serious illness or disability. However, when a serious problem does occur in these early months, the family may have to adjust to a permanent mental or physical disability. Several conditions are known to place the fetus or infant in a position of high risk for development of serious illness or permanent disability.

The Fetus and Infant at Risk: Birth Weight and Gestational Age

Core Concept 1   Inadequate birth weight and incomplete gestation, both of which can be caused by a number of factors, are the most prevalent conditions that place an infant at developmental risk.

Many different problems may occur during the prenatal and neonatal periods. Each of the difficulties discussed here is a condition that places the infant in a risk category. The most prevalent of these disorders are inadequate birth weight and incomplete gestation. Although these problems do occasionally exist alone, there is usually an accompanying problem of some maternal, genetic, or traumatic condition.

GRAMS

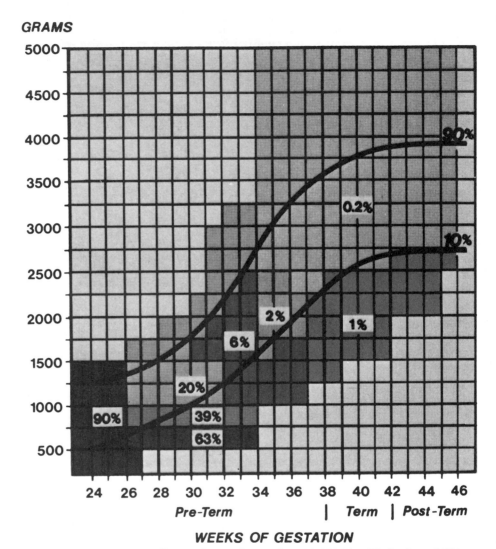

WEEKS OF GESTATION

Figure 6–1. Neonatal Mortality Risk Based on 14,413 Live Births from 1974 to 1980 at the University of Colorado Health Sciences Center
From "Neonatal mortality risk in relation to birth weight and gestational age: Update" by B. L. Koops, L. J. Morgan, and F. C. Battaglia, 1982, *The Journal of Pediatrics, 101(b)*, p. 972. Copyright 1982 by the authors. Reprinted by permission.

Infants with problems related to gestational age and birth weight were classified in the past by a simple designation of prematurity which was based on either birth weight or on estimated gestational age. Because of inadequacies encountered with this approach, a classification based on both weight and age has been more recently adopted (Koops, Morgan, & Battaglia, 1982). The graph in Figure 6–1 indicates the system of classification and the mortality risk associated with infants in the various classification sectors. The range of birth weight occurring between the tenth and ninetieth percentiles during weeks 24 through 46 of gestation has been plotted. Infants who are born before the thirty-eighth week of gestation are referred to as preterm, those born within the thirty-eighth to forty-second weeks are referred to as term, and those born beyond the forty-second week are known as post-term infants. In addition, weight is indicated as "small for gestational age," "appropriate for gestational age," or "large for gestational age." These classifications indicate that both age and weight have been taken into account. In the past an infant who was about the size of a normal term infant might in reality be suffering the disadvantages of a preterm infant. Since it is now possible to estimate the gestational maturity of an infant by physical signs, care for the infant can be appropriate for the particular needs that occur according to gestational age. Such improved care has led to a decrease in total neonatal mortality in the United States even though the incidence of infants with low birth weight has not changed (Babson, Pernoll, Benda, & Simpson, 1980).

Predisposing Factors. Several causative factors have been identified as related to low birth weight and gestational age. Each of the problems discussed in later sections (e.g., infant chromosomal aberrations, maternal-infant interaction problems, early pregnancy trauma) can be associated with early termination of pregnancy. However, there are several other conditions that also appear to lead to early pregnancy termination and inadequate birth weight.

Maternal age and the number of previous pregnancies are a significant factor. Very young mothers or mothers over 40, especially those who have had a number of previous pregnancies, are most likely to have infants who suffer early pregnancy termination (Berger, 1983). Socioeconomic factors are related to the incidence of preterm and low gestational weight infants. For example, the father's occupation has been related to substantial differences in the incidence of prematurity and infant mortality as indicated in Table 6–1.

Premature births have also been associated with ethnicity, although this factor is probably related to lower socioeconomic status more than to ethnic differences per se. The percentage of infants born prematurely among white Americans is consistently about half the percentage born prematurely in nonwhite Americans. Fifty-one percent of all nonwhites (low incomes are more prevalent as a group) have birth complications of some sort whereas only 5% of white upper class births are so affected (U. S. Bureau of the Census, 1982).

Multiple pregnancies account for a great percentage of infants born with problems associated with gestational age and birth weight. The reasons are complex and numerous, including primarily placental insufficiency, which

Table 6–1. Premature Birth Rate According to Father's Occupation

Occupation	Incidence per 1,000 Live births
Farmer	33.8
Professional	49.1
Laborer	71.8
Service worker	78.3
Farm laborer	88.1

From "Patterns of prematurity in Oregon." by C. Kernek, H. Osterud, and B. Anderson, 1966, *Northwest Medicine, 65,* p. 639. Copyright 1966 by the authors. Reprinted by permission.

leads to ineffective transfer of nutrients across the placenta late in pregnancy and ultimately to fetal malnutrition. Labor and delivery often commence before term, and the infants are usually small for their gestational age.

Placental problems are not clearly understood and, when no other cause can be identified, are often attributed to inadequate intrauterine growth. Placental insufficiency implies an impaired exchange between the mother and fetus through the placenta. Several well-defined placental lesions can be definitely associated with fetal and infant disorders (e.g., blockage of fetal vessels in the placenta, early placenta separation, a single umbilical artery).

Maternal smoking is another factor that has been associated with inadequate growth during fetal life (Birren, Kinney, Schaie, & Woodruff, 1981). Mothers who smoke more than 20 cigarettes a day give birth to growth-retarded (but not necessarily preterm) infants two to three times as often as do nonsmoking mothers (Korones, 1981). The reason for this difference has not yet been delineated, and other related factors may be as important as the maternal smoking itself.

Serious damage to the fetus may also be inflicted by maternal alcohol consumption. Known as "fetal alcohol syndrome," it causes a variety of problems including facial abnormalities, cardiac defects, and defects in joints and limbs, as well as low brain weight and mental retardation (Streissguth, Herman, & Smith, 1978; Streissguth, Martin, Martin, & Barr, 1981). Even moderate consumption by pregnant women may result in fetal problems (Hanson, Streissguth, & Smith, 1978). Difficulties associated with maternal alcohol consumption have been recognized for many years (e.g., Sullivan, 1899), but research on the problem was quite rare for a considerable period, and the term "fetal alcohol syndrome" was not used until the early 1970s (e.g., Jones, Smith, Ulleland, & Streissguth, 1973).

Maternal nutrition is another incompletely understood factor, although evidence indicates that it may be very important in relation to fetal outcome. Many families who eat poorly also suffer from socioeconomic limitations and are often influenced by the dietary practices of a subculture. Thus it seems difficult to delineate which of the factors in this complex set of interacting variables has primarily contributed to the occurrence of increased rates of low birth weight and gestational age problems. It is generally known that the pregnant woman has greater nutritional requirements than a woman who is not pregnant. For example, the usual increase in caloric requirements by about 200 kilocalories per day results in about a 25-pound maternal weight gain. Additionally, both protein and calcium requirements of a pregnant mother will be increased by approximately 13% (P. L. Chinn, 1979). Maternal malnutrition, which frequently is part of the mother's life-long state of nutritional inadequacy, has been implicated as exerting potentially damaging influences on the fetus, particularly on the developing central nervous system. However, such findings are difficult to evaluate and substantiate because of the inability to examine the direct transfer of nutrients to the fetus and of difficulties in studying the exact nutritional requirements of the fetus (Gluck, 1971).

Finally, unwed mothers tend to have preterm infants with greater frequency than do married mothers. A rate of premature births of 93.6% was reported for one group of unwed mothers in Oregon in the 1960s (Kernek, Osterud, & Anderson, 1966). The reason for this startling rate of premature infants born to unwed mothers is not known, but again several socioeconomic factors may be involved.

Associated Problems. Infants at risk, especially those with inadequate birth weight and gestational age, tend to be susceptible to serious stress after birth which is manifested primarily as respiratory and cardiac failure or complications, infection, and nutritional disorders. These, rather than the problems of birth weight or gestational age alone, may account for many of the sequelae associated with birth weight and gestational age inadequacies.

Respiratory and cardiac failure complications lead to serious interference with the delivery of oxygen to the growing and developing tissues. Tissues of the central nervous system are particularly vulnerable, for even though it is known that a newborn can tolerate longer periods of anoxia (low oxygen level) than can an adult, a continued low level of oxygen to the tissues interferes with critical development occurring during the forty weeks after conception. Central nervous system tissue cells are still developing until about the forty-second or forty-sixth week of gestation and the tissue depends on an adequate supply of oxygen for sufficient development to occur. An infant who is born at risk before term and who develops such oxygen delivery interference is particularly jeopardized with respect to developing adequate neural tissue. The relationship between such interference and future development has yet to be fully explored. However, continuing improvements in neonatal care, including prevention of respiratory and cardiac complications and improved care for the infant with these complications, have been made with the expectation of reducing the serious neurological sequelae of prematurity.

Infection is another serious complication for infants who suffer birth weight or gestational age problems. The fetus and preterm infant are extremely susceptible to infection from organisms that ordinarily do not cause illness for older individuals, and infants have few physiological mechanisms with which to combat infection. Infection that begins in the skin may rapidly progress to a serious illness such as pneumonia, septicemia (widespread infection of the blood), or meningitis (infection of the central nervous system). Further, an infant does not exhibit the usual signs of infection, such as fever, and detection of an infectious process may be difficult or impossible until it has progressed to a serious stage. Infection of the central nervous system may lead to particularly serious permanent sequelae that affect the child's neurological capacity in later life.

Inadequate nutrition and insufficient oxygen intake is another problem of magnitude for infants of low birth weight and incomplete gestational age. Such infants miss the optimal nutrition normally received through the placenta, and they suffer from inadequate intake of basic metabolic nutrients. Of particular importance during the last few months of gestation is acquisition of glucose, proteins, and oxygen through the placenta, for these materials nourish all growing tissues, particularly those of the central nervous system. Central nervous system tissue depends on each of these nutrients not only for growth and development but also for survival. When an infant is born with fetal malnutrition from placental insufficiency, nutrition therapy must be incorporated into the routine care. Oxygen administration is most complicated for infants of low birth weight or inadequate gestational age, because transfer of the ambient oxygen across the lung-blood barrier cannot be directly measured. As a result an infant may be underoxygenated while receiving large percentages of oxygen or, conversely, overoxygenated while receiving relatively low concentrations of oxygen. Excessive oxygen delivered to the tissues causes damage to the retina of the eye, with ultimate blindness, a condition known as retrolental fibroplasia.

Psychological and Educational Sequelae. It has been extremely difficult to determine precisely the psychological and educational sequelae of birth weight and gestational age inadequacies. There are many factors contributing to the complexity of these difficulties. There are the compounding variables of low socioeconomic status and membership in racial minority groups that consistently have a greater occurrence of births in this category. These same groups also are known to have an increased percentage of educational and psychological problems among their young children (Caputo & Mandell, 1970; Eaves, Nuttall, Konoff, & Dunn, 1970; Parmalee & Schulte, 1970). Further, comparison among various investigations is difficult because of the varying definitions of prematurity, low birth weight, and gestational age classifications. In addition, findings of long-term studies, which are necessary in order to determine educational sequelae, are often outdated by the time the data can be collected. That is, by the time a child who was born prematurely reaches 6 years of age or older, medical and nursing care for preterm infants has progressed so dramatically that there can be little application of the current findings to infants born several years earlier. For example, 20 years ago little was known about the administration of oxygen to preterm infants for the treatment of lung disorders or prevention of anoxia. Today, on the other hand, great advances have been made in these and other related areas, so that most infants cared for in a high-risk specialty center are treated in such a manner that optimal oxygenation of body tissues is maintained throughout the critical period of instability. We now are able greatly to offset the seriously detrimental effects of anoxia, which may have caused many of the psychological and educational sequelae reported for children born in the previous two or three decades (Babson et al., 1980; Lasky et al., 1983; Korones, 1981).

An older interesting investigation conducted by Rubin, Rosenblatt, and Balow (1973) studied psychological and educational sequelae of prematurity and outlined a number of difficulty areas that have received further attention. Infants in this study were born at the University of Minnesota Hospital between 1960 and 1964, and the factor of socioeconomic status was controlled. The investigation included only infants from the urban population of the north-central United States, and from an almost exclusively Caucasian racial background. The infants were classified according to both gestational age and birth weight. The major findings reported by Rubin et al. (1973) suggested that preterm males of low birth weight and full-term infants of both sexes with low birth weight constitute "high-risk" groups of children with regard to eventual impairment in school functioning. Their generic conclusions that prematurely born youngsters represent a high- risk group in several fashions has been continually supported (Cohen & Parmelee, 1983; Silva, McGee, & Williams, 1984). Rubin et al. (1973) found that low birth weight was associated with a number of abnormal conditions, such as low Apgar scores and elevated bilirubin levels during the neonatal period; further, birth weight rather than gestational age was the major correlate of neurological, psychological, and educational impairment. Low birth-weight males and low birth-weight full-term children of both sexes experience a significantly higher incidence of school problems warranting special school services than do full-term children (Rubin et al., 1973). Low birth-weight children also score lower than do full birth-weight peers on measures of cognitive and language development (Crnic, Ragozin, Greenberg, Robinson, & Basham, 1983; Rocissano & Yatchmink, 1983; Rose, 1983; Silva et al. 1984; Ungerer & Sigman, 1983). Rubin et al. (1973) also found that at the age of 7, low birth-weight children were smaller in stature and had a higher incidence of diagnosed neurological abnormalities than normal birth-weight children. These are examples of the mounting evidence that low birth-weight and gestational age present considerable difficulties that are related to mental retardation (Kiely, Paneth, & Susser, 1981).

Chromosomal Aberrations and Genetic Errors

Core Concept 2   Chromosomal abnormalities and genetic errors cause a
number of mental retardation syndromes.

A number of problems occur, particularly during the prenatal period, as a
result of chromosomal and genetic errors. In many cases mental retardation
that results from these difficulties represents the well-known syndrome
classes of retardation.

Chromosomal Aberrations.   Chromosomal aberrations occur when there is
an incorrect number or configuration of the chromosomes in the body. Figure
6–2 illustrates a karyotype or standardized classification of human chromosomes photographed from a blood or skin sample. Such a karyotype is
arranged in a certain manner, and by use of this technique determinations
of some particular chromosomal abnormalities causing an abnormal condition can be identified. The karyotype shown in Figure 6–2 represents a
normal chromosomal configuration with 44 autosomes and two sex chromosomes. Two kinds of abnormalities involve extra chromosomes, such as
three chromosomes in position 21 or two or more X or Y chromosomes.
Another type of common aberration involves abnormally shaped chromosomes, such as an excessively long "arm" on number 15 or another chromosome in the karyotype.

Where there is a total of 45 chromosomes present with only a single X
sex chromosome, the child has a condition termed Turner's syndrome, or
gonadal aplasia. The child is nearly always female, since the Y chromosome
conveys maleness to the individual. The gonads are rudimentary, no secondary sex characteristics develop at puberty, and there may or may not be
other physical characteristics such as bowleggedness, webbed neck, or abnormalities of the kidneys and heart. It is estimated that approximately 20%
of individuals with this problem are mentally retarded (Jones & Grumbach,
1968).

Klinefelter's syndrome, which occurs in males, involves two or more X
and one or more Y chromosomes in at least some cells. Older maternal age
seems to be a predisposing factor to the occurrence of extra X chromosomes
in the infant. At puberty the boy may begin to develop secondary sex characteristics typical of the pubescent girl, and the male gonads are often under-
developed, rendering the individual sterile. Mental retardation occurs
frequently, but not invariably (Grumbach, 1968).

Many aberrations occur on the chromosomes occurring in groups A
through G; known as the autosomal chromosomes, they contain genetic
material that does not involve sexual characteristics. Autosomal problems

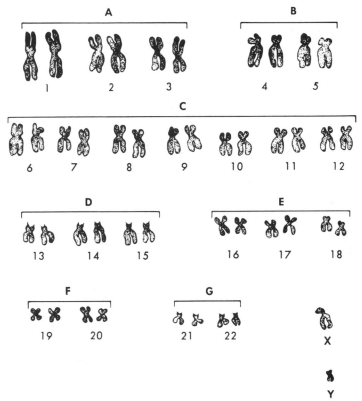

Figure 6–2. Reproduction of Human Chromosomes during Metaphase. The chromosomes are arranged according to a standard system known as karyotype. This is often provided as a tool in genetic counseling.

From *Child Health Maintenance: Concepts in family centered care* (2nd ed.) by P. L. Chinn, 1979, St. Louis: Mosby. Copyright 1979 by C. V. Mosby Co. Reprinted by permission.

occur with Down syndrome and may involve any one of three different chromosomal aberrations. The first type is that of trisomy, or nondisjunction, in which there is an extra copy of chromosome 21 in the G group. This is the most common cause of Down syndrome, and there is a definite correlation of this condition with maternal age as suggested in Table 6–2.

A second type of chromosomal difficulty resulting in Down syndrome is translocation, which occurs in 9% of affected infants born to mothers under the age of 30 and in 2% of affected infants born to mothers over the age of 30. In translocation some of the chromosomal material designated as one of the twenty-first pair of the G group detaches and becomes attached to one of the chromosomes of the fifteenth pair in the D group, causing an extra-long chromosome in the karyotype. This type of chromosomal aberration may be inherited from a parent who is a carrier of the condition, and

Table 6–2. Maternal Age Correlation with Incidence of Down Syndrome

Age of Mother (years)	Incidence per 1,000 Live births
Younger than 20	0.5
20 to 24	0.7
25 to 29	0.7
30 to 34	1.1
35 to 39	3.5
40 to 44	10.0
45 and older	16.0

From "Mental Subnormality and Mongolism" by H. G. Birch and L. T. Taft, in *The biologic basis of pediatric practice* edited by R. E. Cooke, 1968, New York: McGraw-Hill. Copyright 1968 by McGraw-Hill. Reprinted by permission.

such a case can be determined through genetic studies of each parent and their child. When inheritance is not established, the condition has occurred as a result of a chance chromosomal error.

The third condition resulting in Down syndrome is mosaicism. In this case, the cells of the affected individual's body are identified as mixed, some reflecting a trisomy condition and others reflecting the normal complement of chromosomes. This error occurs during the very early cell division phases after fertilization, with some cell groups being formed normally before the occurrence of the error. Such individuals tend to exhibit milder manifestations of the condition; this may reflect the stage of development at which the chromosomal error occurred.

The clinical characteristics of Down syndrome vary but are similar to the extent that most individuals with Down syndrome resemble one another more than they resemble family members. They exhibit a lateral upward slope of the eyes; a protruding tongue because of a small oral cavity; a short nose with flat bondage due to underdevelopment of the nasal bone; a head flattened both in front and in back; shortness of fingers, especially the fifth; wide space between the first and second toes; and short, stocky stature. These children are more likely than the general population to have congenital heart defects and leukemia, and they are more susceptible to respiratory infections. There is almost always mental deficiency, with IQ scores in the moderate to severely retarded ranges. A few individuals have been reported in the normal range, and the effect of early stimulation and education programs may be demonstrated to result in improvement of mental and neurological functioning for some with Down syndrome (Birch & Taft, 1968). Considerable research continues on Down syndrome and includes study of racial factors (Ershow, 1986) and of chromosomal abnormalities involved (e.g., Cox & Epstein, 1985; Davidson, Rumsby, & Niswander, 1985). Some work in this area includes examination of the trisomy 21 condition by using animal models (such as mouse trisomy 16) (Cox & Epstein, 1985; Epstein, Cox, & Epstein, 1985).

Genetic Errors. Genetic errors are those conditions that occur as a result of inheritance factors involving specific genes. Such disorders are rather poorly understood, and investigation of these problems is somewhat restricted because of the limitations on studying human genetic material. Genetic disorders sometimes can be identified through study of family inheritance patterns, but the examination and identification of these problems are difficult. Such conditions cannot be studied in the same manner as the chromosomal disorders, for it is not presently possible to obtain information about genetic material from study of the chromosomes. Most genetic errors are rare, but a few that result in mental retardation occur with sufficient frequency that diagnostic and treatment approaches have been developed. One example of such a condition is phenylketonuria (PKU), which has become one of the most thoroughly studied genetic defects. It occurs about once in every 10,000 live births and accounts for about 0.5 percent of patients in institutions for the mentally retarded. It is transmitted by an autosomal recessive gene that has its highest frequency among northern European ethnic groups but is rare among black and Jewish groups. For affected individuals there is a decrease in the essential enzyme necessary for metabolism of phenylalanine, which then accumulates in the serum, cerebrospinal fluid, tissues, and urine. The effect of this metabolic malfunction on the central nervous system is severe, and all untreated individuals become severely mentally retarded within the first few months of life. Elevated phenylalanine in the blood or urine can be detected within a few weeks after consumption of milk, which contains the substance. Consequently many states have instituted mandatory screening procedures for all infants in order to institute early treatment measures and to minimize or prevent the serious effects of the untreated condition. In addition to the effect of mental retardation, the child develops some degree of microcephaly and has blond hair, blue eyes, and very sensitive skin.

There are a number of other disorders that occur due to specific recessive genes. In these cases the parents are carriers of a deficient gene but are phenotypically normal. However, children who receive the recessive genetic material from each parent may develop conditions that result in mental retardation. One such disorder is galactosemia, which occurs when an infant cannot properly metabolize galactose, a chemical generated from digesting milk products. Affected newborns who are on milk diets will rapidly develop symptoms that can become life threatening such as jaundice, vomiting, and a vastly heightened vulnerability to infection. Intellectual development may also be detrimentally influenced. Early detection of galactosemia and rapid treatment with strict dietary restrictions may dramatically improve the infant's potential development, although some difficulties may persist. Research of a longitudinal nature on treatment effectiveness remains inexact because of the disorder's relative rarity; this is a common difficulty with such genetic problems.

Influences from Maternal-Fetal Interaction

Core Concept 3   Various interactions between the mother and fetus can cause damage resulting in mental retardation.

There are several conditions of abnormal maternal-fetal interactions that lead to serious consequences for the infant. Infants of diabetic mothers, for example, are always high-risk babies because of excessive birth weight for gestational age, which is often low. In addition, there is an increased incidence of physical anomalies among infants of diabetic mothers, and the infants are prone to several serious illnesses during the neonatal period, such as lung disorders, seizures, hypoglycemia (low blood glucose), and hyperbilirubinemia (resulting in jaundice). A mother's diabetic condition can affect the fetus and infant in such a manner that the child is placed at serious risk from several standpoints. The incidence of neurological sequelae is largely dependent on the severity of the maternal diabetes and the neonatal course, including the gestational age and accompanying complications during this period (Babson et al., 1980).

Maternal-fetal Rh factor incompatibility has a very direct effect on the neurological capacity of an infant. This is a case of the mother having a negative Rh blood factor and the fetus a positive Rh factor. The mother reacts to the fetal positive factor by developing antibodies that destroy the fetus's blood cells, leading to serious consequences during fetal life and the neonatal period. The infant's condition is known as erythroblastosis fetalis. The higher the level of antibodies in the mother's blood, the more serious the effect on a fetus. In its the most severe form, known as fetal hydrops, the fetus begins to develop severe anemia, enlargement of the heart, liver, and spleen, and deterioration of the body tissues. In most cases the fetus dies during the late second or early third trimester and is stillborn. If the child is born alive, survival during the neonatal period is unlikely. A moderate form of erythroblastosis fetalis, known as icterus gravis, occurs more frequently, since in many instances the infant's delivery is induced before term to prevent progression of the disease to the more severe form. When this occurs, an infant is placed in a disadvantageous position of being de-livered preterm, but hazards of this condition are less than those of a more severe form of erythroblastosis fetalis. Such an infant may also be of low birth weight because of the condition's effect in utero. The infant is typically anemic and jaundiced, with an enlarged spleen and liver. The high level of bilirubin, occurring from the metabolism of red blood cells, accounts for the jaundice and for the central nervous system damage that may result. As the bilirubin level rises rapidly, adequate excretion cannot occur, and the molecules enter the skin tissue and render a toxic effect, a condition known as kernicterus. If the infant survives the first week of life, outlook for survival is good. However, the possibility of neurological sequelae depends on the severity of hyperbilirubinemia and accompanying illnesses occurring during the neonatal period. When the blood factor incompatibility effects are min-imal, which is usual for the first or second infants of most Rh-negative mothers, neonatal problems are minimal, and there are no neurological sequelae (P. C. Chinn & Mueller, 1971).

Other Trauma During Early Pregnancy

Core Concept 4   Fetal damage causing reduced mental functioning may result from such factors as maternal infection and drug ingestion.

Trauma can occur to the fetus during the first trimester from a variety of causes, including drug or chemical ingestion by the mother and maternal infection. The teratogenic effects of such exposure are poorly understood, but it is known that, while the exact effect of most teratogens is not spec-ified, the timing of exposure likely leads to specific kinds of anomalies. Thus when a mother contracts rubella during the first trimester, the specific anomalies that occur are probably related more to the timing of exposure than to the specific effects of the virus. Teratogenic effects on the fetus include intrauterine growth retardation, central nervous system infection, microcephaly, congenital heart disease, sensorineural deafness, cataracts and/ or glaucoma, and anomalies of the skin. There is a wide range of severity of these conditions, as well as variability in the occurrence of each of the possible conditions. Again, range of severity is probably related to the timing of the infection, as well as to the individual susceptibility of a particular mother and fetus to the effects of the infection. The infant is likely to have a number of physical, behavioral, and intellectual handicaps (Babson et al., 1980).

The Birth Process

Core Concept 5   Problems occurring during the delivery of a baby may cause damage that results in mental retardation.

As noted earlier, mental retardation may result from a variety of influences that take many specific forms of physical trauma and developmental deviation. The preceding section discussed influences and causes of mental retardation during the prenatal period from the time of conception to the initiation of the birth process. This section focuses on influences operative during the birth process itself.

The birth process has long been characterized as an extremely traumatic event in the life of the human organism. In fact "birth trauma" has been described as the basis for many psychological problems in later life. Early proponents of the psychoanalytical school (e.g., Sigmund Freud) attributed all anxiety in later life to the separation shock caused by birth. A variety of other phenomena, such as the content of adult dreams, have been thought at times to reflect birth trauma. Although there is little doubt that birth represents a stressful occurrence, recent thinking places much more emphasis on the physical aspects of this stress than on the psychoanalytical orientations.

Chapter 5 outlined briefly the sequence of events that occurs during the birth of a baby. Although the process is a stressful one, there is minimal danger if the baby is positioned head first and facing downward, and if the mother's pelvic opening is large enough for the child to pass through. This, of course, assumes that fetal development has progressed without mishap to this point. Two general types of problems may result in mental retardation during birth: (1) physical trauma or mechanical injury and (2) anoxia or asphyxia. The first is almost self- explanatory. Physical trauma or mechanical injury refers to some occurrence during birth that physically injures or damages the baby in such a way that mental functioning is impaired. The second type of problem, anoxia or asphyxia, refers to a situation in which the baby is deprived of an adequate oxygen supply for a period long enough to cause brain damage that reduces mental functioning. A variety of conditions, to be discussed in more detail, may be responsible. Although these problems are given different labels and appear to be quite dissimilar, they are frequently interrelated.

It has been mentioned that the danger of birth injury is relatively low if the fetus is positioned correctly. When labor begins, the most favorable position is head first and face down (assuming the mother is lying on her back). Other fetal positions are considered somewhat abnormal and may result in a variety of problems, depending on the situation. Both mechanical

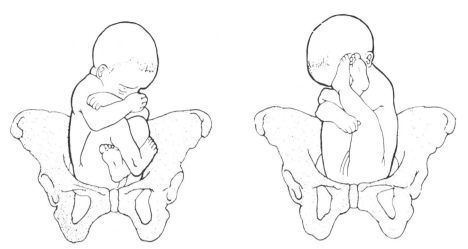

Figure 6–3. Examples of Breech Fetal Position
From *Childbirth: Family centered nursing* (3rd ed.) by J. Iorio, 1975, St. Louis: Mosby. Copyright 1975 by C. V. Mosby Co. Reprinted by permission.

injury and anoxia may result from abnormal fetal presentation. Some of the more common presentation abnormalities and their resulting problems are discussed briefly.

One rather well-known abnormal position involves a breech presentation of the fetus. Breech presentation occurs when the buttocks rather than the head present first. Figure 6–3 illustrates a breech presentation which can be compared with the more normal presentation illustrated in Figure 5–3.

Physicians are becoming increasingly reluctant to deliver babies in a breech position through the birth canal. Except when the delivery is conducted by extremely skilled personnel, the danger to the baby is substantial. More and more frequently a baby lying breech within the uterus is delivered via cesarean section, which involves abdominal surgery and extraction of the baby through the uterine wall.

Numerous difficulties are encountered in breech birth if delivery is executed through the birth canal. Since the head is presented last, it reaches the pelvic girdle (the bony hip structure of the mother) during the later, more advanced stages of labor. Contractions occur rather rapidly at this point, and the head does not have an opportunity to proceed through the slower molding process possible in earlier labor. Additionally, the molding may occur in an abnormal and damaging fashion since the various solid portions of the skull are receiving pressure in an atypical manner.

The abnormal pressure generated by these processes may result in mechanical injury to the brain matter in at least two general ways. First, since the skull is still quite soft, there may be an injury caused by rapid compression, which crushes a portion of the brain. Such damage is less likely in normal presentation since the skull is molded more gently, permitting protective fluid to absorb the pressure. Second, rapid pressure and shifting of cranial bones may be severe enough to damage the circulatory system around the brain. This can result in a hemorrhage in the skull, which in turn damages brain tissue.

A breech birth may also result in fetal anoxia. Because the skull is the last part of the body to be delivered, the baby must depend entirely on the umbilical cord as a source of oxygen until birth is complete. In a breech presentation the cord is occasionally too short to remain attached while the head is expelled. If this is the case, the placenta may become partially or completely detached while the head is still in the birth canal. This separation eliminates the oxygen supply, which may result in oxygen deprivation if delivery is not completed rather quickly. Severe tissue damage can result if the head is not expelled and oxygen supplied through the baby's lungs. This presents an extremely serious problem if the head becomes lodged in the pelvic girdle, preventing or substantially slowing progress down the birth canal. Anoxia may also occur even if the cord is sufficiently long to remain attached throughout the delivery. It has already been noted that the head is the tightest fit as the baby moves through the pelvic girdle. At the beginning of this period, a section of the umbilical cord is necessarily drawn through at the same time. Depending on how tight the skull fits into the bony pelvic structure, the cord may become pinched and the oxygen supply may thus be effectively shut off. If the supply is eliminated in this manner for an extended period (such as the situation of the lodged skull noted earlier) an anoxic condition will result just as if the cord were cut.

These descriptions present only a brief consideration of the difficulties involved in breech delivery and how they may result in damaged tissue and reduced mental functioning. Such problems, as well as numerous variations, are the reason why cesarean delivery is becoming to some degree favored in breech presentations over delivery through the birth canal.

The transverse position is another abnormal fetal position presenting severe problems, and is illustrated in Figure 6–4. The fetus lies across the birth canal rather than longitudinally. All of the injury problems noted with the breech position are potential difficulties with this presentation, depending on how delivery proceeds. Additionally, there are a multitude of other problems that face the attending physician. If it is possible to rotate the fetus safely, then delivery through the birth canal may be attempted. This is particularly true if the baby can be moved into a normal or near normal head-down position. If the fetus cannot be satisfactorily rotated into a longitudinal position, a cesarean section is performed.

It is evident that abnormalities of fetal presentation can cause a variety of difficulties during the birth process. Such problems may result in reduced mental functioning because of mechanical injury, or anoxia, or both. Ab-

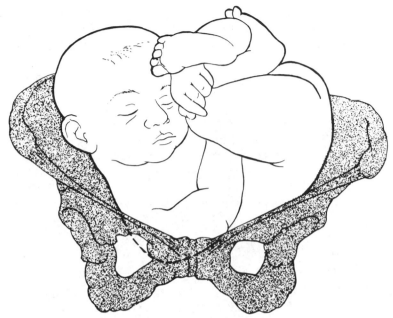

Figure 6—4. An Example of Transverse Fetal Position
From *Childbirth: Family centered nursing* (3rd ed.) by J. Iorio, 1975, St. Louis: Mosby. Copyright 1975 by C. V. Mosby Co. Reprinted by permission.

normal presentation, however, is not the only type of problem that may occur during the birth process. The initial stages of labor are important for several reasons. As the fetus proceeds into the birth canal, the pelvic girdle begins to stretch. With a normally positioned fetus, the head is also molded somewhat to permit passage through the bony pelvic structure. This process occurs during early labor when uterine contractions are less intense and less frequent than they are in later labor. Consequently normal molding and stretching occur without developing stress to cause injury to the baby. It requires a certain amount of time for the baby's head to be molded gently enough to avoid injury. Delivery of a baby after labor of less than about two hours is known as precipitous birth, and it causes considerable concern about the adequacy of time for gentle skull molding. Precipitous birth increases the tissue damage risk and raises the probability of resulting mental retardation.

Time is also important on the other end of the continuum— when labor is unusually prolonged (24 hours or more). Most deliveries do not approach 24 hours in length; 7 to 12 hours is average. A variety of conditions may accompany prolonged labor. Under certain circumstances the uterine conditions deprive a fetus of oxygen, which, after a lengthy labor, results either in an anoxic or a stillborn baby. This is particularly a problem if the membranes have ruptured early and labor is prolonged without delivery. Additionally, with a long period of advanced labor, the fetal skull is under an unusual amount of pressure, which raises the possibility of intracranial hemorrhage. In either case the probability of tissue damage and resulting mental retardation is substantially increased.

This section has briefly reviewed influences and causes of mental retardation that primarily occur at birth. A comprehensive examination of this complex process is beyond the scope of an introductory text. Consequently we have only given examples of conditions that are most prevalent, more well known, and more easily understood. Even this abbreviated presentation generates considerable uneasiness in readers who are still in the initial stages of studying mental retardation, but perspective must be maintained. The vast majority of babies are born normally and reach this point in their lives capable of assuming the challenges of the postnatal world.

PROFESSIONAL INTERVENTION

Core Concept 6   Professional intervention during the prenatal and neonatal periods may prevent or minimize mental retardation.

We have examined a few conditions that may result in mental retardation. In many instances various types of professional intervention can prevent or at least curtail mental retardation.

Children who are born at high risk because of their inappropriate birth weight or gestational age are frequently predisposed to mental retardation. As we have seen, problems often arise when prenatal care is either inadequate or nonexistent. The inadequacy or lack of availability of prenatal care is often related to lack of financial resources, ignorance, a value system that does not include high regard for prenatal care, inefficient health care plans, or a combination of any of these factors.

Limitations in financial resources may result in inadequate prenatal dietary intake, lack of necessary drugs and vitamins, and lack of supervision by health care specialists. Many mothers are uneducated about the necessity of prenatal care (Zill, 1983). Others, who may be informed, have not incorporated good prenatal care into their value systems, ignoring advice from health care specialists. Governmentally supported health-care programs frequently are overburdened and inadequately staffed. Expectant mothers, frustrated by long waits and impersonal prenatal care, may become too discouraged to continue seeking that care. Generally speaking, enhancing the mother's health has positive influences on the unborn child's well-being (Albino, 1984).

Professional intervention can greatly reduce the incidence of high-risk children. Low-income families lacking the financial resources for adequate prenatal care need to be directed to the proper agencies that can provide governmentally supported health care. In addition, these families should be directed to various sources to obtain supplemental foods; there are agencies that distribute food stamps, maintain surplus food programs, and provide other types of resources to improve the diet of the entire family and especially that of the expectant mother. Information of this type can be provided by social workers, public health staff, and other individuals working directly with the families. It is imperative that these families be advised how and where to apply for aid. Such supplemental nutrition and care programs significantly improve many high-risk infants, and benefits extend to other family members (Christiansen, 1984). Many agencies require extensive documentation to verify need for financial assistance. These families may be tutored in skills necessary to complete application forms as well as how to obtain documentation of financial need. In addition, the heavy case loads of physicians involved in governmentally supported programs could be eased considerably by utilization of other health care specialists, such as certified nurses and midwives. Postnatal care can also be increased and enhanced by effectively using the growing corps of pediatric nurse practitioners.

Some of the genetic conditions and chromosomal aberrations mentioned can be dealt with effectively through professional intervention. Since the majority of Down syndrome cases are of the nondisjunctive, or trisomy, variety, a high percentage tend to be related to advanced maternal age. Health-care specialists and social workers can encourage couples to have their children at an earlier age, preferably before the maternal age of 35. Older couples might be urged to exercise birth control methods, or at least be informed of the possible consequences of having children at more advanced ages. Young mothers who have children with Down syndrome should be advised to have a chromosomal analysis to determine if the condition is related to translocation. If a translocation exists, then the likelihood of a genetic, or inherited, etiology is high. These parents can be counseled and advised of the risks involved in having other children. Under such conditions sterilization or other forms of birth control may be considered. Parents could also be advised that a biopsy can be performed by drawing a sample of the amniotic fluid during subsequent pregnancies. Should a translocation exist in the fetus, the parents may decide to terminate the pregnancy via therapeutic abortion. The general issue of abortion is highly controversial and is discussed at length in chapter 13 in relation to social and ethical issues. Although such alternatives may or may not be acceptable to the counselor, care should be exercised to avoid the imposition of personal values on the parents, who are entitled to know what their alternatives are and that the decision regarding the alternatives is rightfully theirs (Moroney, 1986).

Certain disorders such as phenylketonuria (PKU) may be diagnosed early by routine screening. Several states have mandatory legislation requiring the testing of all newborn children. Screening for PKU can be accomplished by the "stick test," which can determine abnormal levels of phenylalanine in the urine. The Guthrie test (Carter, 1979) also determines abnormal presence of phenylalanine through the examination of the patient's blood.

Prevention of PKU-caused mental retardation frequently can be accomplished through dietary restrictions. As early as possible, the child is placed on a diet that is essentially free of phenylalanine. Suitable commercially prepared diets are available and marketed under such names as Ketonil and Lofenalac. The earlier a child is placed on a restricted diet, the greater are the chances of avoiding mental retardation. While there is evidence suggesting a child with PKU may eventually be removed from the restricted diet, the appropriate time is specific to the individual. At any rate, through early detection and intervention, mental retardation can either be avoided or at least the degree minimized.

Rh factor incompatibility between mother and fetus can frequently lead to erythroblastosis fetalis and hyperbilirubinemia, which can cause brain damage and mental retardation. The bilirubin levels can be monitored effectively by periodic testing with a Coombs's test or through amniocentesis, which samples the bilirubin level in the amniotic fluid (P. C. Chinn & Mueller, 1971). When the fetus is affected by a high bilirubin content, professional intervention may take the form of induced labor to deliver the child before the bilirubin level has reached a critical point. There have also been some efforts toward exchange transfusion through a fetal leg extended by surgery. Exchange transfusion immediately after birth has been effective in many instances. One of the most dramatic breakthroughs in medical intervention has been the development of the procedure of intrauterine transfusions. Guided by x-ray films, the surgeon extends a long needle through the mother's abdomen into the peritoneal cavity in the abdomen of the fetus. Blood of the sample type as the mother's is then transfused into the fetus. Thus the incompatibility factor is eliminated and the fetal blood is immune from the mother's antibodies.

Rh_o immune globulin (RhoGAM), a desensitizing drug, was introduced to the general public in 1968. Injected into the mother within 72 hours of the first child's birth, it desensitizes the mother from the antibodies and she can begin her next pregnancy without the presence of antibodies. The procedure can be continued after the birth of each child and will largely preclude the development of antibodies, provided it is followed faithfully after each birth. Between the intrauterine transfusions and desensitization through RhoGAM, there should be few incidents in the future of death or mental retardation resulting from Rh factor incompatibility.

As indicated earlier, the first trimester of pregnancy is critical with respect to any type of fetal insult or injury. During this period expectant mothers must exercise extreme caution to avoid any exposure to radiation, which may affect the fetus, or to infectious diseases. Rubella immunization is now available that can and should eliminate the possibility of widespread rubella epidemics. Parents can greatly reduce the possibility of rubella in their homes by immunizing all children in the family. This also protects mothers of the future from contracting the disease while pregnant.

Prevention of trauma during delivery is the major concern of obstetrical management. The primary concerns include maintaining adequate fetal oxygenation during labor and delivery, ensuring appropriate delivery if there is a fetus-pelvis size disproportion, and providing adequate observation and care of the infant during the first hour of life. Regional high-risk care centers for mothers have been developed to provide an extremely high level of specialized care for both mothers and infants who are known to be in one of the risk categories described. These centers have significantly decreased maternal and infant mortality. Thus one of the most important contributions that can be made in the prevention of threatening situations is early identification of mothers and infants at risk, which allows the rapid transfer of these individuals to a specialized center.

Core Questions

1. What factors appear to contribute to inadequate birth weight and gestational age problems, and how do they place an infant at developmental risk for mental retardation? Give examples.
2. How do different types of Down syndrome occur and why might they relate to differing levels of intellectual functioning?
3. Why is the mother-fetus interaction important? How can it contribute to the proper development of a baby, and how may it contribute to mental retardation? Give examples.
4. Why is the first trimester of pregnancy so important to the developing fetus, and how might maternal infection during this period influence the fetus?
5. Why is fetal positioning important in normal delivery of a baby, and how might abnormal presentation cause mental retardation?
6. How might professional intervention with respect to maternal nutrition during the first trimester of pregnancy be important in preventing mental retardation?

ROUND TABLE DISCUSSION

Prenatal development represents a very important phase in the life cycle of an individual, and there are a number of processes that can malfunction and cause mental retardation. There has been rising concern regarding drug and alcohol use, particularly among young people. Some claim that programs aimed at curtailing abuse of such substances are moralistic "hype" and intrude on an individual's right to privacy. Others argue that even if there were no moral dimension to consider, such programs provide important knowledge related to health of those involved as well as that of their future children.

In your study group or on your own, examine the information provided in this chapter regarding early development and mental retardation. Consider this material in light of substance abuse and discuss the pros and cons of educational/awareness information such as you see on television.

REFERENCES

Albino, J. E. (1984). Prevention by acquiring health-enhancing habits. In M. C. Roberts & L. Peterson (Eds.), *Prevention of problems in childhood* (pp. 34–62). New York: Wiley.

Babson, S. G., Pernoll, M. L., Benda, G. I., & Simpson, K. (1980). *Diagnosis and management of the fetus and neonate at risk* (4th ed.). St. Louis: Mosby.

Berger, K. S. (1983). *The developing person through the life span.* New York: Worth.

Birch, H. G., & Taft, L. T. (1968). Mental subnormality and mongolism. In R. E. Cooke (Ed.) *The biologic basis of pediatric practice* (pp. 1289–1299). New York: McGraw- Hill.

Birren, J. E., Kinney, D. K., Schaie, K. W., & Woodruff, D. S. (1981). *Developmental psychology: A life-span approach.* Boston: Houghton Mifflin.

Caputo, D., & Mandell, W. (1970). Consequences of low birth weight. *Developmental Psychology, 3,* 363–369.

Carter, C. H. (1979). *Handbook of mental retardation syndromes* (3rd rev. ed.). Springfield, IL: Charles C. Thomas.

Chinn, P. C., & Mueller, J. M. (1971). Advances in treatment of Rh negative blood incompatibility of mothers and infants. *Mental Retardation, 9,* 12–25.

Chinn, P. L. (1979). *Child health maintenance: Concepts in family centered care* (2nd ed.). St. Louis: Mosby.

Christiansen, N. (1984). Social effects of a family food supplementation and a home stimulation program. In J. Brozek & B. Schurch (Eds.), *Malnutrition and behavior: Critical assessment of key issues* (pp. 55–81). Lausanne: Nestle Foundation.

Cohen, S. E., & Parmelee, A. H. (1983). Prediction of five-year Stanford-Binet scores in preterm infants. *Child Development, 54,* 1242–1253.

Cox, D. R., & Epstein, C. J. (1985). Comparative gene mapping of human chromosome 21 and mouse chromosome 16. *Annals of the New York Academy of Sciences, 450,* 169–177.

Crnic, K. A., Ragozin, A. S., Greenberg, A. S., Robinson, N. M., & Basham, R. B. (1983). Social interaction and developmental competence of preterm and full-term infants during the first year of life. *Child Development, 54,* 1199–1210.

Davidson, J. N., Rumsby, G., & Niswander, L. A. (1985). Expression of genes on human chromosome 21. *Annals of the New York Academy of Sciences, 450,* 43–54.

Eaves, L., Nuttall, J., Konoff, H., & Dunn, H. (1970). Developmental and psychological test scores in children of low birth weight. *Pediatrics, 45,* 9–20.

Epstein, C. J., Cox, D. R., & Epstein, L. B. (1985). Mouse trisomy 16: An animal model of human trisomy 21 (Down syndrome). *Annals of the New York Academy of Sciences, 450,* 157–168.

Ershow, A. G. (1986). Growth in black and white children with Down syndrome. *American Journal of Mental Deficiency, 90,* 507–512.

Gluck, L. (1971). Appraisal of the fetus and neonate: Growth, development, nutrition. In H. Abramson (Ed.), *Symposium on the functional physiopathology of the fetus and neonate* (pp. 69–82). St. Louis: Mosby.

Grumbach, M. M. (1968). Anatomic and physiologic considerations (male). In R. E. Cooke (Ed.), *The biologic basis of pediatric practice* (p. 1058). New York: McGraw-Hill.

Hanson, J. W., Streissguth, A. P., & Smith, D. W. (1978). The effects of moderate alcohol consumption during pregnancy on fetal growth and morphogenesis. *The Journal of Pediatrics, 92,* 457–460.

Jones, H. W., Jr., & Grumbach, M. M. (1968). Developmental disorders (female). In R. E. Cooke (Ed.), *The biologic basis of pediatric practice* (pp. 1087–1093). New York: McGraw-Hill.

Jones, K. L., Smith, D. W., Ulleland, C. N., & Streissguth, A. P. (1973). Pattern of malformation in offspring of chronic alcoholic mothers. *Lancet, 1,* 1267–1271.

Kernek, C., Osterud, H., & Anderson, B. (1966). Patterns of prematurity in Oregon. *Northwest Medicine, 65,* 639–642.

Kiely, J. L., Paneth, N., & Susser, M. (1981). Low birth weight, neonatal care and cerebral palsy: An epidemiological review. In P. J. Mittler & J. M. de Jong (Eds.), *Frontiers of knowledge in mental retardation: Vol. II. Biomedical aspects* (pp. 541–566). Baltimore: University Park.

Koops, B. L., Morgan, L. J., & Battaglia, F. C. (1982). Neonatal mortality risk in relation to birth weight and gestational age: Update. *The Journal of Pediatrics, 101,* 969–977.

Korones, S. B. (1981). *High-risk newborn infants: The basis for intensive nursing care* (3rd ed.). St. Louis: Mosby.

Lasky, R. E., Tyson, J. E., Rosenfeld, C. R., Priest, M., Kransinski, D., Heartwell, S., & Gant, N. F. (1983). Differences on Bayley's Infant Behavior Record for a sample of high-risk infants and their controls. *Child Development, 54,* 1211–1216.

Lilienfeld, A. M., & Pasamanick, B. (1956). The association of maternal and fetal factors with the development of mental deficiency, II: Relationship to maternal age, birth order, previous reproductive loss and degree of mental deficiency. *American Journal of Mental Deficiency, 60,* 557–569.

Moroney, R. M. (1986). Family care: Toward a responsive society. In P. R. Dokecki & R. M. Zaner (Eds.), *Ethics of dealing with persons with severe handicaps: Toward a research agenda* (pp. 217–232). Baltimore: Brookes.

Parmalee, A., & Schulte, F. (1970). Developmental testing of preterm and small-for-date infants. *Pediatrics, 45,* 21–28.

Rocissano, L., & Yatchmink, Y. (1983). Language skill and interactive patterns in prematurely born toddlers. *Child Development, 54,* 1229–1241.

Rose, S. A. (1983). Differential rates of visual information processing in full-term and preterm infants. *Child Development, 54,* 1189–1198.

Rubin, R. A., Rosenblatt, C., & Balow, B. (1973). Psychological and educational sequelae of prematurity. *Pediatrics, 52,* 352–363.

Silva, P. A., McGee, R., & Williams, S. (1984). A longitudinal study of the intelligence and behavior of preterm and small for gestational age children. *Journal of Developmental and Behavioral Pediatrics, 5,* 1–5.

Streissguth, A. P., Herman, C. S., & Smith, D. W. (1978). Intelligence behavior and dysmorphogenesis in the fetal alcohol syndrome: A report on 20 patients. *Journal of Pediatrics, 92,* 363–367.

Streissguth, A. P., Martin, D. C., Martin, J. C., & Barr, H. M. (1981). The Seattle longitudinal prospective study on alcohol and pregnancy. *Neurobehavioral Toxicology and Teratology, 3,* 223–233.

Sullivan, W. C. (1899). A note on the influence of maternal inebriety on the offspring. *Journal of Mental Science, 45,* 489–503.

Ungerer, J. A., & Sigman, M. (1983). Developmental lags in preterm infants from one to three years of age. *Child Development, 54,* 1217–1228.

Zill, N. (1983). *Happy, healthy and insecure.* Garden City, NY: Doubleday.

7

The Mentally Retarded Child During Infancy and Early Childhood

Core Concepts

1. Physiological growth during infancy and early childhood plays a central role in the general development of an individual, laying the foundation for a wide variety of skills and behaviors.
2. Early intervention often involves an important partnership between professionals and parents.
3. Language development is an area in which mental retardation is likely to become evident during the early childhood years.
4. Cognitive development during infancy and early childhood involves many complex processes and includes areas where mentally retarded children have great difficulty.
5. Developmental problems expressed in social and emotional functioning can have a serious impact on a young child's ability to adapt and chances to succeed.

Development during infancy and early childhood is vital to the continued growth and well-being of an individual as mentioned before. This period can hardly be overemphasized in terms of its importance to the overall developmental process for all children. Experiences during infancy and early childhood can either promote or prevent the attainment of optimal development potential. In the former situation, intellectual functioning may be enhanced to such a degree that the child operates in the upper ranges of capability. In the latter, the experiences may affect the developmental process so that permanently lowered functioning may result. Environmental influences often have more lasting and pervasive effects during infancy and early childhood than during any later phase of the life cycle. Likewise, it is not surprising that this period produces a variety of stressors that produce responses in the families of mentally retarded youngsters (Affleck, Tennen, & Gershman, 1985; Goldberg, Marcovitch, MacGregor, & Lojkasek, 1986).

This chapter focuses on development during infancy and the preschool years and the environmental influences during this period that promote or detract from the fulfillment of potential. Four broad areas of development will be examined: (1) physical, (2) language, (3) cognitive, and (4) psychosocial. Although these are interrelated, they also represent distinct areas of development that have received considerable research attention and, consequently, pertain to our consideration of developmental problems. Each of the four areas is critical in one fashion or another because a child's ability to learn is vulnerable to environmental influence during the early years. Pertinent research will be reviewed with regard to expected traits of development, traits evident in mentally retarded children, and environmental influences.

PHYSICAL DEVELOPMENT

Core Concept 1   Physiological growth during infancy and early childhood
plays a central role in the general development of an
individual, laying the foundation for a wide variety of skills
and behaviors.

Several major body systems are involved in a discussion of physical development. The ones most often considered important to a generic conception of physical development include the gastrointestinal, renal, endocrine, skeletal, reproductive, neurological, and muscular systems (Chinn, 1979). Of these, the ones most closely related to the learning process are the neurological and musculoskeletal systems. These two systems are integrally related from a functional standpoint and are occasionally thought of as one—the neuromotor system. Neurological and motor (i.e., neuromotor) functions are also influenced by important stimuli and responses provided by the endocrine system. For purposes of this text, we will examine neuromotor development in order to become familiar with the physical dimensions of learning and with the influences of the environment on this particular aspect of development.

Neuromotor Development

A number of components are included in the neurological system that must be considered in an examination of physical development. This system is composed of the brain, spinal cord, and peripheral neurons, and includes the autonomic system, which is functionally related to the endocrine system. Neurological pathways extend to the muscle and skin tissues and provide for the transmission of neurological sensations from the environment to the central nervous system. These pathways also serve as media for neurological control and response between the central nervous system and the muscles that permit movement and vocalizations appropriate to various environmental stimuli. The processes involved in stimulus reception and neurological functioning cannot typically be studied directly, but they may be investigated indirectly by observing a variety of performance areas and comparing a given child's functioning with levels that are age appropriate. Neurological maturation represents a critical dimension of the child's overall development and plays a particular role in the areas of cognitive, language, and psychosocial development. More complete attention will be given to these areas in later portions of this chapter. Initially we will focus directly on the development of neuromotor system and examine certain physical development conditions that may be detected in mentally retarded children.

Head and Brain Characteristics. A child's neurological development and capacity are known to be related to head and brain size. As noted earlier, the brain grows very rapidly during the prenatal period. This rapid growth continues after birth; approximately 90 percent of the adult brain size is attained by the time a child is 2 years old. Although brain growth cannot be directly observed, it can be assessed indirectly by measuring the head circumference. Normal circumference ranges have been established for each developmental stage, and they differ somewhat between the sexes. For example, the mean head circumference for male infants at birth is 34.5 cm and reaches 49 cm by the age of 2. Female infants, on the other hand, have a mean head circumference of 34 cm at birth and reach 48 cm by the age of 2. A difference of ± 2 standard deviations from the expected mean head circumference at any age is a variation sufficient to warrant concern. If such a condition occurs, the child must receive extensive medical diagnosis to determine if there is a serious pathological condition present that threatens physical health and that may threaten intellectual functioning. An example of such a condition is found in microcephaly, in which the head circumference exceeds minus 2 standard deviations. (Children with microcephaly also are characterized by several other physical abnormalities and are typically severely retarded.) In this condition the child's brain size is limited, and abnormalities of brain tissue formation may also be present. Limited brain size, tissue abnormalities, or a combination of both may result from a genetic condition or may arise from a condition affecting the skeletal tissue surrounding the brain that arrests the brain tissue growth. In either case the functional status of the neurological system is seriously impaired, and mental retardation results.

Certain other conditions may result in a head circumference that is significantly larger than the expected mean and may indicate a situation that is of serious concern. Hydrocephalus, for example, is a syndrome characterized by an exceptionally large head size even though the brain may be inadequately developed or normal (depending on the precise cause of the condition). This syndrome is related to an increase in the amount of cerebrospinal fluid that circulates in the brain cavity and spinal column. The excess fluid creates an increased pressure on surrounding structures and, in turn, leads to damage of the brain tissue and ultimately to mental retardation, regardless of the initial functional capacity.

Other brain developments also occur at a rapid rate during the early years. Sulci, the grooves between the convolutions in the lobes of the brain, deepen and become more prominent and numerous during this period. They continue to develop throughout life but at a slower rate than during the early years. Sulcus development is thought to reflect processes of learning, memory, and the ability to reason and form conceptualizations. A child exhibiting inadequate neuromotor control and function, or who evidences a developmental delay, may suffer from some abnormality of form or function of the brain, although such a defect is not typically detectable directly. Some information concerning the size and shape of the brain can be obtained using x-ray procedures, but the primary cause of the child's lack of coordination, speech difficulty, and limited ability to learn usually cannot be identified with certainty as a defect of the brain tissue itself. Frequently, direct evidence of brain abnormality must await autopsy; even that usually provides only limited information, such as evidence of identifiable brain tissue lesions. There may, however, be indications that the tissue of the nervous system has not been adequately stimulated at an ideal period of development in order to reach an optimal level of functioning—a process that is imperative for development of adequate neuromotor function (Penfield, 1972).

Myelinization. Myelinization, discussed in chapter 5, is commonly accepted as an important developmental process, although information about the precise nature of both its function and growth remains inexact. Myelinization is the development of the protective insulating sheath that surrounds the brain and neurological pathways. This sheath presumably operates somewhat like insulation on an electrical wire and allows nerve impulses to travel along the nerve pathway rapidly and without diffusion. The newborn has an incomplete myelin sheath, which accounts for nonspecific reactions to stimuli and for a lack of motor coordination. For example, the infant's response to a painful stimulus to the foot is generalized body movement and crying rather than specific withdrawal of the foot, attention to the source of the stimulus, and specific vocalizations indicating pain. As with other growth patterns, myelinization proceeds in a cephalocaudal and proximodistal fashion, which explains the pattern of acquisition of gross motor control before fine motor control. By the age of 2 a major portion of the myelin sheath is formed, and the child's motor capacity is relatively mature.

Reflexes and Voluntary Behavior. Reflex behavior represents a human response which is primitive in comparison to many that are characteristic of general human functioning. Development of human reflex behavior is thought to have evolved out of necessity for protection in a harsh environment before development of sophisticated cognitive skills that provided for ingenuity or voluntary action directed toward protection of the individual. Much of the reflexive behavior of early infancy gradually fades as voluntary control develops through association pathways of the nervous system. Some reflexes persist throughout life, such as the knee jerk, eye blink, and reaction of the eye pupil to light. During early childhood, voluntary movement becomes predominant for the child who is neurologically healthy, although involuntary movement on one side of the body may be exhibited that mirrors voluntary movement on the opposite side. This involuntary mirroring action is pronounced in children who suffer damage to the central nervous system, but the phenomenon itself does not suggest damage unless it persists beyond the preschool years or is so pronounced that it interferes with the child's voluntary movements. Predominance of the one-sided voluntary function is generally established fully by the age of 4, and a child typically demonstrates a preference for right or left hand use in performing motor tasks.

Emotions and the Central Nervous System. The limbic system is located in the central portion of the brain and surrounds the hypothalamus. This system functions specifically to mediate emotional and temperamental dimensions of behavior. Sensations such as pleasure or discomfort and the individual meaning associated with them originate and are stored in this system. Other sensations and behaviors known to be related to limbic function include excitement, anger, fear, sleep, and wakefulness. Maturity in these response areas progresses as young children begin to experience a wider range of environmental stimuli and are able to exercise more control over their own behavior as well as over the behavior of others. Response according to feelings predominates to determine behavior in early childhood, indicating that the limbic system is functioning and that associations with voluntary control areas are not fully accomplished. As growth continues and these associations mature, children become more effective in disguising and voluntarily controlling the emotional components of behavior (Guyton, 1971).

Sensory Organs and Cranial Nerves. Development and integrity of cranial nerves and specialized sensory organs also play an important role in a young child's general functioning status. These maturational processes are essential to a child's ability to receive stimuli from the environment and integrate them into perceptual and memory components of the central nervous system. Cranial nerves are distinct nerve pathways that permit the specialized sensory function and motor performance of the sensory and other essential organs and surrounding muscular structure. These nerves approach functional maturity by the age of 3 and can be tested specifically by assessing the sensory organ functions. Sensory functions, such as smell, taste, touch, and the sense of movement, are important in providing essential neurological stimulation, but ears and eyes are particularly crucial for receiving stimuli related to learning.

Optimal functioning levels are attained during infancy for the capacities of taste and smell, which also come under the influence of voluntary control and association with other sensory areas. Consequently, young children are able to, and often will, refuse to taste a food that appears unpleasant or about which they have heard negative comments. A child responds accurately to the sensation that a taste or smell arouses and begins to learn conditioned associations between certain tastes and smells and culturally accepted values. Preferred foods in a child's culture become palatable, and foods that are not acceptable become displeasing. The role of these sensory capacities in terms of learning problems is not currently understood, but it does appear that significant learning stimuli are provided through these channels.

Hearing is often thought to be the most critical sense with regard to the learning process. Children with hearing deficits seem to have a greater degree of interference with learning than children with other types of sensory disturbances. This effect obviously varies substantially, depending both on the child and on the nature and severity of the deficit. The sense of hearing is dependent on intact tissue structures between the external ear and the brain cortex, which include the important cranial nerves involved in hearing functions. Functional structures of the ear also have much to do with the sense of kinesthetic balance and movement.

An infant's hearing apparatus is mature at birth with the exception of two areas that remain to be completed: myelinization of the cortical auditory pathways beyond the midbrain, and resorption of the connective tissue surrounding the ossicles of the middle ear. The infant obviously can hear and respond differentially to loud noises (by crying) and soft, soothing sounds (by relaxing and becoming calm). These are the characteristic newborn's reactions to most stimuli, generalized and tending to involve movements of the entire body. Typically, these movements are predominantly of a gross motor nature and are nonspecific (that is, they tend to be characterized by a thrashing of the arms, body, and legs or by a generalized calming). As myelinization proceeds, the child begins to exhibit an ability to localize sound direction. By the age of 2 to 3 months the child responds by turning the head toward the direction of the sound stimulus.

This discussion should not be interpreted as meaning that an infant has fully developed, adult-like hearing. This does not occur until about 7 years of age and involves complex cortical functioning, including the ability to listen, to respond with discrimination, to imitate sounds accurately, and to integrate the meaning of sounds. Identification of hearing deficits during the first year of life is vital for maximally effective treatment to be undertaken and optimal learning capacity to be maintained. If a child with a hearing deficiency can be identified at this time and some means of providing auditory stimulation can be instituted, the ability to integrate the meaning of auditory stimuli later in life and to maintain and use these neurological pathways as an avenue for learning is substantially enhanced.

An infant has rather limited visual acuity at birth, which is not fully developed until the age of 6. At birth an infant is able to differentiate only generally between light and dark. Visual acuity development progresses rather rapidly during the neonatal period, and by the age of 6 months, an infant is generally able to recognize objects and people. An ability to follow movement in the environment also begins to develop during the first months of life, and completely coordinated eye movements should be evident by the sixth month. A preschool child who does not establish the ability to perceive a single object when viewing the item with both eyes (the establishment of binocularity) can develop some unique difficulties with regard to perceptual behavior. Lack of effective binocular vision produces the impression of two separate overlapping objects instead of a single unified perception; the child begins to "block" the perception of one eye in order to perceive a single object through the preferred eye. This is the condition of amblyopia, or "lazy eye." The lack of use and stimulation of the unused eye eventually results in gradual deterioration of the neural pathways from the eye to the central nervous system. A permanent loss of eye function may result if the condition is not corrected. This phenomenon illustrates the vital role of adequate stimulation in order for neurological tissue to develop and maintain adequate function.

Integration of incoming visual stimuli with existing neurological functions is an extremely important factor in early learning. By about 2 to 3 years of age the child begins to be able to remember and recall visual images. The child begins to be interested in pictures and to enjoy producing geometric shapes and figures. These abilities lead to a readiness to recognize symbols or to read, which typically will appear by the time the child is 4 years of age. A further visual discrimination, color recognition, has important implications for early learning processes. Color recognition usually is well established by the time the child is 5 years of age.

Summary. Many complex factors contribute to the advances in development during early childhood. Growth of muscle size, practice of motor skills, continuing organization of associations between established neural pathways, and establishment of new pathways represent only a portion of the developmental process that is under way. In addition, it is during this period that the ability to maintain focal attention, a hallmark of early childhood, emerges. Incredible gains are evident in cognitive and intellectual function, memory, consciousness, and thought. The role of each structure in the nervous system and its possible relationship to the various forms of mental retardation is not well understood. It is apparent, however, that an inadequacy in one dimension of the development of the nervous system is typically accompanied by inadequacies in the system as a whole. Thus the child who evidences developmental delays in motor performance during early childhood frequently also exhibits delays in emotional development, language development, and cognitive development (Smith & von Tetzchner, 1986), since each of these dimensions of performance depends on the general adequacy of the nervous system. Table 7–1 summarizes selected developmental landmarks during the first 2 years of life in terms of a few motor, psychosocial, and verbal developmental features. Because delay in one area of development is likely also to be associated with delay in others, the behavior of an affected child may be generally more like that of children who are chronologically younger.

Effects of the Environment

Several processes in a child's development have been discussed, with each capability and each function having an optimal time during the developmental cycle for appearance and integration into the system as a whole. The child's development of these specific capabilities during such periods appears to be vulnerable to disruption, which may result in either temporary or permanent problems. Some of these disruptions result from environmental influences. The effects of environmental conditions or stimuli on a young child are generally recognized to be great, although the exact nature of influences by specific conditions remains poorly understood (Wright, 1971). An early theory developed by Hebb (1949) contains some interesting notions about the possible effects of either deprivation or stimulation of the developing neurological system and its effects on later intellectual functioning.

Hebb postulated that the human brain is comprised of two interrelated types of tissue: sensorimotor, which is primarily determined genetically and provides for the reflexive, sensory, and motor functions of the body; and associative, which is partially determined by genetic endowment but must be developed and established through environmental stimulation, mainly occurring during the first 2 years of life. Hebb believed that the nature of the development of associative functions would determine the limits of an individual's future intellectual capacity. The manner in which this stimulation and development transpire was thought to underlie the higher cognitive functions of the brain. The major portion of the child's behavioral repertoire during the first 2 years, less complex than in later life, is largely supported by the sensorimotor functions of the brain. Consequently, it is a wealth of sensorimotor experiences that substantially contribute to the development of associative tissues and functions in the first 2 years. Because Hebb's theory has not been subject to direct empirical testing, it has not been demonstrated to represent an accurate account of actual neurological development during early life. It has stimulated investigation aimed at examining the influence of early environmental experiences, which are an important field of inquiry concerning mental retardation and behavioral science in general. Such studies that have supported the importance of early stimuli have not accumulated enough evidence to draw definitive conclusions, although certain trends are beginning to emerge. For example, extreme environmental deprivation, particularly during the early childhood period, appears to be a potent, detrimental influence. It has been observed to result

Table 7–1. Selected Developmental Landmarks

	Months							
	1	2	3	4	5	6	7	8
MOTOR								
Sitting				‹		‹	Supported	
Walking								
Sucking								
Standing								‹
Crawling							‹	
Creeping								
Bowel control						‹		
Bladder control								
Head: prone		‹	Lifts head	›				
sitting			‹	Bobs	›			
PSYCHOSOCIAL								
Smiling				Spontaneous	›		Mirror image	
Reacting to others			‹	Follows moving people		›	Discriminates	
Feeding					Solids			Holds
Socialization		‹						
VERBAL								
Crying								
Cooing			‹			›		
Babbling, resembles one syllable							‹	Tone
Imitation of word sounds								
Some word understanding (dada, mamma)								
Word repertoire								

Table 7–1. Selected Developmental Landmarks—Cont'd

							Months								
9	**10**	**11**	**12**	**13**	**14**	**15**	**16**	**17**	**18**	**19**	**20**	**21**	**22**	**23**	**24**

Without support

Supported · Without support

(Utility decreases with use of other feeding means)

Supported · Without support

(Sex differences)

Sustains raised head

Steady

strangers · Waves goodbye

bottle · Cup · Part. self-feed

Forms primary social relations and emotional attachments

differentiation)

3 to 50 words · 50+ begin phrases

in pervasive developmental delays and mental retardation (Zubek, 1969). Perhaps the most dramatic of this evidence involved observations of children who, early in life, were subjected to conditions that resulted in extreme deprivation (Gesell, 1941, Mason, 1942).

There is considerable evidence about sensory deprivation during early life in terms of visual stimuli. This information has resulted largely from studies involving the restoration of vision after the early developmental period, during which the child was blind (Gregory & Wallace, 1963; London, 1960). In this research, individuals of various ages beyond the preschool period received visual stimuli for the first time. This unique investigation has been made possible mostly by surgical removal of congenital cataracts and by corneal transplants. After surgery and a period of study to learn the meaning of the visual stimuli, subjects continued to experience difficulty in pattern discrimination and ability to generalize. Despite the fact that subjects understood that a particular symbol was a triangle or a square, they had great difficulty perceiving the image as such without relying on ancillary aids to recognition (e.g., counting the number of corners). Futher, subjects might recognize a geometric shape representing a square on paper, but could not recognize the same shape in another format (such as a box).

It is difficult to determine the meaning of such extreme evidence for less extreme instances of sensory deprivation that may occur with young children in relatively deprived environments. It seems reasonable to expect that a child who does not have an opportunity to experience and practice certain sensorimotor skills will not have the opportunity to develop such specific motor capacities, but the effects of such a situation on later development of intellectual functioning remain uncertain. Hebb's position would suggest that a wealth of sensory stimulation during the first 2 years, regardless of the type or nature of such stimulation, would promote favorable development of the cognitive and intellectual skills of the individual. Some evidence suggests that the greater the variety of stimuli and the number of situations that promote modification of conceptualization, the more mobile and differentiated the mental structure becomes (Whiteman & Deutsch, 1968). Limited environmental stimulation, a lack of systematic or ordered interpretation and mediation, or limited motivation may bring about stimulus deprivation and, with it, limitations in the development of intelligence.

Several limitations prevent the systematic accumulation of data on the effects of deprivation. Ethical considerations regarding the use of human subjects clearly prevent the experimental manipulation of stimulus deprivation in a manner that may be harmful to the subjects. Occurrences of natural events that result in environmental deprivation are unsystematic and involve such situational variation that investigation of these instances provides data of only limited value. Studies on early visual deprivation have been few in number and have become even rarer because of advances in medical technology. Because of these serious limitations, many researchers have turned to the study of stimulus enrichment in an effort to gather evidence about the effects of environmental sensory stimuli on the development of intellectual functioning. One approach compares the functioning of young children who, as infants, received a natural wealth of sensory stimulation with that of children who were relatively deprived of such environmental stimulation. Although the evidence appears to suggest some differential effect, the data are too general to draw definitive conclusions. Such investigations also are not free of difficulties since, in many cases, it is unclear that the relative presence or absence of environmental stimuli is the only influential variable.

A classic study on early stimulation effects was reported by Skeels and Dye in 1939. These investigators, studying the influences of stimulation on children under 3 years of age, compared two groups of institutionalized infants in two different types of environments. Thirteen infants with IQ scores ranging from 35 to 89 were placed in wards of an institution for retarded children where attendants and older retarded females provided them with a great deal of attention and stimulation. Following a year and a half of this type of treatment, the IQ scores of the children had increased 27.5 points. The comparison group (12 infants with IQ scores ranging from 50 to 103) remained in the orphanage, where attention and stimulation were minimal. These children evidenced a drop of 26.2 IQ points during the same period of time. As noted, however, it is not clear in studies such as this whether differences between the two groups are caused by the sensory stimulation itself or by other related factors in combination with the stimulation. Additionally, while it seems apparent that stimulation may influence the rate of development, it is not clear whether stimulation is responsible for any lasting effect on the quality of function for normal children.

There have been investigations that attempted to experimentally manipulate sensory stimulation during the first few years of life (Burns, Deddish, Burns, & Hatcher, 1983; Greenberg, Uzgiris, & Hunt, 1968; Ottinger, Blatchley, & Denenberg, 1969; White, 1967). These studies have focused mostly on the influences of visual stimulation during the early months of life and have demonstrated significant effects of controlled stimulation on the rate and quality of specific aspects of development. Once again, it is not known if such effects are lasting or significant with respect to the quality of future intellectual function. Additionally, investigations that experimentally manipulate environmental stimuli are not without problems. Although fundamentally more sound from a research design standpoint, such studies have raised certain ethical questions about the experimental manipulation itself, such as the propriety of providing stimulation to one group while not providing (thus denying) such treatment to the comparison group(s). These are questions without easy solutions, and they present significant problems for the accumulation of a solid data base.

One notable long-range study, the Milwaukee Project, which focused on early, intensive stimulation, has received considerable attention (Garber & Heber, 1977; Heber, Dever, & Conry, 1968; Heber & Garber, 1971; Heber, Garber, Harrington, Hoffman, & Falendar, 1972; Strickland, 1971). Data from this investigation provide substantial evidence demonstrating the effectiveness of an early, intensive stimulation program on the development of disadvantaged infants in Milwaukee, Wisconsin. The infants, born to mothers who were assessed as having IQ scores of less than 75, were placed randomly in experimental and control groups. The experimental program of sensory stimulation began in the home shortly after birth, and then the child was brought daily to a center for a regular, planned stimulation program continuing over a period of 5 years. At the study's conclusion, there was a significant difference in intellectual functioning level between experimental and control groups, with the experimental infants estimated to have an average IQ scores that were 33 points higher than those in the control group.

As additional research emerges regarding the effects of stimulation of the nervous system during the first 2 years of life, it may be possible to draw more accurate conclusions about the relationship of the development of this system to the nature of intellectual function later in life and to determine the vulnerability of the system to the environment during the first 2 years of life. It appears to be a reasonable conclusion that sensory stimulation is beneficial in affecting the rate and perhaps the quality of all developmental traits that depend on the neurological system development.

Professional and Parental Intervention

Core Concept 2   Early intervention often involves an important partnership between professionals and parents.

Concerns among professionals working with infants and young children include identification of children who begin to display developmental delays, prevention of the occurrence of delays when possible, and assistance to the child and family when a developmental problem is present. The professionals who have the most contact with children during the infancy and preschool years are health care workers, particularly physicians and public health nurses. These professionals frequently depend on the aid and cooperation of social workers, nutritionists, and dietitians to assist in providing comprehensive services to families with multiple problems and needs.

Screening is a very important process in the overall evaluation schema described in Chapter 4. This is particularly crucial in terms of identifying children who may be exhibiting delays in rate and quality of development.

The American Academy of Pediatrics (1971) has established standards for child health care that include monthly screening for all infants during the first 6 months of life, with intervals increasing gradually until the child is seen yearly by the end of the preschool period. These health care visits should include an assessment of the child's health status, eating patterns, and behavior at home since the last visit. The child's physical systems are evaluated, including the neurological system, in order to determine the adequacy of development, and behavioral observations are recorded to confirm the appearance of behavioral landmarks at each appropriate age. Each visit should also include discussion and guidance sessions pertaining to developmental and health status with the child's parents. Finally, the child is given immunizations to prevent serious contagious disease, and laboratory testing of the blood and urine is taken at regular intervals. Developmental guidance should be given to the family in an effort to prevent accidental problems and to alleviate conditions that may lead to problems.

Such routine health care is important as a means of identifying unexpected developmental problems, but it becomes even more crucial for the family of a child when a problem has been identified. Both the mentally retarded child and the family need a great deal of support and assistance to meet the challenges of daily care and health maintenance. The health care team is well equipped to provide such assistance.

Prevention of mental retardation has always been a matter that professionals in the field have sought to achieve. It is not, however, a subject that can easily be conceptualized or one that is without some controversy (as we will see in chapter 13). One of the major difficulties in conceptualizing prevention is the field of mental retardation itself. Mental retardation, as a condition, is an extremely heterogeneous phenomenon. It varies greatly in terms of causation, severity, environmental circumstances, and professional disciplines concerned with the problem. By now it is clear to the reader that mental retardation is a problem with many faces; it is sociocultural, psychological, and biomedical, to name only a few. Given this brief recount of the complex nature of the problem, it is not surprising that prevention, conceptualized in any sort of all-encompassing fashion, is most difficult. There have, however, been some notable successes in prevention, if only in a limited way.

Screening and treatment for the enzyme-deficiency disease phenylketonuria (PKU) (see chapter 6) is a classic example of an instance in which a definitive problem and subsequent treatment can result in prevention or reducing the effects of mental retardation (Pennington, van Doorninck, McCabe, & McCabe, 1985). This also represents a situation in which continued assistance for the family from the health care team is critical. The child must be placed on an extremely restricted and expensive diet in order to offset the enzyme deficiency. This may place certain pressures on the family, and maintenance of adequate balanced nutrition for the child and for the entire family may be a serious problem. Additionally, the child's health may be jeopardized in other ways, such as by increased susceptibility to infection.

Well defined prevention programs, such as that implemented with PKU, are scarce. However, theories like Hebb's and the results of research such as that described previously in this chapter have stimulated considerable interest among health care workers who are interested in the identification of families and children who are at risk because of inadequate environmental stimulation. Health care workers are often the only professional people who are in contact with such families on any sort of widespread basis. The task of identification of such problems is therefore most logically approached from a health care standpoint if significant impact is to be expected. Nurses and child development specialists have begun to institute programs of environmental stimulation and enrichment in many communities. As the programs develop, research evidence will be forthcoming and will, it is hoped, add to our understanding of the effectiveness of this type of intervention.

Enhanced stimulation is also generating increased interest in terms of intervention beyond the prevention arena. As soon as a child is identified as already being mentally retarded and developmentally disabled, health care workers and child development specialists have often begun infant stimulation programs as a means of assisting the child in developmental progress. Children whose physical neuromotor development would otherwise be expected to be significantly delayed have shown impressive acceleration of physical development. For example, children with Down syndrome and other retarded youngsters are typically delayed by several weeks or months in all aspects of neuromotor development such as sitting, crawling, walking, talking, eating, and even social behaviors such as smiling and peer interaction (Berger & Cunningham, 1986; Strain, 1985). Research findings suggest that intervention in field settings has resulted in rather notable progress (Casto & Mastropieri, 1986).

Infant stimulation programs focus on systematic, planned stimulation of the infant in all sensory modalities. The desired result of such programming is acceleration of the child's development so that these skills appear at a time more nearly consistent with that expected of normal children of the same chronological age. It is believed that all six perceptual systems must be stimulated. This multiple stimulation may not be undertaken at any single session; for example, one perceptual system at a time may be involved in the stimulation being provided on a given occasion. This is often done to enhance clarity and specificity for parents who frequently may be involved heavily in program implementation and have been shown to be important interveners (Bruder, 1987; McConkey & Martin, 1983; Slater, 1986). However, at some point during the program each of the senses (vision, hearing, touch, kinesthetic movement, smell, and taste) is the focus of stimulation. Thus the parent may be instructed to strike a particular kitchen pot with a spoon near the infant, to rattle a toy, and generally to present as many hearing stimuli as possible to attract the infant's attention. As the infant responds, other perceptual systems may be stimulated, and the same stimuli are repeated but at different distances from the child. The next step frequently involves engaging the infant in active participation in the stimulation program. As this is undertaken, the child may be encouraged to hold the sound-producing spoon, move the rattle, manipulate soft cotton or a hard rock, and so on.

Most children born into families with sufficient economic resources receive a wealth of stimulation in all sensory modalities. Stimulation is a routine part of their environment and results from ordinary interactions and activities of the family. For the most part these infants are wanted and loved; they are held and carried, cuddled, talked to, placed near the activities of the other children and adults in the family, and taken in the car for trips into the community. These are all a natural part of each day's activities. However, many infants are born into environments lacking some or all the features often taken for granted by the average middle-class family. The world of such children may have substantially less stimulation than is characteristic of many middle-class environments (Allen, Affleck, McGrade, & McQueeney, 1984). During their early months, they may spend a great deal of time alone in a room with little color and may have limited reaction with other people. When they are fed or changed, they may be handled only briefly, and the bottle often may be propped for feeding. Early experience outside this meager environment may not exist at all.

Instances of reduced stimulation may also be found in other situations. For example, a relative lack of stimulation may be offered the child who is born with a significant physical handicap, even if the family is not of limited means. Such a child may be difficult for the family to look at or to interact with and, consequently, may be excluded to a considerable extent from the activities of the family. This child is not the beautiful baby the family anticipated and therefore may not be carried into the community to participate in routine activities.

Establishment of a planned sequence of stimulation programming for such infants reflects an effort to provide an environment that more closely resembles the rich experience children most enjoy. It should be emphasized that the justification of such a program does not rest on the valuation of a certain life-style found in "middle" America; it is based on the belief, reinforced by accumulating evidence, that such stimulation and early intervention are of benefit to the intellectual development of a child (e.g., Casto & Mastropieri, 1986; Sharav & Shlomo, 1986). Stimulation programs draw heavily on the environment of the child's home, regardless of socioeconomic level. A family of limited income in a home with modest furnishings can provide interaction patterns and sensory stimulation that are as significant as those found in a family of greater income.

LANGUAGE DEVELOPMENT

Core Concept 3   Language development is an area in which mental retardation is likely to become evident during the early
childhood years.

Mental retardation may manifest itself in a variety of ways and in a variety of behavioral domains. Perhaps the most serious and obvious deficit that is often evident is delayed language development. Depending on the specific situation, there may even be a total absence of expressive language. It is quite common for parents and teachers to attribute most, if not all, of the retarded child's learning problems to language deficiencies. Several authorities seem to share this perception or at least to highlight the apparent interrelationship between language and intellectual functioning. For example, Berry and Eisenson (1956, p. 23) noted that "low intelligence undoubtedly is responsible for many cases of delay in speech, but speech delay is the cause for such apparent low intelligence." Another early statement was presented by Van Riper (1972):

> It is quite possible that many children appear, or even become, mentally retarded, because they never learn to speak. Thinking, perceiving, remembering, predicting—all of these require the use of symbols. . . . It is true that mental deficiency can cause delayed speech; it is also true that delayed speech can contribute to mental retardation.

Normal Language Development

Language development is discussed in earlier parts of this book. Table 7–1 also provides some limited guidelines to normal development landmarks, including language and prelanguage behaviors. It is commonly agreed that the normal progression of language development represents an important indicator of general cognitive maturation. Menyuk (1972) summarized ages at which gross linguistic behaviors appear in normal children in the following manner:

Birth	Crying and making other physiological sounds
1 to 2 months	Cooing as well as crying

3 to 6 months	Babbling as well as cooing
9 to 14 months	Speaking first words as well as babbling
18 to 24 months	Speaking first sentences as well as words
3 to 4 years	Using all basic syntactical structures
4 to 8 years	Articulating correctly all speech sounds in context

This progression suggests that, for a normal child, the basic language structure is largely intact somewhere between 4 and 8 years of age. Certainly as maturation continues beyond this point, language facility also tends to grow and expand but appears largely to represent an embellishment of existing structures.

The process involved in language development has been the source of considerable theoretical debate. A substantial portion of this debate began in 1957 with the publication of B. F. Skinner's *Verbal Behavior.* It was Skinner's contention that verbal behavior is reinforced through the mediation of other people who themselves must have a prolonged history that has conditioned them in ways of "precisely" reinforcing the speaker (Skinner, 1957). Additionally, the mediation of others and the reinforcing consequences are continually important to maintenance of the verbal behavior after initial acquisition. This view of language development is at variance with the beliefs of Chomsky (1957) and Lenneberg (1969), who maintain that language is an innate capacity that is species-specific to humans and dependent on the maturation of the brain and nervous system.

Lenneberg (1969) appeared to be diametrically opposed to Skinner's position and discarded learning theory as a relevant explanation for language development. His basis for this view was that the onset of language occurs in children at a similar age in all cultures of the world despite vast differences among cultures. Lenneberg also noted that language may be impaired by specific brain lesions that leave other mental and motor functions intact. He asserted that teaching cannot result in language acquisition unless the individual has the innate biological propensity for language.

Chomsky (1957) assumed a position that is somewhat more of a theoretical compromise and recognized that reinforcement may play some role in language development. However, the role of reinforcement, according to Chomsky, operates along with natural inquisitiveness, casual observation, a strong tendency to imitate, and requires an extraordinary capacity to generalize, hypothesize, and process information. These latter capacities are viewed as operating in a very complex manner that may be largely innate or may develop through some sort of learning or maturation of the nervous system. From Chomsky's position, language results from rule-governed processes, and these processes account for the suddenness and complexity of the child's language development.

The theoretical debate concerning language development has vastly enriched the basis for consideration of the problems in delayed language acquisition and its relationship to mental retardation. Although it is somewhat unfortunate that so much energy has been expended in controversy and refutation, the value of diverse thinking should not be overlooked. Each of these theorists contributed substantially from very different positions, and the various hypotheses will likely blend in some fashion in the future as we unravel the process of normal language development.

Delayed Language Development

There is little question that language development is commonly delayed among those who are mentally retarded (e.g., Cardoso-Martins, Mervis, & Mervis, 1985). Although scales to specifically measure language development of the mentally retarded child have not yet been developed, normative language development instrumentation is useful insofar as it helps to identify the extent to which delay or deficiency exists. A variety of language development scales have been constructed over the years (Clark, 1973; Hedrick & Prather, 1970; Lillywhite, 1968; Murdock & Hartmann, 1974). Some of these scales include those that evaluate phonological (sounds), semantic (meaning), morphological (word forms), and syntactical (word order) skills acquired by normal children. These areas of assessment are important to an evaluation of language development both for children who appear to be progressing normally and for those who exhibit delay. For the most part, language development scales focus on the periods from birth to 5 or 10 years of age, which seems appropriate in terms of general child development processes. Such instrumentation, in addition to that discussed in chapter 4, provides a significant armory for those concerned with language development and, particularly, with delayed or deficient language development.

Delayed language development presents a difficult problem, especially in our contemporary society. The precise manner in which delayed language relates to reduced intellectual functioning, or mental retardation, is unclear although analytical research is emerging (e.g., Smith & von Tetzchner, 1986). Delayed language development is a characteristic that cannot be simply analyzed as suggested by the quotations by Berry and Eisenson (1956) and Van Riper (1972). Hass and Hass (1972) drew some analogies that may be enlightening, if not accurate. They suggested that the communicative plight of the severely retarded 10-year-old child who has been institutionalized for several years might be likened to that of an English-speaking college student in France who finds that school-acquired French is not adequate for satisfactory communication, or that of an anthropologist who cannot establish effective communication with a newly discovered culture. The authors indicated that (1) all the college student must do is master some of the surface features of French, since the semantic representation and basic communication skills are already functional, and (2) the anthropologist may make significant progress based on theoretical background and experience. The retarded child, however, may well be faced with a very different problem. Such a child may have to construct the entire experiential organization and content on which linguistic and/or cognitive variations are based, which may represent a task that is vastly more complex and difficult than that faced by the college student or the anthropologist.

Efforts have been made that are aimed at counteracting language delay with mentally retarded youngsters. Unfortunately, language rehabilitation efforts with this population in general lagged for many years because of attitudes and perceptions held by many speech and language specialists, a substantial number of whom have opposed working with the mentally retarded population on the grounds that speech and language rehabilitation is almost impossible for these individuals. Such attitudes, although regrettable, are somewhat understandable in view of some of the theoretical formulations concerning language development. For example, if the position that language development is "innate" to humans is accepted, many retarded children would have to be rejected for speech and language therapy since language may not appear to be "innate" for them. Other theoretical schemes seem to provide a more optimistic outlook for mentally retarded children; B. F. Skinner's research, for example, provides a strong theoretical basis for working with children whose language skills fail to develop normally. Evidence is accumulating that language development during the early years is directly influenced by learning and social- experiential factors for mentally retarded children as it is for their nonretarded peers (Leifer & Lewis, 1984).

Some efforts under way with regard to language rehabilitation with mentally retarded youngsters have been based on Skinner's approach. Several research projects have focused on the establishment of imitative repertoires in retarded children in order to facilitate speech and language development (Baer & Guess, 1971; Baer, Peterson, & Sherman, 1967; Garcia, Guess, & Byrnes, 1973; Schumaker & Sherman, 1970). These investigations have resulted in a number of outcomes that appear promising. Although the details varied among studies, the major conclusions include the following:

1. Imitation apparently can be learned by children who initially did not have significant imitative behavioral repertoires.
2. Imitation combined with differential reinforcement can be used to train for both simple naming or labeling as well as for generative repertoires of plurality, simple sentences, and verb tense usage.
3. Imitation can be regarded as a particular type of learning set that exemplifies the rule "do as the model does."
4. Language development and consequent behavior that is "rule governed" can be rather directly related to simple training procedures of differential reinforcement and fading, which teach a child to match a series of different behaviors that are modeled.

5. A child with a widely generalized imitative repertoire can be significantly influenced by language models in the environment. Such generalization is essential to the normal acquisition of speech and language.

Some of these results have prompted the development of programming approaches to language development stimulation that may well alter the course of progress for the mentally retarded child (Bricker & Bricker, 1974; Gray & Ryan, 1973; McLean, Yoder, & Schiefelbusch, 1972; Schiefelbusch, 1972 and 1978; Sloane & MacAulay, 1968).

COGNITIVE DEVELOPMENT

Core Concept 4   Cognitive development during infancy and early childhood involves many complex processes and includes areas where mentally retarded children have great difficulty.

Cognitive development generically refers to an individual's developing capacity to formulate mental patterns. Ordinarily, perception refers to sensory experiences received from the environment, whereas cognition refers to the meaning and thought patterns that emerge as a result of combinations of perceptions. Our purpose is well served by these definitions although the explanations vary depending on context and the authority consulted. In this section we discuss the work of selected theorists who have examined cognitive development and implications for mental retardation.

Theoretical Formulations

One individual who has contributed significantly to the theoretical consideration of cognitive development is Jean Piaget. It has already been noted that his work, reviewed in previous chapters, is currently under heavy criticism (Flavell, 1982, 1985). However, his theoretical formulations remain worthy of discussion, particularly in the context of cognitive development. Unlike most theorists, Piaget was primarily interested in the functions and structures of intelligent activity rather than the content of intelligence per se. He outlined stages of intelligence development that change both quantitatively and qualitatively throughout the developmental period. It was Piaget's contention that, although different children progress through various stages at different rates, the sequence of progression is always the same.

Piaget's developmental stages are marked by the most recently emerging capability of the child. It is important to remember, however, that behaviors and processes preceding the currently emerging stage continue to occur and may be more intense and frequent than the newly emerging function.

Piaget's formulations provide an interesting framework in which to consider the cognitive development of mentally retarded children. It is speculated that retarded children, particularly those who are only mildly handicapped, progress through Piaget's developmental stages in structural terms, although their rate of progress is somewhat slower than that of normal children. This progression is largely demonstrable despite the fact that most retarded individuals do not seem to develop spontaneously beyond the first two periods of sensorimotor and concrete operations. Thus mentally retarded children often appear to possess a cognitive structure resembling that of children who are younger in terms of chronological age.

From Piaget's perspective a child's cognitive capacities unfold naturally, although the influence of the environment is substantial. It is through adaptation to the environment that the child shapes the exact nature of structures that unfold. A child's readiness to develop the next sequence of intellectual structure is governed largely by the neurological capacity or readiness of the neurological system, whereas the stimulus for actual progression into the next stage is provided by the environment. This view of cognitive development appears to have substantial implication for teaching retarded children, since the purpose of education is to present an environment that will stimulate development of maximum potential. For Piaget, conceptualization of an idea precedes verbalization. In other words, children must experience and understand a phenomenon actively in the real world before they are able to put the event into words and demonstrate mastery of the problem. Children given opportunities to encounter life experiences appropriate to their stage of cognitive development can be assisted in growth and development of cognitive potential through appropriate environmental stimulation (Sharav & Shlomo, 1986). As we continue to unravel the interactions between system maturation and the environment, we may find that developing cognitive abilities can be a more central focus of the teaching process than in the past (Valett, 1978).

Cognitive development in mentally retarded individuals has been of particular interest to behavioral scientists for many years. In 1944 Inhelder, for example, proposed a system of classifying retarded people according to their cognitive development. It was Inhelder's view that severely retarded individuals are fixated at the level of sensorimotor intelligence. This interpretation would suggest that such individuals simply repeat over and over again the innate behaviors that are observed at birth with very little knowledge about the objects with which they interact. Those who advance further within the sensorimotor stage are more closely oriented to the world around them, recognize familiar objects, and demonstrate intentionality in their behavior. They may be able to use trial and error experimentation with objects in their environment in order to produce a novel effect. Assimilation and accommodation may be clearly differentiated, and the individual may actively seek new accommodational experiences. A limited ability to use symbols to represent events that are not directly in the individual's perceptual field may also emerge, as well as the capacity to manipulate and combine these images or symbols. Such abilities may permit the use of rudimentary language and a beginning level of thinking and anticipation of events in the environment. Thus even though such individuals may be severely handicapped when compared to those of normal intelligence and similar chronological age, they possess certain rather remarkable capacities that provide some potential for interacting with the environment and for learning.

Inhelder's classification scheme viewed moderately retarded people as incapable of progressing beyond the preoperational intuitive subperiod. From this perspective such an individual might evidence some functions similar to a normal child who is about 4 to 7 years old. These functions might include the ability to mentally grasp a complex of distinct and spatiotemporally separate events in succession. Inhelder would envision moderately retarded individuals as being aware of their own thought processes and able to distinguish truth from fantasy. At this level the cognitive system is thought to be capable of transcending time, space, and reality, permitting at least a limited capacity to think of past, present, and future. The moderately retarded are generally unable to conceptualize any other point of view than their own and thereby remain basically egocentric. Their conceptualization of the symbols used to represent reality remains concrete, and they depend substantially on perceptual experiences to provide mental representation of events. Attention is typically focused on the most immediate, interesting, and compelling attribute of an event, and there is a very limited ability to voluntarily transfer attention to another dimension of the situation. Similarly, the moderately retarded person usually cannot mentally reverse an operation or an event in order to examine its components and also exhibits a very limited capacity to reason logically. In general, the person functioning at this level of development has many signs of the ability to think and function much like an older child, such as using language with reasonable effectiveness, getting along socially, adapting, and solving some problems (Strain, 1985). These abilities are significantly limited, however, and the descriptions by Inhelder and Piaget have contributed to the understanding of cognitive difficulties encountered by individuals in this particular stage of development.

The child who is chronologically of preschool age and who exhibits some of the linguistical or cognitive behaviors typical of this developmental stage is tolerated well by society. The cognitive "mistakes" of such a child are deemed amusing or something that time will correct. The retarded adult, on the other hand, who functions at the preoperational subperiod and has similar cognitive traits will be tolerated to a much lesser degree. Such a person is socially expected to function at a much more advanced cognitive level, and the limitations frequently become distressing to others. More often than not, the abilities that have been developed or can be developed are overlooked.

From Inhelder's perspective the mildly retarded individual may be viewed as being able to progress beyond the level of concrete operations, and those who previously were classified as borderline retarded may be able to use simpler forms of formal operations when they reach adulthood. A person functioning at this level is able to move beyond what is expected for the normal preschool-age child and to use well-organized cognitive systems that permit more effective environmental coping. One significant development involves overcoming the tendency to stumble into perplexity and contradiction in thought—a characteristic typical of the preschool child. Cognitive operations develop, whereby the individual can engage in a more advanced level of logic, establishing concepts and events of reality more systematically.

Implications for Professional Intervention

The specialist in early childhood education is perhaps the professional most intimately concerned with the cognitive development of the preschool child, whether retarded or of normal intelligence. The generic goal of early childhood education is primarily to provide an environment that stimulates maximum social and cognitive development. We have already examined the important implications of early environmental stimulation for the development of optimal intellectual functioning later in life. As a child progresses beyond the age of 2, environmental stimulation appears to play a different role in the child's development. During the first 2 years, general stimulation in a wide variety of areas seems to affect the individual's ultimate level of functioning. For example, factors such as parental behavioral style and attitude, particularly the mother's, are significantly related to cognitive development (Berry & Gunn, 1984; Crockenberg, 1983; Mahoney, Finger, & Powell, 1985; McConachie & Mitchell, 1985; Rosenberg, Robinson, & Beckman, 1986).

However, as the child enters the preschool period of 3, 4, and 5 years of age, general sensory stimulation does not appear beneficial in the same manner. Instead, rather specific experiences with particular and focused stimulation seem to become influential in the child's developmental progress. As expressed in Piaget's notions, conceptualization grows out of reality experiences, and then the child develops the capacity to represent this event symbolically both in thought and language. The objective of the early childhood education specialist is to provide specific tangible experiences that are consistent with the cognitive capacity of the child and that stimulate the development of the cognitive structures. The initial challenge for the educational specialist working with a mentally retarded preschooler is to understand the level of cognitive development of the child. If, for example, the child is functioning at the sensorimotor stage and is thought to have potential for development into the preoperational thought period, the specialist may direct efforts toward preparing the child for preoperational thinking. This child may be given experiences with a variety of spatial problems, such as physical activities that provide a contrast between objects in the environment and the child, and a recognition of how these objects can be manipulated and experienced in a consistent, predictable manner. Through such techniques the education specialist may build a program for the young child that facilitates progression into the next cognitive stage of development. Early intervention programs are important to the developmental progression for young mentally retarded children (Casto & Mastropierei, 1986).

PSYCHOSOCIAL DEVELOPMENT

Core Concept 5   Developmental problems expressed in social and emotional functioning can have a serious impact on a young child's ability to adapt and chances to succeed.

It is evident that the overall growth and development of a young child involve many different components, each of which is essential to the integrated whole with respect to development and is interrelated in a variety of complex fashions. Social-emotional development is one of these processes vital for young children, regardless of their intellectual capacity. The development of social and emotional functioning has pervasive effects on intellectual functioning to the extent that when a child has a serious problem in psychosocial development, there is likely to be an inability to fulfill the intellectual potential that may be present. Thus the development of psychosocial functioning is a central concern for the young child. We will explore several theoretical positions that have particular implications for the preschool period of development. Emphasis will be placed on the implications of each theory for the potential intellectual functioning of the child with normal intelligence as well as the preschool-aged, mentally retarded child.

Theoretical Formulations

Theoretical formulations in the area of psychosocial development are somewhat different from those we have examined in other behavioral domains.

In many cases the topics under discussion represent concepts that are extremely abstract and have been difficult (some contend impossible) to measure. This does not detract from the importance of considering their development; few would deny that these concepts, although abstract, have reality in terms of behavior.

Development of Trust, Autonomy, and Initiative. E. H. Erikson viewed child development primarily from a psychoanalytical perspective. Erikson (1968) hypothesized that infancy is the time in a child's life when the first social achievement is accomplished—that of basic trust. To the extent that the child's parents provide nurturance, familiarity, security, and continuity of experience, an infant is able to develop a basic sense of trust in both the immediate environment and the people in it. An infant's behavior reflects constant testing, experimenting, and exploring of the world in order to discover its predictability or the extent to which it can be trusted. It was Erikson's notion that when an adequate mothering relationship is not present, an infant develops a sense of mistrust for the environment and the people in it. It was also his contention that such an experience is irrevocable and influences the manner in which all subsequent stages evolve. Clearly all infants experience some degree of trust and mistrust. It is the predominance of the one over the other that seems critical in determining successful completion of this stage.

The development of autonomy and initiative are involved in Erikson's depiction of emotional development during early childhood. Initially the child undergoes a struggle to attain autonomy and a sense of self and of separateness. As part of this process, a child must overcome the hazards of doubt and shame. The child learns to exercise control over the processes of having and letting go. The family environment, in turn, offers both restraint and freedom in an appropriate balance to permit a young child to experiment without being the victim of indiscriminate use of the abilities to hold on and to let go. As this process evolves, the child begins to develop a sense of autonomy, which is important in further development of independent functioning.

Erikson also postulated a second stage in early childhood that begins at about the end of the third year. This stage involves the struggle to gain a sense of initiative and to overcome the perils of guilt. The difference between this stage and the establishment of autonomy is likened to the difference between knowing oneself and knowing one's potential. In this process a child develops a sense of conscience, which is the regulatory or control function of the personality. If this function becomes overdeveloped, an individual may become overly inhibited and even self-destructive with a diminished capacity for creativity and initiative. As with all developmental processes, the desirable outcome is dominance of the positive task accomplishment over the hazards of the stage.

Development of Attachment.   Attachment behavior is also thought to be an important emotional component of personality with considerable implication for future development. Bowlby (1969) viewed infancy as a crucial period for the emergence of this behavior. As attachment evolves, the reciprocal behaviors of the mother and other significant individuals are often caretaking behaviors. The infant's behavior reflects efforts to maintain proximity first to the mother and then to other members of the family who, in turn, reciprocate the expressed needs for proximity. There are many specific ways in which an older infant maintains proximity, although they seem to emerge in five basic patterns: sucking, clinging, following, crying, and smiling. Some of these behaviors are evident at birth but are manifested as the infant's self-directed attachment behavior at about the age of 4 months. As development progresses, an infant exhibits rather sophisticated goal-directed systems of behavior that maintain proximity to the mother. These systems of behavior usually become apparent between the ages of 9 and 18 months.

   Visual and tactile contact are viewed as crucial for the development of attachment behavior. The nature of visual and tactile interactions provides an important indication of the adequacy of attachment formation. Using the mother as a base of security from which to operate, an infant explores the larger world but maintains visual contact during the process. Tactile contact is periodically reestablished, and then exploration continues. When the child becomes frightened, distressed, or uncomfortable for any reason, there is a tendency to establish contact that retains proximity to mother, such as clinging and following. When a serious threat of separation occurs, intense anxiety, anger, and violent distress result. These feelings and behaviors are strong throughout infancy and still apparent throughout early childhood, although they begin to lessen in intensity.

Environmental Antecedents to Self-esteem.   There has been considerable interest in developing a better understanding of the influence of environmental factors on emotional and social development. Theoretical formulations typically have not been oriented toward child development, although the implications for infants and young children are substantial. Further, such theories highlight the essential aspects of the environment that developmentally oriented theorists also discuss. The eminent therapist Carl Rogers (1951) suggested that individuals need a psychological atmosphere of unconditional positive regard in order to develop to their full potential. This type of atmosphere logically must come from the significant others in one's environment and involves total and unconditional acceptance of the feelings and values of a young child. This does not, however, mean that others must always agree with a child; they must only accept the child's feelings and values as real. Evaluative comparison, rejection judgments, lack of trust, and harsh punishment lead to the development of underlying doubts of worthiness and competence on the part of the child and may block the development of self-esteem, acceptance, and assurance.

Somewhat more recently, Coopersmith studied the development of self-esteem and formulated some theoretical propositions about young children (1967). His work focused on factors involved in a child's social relationships that lead to optimal development of self esteem in later life. It appears that children who feel that they are significant to their parents tend to develop high levels of self-esteem. Such feelings can be conveyed by parental attention and concern as well as by restrictions imposed regarding behavioral limits. In this type of familial environment the children are made aware of their successes, and they experience frequent success in their efforts toward development and learning; but they also are made aware of situations when success has not occurred and are encouraged to develop behavioral changes needed to achieve success and approval. Additionally, high self-esteem seems to be related to a high level of stimulation, activity, and vigor in the family. A high level of communication among family members is usual and includes differences of opinion, dissent, and disagreement, all leading to the development of mutual knowledge and respect.

Implications for Intellectual Functioning

This discussion suggests that many of the factors of major concern in psychosocial development are also recognized as important components in intellectual functioning. For example, the role of early stimulation is immediately apparent in both psychosocial and intellectual domains. Personality theorists focus on the crucial relationship between the infant or young child and at least one significant adult who provides necessary care and love for the child. This adult's attention and affection are received by a child primarily through the sensory channels that are so critical in the development of intellectual functioning. It appears that there must be a significant interaction or interdependence between the development of psychosocial and intellectual functions, although the precise nature of this relationship is not currently understood. Children whose intellectual development may suffer because of environmental deprivation are also likely to exhibit signs of attenuated emotional development. Such developmental inadequacies may be evident simply because of the lack of sensory stimulation required for proper development of these areas. Additionally, a child who is unable to develop adequate emotional security, self-esteem, or social relationships with family members and peers is likely to inhibited in intellectual performance. Whether the inhibiting influence becomes permanent or significant is probably a result of an interaction of a number of factors that have not been investigated sufficiently to draw reliable conclusions. It seems reasonable, however, to state that healthy psychological development in early life probably has a favorable influence on the child's ability to function intellectually.

There is relatively little understanding of specific psychosocial development in the mentally retarded infant or preschooler. It does seem that these children exhibit developmental lags in the psychosocial features examined, remaining dependent and relatively immature in social interactions for a prolonged period. It is not clear, however, whether this developmental lag arises from the neurological deficiencies or from the lack of interaction with significant adults. Evidence does suggest that sociometric status ratings by preschoolers' nonhandicapped peers are related to their prosocial behavior (Strain, 1985). It seems reasonable to assume that the young retarded child might exhibit a developmental delay similar to that described cognitively by Piaget's theory. However, all possible efforts should be made to sustain an optimal level of psychosocial development for the retarded child.

Professional Intervention

The psychosocial development is as important for the mentally retarded child as for the child of normal intelligence. Professionals working with retarded children must be as concerned with this area of development as they are with cognitive domains. The emotional development of such a child may be particularly at risk because of unfavorable parental reactions. The family may need assistance from mental health specialists (psychologist, psychiatrist, psychiatric social worker) to maintain optimal mental health and development for all family members. The parents, as well as the retarded child, may have particular needs. Such professionals may provide short-term assistance and intervention during periods of crisis, such as at the time of the child's birth, when the diagnosis of mental retardation is confirmed, or during periods of intense physical, social, or emotional stress in the family. Long-term assistance or intervention may be needed if unusual or prolonged stress affects the family unit. It may be difficult for the family to accept such assistance, which threatens the emotional integrity of the family unit and of the individual members. Accepting assistance often means recognizing a need that is difficult to acknowledge and which many families interpret as a weakness or failure. Friends, health care professionals, and educators should be alert to signs of a need for mental health intervention and should help the family to admit the problem and to accept such assistance.

In many cases mental retardation is not apparent at birth. Under such circumstances the family often becomes aware of the child's handicap during the first months or years of life. It is not uncommon for the family to experience particular stress and crisis as members seek to allay their fears, restore their hopes for the normal, healthy baby they believed to exist, and reach some level of resolution concerning the reality of the situation. The longer the family has lived with a child believing that the baby is healthy and normal, the more difficult the adjustment when the family becomes aware of mental retardation. Chapters 8 and 13 discuss further the difficult emotional complexities that families of retarded children experience.

Intervention during infancy and early childhood has been examined in several areas within this chapter. Such efforts are clearly important to the overall development of a child although systematic and comprehensive programs have seldom been available on a widespread basis. However, the enactment of Public Law 99-457, Education of the Handicapped Amendments of 1986, holds promise for change in this regard. These amendments essentially extended provisions of P.L. 94-142 and provided for full service programs to young children aged birth to 2 years of age as well as at the preschool level, ages 3 to 5 (see chapter 14). It is hoped that future research will be able to evaluate the effectiveness of such programming.

Core Questions

1. What developments occur during infancy and the early years with respect to the brain?
2. How can one trace the development of myelinization from a behavioral standpoint in very young children?
3. How does the early development of sensory organs influence a young child's learning?
4. How might environmental deprivation of stimuli affect the cognitive development of young children and result in mental retardation?
5. How are parents potentially important in early childhood intervention programs?
6. How are Chomsky, Lenneberg, and Skinner different in their theoretical formulations of language development?
7. How is early sensory stimulation important for both emotional and intellectual development?
8. How do Rogers and Coopersmith view environmental antecedents to the development of self-esteem? What are their differences and similarities?
9. In what manner does Inhelder's view of mental retardation limit the development of moderately retarded individuals?
10. In what respects would Piaget see the cognitive developmental progress of mentally retarded and nonretarded individuals as being the same?

ROUND TABLE DISCUSSION

Human development during infancy and early childhood is extremely important. Much that occurs at this stage of life provides a foundation for many later skills and abilities. Physiological systems are developing and interact with aspects of cognition, language, and social development in a complex fashion that ultimately results in an individual's total potential.

In your study group or on your own, examine how physiological growth and development relate to language, cognition, and social competence. Explore the role of the environment during this time, including aspects of parental interaction and behavior. Discuss how parents can contribute both to proper emotional health and also to mental retardation in a child. Describe how you might discuss early child development with potential parents in order to facilitate their effectiveness as parents and as developmental specialists.

REFERENCES

Affleck, G., Tennen, H., & Gershman, K. (1985). Cognitive adaptations to high-risk infants: The search for mastery, meaning, and protection from future harm. *American Journal of Mental Deficiency, 89,* 653–656.

Allen, D. A., Affleck, G., McGrade, B. J., & McQueeney, M. (1984). Factors in the effectiveness of early childhood intervention for low socioeconomic status families. *Education and Training of the Mentally Retarded, 19,* 254–260.

American Academy of Pediatrics (1971). *Standards of child health care, council on pediatric practice.* Evanston, IL: Author.

Baer, D. M., & Guess, D. (1971). Receptive training of adjectival inflections in mental retardates. *Journal of Applied Behavior Analysis, 4,* 129–139.

Baer, D. M., Peterson, R. R., & Sherman, J. A. (1967). The development of imitation by reinforcing behavioral similarity to a model. *Journal of the Experimental Analysis of Behavior, 10,* 405–416.

Berger, J., & Cunningham, C. C. (1986). Aspects of early social smiling by infants with Down's syndrome. *Child Care, Health and Development, 12,* 13–24.

Berry, M. C., & Eisenson, J. (1956). *Speech disorders: Principles and practices of therapy.* New York: Appleton-Century-Crofts.

Berry, P., & Gunn, P. (1984). Maternal influence on the task behaviour of young Down's syndrome children. *Journal of Mental Deficiency Research, 28,* 269–274.

Bowlby, J. (1969). *Attachment and loss* (Vol. 1). New York: Basic.

Bricker, W. A., & Bricker, D. D. (1974). An early language training strategy. In R. L. Scheifelbusch & L. L. Lloyd (Eds.), *Language perspectives: Acquisition, retardation, and intervention,* pp. 431–468. Baltimore: University Park.

Bruder, M. B. (1987). Parent-to-parent teaching. *American Journal of Mental Deficiency, 91,* 435–438.

Burns, K. A., Deddish, R. B., Burns, W. J., & Hatcher, R. P. (1983). Use of oscillating waterbeds and rhythmic sounds for premature infant stimulation. *Developmental Psychology, 19,* 746–751.

Cardoso-Martins, C., Mervis, C. B., & Mervis, C. A. (1985). Early vocabulary by children with Down syndrome. *American Journal of Mental Deficiency, 90,* 177–184.

Casto, G., & Mastropieri, M. A. (1986). The efficacy of early intervention programs: A meta-analysis. *Exceptional Children, 52,* 417–424.

Chinn, P. L. (1979). *Child health maintenance: Concepts in family centered care* (2nd ed.). St. Louis: Mosby.

Chomsky, N. (1957). *Syntactic structures.* The Hague: Mouton.

Clark, P. M. (1973). *Communication sequences (language).* Los Angeles: Los Angeles Unified School District, Title III ESEA, P.L. 89–10.

Coopersmith, S. (1967). *The antecedents of self-esteem.* San Francisco: Freeman.

Crockenberg, S. (1983). Early mother and infant antecedents of Bayley Scale performance at 21 months. *Developmental Psychology, 19,* 727–730.

Erikson, E. H. (1968). *Identity, youth and crisis.* New York: Norton.

Flavell, J. H. (1982). Structures, stages, and sequences in cognitive development. In W. A. Collins (Ed.), *The concept of development: The Minnesota symposia on child psychology* (Vol. 15, pp. 1–28). Hillsdale, NJ: Erlbaum.

Flavell, J. H. (1985). *Cognitive development.* Englewood Cliffs, NJ: Prentice-Hall.

Garber, H., & Heber, R. F. (1977). The Milwaukee Project: Indications of the effectiveness of early intervention in preventing mental retardation. In P. Mittler (Ed.), *Research to practice in mental retardation: Care and intervention* (Vol. 1, pp. 119–127). Baltimore: University Park.

Garcia, E., Guess, D., & Byrnes, J. (1973). Development of syntax in retarded girls using procedures of imitation, reinforcement and modeling. *Journal of Applied Behavior Analysis, 5,* 299–310.

Gesell, A. (1941). *Wolf child and human child.* New York: Harper.

Goldberg, S., Marcovitch, S., MacGregor, D., & Lojkasek, M. (1986). Family responses to developmentally delayed preschoolers: Etiology and the father's role. *American Journal of Mental Deficiency, 90,* 610–617.

Gray, B., & Ryan, B. (1973). *A language program for the non-language child.* Champaign, IL: Research Press.

Greenberg, D., Uzgiris, I. C., & Hunt, J. McV. (1968). Hastening the development of the blink response with looking. *Journal of General Psychology, 113,* 167–176.

Gregory, R. L., & Wallace, J. G. (1963). Recovery from early blindness. *Experimental Psychology Monograph* (No. 2), Cambridge, England.

Guyton, A. C. (1971). *Textbook of medical physiology* (4th ed.). Philadelphia: Saunders.

Hass, W. A., & Hass, S. K. (1972). Syntactic structure and language development in retardates. In R. L. Schiefelbusch (Ed.), *Language of the mentally retarded* (pp. 321–342). Baltimore: University Park.

Hebb, D. O. (1949). *The organization of behavior.* New York: Wiley.

Heber, R. F., Dever, R. B., & Conry, J. (1968). The influence of environmental and genetic variables on intellectual development. In H. J. Prehm, L. A. Hamerlynck, & J. E. Crosson (Eds.), *Behavioral research in mental retardation,* pp. 1–23. Eugene: University of Oregon.

Heber, R. F., & Garber, H. (1971). An experiment in prevention of cultural-familial mental retardation. In D. A. Primrose (Ed.), *Proceedings of the Second Congress of the International Association for the Scientific Study of Mental Deficiency* (pp. 31–35). Warsaw, Poland: Polish Medical Publishers.

Heber, R. F., Garber, H., Harrington, S., Hoffman, C., & Falendar, C. (1972). *Rehabilitation of families at risk for mental retardation: Progress report.* Madison: University of Wisconsin.

Hedrick, D. L., & Prather, E. M. (1970). *Sequenced inventory of language development.* Seattle: Child Development and Mental Retardation Center.

Inhelder, B. (1944). *Le diagnostic du raisonnement chez les debiles mentaux.* Neuchatel, Switzerland: Delachaux et Niestle.

Lenneberg, E. H. (1969). On explaining language. *Science, 164*, 635–643.

Leifer, J. S., & Lewis, M. (1984). Acquisition of conversational response skills by young Down syndrome and nonretarded children. *American Journal of Mental Deficiency, 88*, 610–618.

Lillywhite, H. (1968). Doctor's manual of speech disorders. *Journal of the American Medical Association, 167*, 850–851.

London, I. A. (1960). Russian report on the post-operative newly seeing. *American Journal of Psychology, 73*, 478–482.

Mahoney, G., Finger, I., & Powell, A. (1985). Relationship of maternal behavioral style to the development of organically impaired mentally retarded infants. *American Journal of Mental Deficiency, 90*, 296–302.

Mason, M. K. (1942). Learning to speak after six and one-half years of silence. *Journal of Speech Disorders, 7*, 295–304.

McConachie, H., & Mitchell, D. R. (1985). Parents teaching their young mentally handicapped children. *Journal of Child Psychology & Psychiatry & Allied Disciplines, 26*, 389–405.

McConkey, R., & Martin, H. (1983). Mothers' play with toys: A longitudinal study with Down's syndrome infants. *Child Care, Health and Development, 9*, 215–226.

McLean, J. E., Yoder, D. E., & Schiefelbusch, R. L. (Eds.) (1972). *Language intervention with the retarded.* Baltimore: University Park.

Menyuk, P. (1972). *The development of speech.* Indianapolis: Bobbs-Merrill.

Murdock, J. Y., & Hartmann, B. (1974). *A language development program: Imitative gestures to basic syntactic structures.* Salt Lake City: Word Making.

Ottinger, D. R., Blatchley, M. E., & Dennenberg, V. (1969). *Stimulation of human neonates and visual attentiveness.* Paper presented at the meeting of the American Psychological Association, Washington, DC.

Penfield, W. (1972). The uncommitted cortex, the child's changing brain. In H. W. Bernard & W. C. Huckins (Eds.), *Exploring human development: Interdisciplinary readings* (pp. 63–78). Boston: Allyn & Bacon.

Pennington, B. F., van Doorninck, W. J., McCabe, L. L., & McCabe, E. R. B. (1985). Neuropsychological deficits in early treated phenylketonuric children. *American Journal of Mental Deficiency, 89*, 467–474.

Rogers, C. R. (1951). *Client-centered therapy: Its current practice, implications and theory.* Boston: Houghton Mifflin.

Rosenberg, S. A., Robinson, C. C., & Beckman, P. (1986). Measures of parent-infant interaction: An overview. *Topics in Early Childhood Special Education, 6* (2), 32–43.

Schiefelbusch, R. L. (Ed.) (1972). *Language of the mentally retarded.* Baltimore: University Park.

Schiefelbusch, R. L. (Ed.) (1978). *Bases of language intervention.* Baltimore: University Park.

Schumaker, J., & Sherman, J. A. (1970). Training generative verb usage by imitation and reinforcement procedures. *Journal of Applied Behavior Analysis, 3*, 273 287.

Sharav, T., & Shlomo, L. (1986). Stimulation of infants with Down syndrome: Long-term effects. *Mental Retardation, 24*, 81–86.

Skeels, H. M., & Dye, H. B. (1939). A study of the effects of differential stimulation. *Proceedings of the American Association on Mental Deficiency, 44*, 114–136.

Skinner, B. F. (1957). *Verbal behavior.* New York: Appleton-Century- Crofts.

Slater, M. A. (1986). Modification of mother-child interaction processes in families with children at-risk for mental retardation. *American Journal of Mental Deficiency, 91,* 257–267.

Sloane, H. N., & MacAulay, B. D. (Eds.) (1968). *Operant procedures in remedial speech and language training.* Boston: Houghton Mifflin.

Smith, L., & von Tetzchner, S. (1986). Communicative, sensorimotor, and language skills of young children with Down syndrome. *American Journal of Mental Deficiency, 91,* 57–66.

Strain, P. S. (1985). Social and nonsocial determinants of acceptability in handicapped preschool children. *Topics in Early Childhood Special Education, 4* (4), 47–58.

Strickland, S. R. (1971). Can slum children learn? *American Education, 7* (6), 3–7.

Valett, R. E. (1978). *Developing cognitive abilities: Teaching children to think.* St. Louis: Mosby.

Van Riper, C. (1972). *Speech correction: Principles and methods* (5th ed.). Englewood Cliffs, NJ: Prentice-Hall.

White, B. L. (1967). *An experimental approach to the effects of experience on early human behavior.* Paper presented at the meeting of the Minnesota Symposium on Child Psychology, Minneapolis.

Whiteman, M., & Deutsch, M. (1968). Social disadvantage as related to intellective and language development. In M. Deutsch, I. Katz, & A. R. Jensen (Eds.), *Social class, race, and psychological development.* New York: Holt, Rinehart & Winston.

Wright, L. (1971). The theoretical and research base for a program of early stimulation care and training of premature infants. In J. Hellmuth (Ed.), *Exceptional Infant* (Vol. 2). New York: Brunner/Mazel.

Zubek, J. P. (Ed.) (1969). *Sensory deprivation: Fifteen years of research.* New York: Appleton- Century-Crofts.

THREE

THE RETARDED CHILD DURING SCHOOL YEARS

8

The Elementary-Age Retarded Child

Core Concepts
Cognitive Development
Learning Characteristics
  Memory
  Distribution of Practice
  Learning Concrete and Abstract Concepts
  Learning Sets and Transfer of Training
  Educational Achievement
Adaptive Behavior
Personality and Emotional Development
  Motivational Problems
Physical and Health Characteristics
  Physical Differences
  Health Differences
Alternatives for Educational Placement
  Regular Class Placement with Support Services
  The Special Education Classroom in the Regular School
  The Special School
Instructional Approaches
  Teaching Academic Skills
  Teaching Adaptive Skills
Educating the Culturally Different Retarded Child
Core Questions
Round Table Discussion
References

Core Concepts

1. The problems associated with mental retardation become a reality for mildly retarded children during the school years.

2. For children with moderate to profound mental retardation, deficits in intellectual and social functioning are evident prior to the school years.

3. Piaget described the cognitive development of the child in terms of stages or periods of intellectual growth.

4. Mentally retarded children move through the same stages of development as their nonretarded peers, but at a slower rate.

5. The memory capabilities of children with mental retardation are deficient in comparison with their nonretarded peers.

6. Distributed practice in a learning situation enhances the learning performance of retarded children.

7. Mentally retarded children are able to grasp concrete and meaningful concepts in a learning situation much better than they grasp abstract concepts.

8. Mentally retarded children develop learning sets at a slower rate than their nonretarded peers.

9. Most mentally retarded children will benefit from instruction in the basic academic tool subjects.

10. Adaptive behavior deficiencies in school settings are associated with coping behavior, social skills, language development, emotional development, self-care, and applied cognitive and academic skills.

11. A mentally retarded child's problems in school-related settings are often compounded by inadequate social development.

12. Mentally retarded individuals are able to participate, and be actively involved, in their own local communities.

13. The more severe the mental retardation, the greater the probability that the child will exhibit corresponding physical problems.

14. Several environmental factors may contribute to health problems for children with mental retardation.

15. The national mandate for the education of handicapped children clearly indicates placement in the least restrictive environment.

16. Regular class placement with support services includes both the consulting teacher and resource room models.

17. Mentally retarded students may be educated in either part-time or full-time special education classrooms in the regular school building.

18. Special schools, although administratively convenient, do not provide critical opportunities for interaction between retarded children and their nonretarded peers.

19. For students with mental retardation, learning in the school setting is a continual process of adaptation.
20. Instruction in the academic areas may include both a "foundation" and a "functional" approach to learning.
21. Adaptive skills are necessary to decrease an individual's dependence on others and to increase opportunities for school and community participation.
22. Culturally different children who are mentally retarded need an educational experience that focuses on learning how to learn.

Core Concept 1

The problems associated with mental retardation become a reality for mildly retarded children during the school years.

The beginning of elementary school is generally an exciting time for both children and their parents. It is a time to make new friends and associations. Even for the nonretarded child, the beginning of school is filled with many uncertainties as well as anticipation. For mentally retarded children and their families, this may be the beginning of their difficulties related to mental retardation. For many parents, the problems of mental retardation may become a reality as their child enters school. According to the AAMD classification system (Grossman, 1983), the six-year-old mildly retarded child may have a developmental lag of only about one year when compared with nonretarded age-mates. This maturational lag may have been so slight during the early childhood years that it was viewed as insignificant or not even noticed by the parents and family physician. This is often the result of an absence of corresponding physical or health problems. The child's difficulties first surface in response to the academic and social demands of the school environment. Such problems may become even more compounded without proper educational assessment. A teacher may attribute the difficulties to immaturity, for example, and not refer the child for specialized services during early primary grades.

Core Concept 2

For children with moderate to profound mental retardation, deficits in intellectual and social functioning are evident prior to the school years.

Whereas deficits associated with mild mental retardation may not be apparent by the time the child enters school, problems characterizing moderate, severe, and profound retardation are clearly evident. The term "education" takes on an entirely different meaning for these children. Before legislative mandates of the 1970s, many children with moderate to profound retardation were excluded from public education programs because they were unable to meet the system's academic or social requirements. However, a different set of values has emerged for the 1980s that establishes a new definition for public education: to raise the functioning level of the child to the next highest developmental level regardless of the severity of the disorder. For more severely retarded children the emphasis is not on academic learning, but on the development of skills that will increase independence within the school, home, and community (e.g., self-help skills, mobility, and communication).

Cognitive development, learning, personality, emotional development, motivational problems, and physical health characteristics of mentally retarded children and related theories will be discussed in this chapter. In most instances these characteristics and theories are not limited to elementary-age retarded children but, rather, may follow the retarded individual throughout life. We have elected to present these concerns in this chapter, however, since it is often at the beginning of the school program that many of them are initially manifested to the professional working with the retarded individual.

COGNITIVE DEVELOPMENT

Core Concept 3   Piaget described the cognitive development of the child
in terms of stages or periods of intellectual growth.

To gain some understanding of the cognitive development of the elementary-age child, turn to the theory of Jean Piaget. Piaget referred to the span of 2 to 7 years as the period of preoperational thought and the span from 7 to 11 years of age as the period of concrete operations. A few of the younger elementary-age children will be completing the preoperational thought period, and most will be functioning in the concrete operations period.

During the preoperations subperiod, perceptions are the dominant mental activity of the child. At about the age of 7 years, the child begins to move into a period in which perceptions are dominated by intellectual operations, the dominant mental activity of the concrete operations period (P. L. Chinn, 1979). The ability to order and relate experiences to an organized whole begins to develop. Rather than being bound to irreversibility as before, the child begins to develop mobility in thought processes and can reverse some mental operations and return to the starting point.

By the age of 4 years, the child is less self-centered and more able to take into account another person's point of view. Instead of centering on a one-dimensional property of a situation, the child is able to focus on several properties in sequence and move quickly from one to another.

This period is termed concrete because the child's mental operations still depend on the ability to concretely perceive what has happened. Mental experimentation cannot be performed without dependence on perception. Chinn stated that the basic ability from which concrete operations develop is the ability mentally to form ordering structures, which Piaget termed groupings and lattices. Lattices are a special form of groupings in which the focus is on the connection between two or more objects and the objects that are connected. This allows the development of a classification hierarchy system in which the child can understand, for example, that all humans are animals, but not all animals are human.

During the preoperational period the child's egocentrism is evident in conversations with other children. During this developmental period conversations with other children the same age will consist of collective monologues. Each child pursues a private, personal conversation regardless of what the other child says. During the concrete operational period, however, these children begin to take into account the other child's point of view and begin to incorporate these views into their own conversations. Thus more meaningful communication emerges, and the children carry on dialogue, with each responding to what the other has just said (Piaget, 1969; Pulaski, 1971).

Core Concept 4 Mentally retarded children move through the same stages of development as their nonretarded peers, but at a slower rate.

Elementary-age mildly retarded children will be slower in progressing from the preoperational stage into concrete operations. Delay in development may be as much as three to four years. Even when the period of concrete operations is reached, only the lower stages may be attained during the elementary school years and higher functioning in the period will not be attained until adolescence. Moderately retarded children may fixate at the preoperational level and not reach even the most basic stages of the concrete operational period until later adolescence. Severely and profoundly retarded children may fixate at the sensorimotor and preoperational stages and never develop cognitively into the more advanced periods, regardless of chronological age. Professionals must be aware of these differences in cognitive functioning across the various severity levels associated with mental retardation so that they will structure learning experiences commensurate with individual levels of development.

LEARNING CHARACTERISTICS

When we compare mentally retarded children with their nonretarded agemates, we find that the very nature of retardation makes mentally retarded children perform more poorly on task of learning and retention. Research on learning and mental retardation has expanded dramatically since the early 1950s. Zeaman (1974) estimated that more than 1,500 studies that were published on learning involved mentally retarded persons. Even with this impressive number of studies, however, our knowledge base still needs considerable expansion.

One critical problem with research on learning has been the failure of many investigators to clearly differentiate between mild, moderate, severe, and profound retardation when reporting their results. Other problems include the underutilization of research knowledge in practice (Drew & Buchanan, 1979), the lack of replicated research investigations across geographical regions (Prehm, Logan, & Towle, 1972), and insufficient funding for research, which has resulted in extremely few comprehensive investigations in specific areas of learning and retention (Gallagher, 1979).

Keeping these limitations in mind, we will discuss the learning characteristics of mentally retarded children. In addition, our attention will be directed to not only the pertinent research in this area but also some of the implications for classroom practice.

Memory

Core Concept 5   The memory capabilities of children with mental retardation are deficient in comparison with their nonretarded peers.

The greater the severity of intellectual deficit, the greater the deficits in memory. Memory problems in mentally retarded children have been attributed to several factors. Mercer and Snell (1977) have suggested that these deficits are associated with an inability to focus on relevant stimuli in a learning situation. Denny (1964) indicated that retarded children may be deficient in the development of learning sets. Frank and Rabinovitch (1974) stated that these children have inefficient rehearsal strategies that interfere with memory abilities. Hardman and Drew (1975) suggested that retarded children are unable to benefit from incidental learning cues in their environment. Stephens (1972) found that retarded children do not effectively transfer knowledge to new tasks or situations. Ellis (1963) theorized that mentally retarded children have a stimulus trace deficit as a result of a poorly developed central nervous system. The stimulus trace deficit reduces their ability to retain stimuli and recall them when needed. These are but a few of the many factors associated with memory problems in retarded children.

The literature regarding the memory of learned material strongly indicates that ability is related to the type of retention task involved. The short-term memory of mentally retarded individuals, that is, the ability to recall material over a period of seconds and minutes, has long been a topic of interest. Early work in the area provides a confusing picture. Some evidence suggested that the short-term memory performance of mentally retarded children is no different from that of nonretarded individuals (Drew & Prehm, 1970; Logan, Prehm, & Drew, 1968), whereas other researchers obtained results that indicate inferior performance by the retarded (Brown, 1974; Butterfield, Wambold, & Belmont, 1973; Ellis, 1970). Probably the most programmatic research on short-term memory has been conducted in the laboratories at the University of Alabama. This work has rather consistently indicated difficulties in short-term memory for mentally retarded individuals across the various levels of severity (Ellis, 1970). Zeaman and House (1979) have suggested that a high level of distractibility by external and irrelevant stimuli is also associated with the retarded person's short-term memory difficulties. The retarded child may take longer to understand the nature of a task than nonretarded age-mates. Several authors have suggested procedures that could be used in the classroom to compensate for these deficiencies (Clinton & Evans, 1972; Fisher & Zeaman, 1973; Mercer & Snell, 1977; Smith, 1968). The following procedures (Smith, 1968) may be adopted in the classroom to facilitate short-term memory in retarded children:

1. Reduce extraneous environmental stimuli, which tend to distract students
2. Present each component of stimuli clearly and with equivalent stimulus value initially
3. Begin with simpler tasks, moving to the more complex
4. Avoid irrelevant materials within the learning task
5. Label stimuli
6. Minimize reinforcement to avoid the interfering anticipation of reward
7. Provide practice in short-term memory activities

8. Integrate practice material with new subject fields, making use of successful experiences of the child
9. Dramatize skills involving short-term memory, making them methodologically central to the program

Studies involving long-term memory of mentally retarded persons are even less firm with regard to result than are those on short-term memory. Several researchers have obtained results suggesting that, on long-term memory tasks, retarded and nonretarded subjects do not perform differently (Cantor & Ryan, 1962; Jensen & Rohwer, 1963). Ellis (1963, 1970) has consistently contended that long-term memory is equal between retarded and nonretarded persons, although his attention to this area has been secondary to his major research on short-term memory. Other research has indicated that long-term memory performance is inferior for retarded persons (Drew & Prehm, 1970; Logan, Prehm, & Drew, 1968). Probably the best summary of the status of long-term memory research with mentally retarded individuals was provided by Belmont (1966). Although improvements have been evident since 1966, Belmont's serious criticisms are essentially still appropriate concerning the lack of sophistication of research methods. Thus he noted that, because of the primitive research methods, there is almost no solid evidence either to support or to contradict a retarded person's long-term memory deficit. Smith (1968) suggested that to ensure retention in long-term learning situations, we should provide retarded individuals with opportunities to overlearn material beyond criterion level and also to have ample opportunity to use the learned material.

As is evident from the preceding discussion, a substantial portion of the memory research with retarded children has been couched in terms of short-term and long-term memory. Much of the current thinking in cognitive psychology has moved away from a simple view focusing on memory time interval toward an information processing model. Linton (1980) described information processing in the following manner:

> These (current) theories focus on the successive processing steps that information entering an organism undergoes. As you read the words on this page, for example, you are acting as an information processor. Words are perceived and attended to, patterns are recognized, meanings are accessed/retrieved, and some material is stored. Throughout such normal processing, information must be stored, sometimes only for a few moments (so that further processing can occur) and sometimes relatively permanently. (pp. 105–106)

Bray (1979) reviewed research on mentally retarded individuals in the context of an information processing framework. He found that much of the cognitive research in mental retardation has been conceptualized in an information-processing perspective despite the fact that early investigators were working without the benefit of such a model in a formalized sense. Future research on the memory functions in mentally retarded individuals will probably be pursued more directly in the context of information processing.

Distribution of Practice

Core Concept 6   Distributed practice in a learning situation enhances the learning performance of retarded children.

Whereas many nonretarded individuals appear to be able to function well by using massed practice, such as cramming for examinations, the literature suggests that distributed practice enhances the learning performance of retarded children more than does mass practice, and to a greater extent than it does for normal individuals (Madsen, 1963). Thus the teacher should provide the retarded child with short but frequent practice sessions on day-to-day tasks. Additionally, the teacher should allow for practice in a variety of situations and contexts and allow for the meaningful introduction of overlearning. This should result in both an increased rate of acquisition and a greater degree of retention.

Learning Concrete and Abstract Concepts

Core Concept 7   Mentally retarded children are able to grasp concrete and meaningful concepts in a learning situation much better than they grasp abstract concepts.

The more meaningful and concrete the material, the more apt the retarded child is to learn. The teacher or parent may be advised to teach nothing with inanimate objects if the real, living object is available. Likewise it might be said figuratively that we should teach nothing indoors if we can teach the same thing outdoors; the retarded child will grasp concepts more readily if the real object is present rather than a picture of the object. Rather than reading and looking at pictures of fire fighters and their equipment, the retarded child may learn faster and to a greater extent if taken on a field trip to a fire station.

Learning Sets and Transfer of Training

Core Concept 8   Mentally retarded children develop learning sets at a slower rate than their nonretarded peers.

Learning set and transfer of training appear to be interrelated in a person's ability to solve problems. Whereas learning set refers to an individual's ability to learn how to learn, transfer is generally regarded as the ability to apply learned responses and experiences from previous problems to new problems with similar components. Mentally retarded children develop learning sets at a slower rate than nonretarded children of comparable chronological age (Stevenson, 1972), but the formation of learning sets can be facilitated in the classroom setting. Payne, Polloway, Smith, and Payne (1981) provided the following suggestions:

1. Prevent the development of failure sets that interfere with learning by providing for success experiences
2. Present content to be learned in easy-to-hard progressions
3. Present factual and conceptual information in sequence
4. Assist the child in developing rules and generalizations (mediation strategies) to transfer learned information to new experiences
5. Reinforce correct responses to stress successful experiences (p. 29)

Although transfer of training is an essential component in human learning, there is a paucity of research about transfer as it relates to persons with mental retardation. The evidence that does exist suggests that for the mildly retarded child the ability to transfer is not significantly impaired (Evans & Bilsky, 1979), but children who are moderately to profoundly retarded will exhibit deficiencies in this area (Stephens, 1972). The following are some suggestions for working with the mentally retarded child who is deficient in the development of generalization skills:

1. Age seems to make a difference in the ability to transfer learning for both retarded and nonretarded individuals. Younger children transfer learning with greater ease than do older children.
2. Research also suggests that the retarded individual can transfer learning best when both the initial task and the transfer task are very similar. Transfer is most effective if a considerable number of the operations involved in the first task can be performed as a unit in the transfer task.
3. Meaningfulness seems extremely important to the retarded person's ability to transfer, with a more meaningful task being easier to learn initially as well as to transfer to a second setting.

4. Retarded individuals seem to be able to transfer learning more effectively if instructions are more general rather than detailed and specific. This seems to be an opposite trend to that found with nonretarded children, who perform better if more detail is involved.

These suggestions have several implications for working with the retarded child in an educational setting. Initially it appears that transfer of training ought to be an important consideration in planning a retarded child's early learning. Often such consideration is left unattended until quite late in the curriculum (e.g., vocational training). It seems that transfer of learning by retarded children will be most effective if the initial learning problem is a simulation of the transfer task. This appears to be an important point when one is involved in planning the activities and designing the materials to be used in educating retarded children.

Since meaningfulness seems so important to both the effective learning and transfer of material, this area must receive particular attention by the person working with retarded children. Often the meaning of a given activity is not readily evident, and children may then encounter more difficulty than would be the case if they were aware of how the task will help them. The teacher and others working with retarded children may find both learning and transfer facilitated if they make special effort to show children how the task will be relevant to their later performance, to their lives, or even to current interests. This must be done carefully, however, to avoid the explanation becoming too long and detailed. If verbal instructions become too detailed or laboriously specific, the retarded child encounters greater difficulty in transferring learning. Thus the person working with the retarded child must be clinically sensitive to finding the most effective level of detail.

Educational Achievement

Core Concept 9   Most mentally retarded children will benefit from instruction in the basic academic tool subjects.

Mildly retarded children require an extremely systematic instructional program that accounts for differences in the rate of learning, but they may achieve as high as fourth or fifth grade level in reading and arithmetic. However, research on reading achievement for mildly retarded learners indicates that they will develop poor reading mechanics and comprehension when compared with the norm. Most mildly retarded children read below their mental age (Carter, 1975).

A significant relationship appears to exist between measured IQ and reading achievement (Carter, 1975). This seems to suggest that reading instruction be limited to only higher functioning retarded children. However, a growing body of research indicates moderately and severely retarded individuals can be taught to read at least a protective, or survival, vocabulary (Snell, 1983). Kirk (1972) suggested that the ability of moderately retarded children is "limited to reading and recognizing their names, isolated words and phrases, common words used for their protection, such as 'danger,' 'stop,' 'men,' 'women,' and other signs which they encounter in the community" (p. 231).

Mentally retarded children are also deficient in arithmetic skills, but the performance of mildly retarded children on computation tasks is more consistent with their mental age (Whorton & Algozzine, 1978). Frank and McFarland (1980) indicated that arithmetic skills are most efficiently taught through the use of money concepts. The immediate practical application is motivating to the student. Regardless of the approach used, arithmetic instruction must be concrete and practical to compensate for the child's deficiencies in reasoning ability.

ADAPTIVE BEHAVIOR

Core Concept 10   Adaptive behavior deficiencies in school settings are associated with coping behavior, social skills, language development, emotional development, self-care, and applied cognitive and academic skills.

For educational purposes, adaptive behavior for the elementary age child is defined as the ability to apply the basic academic skills learned in school to daily activities. A child must also develop appropriate reasoning, judgment, and social skills that promote the development of positive interpersonal relationships. The State of Iowa Department of Public Instruction (1981) provided some excellent examples of in-school adaptive behavior deficiencies that may be associated with mental retardation:

1. *Lack of school coping behaviors* related to attention to learning tasks, organizational skills, questioning behavior, following directions, maintaining school supplies, and monitoring time use.
2. *Poor social skills* as related to working cooperatively with peers, social perceptions, response to social cues, use of socially acceptable language, and acceptable response to teacher.
3. *Poor language skills* as related to the ability to understand directions, communicate needs, express ideas, listen attentively, and voice modulation.

Maintaining personal belongings is an important part of adaptive behavior.

4. *Poor emotional development* related to avoidance of school work and social experiences as exemplified by tardiness, chronic complaints of illness, sustained or frequent idleness, aggressiveness under stress, classroom disruption, and social withdrawal.
5. *Poor self-care skills* related to personal hygiene, dress, maintaining personal belongings, and mobility in and about the school.
6. *Limited success in applied cognitive skills* related to initiating age-appropriate tasks, solving non-academic problems, drawing conclusions from experience, and planning activities.
7. *Delayed academic development* related to ability to form letters, blend letter sounds, recall content from reading and listening, make mathematical computations, and repeat information in a logical sequence. (pp. 15–16)

Each of the above areas contributes to a child's adaptation (or maladaptation) within the school setting. In the following section we will examine further the area of emotional development.

PERSONALITY AND EMOTIONAL DEVELOPMENT

Core Concept 11   A mentally retarded child's problems in school-related settings are often compounded by inadequate social development.

When mentally retarded children enter school, they are confronted with an environment that often tends to magnify their intellectual differences. This situation is compounded for mildly retarded children, who, before the beginning of school, may be unaware that they are different. Intellectually inadequate and academically unsophisticated, many of these children fail to adjust to the academic world. Their academic problems are compounded by social development that is commensurate with their mental age but not with their chronological age. Thus many find rejection on two fronts—from the teacher frustrated with their academic limitations and from their normal peers frustrated with their social inadequacies. Failing in their efforts and sensing rejection, retarded children are very susceptible to emotional problems.

There appears to be little disagreement with the notion that there is a higher incidence of emotional problems among retarded persons than among the general population. As much as 40 percent of retarded people may have emotional or personality deviations, compared with about 20 percent for the nonretarded population. It appears, however, that the emotional difficulties of the majority of retarded individuals are milder and more transient in nature than are those of the nonretarded (Beier, 1964; Menolascino & Egger, 1978).

Maladaptive behaviors may also be characteristic of moderately and severely retarded children. These behaviors include head rolling, body rocking, twirling, teeth grinding, and inappropriate vocalizations. Garrard and Richmond (1975) reported that some severely retarded children may also engage in self-injurious acts such as self-biting, head banging, and face slapping.

Several explanations have been offered for a higher frequency of emotional problems among retarded children. Retarded children may be subject to greater stress, frustration, and conflict as a result of their intellectual deficiencies. Beier (1964) stated that the most frequently mentioned problems appear to concern either rejection or overprotection. Many parents consider their children to be an extension of themselves. When a child falls short of parental expectations, as do the mentally retarded, the situation may be too ego-damaging for the parents to cope. When a retarded child is born into a family with intellectually limited parents, there may be little if any reaction. If, however, the child is born into other situations, parents may meet the feelings of frustration and failure either by rejecting the child or by developing strong feelings of guilt that may lead them to overprotection.

Retarded children often become dependent on other individuals for survival. They may have little control of the environment and, consequently, they may have difficulty in finding and preserving their identity and integrity. Many retarded children become frustrated and choose to resist. By doing so, they create problems for themselves and others. Sensing futility, they may become passive and submissive. Feelings of shame and guilt associated with consistent failures are often coupled with frustration and hopelessness.

The retarded individual's emotional adjustment may be to a great extent a function of the public attitude toward retarded children. It has been well documented that nonretarded children hold negative attitudes toward their retarded peers (Siperstein & Bak, 1985). However, in a questionnaire administered to 430 adults regarding their attitudes toward retarded children, Gotlieb and Corman (1975) found some revealing attitudes. While 88 percent of the respondents expressed an accepting attitude toward retarded children, agreeing that parents should allow their normal children to play with a mentally retarded child, this acceptance was not accompanied by equally strong support for integrated educational placement. Only 37 percent agreed that retarded children would learn more if they were integrated into regular classes. Older respondents, parents of school age children, and people with no previous contact with retarded persons tended to favor segregation of retarded children in the community. Peterson (1975) investigated the attitudes of nonretarded children toward their mildly retarded peers and found that subjects who had contact with mildly retarded children had more favorable attitudes toward them than did those who had no such contact. Older subjects had more favorable attitudes toward younger subjects, and subjects whose parents had attained higher levels of education had more negative attitudes. These studies suggest that the development of more positive attitudes is essential for acceptance of retarded children and for the development of the retarded child's individual self-concept. Two investigations (Gresham, 1982; Siperstein & Bak, 1985) suggested that the social behavior of handicapped children can be improved if they are directly taught social skills prior to, as well as during, integration into the regular classroom.

Motivational Problems

Core Concept 12	Mentally retarded individuals are able to participate, and be actively involved, in their own local communities.

Individuals with normal intelligence will excel in nearly all dimensions of human behavior when compared with mentally retarded children. However, there is remarkable evidence of retarded individuals' ability to achieve. When motivated and producing at optimal levels, many retarded people are able to be competitively employed and become useful and integral parts of society.

With a goal of useful, integrated functioning in mind, many parents and professionals have sought to bring about maximum realization of the potential within retarded individuals. Maslow (1954) emphasized the natural and sequential development of the individual through basic stages of needs until he or she progresses to higher levels of motives and organization. The eventual goal for the individual is self-actualization, which reflects the developmental stage of maximum potential. Typically, limited numbers of individuals are thought to have reached self-actualization. Individuals such as Albert Schweitzer, humanitarian, physician, theologian, and accomplished musician, and Leonardo da Vinci, artist and inventor, are sometimes mentioned as possibly having been self-actualized individuals.

Kolstoe and Frey (1965) have discussed the possibility of self-actualization among retarded individuals, but only after they have progressed through the basic stages of needs. Maslow (1954) conceived of the five levels of needs arranged in a sequence from lower needs to higher needs:

1. Physiological needs (for example, to satisfy hunger and thirst)
2. Safety needs (for example, to maintain security, order, and stability)
3. Belongingness and love needs (for example, to receive affection and identification)
4. Esteem needs (for example, to experience prestige, success, and self-respect)
5. Self-actualization needs

The prepotency of needs has important implications for parents and professionals (such as the special education teacher or rehabilitation counselor) who work with retarded persons. The retarded child of elementary school age may have very real physiological needs. Some may come to school with severe nutritional deficiencies such as improper diet or insufficient amount of food. They can come hungry because of lack of food, tired because of lack of sleep and rest, cold because of lack of adequate clothing, or in physical discomfort because of lack of medical or dental attention. The observant teacher can identify these problems and make sure that proper attention is given to them. A bowl of milk and cereal before the start of school may be sufficient to turn the child's mind away from a growling stomach to a math lesson. Likewise, providing for a child's clothing and medical and dental needs can change his or her perceptions of what is immediately important. P. L. Chinn (1973) found a relationship between health problems and academic and social problems in the classroom.

The professional can provide for many of the safety needs of a retarded child. If the teacher notices that the child has been physically abused, this should be reported immediately to the proper authorities. Some schools may be justly criticized for their rigidity, but others may provide the order and stability that possibly are lacking in the homes of some children. The security of knowing that for 5 days a week he or she can expect a warm meal during the noon hour and a certain amount of order within the day may be vital to the life and development of a retarded child.

Nearly every child wants to be identified in a special way with someone or something. Except in unusual circumstances, most children need affection and a sense of belonging to a group or to an individual. For retarded children lacking in social skills, this need may be difficult to fulfill. The special education teacher can sometimes facilitate group acceptance; even if this cannot be accomplished immediately, teachers can provide a sense of belonging if they can accept children as they are, as individuals worthy of concern and affection.

The retarded child may never progress beyond needing a sense of belonging and love. Prestige, success, and self-respect, which fulfill esteem needs, may be formidable goals for these individuals. If the parent and professional will look hard enough, somewhere buried amidst all the disabilities of the most lacking child in the classroom they will find some hidden ability to do something as well as, if not better than, the rest of the children in the class. By capitalizing on this ability and drawing attention to it, they may be able to help the child attain the respect of peers in the classroom. Even if this cannot be achieved, the self-respect that comes with worthy accomplishment may suffice to meet this basic need.

When the first four basic needs have been met, retarded persons may then look toward the final goal of self-actualization. Although they may never be able to match the accomplishment of their normal peers, retarded individuals may find considerable satisfaction and contentment in being the best at whatever they are capable of doing, being well liked by their peers, and contributing to a better life for themselves and their families.

PHYSICAL AND HEALTH CHARACTERISTICS

Physical Differences

Core Concept 13	The more severe the mental retardation, the greater the probability that the child will exhibit corresponding physical problems.

The vast majority of mentally retarded children do not differ from nonretarded children in their physical appearance. However, there is a positive correlation between severity of intellectual deficit and degree of physical anomalies (Hardman & Drew, 1977). With more severe mental retardation, there is a greater probability that the child will exhibit physical problems. Among mildly retarded children, there may be no noticeable differences because the retardation is not usually associated with genetic factors. For more severely involved children, physical differences are more evident and may be traced to biomedical conditions (e.g., Down syndrome, hydrocephaly).

Motor development of mentally retarded children may be significantly below the norms of nonretarded children. Rarick and Dobbins (1972) indicated that these differences are not as evident if the comparison is limited to mildly retarded and nonretarded children. However, Bruininks (1974) reviewed studies on motor performance of mildly retarded children and concluded that these children were inferior on measures such as equilibrium, locomotion, and manual dexterity. A study by Bruininks (1977) confirmed that physiological development is associated with severity of retardation. Bruininks found that nonretarded children were superior to both mildly and moderately retarded children on motor skill proficiency, and the performance of moderately retarded children was inferior to that of the more mildly retarded group. Bunker (1977) indicated that moderately and severely retarded children exhibit significant delays in several areas of motor skill development:

> Problems in body management skills may include general body awareness, mobility, the development of spatial concepts, an awareness of body postures, and control of body actions, body image, and self-help skills. . . . In addition to these basic skills, these children may also have difficulty with efficient locomotor patterns, such as skipping, hopping, and jumping and with both gross and fine motor manipulative skills such as writing, drawing, throwing, striking, kicking, and catching. (p. 181)

Francis and Rarick (1960) suggested that mental retardation need not cause motor retardation. Motor deficiencies among retarded persons may be more a function of deprivation in learning and practice opportunities than of the retardation.

Two investigations conducted in the 1960s suggested that mentally retarded individuals are generally deficient in height and weight when compared with nonretarded children (Fishler, Share, & Koch, 1964; Mossier, Grossman, & Dingman, 1965). Research studies have also suggested a higher prevalence of vision and hearing impairments among mentally retarded children (Bensberg & Siegelman, 1976; Lloyd, 1970). Speech problems are also more prevalent among retarded children (Fawcus & Fawcus, 1974). Fink (1981), in a survey of Oregon service providers, reported severe speech delays in nearly 90 percent of 1,700 moderately retarded children. Most severely and profoundly retarded children have multiple handicaps, exhibiting deficits in nearly every aspect of cognitive and physical development.

Health Differences

Core Concept 14   Several environmental factors may contribute to health problems for children with mental retardation.

There is a positive correlation between low socioeconomic status and mental retardation, particularly mild mental retardation. This means that retarded children may be subjected to conditions that contribute to their deficiencies; such conditions may include poor nutrition, inadequate sanitation, and greater susceptibility to infections. Families from low socioeconomic backgrounds must often depend on governmentally supported medical care. For others, health services may be minimal or nonexistent. During the school years, these conditions can result in more illness and, consequently, absence from school.

Health and sanitation problems are often difficult to overcome. Retarded children may exist in a way of life that is accepted by their parents, members of a particular subculture. The parents may feel little, if any, need to change their life-style. Refinements in health delivery services to make medical and nursing services more readily accessible are necessary. This should include not only services to expectant mothers and to the ill, but also preventive medicine and educational services available from both public health and social service workers. The remediation of substandard housing, which promotes health hazards, needs priority consideration as one of the more popular and publicized social issues. Unfortunately, the needs of a minority population do not often coincide with social conscience and adequate funds. Professionals must therefore teach retarded children to protect themselves from potential hazards and to become resourceful enough to find the best medical services available.

ALTERNATIVES FOR EDUCATIONAL PLACEMENT

Core Concept 15   The national mandate for the education of handicapped children clearly indicates placement in the least restrictive environment.

Special education for mentally retarded children historically has meant segregated education. Before the 1960s, the vast majority of special education services available were administered in self-contained classrooms that completely segregated the retarded child from nonretarded peers. Additionally, these special education services were available primarily to the more mildly retarded child who was defined as "educable," a term which implied that, although the child was retarded, he or she could still benefit from some of the traditional academic curricula taught in the public schools. Children functioning at lower levels (as determined by IQ tests) were generally excluded from public schools, because they required "training" in such areas as self-help, language development, gross motor skills, and academic readiness. The needs of "trainable" mentally retarded children were not within the purview of the public education curriculum. For more severely retarded children, exclusion from the public schools was automatic. These children needed habilitation, not education. Severely and profoundly retarded children were often labeled as "custodial," an obvious implication of a minimal functioning level.

The passage of the Education for All Handicapped Children Act (Public Law 94–142) in 1975 was the culmination of years of litigation dealing with the discrimination against handicapped children in this nation's schools. (Public Law 94–142 is discussed in detail in chapter 13.) This law mandates that handicapped children must be educated in the "least restrictive environment" (LRE). The LRE concept mandates that the educational experience must meet the developmental needs of all retarded children regardless of severity. Deno (1970) envisioned a continuum to meet these needs even before LRE became national policy (Fig. 8–1). Deno's cascade of educational services ranged from integration in a regular classroom setting with no support to segregation in a special school facility.

Levels I through III of the cascade involve integration, or "mainstreaming," of retarded children with their nonretarded age-mates. Mainstreaming does not merely imply placement in regular classrooms or spending time with handicapped peers. Mainstreaming refers to the following (Kaufman, Gotlieb, Agard, & Kukic, 1975):

> [The] temporal, instructional, and social integration of eligible exceptional children with normal peers based on an ongoing, individually determined educational planning and programming process and requires clarification of responsibility among regular and special education administrative, instructional, and supportive personnel. (pp. 40–41)

Some advocates and professionals have emphasized integration, even the total integration of moderately and severely retarded students into regular education classrooms.

Properly placed retarded students in mainstreamed situations profit from such experiences (Brinker, 1985; Stainback & Stainback, 1985). Budoff and Gottlieb (1976) compared a group of special-class mildly retarded children who were assigned randomly to regular classes with a group who were retained in special classes. They found that after one school year the main-

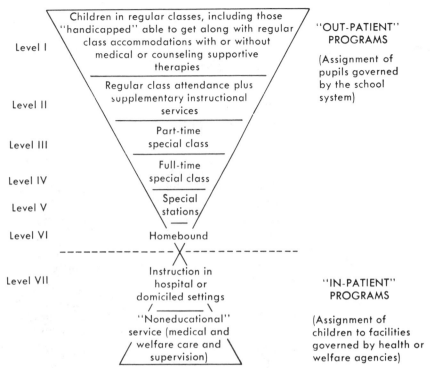

Figure 8–1. The Cascade System of Special Education Service. The tapered design indicates the considerable difference in the numbers involved at the different levels and calls attention to the fact that the system serves as a diagnostic filter. The most specialized facilities are likely to be needed by the fewest children on a long-term basis. This organizational model can be applied to development of special education services for all types of disability. From "Special education as developmental capital" by E. Deno, 1970, *Exceptional Children, 37,* pp. 229–337. Copyright 1970 by the Council for Exceptional Children. Reprinted by permission.

streamed students were more internally controlled, expressed more positive attitudes toward school and themselves, believed others perceived them as more competent, and were more reflective in their behavior than were the students assigned to a special class. McEvoy, Nordquist, and Cunningham (1984) emphasized, however, that if mainstreaming is to be successful regular classroom teachers may require extensive training and experience in assessing the behavioral characteristics of retarded children.

We now turn our attention to some of the alternative placements available to mentally retarded children in our public schools. In this section we will discuss regular classroom placement with support services, the special education classroom in the regular school, and the special day school for mentally retarded students.

Regular Class Placement with Support Services

Core Concept 16	Regular class placement with support services includes both the consulting teacher and resource room models.

As depicted in Figure 8–1, placement at level I means that the student remains in the regular classroom with minimal or no support services. The regular classroom teacher is responsible for any adaptation that may be necessary for the student's success in this environment. Consequently, this teacher must have the skills to develop and adapt curricula to meet individual needs.

Since regular teachers are an integral part of a successful educational experience for the retarded child, it is important that they receive expanded university preparation in the education of handicapped children. This premise has been supported by the National Council for the Accreditation of Teacher Education (NCATE) and the National Advisory Council on Education Professions Development. Necessary skills for the regular classroom teacher include an understanding of how a handicapping condition can affect the ability to learn academic skills or to adapt in social situations. The teacher must also be able to recognize a learning or behavior problem and seek out appropriate resources within the school to facilitate the implementation of an appropriate individualized program. School districts also have a responsibility to the teacher and the child. Appropriate resources and support personnel must be available to assist the teacher, and time must be set aside for planning and coordinating activities for the child.

A student placed at level II in the cascade of services will either remain in the regular classroom for the entire school day and also receive consultive services or will go to a special education resource room for a portion of the instructional programming. Both of these service models require collaboration between regular classroom teachers and other consulting professionals. Services may range from assisting a teacher in the use of tests or modification of curriculum to directly instructing students in the classroom. The regular classroom teacher must be able to participate as a member of a multidisciplinary team involved in planning appropriate educational services for the child. This team may include special educators, communication specialists, occupational or physical therapists, school psychologists, social workers, physical education specialists, and the child's parents.

The Consulting Teacher. The consulting teacher (sometimes referred to as a curriculum specialist, itinerant teacher, or master teacher) provides assistance to the regular classroom teacher or the child while the child remains in the regular classroom. This specialist may help a teacher to identify specific problem areas for the child and recommend appropriate assessment techniques and educational strategies. Reynolds and Birch (1982) suggested that there are several positive features of a consulting teacher service. Regular classroom teachers are trained and supported in their own backyard while the emphasis is on adapting the classroom environment to the needs of the retarded child. However, if the child requires more support than can be provided through a consultant model, a more restricted setting such as a resource room may be necessary.

The Resource Room. The resource room also reflects a philosophy of sharing of responsibility between regular education and special education for the retarded children in a particular school. This program reflects an effort to integrate children as much as possible into regular education and still provide them with special education support services when they are needed. The child is able to remain with nonretarded age-mates for the majority of the school day, which removes a great deal of the stigma associated with separate full-day special education classrooms (Jenkins & Mayhall, 1973).

In the resource room program, retarded children are assigned to a regular education teacher in elementary grades or to a regular education homeroom teacher in the upper grades. These children are primarily in regular education and will participate in as many regularly scheduled activities as possible. Assignments, possibly with modifications, will approximate those of all other children. At designated times arranged between the two teachers, the children in resource programs meet with the special education resource teacher.

The resource teacher maintains a room within the school building and is a regular member of the school faculty. The special education teacher's function is essentially twofold. The first responsibility is to provide instructional support services to the handicapped child. These services may include orientation to the school for new students, tutorial services, counseling, and the development of instructional aids if needed. A second major function for the resource room teacher is to serve as a liaison between the regular classroom teacher and the child. It is the responsibility of the resource room teacher to facilitate understanding between regular class teachers and the retarded child, to aid regular class teachers in understanding the needs and nature of retarded children, and to support the retarded child both academically and in areas of personal and social adjustment.

The Special Education Classroom in the Regular School

Core Concept 17 Mentally retarded students may be educated in either part-time or full-time special education classrooms in the regular school building.

Part-Time Special Class. The part-time special class approach involves the sharing of responsibility for the retarded child by both the regular and special education teacher. The major difference between a part-time special class and a resource room rests in the area of primary responsibility. In the resource room situation the retarded child is a regular class student most of the time, having support services from special education. In the part-time special class the students are assigned to a special education teacher and class, remaining in the same room with the same teacher for a large portion of the day. During the remainder of the day these students are integrated into as many regular education activities as possible. In most instances the retarded child remains in the special classroom for the academically oriented subjects. The integrated classes are typically less academically oriented, including subjects such as music, shop, home economics, physical education, and art. If the part-time special class functions as planned, a student will have the advantage of an unthreatening academic setting along with integration into the social mainstream. It should be noted that in some school districts, programs referred to as resource rooms actually function as part-time special classes as we have described them.

Full-Time Special Class. A traditional approach to providing educational services to mildly retarded children is the full-time special class in the neighborhood school. This approach has also been used more recently for both moderately and severely retarded children. The full-time special class has been criticized because it totally segregates students from their non-retarded age- mates, but it also has had its share of supporters. Some research in the 1950s indicated that social adjustment for the retarded children in full-time special education classrooms may exceed that of retarded children in regular education classes, although there may be no differences in academic performance between the two groups (Cassidy & Stanton, 1959). There are indications that retarded children in special classes have less fear of failure than retarded children in regular grades (Jordan & deCharms, 1959). It has also been suggested that children in special classes have a greater opportunity to excel and to become a "star" (Baldwin, 1958). Proponents will also argue that the self- contained class has a teacher who is thoroughly prepared and fully understands the needs and nature of retarded children.

The Special School

Core Concept 18   Special schools, although administratively convenient, do not provide critical opportunities for interaction between retarded children and their nonretarded peers.

Many classes for moderately and severely retarded children are located in special schools exclusively for handicapped children. Proponents of this arrangement argue that special schools provide services for large numbers of retarded children and therefore provide greater homogeneity in the grouping and programming for children. They also support this type of arrangement because it allows teachers to specialize in their teaching areas. For example, one individual might decide to specialize in art for the retarded, another in physical education, and a third in music. In smaller programs in which there are only one or two teachers, these individuals may be required to teach everything from art and home economics to academic subjects.

Special schools also provide for the centralization of supplies, equipment, and special facilities for the retarded. Smaller isolated programs may not be able to justify the purchase of expensive equipment used only occasionally, but the special school may be able to justify the expenditure because of more frequent use by a larger number of classes.

Research studies on the efficacy of special schools do not support the above rationale. Several authors (Brinker, 1985; Stainback & Stainback, 1985; Wehman & Hill, 1982; Wilcox & Bellamy, 1982) contend that, regardless of the severity of their handicapping condition, children with mental retardation definitely benefit from placement in a regular education facility where "opportunities for integration with nonhandicapped peers are systematically planned and implemented (Hardman, Drew, & Egan, 1987, p. 89). Several studies have indicated that educational outcomes for students in an integrated setting are significantly improved (Pumpian et al., 1980; Schutz, Williams, Iverson & Duncan, 1984; Ziegler & Hambleton, 1976). Additionally, in appropriately implemented integrated services, there have been no substantiated detrimental outcomes for students with severe handicaps (Guralnick, 1978; Schutz et al., 1984; Stainback & Stainback, 1981). Systematically planned interactions between severely handicapped and nonhandicapped peers yield improved attitudes and interaction patterns (Schutz et al., 1984; Stainback & Stainback, 1981; Voeltz, 1982). Finally, integrated services can provide equal or superior quality educational opportunities at a lower cost (Fink, 1979; U.S. Office of Education, 1985).

The courts (Armstrong v. Kline, 1980; Campbell v. Talladega County Board of Education, 1981; Roncker v. Walters, 1983; Fialkowski v. Shapp, 1975) have also affirmed the application of the least restrictive environment clause of P.L. 94–142 to students with severe handicaps. Specifically, severely handicapped students are to be educated to the maximum extent possible with their nonhandicapped peers, which includes attending regular school buildings, unless extenuating individual circumstances preclude this as an appropriate placement decision (Rostetter, Kowalski, & Hunter, 1984).

Critics argue that although administratively convenient to operate, special schools deprive retarded children of many of their basic rights. First, these schools are quickly identified as being different and exclusively for retarded children. Because of the stigma that is attached to such schools, both the children and their parents may suffer. Critics also argue that the real world of society is not naturally segregated, and special schools remove children from the mainstream of society and education, depriving them of valuable experiences with nonretarded peers.

It should be noted that physical proximity (locating a class for severely retarded children in a regular education school) does not necessarily lead to integration. The integration of these students will require a systematic effort on the part of all school personnel. What level of integration is possible for severely retarded students? Stainback and Stainback (1982) suggested that these students can be integrated for several kinds of activities, including the following:

> Homeroom, art, music, recess, Thanksgiving and birthday parties, show and tell times, and rest periods. Nonhandicapped students could be encouraged to visit the special education classroom to work as tutors or simply to spend a little time with a severely retarded friend. In addition, teachers can facilitate interactions between nonhandicapped and severely retarded students in the school cafeteria, at assembly programs, in the hallways, and at the bus loading and unloading zones. (p. 88)

These authors also reported that prospective elementary education teachers who had the opportunity to interact with severely retarded children, in contrast to those teachers who did not have such an opportunity, were not fearful of or intimidated by their presence.

INSTRUCTIONAL APPROACHES

Core Concept 19   For students with mental retardation, learning in the school setting is a continual process of adaptation.

Mentally retarded students can and will learn if provided with an appropriate instructional program and a teaching process that is oriented to their individual needs. The Individualized Education Program (IEP) includes an assessment of the child's current level of educational performance, statement of prioritized annual goals, short-term objectives, specification of educational services necessary to accomplish goals and objectives, and timelines for the implementation of services. The specific course of study, based on annual goals, is a critical factor in the implementation of an appropriate educational program. However, the selection of curricula for retarded learners has been a problem for educators because of the heterogeneous needs of these students. Since retarded learners do not learn as quickly or as effectively as their nonretarded age-mates, the traditional approach to teaching basic academic skills may not be appropriate for these students. For the moderately and severely retarded, academic skills such as reading, writing, and arithmetic may not be a priority. Given the limited instructional time available in the schools, the course of study for these children may necessarily be oriented more toward adaptive living skills. In the following section, instructional approaches for retarded children that emphasize the acquisition of both academic and adaptive skills will be discussed.

Teaching Academic Skills

Core Concept 20   Instruction in the academic areas may include both a "foundation" and a "functional" approach to learning.

The primary instructional approach in the public schools emphasizes learning of "foundation" skills in the basic academic areas. For example, reading is learned as a set of sequenced skills that can be divided into three phases: (1) the development of readiness skills (e.g., left-to-right sequencing, visual and auditory discrimination skills, and memory skills), (2) word recognition or decoding skills (breaking the code and correctly identifying the abstract symbols in sequence), and (3) reading comprehension (giving symbols meaning). Each step in the process is a prerequisite for the next, so that a foundation is laid for higher levels of functioning. However, the retarded learner may not efficiently acquire the necessary prerequisites within the time frame prescribed by the schools. For many children with mental retardation, having more time to learn the skills may be all that is necessary for an instructional approach to be effective. For others, the investment of time and energy may be better directed toward areas such as self-care, mobility, or communication (Hirshoren & Burton, 1979).

Another approach to learning academic skills, often termed "functional," is consistent with an adaptive learning curriculum. In this approach the basic academic tools are taught only in the context of daily living activities. A functional life program in the area of reading would primarily focus on only those words that facilitate adaptation in the child's environment, such as:

A Functional Reading Vocabulary

Go	Up	Dynamite	School
Slow down	Down	Explosives	School bus
Stop	Men	Fire	No trespassing
Off	Women	Fire escape	Private property
On	Exit	Poison	Men working
Cold	Entrance	Wet paint	Yield
Hot	Danger	Police	Railroad crossing
In	Be careful	Keep off	Boys
Out	Caution	Watch for children	Girls

Functional math skill development may relate more to environmental needs such as telling time or counting money. Whatever the academic area, a functional approach pairs the skill being taught with an environmental cue. Snell (1983) stressed that when attempting to "functionalize" learned skills the teacher must use instructional materials that are realistic. Traditional materials, such as workbooks, basic readers, flash cards, etc., are not practical because the student is unable to relate them to his or her world.

It should be noted that the curricular approaches discussed above are not necessarily mutually exclusive. A foundation approach can incorporate many functional elements to reduce the abstract nature of the academic subjects, which facilitates efficient learning for the mentally retarded student.

Teaching Adaptive Skills

Core Concept 21   Adaptive skills are necessary to decrease an individual's dependence on others and to increase opportunities for school and community participation.

The public schools, which excluded many retarded children for the better part of this century, are now faced with the challenge of providing an educational experience that is consistent with the developmental needs of these children. Educational programming has been expanded to include the learning of adaptive skills necessary to decrease an individual's dependence on others and to increase opportunities for school and community participation. The teaching of adaptive skills to retarded children is based on the premise that if these skills are not taught through formal instruction, they will not be learned. For children who are not mentally retarded, the teaching of these skills is unnecessary because they are acquired through daily experiences.

Adaptive skill content areas for elementary age retarded children include motor, self-care, social, communication, and functional academic skills. The development of gross and fine motor skills is a prerequisite to successful learning in other adaptive areas. Gross motor skills development relates to general mobility such as balance and locomotor patterns and includes neck and head control, rolling, body righting, sitting, creeping, crawling, standing, walking, running, jumping, and skipping. Fine motor training includes learning to reach for, grasp, and manipulate objects. Motor development requires that the child be able to visually "fix" on an object and "track" a moving target (Mori & Masters, 1980). The coordination of fine motor skills and visual tracking (eye-hand coordination) is a prerequisite to object control skills that are required in vocational situations and is a basis for learning leisure time activities.

Self-care skills are essential to the independence of the retarded child in the home and school setting. The primary self-care areas are feeding, dressing, and personal hygiene. Feeding skills include learning to finger feed, use proper utensils, drink from a cup, and serve food. An example of a sequence for teaching feedings skills may be found in the analysis by Barnard and Powell (1972, pp. 97–98) of the 18 steps for proper use of a spoon.

1. Orients to food by looking at it.
2. Looks at spoon.
3. Reaches for spoon.
4. Touches spoon.
5. Grasps spoon.
6. Lifts spoon.
7. Delivers spoon to bowl.
8. Lowers spoon into food.
9. Scoops food into spoon.
10. Lifts spoon.
11. Delivers spoon to mouth.
12. Opens mouth.
13. Inserts spoon into mouth.
14. Moves tongue and mouth to receive food.
15. Closes lips, removes spoon.
16. Chews food.
17. Swallows food.
18. Returns spoon to bowl.

Dressing skills involve learning to button, zip, buckle, lace, and tie. A test of dressing skill development is found in Figure 8–2. Personal hygiene skills include toileting, washing face and hands, bathing, toothbrushing, and shampooing and combing hair.

Instruction in social skills applies many of the self-care areas to the development of positive interpersonal relationships. Social skill training stresses appropriate physical appearance, etiquette, use of leisure time, and sexual behavior. Communication is closely related to social skill development, because without communication there is no social interaction. The communication may be verbal or manual (e.g., sign language or language boards), but the important factor is that some form of communication must be present.

EDUCATING THE CULTURALLY DIFFERENT RETARDED CHILD

Core Concept 22   Culturally different children who are mentally retarded need an educational experience that focuses on their learning how to learn.

Child's name: Date: Pretest of dressing skills	Independent	Verbal assistance	Physical assistance	Description of method child uses to complete the test

Undressing trousers, skirt
  1. Pushes garment from waist to ankles
  2. Pushes garment off one leg
  3. Pushes garment off other leg				

Dressing trousers, skirt
  1. Lays trousers in front of self with
     front side up
  2. Inserts one foot into waist opening
  3. Inserts other foot into waist opening
  4. Pulls garment up to waist				

Undressing socks
  1. Pushes sock down off heel
  2. Pulls toe of sock pulling sock off foot				

Dressing socks
  1. Positions sock correctly with heel-side down
  2. Holds sock open at top
  3. Inserts toes into sock
  4. Pulls sock over heel
  5. Pulls sock up				

Undressing cardigan
  1. Takes dominant arm out of sleeve
  2. Gets coat off back
  3. Pulls other arm from sleeve				

Dressing cardigan flip-over method
  1. Lays garment on table or floor in front of self
  2. Gets dominant arm into sleeve
  3. Other arm into sleeve
  4. Positions coat on back				

Undressing polo shirt
  1. Takes dominant arm out of sleeve
  2. Pulls garment over head
  3. Pulls other arm from sleeve				

Dressing polo shirt
  1. Lays garment in front of self
  2. Opens bottom of garment and puts arm
     into sleeves
  3. Pulls garment over head
  4. Pulls garment down to waist				

Undressing shoes
  1. Loosens laces
  2. Pulls shoe off heel
  3. Pulls front of shoe to pull shoe off of toes				

Dressing shoes
  1. Prepares shoe by loosening laces and
     pulling tongue out of shoe out of the way
  2. Inserts toe into shoe
  3. Pushes shoe on over heel				

Figure 8–2. Pre-test of Dressing Skills

From *Occupational therapy for mentally retarded children* (p. 95) by M. Copeland, L. Ford, and N. Solon, 1976, Baltimore: University Park Press. Copyright 1976 by University Park Press. Reprinted by permission.

Because there are disproportionately large numbers of ethnic minority children in some classes for retarded children (P. C. Chinn & Kamp, 1982; Hurley, 1975), there is a critical demand for teachers who are sensitive to needs of these children. Bessant-Byrd (1981) indicated that teachers must develop an understanding of the philosophies of various cultures and be able to use classroom materials that are characteristic of differing life-styles. Hurley (1975) suggested that to meet the educational needs of culturally different retarded children the teacher needs to focus on teaching these children how to learn in addition to the usual memorization of facts and acquisition of basic skills. These children may have linguistic limitations both in their native language or dialect and in standard English. Thus reading material should be primarily experience oriented so that the child can draw from his or her own perceptions and experiences.

P. C. Chinn (1979) suggested several topics that should be considered in curriculum development for the culturally different child, including the value of education, ethnic studies, poverty, health, and cultural pluralism. Since about 800,000 minority children and youth drop out of school every year, the curriculum must convince these students that school is a positive social institution in which they are valued by teachers and age-mates. Ethnic studies should focus on the use and meaning of societal labels and on the image of culturally diverse people that is portrayed through the media. The curriculum for the culturally different retarded child living in a poverty situation should include instruction on available resources for food assistance and medical care. Given the limited financial resources of the family, effective use of money management and consumer skills must also be emphasized. Finally, classroom teachers must believe in and communicate the basic tenet that people in this society exist in a pluralistic culture that values the intrinsic worth of every individual.

Core Questions

1. Discuss Piaget's stages of development as they relate to children with mental retardation.
2. How do the memory capabilities of retarded children compare with those of their non-retarded peers?
3. Compare mass and distributed practice in relationship to the learning performance of children with mental retardation.
4. Discuss several suggestions for working with retarded children who are unable to adequately transfer learning from one situation to another.
5. What are some examples of in-school adaptive behavior deficiencies that may be exhibited by children with mental retardation?
6. Discuss possible explanations for the higher frequency of emotional problems associated with children who are mentally retarded.
7. Discuss the cascade of educational services for children with mental retardation.

8. Why are segregated educational environments criticized for failing to meet the educational needs of children with mental retardation?
9. Describe adaptive skill content areas for children with mental retardation.

ROUND TABLE DISCUSSION

This chapter has discussed several perspectives related to the education of retarded children in both integrated and segregated environments. We have also emphasized the need to provide for systematic and planned opportunities for interaction between retarded and non-retarded children if integration is to be successful.

In your study group or on your own, discuss the rationale for integrating retarded children into both regular school and regular classroom environments. Given support for the integration of retarded children in the regular school, discuss ideas for planning appropriate interactions, both in and out of the school, between retarded and non-retarded children.

REFERENCES

Armstrong v. Kline, 476 F. Supp. 583 (E.D. Pa. 1979), Aff's CA 78–0172 (3rd cir. July 15, 1980).

Baldwin, W. D. (1958). The social position of the educable mentally retarded in the regular grades in the public schools. *Exceptional Children, 25,* 106–108.

Barnard, K. E., & Powell, M. L. (1972). *Teaching the mentally retarded child: A family care approach.* St. Louis: Mosby.

Beier, D. C. (1964). Behavioral disturbances in the mentally retarded. In H. A. Stevens and R. Heber (Eds.), *Mental Retardation* (pp. 454–482). Chicago: University of Chicago.

Belmont, J. M. (1966). Long-term memory in mental retardation. *International Review of Research in Mental Retardation, 1,* 219–255.

Bensberg, G., & Siegelman, C. (1976). Definitions and prevalence. In L. Lloyd (Ed.), *Communication, assessment, and intervention strategies.* Baltimore: University Park.

Bessant-Byrd, H. (1981). Competencies for educating culturally different exceptional children. In J. N. Nazzaro (Ed.), *Culturally diverse exceptional children in school.* Reston, VA: ERIC Clearinghouse on Handicapped and Gifted Children.

Bray, N. W. (1979). Strategy production in the retarded. In N. R. Ellis (Ed.), *Handbook of mental deficiency, psychological theory and research* (2nd ed.) (pp. 699–726). Hillsdale, NJ: Erlbaum.

Brinker, R.P. (1985). Interactions between severely mentally retarded students and other students in integrated and segregated public school settings. *American Journal of Mental Deficiency, 89*(6), 587–594.

Brown, A. L. (1974). The role of strategic behavior in retardate memory. In N. R. Ellis (Ed.), *International review of research in mental retardation* (Vol. 7). New York: Academic Press.

Bruininks, R. H. (1974). Physical and motor development of retarded persons. In N. R. Ellis (Ed.), *International review of research in mental retardation* (Vol. 7). New York: Academic Press.

Bruininks, R. H. (1977). *Manual for Bruininks-Ostertsky Test of Motor Proficiency.* Circle Pines, MN: American Guidance Service.

Budoff, M., & Gottlieb, J. (1976). Special-class EMR children mainstreamed: A study of an aptitude (learning potential) X treatment interaction, *American Journal on Mental Deficiency, 81*(1), 1–11.

Bunker, L. K. (1978). Motor skills. In M. E. Snell (Ed.), *Systematic instruction of the moderately and severely handicapped.* Columbus, OH: Merrill.

Butterfield, E. C., Wambold, C., & Belmont, J. M. (1973). On the theory and practice of improving short-term memory. *American Journal of Mental Deficiency, 77,* 654–669.

Campbell v. Talladega Board of Education, U.S. District Court (1981).

Cantor, G. N., & Ryan, T. J. (1962). Retention of verbal paired-associates in normals and retardates. *American Journal of Mental Deficiency, 66,* 861–865.

Carter, J. L. (1975). Intelligence and reading achievement of EMR in three educational settings. *Mental Retardation, 13*(5), 26–27.

Cassidy, V. M., & Stanton, J. E. (1959). *An investigation of factors involved in educational placement of mentally retarded children: A study of differences between children in special and regular classes in Ohio* (Project No. 043). U. S. Office of Education Cooperative Research Program, Columbus, OH: Ohio State University.

Chinn, P. C. (1979). Curriculum development for culturally different exceptional children. *Teacher Education and Special Education, 2*(4), 49–58.

Chinn, P. C., & Kamp, S. H. (1982). Cultural diversity and exceptionality. In N. G. Haring (Ed.), *Exceptional children and youth* (3rd ed.) (pp. 371–390). Columbus, OH: Merrill.

Chinn, P. L. (1973). A relationship between health and school problems: A nursing assessment. *Journal of School Health, 43*(2), 85–92.

Chinn, P. L. (1979). *Child health maintenance: Concepts in family centered care* (2nd ed.). St. Louis: Mosby.

Clinton, L., & Evans, R. A. (1972). Single alternation discrimination learning in retarded adolescents as a function of within-trials variability. *American Journal of Mental Deficiency, 76,* 434–439.

Copeland, M., Ford, L., & Solon, N. (1976). *Occupational therapy for mentally retarded children.* Baltimore: University Park.

Denny, M. R. (1964). Research in learning and performance. In H. A. Stevens & R. Heber (Eds.), *Mental retardation: A review of research* (pp.100–142). Chicago: University of Chicago.

Deno, E. (1970). Special education as developmental capital. *Exceptional Children, 37,* 229–237.

Drew, C. J., & Buchanan, M. L. (1979). Research on teacher education: Status and need. *Teacher Education and Special Education, 2,* 50–55.

Drew, C. J., & Prehm, H. J. (1970). Retention in retarded and nonretarded children as a function of direction of recall and material associative strength. *American Journal of Mental Deficiency, 75,* 349–353.

Ellis, N. R. (1963). The stimulus trace and behavioral inadequacy. In N. R. Ellis (Ed.), *Handbook of mental deficiency* (pp. 134–158). New York: McGraw-Hill.

Ellis, N. R. (1970). Memory processes in retardates and normals. In N. R. Ellis (Ed.), *International review of research in mental retardation* (Vol. 4) (pp. 1–32). New York: Academic Press.

Evans, R. A., and Bilsky, L. H. (1979). Clustering and categorical list retention in the mentally retarded. In N. R. Ellis (Ed.), *Handbook of mental deficiency: Psychological theory and research* (2nd ed.) (pp. 533–567). Hillsdale, NJ: Erlbaum.

Fawcus, M., & Fawcus, R. (1974). Disorders of communication. In A. M. Clarke & A. D. B. Clarke (Eds.), *Mental deficiency* (pp.592–628). New York: Free Press.

Fialkowski v. Shapp, 405 F. Supp. 946 (E.D. Pa. 1975).

Fink, W. (1979). *Evaluation of the rural model program for severely handicapped students.* Salem, OR: Programs for Mental Retardation and Developmental Disabilities.

Fink, W. (1981). *The distribution of clients and their behavioral characteristics in programs for the mentally retarded and other developmentally disabled throughout Oregon.* Eugene, OR: Oregon Mental Health Division.

Fisher, M. A., & Zeaman, D. (1973). An attention-retention theory of retardate discrimination learning. In N. R. Ellis (Ed.), *The international review of research in mental retardation* (Vol. 6) (pp. 171–256). New York: Academic Press.

Fishler, K., Share, J., & Koch, R. (1964). Adaptation of Gesell Developmental Scales for evaluation of development in children with Down's syndrome (Mongolism). *American Journal of Mental Deficiency, 68,* 642–646.

Francis, R. J., & Rarick, G. L. (1960). *Motor characteristics of the mentally retarded.* Cooperative Research Monograph, No. 1, Washington, DC: U.S. Department of Health, Education, and Welfare.

Frank, A. R., & McFarland, T. D. (1980). Teaching coin skills to EMR children: A curriculum study. *Education and Training of the Mentally Retarded, 15,* 270–278.

Frank. H. S., & Rabinovitch, M. S. (1974). Auditory short-term memory: Developmental changes in rehearsal. *Child Development, 45,* 397–407.

Gallagher, J. J. (1979). Organizational needs for quality special education. In M. C. Reynolds (Ed.), *Futures of education for exceptional children* (pp. 133–150). Minneapolis: National Support Systems.

Garrard, S. D., & Richmond, J. C. (1975). Mental retardation. I. Nature and manifestations. In M. F. Reiser (Ed.), *American handbook of psychiatry* (2nd ed.) (pp. 437–452). New York: Basic.

Gotlieb, J., & Corman, L. (1975). Public attitudes toward mentally retarded children. *American Journal on Mental Deficiency, 80*(1), 72–80.

Gresham, F.M. (1982). Misguided mainstreaming: The case for social skills training with handicapped children. *Exceptional children, 48,* 422–433.

Grossman, H. J. (Ed.). (1983). *Classification in mental retardation.* Washington, DC: American Association on Mental Deficiency.

Guralnick, M. J. (1978). Integrated preschools as educational and therapeutic environments: Concepts, designs, and analysis. In M. J. Guralnick (Ed.), *Early intervention and the integration of handicapped and nonhandicapped children* (pp.115–145). Baltimore: University Park Press.

Guralnick, M. J. (1981). Programmatic factors affecting child-child social interactions in mainstreamed preschool programs. *Exceptional Education Quarterly, 1*(4), 71–91.

Hardman, M. L., & Drew, C. J. (1975). Incidental learning in the mentally retarded: A review. *Education and Training of the Mentally Retarded, 10*(1), 3–9.

Hardman, M. L., & Drew, C. J. (1977). The physically handicapped retarded: A review. *Mental Retardation, 15*(5), 43–48.

Hardman, M. L., Drew, C. J., & Egan, M. W. (1987). *Human exceptionality: Society, school, and family (2nd ed.).* Boston: Allyn & Bacon.

Hirshoren, A., & Burton, T. A. (1979). Teaching academic skills to trainable mentally retarded children: A study in tautology. *Education and Training of the Mentally Retarded, 17*(3), 177–179.

Hurley, O. L. (1975). Strategies for culturally different children in classes for the retarded child. In E. L. Meyen, G. A. Vergason, & R. J. Whelan (Eds.), *Alternatives for teaching exceptional children* (pp. 122–134). Denver: Love.

Jenkins, J., & Mayhall, W. (1973). Describing resource teacher programs. *Exceptional Children, 40,* 35–36.

Jensen, A. R., & Rohwer, W. D., Jr. (1963). The effect of verbal mediation on the learning and retention of paired associates by retarded adults. *American Journal of Mental Deficiency, 68,* 80–84.

Jordan, T. E., & deCharms, R. (1959). The achievement motive in normal and mentally retarded children. *American Journal of Mental Deficiency, 64,* 80–84.

Kaufman, M. J., Gottlieb, J., Agard, J. A., & Kukic, M. B. (1975). Mainstreaming: Toward an explication of the concept. In E. L. Meyen, G. A. Vergason, & R. J. Whelan (Eds.), *Alternatives for teaching exceptional children* (pp. 35–54). Denver: Love.

Kirk, S. A. (1972). *Educating exceptional children* (2nd ed.). Boston: Houghton Mifflin.

Kolstoe, O. P., & Frey, R. (1965). *A high school work-study program for the mentally subnormal student.* Carbondale: Southern Illinois University.

Linton, M. (1980). Information processing and developmental memory: An overview. In R. L. Ault (Ed.), *Developmental perspectives* (pp. 104–155). Santa Monica, CA: Goodyear.

Lloyd, L. L. (1970). Audiologic aspects of mental retardation. In N. R. Ellis (Ed.), *International review of research in mental retardation* (Vol. 4) (pp. 311–374). New York: Academic Press.

Logan, D. R., Prehm, H. J., & Drew, C. J. (1968). Effects of unidirectional training on bidirectional recall in retarded and non-retarded subjects. *American Journal of Mental Deficiency, 73,* 493–495.

Madsen, M. C. (1963). Distribution of practice and level of intelligence. *Psychological reports, 13,* 39.

Maslow, A. H. (1954). *Motivation and personality.* New York: Harper.

McEvoy, M. A., Nordquist, V. M., & Cunningham, J. L. (1984). Regular- and special-education teachers' judgments about mentally retarded children in an integrated setting. *American Journal of Mental Deficiency, 89*(2), 167–173.

Menolascino, F. J., & Egger, M. L. (1978). *Medical dimensions in mental retardation.* Lincoln: University of Nebraska.

Mercer, C. D., & Snell, M. E. (1977). *Learning theory research in mental retardation: Implications for teaching.* Columbus, OH: Merrill.

Mori, A. A., & Masters, L. F. (1980). *Teaching the severely mentally retarded*. Rockville, MD: Aspen.

Mossier, H. D., Grossman, H. J., & Dingman, H. F. (1965). Physical growth in mental defectives. *Pediatrics, 36,* 465–519.

Payne, J. S., Polloway, E. A., Smith, J. E., & Payne, R. A. (1981). *Strategies for teaching the mentally retarded* (2nd ed.). Columbus, OH: Merrill.

Peterson, G. (1975) Factors related to the attitudes of nonretarded children toward their EMR peers. *American Journal of Mental Deficiency, 79,* 412–416.

Piaget, J. (1969). *The theory of stages in cognitive development*. New York: McGraw-Hill.

Prehm, H. J., Logan, D. R., & Towle, M. (1972). The effect of warm-up on rote learning performance. *Exceptional Children, 38,* 623–627.

Pulaski, M. A. (1971). *Understanding Piaget: An introduction to children's cognitive development*. New York: Harper & Row.

Pumpian, I., Baumgart, D., Shiraga, B., Ford, A., Nisbet, J., Loomis, R., & Brown, L. (1980). Vocational training programs for severely handicapped students in the Madison Metropolitan School District. In L. Brown, M. Falvey, I. Pumpian, D. Baumgart, J. Nisbet, A. Ford, J. Schroeder, R. Loomis (Eds.), *Curricular strategies for teaching severely handicapped students functional skills in school and non-school environments* (pp. 61–101). Madison, WI: University of Wisconsin & Madison Metropolitan School District.

Rarick, G. L., & Dobbins, D. A. (1972). *Basic components in the motor performance of educable mentally retarded children: Implications for curriculum development*. Washington, DC: U.S. Office of Education.

Reynolds, M. C., & Birch, J. W. (1982). *Teaching exceptional children in all America's schools*. Reston, VA: Council for Exceptional Children.

Roncker v. Walters, 700 F.2d 1058 (6th Cir. 1983).

Rostetter, D., Kowalski, R., & Hunter, D. (1984). Implementing the integration principle of PL 94-142. In N. Certo, N. Haring, & R. York (Eds.), *Public school integration of severely handicapped students: Rational issues and progressive alternatives* (pp. 293–320). Baltimore: Brookes.

Schutz, R. P., Williams, W., Iverson, G. S., & Duncan, D. (1984). Social integration of severely handicapped students. In N. Certo, N. Haring, & R. York (Eds.), *Public school integration of severely handicapped students: Rational issues and progressive alternatives* (pp. 15–42). Baltimore: Brookes.

Siperstein, G. N., & Bak, J. J. (1985). Effects of social behavior on children's attitudes toward their mildly and moderately mentally retarded peers. *American Journal of Mental Deficiency, 90*(3), 319–327.

Smith, R. (1968). *Clinical teaching: Methods of instruction for the retarded*. New York: McGraw-Hill.

Snell, M. E. (1983). Functional reading. In M. E. Snell (Ed.), *Systematic instruction of the moderately and severely handicapped* (2nd ed.) (pp. 445–487). Columbus, OH: Merrill.

Stainback, S., & Stainback, W. (1981). A review of research on interactions between severely handicapped and nonhandicapped students. *The Journal of the Association for the Severely Handicapped, 6,* 23–29.

Stainback, S., & Stainback, W. (1982). Influencing the attitudes of regular class teachers about the education of severely retarded students. *Education and Training of the Mentally Retarded, 17*(2), 88–92.

Stainback, S., & Stainback, W. (1985). *Integration of students with severe handicaps into regular schools*. Reston, VA: Council for Exceptional Children.

State of Iowa Department of Public Instruction. (1981). *Assessment, documentation and programming for adaptive behavior: An Iowa Task Force Report*. Des Moines: Author.

Stephens, W. E. (1972). Equivalence formation by retarded and nonretarded children at different mental ages. *American Journal of Mental Deficiency, 77*, 311–313.

Stevenson, H. W. (1972). *Children's learning*. Englewood Cliffs, NJ: Prentice-Hall.

U.S. Office of Education (1985). *Seventh annual report to Congress on the implementation of The Education of the Handicapped Act*. Washington, DC: U.S. Government Printing Office.

Voeltz, L. M. (1982). Effects of structured interactions with severely handicapped peers on children's attitudes. *American Journal on Mental Deficiency, 86*, 380–390.

Wehman, P., & Hill, J. W. (1982). Preparing severely handicapped youth for less restrictive environments. *The Journal of the Association for the Severely Handicapped, 7*(1), 33–39.

Whorton, J. E., and Algozzine, R. F. A. (1978). Comparison of intellectual, achievement, and adaptive behavior levels for students who are mildly retarded. *Mental Retardation, 16*, 320–321.

Wilcox, B., & Bellamy, T. (1982). *Design of high school programs for severely handicapped students*. Baltimore: Brookes.

Zeaman, D. (1974, August). *Experimental psychology of mental retardation: Some states of the art*. Invited address to a meeting of the Annual Convention of the American Psychological Association, New Orleans, LA.

Zeaman, D., & House, B. J. (1979). A review of attention theory. In N. R. Ellis (Ed.), *Handbook of mental deficiency: Psychological theory and research* (2nd ed.) (pp. 63–120). Hillsdale, NJ: Erlbaum.

Ziegler, S., & Hambleton, D. (1976). Integration of young TMR children into regular elementary school. *Exceptional Children, 42*(8), 459–461.

9

The Retarded Adolescent

Core Concepts
Expected Outcomes of Secondary Education Programs
Vocational Preparation
    Legislative Mandates for Vocational Training
    Work-Study Programs
    Career Education
    Work Experience
    Community-Referenced Training
Teaching Adaptive Skills
    Socialization
    Personal Appearance and Sexuality
    Recreation and Leisure
Teaching Academic Skills
Transition Planning
    Coordinating Transition Planning
    Determining Individual Need
    Developing a Transition Plan
    Involving Parents in Transition Planning
    Integration with Non-retarded Peers
Core Questions
Round Table Discussion
References

Core Concepts

1. Components of an effective high school program for retarded adolescents include: (*a*) a comprehensive curriculum that focuses on vocational preparation, (*b*) the teaching of adaptive skills, and (*c*) instruction in functional academics where appropriate.

2. Work is important not only for monetary rewards, but for personal identity and status.

3. The Vocational Rehabilitation Act and the Education for All Handicapped Children Act are two pieces of legislation that have had a significant impact on vocational training for mentally retarded adolescents.

4. Work-study programs provide the student with integrated work and classroom experiences.

5. Career education focuses on preparation for life and includes personal social skills, as well as occupationally related instruction.

6. In the work experience method of training, the student may participate in occupational activities in the community under actual working conditions.

7. In a community-referenced training approach, goals and objectives are determined according to both the demands of the community work setting and the functioning level of the individual.

8. Socialization training includes the development of positive interpersonal relationships with family and peers as well as the acquisition of behaviors that are appropriate in a variety of community settings.

9. Many retarded adolescents lack the financial resources or the necessary skills and sophistication needed to maintain their personal appearance adequately.

10. The greatest value of recreation/leisure activities may be their contribution to the emotional and psychological development of retarded individuals.

11. Academic tool subjects are taught to enhance the retarded adolescent's future opportunities for independence in the classroom setting, family unit, and community.

12. Although effective educational and adult service models have been designed to provide greater opportunities for retarded inividuals in community settings, no significant long-term changes will result without the inclusion of a transition planning process.

13. Effective transition planning is an ongoing process which begins with goals and objectives established at the time the student enters school.

14. The needs of mentally retarded adults are diverse and will vary according to both the severity of the condition and the demands imposed by the environment.

15. The purposes of transition planning are to establish a working relationship between parents and adult service agencies, identify resources for employment and community participation, access services prior to graduation, and identify systems that will help maintain needed services.

16. Parents must have the opportunity of learning as much as possible about adult service systems prior to their child's leaving school.

17. The successful transition of the mentally retarded adult to life in an integrated community setting begins with integration during the school years.

Adolescence is truly a period of transition that encompasses the personal, social, and educational life of the individual. Adolescents are between childhood and adulthood for several years, attempting to free themselves from the role of a child but not yet ready to assume the responsibilities of an adult. They work toward emancipation from the primary family unit while developing social and educational characteristics that will provide greater acceptance into society. Educational goals during this period are directed toward employment opportunities and preparation for life as an adult.

For the individual with mental retardation, the challenges of adolescence are obviously intensified. Many retarded adolescents have the physical attributes of their nonretarded peers but not the capacity to fully cope with the demands of their environment or with their own desires for emancipation from childhood. For the moderately and severely retarded adolescent whose physical and cognitive differences may be readily apparent, the focus is on the level of social and occupational independence that may be possible in our society.

In this chapter we will consider the educational and vocational programs available for retarded adolescents in the public schools. We will discuss the expected outcomes of secondary education programs for students with mental retardation and analyze the components of an effective high school experience. During the adolescent years, educational programs for mentally retarded individuals primarily focus on the skills necessary to successfully make the transition from school to adult life. Beginning in junior high school, mildly retarded individuals need a greater emphasis on applying academic tools, such as reading and arithmetic, to vocational and functional life needs. For moderately and severely retarded children, many of these skill areas are a central focus of the curriculum from the time they enter school.

Reaching adolescence opens many new areas for consideration for retarded youngsters.

EXPECTED OUTCOMES OF SECONDARY EDUCATION PROGRAMS

Core Concept 1   Components of an effective high school program for retarded adolescents include: (*a*) a comprehensive curriculum that focuses on vocational preparation, (*b*) the
teaching of adaptive skills, and (*c*) instruction in functional academics where appropriate.

A critical measure of the effectiveness of any educational program is the success of its graduates. Although 1986 marked the 10th anniversary of the passage of Public Law 94–142, the educational opportunities afforded by this landmark legislation had not yet allowed special education graduates to be fully integrated in the social and economic mainstream of their local communities (Hardman & McDonnell, 1987). Several follow-up studies of special education graduates suggested that these handicapped adults were unable to participate fully in community activities, had little or no social life outside the family unit or primary caregivers, were isolated from both handicapped and non-handicapped peers, and were not employed (Brodsky, 1983; Hasazi, Gordon, & Roe, 1984; Mithaug, Horiuchi, & Fanning, 1985; Wehman, Kregel, & Seyfarth, 1985). Other authors (Bellamy, Rhodes, Borbeau, & Mank, 1982; Bruininks & Lakin, 1985; Buckley & Bellamy, 1985; Department of Labor, 1979; Whitehead, 1981) reported that service programs available to students with severe handicaps, including mental retardation, were not successful in producing meaningful outcomes nor moving individuals to less restrictive living or vocational options.

Given that special education graduates are not fully accessing community services and programs, there is a need to identify what outcomes high school programs are expected to produce. These outcomes may be described in terms of independence from primary caregivers, of access to services and activities within the local community, and of involvement in the economic life of the community (Hardman & Rose, 1984; Wilcox & Bellamy, 1982). A secondary program for mentally retarded students must be directed toward meeting each of these outcomes if it is to be effective. Components of an effective high school program include a comprehensive curriculum that focuses on vocational preparation, the teaching of adaptive skills, and instruction in functional academics where appropriate. Additionally, secondary education programs should incorporate integration with non-retarded peers, consistent parental involvement, and the implementation of a systematic transition planning system (Hardman & McDonnell, 1987; Hardman & Rose, 1984; Wilcox & Bellamy, 1982).

VOCATIONAL PREPARATION

Core Concept 2   Work is important not only for monetary rewards, but for personal identity and status.

The mentally retarded individual is often characterized as one who consumes services rather than one who contributes to the community. A con-

Vocational preparation for mentally retarded individuals often involves complex settings and circumstances.

sumer of services is always viewed as being dependent upon the charity of others. Employment assists in removing this image and placing the individual in the role of contributor. Work is important as a means to earn wages, and through wages we are able to access material goods that contribute to our quality of life. Work also means personal identify and status.

From the time the first settlers arrived in the United States, there has always been the strong belief that "individuals should be free to earn their livelihoods in whatever way that proves most profitable" (Calhoun & Finch, 1976, p. 31). However, this belief has not been applied equally for all people. For persons with mental retardation, access to vocational training and employment has been negligible throughout most of this country's history. Even today many persons with mental retardation are unemployed or underemployed in spite of the dramatic increase in vocational research and development that has taken place in the 1970s and 1980s (Bellamy, O'Connor, & Karan, 1979; Bellamy, Rhodes, & Albin, 1985; Brolin, 1976; DuRand & DuRand, 1978; Moon, Goodall, & Wehman, 1985; Revell, Wehman, & Arnold, 1985). There are many explanations for this problem, some of which are explained by Payne and Patton (1981):

> Vocational training programs for retarded persons have often been narrowly focused; that is, these programs are often predicated upon the development of only one or two specific skill areas. Some programs have prepared their clients for a job market that no longer exists. In some extreme cases, there is no career and/or vocational program at all. (p. 265)

In this section we will examine the issues relating to vocational preparation for persons with mental retardation. We will review various approaches to vocational training, including work-study, career education, work experience, and community-referenced training. Our discussion begins with the legislative mandates that have played such a vital role in the development of vocational services for retarded citizens.

Legislative Mandates for Vocational Training

Core Concept 3	The Vocational Rehabilitation Act and the Education for All Handicapped Children Act are two important pieces of legislation that have had a significant impact on vocational training for mentally retarded adolescents.

Federal legislation has widely supported comprehensive vocational preparation that is accessible to all persons with mental retardation. Chapter 13 of this volume provides a description of this legislation within the context of the broad scope of legal mandates concerning mentally retarded persons. We will briefly examine the Vocational Rehabilitation Act and the Education for All Handicapped Children Act, which have had a significant impact on the development and quality of vocational services to mentally retarded individuals.

Persons with mental retardation have been eligible for vocational services for 40 years under the Barden-LaFollet Act of 1943. However, as Brolin (1976) pointed out, few persons with mental retardation received any services until the 1960s. Access to vocational rehabilitation services was greatly enhanced with the passage of the Vocational Rehabilitation Act of 1973 (P.L. 93–112). This act established vocational training as a service that must be made available to all qualified handicapped persons. This act contains Section 504, the basic civil rights legislation for the handicapped. Section 504 makes it illegal to discriminate against handicapped individuals in providing access to vocational training and employment. Subsection 84.11 of the Federal Regulations for Section 504 states: "No qualified handicapped person shall, on the basis of handicap, be subjected to discrimination in employment under any program or activity to which this part applies" (*Federal Register*, May 4, 1977). Discrimination is prohibited in:

1. Recruitment, advertising, and the processing of applications
2. Hiring, alterations in job status, rehiring
3. Rates of pay and other forms of compensation
4. Job assignments and classifications, lines of progression, and seniority
5. Leaves of absence and sick leave
6. Fringe benefits
7. Selection and financial support for training, conferences, and other job-related activities
8. Employer-approved activities, including social and recreational programs

The passage of P.L. 93–112 did not mean that the negative attitudes that have long been in existence toward handicapped persons would by any means change immediately. It was, however, a first step toward opening new vocational doors for handicapped people generally and for retarded persons specifically. Career and vocational education for retarded persons became even more important than ever. Section 503 also emphasizes the regulations for affirmative action to employ handicapped people. Thus, if retarded individuals are properly educated and are able to perform competitively for jobs, the federal government stands behind these individuals both in promoting affirmative action in their employment as well as in prohibiting any discrimination in their hiring. It is, however, critical that retarded persons be educated and trained as competent employees. Although laws facilitate employment of the handicapped, they do not obligate an employer to employ or retain those who cannot demonstrate competence.

In addition to reaffirming the civil rights of persons with a handicap, the law has several other objectives (Meers, 1980):

- To promote expanded employment opportunities for the handicapped in all areas of business and industry
- To establish state plans for the purpose of providing vocational rehabilitation services to meet the needs of the handicapped
- To conduct evaluations of the potential rehabilitation of handicapped clients and to expand services to them as well as to those who have not received any or received inadequate rehabilitation services
- To increase the number and competence of rehabilitation personnel through retraining and upgrading experiences. (p. 33)

Current provisions of the Rehabilitation Act mandate services on a priority basis, with the most severely handicapped having the highest priority. However, research studies published in the 1970s indicated that many of these people continued to be excluded from vocational rehabilitation services

(Bellamy, Horner, & Inman, 1979; Halpern, 1974; Sowers, Thompson, & Connis, 1979). In 1986 Congress passed new amendments to the Vocational Rehabilitation Act (Rehabilitation Act Amendments of 1986, P.L. 95–506), which strengthened the mandate to serve the most severely handicapped individuals. These amendments include provisions for "supported employment," a new dimension in employment models for persons with mental retardation. Supported employment as defined in P.L. 95–506 means

> competitive work in integrated work settings for individuals with severe handicaps for whom competitive employment has not traditionally occurred, or for individuals for whom competitive employment has been interrupted or intermittent as a result of a severe disability, and who because of their handicap, need on-going support services to perform such work. (Section 103)

Chapter 10 contains a more in-depth explanation of the supported employment concept.

The Education for All Handicapped Children Act (P.L. 94–142) of 1975 requires that all individuals with handicapping conditions who are between the ages of 3 and 22 years receive a free and appropriate education, including a vocational education (Meers, 1980). As Laski (1979) suggested, the provisions of this act are the basis for vocational training for severely retarded children and youth. The need for an appropriate vocational training program for severely retarded persons has been well substantiated by several investigators (Brolin, 1972; Gold, 1974; Martin, Flexer, & Newbery, 1979; Wehman et al. 1982; Wehman & Kregel, 1985).

Work-Study Programs

Core Concept 4	Work-study programs provide the student with integrated work and classroom experiences.

Under a work-study program, the responsibility for the student's program is usually shared by a special education teacher and a vocational rehabilitation counselor. For a portion of the day the student spends time in the classroom setting while increasing tool subject skills that will facilitate independent adult living (e.g., budgeting, transportation, and interpersonal relationships). During the remainder of the day the student leaves the campus and receives training (e.g., clerical, food service, custodial, auto repair, etc.) in an on-the-job training facility somewhere in the community. These employment settings range from sheltered to competitive. The kind of placement will depend on the student's aptitude, ability, and readiness. The actual amount of time spent in each component of a work-study program varies considerably between programs. At the end of 3 to 4 years, most schools have provisions for a high school diploma, and the student is released from school and placed in some form of gainful employment.

Attempts to determine the efficacy of work-study programs have been made by several investigators (Brimer & Rouse, 1978; Chaffin, Davidson, Regan, & Spellman, 1971; Halpern, 1973, 1974; Howe, 1967). These investigations have produced inconsistent findings regarding the efficacy of work-study programs.

Brimer and Rouse (1978) conducted a follow-up of high school graduates who had participated in work-study and reported that the vast majority of

Work-Study programs are often a shared responsibility between the special education teacher and a vocational rehabilitation counselor.

program graduates were working and earning salaries above minimum wage. These positive results were attributed to the well-organized and collaborative efforts of the schools and vocational rehabilitation agency. Halpern (1973) reported similar results in a follow-up of high school graduates in Oregon who had also participated in work-study. However, in a follow-up published in 1974, Halpern found differences among students who were in full-time and part-time work-study programs. Of those students in full-time work-study, 75 percent were employed, but only 52 percent of the part-time work-study participants were working.

In Howe's (1967) investigation, work-study programs were compared with more traditional classrooms without the work-study component. No significant differences could be determined in either group in terms of overall adjustment in life as adults. The group educated in the traditional special education program achieved as well in the adult community as the group with work-study experience. Although nothing was found to indicate that a work-study program is detrimental to later adjustment, the findings of this study suggest that not all mentally retarded students in vocational level classes need off-campus placement as part of their training program. This finding was corroborated in a study by Chaffin et al. (1971). These authors reported, in a follow-up study conducted 2 years after graduation, that no statistically significant differences were found between the percentages of work-study and non-work-study students who were gainfully employed. The work-study group did, however, earn significantly higher salaries.

In addition to the above inconsistencies in studies focusing on work-study programs, methodological problems also appear in the research. One variable that must be considered is sampling bias. In a review of the literature on work-study programs, Peck, Apolloni, and Cooke indicated that "the selection of potential candidates for work-study . . . has been systematically biased toward serving those with the greatest prospects for gainful occupation. Such a sampling bias would greatly threaten the validity of studies that have compared served and unserved populations of students" (1981, p. 13). Another important variable that always needs to be considered in such studies but cannot always be assessed accurately is that of competence of the professionals working with the retarded in various capacities during the training period. Training and educational programs that are sound in terms of curriculum can be effective only if the professionals employed are competent in their work. This statement in no way reflects our opinions of the competence of the professionals working with the retarded subjects in the above-mentioned studies. Rather, we are drawing attention to the importance of carefully assessing all possible variables in any research that may have a bearing on the findings. In the above-mentioned studies, many different individuals may have had an effect on the outcome of the research. Students are very much affected both by the teachers and by the quality of vocational preparation received by the mentally retarded students before the actual work experience. Vocational rehabilitation counselors also have a primary role in the development of student competencies, and the employers providing the work training are an integral part of the rehabilitation process. Finally, the attitudes of the parents may be reflected in the performance of their children. We may conclude that the preparation of retarded students for effective and competitive functioning in an adult society can be facilitated by a concerted team effort, including work experience in the real world.

In any case, regardless of program biases, the curriculum in recent years for mild to moderately retarded adolescents at the high school level appears to have moved in the direction of work-study or some type of vocational experience. By the time these students reach a vocational level class, they usually have become eligible for assistance through vocational rehabilitation. If they meet eligibility requirements, a number of services become available that can enhance their chances to become vocationally competent. To be eligible for vocational rehabilitation services in most states an individual must (1) have a disability, (2) have a disability that represents a vocational handicap, or (3) represent reasonable feasibility for rehabilitation.

In the past, rehabilitation counselors working under rigid case closure quotas were hesitant to certify and accept as clients retarded individuals who were considered difficult to rehabilitate. In most states, quotas for rehabilitation counselors working with retarded persons have now either been eliminated or modified to realistic levels. In many instances the counselors come into the public schools and work closely with the special education teacher. The basic responsibilities of the vocational rehabilitation counselor working with retarded students are as follows:

1. Certification of all trainees for vocational rehabilitation services
2. Consultation with school officials on training arrangements within participating school districts
3. Provision of vocational rehabilitation services for the individual trainees when extended services are needed (e.g., psychotherapy or surgery)
4. Evaluation of public school records pertaining to those individuals referred for rehabilitation services
5. Initiation of and conducting joint conferences with the work-study teachers
6. Approval of all job training; evaluation of training facilities, arrangement of training schedules and agreements, and consultation with the trainee and work-study teacher
7. Approval of all expenditures for client services
8. Approval of all individual vocational rehabilitation plans for clients accepted for vocational rehabilitation services

9. Maintenance of individual case records of the vocational
   rehabilitation clients

In addition to providing these services, vocational rehabilitation counselors can initiate other traditional rehabilitation services, such as the fitting
of prosthetic devices, the provision for corrective surgery, and the payment
of training fees. Rehabilitation counselors can also provide another important service by issuing subminimum wage exemption certificates when
deemed necessary. Many employers who are interested in hiring handicapped
individuals are hesitant to do so when the worker's production level does
not meet the criterion set for other employees and when minimum wage
restrictions are nevertheless imposed. Under such circumstances, the vocational rehabilitation counselor can issue a subminimum wage exemption
certificate that will allow for payment of wages commensurate with the
level of productivity.

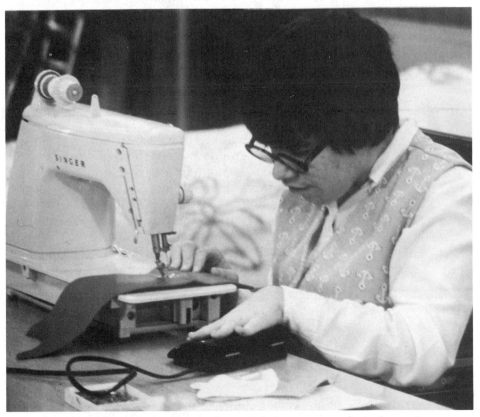

Career education is important for retarded young people and coordinates
many aspects of occupational and independent living skills.

Career Education

Core Concept 5   Career education focuses on preparation for life and includes personal social skills as well as occupationally related instruction.

Brolin (1976, 1977, 1982) suggested that although the work-study programs instituted in the 1960s were a marked improvement over exclusively academically oriented curricula, they were still not enough to assure community adjustment for the retarded adult. There is a need for a broadened concept, such as that offered through career education. Clark (1979) indicated that this concept includes preparation for life and personal social skills in addition to occupationally-related instruction. He developed a school-based career education model for handicapped students that begins at the elementary-age level and continues into the adult years (See Figure 9–1).

Career education is a total educational concept that systematically coordinates all school, family, and community components, thus facilitating the individual's potential for economic, social, and personal fulfillment. Brolin (1982) suggested six areas of primary responsibility for special educators in developing occupational guidance and preparation for mentally retarded persons:

1. Knowing and exploring occupational possibilities
2. Making appropriate occupational decisions
3. Exhibiting appropriate work behaviors
4. Exhibiting sufficient physical and manual skills
5. Acquiring a specific saleable job skill
6. Seeking, securing, and maintaining satisfactory employment

D'Alonzo (1977) suggested that most elementary and middle school curricula fail to provide those learning experiences that have a direct relationship to career or prevocational development. The lack of these experiences at earlier levels creates a problem for those attempting to develop career education skills at the secondary level.

Work Experience

Core Concept 6   In the work experience method of training, the student may participate in occupational activities in the community under actual working conditions.

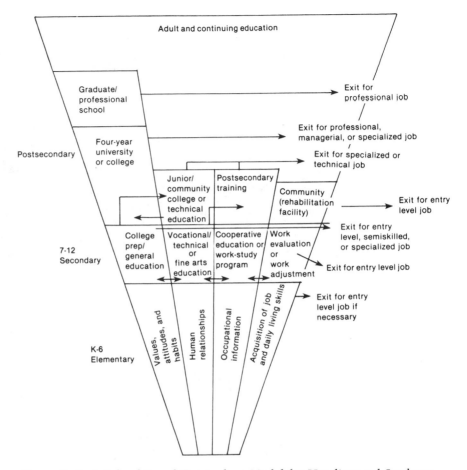

Figure 9–1. A School-Based Curriculum Model for Handicapped Students
From Clark, G.M. *Career education for the handicapped child in the elementary classroom.*
Denver: Love Publishing Co., 1979.

The nature of the work experiences will vary somewhat according to the philosophy of each particular program. Some programs begin work experience within the school setting and eventually introduce the student to community settings. Other programs may begin the experiences in the community immediately. The nature of the experience, its difficulty, and the actual type of assignment are usually dependent on the needs and the nature of each student. Before placements are made, each student is carefully evaluated to establish ability and interests. During the years spent in the vocational level class, students may have an opportunity to work in a variety of settings to maximize exposure to different types of vocational experiences that may be encountered, which may allow them to find the permanent placement they would like at the completion of school. The primary purpose

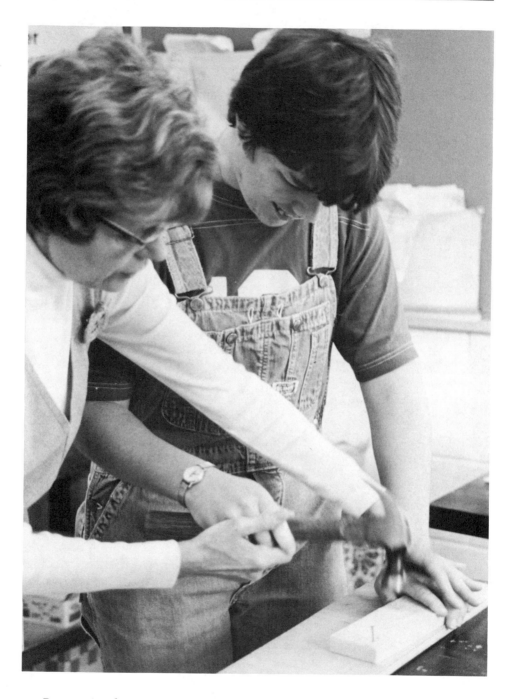

Prevocational instruction and experience are important for the success of education at the secondary level.

of the work experience, however, is not to develop specific vocational skills, but to enable the student to develop the work habits and interpersonal skills necessary to acquire and maintain any job. If specific skills are acquired in the course of training, they naturally could be helpful in obtaining specific jobs at the end of school, but specific skill competencies are not emphasized at the expense of the emotional dimensions of vocational behavior.

The professional working with retarded adolescents in work-experience programs frequently encounters problems that may hinder and even preclude the development of effective programming for the student. As discussed in earlier chapters, the majority of retarded persons come from lower socio-economic backgrounds; and work-related motivational problems sometimes develop when the student's family has existed for a number of years, if not generations, on public assistance. Difficulties may arise when students in training or their parents come to the realization that employment following school may take the form of a relatively low-paying job. When remuneration is low, there may be little incentive to work unless work values have been emphasized. Another situation affecting the retarded is that handicapped individuals frequently are vocationally stereotyped. Retarded employees are often ushered into entry level jobs only, for example, as dishwashers or janitors. Although these occupations may be personally satisfying and rewarding to some handicapped individuals, they too frequently represent the lack of consideration for the individual's interest and aptitude. The limitations of each individual must be considered, but training programs and vocational placements that consider only administrative convenience are inexcusable. Several researchers (e.g., Brimer and Rouse, 1978; Brolin, DuRand, Kromer, and Muller, 1975; Halpern, 1973) have found retarded individuals employed in positions paying well over the national mean.

Some retarded people have vocational goals inappropriate to their abilities, which can raise another problem regarding work-experience. Sometimes they tend to set vocational goals for themselves that cannot be realized. Sometimes problems are created by parents who set inappropriate expectations for their children; these expectations carry with them educational requirements beyond the capabilities of the students. For whatever reason, and whether these students are fantasizing or really believe that they possess greater capabilities than they have, problems do develop if they consider the work to which they have been assigned to be demeaning. In situations of this nature the task for parents, teachers, and counselors is to help these retarded individuals realize their limitations while not jeopardizing their fragile self-concept. The task then is to help the student to exchange unrealistic vocational choices for those that are functional and still satisfying. The student aspiring to become a nurse may be led into a nurse's aide position, while the aspiring airline pilot is led into a position in the airline industry loading baggage or maintaining aircraft. Effort should be directed toward finding acceptable alternatives without the loss of personal dignity.

Community-referenced Training

Core Concept 7	In a community-referenced training approach, goals and objectives are determined according to both the demands of the community work setting and the functioning level of the individual.

The community-referenced approach to vocational training, although similar to work experience programs in many ways, has some very notable differences. The idea that retarded individuals must "get ready" to go into community work settings is not acceptable under this approach. The vocational instruction must focus directly on the activities to be accomplished in the community work setting rather than on the development of isolated skills in the classroom setting. Consequently, the goals and objectives are developed from the demands of the community work setting in conjunction with the functioning level of the individual. Research has clearly indicated that retarded individuals, including those with moderate and severe differences, can work in community employment settings if provided adequate training and support (Bellamy, Rhodes, & Albin; 1985; Wehman, Hill, Goodall, Cleveland, Brooke, & Pentecost, 1982; Wehman & Kregel, 1985).

Effectively preparing adolescents for community work settings will require a comprehensive vocational program in the high school. The critical characteristics of a vocational program based upon a community-referenced approach to instruction were addressed by McDonnell, Hightower, and Hardman (1987) and include:

1. A vocational curriculum reflecting the job opportunities available in the local community
2. Vocational training taking place in actual job sites
3. Training designed to sample the individual's performance across a variety of economically viable alternatives
4. Students being provided with ongoing opportunities to interact with non-handicapped peers in the work setting
5. Vocational training culminating in specific job training and placement
6. Job placement linked to comprehensive transition planning that focuses on establishing interagency agreements that support the individual's full participation in the community

The components of a community-referenced vocational preparation approach may be found in Figure 9–2.

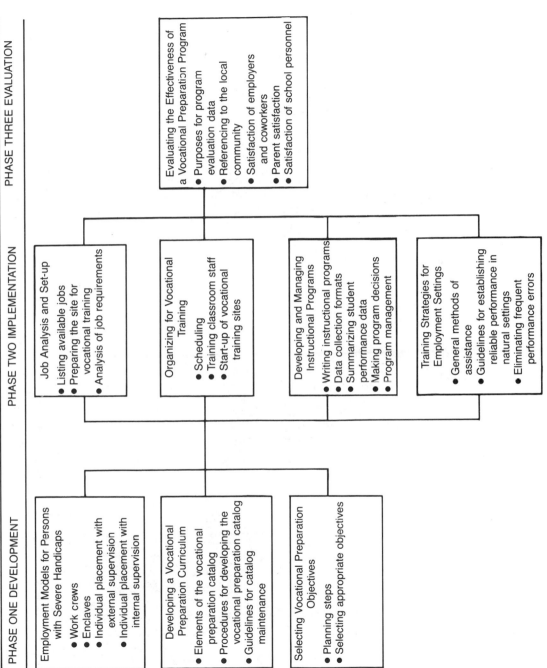

Figure 9–2. Components of a Community-Referenced Vocational Preparation Program

Adapted from *The Utah community-based vocational preparation manual* by J. McDonnell, J. Hightower, and M. L. Hardman, Salt Lake City: University of Utah, Department of Special Education.

TEACHING ADAPTIVE SKILLS

Socialization

Core Concept 8	Socialization training includes the development of positive interpersonal relationships with family and peers as well as the acquisition of behaviors that are appropriate in a variety of community settings.

Adaptive skills teaching generally fall into three categories: socialization, personal appearance, and recreation/leisure time. First we will discuss socialization training, which includes the development of positive interper-

Socialization for later independent living is essential.

sonal relationships and appropriate behaviors. It is important for retarded adolescents to become aware of both their strengths and limitations as they interact with adults and their age-mates in a social context.

One of the greatest needs in the area of socialization for retarded adolescents is access to social outlets. Retarded adolescents lack the necessary social sophistication that nonretarded children gain by observation, so many retarded adolescents are unable to plan and carry out social activity successfully. Their social problems include dealing with such aspects as transportation, planning parties, asking for and accepting dates, behavior on dates, and financing social activities.

Transportation is a problem for many teenagers. Some are unable to drive because they are not old enough or because they lack access to an automobile. If the retarded adolescent is unable to drive because of age, or inability to pass driver's training, instruction in the use of public transportation can be provided by parents and teachers. The ability to use public transportation may be important not only for social but for vocational reasons as well. If public transportation is not available, then transportation must be provided by parents, schools, or volunteers. For those young people able to profit from driver's education and successfully fulfill state requirements, it should be made available in the public schools when legal age is reached. Driver's education is a debatable issue for the retarded adolescent. It can be argued that only the most capable mentally retarded students should be encouraged to drive. These would include those who possess the coordination and ability to think critically in emergencies.

Since the retarded adolescent may not be capable of taking the initiative for planning social activities, such responsibilities rest with volunteer groups, local associations for retarded persons, and parents. Many social functions can be planned at school with the aid of the teacher. If a university is in proximity, special education and recreation therapy majors might be available to assist in planning and supervising these social functions.

Proper social behavior and personal interaction skills should begin early in the home and continue throughout the school years. Most retarded adolescents are eager to learn, because they wish to be as much like their normal peers as possible and prefer to avoid any behavioral patterns that draw attention to their limitations.

Retarded adolescents who are eager to show their affection for others of the opposite sex may lack the skills to do so in socially acceptable ways. Many try to emulate what they have seen on the television or movie screen or what they have heard their peers discussing, but unfortunately are unable to distinguish reality from fantasy. They are frequently unable to "read" their environment to determine what is really acceptable and what is not. It is the responsibility of both parents and professionals to help the retarded individual developing through adolescence and adulthood to learn acceptable behavioral patterns.

Personal Appearance and Sexuality

Core Concept 9   Many retarded adolescents lack the financial resources or the necessary skills and sophistication needed to maintain their personal appearance adequately.

By the time children reach adolescence, many become acutely aware of their personal appearance in relationship to sex role expectations. At this time many adolescents develop heterosexual interests and become concerned with enhancing themselves in order to make a positive impression on the opposite sex. Adolescents typically conform to peer opinions, activities, and appearances. Girls become increasingly aware and interested in the use of cosmetics, fashionable hair styles, and stylish clothing. They are concerned with their height and weight. Boys, too, are concerned with their clothing, hair styles, and physical attributes.

Many retarded adolescents lack the financial resources or the necessary skills and sophistication needed to maintain their personal appearance adequately. Most adolescents learn from peers or siblings the methods of hair styling, use of cosmetics, and coordination of clothing styles, but retarded adolescents frequently have little, if any, help. They may be unable to learn from observing the examples set by others and experimenting on their own.

The onset of puberty brings about many changes in the adolescent. These changes include physiological and behavioral differences, such as the attainment of sexual function. When these physical changes begin to occur, production levels increase for estrogen, progesterone, and testosterone, the hormones essential for secondary sex characteristics (such as broadening of the shoulders and increased muscle mass for boys and widening of the hips for girls). Changes occur in reproductive systems and in the distribution of both body hair and adipose tissue. The rate and the time of these changes are variable: girls begin pubertal changes generally between the ages of 10 and 14 years; boys usually begin later, between age 12 and 16 years (Timiras, 1972).

The beginning of reproductive capabilities is evident with the beginning of menstruation for girls and seminal emission for boys. Menstruation usually is irregular and not accompanied by ovulation for several months. Likewise, the mature sexual capabilities for boys may not occur for several months after the first indications of development.

Unless retarded adolescents are prepared for the gross physiological changes brought about by puberty, these changes may come as a traumatic experience. The adolescent retarded girl who has not been prepared for menstruation may find her initial experience frightening or may be too embarrassed to seek help. The responsibility for providing sex education has been

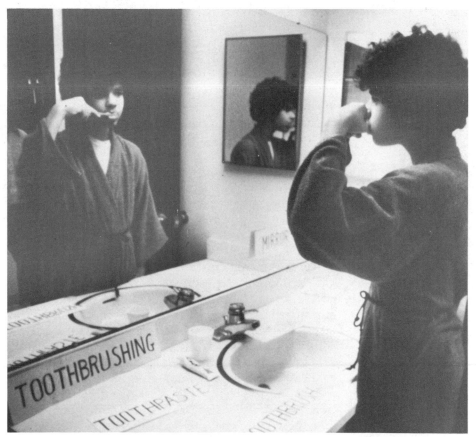

Personal appearance becomes important for the mentally retarded youngster during adolescence.

a widely debated issue. Whereas some individuals believe that sex education belongs in the school, others contend that sex education is primarily if not exclusively the responsibility of the parents (Kempton, 1983). Rauh, Johnson, and Burket (1973) contend that, next to school tax levies, sex education is probably the most controversial subject confronting American public schools today. Several school districts that have developed sophisticated, sequential sex education programs have given them up because of public pressure.

It would be fine if either the school, the home, or the church would assume the responsibility for sex education. Unfortunately, in many instances no one is willing to assume this responsibility. Teachers are hesitant to do so without authorization. Peers are sometimes the only source from which the young people can obtain any information, which is often distorted or highly inaccurate. This problem is not unique to retarded persons but is even greater for them, because their accessibility to accurate information may be even more remote. The nonretarded adoelscent can seek and find information in a library. The retarded adolescent may not be able to read or comprehend the written information even if it is made available.

Parents often have difficulty discussing their child's sexual maturation with their pediatrician. Even though they may recognize the need for information to deal effectively with their child, parents may be reluctant to ask questions. Not until the natural course of physical development forces the issue of sex education into the open do many parents of mentally retarded individuals seek counsel (Fischer and Krajicek, 1974). In Hammer and Bernard's study of retarded adolescents (1966), sexual behavior appeared to be one of the greatest concerns of parents. The parents generally considered themselves ill prepared to provide adequate sex education and even considered institutionalization as the only means of avoiding pregnancies and sexual deviancy. It is interesting to note that professional observers did not perceive the problem to be of the magnitude that the parents did.

Kempton (1983) suggested that a retarded child's general attitude toward accepting himself as a sexual being will tend to reflect the attitude of important adults in his environment. If the adults are comfortable with all facets of themselves, so also will the child be. It is common advice that adults should answer only those specific questions that the child asks about sex, but Fisher and Krajicek (1974) suggest that this is not generally applicable to retarded children, some of whom have inadequate verbal skills. Adults must therefore take the initiative in matters relating to sex education. Success in dealing with the retarded in sex education depends greatly on adults' willingness to "give the child permission" to ask questions or to "wonder" about sexually related matters. Cultural implications that sex is something dirty and should not be discussed tend to restrict adequate parent-child interactions.

There is little doubt that sexual activity among adolescents is on the increase. Related to the increase of sexual activity among adolescents is the increasing incidence of venereal disease. Adolescents, including retarded persons, will continue to engage in sexual activity with or without the approval of society. Unless they receive adequate sex education, both unwanted pregnancies and venereal diseases are inevitable. While school boards, parents, and the public argue over the responsibility of sex education, many retarded adolescents continue to be sexually active and ignorant, victims of our indecision.

In addition to changes in sexual function, puberty may also bring about cosmetic changes, such as problems with acne. Acne frequently causes emotional scarring that is far more significant and permanent than the physical scarring that occurs with this condition (Reisner, 1973). Nonretarded adolescents have the advantage of being able to read and ask questions. Some have access to a dermatologist to help protect or improve cosmetic appearance. The retarded adolescent may have difficulty locating the necessary help or lack the financial resources to consult a dermatologist. Unable to groom themselves adequately and maintain an acceptable cosmetic appearance, retarded adolescents may find social acceptance nearly impossible.

Unfortunately, some parents of retarded children make the assumption that, because of a retarded child's intellectual limitations, physical appearance is of little consequence. Yet most retarded children strive constantly to be as much like their normal peers as possible and want nothing to draw any attention to the fact that they are somewhat different from other children. Adverse physical appearance does draw attention and hinders or precludes social acceptance. Parents and teachers must be aware that how an individual looks usually has a bearing on self-concept. Thus programs and curricula must consider appearance and grooming in the education of retarded adolescents.

Parents may lack the ability or the desire to teach their retarded children adequate grooming skills; in such situations, the responsibility may fall heavily on the schools. The manner in which the students are taught may take several different forms. Positive discussions in a class are one possible means. Guest speakers from clothing stores can usually be brought into the schools, or the students can be taken to the stores for a demonstration. Likewise, the people in cosmetic sales are usually very cooperative and often will teach and demonstrate the proper use of cosmetics for the girls. If a dermatologist is not available, then the school nurse should be able to provide the necessary information on skin care and the treatment of acne. Beauty colleges that train cosmetologists frequently are willing to provide their services, teaching the retarded students how to shampoo and take care of their hair.

Even if the students are able to learn how to groom themselves properly, the problem of financial resources sometimes presents an obstacle to mentally retarded individuals, many of whom come from lower socioeconomic backgrounds in which resources are insufficient to purchase the necessary clothing and supplies. There are several alternatives to addressing this problem. First, the students can learn to make their own clothing. Even the boys can learn how to sew in order to repair and make clothing. This can be taught by the teacher or, perhaps, through a cooperative arrangement with the school home economics program. This process can both provide clothing at a substantially lower cost than retail purchase and develop a leisure-time activity. Other benefits can be derived from the making of their own clothing. Students usually gain a certain amount of pride from creating and making something of value, and there is also the benefit of learning to measure and to follow directions, both of which sewing requires.

Recreation and Leisure

Core Concept 10   The greatest value of recreation/leisure activities may be their contribution to the emotional and psychological development of retarded individuals.

Recreation and leisure activities are also essential components of the adolescent's social world. The adolescent may spend anywhere from 30 to 40 hours a week in school or in a job situation today. However, it has been estimated that by the year 2000, working adults will be spending only about 32 hours in occupationally related activities (Bucher & Bucher, 1974). Obviously there will be a real need to develop expanded recreation and leisure activities for all of society. For retarded individuals the need for recreation/leisure education is critical because they have a significantly large amount of leisure time (Verhoven, 1975). Staley and Miller (1972) suggested that those having the most leisure time are often least able to cope with it. Frustrated with the inability to find legitimate forms of leisure expression, individuals may adopt deviant solutions to this problem. The amount of free time has in some instances led to increased crime and violence (Murphy, 1975).

Without minimizing the importance of psychomotor contribution of recreational activities, Wright (1974) suggested that perhaps the greatest value of these activities may be their contributions to the emotional and psychological development of retarded individuals. The involvement in a recreational activity may be one of the few times these individuals view themselves as successful (Brackey, 1971). In terms of physical education and recreation, the picture today for retarded adolescents is encouraging. Some agencies and communities are initiating new programs specifically for retarded persons. Many colleges and universities have developed special or adaptive physical education, recreation, and therapeutic recreation programs that prepare students majoring in these fields to work with handicapped persons. Other programs, such as The Special Olympics, sponsored by the Joseph P. Kennedy, Jr., Foundation, have provided for athletic competition for retarded children and adolescents.

Although the development of structured leisure time programs for retarded students is encouraging, much remains to be done. Several authors have reported that typical free-time activities for retarded adolescents were napping and watching television (Bjaanes & Butler, 1974; Gollay, 1977). Yet training procedures for developing leisure time skills can be effective. Wehman, Renzaglia, Berry, Schutz, and Karan (1978) effectively taught severely retarded individuals how to exercise and enjoy table games. Johnson and Bailey (1977) increased the leisure skills of women with mental retardation living in a halfway house through developmental training procedures. Day and Day (1977) developed a comprehensive curriculum for people with mental retardation. All these authors reported that their subjects not only learned these basic skills but also were able to transfer them after instruction was terminated.

TEACHING ACADEMIC SKILLS

Core Concept 11 Academic tool subjects are taught to enhance the retarded adolescent's future opportunities for independence in the classroom setting, family unit, and community.

The objectives of an academic skill program for retarded adolescents are primarily functional and directly oriented to daily living activities, leisure time, and vocational preparation. These objectives are constant regardless of the severity of the individual's retardation. However, the means to achieve these objectives will differ across the various severity levels. For the mildly retarded adolescent, academics may be of higher priority than for the student who is more severely retarded. This is because mildly retarded adolescents may be able to better assimilate functional academic skills into their daily living and vocational activities. Given that moderately and severely retarded adolescents have a somewhat diminished capacity for applying academic tools to daily living, these students may require more emphasis on adaptive skill training. This is particularly evident in light of the limited instructional time available for these students during their school years.

A functional academic program includes instruction in reading, language, and arithmetic. A functional reading program focuses on reading for protection and information (Baroff, 1974). A protective (sometimes referred to as survival) vocabulary will allow the student to read building signs (e.g., push/pull, men/women, entrance/exit), street signs (e.g., walk/don't walk, stop, caution, railroad crossing), and other common environmental safety words (e.g., keep out, danger, poison, hazard, do not enter). An informational reading program teaches functional skills related to vocational proficiency (e.g., components of a job application form, reading classified ads), and the use of maps, telephone directories, and catalogs. From a survey of professionals in career education, Schilit and Caldwell (1980) compiled a list of career/vocational words as a means to assist teachers in more effectively preparing retarded adolescents to enter the working world (see Figure 9–3). A reading program that is more oriented toward leisure time activities will assist the student in gaining the most out of television, magazines, and newspapers (e.g., movie listings).

1. Rules	35. Employee	69. License
2. Boss	36. Layoff	70. Poison
3. Emergency	37. Take-home-pay	71. Office
4. Danger	38. Unemployed	72. Power
5. Job	39. Cost	73. Qualifications
6. Social security	40. Deduction	74. Earn
7. First-aid	41. Fired	75. Transportation
8. Help wanted	42. Closed	76. Withholding
9. Safety	43. Parttime	77. Vote
10. Warning	44. Correct	78. Break
11. Signature	45. Foreman	79. Cooperation
12. Time	46. Time-and-a-half	80. Dependable
13. Attendance	47. Worker	81. Money
14. Absent	48. Buy	82. Physical
15. Telephone	49. Raise	83. Hazardous
16. Bill	50. On-the-job	84. Net income
17. Hired	51. Entrance	85. Strike
18. Overtime	52. Responsible	86. Owner
19. Punch in	53. Hospital	87. Repair
20. Directions	54. Hourly rate	88. Alarm
21. Paycheck	55. Schedule	89. Gross income
22. Wages	56. Instructions	90. Manager
23. Appointment	57. Save	91. Reference
24. Income tax	58. Union	92. Uniform
25. Interview	59. Credit	93. Hard-hat
26. Supervisor	60. Elevator	94. Authority
27. Vacation	61. Punctuality	95. Training
28. Apply	62. Rights	96. Holiday
29. Fulltime	63. Hours	97. Late
30. Income	64. Payroll	98. Personal
31. Quit	65. Attitude	99. Tools
32. Check	66. Reliable	100. Area
33. Careful	67. Work	
34. Dangerous	68. Caution	

Figure 9–3. One Hundred Most Essential Career/Vocational Words
From "A word list of essential career/vocational words for mentally retarded students" by J. Schilit and M. L. Caldwell, 1980, *Education and Training of the Mentally Retarded, 15* (2), pp. 113–117.

Functional language programs focus on the use of expressive and receptive skills. Instruction in expressive language includes effective oral skills in carrying on a conversation, talking on the telephone, and responding to questions. Some degree of writing proficiency may also be necessary to enhance community and vocational independence. These skills range from the basic ability to write one's name to the more complex task of filling out a job application form. Receptive skills are also needed for daily conversations and job interviews. Good oral skills will be useless if the individual has not acquired some ability to listen and comprehend what others are communicating.

The intended outcomes for a functional arithmetic program are generally basic management of personal finances, consumer skills, and telling time. A personal finance program instructs the adolescent in several areas, including budgeting money, establishing and using credit, taxes, insurance, and wages. Consumer skills include both the identification of coins and bills of all denominations and making change, and the reading of bus or train schedules and timetables.

TRANSITION PLANNING

Core Concept 12	Although effective educational and adult service models have been designed to provide greater opportunities for retarded individuals in community settings, no significant long-term changes will result without the inclusion of a transition planning process.

Each year approximately 60,000 mentally retarded adolescents leave school and face life as adults in their local communities. The transition from school to adult life is not easy. Many retarded adults find that they are unable to access the critical services necessary to succeed in their own local communities (Brodsky, 1983; Hasazi et al., 1985), and these individuals may face long waiting lists for vocational and housing services (McDonnell, Wilcox, & Boles, 1985). Transition planning must facilitate the coordination and expansion of services within a community for each retarded adult. (Schalock, 1985; Wehman, Kregel, & Barcus, 1985). Given this information, professionals and parents have come to the realization that there is a need for a systematic effort to put in place a transition planning process that begins during the school years and carries over into adulthood.

Federal and state initiatives for transition planning were begun in 1983 and focused on the development of new programs to facilitate transition from school to adult life. The critical components of transition planning were identified: (a) effective high school programs that prepare students to work and live in the community, (b) a broad range of adult service programs that can meet the various support needs of individuals with handicaps in employment and community settings, and (c) comprehensive and cooperative transition planning between educational and community service agencies in order to develop needed services for graduation (Will, 1984). The remainder of this section will focus on a process designed to address the critical components of transition planning, and facilitate the coordination and expansion of services within the community for each retarded individual.

Coordinating Transition Planning

Core Concept 13 Effective transition planning is an ongoing process which begins with goals and objectives established at the time the student enters school.

The foundation for a formal transition planning process is initiated in the high school program. High schools must organize their programs and activities to produce those outcomes that facilitate success for the individual during the adult years. These outcomes for the retarded adult include being able to function as independently as possible in daily life. This individual should also be involved in the economic life of the community, which should provide opportunities for both paid and unpaid work. The handicapped adult should also be able to participate in social and leisure activities that are an integral part of community life. The school's roles in the transition process include the assessment of individual needs, developing transition plans for each student, coordinating transition planning with adult service agencies, and participating with parents in the planning process (Hardman, Drew, & Egan, 1987; Hardman & McDonnell, 1987; McDonnell & Hardman, 1985).

Determining Individual Need

Core Concept 14 The needs of mentally retarded adults are diverse and will vary according to both the severity of the condition and the demands imposed by the environment.

For many mildly retarded adults, no assistance may be necessary following school; for others, a short-term support system may have to be developed. For moderately to severely retarded adults, the assistance necessary to ensure appropriate access to community services may have to be long-term and intense. An effective transition planning system must then take into account both the short and long-term service needs of the individual. Hardman and McDonnell (1985) suggested that in order to identify the levels of support that an individual will require, parents and the schools must be able to view the individual during the high school years in a variety of performance areas (i.e., self-care, work, residential living, recreation and leisure time). Assessment in self-care would include such activities as grocery shopping, riding public transportation, crossing streets, maintaining a schedule, etc.

Developing a Transition Plan

Core Concept 15   The purposes of transition planning are to establish a
working relationship between parents and adult service
agencies, identify resources for employment and community participation, access services prior to graduation,
and identify systems that will help maintain needed
services.

Approximately two years before the student is expected to leave school, the
development of a formal transition plan should be initiated. There are several
purposes for this plan: (1) establishment of a formal working relationship
among parents, post-school case managers, and adult service providers, (2)
identification of the services and resources that will ensure meaningful
employment and community participation, (3) access to these services prior
to graduation, and (4) identification of the systems that will facilitate the
maintenance of needed services (McDonnell, Hightower, & Hardman, 1987).
In order to address each of these concerns, parents and professionals must
work together to review the services that are potentially available both
during and after leaving school, and then to identify activities that will
facilitate access to these services and to establish timelines and responsibilities for completion of the activities.

The components of the transition plan as outlined by McDonnell, Hightower, & Hardman include:

1. Vocational placement or program. Specify the type of placement or
   program that is most appropriate for the student. Determine how the
   resources between the school and post-school service programs will
   be coordinated to ensure that appropriate jobs are identified, and the
   student is trained for that placement.
2. Residential placement. Determine which residential alternative is the
   most appropriate for the student. If the family feels it is in the best
   interests of the retarded adult that he or she remain home for a period
   of time after leaving school, then appropriate family support services
   need to be in place. If the individual is to move into a residential
   placement immediately following school, then alternative living
   arrangements need to be considered.
3. Leisure alternatives. Identify those leisure alternatives that are most
   important to the student. Activities should be planned to ensure that
   the student has the necessary resources or skills to participate in such
   activities regardless of where the individual chooses to live following

school. Such resources or skills may include financing the activity, transportation, arranging for a peer to attend the activity with the student, etc.

4. Income and medical support. Balance the potential array of service alternatives with the individual's supplemental security income program. Ensure that needed cash awards or medical benefits are not jeopardized by other services.

5. Transportation. The specific transportation mode giving access to vocational, residential, and leisure alternatives should be determined. Identify the specific alternatives for each activity, the method of financing transportation, and strategies to coordinate transportation issues between school and adult service providers.

6. Long-term support and care. Identify the need for guardianship and/or specific trusts or wills. Specific services or agencies need to be identified that can assist parents in establishing these legal documents. Figure 9–4 presents a format for the development of a written transition plan.

Student: _____ Bob Robins _____   Meeting Date: _____ 10/15/85 _____
     Graduation Date: _____ 6/7/87 _____

Participants:
     Parent(s) _____ Mrs. Robins _____
     School _____ William B. _____
     DSH Casemanager _____ Susan L. _____
     DVR Casemanager _____ N/A _____

Planning Area: Vocational Services	*Responsible Person*	*Timelines*
Transition Goal		
Bob will initiate work training in Wasatch Work Crew Program	William B.	12/15/85
Support Activities		
1. Complete application process	Mrs. Robins Susan L.	11/1/85
2. Obtain UTA bus pass	Mrs. Robins	11/1/85
3. Teach bus route to Wasatch business office	William B.	11/14/85
4. Establish planning meeting with Wasatch WCP director	Susan L.	1/10/86

Figure 9–4. High School Transition Plan for a Severely Handicapped Student
From "Planning the Transition of Severely Handicapped Youth from School to Adult Services: A Framework for High School Programs" by J. McDonnell and M. L. Hardman, December 1985. *Education and Training of the Mentally Retarded.* Copyright 1985 by the Council for Exceptional Children. Reprinted by permission.

Involving Parents in Transition Planning

Core Concept 16 Parents must have the opportunity of learning as much
as possible about adult service systems prior to their
child's leaving school.

Parent education during the high school years should include the characteristics of adult service agencies, criteria for evaluating adult service programs, and potential as well as current service alternatives for the adult
with mental retardation. School districts need to offer ongoing educational
programs for parents to acquaint them with the issues involved in the transition from school to adult life. Every school district should develop and
use a transition planning guide to help parents complete critical planning
activities (McDonnell & Hardman, 1985).

Integration with Non-retarded Peers

Core Concept 17 The successful transition of the mentally retarded adult
to life in an integrated community setting begins with
integration during the school years.

Integration is an affirmation of the importance of learning and performance
opportunities provided by social interaction with academic peers. During
the high school transition years, the integration of mentally retarded students with their non- retarded peers may take place in several contexts. The
mentally retarded student may participate in a variety of academic or non-
academic classes (e.g., physical education, shop, art, music, etc.) within the
regular classroom environment. In addition, although they receive much of
their formal education within a self-contained special education classroom,
they may also participate in "normal" activities of the school (e.g., school
assemblies, lunch, hall interaction). The mentally retarded student may also
have the opportunity to interact with non-retarded students through such
programs as peer tutoring, in which non-retarded peer tutors volunteer to
assist mentally retarded students as part of their high school educational
experience. Peer tutors may assist in any context within the special education classroom, such as vocational education, adaptive learning, or rec-
reation/leisure activities. In a review of "best practice indicators" for
educating learners with severe handicaps, Fox et al. (1986) suggested that

handicapped students must have access to the same environments as their non-handicapped peers. "A primary goal of social integration should be to increase the *number* of integrated community and school environments in which learners can participate" (p. 4). Figure 9–5 highlights the best practice indicators for social integration.

Core Questions

1. Identify three components of an effective high school program for adolescents with mental retardation.
2. What basic civil rights were established under Section 504 of the Vocational Rehabilitation Act?
3. Distinguish between work-study, career education, and work experience programs.

---

1. A number of current and future age-appropriate integrated school and community environments have been identified for each individual learner   YES   NO
2. Ecological analyses are used to identify barriers and facilitators to participation in identified school and community environments   YES   NO
3. A plan for increasing participation in identified age-appropriate school and community environments should be reflected in the IEP   YES   NO
4. Learners with severe handicaps have opportunities to interact with age-appropriate peers and other community members within identified school and community environments   YES   NO
5. The learner's educator or related services personnel functions as a trainer/advocate to age-appropriate non-handicapped peers, other teachers, and community members   YES   NO

OVERALL BEST PRACTICE SCORE: SOCIAL INTEGRATION

NOT IMPLEMENTED		PARTIALLY IMPLEMENTED		TOTALLY IMPLEMENTED
1	2	3	4	5

The LEA has a written policy statement addressing social integration of learners with severe handicaps   YES   NO

Figure 9–5. Best Practice Indicators for Social Integration

From *Best educational practices '86: Educating learners with severe handicaps* (p. 5) by W. Fox, J. Thousand, W. Williams, T. Fox, P. Towne, R. Reid, C. Conn-Powers, & L. Calcagni, 1986, Burlington, VT: University of Vermont, Center for Developmental Disabilities. Copyright 1986 by W. Fox. Reprinted by permission.

4. Identify the components of a community-referenced vocational preparation program.
5. Discuss the barriers to socialization facing the retarded adolescent.
6. What difficulties face the retarded adolescent in attempting to maintain an appropriate personal appearance?
7. What is the value of recreation and leisure activities?
8. Discuss the objectives of a functional academics program for a high school-age mentally retarded student.
9. Discuss the school's role in the transition planning process.
10. Why is integration with non-handicapped peers an important aspect of a quality educational experience for adolescents with mental retardation?

ROUND TABLE DISCUSSION

The principle of normalization emphasizes that the person with mental retardation should have the same opportunities and access to services as non-handicapped individuals in a community setting. More than just providing the opportunity for a person with mental retardation to live or work in the community, it means providing the necessary support services to assist the individual in successfully meeting the demands of adult life.

In your study group or on your own, discuss the range of activities and services that must be available for the adult with mental retardation to live and work successfully in a community setting. How would you ensure that these services are available to people with mental retardation?

REFERENCES

Baroff, G. A. (1974). *Mental retardation: Nature, cause, and management.* New York: Halsted.

Bellamy, G. T., Horner, R. H., & Inman, D. P. (1979). *Vocational rehabilitation of severely retarded adults: A direct service technology.* Baltimore: University Park.

Bellamy, G. T., O'Connor, G., & Karan, O. (1979). *Vocational rehabilitation of severely handicapped persons: Contemporary service strategies.* Baltimore: University Park.

Bellamy, G. T., Rhodes, L., & Albin, J. M. (1985). *Support employment.* Unpublished manuscript, University of Oregon, Eugene, Oregon.

Bellamy, G.T., Rhodes, L.E., & Borbeau, P., & Mank, D.M. (1982). *Mental retardation services in sheltered workshops and day activity programs: Consumer outcomes and policy alternatives.* Unpublished manuscript, University of Oregon, Specialized Training Program, Eugene, OR.

Bjaanes, A., & Butler, E. (1974). Environmental variation in community care facilities for mentally retarded persons. *American Journal of Mental Deficiency, 78,* 429–439.

Brackey, L. (1971). How our flowers grow. In American Alliance of Health, Physical Education and Recreation, *The best of challenge.* Washington, DC: The Alliance.

Brimer, R., & Rouse S. (1978). Post-school adjustment: A follow-up of a cooperative program for the educable mentally retarded. *Journal for Special Educators of the Mentally Retarded, 14,* 131–137.

Brodsky, M. (1983). *Post high school experiences of graduates with severe handicaps.* Unpublished doctoral dissertation, University of Oregon, Eugene, OR.

Brolin, D. E. (1972). Value of rehabilitation services and correlates of vocational success with the mentally retarded. *American Journal of Mental Deficiency, 76,* 644–651.

Brolin, D. E. (1976). *Vocational preparation of retarded citizens.* Columbus, OH: Merrill.

Brolin, D. E. (1977). Career development: A national priority. *Education and Training of the Mentally Retarded, 12*(3), 154–156.

Brolin, D. E. (1982). *Vocational preparation of persons with handicaps* (2nd ed.). Columbus, OH: Merrill.

Brolin, D. E., DuRand, R., Kromer, K., & Muller, P. (1975). Post-school adjustment of educable retarded students. *Education and Training of the Mentally Retarded, 10,* 144–148.

Bruininks, R. H., & Lakin, K. C. (1985). *Living and learning in the least restrictive environment.* Baltimore: Brookes.

Bucher, C. A., & Bucher, R. D. (1974). *Recreation for today's society.* Englewood Cliffs, NJ: Prentice- Hall.

Buckley, J., & Bellamy, G. T. (1985). *A national survey of day and vocational programs for adults with severe disabilities: A 1984 profile.* Unpublished manuscript, University of Oregon, Specialized Training Program, Eugene, OR.

Calhoun, C. C., & Finch, A. V. (1976). *Vocational and career education concepts and operations.* Belmont, CA: Wadsworth.

Chaffin, J., Davidson, R., Regan, C., & Spellman, C. (1971). Two follow-up studies of former mentally retarded students from the Kansas work study project. *Exceptional Children, 37,* 733–738.

Clark, G. M. (1979). *Career education for the handicapped child in the elementary classroom.* Denver: Love.

D'Alonzo, B. J. (1977). Trends and issues in career education for the mentally retarded. *Education and Training of the Mentally Retarded, 12*(2), 156–158.

Day, R., & Day, M. (1977). Leisure skills instruction for the moderately and severely retarded: A demonstration program. *Education and Training of the Mentally Retarded, 12,* 128–131.

Department of Labor. (1979). *Study of handicapped clients in sheltered workshops, Vol. 2.* Washington, DC: Author.

DuRand, L., & DuRand, J. (1978). *The affirmative industry.* St. Paul: Diversified Industries.

Fischer, H. L., & Krajicek, M. J. (1974). Sexual development of the moderately retarded child. *Clinical Pediatrics, 13*(1), 79–83.

Fox, W., Thousand, J., Williams, W., Fox, T., Towne, P., Reid, R., Conn-Powers, C., & Calcagni, L. (1986) *Best educational practices '86: Educating learners with severe handicaps.* Monograph Series. Burlington, VT: University of Vermont, Center for Developmental Disabilities.

Gold, M. W. (1974). Redundant cue removal in skill training for the mentally retarded. *Education and Training of the Mentally Retarded, 9*(1), 5–8.

Gollay, E. (1977). Deinstitutionalized mentally retarded people: A closer look. *Education and Training of the Mentally Retarded, 12*(1), 137–144.

Halpern, A. S. (1973),. General unemployment and vocational opportunities for EMR individuals. *American Journal of Mental Deficiency, 78,* 123–127.

Halpern, A. S. (1974). Work-study programmes for the mentally retarded: An overview. In P. L. Browning (Ed.), *Mental retardation: Rehabilitation and counseling.* Springfield, IL: Thomas.

Hammer, S. L., & Bernard, K. E. (1966). The mentally retarded adolescent. *Pediatrics, 38,* 845–857.

Hardman, M. L., Drew, C. J., & Egan, M. W. (1987). *Human exceptionality* (2nd ed.). Boston: Allyn & Bacon, Inc.

Hardman, M. L., & McDonnell, J. (1987). Implementing federal transition initiatives for youths with severe handicaps: The Utah Community-based Transition Project. *Exceptional Children, 53*(6), 493–498.

Hardman, M. L., & Rose, E. (1984). *The Utah Community-based Transition Project* (Grant No. GOO 8430010). Washington, DC: US Department of Education, Office of Special Education and Rehabilitative Services.

Hasazi, S. B., Gordon, L. R., & Roe, C. A. (1984). Factors associated with the employment status of handicapped youth exiting high school from 1975 to 1983. *Exceptional Children, 51,* 455–469.

Howe, C. D. (1967, September). *A comparison of mentally retarded high school students in work-study versus traditional programs.* Long Beach, CA: US Department of Health, Education and Welfare, Office of Education, Bureau of Education for the Handicapped.

Johnson, M. S., & Bailey, J. S. (1977). The modification of leisure behavior in a halfway house for retarded women. *Journal of Applied Behavior Analysis, 10,* 273–282.

Kempton, W. (1983, April). Teaching retarded children about sex. *PTA Today,* 28–30.

Laski, F. (1979). Legal strategies to secure entitlement of services for severely handicapped persons. In G. T. Bellamy, G. O'Connor, & O. Karan (Eds.), *Vocational rehabilitation of severely handicapped persons* (pp. 1–32). Baltimore: University Park.

Martin, A., Flexer, R., & Newbery, J. (1979). The development of a work ethic in the severely retarded. In G. T. Bellamy, G. O'Connor, and O. Karan (Eds.), *Vocational rehabilitation of severely handicapped persons* (pp. 137–159). Baltimore: University Park.

McDonnell, J., & Hardman, M. L. (1985). Planning the transition of severely handicapped youth from school to adult services: A framework for high school programs. *Education and Training of the Mentally Retarded, 20*(4), 275–286.

McDonnell, J., Hightower, J., & Hardman, M. L. (1987) *The Utah community-based vocational preparation manual.* Salt Lake City: University of Utah, Department of Special Education.

McDonnell, J., Wilcox, B., & Boles, S. M. (1985). Do we know enough to plan for transition? A national survey of state agencies responsible for services to persons with severe handicaps. Unpublished manuscript. University of Oregon, Eugene, OR.

Meers, G. D. (1980). *Handbook of special vocational needs education.* Rockville, MD: Aspen Systems.

Mithaug, D. E., Horiuchi, C. N., & Fanning, P. N. (1985). A report on the Colorado statewide follow-up survey of special education students. *Exceptional Children, 51*(5), 397–404.

Moon, S., Goodall, P., & Wehman, P. (1985). *Critical issues related to supported competitive employment.* Richmond, VA: Rehabilitation and Training Center, Virginia Commonwealth University.

Murphy, J. F. (1975). *Recreation and leisure service.* Dubuque, IA: Wm. C. Brown.

Payne, J. S., & Patton, J. R. (1981). *Mental retardation.* Columbus, OH: Merrill.

Peck, C. A., Apolloni, T., & Cooke, T. P. (1981). Rehabilitation services for Americans with mental retardation: A summary of accomplishments in research and development. In E. L. Pan, T. E. Backer, and C. L. Vash (Eds.), *Annual review of rehabilitation* (Vol. 2). New York: Springer.

Rauh, J. L., Johnson, L. B., & Burket, R. L. (1973). The reproductive adolescent. *Pediatric Clinics of North America, 20,* 1005–1020.

Reisner, R. M. (1973). Acne vulgaris. *Pediatrics Clinics of North America, 20,* 851–864.

Revell, W. G., Wehman, P., & Arnold, S. (1985). A supported work approach to competitive employment of individuals with moderate and severe handicaps. In P. Wehman and J. W. Hill (Eds.), *Competitive employment for persons with mental retardation: From research to practice* (pp. 46–64). Richmond, VA: Rehabilitation Research and Training Center, School of Education, Virginia Commonwealth University.

Schalock, R. L. (1985). Comprehensive community services: A plea for interagency collaboration. In R.H. Bruininks & K.C. Lakin (Eds.) *Living and learning in the least restrictive environment* (pp. 37–64). Baltimore: Brookes.

Schilit, J., & Caldwell, M. L. (1980). A word list of essential career/vocational words for mentally retarded students. *Education and Training of the Mentally Retarded, 15*(2), 113–117.

Sowers, J., Thompson, L., & Connis, R. (1979). The food service vocational training program: A model for training and placement of the mentally retarded. In G. T. Bellamy, G. O'Connor, & O. Karan (Eds.), *Vocational rehabilitation of severely handicapped persons* (pp. 181–205). Baltimore: University Park.

Staley, E., & Miller, N. P. (1972). *Leisure and the quality of life: A new ethic for 1970's and beyond.* Washington, DC: American Alliance for Health, Physical Education and Recreation.

Timiras, P. S. (1972). *Development physiology and aging.* New York: Macmillan.

Verhoven, P. J. (1975). *A proposal for the development and pilot testing of a leisure education program model in select school systems.* Washington, DC: National Recreation and Park Association.

Wehman, P., Hill, M., Goodall, P., Cleveland, P., Brooke, V., Pentecost, J. (1982). Job placement and follow-up of moderately and severely handicapped individuals after three years. *Journal of Association for Severely Handicapped, 7,* 5–16.

Wehman, P., & Kregel, J. (1985). A supported work approach to competitive employment of individuals with severe handicaps. In P. Wehman and J. W. Hill (Eds.), *Competitive employment for persons with mental retardation: From research to practice* (pp. 20–45). Richmond VA: Rehabilitation Research and Training Center, School of Education, Virginia Commonwealth University.

Wehman, P. Kregel, J., & Barcus, J. M. (1985). From school to work: A vocational transition model for handicapped students. In P. Wehman & J. W. Hill (Eds.), *Competitive employment for persons with moderate and severe mental retardation: From research to practice* (pp. 169–198). Richmond, VA: Rehabilitation Research and Training Center, Virginia Commonwealth University.

Wehman, P., Kregel, J., & Seyfarth, J. (1985). Transition from school to work for individuals with severe disabilities: A follow-up study. In P. Wehman and J. W. Hill (Eds.), *Competitive employment for persons with mental retardation: From research to practice* (pp. 247–264). Richmond, VA: Rehabilitation Research and Training Center, School of Education, Virginia Commonwealth University.

Wehman, P., Renzaglia, A., Berry, G., Schutz, C., & Karan, O. (1978). Developing a leisure skill repertoire in severely and profoundly handicapped persons. *AAESPH Review, 3*, 162–172.

Whitehead, C. (1981). *Final report: Training and employment services for handicapped individuals in sheltered workshops.* Washington, DC: Office of Social Services Policy, Office of the Assistant Secretary for Planning and Evaluation, US Department of Health and Human Services.

Wilcox, B., & Bellamy, G. T. (1982). *Design of high school programs for severely handicapped students.* Baltimore: Brookes.

Will, M. (1984). *OSERS program for the transition of youth with disabilities: Bridges from school to working life.* Report from the Office of Special Education and Rehabilitative Services. Washington, DC.

Wright, B. (1974). Success breeds success. In American Alliance of Health, Physical Education and Recreation, *The best of challenge* (Vol. 2). Washington, DC: Author.

FOUR

THE RETARDED ADULT

The Retarded Adult

Core Concepts

1. The successful adjustment of the adult with mental retardation to community living depends upon vocational opportunities, access to public transportation and buildings, and adequate housing, medical services, and recreation and leisure.

2. Small community residential models for mentally retarded adults include group homes, semi-independent apartments, and foster care.

3. To become an integral part of society, the mentally retarded adult must abide by the rules and mores of the social order and participate in the functions required of citizenship.

4. The treatment of mentally retarded persons by law enforcement agencies and the judicial system will vary from one community to another.

5. Leisure time and recreation activities provide an important source of pleasure and relaxation for the mentally retarded adult.

6. Many individuals with mental retardation desire and value marriage and sexual intimacy.

7. Many mentally retarded adults are capable of self-sufficiency and social adaptation within a community setting.

8. Institutional living is widely viewed as a detriment to the intellectual, psychological, and physical development of mentally retarded individuals.

9. Competitive employment for persons with mental retardation can be described in terms of three service alternatives: (*a*) employment with no support services, (*b*) employment with time-limited support services, and (*c*) employment with ongoing support services.

10. The purpose of a sheltered workshop is to prepare the retarded person for competitive employment or to provide a terminal sheltered job.

The study of the life cycle of mentally retarded individuals is a relatively new phenomenon. Professionals have devoted most of their attention to development during childhood, because early development progresses so rapidly, is easily categorized into stages, and is so clearly significant for later life. Thus, while adulthood constitutes the major portion of an individual's life, it has received little attention until very recently (Bellamy & Horner, 1987).

Various cultures and religious groups have their own criteria for reaching adulthood. For example, a Jewish male becomes a bar mitzvah at 13, and a ceremony at that time signifies his admission into the adult religious community. Puberty, the biological coming of age, is observed as a social coming of age by many religious communities and traditional societies (Bradbury, 1975).

Adulthood generally is considered the period in life when a person has made a transition from a life of relative dependence to one of increasing independence and responsibility. Agreement among the various professions tends to be lacking as to when adulthood formally takes place. From a legal standpoint, an individual becomes an adult upon reaching a specific age, which varies from 18 years in some states to 21 years in others. Thus an individual may be instantaneously transformed from adolescent to adult on a specified birthday. A person may also be transformed from adolescent to adult or vice versa by crossing from one state to another.

Many public school officials have tended to view either the completion of a high school program or the exclusion from school because of age (often 21 years) as the point at which the responsibility of the school ends and the individual presumably has reached some semblance of adulthood. Professionals in the health sciences tend to equate specific levels of physical development with adulthood. Those with certain physiological deviancies may never be considered to be adults, regardless of their intellectual or social competencies. A behavioral science view that emphasizes specific behavioral patterns to meet adulthood standards simply adds to the frustrating lack of uniformity in criteria.

Mentally retarded adults exist as a paradox. They have achieved the status of adulthood because they have lived long enough to deserve the distinction. However, some of these adults are unable to attain a level of total independence; they lack the intellectual skills to meet typical high school graduation requirements and may lack behavioral characteristics considered essential for adequate adult functioning.

Many individuals who are mildly or moderately retarded endure the frustrations of childhood and adolescence with the hope and expectation that adulthood will bring an emancipation from the many problems associated with school. While academic pressures and certain intellectual demands tend to subside on completion of school, other demands find their way into the life of a retarded adult. What are the expectations for an adult in our society? An adult works, earns money, and buys the necessities of life and as many of the pleasures as can be afforded. An adult socializes, often marries and has children, and tries to live as productively and happily as possible. The retarded adult, however, may be unable to find or hold a job. Even if jobs are available, the wages may be so low that even the necessities of life may be out of reach. What if the retarded adult has no one to socialize with, no one to love or be loved by? What if the retarded adult must become dependent on parents for mere existence and the parents become too old to help or they die? There are many "what ifs" for retarded adults; the frustrations of earlier life are exchanged for newer and sometimes harsher ones.

There is a paucity of available research that focuses on the retarded adult (Hardman, Drew, & Egan, 1987). Most studies are concerned with retarded children in the educational system, because it is in the schools that the deficiencies of mentally retarded persons tend to be the most evident. It was not until 1973 that the Association for Retarded Children appropriately changed its name to the Association for Retarded Citizens. Although this association has long campaigned for the rights for all retarded persons, the change is indicative of a growing recognition of the need to emphasize programming at all stages of life. We support the emphasis of children and youth; however, we are also concerned with the lack of emphasis on appropriate opportunities, programs, and services for retarded adults. If average life expectancy is reached, the individual will live three times as many years as an adult than as a child and adolescent. It seems only appropriate that we devote more time to the needs and nature of retarded adults.

COMMUNITY LIVING

Core Concept 1   The successful adjustment of the adult with mental retardation to community living depends upon vocational opportunities, access to public transportation and buildings, and adequate housing, medical services, and recreation and leisure.

The availability of appropriate services within the community permits a greater opportunity for the mentally retarded individual to achieve what has become commonly referred to as "normalization." The principle of normalization was first articulated by Nirje (1969) and Bank-Mikkelsen (1969) and was expanded and advocated in the United States by Wolfensberger (1972). Normalization means "making available to the mentally retarded patterns and conditions of everyday life which are as close as possible to the norms and patterns of mainstream society" (Nirje, 1969, p. 181). Normalization does not mean the mere provision of a normative situation, such as a home in the community. Without the needed support services, the retarded individual may not be able to meet the demands of the community. Nirje stated that:

> normalization will not make a subnormal normal, but will make life conditions of the mentally subnormal as close as possible, bearing in mind the degree of his handicap, his competence and maturity as well as the need for training activities and availability of services. . . . The awareness that mostly only relative independence and integration can be attained (is) implied and stressed by the words "as close as possible." (1969, p. 63)

Wolfensberger (1983) suggested rethinking the term normalization and introduced the concept of "social role valorization"—giving value to the individual with mental retardation. He indicated that "the most explicit and highest goal of normalization must be the creation, support, and defense of valued social roles for people who are at risk of social devaluation" (p. 234). We must attempt to establish socially valued roles and life conditions for people who are devalued by society. Strategies to accomplish this goal might include enhancing the mentally retarded individual's social image or perceived value in the eyes of others and increasing the mentally retarded individual's competence within society.

The principles of normalization and social valorization have brought with them a strong emphasis on deinstitutionalization, which refers to the process of returning persons residing in large centers for the mentally retarded to community and home environments. However, the principles apply not only to those retarded individuals moving from an institution to a less restrictive setting but also to those retarded individuals living in the community for which a more "normal" life-style is a worthy goal.

Turnbull and Turnbull (1975) suggested that the decisions involving residential living frequently are made by the parents or guardians and administrators of the retarded person, who often has no opportunity to voice opinions or preferences in the decision making process. This has been based on the assumption that the retarded individual is incompetent to participate in these decisions.

There are many areas of everyday living that most individuals take for granted, such as shopping, crossing streets, making daily purchases, and getting transportation. Yet unless deliberate efforts are made to provide instruction in these areas, a number of problems can develop. For example, a group of young retarded adults living in a community-based home had not had any instruction regarding the use of traffic lights to cross streets, and they did not stop for red lights. The residents did not receive appropriate training until the trainers within the group home recognized the problem.

In the following sections, we will discuss various aspects related to community living. These include residential alternatives, community participation, marriage and sexuality, and adjustment to community life.

Community-Based Residential Living

Core Concept 2   Small community residential models for mentally retarded adults include group homes, semi-independent apartments, and foster care.

As we move into the 1990s, the vast majority of families and professionals concerned about people with mental retardation are advocating a nationwide expansion of small, community-based residences, placed within local neighborhoods and staffed with trained support personnel. Residents in these settings would use existing services in the community for education, work, health care, and recreation. Other alternatives might also be appropriate, such as living with a local family, foster care, or adoption.

Sarason (1974) emphasized "a psychological sense of community." Sarason contended that the main criterion by which any program should be developed and assessed is whether it promotes a sense of belonging, mutual responsibility and purpose, and the opportunity for persons to be part of a group on which they can depend and to which they can contribute.

Mentally retarded people in community-based living circumstances are able to experience important growth activities not available in other settings.

Another view is that a setting should provide community training for the resident. These programs emphasize providing opportunities for activities to develop skills for independent functioning in daily activities.

Several systems for classifying community residential programs have been developed over the years (Baker, Seltzer, & Seltzer, 1977; Campbell & Bailcy, 1984). Tablc 10–1 presents a summary of current program models

Table 10–1. Residential Program Models

Original Definition	**Proposed Definition**
Residential Facility	
Any living quarters which provided 24-hour, 7-days-a-week responsibility for room, board, and supervision of mentally retarded people as of (date), with the exception of: (a) single family homes providing services to a relative; (b) nursing homes, boarding homes, and foster homes that are not formally state licensed or contracted as mental retardation service providers; and (c) independent living programs which have no staff residing in the same facility.	
Program models	
A home or apartment owned or rented by a family, with one or more retarded people living as family members (e.g., foster homes)	A residence owned or rented by a family as their own home, with one or more mentally retarded people living as family members (e.g., foster home)
A residence with staff who provide care, supervision, and training of one or more mentally retarded people (e.g., group residence)	A residence with staff who provide care, supervision, and training of one or more mentally retarded people (e.g., group residence)
A residence consisting of semi-independent units or apartments with staff living in a separate unit in the same building (e.g., supervised apartments)	A residence consisting of semi-independent units or apartments with staff living in a separate unit in the same building (e.g., semi-independent living program)
A residence which provides sleeping rooms and meals, but no regular care or supervision of residents (e.g., boarding home)	A residence with staff which provide sleeping rooms, meals, and supervision, but no formal training or help with dressing, bathing, etc. (e.g., board & supervision facility)
A residence in which staff provide help with dressing, bathing, or other personal care, but no formal training of residents (e.g., personal care home)	A residence with staff who provide help with dressing, bathing, or other personal care, but no formal training of residents (e.g., personal care facility)
A nursing home (e.g., ICF or SNF)	A facility that provides daily nursing care with primary emphasis on residents' health care needs (e.g., nursing home)

From "Classification of Residential Facilities for Individuals with Mental Retardation" by B. K. Hill and K. C. Lakin, 1986, *Mental Retardation, 24* (2), 109. Copyright 1986 by the American Association on Mental Deficiencies. Reprinted by permission.

as described by Hill and Lakin (1986). In this chapter we will discuss three widely used residential models for adults with mental retardation living within the community: group homes, semi-independent apartments, and foster care.

Group Homes. There is considerable variation in organization patterns and alternatives within the group home model. *Small group homes* are usually a community residence with up to four persons living in a single dwelling. *Large group homes* may have as many as 8 to 12 residents. These homes are staffed by trained house parents or professionals; they often have an assistant to serve as a relief person for their days and times off. In some instances a house director is employed on a full- or half-time basis to handle administrative matters. Many group homes are now employing shift workers who are on duty as a team for 4 to 7 days at a time. Small group homes are usually integrated into residential neighborhoods. The homes emphasize programs that provide daily living experiences as similar as possible to those of nonretarded individuals. Day placements for work skill training is typical of these programs.

These homes are typically financed by state funds supplemented by fees paid by the residents. As might be expected, a fairly high percentage of these homes meet with some opposition from the community, usually from neighbors. Baker, Seltzer and Seltzer (1977) found in their study of group homes that 19% of the residents in the study returned to institutions or hospitals, 24% went on to live in an apartment, 26.5% returned to live with their families, and 5% were placed in foster homes. In some instances group homes serve as a permanent residence for certain individuals, and in other instances they serve as an intermediate step for a more normalized situation. In some group homes residents contribute to group decision making, which may produce decisions superior to those made individually. Peer group discussions and decision making of day-to-day administrative issues may have a beneficial learning experience for retarded residents (Heller, 1978).

The availability of group homes was the subject of a survey conducted by Janicki, Mayeda, and Epple (1983). These authors found that in the 1970s there was a dramatic increase in the availability of group homes in the United States. The survey indicated that there were more than 5,700 group homes in this country, an increase of over 900% since 1973. They also reported that approximately 23,500 persons were living in group homes for the mentally retarded at the time of the survey, representing a growth rate of 183%. However, these authors conclude that although there has been considerable expansion in the development of group homes, "there still appears to be an outstanding need for more group home beds nationally" (p. 50).

In a study of 132 group homes, Baker, Seltzer and Seltzer (1977) found that 21% of the residents were engaged in competitive employment, 51% in sheltered workshops or educational programs, and 16% in day activity centers. The mean age of these residents was 29 years, with 35% of the group listed as mildly retarded, 48% as moderately retarded, 13% as severely retarded, and the remaining were handicapped, nonretarded individuals.

Semi-independent Living Apartment. The semi-independent apartment represents the least supervised, least restrictive setting of all residential models in which some degree of supervision is provided. Three variations of semi-independent apartment living are suggested by Fritz, Wolfensberger, and Knowlton (1971):

1. *Apartment clusters.* Apartment clusters consist of several apartments in relative physical proximity to one another, functioning to some extent as a unit, and supervised by a resident staff member residing in one of the apartment units.
2. *Single co-residence apartment.* Single apartments in which an adult staff member (usually a college student) shares an apartment with two or three retarded roommates.
3. *Single apartment.* The maximum independence is an apartment, occupied by two or more retarded adults who are given assistance by a nonresident staff member.

These three variations provide varying degrees of independence, and individuals living in apartments usually are less retarded than those living in other residential models. In this arrangement most residents are responsible for or contribute to apartment maintenance, meal preparation, and transportation to place of employment.

Foster Family Care. The purpose of *foster family care* is to provide a surrogate family for the retarded individual. A goal of foster family care is to integrate the individual into the family setting. In a normal family environment and with the foster family's understanding, the individual presumably will learn behavior acceptable to the family; and, if it is feasible, will work. One possible problem related to this foster home model is that a retarded person may assume a dependent, childlike role and, as a result, be overprotected. Generally these placements provide residents with adequate productive daytime activities and adequate opportunity to manage their physical environment, both of which are fundamental components of normalization. These settings accommodate from one to six adults, and activities and quality of care to some extent are discretionary with the operators of these homes. Furthermore, in most instances, those who operate the foster homes receive a per capita fee from the state. If their goal is to make a profit, there is a danger that they will spend too little on their foster residents in order that they may increase profits.

One other setting that is considered by some to be a community residential alternative is the *sheltered village.* Sheltered villages for retarded adults are usually located in rural areas and are secluded and spread out over several buildings. Although rules, activities, and relative freedom vary from one village to another, the villages do have one common characteristic: they are intended to isolate the retarded individual from the outside community. It is believed that these residents are better off in isolation than exposed to the potential failure, frustrations, and demands of the outside world. Most of these facilities are private, and a number are church sup-

Community participation by those with mental retardation may include many daily activities undertaken by nonretarded individuals.

ported. Fees are generally high, nearly double the cost of fees in other residential alternatives.

Of the community models we have discussed, this alternative appears to be in greatest conflict with the principle of normalization. Proponents of these settings argue that the individual is better off protected and sheltered from the chaos, prejudice, and demands of society.

Community Participation

Core Concept 3	To become an integral part of society, the mentally retarded adult must abide by the rules and mores of the social order and participate in the functions required of citizenship.

Active Citizenship. Although special education classes may emphasize participation in social and civic activities, many retarded adults either do not internalize what they have learned or, perhaps, find participation in activities such as voting to be confusing. Edgerton (1967) found that none of his subjects had ever voted. Gozali (1971) investigated the degree of knowledge and participation of 68 mildly retarded individuals in democratic political processes. The subjects ranged in chronological age from 21 to 28 years and in IQ from 68 to 82, and all had attended special education programs. Each individual was verbally given 60 questions relating to citizenship. Gozali found that most did poorly on the test and none had even registered to vote.

Perhaps voting is not an important function for retarded persons, or they do not perceive it as such. If it is not a useful and worthwhile function for these people, then instruction in casting a ballot may be a useless exercise. If, however, mentally retarded persons are not participating in this basic right and responsibility because of their lack of sophistication, efforts could be increased to facilitate their active participation. Curricula could include not only an academic understanding of voting, but also some practical experience in simulation voting for public officials and even real voting within the classroom for various types of responsibilities. Groups such as the local association for retarded citizens could provide transportation and help on voting registration and other related procedures. Mentally retarded persons are often on the lower end of the economic continuum. Changes in government frequently have a profound effect on their lives. Voting has as much relevancy for their lives as for the lives of other citizens in the community.

Core Concept 4 The treatment of mentally retarded persons by law enforcement agencies and the judicial system will vary from one community to another.

The Mentally Retarded Offender. Throughout the years various studies have found a disproportionately high number of mentally retarded individuals involved in delinquent or criminal activity (Goddard, 1914; Kvaraceus, 1945; Moore, 1911; Peterson and Smith, 1960). Presently, there are well over 20,000 mentally retarded persons incarcerated in prisons, which represents nearly 10% of the total prison population (DeSilva, 1980; Reichard, Spencer, and Spooner, 1980). These data are consistent with a study conducted in 1969 by Allen in which he polled correctional institutions across the United States. His surveys revealed that the percentage of mentally retarded persons (using an IQ of 70 as a cutoff) in correctional institutions was triple that in the general population. In other words, approximately 9% of the inmate population had IQs of 70 or below compared with 3% in the general or noncorrectional institutionalized population. Nearly 1,500 inmates (1.6%) were reported to have IQs ranging downward from 55 to 17. The study also found a general lack of mental health resources personnel within the institutions and few special programs for retarded persons. Over half the institutions had no programs of any kind, not even a special education class.

Allen (1970) examined correctional institutions in six states and found that in most instances disclosure of mental retardation was not made before judgment. He maintained that the disclosure of mental retardation is a relevant issue in determining the individual's competency to stand trial, in considering the admissibility of the confession, and in resolving the issue of criminal responsibility (insanity). Most prisoners in the sample were poor and black and whose appointed counsel had spent little time with them. The trial was often a mere formality, with 95% of the defendants either confessing or pleading guilty.

The study also found a significantly larger proportion of retarded subjects convicted for violent crimes than the nonretarded group. Allen suggested that this finding should be qualified by pointing out that the retarded are, as a group, easier to apprehend, more likely to confess, easier to convict,and expected to be incarcerated longer than the nonretarded offenders. Allen further pointed out that retarded offenders of less severe crimes are often committed to institutions for the retarded, thus inflating the proportion of retarded persons involved in violent crimes within the prison.

The results of Allen's study suggests that our judicial system is not equal for all. Retarded persons seldom can afford private defense lawyers and therefore must make do with court appointed attorneys. The quality of such legal defense is a debatable issue, although we recall that Allen's researchers found the entire trial process to be a mere formality.

The results reported by Allen (1969, 1970) are consistent with those found in a study by Schilit (1979). In a survey of police officers, lawyers, and judges, Schilit found that 91% of these people did not have any formal training in mental retardation and consistently underestimated the functional capabilities of mentally retarded individuals. He discussed the implications that this study has for the criminal justice system:

1. The mentally retarded person who comes into contact with the criminal justice system is at a definite disadvantage due to the criminal justice system's unfamiliarity and uncertainty in dealing with mentally retarded individuals.
2. Preservice and inservice education for criminal justice system personnel is needed on the topic of mental retardation and the mentally retarded offender.
3. Mentally retarded individuals need to be trained about the criminal justice system and what to do if they come into contact with the criminal justice system.
4. There is a need for community agencies to begin dealing with this area of concern, that is, the mentally retarded offender and the criminal justice system.
5. The criminal justice system might need to reorganize itself to establish a system within itself to handle mentally retarded offenders. (p. 22)

In some communities law enforcement officers are sympathetic to retarded persons, whereas in others they are viewed as a nuisance. Retarded persons, who often lack financial resources and people to represent them, may suffer greatly in our judicial system. There appears to be a great need for the development of a system in which retarded persons can receive adequate legal help when they are in difficulty. The American Civil Liberties Union has long served as an advocate for oppressed groups. The ACLU, along with protection and advocacy systems for developmentally disabled persons in every state, local associations for retarded citizens, and local bar associations, can serve as effective advocates for retarded people. Most mentally retarded people have demonstrated their positive capabilities within the social system. A concerted effort will increase the number of responsible retarded individuals and decrease their number in correctional institutions.

Core Concept 5   Leisure time and recreation activities provide an important source of pleasure and relaxation for the mentally retarded adult.

Leisure Time and Recreation. Many adults who are mentally retarded have busy and active work schedules. For these individuals leisure time and recreational activities provide a much-needed change from daily work schedules. Other mentally retarded adults have little, if any, work or regular daily activity. These individuals need recreation activities as a means to achieve more satisfaction and independence in their lives. However, as Schleien, Kiernan, and Wehman (1981) pointed out, "remarkably few studies have investigated the leisure skill behaviors of mentally retarded adults living in community based residences" (p. 13).

Shannon (1985) found that mentally retarded adults spend significant amounts of time in solitude within their homes. Typical activities included watching television, listening to music, and looking at books and magazines. An earlier study (Stanfield, 1973) indicated that walking idly around the neighborhood was a frequent activity of many retarded adults. Stanfield reported that 44% of his subjects did not participate in postschool or rehabilitation programs. This left a large number of subjects with basically no structured daily activity. Stanfield (1973, p. 522) quotes one mother as saying: "At first it wasn't too bad. He enjoyed his vacation as he called it— and then he began to ask when school would start again. I don't have the

Many forms of recreation and leisure are being recognized as being relevant for retarded individuals.

time it takes—and I don't always know what to do for him." Stanfield concluded that the vast majority of adults with mental retardation had no social or recreational life apart from that with the immediate family. The findings of the Shannon and Stanfield studies have been corroborated by Bjaanes and Butler (1974), who found that residents living in community residences spent only 3% of their free time in structured leisure activities.

Too often retarded adults are left with a lonely inactive life when, in fact, meaningful leisure activities should be an integral part of their lives (Fain, 1986). Peck, Appolloni, and Cooke (1981) suggested that successful training in leisure time can be accomplished through the incorporation of systematic assessment, highly structured training procedures, and rigorous evaluation components. The retarded adult is fully entitled to the pleasures that well-planned recreational activities afford. Efforts in this direction by recreation therapists, churches, schools, and family can help make life for the mentally retarded adult more meaningful.

Marriage and Sexuality

Core Concept 6	Many individuals with mental retardation desire and value marriage and sexual intimacy.

A considerably smaller percentage of all mentally retarded adults marry in contrast to their nonretarded peers. Peterson and Smith (1960) found that marriage rates are two and one-half times higher for nonretarded men and three times higher for nonretarded women. Divorce figures were four times higher for the retarded group. As a group, 50% of the retarded adults remained unmarried, compared to 20% in the nonretarded group.

Edgerton (1967) and Edgerton and Bercovici (1976) found that marriage was highly valued among retarded adults and was considered a highly meaningful status to achieve. They interviewed a number of former hospital patients and found that marriage, particularly to someone not from the institution, was of paramount importance to retarded adults. One retarded woman indicated that every girl wanted to marry an individual not associated with the hospital. She indicated that she had done everything to enhance her chances such as "speaking properly," buying nice clothing, and going to nice places. She avoided "hospital guys" (males released from the institution from which she herself had been released). A male adult indicated that the men in his group of former institutional subjects, including himself, had remained single because of their inability to meet nonretarded girls. He further stated that the only girls available to the men released from the institution were "hospital girls" or prostitutes.

Heshusius (1982) reviewed the literature for perceptions on marriage and sexuality of persons labeled as mentally retarded and then sorted the statements of mentally retarded persons according to some common elements. These generalized statements reflected a desire for, and enjoyment of, sexual contact as well as a fear of sexual intimacy. Many retarded persons felt that sexual intimacy belonged with marriage. There was also some ignorance of the basic facts on sexual relations. Heshusius stressed the need for more sensitivity on the part of society to a retarded person's need for sexual intimacy.

According to the available literature it appears that mentally retarded persons do desire and value marriage and sexual intimacy. As a group, however, they are apparently not successful in finding mates; this may result partly from their desire to marry nonretarded individuals or, at least, individuals who had no previous association with an institution. This wish may indicate an overall desire to assume as normal an existence as possible.

The area of sex education is a major concern, but it is sometimes deliberately ignored. However, as adults in the community, these persons will be to a certain extent free to conduct their personal lives as they choose. How they do so, and what the results of their interpersonal relationships are, may depend on the instruction and training that they receive in sex education. Deisher's study (1973) on institutional staff attitudes regarding the sexuality of retarded individuals suggested that there may be a substantial number of staff members who believe that residents should be permitted either limited expression of sexual feeling or no expression at all. Although more liberal attitudes may have developed since this study, there remains the concern that those staff members who view retarded individuals primarily as asexual will not provide these individuals with adequate sex education before deinstitutionalization. Yet, several authors have demonstrated that retarded individuals can learn new social/sexual skills (Foxx, McMorrow, Storey, & Rogers, 1984).

Another issue concerning the sexuality of mentally retarded persons is the practice of *sterilization*. In past years sterilization has been viewed as a means of eliminating or curtailing mental retardation by preventing the birth of children who may be retarded, preventing retarded individuals from having unwanted children, or preventing retarded individuals from having children for whom they are allegedly incompetent to care. In 1927 Justice Holmes issued his famous opinion for the Supreme Court, which upheld a state compulsory sterilization law. He stated that "three generations of imbeciles are enough" (Buck v. Bell, 1927). The practice of the sterilization of retarded individuals has decreased considerably in more recent years. Ferster (1966) reports that compulsory sterilization decreased from 1,643 cases in 1943 to 643 cases in 1963.

The prime targets for compulsory sterilization appear to be retarded individuals who are in the process of being released from institutions (Burt,

1973; Edgerton, 1969). In Edgerton's study of former patients of Pacific State Hospital, he found that 44 of the 48 subjects had undergone "eugenic" sterilization. During the period of their institutionalization, sterilization was considered a prerequisite to release. Form letters were sent to parents or guardians to gain consent for the procedure. These letters strongly implied that sterilization could permit parole and would be in the best interest of the individual. Therefore unless there was strong objection, the surgery was routinely performed.

By 1935 mentally retarded persons constituted 44% of those sterilized in this country; by 1946 this had increased to 69%. The rate of sterilization increased through 1937 and leveled off by 1942. The leveling off was attributable to the shortage of medical personnel during the war years (Goldstein, 1964). Gamble (1951) reported that through 1950, 26,000 retarded individuals had been rendered parolable from institutions by sterilization.

Follow-up studies of sterilized retarded individuals have generally reported favorable adjustment or at least no noticeably negative effects from the operation (Craft, 1963; Johnson, 1946). Adjustment in these studies was gauged by marriage, sexual changes, and incidence of sex offenses. It is interesting to note that while the subjects of the Craft study experienced no change in sexual habits or behaviors, the incidence of sex offenses decreased dramatically. Although the findings appear contradictory, they may be a function of maturity that the subjects could have developed during institutionalization or of changes in criteria defining a sex offense. It is possible that what was considered promiscuous behavior for younger, virile retarded persons may be considered the private business of sterilized consenting adults in a later period of life.

In Edgerton's initial study (1967) the majority of the interviewed group held negative feelings regarding the sterilization that had been imposed on them to preclude the possibility of bearing children. The objections tended to center around three areas of concern. First, the sterilization was an indelible mark of their previous institutionalization. Second, some individuals felt deprived of the children they wanted. Third, there appeared to be fear on the part of many individuals that their partners would discover their infertility when no offspringwere produced after a period of time.

Some of the issues regarding sterilization of mentally retarded individuals are readily apparent. Resolution of these issues is far more complex and difficult than their identification. Some retarded individuals are either not able or unwilling to exercise birth control to avoid unwanted pregnancies. The result of some of these unwanted pregnancies may be neglected and abused children or children for whom parents must seek external financial assistance to provide minimal support in terms of food, clothing, and health care. In some instances pregnancy results in the birth of other retarded children. The retarded individuals most frequently sterilized have tended to be those who are residents in institutions, particularly residents in the process of being released.

A number of institutionalized retarded persons are wards of the state. This condition permits the institution greater flexibility with matters regarding sterilization, because parental consent may be unnecessary. Thus it appears that the institutionalized are prime targets for sterilization. This practice appears to be both ironic and discriminatory. It is ironic since institutionalized retarded persons represent the segment of the retarded population that should be least likely to present birth control problems. Not only are many of these individuals so socially and physically incompetent that sexual relationships represent remote possibilities, but they are among the most closely and carefully supervised members of our retarded population. The practice of sterilizing institutionalized retarded persons as a prerequisite to release appears to be highly discriminatory. Such persons represent no greater threat to themselves and to society than the majority of the retarded individuals who are not under the jurisdiction of an institution. Yet, because they have lived in institutions, they are singled out and prevented even from choosing or demonstrating their relative competence as parents.

The concern of discriminatory sterilization laws should not be limited to the institutional group exclusively. The question of whether or not society has the right to impose sterilization on any retarded individual has great relevancy to parents, to professionals, and to the retarded individuals themselves. Prominent jurists such as Burt (1973) and Allen (1969) suggest that involuntary sterilization of a mentally retarded person violates that person's basic rights. It is interesting to note that two of the four unsterilized subjects in Edgerton's study were considered successful mothers of normally intelligent children.

A primary issue in the matter of sterilization is who decides, and by what criterion, who must be sterilized. Should we sterilize all retarded individuals in institutions and in the community? What are the criteria to be used for determining sufficient retardation to warrant compulsory sterilization? Should we sterilize all individuals at the moderate level or below? Should we use a cutoff of 70 or 75 IQ, which includes all mildly retarded persons as well? Perhaps the strong advocates of sterilization could find justification for using 100 IQ as a minimum criterion for the right to have children, since 100 IQ represents the mean or average IQ. Obviously the setting of arbitrary criteria can be both unfair and potentially dangerous to the civil rights of every individual.

As rational individuals, we must be cognizant of the realities of different life-styles and different standards of living. The standards of a good life are relative to the individual. Many middle-class individuals may consider the life-style of mildly retarded individuals as totally unacceptable. Mildly retarded persons may themselves be dissatisfied with their present life-style, but no more so than many middle-class families.

When certain genetic disorders exist, sterilization may be a viable alternative. However, capricious and prejudicial decisions that disregard the rights of mentally retarded individuals and preclude their self-fulfillment must be carefully examined and challenged by responsible parents, professionals, and advocates for retarded persons.

Research on Adjustment to Community Living

Core Concept 7   Many mentally retarded adults are capable of self-sufficiency and social adaptation within a community setting.

The 1980s has been a decade of expansion in community living alternatives for persons with mental retardation. We have made significant advances in the knowledge of factors affecting community adjustment (Bruininks & Lakin, 1985; Peck, Apolloni, & Cooke, 1981; Tessler & Manderscheid, 1982). However, much remains to be done to use effectively the available information and to identify further those variables that are associated with success in community programs (Eyman & Borthwick, 1980; Hitzing, 1980; O'Conner, 1976).

The literature concerning follow-up studies of retarded individuals dates back to 1919. Fernald (1919) studied individuals discharged from an institution over a 25-year period and found considerable variability in adjustment to community life. In the 1930s and 40s, several studies compared the community adjustment of mentally retarded individuals with control groups of nonretarded individuals. These include the studies of Fairbanks (1931), Baller (1936), and R. J. R. Kennedy (1948). Fairbanks and Kennedy conducted their studies during periods when economic and general employment conditions were generally favorable. Baller's study was conducted during a period of severe economic depression. When economic conditions are poor, mentally retarded individuals are frequently among those most severely affected. Employers may consider them the most dispensable of their employees, often the first to be laid off. This is particularly evident in Baller's study—only 20% of the retarded subjects were gainfully employed as opposed to 50% of the control group (normal subjects). In Fairbanks's and Kennedy's studies, however, the retarded compared very favorably with the controls with respect to gainful employment. In all three studies, the marital status of the retarded group appeared to be comparable with the control group. Home ownership, as reported by Fairbanks and Kennedy, also appeared comparable. These studies suggest that the majority of retarded persons were able to make acceptable adjustments to community life. The majority were employed in semiskilled and unskilled jobs. Economic conditions and the type of community may have had some effect on their ability to adjust.

Follow-up studies of the subjects suggest that even in later years, community adjustment of these individuals can be considered successful (Baller, Charles, & Miller, 1966; R. A. Kennedy, 1966). Another study in the 1960s (Edgerton, 1967) examined the posthospital lives of a number of individuals released from Pacific State Hospital, a California residential institution. The subjects of Edgerton's study were mildly retarded individuals who had received the benefit of vocational rehabilitation training programs both in the hospital and in the community. These individuals were considered among the more intellectually, socially, and emotionally capable within the institution. As a group, Edgerton found the subjects generally living comfortably, with most of them married and enjoying various leisure activities. By and large their existence was relatively inconspicuous. Edgerton suggested that one of the greatest problems faced by this group was the stigma of being labeled mentally retarded. These individuals could not and would not accept the "fact" that they were or had ever been mentally retarded. To do so would be humiliating and would devaluate their feelings of self-worth. Thus, much of their effort was in the direction of attempting to convince others, as well as themselves, that they were normal individuals. Many blame their relative incompetence on the years spent in the institution, when they were locked up and deprived of the knowledge and experience required for competent living and functioning in the larger community.

In a follow-up to the 1967 study, Edgerton and Bercovici (1976) examined the lives of many of the same individuals several years later to determine what effect the passage of time had on their community adaptation. Thirty of the original 48 subjects were located. In this follow-up, the subjects expressed far less concern for passing as "normal," and concern about stigma was less evident. Additionally, the authors found that "normal" benefactors played a less significant role. Overall, dependence on benefactors lessened over time. This may have been the result of either less need for these benefactors or the lessening availability of them. Edgerton and Bercovici concluded that what the subjects perceived as reduced stigma may have helped to reduce the need for benefactors, and the additional years of experience in community living may have reduced the need for assistance. While Edgerton and Bercovici rated the life circumstances for the total group as slightly worse compared with their status in the earlier study (1967), in general the subjects themselves considered their circumstances to be happier. Their happiness was not necessarily a function of vocational success. Rather, happiness may have been more a function of perceiving themselves as normal, and in periods of high unemployment, many normal people may not be working.

A second follow-up to Edgerton's 1967 study was conducted in 1982 (Edgerton, Bollinger, & Herr, 1984). This follow-up study focused on personal and social resources of the 15 mildly retarded persons originally studied in 1960 and 1961. These authors found less dependence on others than reported in the previous investigations. Additionally, these 15 individuals, now ranging between 47 and 68 years of age, were described as more hopeful, confident, and independent by the investigators.

In the 1970s, several authors (e.g., Bellamy, O'Conner, & Karan, 1979; Close, 1975; Gold, 1973) demonstrated that under carefully controlled conditions severely and profoundly retarded persons are capable of self-sufficiency and social adaptation within a community setting. More recent investigations (Bruininks, Meyers, Sigford, & Lakin, 1981; Conroy & Bradley, 1985; Eyman & Borthwick, 1980; O'Neill, Brown, Gordon, & Schonhorn, 1985) have focused on the feasibility of small, community living situation for people with moderate and severe mental retardation. Over a five-year period, Conroy and Bradley (1985) monitored the transfer of mentally retarded residents from a large institution to small community living programs. They found that during the period of institutionalization only minimal developmental growth occurred, but substantial growth was found during the period of community living. Eyman and Borthwick (1980) compared the adaptive behavior of severely and profoundly retarded persons residing in an institution with the behavior of those living in a community setting. They reported that more than 80% of those severely and profoundly retarded persons residing in an institution exhibited maladaptive behavior, whereas less than half of those living in community settings did so.

INSTITUTIONAL LIVING

Core Concept 8   Institutional living is widely viewed as a detriment to the intellectual, psychological, and physical development of mentally retarded individual.

An institution is defined as an establishment or facility governed by a collection of principles or fundamental rules. Institutions for persons with mental retardation have been subsumed under many different labels, such as school, hospital, and colony. The characteristics of an institution include: (1) all aspects of life are conducted in the same place and under the same single authority; (2) activities that are carried on in the immediate company of any others, all of whom are treated alike and required to do the same thing together; (3) tightly scheduled activities governed by a system of explicit formal rulings and a body of officials; (4) grossly restricted social mobility; (5) a work ideology defined as treatment, punishment, or rehabilitation; and (6) a rewards and punishment system that takes in the total life situation of the individual (Goffman, 1975).

The deinstitutionalization movement in the United States came about because many institutions for the mentally retarded had become dehumanizing warehouses with no adequate treatment programs (Balla, 1976; Blatt, Ozolins, & McNally, 1979; *Staff Report*, 1985; *Wyatt v. Stickney*, 1972; Zigler, 1973). For persons with mental retardation, institutional living is widely viewed as a detriment to intellectual, psychological, and physical development.

Menolascino, McGee, and Casey suggested that there is an abundance of information and research data available indicating that:

> (1) Prolonged institutionalization has destructive developmental consequences . . . (2) appropriate community-based residential settings are generally more beneficial than institutional placements . . . and (3) mentally retarded individuals with a widespectrum of disabilities—including the severely and profoundly retarded—can be successfully served in community-based settings. (1982, p. 65)

The most harmful aspect of institutional living is the emphasis on a restrictive regimen with no attempt to personalize programs or living conditions to the needs of the residents (Hardman, Drew, & Egan, 1987).

The legal and moral debate regarding what is a good or bad institution or whether there is a need for any large residential facility for mentally retarded persons continues in the 1980s. Some institutions for the mentally retarded have attempted in recent years to provide a more family-like environment for the retarded person instead of the more restricted dormitory living conditions. The changes include efforts to provide private or semiprivate bedrooms, family-like dining facilities, individual clothing and hairstyles, and private possessions.

A criterion for determining whether the institution is an appropriate living and learning environment for any person with mental retardation (e.g., the profoundly retarded) has not been agreed on by parents or professionals. We can say, however, that the accomplishments of institutions in the past 80 years add up to very little. The institution of the twentieth century has been more concerned with social management than with the physical and psychological growth of the mentally retarded person. As such, across the United States these large public facilities continue to depopulate at rate of about 6,000 residents per year. They are being replaced by smaller, community-based programs (Hill, Lakin, & Bruininks, 1984).

EMPLOYMENT

From childhood through our adult lives, we fantasize about vocational choices. Fantasy may accompany a person through life, but aspirations tend to become more congruent with actual abilities as the individual matures. Since an individual's life-style and ultimate personal satisfaction are often

A variety of employment options should be explored for retarded individuals.

related to vocational satisfaction, counselors attempt to direct and aid students in finding acceptable vocational choices.

People with mental retardation are like the nonretarded in that they, too, have vocational aspirations. However, because of their intellectual limitations, these individuals may find it more difficult to obtain vocational positions congruent with their aspirations. These difficulties and limitations may be caused not only by their own limitations but also by the lack of imagination and creativity and by the stereotyping tendencies of professionals.

Competitive Employment

Core Concept 9   Competitive employment for persons with mental retardation can be described in terms of three service alternatives: (a) employment with no support services, (b) employment with time-limited support services, and (c) employment with ongoing support services.

Sustained competitive employment for persons with mental retardation is a laudable societal goal. Employment is important beyond the economic aspect for many reasons, including adult identity, social contacts, integration with peers, and the perception of contributing to society. Yet, research on employment of persons with mental retardation clearly indicates that many more persons with mental retardation could be working competitively than currently are employed (Wehman & Moon, 1985). Studies by the U.S. Department of Labor (1979) and the U.S. Commission on Civil Rights (1983) indicate the disabled individuals have unemployment rates between 50 and 75%. These unacceptably high rates are due to a number of factors. First, traditional employment models have been oriented either to no training for the individual after exiting school or to short- term training programs with the expectation the individual will need no ongoing support while on the job. Another factor associated with underemployment is related to an emphasis on sheltered or protected work settings, where the individual is placed for training but does not earn significant wages. The average annual wage in sheltered work settings and work activity centers is about $400 (Whitehead & Rhodes, 1985). The retarded adult may remain in such settings for most, if not all, of the adult years.

There are, however, some good reasons to be optimistic regarding competitive employment for people with mental retardation. We are now seeing significant emphasis upon improvement of employment services. Research knowledge is expanding, and there is a greater emphasis upon employment with both state and national policy makers (Ferguson & Ferguson, 1986;

Stark & Kiernan, 1986). The concept of competitive employment for persons with mental retardation has changed dramatically in recent years (Hill et al., 1985; O'Neill & Stern, 1985; Vogelsberg, 1985; Will, 1985). Competitive employment can now be described in terms of three service alternatives: (a) employment with no support services, (b) employment with time-limited support services, and (c) employment with ongoing support services.

Employment with No Support Services. The adult with mental retardation may be able to locate and maintain a community job with no additional support services from public or private agencies. The individual finds a job independently either through contacts made during school vocational preparation programs or through such sources as job service, classified ads, family sources, friends, etc. For the mildly retarded person, competitive employment without support is possible if adequate vocational training and experience are available during the school years (Brolin, DuRand, Kromer, & Muller, 1975).

A major concern of professionals preparing retarded individuals for competitive employment is the identification of those characteristics related to vocational success. If they can be identified, vocational training programs and early educational programs can be developed to emphasize the positive characteristics that tend to enhance vocational success.

In a study of variables influencing work success for retarded individuals in Israel, Sali and Amir (1970) found that personality characteristics appeared to influence performance and output to a greater extent than did IQ or specific abilities. Perseverance was the personality characteristic that showed the greatest relationship to the performance level. This suggests that motivational factors may be among the greatest influences on success at work for the retarded. Other variables that were highly related to work success included good motor coordination and good social adjustment.

Employment with Time-Limited Training and Support Services. After the mentally retarded exit school, they may have access to several services on a short-term basis, including vocational rehabilitation, vocational education, and on-the-job training. As Will (1985, p. 21) suggested, "Access to such time-limited services is generally restricted to individuals thought capable of making it on their own after services are completed." Vocational rehabilitation is the most well known of all time-limited employment services. Under the vocational rehabilitation model, the individual must have an employment-related disability in order to qualify for assistance. There is also the expectation that the individual will be independently employed following rehabilitation training. After the individual completes the training, rehabilitation services are terminated unless the individual fails on the job and has to be re-trained.

Upon examination of the various reasons for occupational failure among adult retarded individuals, it appears evident that few individuals lose their jobs because of actual inability to perform the specific tasks to which they have been assigned. Rather, failure seems to be more related to personality factors and the inability to adjust to the job situation.

Hill et al. (1985) found that the lack of academic skills did not preclude job placement or retention. Of the 155 mentally retarded employed clients in their study, the majority had very limited math or reading skills, and half could not tell time.

Employment with On-going Support Services: The Supported Employment Model. The vast majority of persons with mental retardation, including those moderate and severe disabilities, can work in competitive employment situations. However, "some on-going support for retraining, contingency management, or crisis intervention is typically needed—support that is seldom available in the truly competitive work setting" (Bellamy & Horner, 1987, p. 495). This ongoing assistance is embedded in the concept of "supported employment." As defined by Public Law 98–527, supported employment is:

> paid employment which (i) is for persons with developmental disbilities for whom competitive employment at or above the minimum wage is unlikely and who, because of their disabilities, need intensive ongoing support to perform in a work setting; (ii) is conducted in a variety of settings, particularly worksites in which persons without disabilities are employed; and (iii) is supported by any activity needed to sustain paid work by persons with disabilities, including supervision, training, and transportation. (Developmental Disabilities Act of 1984)

The following are some key issues and concepts of the supported employment model.

What Are the Supported Employment Placement Models? The models are individual placement, community mobile work crew, and industry-based enclaves. Under the individual placement model, a single individual is trained to perform jobs within local businesses while being provided with ongoing support and follow-up. In the community mobile work crew, a group of workers and a supervisor perform one or more contracted jobs with businesses, industry, or private individuals. The industry-based enclave provides employment to a small group of disabled adults in a host business or industry.

What Are the Unique Features of Supported Employment? Supported employment provides employment opportunities that integrate handicapped and non-handicapped individuals, has an emphasis upon meaningful wages, includes long-term support, and provides for individual vocational choice.

Who Would Benefit from a Supported Employment Program? Any individual who needs on-going support in order to work, and whose work may not meet productivity requirements for payment above minimum wage would benefit from supported employment.

Who Would Not Benefit from Supported Employment? Any disabled individual who can work independently in a competitive employment situation with a time-limited training service does not need supported employment. Additionally, some severely disabled individuals should not be forced into work roles (e.g., persons of retirement age, medically fragile individuals).

Sheltered Employment

Core Concept 10   The purpose of a sheltered workshop is to prepare the retarded person for competitive employment or to provide a terminal sheltered job.

Sheltered workshops provide both occupational training and remunerative employment opportunities for mentally retarded persons. Payne and Patton described several common characteristics of sheltered workshops:

1. Clients/employees usually work on contractual jobs.
2. These contract jobs are usually of short duration; therefore, a staff person is needed to bring in new jobs.
3. Most tasks are broken into small steps.
4. Jobs usually proceed in an assembly line fashion; one part is added at each step of the process until a final product is completed.
5. The facility may or may not provide vocational assessment and training for persons outside of the center. (1981, p. 278)

Some sheltered workshops operate exclusively for mentally retarded clients, whereas others operate for a wider variety of handicapped individuals, such as the visually impaired, the cerebral palsied, and the emotionally disturbed. Some are operated by national programs such as the Goodwill Industries of America, Inc., which has more than 100 centers, and the Jewish Vocational Service agencies, with more than 20 locations. Other workshops are community based and may be supported by United Fund, religious groups, private endowments, or, more recently, public schools.

Typically, sheltered workshops are involved with the restoration or renewing and sale of usable clothing or household articles. These items are usually contributed through collections or strategically located depositories.

Other workshop revenue comes from contracts with various businesses or industries.

Workshop clients are typically compensated on a piecework basis on a rate comparable with that of industry workers. Thus if the typical industry worker is paid $4 for 10 units of work an hour, the workshop client should be paid $2 if production reaches five units during the entire day. Some workers are relatively productive and may earn in excess of $10 per day. Others are less capable and may earn less than a dollar per day. In regard to fair wage practices for persons in sheltered employment, Whitehead indicated that "Department of Labor compliance investigations have regularly revealed underpayments of wages to workshop clients" (1981, p. 7).

Over the years the sheltered workshop model has been criticized. Questions have been raised regarding the efficacy of providing terminal placement for those individuals earning relatively low levels of pay. From a purely economic standpoint, justification for maintaining services for these individuals may be questionable. Their wages are so low as to be of almost negligible value to themselves. Their productivity level is so low that their contribution to the employment field may also be considered nearly negligible.

Gold (1973) criticized the lack of consistent remunerative work and challenging tasks in sheltered workshops. These workshops have also been criticized for a lack of systematic procedures to evaluate the production capabilities of clients and failure to provide a broad scope of vocational tasks that are consistent with the range of capabilities exhibited by retarded persons.

In many respects the sheltered workshop stands as a contradiction to a focus on community living and gainful employment. In industry, workers are employed to produce a product. In the sheltered workshop, the product is often the means to produce workers. However, for many workers that sheltered setting becomes the permanent work setting. Bellamy and Horner summed up the need for a changing emphasis regarding the sheltered workshop of the 1980s: "Segregation in large sheltered facilities appears quite unnecessary when current procedures for developing work and work supported behaviors are used" (1987, p. 496).

Core Questions

1. Define and discuss the principle of normalization.
2. Describe three widely used community residential models for mentally retarded adults.
3. Discuss some of the reasons why a disproportionate number of adults with mental retardation become involved in delinquent or criminal behavior.
4. Why is sex education important for persons with mental retardation?
5. Summarize the research on the adjustment of persons with mental retardation to community living.

6. Why is institutionalization considered a detriment to the intellectual, psychological, and physical growth of the individual?
7. Discuss some of the reasons for high unemployment among persons with mental retardation.
8. Define and discuss the concept of supported employment.
9. What are some of the criticisms of sheltered employment?

ROUND TABLE
DISCUSSION

The principle of normalization emphasizes that the person with mental retardation should have the same opportunities and access to services as non-handicapped individuals in a community setting. It means much more than just providing an opportunity for a person with mental retardation to live or work in the community. It also means providing the necessary support services to assist the individual in successfully meeting the demands of adult life.

In your study group or on your own, discuss the range of activities and services that must be available for the adult with mental retardation to successfully live and work in a community setting. How would you ensure that these services are available to people with mental retardation?

REFERENCES

Allen, R. C. (1969). *The retarded citizen: Victim of mental and legal deficiency.* Unpublished paper. (Available from Institute of Law, Psychiatry, and Criminology, Washington, DC: George Washington University.) Portions of this paper published in *Legal Rights of the Disadvantaged*, Washington, DC: US Department of Health, Education and Welfare, 1969.

Allen, R. C. (1970). The law and the mentally retarded. In F. J. Menolascino (Ed.), *Psychiatric approaches to mental retardation.* New York: Basic Books.

Baker, B. L., Seltzer, G. B., & Seltzer, M. M. (1977). *As close as possible: Community residences for retarded adults.* Boston: Little, Brown..

Balla, D. (1976). Relationship of institution size to quality of care: A review of the literature. *American Journal of Mental Deficiency, 81,* 117–124.

Baller, W. R. (1936). A study of the present social status of a group of adults who, when they were in elementary schools were classified as mentally deficient. *Genetic Psychology Monographs, 18,* 165–244.

Baller, W., Charles, C., & Miller, E. (1966). *Mid-life attainment of the mentally retarded: A longitudinal study.* Lincoln: University of Nebraska.

Bank-Mikkelsen, N. E. (1969). A metropolitan area in Denmark: Copenhagen. In R. B. Kugel and W. Wolfensberger (Eds.), *Changing patterns in residential services for the mentally retarded* (pp. 227–254). Washington, DC: President's Committee on Mental Retardation.

Barrett, A. M., Relos, R., & Eisele, J. (1965). Vocational success and attitudes of mentally retarded toward work and money. *American Journal of Mental Deficiency, 70,* 102–107.

Bellamy, G. T., & Horner, R. H. (1987). Beyond high school: Residential and employment options after graduation. In M. E. Snell (Ed.) *Systematic instruction of persons with severe handicaps* (pp. 491–510). Columbus, OH: Merrill.

Bellamy, G. T., O'Conner, G., & Karan, O. (1979). *Vocational rehabilitation of severely handicapped persons: Contemporary service strategies.* Baltimore: University Park.

Bjaanes, A., & Butler, E. (1974). Environmental variation in community care facilities for mentally retarded persons. *American Journal of Mental Deficiency, 78,* 429–439.

Blatt, B., Ozolins, A., & McNally, J. (1979). *The family papers: A return to purgatory.* New York: Longman.

Bradbury, W. (1975). *The adult years.* New York: Time-Life.

Brolin, D., DuRand, R., Kromer, K., & Muller, P. (1975). Postschool adjustment of educable retarded students. *Education and Training of the Mentally Retarded, 10,* 144–148.

Bruininks, R. H., & Lakin, K. C. (1985). *Living and learning in the least restrictive environment.* Baltimore: Brookes.

Bruininks, R. H., Meyers, C. E., Sigford, B. B., & Lakin, K. C. (Eds.) (1981). *Deinstitutionalization and community adjustment of mentally retarded people* (AAMD Monograph No. 4). Washington, DC: American Association on Mental Deficiency.

Buck v. Bell. Supreme Court Reports, No. 584, 274, U.S. 200, 1927.

Burt, R. A. (1973). Legal restrictions on sexual and familial relations of mental retardates—old laws, new guises. In F. F. de la Cruz and G. D. LaVeck (Eds.), *Human sexuality and the mentally retarded* (206–214). New York: Brunner/Mazel.

Campbell, V. A., & Bailey, C. J. (1984). Comparison of methods for classifying community residential settings for mentally retarded individuals. *American Journal of Mental Deficiency, 89,* 44–49.

Close, D. W. (1975, May). *Normalization through skill training: A group study.* Paper presented at the annual convention of the American Association on Mental Deficiency, Portland, OR.

Cohen, J. S. (1960). An analysis of vocational failures of mental retardates placed in the community after a period of institutionalization. *American Journal of Mental Deficiency, 65,* 371–375.

Conroy, J. W., & Bradley, V. J. (1985). *The Pennhurst longitudinal study: A report of five years of research and analysis.* Philadelphia: Temple University Developmental Disabilities Center.

Craft, J. H. (1963). The effects of sterilization. *Journal of Heredity, 27,* 379–387.

Deisher, R. W. (1973). Sexual behavior of retarded in institutions. In F. F. de la Cruz and G. D. LaVeck (Eds.), *Human sexuality and the mentally retarded* (pp. 145–152). New York: Brunner/Mazel.

DeSilva, B. (1980, August). Offender: A problem—a program. *Corrections Magazine, 6,* 25–33.

Edgerton, R. B. (1967). *The cloak of competence.* Berkeley: University of California.

Edgerton, R. B., & Bercovici, S. M. (1976). The cloak of competence years later. *American Journal of Mental Deficiency, 80,* 485–497.

Edgerton, R. B., Bollinger, M., & Herr, B. (1984). The cloak of competence: After two decades. *American Journal of Mental Deficiency, 88*(4), 345–351.

Eyman, R. K., & Borthwick, S. A. (1980). Patterns of care for mentally retarded persons. *Mental Retardation, 18,* 63–66.

Fain, G. S. (1986). Leisure: A moral imperative. *Mental Retardation, 24*(5), 261–283.

Fairbanks, R. F. (1931). The subnormal child: Seventeen years later. *Mental Hygiene, 17,* 177–208.

Ferguson, D. L., & Ferguson, P. M. (1986). The new victors: A progressive policy analysis of work reform for people with very severe handicaps. *Mental Retardation, 24*(6), 331–338.

Fernald, W. E. (1919). After-care study of the patients discharged from Waverly for a period of twenty-five years. *Ungraded, 5,* 25–31.

Ferster, E. (1966). Eliminating the unfit: Is sterilization the answer? *Ohio State Law Journal, 27,* 391.

Foxx, R. M., McMorrow, M. J., Storey, K., & Rogers, B. M. (1984). Teaching social/sexual skills to mentally retarded adults. *American Journal of Mental Deficiency, 89*(1), 9–15.

Fritz, M., Wolfensberger, W., & Knowlton, M. (1971, May). *An apartment living plan to promote integration and normalization of mentally retarded adults.* Downsview, Ontario: Canadian Association for the Mentally Retarded.

Gamble, C. J. (1951). The prevention of mental deficiency by sterilization. *American Journal of Mental Deficiency, 56,* 192–197.

Gan, J., Tymchuk, A., Nisihara, A. (1977). Mildly retarded adults: Their attitudes toward retardation. *Mental Retardation, 15*(5), 5–10.

Goddard, H. H. (1914). *Feeblemindedness, its causes and consequences.* New York: Macmillan.

Goffman, E. (1975). Characteristics of total institutions. In S. Dinitz, R. R. Dynes, & A. C. Clarke (Eds.), *Deviance: Studies in definition, management, and treatment.* New York: Oxford University.

Gold, M. W. (1973). Research on the vocational rehabilitation of the retarded: The present, the future. In N. Ellis (Ed.), *International review of research in mental retardation* (Vol. 6, pp. 97–147). New York: Academic Press.

Goldstein, H. (1964). Social and occupational adjustment. In R. Heber and H. Stevens (Eds.), *Mental retardation* (pp. 214–258). Chicago: University of Chicago.

Gozali, J. (1971). Citizenship and voting behavior of mildly retarded adults: A pilot study. *American Journal of Mental Deficiency, 75,* 641.

Hardman, M. L., Drew, C. J., & Egan, M. W. (1987). *Human exceptionality: Society, school, and family* (2nd ed.). Newton, MA: Allyn & Bacon.

Heller, T. (1978). Group decision making by mentally retarded adults. *American Journal of Mental Deficiency, 82,* 480–486.

Heshusius, L. (1982). Sexuality, intimacy, and persons we label mentally retarded: What they think—what we think. *Mental Retardation, 20*(4), 164–168.

Hill, J. W., Hill, M., Wehman, P., Banks, P. D., Pendleton, P., & Britt, C. (1985). Demographic analyses related to successful job retention for competitively employed persons who are mentally retarded. In S. Moon, P. Goodall, & P. Wehman (Eds.), *Critical issues related to supported competitive employment* (pp. 30–56). Richmond, VA: Rehabilitation Research and Training Center at Virginia Commonwealth University.

Hill, B. K., & Lakin, K. C. (1986). Classification of residential facilities for individuals with mental retardation. *Mental Retardation, 24*(2), 107–115.

Hill, B., Lakin, K. C., & Bruininks, R. H. (1984). Trends in residential services for people who are mentally retarded. *The Journal of the Association for Persons with Severe Handicaps, 9*(4), 243–250.

Hitzing, W. (1980). ENCOR and beyond. In T. Apolloni, J. Cappuccilli, & T. P. Cooke (Eds.), *Achievements in residential services for persons with disabilities: Toward excellence.* Baltimore: University Park.

Janicki, M. P., Mayeda, T., & Epple, W. A. (1983). Availability of group homes for persons with mental retardation in the United States. *Mental Retardation, 21*(2), 45–51.

Johnson, B. S. (1946). A study of cases discharged from Laconia State School from July 1, 1924 to July 1, 1934. *American Journal of Mental Deficiency, 50,* 437–445.

Kantner, H. M. (1969). *The identification of elements which contribute to occupational success and failure of adults classified as educable mentally retarded.* Unpublished doctoral dissertation, Arizona State University, Tempe.

Kennedy, R. A. (1966). *A Connecticut community revised: A study of the social adjustment of a group of mentally deficient adults in 1948 and 1960.* Hartford: Connecticut State Department of Health, Office of Mental Retardation. Kennedy, R. J. R. (1948). *The social adjustment of morons in a Connecticut city.* Willport, CT: Commission to Survey Resources in Connecticut.

Kvaraceus, W. C. (1945). *Juvenile delinquency and the school.* Yonkers-on-Hudson, NY: World Book.

Menolascino, F. J., McGee, J. J., & Casey, K. (1982). Affirmation of the rights of institutionalized retarded citizens (Implications of *Youngberg v. Romeo*). *TASH Journal, 8,* 63–71.

Moore, F. (1911). Mentally defective delinquents. In I. C. Burrows (Ed.), *Proceedings of the National Conference on Charities Correction.* Boston: Ellis.

Nirje, B. (1969). The normalization principle and its human management implications. In R. B. Kugel and W. Wolfensberger (Eds.), *Changing patterns in residential services for the mentally retarded* (pp. 227–254). Washington, DC: President's Committee on Mental Retardation.

Nirje, B. (1970). The normalization principle and its human management implications. *Journal of Mental Subnormality, 16,* 62–70.

O'Conner, G. (1976). *Home is a good place,* (Monograph No. 2). Washington, DC: American Association on Mental Deficiency. Olshansky, S., & Beach, D. (1974). A five year follow-up of mentally retarded clients. *Rehabilitation Literature, 35*(2), 48–49.

O'Neill, J., Brown, M., Gordon, W., & Schonhorn, R. (1985). The impact of deinstitutionalization on activities and skills of severely/profoundly retarded multiply handicapped adults. *Applied Research in Mental Retardation, 6,* 361–371.

O'Neill, C., & Stern, J. (1985). State-wide systems change in employment services for individuals with developmental disabilities in the State of Washington. In S. Moon, P. Goodall, & P. Wehman (Eds.), *Critical issues related to supported competitive employment* (pp. 213-229). Richmond, VA: Rehabilitation Research and Training Center at Virginia Commonwealth University.

Payne, J. S., & Patton, J. R. (1981). *Mental retardation.* Columbus, OH: Merrill.

Peck, C. A., Apolloni, T., & Cooke, T. P. (1981). Rehabilitation services for Americans with mental retardation: A summary of accomplishments in research and development. In E. L. Pan, T. E. Backer, and C. L. Vash (Eds.), *Annual review of rehabilitation* (Vol. 2). New York: Springer.

Peterson, L., & Smith, L. L. (1960). A comparison of post school adjustment of educable mentally retarded adults with that of adults of normal intelligence. *Exceptional Children, 26,* 404–408.

Reichard, C. L., Spencer, J., & Spooner, F. (1980, Spring). The mentally retarded defendant-offender. *Journal of Special Education, 14,* 113–119.

Sali, J., & Amir, M. (1970). Personal factors influencing the retarded person's success at work: A report from Israel. *American Journal of Mental Deficiency, 76,* 42–47.

Sarason, S. B. (1974). *The psychological sense of community.* San Francisco: Jossey-Bass.

Schilit, J. (1979). The mentally retarded offender and criminal justice personnel. *Exceptional Children, 46,* 16–22.

Schleien, S. J., Kiernan, J., & Wehman, P. (1981). Evaluation of an age-appropriate leisure skills program for moderately retarded adults. *Education and Training of the Mentally Retarded, 16*(1), 13–19.

Shannon, G. (1985). *Characteristics influencing current recreational patterns of persons with mental retardation.* Unpublished doctoral dissertation, Brandeis University. *Staff report on the institutionalized mentally disabled.* (1985). Washington, DC: United States Senate Subcommittee on the Handicapped, Committee on Labor and Human Resources.

Stanfield, J. S. (1973). Graduation: What happens to the retarded child when he grows up? *Exceptional Children, 39,* 548–552.

Stark, J. A., & Kiernan, W. E. (1986). Symposium overview: Employment for people with mental retardation. *Mental Retardation, 24*(6), 329–330.

Sutter, P. (1980). Environmental variables related to community placement failure in mentally retarded adults. *Mental Retardation, 18*(4), 189–191.

Tessler, R. C., & Manderscheid, R. W. (1982). Factors affecting adjustment to community living. *Hospital and Community Psychiatry, 33*(3), 203–207.

Turnbull, H. R., & Turnbull, A. P. (1975). Deinstitutionalization and the law. *Mental Retardation, 13,* 14–20.

U.S. Commission on Civil Rights. (1983). Accommodating the spectrum of disabilities. Washington, DC: U.S. Commission on Civil Rights.

U.S. Department of Labor. (1979). Study of handicapped clients in sheltered workshops. Washington, DC: U.S. Department of Labor.

Vogelsberg, R.T. (1985). Competitive employment programs for individuals with mental retardation in rural areas. In S. Moon, P. Goodall, & P. Wehman (Eds.), *Critical issues related to supported competitive employment* (pp. 57–81). Richmond, VA: Rehabilitation Research and Training Center at Virginia Commonwealth University.

Wehman, P., & Moon, M. S. (1985). Critical values in employment programs for persons with developmental disabilities. In P. Wehman & J. W. Hill (Eds.), *Competitive employment for persons with mental retardation* (Vol. 1). Richmond, VA: Rehabilitation Research and Training Center.

Whitehead, C. W. (1981, March). *Training and employment services for handicapped individuals in sheltered workshops: Final report.* Washington, DC: U.S. Department of Health and Human Services, Planning and Evaluation.

Whitehead, C., & Rhodes, S. (1985). Guidelines for evaluation, reviewing, and enhancing employment related services for people with developmental disabilities. Washington, DC: National Association of Developmental Disabilities Councils Project.

Will, M. (1985). OSERS programming for the transition of youth with disabilities: Bridges from school to working life. In S. Moon, P. Goodall, & P. Wehman (Eds.), *Critical issues related to supported competitive employment* (pp. 12–29). Richmond, VA: Rehabilitation Research and Training Center at Virginia Commonwealth University.

Wolfensberger, W. (1972). *Normalization: The principle of normalization in human services.* Toronto, Canada: National Institute on Mental Retardation.

Wolfensberger, W. (1983). Social role valorization: Proposed new term for the principle of normalization. *Mental Retardation, 21*(6), 234–239.

Wolfensberger, W. (1969). Will there always be an institution? II: The impact of the new service models—Residential alternatives to institutions. *Mental Retardation, 9*(6), 31–38.

Wyatt v. Stickney, 344 F. Supp, 387, 344 F. Supp, 373 (M. D. Ala. 1972).

Zigler, E. (1973). The retarded child as a whole person. In D. K. Routh (Ed.), *The experimental psychology of mental retardation,* Chicago: Aldine.

11

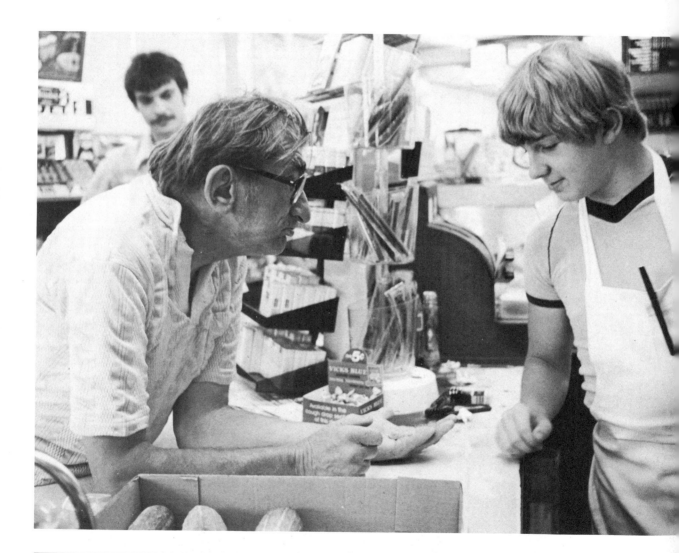

The Retarded Elderly

Core Concepts
1. A number of research methodology problems, some pertaining to aging research generally and others specifically arising from mental retardation, have contributed to the relative sparsity of study on elderly mentally retarded individuals.

2. Identifying the mentally retarded elderly has been a difficult problem, with respect to both agreeing on who is old and actually finding such individuals.

3. Age-related trends in the mental functioning of elderly mentally retarded people are of great interest and are often described in relation to the nonretarded population.

4. Social and personal functioning of the mentally retarded elderly provide some extremely interesting areas of study; evidence is currently confusing and may, in some ways, challenge our notions of the normalization principle.

5. Service programs and living arrangements for the retarded elderly also raise interesting questions from the perspective of normalization.

Study of the retarded elderly continues the progression of the developmental cycle for this population. In some ways the content of this chapter extends the material in chapter 10, although the focus is altered appropriately for the group. Distinguishing between adulthood and the aged is not simple. There are, however, some very legitimate reasons to give special attention to the latter part of adulthood—the final phase of the life cycle. Interest in the process of aging and in the field of geriatrics has grown dramatically in the past few years. Part of this attention perhaps has been the result of a developing society that can afford to be increasingly humanitarian. Another very strong influence has been the visible presence of an increasing number of older persons in our midst (Kaplan, 1979). As our medical sophistication has progressed (and the raw physical demands for survival have diminished), the longevity of the general population has increased.

Aging: What does it mean? Who is an old person? Certainly these are questions to which most can provide some sort of answer. An old person is perhaps one's grandmother or grandfather. An old person may be one who is retired. But an old person as defined by a child will differ greatly from one defined by someone who is 45 years of age. For the most part, people's perceptions of age involve specific examples, probably based on personal experience or on a concept in a personal frame of reference. One does not have to probe very far before it becomes evident that answers vary a great deal: There are nearly as many answers to these questions as there are individuals to be polled. It follows that the conceptual basis on which a behavioral scientist must operate must also vary. If the process of aging and the elderly are considered from a physiological viewpoint, they appear in a very different perspective than if they are viewed from a cultural viewpoint. Different individuals and characteristics will emerge from different definitions of the elderly. The problem is further compounded by different attitudes and philosophies. This chapter will focus on a domain that is very fluid and quite complex, characteristics that become even more pronounced because of the primitive level of knowledge development in the area.

The particular focus of this chapter is on the aging of the mentally retarded population. This brings us to a second reason for providing special attention to this phase of the life cycle of mentally retarded individuals. It has been emphasized throughout this volume that people with mental retardation represent one part of the complete spectrum of humanity. Although they are different from the nonretarded in some respects, they are similar in many others; to ignore this is to be blinded by either attitude or lack of information. The process of aging must be given attention, for the retarded elderly as well as for the population in general. The major emphasis both in research and in service for retarded people has been for their childhood years. One only has to peruse the literature written through the years to note that even for the mentally retarded adolescent, attention by professionals declines dramatically. Retarded children do, however, grow up, and they grow old and die.

RESEARCH ON AGING AND RETARDATION

Compared to many areas of behavioral science, there has been relatively little study specifically focusing on aging in mentally retarded populations (Cotten, Sison, & Starr, 1981; Tymchuk, 1979). In fact, the information available is so limited that it has been characterized in earlier editions of this book as nearly nonexistent. With rare exceptions (e.g., Kaplan, 1943) interest in this area has not been evident until recently. Although there is still an urgent need for additional study, this area is emerging and is increasingly being given greater emphasis and attention (Janicki & MacEachron, 1984; Janicki & Wisniewski, 1985; Seltzer & Seltzer, 1985).

The introductory statement presented earlier suggested a certain lack of clarity regarding who the retarded elderly are. Some of the reasons for this lack of clarity were alluded to and will receive additional attention in this section. Research will be reviewed in an attempt to explore how the mentally retarded elderly differ from and how they are similar to their nonretarded peers. Since there are limited research data on these retarded individuals, the elderly nonretarded population occasionally will be used as a reference group.

Methodological Problems

Core Concept 1   A number of research methodology problems, some pertaining to aging research generally and others specifically arising from mental retardation, have contributed to the relative sparsity of study on elderly mentally retarded individuals.

A number of influences contribute to the relative paucity of research in the area of aging and mental retardation, some of which involve lack of interest in and an uncaring attitude toward the population (Dybwad, 1985), although recent changes appear evident. Other influences involve methodological problems encountered in conducting research on aging in general and with the mentally retarded population in particular (Seltzer, 1985a).

Some of the methodological problems encountered in investigations on aging involve fundamental research design difficulties. Reviewed in depth by Schaie and Gribbin (1975), these difficulties represent very serious impediments to the growth of a knowledge base about the process of aging. Because of their importance, these design problems will be reviewed briefly. They must be considered during attempts to interpret existing data on the elderly and on the process of growing old.

Two of the most common approaches to studying the process of aging involve the cross-sectional design and the longitudinal design. The cross-sectional studies sample subjects from several age levels (e.g., ages 40 to 49, 50 to 59, 60 to 69, and 70 to 79) and compare certain measurements (e.g., behaviors) between groups. Longitudinal studies, on the other hand, select a single group of subjects and follow it through the years to compare behaviors at the different ages. The object of each approach is to compare attributes at different ages to determine how the aging process affects them. Although on the surface these approaches appear appropriate for their purpose, problems have arisen that appear to make interpretation of data difficult or, at least, something to be undertaken cautiously.

The cross-sectional design is by far the most convenient procedure since all subjects can be assessed at approximately the same time. A sample of subjects at each level is selected, and the investigator records the desired data. As noted before, a comparison of the data from the different age levels is made with the presumption that any differences between groups result from age differences (inferring the aging process). The design problem that surfaces relates to this inference or interpretation. Although it may be the case that observed differences are caused by age differences, there also may be other explanations. Differences that appear, for example, between the group that is 40 and the group that is 70 years old, could be the result of sociocultural change over a period of 30 years. The retarded population also may be affected by the enormous changes in treatments discovered and employed in the past 30 years. It is quite obvious (as observations of the past quarter of a century confirm) that many social and cultural changes have occurred. Differences between groups may be due to aging, to different sociocultural influences, or to a combination of the two.

Longitudinal investigations, unlike cross- sectional studies, are not plagued by the problem of sociocultural change. Because the same sample is followed through a period of years (perhaps as long as a life span), the "generation gap" differences are not a potent influence. It cannot be denied, however, that a given person makes certain behavioral changes as sociocultural influences change through time, but these changing influences would probably be felt by all members of the study group at approximately the same time. A serious difficulty encountered during a longitudinal study is sample attrition over the long period involved. Because subjects are inevitably lost during the investigation, the sample still available at, say, age 70 years, is likely to be quite different than the initial sample at 40 years. Thus differences might result from the fact that the sample composition differs between 40 and 70 years rather than from the effects of age. This has been termed *experimental mortality* and is an inherent design problem in longitudinal studies (Achenbach, 1978; Drew & Hardman, 1985; Nesselroade & Baltes, 1979; Schaie & Gribbin, 1975).

An additional difficulty in longitudinal studies is that the investigation may extend beyond the life span of the researcher. This has led to the frequent use of retrospective studies that have not taken direct measurement at the earlier ages but rely instead on retrospective reports based on the memory of the subjects and of others close to them. Such approaches are plagued with serious difficulties having to do with the reliability and accuracy of the retrospective reports.

These methodological problems present serious obstacles to soundness in research on the effects of aging. They do not, however, imply that the study of aging is impossible or that it should not be undertaken. This section has been included to provide the reader with information concerning problems in reading and interpreting research on the elderly. Obviously, there are times when research results must be interpreted cautiously in order not to generalize beyond the data generated or to make unsound inferences based on preliminary findings.

Identifying the Retarded Elderly

Core Concept 2   Identifying the mentally retarded elderly has been a difficult problem, with respect to both agreeing on who is old and actually finding such individuals.

Investigators studying the aging process in the mentally retarded are faced with even more difficulties than are those who study aging in general. Because there has been limited research focusing specifically on this population, there is little information available as a point of departure for further studies. Dickerson, Hamilton, Huber, and Segal (1974) characterized the mentally retarded elderly as somewhat of an invisible group because they have been largely invisible in the literature of both gerontology and mental retardation.

Faced with this situation, researchers are forced to address some fundamental questions as they initiate study of the retarded elderly. One of the first questions to be raised was mentioned earlier in this chapter: Who is an old retarded person? Tymchuk (1979) noted that 40 and 55 years each have been used at different times as a lower limit of old age for mentally retarded people. Segal (1977) suggested that individuals 55 years and older be considered as aged because certain federal agencies use 55 as a guideline with respect to funding programs for the elderly.

Dickerson et al. (1974) speculated that a mentally retarded person who lives to 45 or 50 years of age is probably considered old. This statement is striking primarily because a nonretarded person aged 45 to 50 or even 55 years is not typically considered to be old. However, Dickerson et al. indicated that persons with mental retardation may be in double or triple jeopardy with regard to the normal loss pattern associated with advancing age. This hypothesis should not be interpreted as speculation that the physiological aging process is necessarily more rapid in the retarded population. These authors made it clear that their speculation was based partly on factors such as where the retarded person resides and what minimal services are available for the elderly handicapped, because these factors have an effect on how well they function. Agreeing on who is old among mentally retarded people remains difficult for researchers in the area (Seltzer, 1985b).

We have suggested that identification of the retarded elderly is not a simple task. One related question pertains to the size of the population. Although there is not a great deal of literature on this topic, some attention has been given to it (e.g., Dickerson et al., 1974; Digiovanni, 1978; Kriger, 1975; Tymchuk, 1979). Estimates vary widely depending on the sociocultural nature of the population studied, the age used as a lower limit, and the procedures employed for calculating prevalence. Digiovanni (1978) cited estimates ranging between 50,000 and 315,000 elderly retarded individuals residing in the United States. Tymchuk (1979), using a 2% prevalence figure and the 1970 U. S. Census, suggested that there might be 1.2 million retarded people over 45 years of age. Seltzer (1985b), using a 1% prevalence figure and the 1980 census, estimated a population of 460,000 elderly retarded people. Some writers have focused on institutionalized populations. For example, Payne (1967) found that 18.2% of the institutionalized population sampled (17 institutions in 13 western states) was over 40, but Kriger (1975) found only a very small number of retarded persons older than 40 in her study. A search of available records produced only 110 names in the entire state of Ohio (and only 75 of these individuals actually could be found). These figures are particularly striking considering that over 38,000, based on percentage projections, should have existed.

Results such as Kriger's raise some extremely interesting questions regarding aging and mental retardation. Where are the retarded elderly? Perhaps the use of population percentage projections is inappropriate for this group, although there is no particular reason to think so. It does not seem reasonable, however, that the State of Ohio (or any other state for that matter) would have only 110 retarded individuals over 40. Are they hidden or invisible because there is a lack of services—and therefore they are not on anyone's records? Is there a lower survival rate among the mentally retarded? Have they adapted to the point where it is no longer evident that they are retarded? These questions are central to the study of aging among the mentally retarded, and definitive answers remain forthcoming.

CHARACTERISTICS OF THE RETARDED ELDERLY

It is not surprising that we lack a complete picture of the retarded elderly. Problems encountered in the study of aging generally are compounded by complexities that pertain specifically to the mentally retarded population. Interest in this area is growing, however, and evidence is becoming increasingly available about the characteristics of this population.

Mental Functioning

Core Concept 3   Age-related trends in the mental functioning of elderly mentally retarded people are of great interest and are often described in relation to the nonretarded population.

Decline in mental functioning is a characteristic that is typically associated with the aging process. Most people agree that older people they know frequently are less mentally alert and often not generally as capable as younger individuals. One's perception often compares the functioning of older people with one's recollections of their functioning when younger. Although there are many unanswered questions related to this perception, it is definitely a widely held view that appears to have influenced research on aging generally; there often seems to be an assumption that aging erodes cognitive ability (Baltes & Labouvie, 1973; Labouvie-Vief, 1977; Riegel, 1973;

Schaie & Gribbin, 1975). Decline in mental functioning *may* occur as age increases, but when such a perspective *unduly* influences scientific investigation the results may be biased (Labouvie-Vief, 1977). Caution must be exercised in interpreting results. Other questions are related to the influence of the aging process on older mentally retarded people: Do they experience further decline in mental functioning as they age? Does the rate of mental decline occur in a similar fashion as for nonretarded peers (if, in fact, it occurs at all)? Answers to these questions remain elusive even today when more attention is being paid to older retarded populations (Janicki & Jacobson, 1986).

Another assumption regarding a decline in mental functioning with age has also been present in the field of mental retardation. As Goodman (1977a) noted, "It is commonly supposed that the intelligence gap between retarded and normal individuals widens with age" (p. 199). This suggests not only a general decline of intelligence with age but also that the decline is more rapid in the mentally retarded population. Goodman was basically presenting a question for debate, because the general nature of intellectual change as a function of age remains unclear and controversial (e.g., Baltes & Schaie, 1976; Horn & Donaldson, 1976). Further, Goodman's own research (1977a, 1977b) did not support a more rapid decline of mental functioning in people with mental retardation.

Other researchers have focused specifically on the mental functioning of retarded individuals and have included other subjects in their samples (Bell & Zubek, 1960; Fisher & Zeaman, 1970; Kaplan, 1943; Thompson, 1951). In most cases results were mixed, although there seems to be some evidence of a decline in measured intelligence. Bell and Zubek, for example, conducted a cross-sectional study using subjects from 15 to 64 years of age. They reported that full-scale IQs seemed to hold rather well between 20 and 45 but declined thereafter. Kaplan's early investigation (1943) used a different design and assessed measured intelligence of retarded individuals over 45 years of age. Subjects in his study had been tested previously, and the earlier test scores were compared with the retest performances to determine the degree of change. An average of nearly 15 years had elapsed between testings. Although some decline in measured intelligence was noted, results did not suggest that the subjects' rate of decline was much different than might be expected of their nonretarded counterparts. In fact, certain specific performance areas showed an increased functioning over earlier assessments (e.g., vocabulary performance in males).

There are data that raise some suspicion about what might be conceived of as "early aging" among some subgroups of the mentally retarded population. For example, retarded people with Down syndrome seem particularly vulnerable to Alzheimer's disease, a form of presenile or early onset dementia. Some evidence suggests that Alzheimer's disease symptoms appear in between 20–30% of those with Down syndrome reaching 30 years of age

(Wisniewski & Merz, 1985; Wisniewski & Wisniewski, 1983). This compares with the general aging population where *all* chronic organic brain disorders, including Alzheimer's, are thought to occur in only about 7% of the total population (Levenson, 1983). It is not known why this particular group seems to be susceptible to Alzheimer's disease, although such findings may be of particular importance for the study of aging in general. Brown (1985) noted that Down syndrome, among all developmental disabilities, has the largest number of characteristics suggestive of early aging. It may be that the genes accounting for Alzheimer's disease are important to the process of aging generally. Closer scrutiny of chromosome 21 in the biological investigation of aging may be suggested because of the frequency with which this chromosome is involved in Down syndrome (Wisniewski & Merz, 1985).

Mental functioning was also studied by Fisher and Zeaman (1970) in over 1100 institutionalized mentally retarded subjects. They concluded their paper with the following findings:

> High level retardates continue to grow (although not linearly) in MA for longer periods of their life (at least until the late 30's). The MA growth functions for lower level subjects flatten off earlier.
>
> MAs for all levels show a tendency to decline with advancing age (after CA 60).
>
> Between 5 and 16 years, IQs of retardates fall precipitously despite their linear increase in MA. This is true for measurements made semilongitudinally or cross-sectionally. . . .
>
> Between 16 and 60 years, retardate IQ is relatively stable, with higher levels showing some tendency to gain IQ points with age. (p. 175)

Results of research reviewed indicate a mixture of findings, which is not surprising given the limited attention to the area. In part these varying data may be the result both of different research designs and of the specific samples included in the studies. The evidence does seem to suggest that there is a decline in mental functioning as mentally retarded people grow old—at least in terms of measured intelligence. It is not at all clear how such a decline compares with that of their nonretarded peers, although limited evidence suggests that it is not substantially greater (Janicki & Jacobson, 1986; Kaplan, 1943). It is also unclear how specific areas of functioning that are a part of the global measured intelligence vary with age.

Another point must also be considered regarding the interpretation of these results. It is commonly agreed that situational factors, such as the testing itself, can substantially alter an individual's performance. This may involve either a heightened or decreased performance, depending on the individual and the situation. This influence has also been found by a number of investigators in the field of gerontology (Botwinick, 1969; Fisher, 1973; Furry & Baltes, 1973; Lair & Moon, 1972). One factor that may well result in declining test scores is the increased cautiousness that is observed in older people in general. Botwinick's results, in particular, highlighted the "risk avoidance," or greater cautiousness, in the elderly (1969).

Increased cautiousness tends to influence most prominently tasks where a time limit for responding was involved. It also seems highly evident in situations that have the potential to produce anxiety, such as in the presence of a nonroutine authority figure (e.g., the psychometrician; see following paragraph). Both of these conditions logically can be assumed to exist for aged mentally retarded individuals in a testing situation. If they exhibit the same increased cautiousness as older people in general (and there is no reason to expect that they would not), the timed responses required by testing might have a substantial negative influence on their scores: They simply may fail to respond within the allotted time.

The presence of a psychometrician may create special concern for the retarded elderly. Kaplan (1943) suggested that the event of a mental test is an important occurrence in the life of an older retarded person (recall that nearly all of the data available on these aged retarded people involved in-stitutionalized populations). He specifically indicated that this provided strong motivation for these older patients to do well; to do poorly might result in negative consequences, but a good performance might have favor-able results (such as institutional parole or release). Whereas the logic pre-sented seems appealing, some recent studies have reported certain findings that place this line of reasoning somewhat in doubt.

A part of the investigation by Dickerson et al. (1974) involved individual interviews with older, institutionalized mentally retarded patients, many of whom had resided in the institution for an extended period (20 to 60 years). The overwhelming perception is that these patients would not view parole or release favorably. In large part they were happy in the institution and made many comments such as, "I like it here," "All of my friends are here," "I'd be afraid to go—there is so much crime," and "I'm safe here" (Dickerson et al., 1974, p. 8). These investigators further reported that some patients were reluctant to be interviewed because they were afraid that would mean they would have to live elsewhere. One can certainly argue that these pa-tients' desire to remain in the institution might be based on the wrong reasons, but their perceptions would not seem disputable—they felt com-fortable in the institution and did not wish to move elsewhere, either in fear of the unknown or for other related reasons. Such a perception is def-initely at variance with the interpretation make by Kaplan (1943) and could easily be viewed as an attitude that might promote poorer test performance.

Other factors may also contribute to the apparent decline in mental functioning by older retarded people. It should be noted, however, that these points are largely speculative since research on these topics comes mainly from the general field of gerontology rather than of mental retardation. For example, age deficits are typically evident on tasks that are paced (Kinsbourne, 1973; Taub, 1972), tasks that require a constant switching of attention (Craik, 1971), and tasks that involve free recall rather than recognition (Harwood & Naylor, 1969). Although these findings did not entail studies with retarded subjects, it is conceivable that such results would also be evident with this population. Such tasks as those noted also have a familiar ring as one considers the activities included in an intelligence test.

Age deficits have also been found with tasks that require a change of learning set (Traxler & Britton, 1970). This is another topic that has not been extensively investigated with older retarded subjects. The literature does, however, suggest that retarded subjects (undifferentiated by age) are particularly susceptible to the formation of sets; this diminishes their ability to transfer learning to other situations (Drew & Espeseth, 1968; Kaufman & Prehm, 1966). In view of these findings, it would seem reasonable to expect that older retarded people might be more susceptible to forming sets than both younger retarded and older nonretarded individuals. This, of course, is speculative; specific investigation of the topic remains to be undertaken.

Research on the mental functioning of aged retarded people has been limited in both depth and scope. This perhaps reflects the limited research on the retarded elderly in general rather than a lack of interest in terms of mental functioning specifically. We anticipate that it will become a topic of increased activity in the future.

Social and Personal Functioning

Core Concept 4   Social and personal functioning of the mentally retarded elderly provide some extremely interesting areas of study; evidence is currently confusing and may, in some ways, challenge our notions of the normalization principle.

It is evident from the interviews conducted by Dickerson et al. (1974) that, for the most part, the older retarded individuals in their sample did not want to live outside the institution. Their reasons for wishing to remain varied considerably in terms of specifics, as suggested by their remarks noted earlier. Probably they had very little information concerning what life was like outside the institution; after all, the average length of institutionalization was 38 years. The institution had become their home, and they seemed to view the outside world as a place of uncertainty to be feared. A review of their remarks does seem to reflect a feeling of security in their institutional placement.

An additional theme also seems to emerge. These older mentally retarded patients made repeated reference about being happy and about their friends. One older gentleman (age unknown, institutionalized for 57 years) even made note of having been very active with "his ladies." This raises some very interesting questions about the quality of life experienced by the elderly mentally retarded. What types of social and personal life do they have? As stated before, information on this topic is limited, although there have been some reports that provide a glimpse of what life is like for the mentally retarded of advanced years.

Talkington and Chiovaro (1969) reported on a pilot project, supported by Title III of the Older American Act, aimed at producing programs for the special needs of the elderly retarded person. This project included over 100 older retarded individuals (institutionalized) ranging in age from 50 to 72. The description of these individuals at the beginning of the project varies somewhat from the impressions evident in the findings of Dickerson et al. (1974). Talkington and Chiovaro characterized their subjects as being mostly inactive, showing behavioral patterns that suggested senility and "regressive trends in self care" (p. 29). They also noted that these older retarded patients evidenced a general lack of interest and characteristic feelings of worthlessness. Although these investigators reported substantial progress by patients as a function of their project, the description of their subjects before beginning the program was not a very favorable one. They noted that most of the patients in the project had been forgotten by their families or, in many cases, the family members had died or moved to other locations. Such findings place the all important support networks on relatively unsound grounds (Seltzer, 1985b). A generally low level of adaptive behavior functioning was also found by Silverstein, Herbs, Nasuta, and White (1986) in their study of aging with Down syndrome subjects.

Despite the evident differences, there are some similarities between the findings of Dickerson et al. and the description of Talkington and Chiovaro discussed previously. Dickerson et al. also reported that several of their subjects no longer had close relatives that were alive or active in visiting the institution. One of their subjects, a female, had lived in the institution for 52 years. During the interview this woman reported that when she was initially placed (an arrangement made by her mother), her brother had brought her to the institution. Since that time she had seen neither her brother nor her mother. This particular patient, however, represented an atypical point of view in the Dickerson study—she was the one woman in the sample who desired to live outside the institution.

Information in this chapter clearly indicates that a comprehensive picture of the social and personal functioning of the retarded elderly is not available at this time. Many dimensions of this topic remain unexplored, and the literature that is available presents a picture that is somewhat unexpected, considering the general ideas about growing old held by nonprofessionals. Although they may not have had a life in old age that most of us would choose, aged mentally retarded people do not seem to view their own lot in life as a miserable one. Many interviewed in the Dickerson study, at least, seemed relatively satisfied. This is only one source of data, but it does raise some interesting questions that should provide a fertile topic for future research.

PROGRAMMING AND FUTURE RESEARCH

Core Concept 5	Service programs and living arrangements for the retarded elderly also raise interesting questions from the perspective of normalization.

Providing programs for the retarded elderly has received even less attention than has research on aging and retardation generally. Janicki, Ackerman, and Jacobson (1985) found little consideration given to this population by state plans for developmental disabilities. However, there has been general concern with respect to educating, placing, and treating mentally retarded individuals so that they may have a life as near normal as possible. This popular notion has emerged from the "least restrictive alternative" and the "normalization" concepts. It has kindled an interest in community living arrangements for adult retarded populations (Baker, Seltzer, & Seltzer, 1977; Bank-Mikkelsen, 1969; Nirje, 1969; Wolfensberger, 1969, 1972).

Community living arrangements have raised substantial controversy from time to time. Objections frequently come from neighborhood residents, who are fearful for the physical well-being of their families or who believe their property value will be reduced because there is a nearby facility for retarded people. These arguments have been the most prominent objections to community living placements. However, we must also consider an issue that is considered only occasionally and may relate specifically to the retarded elderly—the well-being of the individual. The evidence available presents a rather confusing picture, particularly if one supports the normalization principle.

Research cited earlier (e.g., Dickerson et al., 1974) suggested that older retarded people are largely comfortable in residential settings and may even fear placement in the larger community. Some evidence also indicates that aged mildly and moderately retarded individuals in state residential facilities (intermediate care facility providing 24-hour supervised residential living) "fared better on almost all measures (medical status, medication consumption, and behavior problems)" than did the nonretarded elderly in general (Cotten et al., 1981, p. 363). Further, the retarded subjects in this study were no different from their nonretarded peers in terms of adaptive behavior, although the retarded individuals tended to function more poorly with respect to communication skills.

Interpretation of this evidence must be undertaken with care because a number of factors are involved. For one thing, the research is very limited and a great deal more investigation is essential. Another point that must be considered is the amount of time that the mentally retarded individuals (in these studies) had spent in residential living placement. The Dickerson et al. (1974) study examined subjects who had spent an average of 38 years in institutions. Cotten et al. (1981) studied retarded subjects with an average of nearly 20 years of institutionalization, whereas their nonretarded subjects had an average of only 1.5 years of residential living. It is logical to conclude that the retarded subjects were more accustomed to such living arrangements than were nonretarded subjects, for whom it was a relatively new experience. The many years of residential living may well have influenced findings in the Dickerson et al. (1974) study. In this case, familiarity may have bred comfort and security, which could have led in turn to the general attitude observed.

Meyers, Borthwick, and Eyman (1985) studied the place of residence in California of nearly 60,000 mentally retarded individuals classified by their age, ethnicity, and level of retardation. These investigators found a decreasing number of their subjects residing in their natural homes as age increased and also, not unexpectedly, as the level of retardation became more severe. Of particular interest in this investigation was the finding that, although the Caucasian group represented the largest part of their sample, there were fewer of them living in their natural homes. Both Hispanic and black clients were much more likely to be residing in their natural home, perhaps due to sociocultural beliefs of these ethnic groups.

Our accumulated evidence on living arrangements for the retarded elderly, although growing, still remains somewhat sparse. However, the general picture can be interpreted cautiously, and projections can be presented. Data to date suggest that some older retarded people are doing satisfactorily in residential settings and that many of them may wish to remain there. The discussion provided earlier indicates why this may be so. We must ask ourselves how these data fit into a normalization perspective. Actually, it fits very well if one considers the *individual* and the past experiences he or she has had. For the elderly retarded subjects we may study, residential living may represent their past to a considerable extent. These individuals may be most comfortable in a residential setting, either a nursing home for the elderly or a similar setting specifically designed for retarded people. Thus normalization placement might be best treated on an individual, case-by-case basis rather than by imposing general external requirements based on a theoretical perspective. There is little question about how matters will stand in the future, if the least restrictive environment is effectively in place for those retarded individuals that are now youngsters. If such programming represents a significant part of their life experience, normalization that is sensitive to individual needs and normalization that is based on theoretical principles may be much more similar when this generation becomes elderly.

Other programming for older mentally retarded individuals has also been largely ignored. For example, such support services as *specialized* counseling and social, medical, and legal services for this population have not emerged in any substantial form. Further, such services should often be different from those required by the general elderly population because of the unique problems presented by the retarded elderly (Tymchuk, 1979).

Research needs in terms of the retarded elderly are massive, as has been suggested by our earlier comments. The empirical knowledge base on this population is extremely scanty. We do not have a firm grasp on how many aged retarded people there are or where they are. Such information, especially in the absence of a clear definition of what "old" means for them, is fundamental to further research. It is difficult to describe characteristics and to prescribe specific programming unless these basic questions are answered.

The aged mentally retarded population is obviously a rich area of study for beginning researchers in mental retardation. It represents an emerging area of specialization that promises an exciting career for future researchers. However, in order to promote this important area of study it will be necessary to initiate research training programs focusing on the topic. Future researchers in this area will have to study both mental retardation and gerontology in general and also to project the synthesis into applications for the retarded elderly. Research needed on the retarded elderly is unlikely to come in substantial form from either mental retardation or gerontology singly.

COMMENTS

Who are the retarded elderly and what are their characteristics? These were general questions with which we began this chapter, and in large part they remain unanswered. The final part of the life cycle of the mentally retarded individual is one that has been examined very little, particularly in comparison to those presented earlier in this volume. We are still faced with the question of whether or not mentally retarded people tend to age more rapidly than their nonretarded peers. In some cases retarded individuals do seem to become prematurely old. Certainly ages under discussion in this chapter (45 to 55 years) are not considered old in the general population. If, in fact, this population does age more quickly, it is not at all clear whether it is the result of factors related to mental retardation or to environmental factors that may be associated with mental retardation, such as poor health care.

It is interesting to note that the mentally retarded group seems to be a segment of the population that does not experience the "middle age" stage of life to any marked degree. They frequently behave like children and are often thought of as being in an extended childhood and adolescent phase for a large part of their lives. Whether this is because of the institutional atmosphere and its consequent expectations (or lack of them) has not been addressed or considered to any degree. Again, the need for research with comparable groups that have not been institutionalized is evident. Although the mentally retarded adult has been receiving greater attention in recent years, this period seems shortened to some degree, because by the age of 45 or 50 they are considered "old." Once again the question is raised as to whether this is a function of mental retardation, the sociocultural environment, or both. Certainly the patterns of services available to mentally retarded people affect this phenomenon to a rather substantial degree. Literature available on this population suggests that aged retarded individuals tend to spend very long periods of time in institutions. Many who are discharged are placed in nursing homes—facilities that society characteristically reserves for the elderly. This very pattern of placement would seem to largely delete the middle age phase from the life of the retarded individual.

A further note of interest emerges regarding the placement of older mentally retarded people in nursing homes. Once in these facilities, they tend to be grouped with elderly patients who are senile. Dickerson et al. (1974) suggested that this is one phenomenon that contributes to the "invisibility" of the retarded elderly. Their behaviors do not seem to be differentiated from those of elderly patients in general, and they "lose" their diagnosis of mental retardation. Obviously one must question whether or not such programming practices are appropriate for and in the best interests of these individuals. However, if they are (a matter not yet determined), it raises the question of the advisability of relabeling these people with a term (i.e., "retarded") that carries such negative connotations. As has been suggested throughout this volume, mental retardation is a complex problem that involves an interaction of many forces and influences. It is a problem that society must address and one that society has at least partially created. The life of the aged retarded individual reflects these interacting variables to no lesser extent than in earlier stages of the life cycle.

Core Questions

1. How have the general methodological problems encountered in conducting gerontological research contributed to investigation of the mentally retarded elderly?
2. Why have aged retarded people have been characterized by some as an "invisible" group?
3. What are some implications for social services to the retarded elderly because of their invisibility?

4. How does the disagreement regarding who is old contribute to research difficulties on elderly retarded people?
5. The general perception of older people is that they have a reduced level of mental functioning. Does this perception hold for older mentally retarded individuals?
6. Do mentally retarded people seem to decline in mental functioning more rapidly than nonretarded people?
7. What factors other than reduced mental functioning may enter the picture in terms of mental performance for older populations?
8. What is life like for older institutionalized retarded individuals from a social and personal standpoint? Do they like their life or are they generally unhappy?
9. If we, the nonretarded professionals, subscribe to the normalization principle, how may some of our views run counter to the desires of older retarded citizens who are currently in institutions? Who is right, and what factors need to be considered in answering this question?
10. Why do some object to community-based living arrangements for older mentally retarded individuals?
11. How do age and ethnicity relate to living placement for mentally retarded people?

ROUND TABLE DISCUSSION

The notions of mainstreaming and normalization at many different stages of the life cycle have been much in evidence throughout this volume. In some ways these principles represent an imposition of what one group (mental retardation professionals) believes is best upon another group (mentally retarded people). Somehow when we reach the level of old age these principles take on some other considerations, such as what people want or what makes them happy.

In your study group or on your own, examine the principles of mainstreaming and normalization as they apply to the mentally retarded elderly. Consider why the notions seem more complicated by the fact that many older retarded people have been institutionalized for many years and how this might influence their perceptions of satisfaction. How might such results be different 20 or 30 years from now? How do these matters influence the manner in which you might plan services for elderly retarded people over the next decade?

REFERENCES

Achenbach, T. M. (1978). *Research in developmental psychology: Concepts, strategies, methods.* New York: Free Press.

Baker, B. L., Seltzer, G. B., & Seltzer, M. M. (1977). *As close as possible: Community residences for retarded adults.* Boston: Little, Brown.

Baltes, P. B., & Labouvie, G. V. (1973). Adult development of intellectual performance: Description, explanation, and modification. In C. Eisdorfer & M. P. Lawton (Eds.), *The psychology of adult development and aging* (pp. 157–219). Washington: DC: American Psychological Association.

Baltes, P. B., & Schaie, K. W. (1976). On the plasticity of intelligence in adulthood and old age: Where Horn and Donaldson fail. *American Psychologist, 31,* 720–725.

Bank-Mikkelsen, N. E. (1969). A metropolitan area in Denmark: Copenhagen. In R. B. Kugel & W. Wolfensberger (Eds.), *Changing patterns in residential services for the mentally retarded* (pp. 227–254). Washington, DC: President's Committee on Mental Retardation.

Bell, A., & Zubek, J. P. (1960). The effect of age on the intellectual performance of mental defectives. *Journal of Gerontology, 15,* 285–295.

Botwinick, J. (1969). Disinclination to venture response versus cautiousness in responding: Age differences. *Journal of Genetic Psychology, 119,* 241–249.

Brown, W. T. (1985). Genetics of aging. In M. P. Janicki & H. M. Wisniewski (Eds.), *Aging and developmental disabilities: Issues and approaches* (pp. 185–194). Baltimore: Brookes.

Cotten, P. D., Sison, G. F. P., Jr., & Starr, S. (1981). Comparing elderly mentally retarded and non-mentally retarded individuals: Who are they? What are their needs? *The Gerontologist, 21,* 359–365.

Craik, F. I. (1971). Age differences in recognition memory. *Quarterly Journal of Experimental Psychology, 23,* 316–323.

Dickerson, M., Hamilton, J., Huber, R., & Segal, R. (1974). *The aged mentally retarded: The invisible client—a challenge to the community.* Paper presented at the annual meeting of the American Association on Mental Deficiency, Toronto.

Digiovanni, L. (1978). The elderly retarded: A little known group. *The Gerontologist, 18,* 262–266.

Drew, C. J., & Hardman, M. L. (1985). *Designing and conducting behavioral research.* New York: Pergamon.

Drew, C. J., & Espeseth, V. K. (1968). Transfer of training in the mentally retarded: A review. *Exceptional Children, 35,* 129–132.

Dybwad, G. (1985). Thoughts on aging among persons with disabilities. In M. P. Janicki & H. M Wisniewski (Eds.), *Aging and developmental disabilities: Issues and approaches* (pp. xi–xii). Baltimore: Brookes.

Fisher, J. (1973). Competence, effectiveness, intellectual functioning, and aging. *The Gerontologist, 13,* 62–68.

Fisher, M. A., & Zeaman, D. (1970). Growth and decline of retardate intelligence. In N. R. Ellis (Ed.), *International review of research in mental retardation* (Vol. 4) (pp. 151–191). New York: Academic Press.

Furry, C. S., & Baltes, P. B. (1973). The effect of age differences in ability-extraneous performance variables on the assessment of intelligence in children, adults, and the elderly. *Journal of Gerontology, 28,* 73–80.

Goodman, J. F. (1977a). IQ decline in mentally retarded adults: A matter of fact or methodological flaw. *Journal of Mental Deficiency Research, 21,* 199–203.

Goodman, J. F. (1977b). Aging and intelligence in young retarded adults: A cross-sectional study of fluid abilities in three samples. *Psychological Reports, 41,* 255–263.

Harwood, E., & Naylor, G. F. K. (1969). Recall and recognition in elderly and young subjects. *Australian Journal of Psychology, 21,* 251–257.

Horn, J. L., & Donaldson, G. (1976). On the myth of intellectual decline in adulthood. *American Psychologist, 31,* 701–719.

Janicki, M. P., Ackerman, L., & Jacobson, J. W. (1985). State developmental disabilities/aging plans and planning for an older developmentally disabled population. *Mental Retardation, 23,* 297–301.

Janicki, M. P., & Jacobson, J. W. (1986). Generational trends in sensory, physical, and behavioral abilities among older mentally retarded persons. *American Journal of Mental Deficiency, 90,* 490–500.

Janicki, M. P., & MacEachron, A. E. (1984). Residential, health, and social service needs of elderly developmentally disabled persons. *The Gerontologist, 21,* 128–137.

Janicki, M. P., & Wisniewski, H. M. (1985). Some comments on growing older and being developmentally disabled. In M. P. Janicki & H. M Wisniewski (Eds.), *Aging and developmental disabilities: Issues and approaches* (pp. 1–5). Baltimore: Brookes.

Kaplan, O. (1943). Mental decline in older morons. *American Journal of Mental Deficiency, 47,* 277–285.

Kaplan, O. J. (1979). Introduction. In O. J. Kaplan (Ed.), *Psychopathology of aging* (pp. 1–6). New York: Academic Press.

Kaufman, M. E., & Prehm, H. J. (1966). A review of research on learning sets and transfer of training in mental defectives. In N. R. Ellis (Ed.), *International review of research in mental retardation* (Vol. 2) (pp. 123–147). New York: Academic Press.

Kinsbourne, M. (1973). Age effects on letter span related to rate and sequential dependency. *Journal of Gerontology, 28,* 317–319.

Kriger, S. F. (1975). On aging and mental retardation. In J. C. Hamilton & R. M. Segal (Eds.), *Proceedings of a consultation-conference on the gerontological aspects of mental retardation* (pp. 20–32). Ann Arbor: University of Michigan.

Labouvie-Vief, G. (1977). Adult cognitive development: In search of alternative interpretations. *Merrill-Palmer Quarterly, 23,* 227–263.

Lair, C. V., & Moon, W. H. (1972). The effects of praise and reproof on the performance of middle aged and older subjects. *Aging and Human Development, 3,* 279–284.

Levenson, A. J. (1983). Organic brain syndromes, other non-functional disorders, and pseudodementia. In R. D. T. Cape, R. M. Coe, & I. Rossman (Eds.), *Fundamentals of geriatric medicine* (pp. 139–150). New York: Raven.

Meyers, C. E., Borthwick, S. A., & Eyman, R. K. (1985). Place of residence by age, ethnicity, and level of retardation of the mentally retarded/developmentally disabled population of California. *American Journal of Mental Deficiency, 90,* 266–270.

Nesselroade, J. R., & Baltes, P. B. (Eds.). (1979). *Longitudinal research in the study of behavior and development.* New York: Academic Press.

Nirje, B. (1969). The normalization principle and its human management implications. In R. B. Kugel & W. Wolfensberger (Eds.), *Changing patterns in residential services for the mentally retarded* (pp. 177–188). Washington, DC: President's Committee on Mental Retardation.

Payne, D. (1967). *1,500,000 bits of information: Some implications for action.* Boulder, CO: Western Interstate Commission for Higher Education.

Riegel, K. F. (1973). An epitaph for a paradigm. *Human Development, 16,* 1–7.

Schaie, K. W., & Gribbin, K. (1975). Adult development and aging. *Annual Review of Psychology, 26,* 65–96.

Segal, R. (1977). Trends in services for the aged mentally retarded. *Mental Retar-dation, 15*(2), 25–27.

Seltzer, M. M. (1985a). Research in social aspects of aging and developmental disabil-ities. In M. P. Janicki & H. M. Wisniewski (Eds.), *Aging and developmental disabilities: Issues and approaches* (pp. 161–173). Baltimore: Brookes.

Seltzer, M. M. (1985b). Informal supports for aging mentally retarded persons. *American Journal of Mental Deficiency, 90,* 259–265.

Seltzer, M. M., & Seltzer, G. B. (1985). The elderly mentally retarded: A group in need of service. *The Journal of Gerontological Social Work, 8,* 99–119.

Silverstein, A. B., Herbs, D., Nasuta, R., & White, J. F. (1986). Effects of age on the adaptive behavior of institutionalized individuals with Down syndrome. *American Journal of Mental Deficiency, 90,* 659–662.

Talkington, L., & Chiovaro, S. (1969). An approach to programming for aged MR. *Mental Retardation, 7*(1), 29–30.

Taub, H. A. (1972). A comparison of young adult and old groups on various digit span tasks. *Developmental Psychology, 6,* 60–65.

Thompson, C. W. (1951). Decline in limit of performance among adult morons. *American Journal of Psychology, 64,* 203–215.

Traxler, A. J., & Britton, J. H. (1970). Age differences in retroaction as a function of anticipation interval and transfer paradigm. *Proceedings of the 78th Annual Convention of the American Psychological Association, 5,* 683–684.

Tymchuck, A. J. (1979). The mentally retarded in later life. In O. J. Kaplan (Ed.), *Psychopathology of aging* (pp. 197–209). New York: Academic Press.

Wisniewski, H. M., & Merz, G. S. (1985). Aging, Alzheimer's disease, and devel-opmental disabilities. In M. P. Janicki & H. M. Wisniewski (Eds.), *Aging and developmental disabilities: Issues and approaches* (pp. 177–184). Baltimore: Brookes.

Wisniewski, K. E., & Wisniewski, H. M. (1983). Age associated changes and dementia in Down's syndrome. In B. Reisberg (Ed.), *Alzheimer's disease* (pp. 319–326). New York: Free Press.

Wolfensberger, W. (1969). Twenty predictions about the future of residential services in mental retardation. *Mental Retardation, 7*(6), 51–54.

Wolfensberger, W. (1972). Will there always be an institution? II: The impact of new service models: Residential alternatives to institutions. *Mental Retardation, 9*(6), 31–38.

FIVE

FAMILY, SOCIAL, AND LEGAL ISSUES

12

Mental Retardation and the Family

Core Concepts

1. Parents of mentally retarded children may progress through a series of stages ranging from awareness to acceptance.
2. Denial is a common parental reaction, especially during the initial stage of adjustment.
3. Parents may project blame for the retarded child onto those individuals whom they believe are responsible for their suffering.
4. Common fears of parents are associated with having other mentally retarded children, loss of friends, a lifetime of caring for the retarded child, and impact on the family unit.
5. When parents of retarded children are unable to blame someone else, they may place the guilt on themselves.
6. When parents begin to realize fully what has happened, they may react with grief or mourning.
7. Parents may choose to isolate themselves because of their feelings of shame and guilt.
8. Parental rejection may be expressed by strong underexpectations of achievement, unrealistic goals, escape, and reaction formation.
9. The parent's final step in adjustment is acceptance that the child has a handicap, acceptance of the child, and self-acceptance.
10. Parents of mentally retarded children must have their own needs and feelings recognized and understood by each other, friends, family, and professionals.
11. The search for a cause is generally in two directions: for either a theological or a medical explanation.
12. When parents have had their basic needs met regarding the cause of their child's condition, they will usually investigate the possibility of remediation or cure.
13. Organizations such as the Association for Retarded Citizens can provide valuable information and services to parents.
14. Families with a child who is mentally retarded must be able to maintain as nearly normal functioning as possible.
15. One of the greatest concerns of parents of a retarded child is what the future will hold for their child when they are no longer able or available to provide care.
16. Among the primary needs of the retarded child is the need for communication.
17. Like all people, individuals with mental retardation need to feel accepted.
18. Every retarded child, no matter how severely handicapped, has the ability to grow and develop.

19. The effect of a retarded child on the normal siblings is receiving increasing attention by professionals.
20. Normal siblings need to be involved in the total family communication process.
21. Normal siblings are often neglected members of the family unit.
22. Normal siblings must be able to acknowledge their feelings without guilt.

The family is the oldest and most enduring of all human institutions. It has survived wars, famine, plagues, depression, recession, the constant changes of social values, and the rise and fall of civilizations and empires. The family is based on both an emotional and a hereditary bond between parents and children. The primary family unit in this country is the nuclear family, which consists of parents and their children; and the extended family includes grandparents, cousins, and even distant relatives. Family systems are developed for various reasons, including the need for security, belonging, and love. The family provides both a socially acceptable vehicle to bring children into the world and the means of enculturating them once they are born. Many individuals see children as an extension of themselves. Some perceive their children as a means to attain some degree of immortality. Still others have children because it appears to be a normal thing to do. Unfortunately, the conception of some children is unplanned, and the children are unwanted.

A child may have a positive or negative effect on the relationship already existing between husband and wife. The child may draw the parents closer together with a commitment toward a common goal, or may cause discord and conflict between the parents. Either way, the arrival of a child usually represents a dramatic change in life-style for a couple. Financial problems may plague new parents. Recreational and social activities may have to be curtailed or modified. Travel over extensive distances or time may become difficult because of expense, inconvenience, and sometimes the uncooperative behavior of the child. Entertainment may become a problem because of the expense or difficulty of obtaining baby-sitters.

Couples with children may find that their childless friends lack sympathetic understanding about the needs and nature of children and parenthood. This may result in a change in friendship patterns and mark an end to a relatively independent and carefree life-style. Housing needs may change significantly: The small but adequate apartment suddenly becomes inadequate; the comfortable and socially convenient "adults only" apartment complex must be vacated for one that is less to their tastes. A two-seat sports car may no longer be practical, since the required additional room for the child and the child's belongings may dictate a larger and more practical, but less enjoyable, mode of transportation.

The list of complications, inconveniences, expenses, and changes in lifestyles brought on by a new child is endless, but many of these negative aspects of parenthood are often overshadowed by the sheer joy and pleasure that the child brings to the new parents. The displeasures of diaper changing and the sleepless nights caused by the infant's crying may fade away with the first smile, the first step, and the first spoken word. With these first accomplishments, parents may begin to envision a fruition of their dreams and hopes of parenthood—healthy, bright, capable, beautiful children doing all the things that the parents did or wished they could have done.

The parents of mentally retarded children, particularly those with children who are more severely retarded, may find few of the joys that compensate for the frustrations and inconveniences imposed by a child (Volpe & Koenigsberger, 1981). The retarded child's delayed maturation may preclude the exhibiting of skills associated with normal development. Developmental delays in these children may retard their abilities to smile at their parents and mimic voices or to take their first steps at the same times as normal infants. Dreams and hopes regarding the child's future are often shattered. The child threatens the parents' self-esteem, dignity, and feelings of self-worth. Many individuals view the procreation of normal, healthy children as one of the main purposes of existence; in producing a mentally disabled child, they may feel that they have failed in what they consider one of their most fundamental purposes in life. For many parents, the feeling of failure and the loss of self-worth are temporary. However, it is important for parents to realize that "fleeting moments of resentment and rejection of the burdens presented by a handicapped child are natural and not indicative that they are bad parents" (Greer, 1975, p. 519).

There is no response, reaction, or feeling that can be considered typical, mature, good, or bad. Because individuals with mental retardation may be able to accomplish realistic goals set by themselves or by their parents, it is important for professionals working with the retarded person and the family to facilitate the recognition of these accomplishments. Parental reactions to the growth and development of the retarded child are unpredictable. Reactions are based on feelings, and the magnitude of the parents' feelings and reactions is as great as they perceive the problem to be. Unless the professionals in the field of mental retardation have already endured such an experience, they are unlikely to predict accurately the parents' responses to having a retarded child. Parental reactions vary because of feelings of frustration, fear, guilt, disappointment, ambivalence, and despair. The feelings and perceptions of the parents may not be congruent with those of professionals.

Chinn, Winn, and Walters (1978) suggested that the professional worker is involved with the retarded child by choice. Interaction is limited. Even for the teacher who may spend a 6-hour day with the retarded child 5 days a week, interaction is comparatively limited. Parents have the child every day and every night. There are no weekends, no Christmas, spring, and summer vacations when they can escape the reality of having a retarded child. Often the parents cannot look to a time or date that signals the child's entry into independent living and their own freedom from parental responsibilities and obligations.

In this chapter we shall address the impact of the retarded child on the family. We will discuss the needs of the child, the needs of the parents, the needs of the siblings in the family, and, finally, the decision regarding institutionalization.

THE IMPACT OF THE RETARDED CHILD ON THE FAMILY

Core Concept 1   Parents of mentally retarded children may progress through a series of stages ranging from awareness to acceptance.

A child with mental retardation will have a profound impact on the family. In cases in which the condition is not readily apparent at birth, it is only with the passage of time that the condition becomes evident. However, many conditions associated with mental retardation are easily recognizable from the time of birth.

Stages from Awareness to Acceptance

Rosen (1955) was one of the first authors to suggest that parents of retarded children may move progressively through a series of stages. He outlined five stages from the time the parents first become aware of a problem until they accept the child. These stages will be referred to throughout this chapter:

1. Awareness of a problem
2. Recognition of the basic problem
3. Search for a cause
4. Search for a cure
5. Acceptance of the problem

The degree of severity is always an important variable. A mildly retarded child may not have any distinguishing physical characteristics that suggest mental retardation, so many parents are unaware that the child is retarded until he or she fails academically in the public schools. However, the degree of impact, frustration, or disappointment does not necessarily correlate directly with the degree of deficiency. Parents of severely retarded children may find it easier to acknowledge their problem than parents whose children are mildly retarded. The mental retardation is obvious to the parents of severely retarded children, and acknowledgment (but not necessarily acceptance) generally comes quickly.

The religious background of the parents may be a variable related to the degree of impact of mental retardation on the family. The etiology and age of onset are also important variables. Physical traumas that may permanently impair a child who has developed normally may be more debilitating to the parents than congenital retardation.

The socioeconomic and intellectual levels of the family are factors in the degree of impact generated by mental retardation. Some families who exist in lower socioeconomic levels may place less emphasis on cognitive development and skills and, at times, more emphasis on the development of physical attributes. This may be particularly true when members of the family work primarily in occupations that have greater physical rather than cognitive demands. However, in a situation in which a family places great emphasis on cognitive development and members of the family work primarily in professional settings requiring a higher level of education, reactions may be quite different. A retarded child born into a family in which education and white-collar jobs are held in high regard may present a greater threat and disappointment to the family.

For the parents of severely and profoundly retarded children, awareness of a general learning problem and recognition that the basic problem is mental retardation may come simultaneously. Moderately and mildly retarded children may not have physically distinguishing characteristics that readily identify them as mentally retarded. With these children the parents gain a gradual awareness of the problem when the child fails to develop or progress as anticipated. The problem may be more obvious if parents have had other children that have developed normally.

Although many parents may notice inconsistent growth and developmental patterns, the actual problem does not manifest itself until the child is in school, fails academically, and is evaluated and declared retarded by the school psychologist. When the parents are informed that their child is retarded, they may acknowledge the condition and recognize it for what it is, or they may resort to a variety of defense mechanisms as a way of coping with the problem. The initial impact may take several forms. It may result in some sort of a transient stress disorder for the parents, or it may even have a permanent debilitating effect on the entire family unit. Featherstone (1980) suggested that the advent of a handicapped child may attack the very foundation of a marriage by inciting powerful emotions in both parents, including feelings of shared failure. Other authors (Cleveland, 1980; M. E. Lamb, 1983) indicated fathers and mothers may react very differently to the handicapped child. The mother may take on the role of physical protector and guardian of the child's needs, while the father is more reserved in his role. He may cope by withdrawing, internalizing his feelings.

The presence of a retarded child need not create a family crisis. How the event is defined by the family will determine whether or not a real crisis exists. There are few families, however, in which the stigma of mental retardation imposed by our society will not cause the event to be interpreted as a crisis. The professional can help the family to cope with the crisis. By examining the resources of the family, including role structure, emotional stability, and previous experiences with stress, the professional can help the family use its strengths to deal effectively with the situation.

Prior to leaving our discussion of parental stages, it should be noted that the concept has come under some criticism. Blacher (1984) suggested that the stage approach should be used with caution by professionals. Research is inconclusive regarding how well stages assist in understanding, predicting, and helping parents cope with the newborn child with disabilities. The stage approach has, however, demonstrated that parents do experience common feelings and reactions that may occur during certain periods of time.

Parental Reactions

Core Concept 2	Denial is a common parental reaction, especially during the initial stage of adjustment.

Denial. Denial provides a form of self-protection against the painful realities. Parents may minimize the degree of handicap or simply deny that any problem exists (Safford & Arbitman, 1975). They close their minds to their child's limitations or may attribute the limitations to the child's laziness, indifference, or lack of motivation. Denial is both useless and destructive. It is useless because the refusal to accept the reality of the handicap will not make the problems disappear. It is destructive because it impedes the child's own acceptance of limitations and may prevent necessary training and therapy.

Denial symptoms are both frustrating and exasperating to the professional. When the parents (sometimes only one parent) refuse to recognize the conditions for what they really are, treatment is frequently delayed and sometimes never receives proper attention. Because federal law requires parental consent before placement of a child in special education, the retarded child whose parents deny that the problem exists may be excluded from any special education programs. Denial may also deprive the child of necessary medical treatment, which only adds to the frustration of professionals endeavoring to help the family.

Although denial strains the relationship between parents and professionals, the latter should always be cognizant of the extreme emotional stress placed on the family and should realize that, for the present time, this immature reaction may be the only one that the parents are capable of exhibiting. With time, patience, and continued support, the professionals may eventually help the parents to face reality and to realize that the birth of the retarded child need neither stigmatize their lives nor cast any doubts on their integrity as adequate parents or human beings.

Core Concept 3   Parents may project blame for the retarded child onto those individuals whom they believe are responsible for their suffering.

Projection of Blame. Another reaction that parents may exhibit is the projection of blame. Frequently, the targets for attack are individuals who are associated with the parents' considerable frustration and agony. Their negative feelings may be understandable in some instances, but they are not reasons to justify projection of blame. Physicians are frequently the object of parental attack. Attacks often directed at an allegedly incompetent obstetrician commonly include the following (Wentworth, 1974):

> If only the doctors had taken better care of my wife (or me) before the baby was born, they would have known something was going wrong and could have prevented it.
>
> If only the doctor had not taken so long to get to the hospital, help would have been there early enough to keep something from happening.
>
> If they'd had enough sense not to use so much anesthesia.

The other allegedly incompetent physician at whom attacks are directed is the pediatrician who "did not attend to the child properly immediately after birth or failed to treat an illness or injury adequately." The majority of these attacks are not justified, since the mental retardation may not be a function of inadequate or incompetent medical care. Parental hostility may be more frequently justified in the inadequate and sometimes even improper counseling on the part of the physician. Although skilled in the medical aspects of their practice, physicians are often ill-equipped to counsel parents adequately, because they lack knowledge of the resources available for the care and treatment of retarded children.

When the retardation is evident and can be diagnosed at birth, it is usually the responsibility of the attending physician, the obstetrician, or the pediatrician to inform the parents of the situation. The task of informing parents that their child is retarded may be considered difficult or unpleasant, and physicians have frequently been criticized for not discharging this professional responsibility adequately. N. W. Farber (1968) suggested that family physicians often feel a sense of guilt or that they are in some way responsible and have failed the family. If Farber's contention is accurate, it may explain in part the numerous incidents in which parents complain bitterly that their physician either resisted or failed to inform them of the true nature of the problem. These parents typically complain that the physician had indicated that their child would eventually catch up. Farber cited two examples of physicians failing to adequately inform parents. In one situation the mother read the diagnosis on the medical chart and found that "mongoloid" had been indicated. In another situation the attending physician recommended that the newborn child remain in the hospital for reasons of health. Six weeks later another physician called the mother over the phone and informed her that the child was retarded. He suggested institutionalization and indicated that he would assist in the placement.

Other professionals who may be subject to parental criticism are the school psychologists or social workers who may have had the primary responsibility of informing parents that their children have been psychologically evaluated and diagnosed as mildly retarded. They may then recommend the child be placed in a special education class. It may also be the responsibility of these individuals to secure the necessary written parental consent for special class placement. Even if the counseling is carried out as professionally as can be expected, frustrated parents may still use the psychologist or social worker as a scapegoat, projecting blame onto them. In the school setting former teachers are most likely to receive the brunt of the projected blame from parents. Parents may place the blame of the child's retardation on the previous teachers for allegedly failing to teach the child adequately. The teachers may indeed be guilty of failing to meet the needs of the child educationally or even of failing to refer the poorly performing child for psychological evaluation.

We have suggested that parents may project the blame for their child's mental retardation onto various professionals. In most instances the attacks are without justification. However, at times frustration and anger toward these professionals may be justified because the needs of the parents of the retarded child were inadequately provided for. When this is the case, the projection of blame may be more of a displacement reaction. In other words, blame may be justified, but not for the expressed reasons.

Core Concept 4   Common fears of parents are associated with having other mentally retarded children, loss of friends, a lifetime of caring for the retarded child, and impact on the family unit.

Fear. The unknown generates anxiety in the individual. Anxiety in turn may generate fear. The parents of retarded children face so many unknowns that fear is a natural and common reaction. Although the professional may be familiar with the etiology, nature, and prognosis of mental retardation and the available resources for dealing with it, many parents may have little knowledge about mental retardation before the birth of the child. Some of the fears and concerns may seem completely absurd to the professional, but they are genuine and must be acknowledged, heard with sensitivity, and responded to appropriately. Until the parents are provided with adequate information, the fears will persist. Unfortunately, answers are not available for all of the questions the parents ask, and a certain amount of anxiety may always be present. Among the common fears are the following:

> What caused this handicap, and if we choose to have other children, will they be retarded too?
> How will our friends and relatives feel about us and the child?
> Will we always have to take care of the child, or are self-care and independence possible someday?
> What will this do to our family?
> Who will take care of the child when we are no longer able to do so?

These are merely a few of the many questions that the parents need to have answered. The parents may lack knowledge of and experience with mental retardation and thus have no conceptual background on which to base their hopes or control their fears. The professional can have many of the answers readily available to respond to the parents' questions. Many of the questions can be anticipated, and professionals must be able either to answer them or to provide sources where they can be found.

When the parents are informed that the child is handicapped, a certain amount of basic information should be provided. There is danger in providing the parents with too much information at the beginning, because they are already so overwhelmed with the fact that the child is handicapped. They may be unable to integrate any more information at that time. There is an equal amount of danger in providing the parents with inadequate information when they need it. As the professional gains experience in working with parents, an ability to sense the needs of the parents will develop. Careful follow-up can provide parents with additional information as warranted.

Core Concept 5   When parents of retarded children are unable to blame someone else, they may place the guilt on themselves.

Guilt. Human nature dictates that blame for wrongdoing be assigned somewhere. To some people the birth of a retarded, or abnormal, child represents wrongdoing. Some people who feel that everything should be orderly and logical maintain that abnormality is wrong, and someone or something must be responsible for this wrong. Parents sometimes follow this line of reasoning, and when they are unable to place blame somewhere else, they turn it on themselves. They begin to look for and eventually find something in their lives or their behavior that may be responsible for this handicapping condition. When they look hard enough, a seemingly logical reason may eventually appear; guilt may then take the form of self-incrimination for past wrongs. Guilt may follow more realistic lines; it is possible that the parent, however unintentionally, may be responsible for the handicapping condition. An example of this is rubella syndrome, in which the mother's development of German measles may lead to the birth of a child with retardation.

Guilt can serve a useful purpose if it prevents the recurrence of inappropriate behavior, but guilt usually is insidious and debilitating. Retardation will not disappear if parents assume the blame, and intense feelings of guilt can erode the parents' positive self-image. Guilty parents are difficult to work with, and guilt is extremely difficult to dispel. Professionals working with parents who are experiencing feelings of guilt can help them channel their energies into more productive activities.

Core Concept 6   When parents begin to realize fully what has happened, they may react with grief or mourning.

Mourning or Grief. Grief is a natural reaction to situations that bring extreme pain and disappointment. We all grieve when we lose something that we cherish or value. The birth of a child with a handicap represents the loss of a dream—a hope for a normal healthy son or daughter. It may also represent the loss of the parents' positive self-image. To the parents, such a birth may seem more like a death. In some instances parents may react to the birth of the retarded child with death wishes. Hart (1970) cited a father's reaction shortly after the birth of a child with Down syndrome: The father stated that he felt as if he were in mourning and should be dressed in black. Other parents either consciously or unconsciously wish for the death of their retarded child. Begab (1966) stated that it is not uncommon for parents to harbor death wishes toward their retarded child, particularly when the child becomes burdensome and they wish to be relieved of this burden. Hart suggested that some parents will institutionalize a retarded child immediately after birth, announce that the child was stillborn, and even place an obituary notice in the newspaper. Some parents unconsciously wish for the retarded child's death, and are preoccupied with thoughts of "when the child dies" or "if the child should die." Many of these parents would deny their death wishes if confronted with them, as they are unable to acknowledge these hidden wishes on a conscious level. Grossman (1972) suggested that death wishes may also be present among normal siblings. Another group of parents, however, are consciously aware of their death wishes and may or may not be willing to indicate these feelings publicly.

More recently, however, a growing number of individuals have been willing to risk public censure by refusing to grant permission for lifesaving surgery or for medical treatment that would prolong the life of their retarded child. Although such decisions raise many moral and ethical questions, only these parents know the true extent of the emotional, financial, and physical hardships they have had to endure. The Judeo-Christian ethic places a high value on human life. The medical profession obligates most physicians to sustain life even when it appears unproductive and futile. The difficult issue of who holds the responsibility for life and death decisions has yet to be resolved. Furthermore, at the time that the critical decision must be made, individuals confronted with such an awesome decision frequently do not have sufficient information regarding the child's potential quality of life.

Core Concept 7	Parents may choose to isolate themselves because of their feelings of shame and guilt.

Withdrawal. There are times when we want and need to be alone. We can be alone physically, or we can have others around us and still be alone. We may choose to shut others out of our thoughts. Being alone gives us a kind of freedom—freedom to think by ourselves, rest, meditate, and do things in our private world. Solitude can be therapeutic.

Although therapeutic in many instances, withdrawal can be potentially damaging; it is a form of isolation, and prolonged isolation can be harmful. Parents of a retarded child may unfortunately withdraw from the friends, relatives, professional workers or from activities that may facilitate the healing process. The withdrawn parent can construct a protective barrier or space and silence against outside pain, even if not against the hurt inside. Staying away from social functions protects against "nosy" questions about the children and the family. Keeping away from restaurants and other public places keeps "critical eyes from staring at the retarded child."

Core Concept 8	Parental rejection may be expressed by strong under-expectations of achievement, unrealistic goals, escape, and reaction formation.

Rejection. One of the most common parental reactions to deal with is rejection. The term "parental rejection" carries with it such a negative connotation that any parent described as rejecting is frequently stereotyped and prejudged, not only as an incompetent parent but also as a person devoid of the humanitarian values that we hold in high regard. As we examine the everyday dynamics between all parents and their children, we find many instances in which the child's behavior exceeds the tolerance level of the parents. Thus if children of normal intelligence frequently elicit negative responses from their parents, we can clearly understand how a retarded child with limitations and additional problems will frequently cause some form of parental negativism. However, it is the extreme degree of rejection that we are considering. There are four common ways in which parental rejection is expressed:

1. *Strong underexpectations of achievement.* In this particular type of rejection, the parents have so devalued the child that they minimize or ignore any positive attributes. The child often becomes aware of these parental attitudes, begins to have feelings of self-worthlessness, and behaves accordingly. This result is often referred to as a "self-fulfilling prophecy."
2. *Setting unrealistic goals.* Parents sometimes set goals so unrealistically high that they are unattainable. When the child fails to reach these unrealistic goals, the parents can then justify their negative feelings and attitudes on the basis of the child's limited performance.
3. *Escape.* Another form of rejection may include desertion or running away. It may be quite open and obvious, as exemplified by the parent who simply leaves the family and moves out of the home entirely. Other types of desertion may be more subtle—the parent becoming so occupied with various responsibilities that there is little, if any, time to be at home with the family. This could take the form of "special projects requiring attention at the office" or perhaps the demands of various "responsibilities at the church." Other parents may seek to place the child in a distant school or institution when comparable facilities are available near the home. We would like to emphasize strongly that placement of a retarded child in an institution should not be equated with parental rejection, however. The majority of institutional placements are made with full consideration of the best interests of both the child and the family.
4. *Reaction formation.* When the parent tends to deny negative feelings and publicly presents completely opposite images, this may be classified as reaction formation. The negative feelings of the parents are contrary to their consciously-held values, and they cannot accept themselves as anything but kind, loving, warm parents. For example,

parents who resent their retarded child may frequently tell friends and relatives how much they love their child. (Gallagher, 1956)

Many parents are in an untenable position when dealing with professionals. If they express their honest feelings of not liking their child, they are condemned as rejecting parents. If they indicate that they like and love their retarded child, they may be suspected of manifesting a reaction formation.

It is important to distinguish between primary and secondary rejection. Primary rejection is the result of the unchangeable nature of the child. In this case it is the personality dynamics of the parents rather than the behavior of the child that determines negative parental attitudes. Secondary rejection, on the other hand, is the result of the behavioral manifestation of the child that results in the negative attitudes of the parents. In secondary rejection, parental rejection may be altered if the child's behavior is modified. Gallagher suggested that if the type of rejection could be readily identified, working with parents would be easier for the professional. Unfortunately, this is not a simple task, and a considerable amount of time may be necessary before the parents reveal their true emotional attitudes and values.

When parents discover that their child is mentally retarded, they commonly undergo a transient stress disorder, which is a form of emotional disturbance. It is a common and natural outcome of an inordinate amount of stress. Experienced by nearly everyone at some time in life, transient stress disorders can develop because of the loss of a loved one or can be caused by other emotional traumas, such as divorce or the loss of a job. Fortunately, they are temporary. We are usually able to adjust to the stressful situation, and the disorder is alleviated. If, however, the problems are not resolved, the disorder may persist. Ideally the reactions we have examined may be symptomatic of a transient stress disorder and will be worked through as the parents have time to resolve their feelings.

Core Concept 9   The parent's final step in adjustment is acceptance that the child has a handicap, acceptance of the child, and self-acceptance.

Acceptance. Acceptance is the final step in the long, difficult road to initial adjustment for the parent. Acceptance can develop in three areas: (1) acceptance that the child has a handicap, (2) acceptance of the child, and (3) acceptance of self. Acceptance of the child is a major and critical step in the healing and growing process, and it implies the recognition that such children are valuable for themselves. First and most important, they are children. They have feelings, wants, and needs like other children. They have the potential to enjoy life and to contribute to the enjoyment of others.

They can set, or their parents can set for them, realistic, attainable goals. The attainment of these goals can bring satisfaction, pride, and pleasure to both the parents and the children. They are people, very real and important people.

The entire process of reaching self-acceptance is a long and difficult one for the parents. It is filled with pain, frustration, self-doubt, and ego-shattering experiences. Somehow, in spite of all the hurts and debilitating experiences, the parents can emerge with the firm conviction that they are parents of a very special child. They are individuals worthy of respect from others and from themselves. Their integrity as worthy members of the human race has not been diminished; instead, it has been enhanced. They have not only endured a major crisis but have grown into stronger, wiser, and more compassionate human beings.

THE NEEDS OF PARENTS

Parents of mentally retarded children exhibit the same range of behavior as do parents of nonretarded children. Most of these parents are well-adjusted people, and others have varying social and intellectual deficiencies. However, as Payne and Patton (1981) indicated, parents of mentally retarded children differ from most parents in that often services "normally afforded by society to nonretarded children and their families have been routinely denied to them. More recently services have been provided, but often these services are not comprehensive" (p. 353).

In this section, we will examine some of these parental needs that often go unmet. As we examine these issues, it is important to remember that, although we speak in general terms about "parents," we are sensitive to the uniqueness within each family. Our generalizations about families with retarded children are for discussion purposes only.

Communication

Core Concept 10 | Parents of mentally retarded children must have their own needs and feelings recognized and understood by each other, friends, family, and professionals.

It is important for parents to know they have the support of those who care about them. For professionals working with families, support implies recognition of individual family needs and assistance in meeting these needs (Seligman & Seligman, 1980).

Parents need to both receive and send messages accurately. They require information presented in a clear, concise manner, in terms that they can understand rather than in what may be to them meaningless professional jargon. Parents often feel ambivalent when receiving information from professionals. They want the truth because they know they must have it to deal with their problems effectively, but at the same time they do not want to hear the truth if it is too painful. Recognizing parental ambivalence can be helpful and can also clarify the professional's own ambivalence.

Unfortunately, in many cases both the parents and the professional may not possess the communication skills necessary for positive interaction (Sawyer & Sawyer, 1981). Too many professionals talk down to parents in a patronizing, authoritarian manner. They sometimes think that the parents lack sufficient experience or background to understand. As a result many professionals communicate poorly or fail to communicate at all. The resulting interaction can be confusing and disappointing to all parties concerned (Hardman, Drew, & Egan, 1987). Occasionally, professionals even withhold pertinent information. Barash and Maury (1985) surveyed 33 parents of children with Down syndrome, asking them how they were informed about their child's condition. The survey indicated that there was considerable variation from professional to professional in the accuracy of the information presented, when and how the parents were told, and the nature of future guidance. Additionally, professionals must remember that parents have the right to question information or decisions made by professionals that are inconsistent with family values (Henley & Spicknall, 1982).

Parents are often concerned about the future development of the child. They want to know how and when the child will develop and what the prognosis is for the future. Gayton (1975) suggested that many professionals take a "don't worry about it now" attitude and label the parents as overanxious if they persist. He warns that if the professional does not provide the parents with reliable information or direct them to responsible sources, they may search on their own. In searching on their own they may find outdated or inaccurate material containing misconceptions about their child's condition. Parents need to be provided with accurate information as early as possible to alleviate their anxiety and to provide them with a feeling that they are doing something to help. Mattson and Agle (1972) suggested that this information-seeking behavior of parents results in "control through thinking," which allows them to master their anxiety and feelings of helplessness.

Understanding the Causes of Mental Retardation

Core Concept 11   The search for a cause is generally in two directions: for either a theological or a medical explanation.

When the retarded child is diagnosed and the parents recognize and acknowledge the condition, frequently they attempt to find the cause of the condition. This search for an explanation may lead them into one of two disciplines—theology or medicine.

Religious Counseling and Theological Explanation. In a time of crisis and difficulty, people frequently turn to religion for comfort, assurance, and sanction. Some seek assurance that they are not to blame, others seek some help in picking up the "broken pieces of their life." It is interesting to note, however, that Wolfensberger and Kurtz (1969) found that in most studies even religious parents of retarded children have found little guidance and comfort from their spiritual leaders. These researchers suggested that the inadequate religious guidance is a function of interpreting mental retardation primarily as a medical problem. The authors suggested that the problem may be partially that the clergy lack the training and information that are necessary to counsel parents of handicapped children.

Mental retardation within a family unit may develop into a theological crisis, the degree of which may be directly related to the religious background of the parents. Although the advent of a retarded child could either weaken or strengthen religious beliefs, the particular faith of the parents may also affect their responses to the event. Their religious orientation may be directly related to the degree of acceptance of their retarded child.

Studies in the late 1950s suggested that religious affiliation may influence a family's reaction to a handicapped child (B. Farber, 1959; Zuk, 1959). These studies suggested that Roman Catholic families tend to be more accepting of a retarded child than are either Protestant or Jewish families. Whereas family acceptance of mental retardation may be a function of religious affiliation, it may be even more closely related to the particular religion's theological explanation for the occurrence of the event. The Catholic church considers redemption as a continual process; thus humanity will continually experience suffering as redemption for its sins. This is not to imply that the advent of a particular child represents atonement for the sins of the particular parents involved, but rather for all humankind (Hutchinson, 1968). The Methodist church believes that the handicapped child is a function of nature missing its mark (Neal, 1968). The Mormon church believes that retarded individuals are part of the divine plan—their premortal existence was as whole spirits, and their presence on earth is merely temporal and for a short period of time in comparison to eternity (Christiansen, 1969). They contend that when they leave their earthly existence, they will again assume a more perfect existence. Jewish rabbis tend to indicate that there is no classical theological explanation: The event simply occurred.

It is not our intention to present a comprehensive overview of theological explanations for mental retardation. Even the explanations within specific denominations or religious groups may vary with the individual theological interpretation of each religious leader. We are indicating, rather, that there are divergent theological views. Often suggested by laymen, but emphatically denounced by the clergy and religious leaders, is the contention that the retarded child represents divine retribution for either or both of the parents' present or past sins. Such a position is emotionally debilitating to parents.

Considering the divergent theological views, one can perhaps understand why reactions of parents with different religious affiliations may vary. Those who have no theological explanation may find acceptance far more difficult than do parents who are convinced that the retarded child is part of a divine plan. Some devout parents view the retarded child as a religious responsibility. Some view themselves as martyrs, ready to accept the responsibility as "a God-given cross to be borne patiently and submissively" (Kravaceus & Hayes, 1969).

Our basic concern is the quality of religious counseling. As stated earlier, the clergy is inclined to view mental retardation as more a medical than a religious problem. This position may be correct, but it does not negate the need for sound religious counseling in relation to mental retardation. It would appear that religious leaders generally need a better grasp of the problems involved in counseling parents of handicapped children. More time during divinity school could profitably be spent on pastoral counseling for handicapped children and their families. In addition, the clergy must clearly conceptualize within their own minds both what their religious body generally and they personally believe about theological implications involved in this matter. As these implications are clarified, a plan must be formulated for counseling the parents to enable them to deal with a guilt-related anxiety. It must be determined how religion can aid them in their time of trauma. To fulfill such a plan, each of the clergy should explore the various programs, facilities, and agencies to which they can refer the parents. Finally, each religious leader should initiate, if it has not already been done, an affirmative action program to provide programs within the religious school, confirmation classes, and so on to accommodate the handicapped individual. If religious institutions are to reflect the social conscience of society, definitive and affirmative actions must be taken to educate their congregations about exceptional children and to provide effective programs for them as well.

Medical Explanations. For many parents, it is the physician who informs them that they have a child with mental retardation. Diagnoses for Down syndrome and physical trauma are made at birth. In other cases parents may learn of the child's condition during the early childhood years or after formal schooling begins. Regardless of when the information is transmitted, medical counseling must be done with great skill to alleviate or minimize feelings of guilt associated with the child's condition. The mother of a child with rubella syndrome should be freed from the anxieties that result from blaming herself for "being responsible."

Unfortunately, physicians have been widely criticized for the way information has been communicated to parents. Wolraich (1982) indicated also that "parents have been unhappy not only about how they are told, but also with what they were told about their child's condition" (p. 324). Parents usually want a medical opinion about the nature of the child's condition, the prognosis for the child, and the possibility of having a second child who is mentally retarded. Parents may listen to an explanation of the mathematical odds of having another retarded child, but often they want the professional to decide whether or not they should have another child. Any professional, whether a physician, geneticist, teacher, or psychologist, who is approached by parents for advice of this nature is taking a risk of being a scapegoat later if the parents do have another retarded child. Any pregnancy involves some degree of risk, and the odds, risks, and possible consequences should be clearly articulated by the professional. After the information is given, the decision whether or not to have another child is rightfully that of the parents. It is they who will share the joy of a normal child or bear the consequences of a handicapped one.

To provide comprehensive medical counseling and services to persons with mental retardation and their families, several considerations must be addressed (Hardman, Drew, & Egan, 1987):

1. The physician in community practice (general practitioners, pediatricians, etc.) must receive more medical training in the medical, psychological, and educational aspects of exceptional populations.
2. Physicians must be more willing to treat disabled patients for common illnesses when the treatment is irrelevant to the patient's disability.
3. Physicians need not become specialists in specific disability areas but must have enough knowledge to refer the patient to an appropriate specialist when necessary.
4. Physicians must not expand their counseling role beyond medical matters but must be aware of, and willing to refer the patient to, other community resources.

Searching for a Cure

Core Concept 12   When parents have had their basic needs met regarding the cause of their child's condition, they will usually investigate the possibility of remediation or cure.

Unfortunately, in the majority of cases of mental retardation, prospects for a complete cure are remote. In some conditions, such as when the retardation is a function of emotional disorders or environmental deprivation, some remediation techniques may be prescribed (e.g., psychotherapy, environmental stimulation and enrichment); if treatment is prescribed early enough, some positive results are possible. In certain types of medical conditions, such as glactosemia or phenylketonuria, dietary controls can minimize the extent of damage. Physical therapy and speech therapy can be prescribed to improve functional level. In many instances the prescribed treatments may improve the intellectual and the functional level, but seldom is it possible to move these children out of the ranges of mental retardation into what we could classify as a normal range of intelligence.

We must be acutely aware of the desperate nature of the feelings of many parents at this particular stage. Some may, if the financial resources permit, take the child from one clinic to another hoping to receive the diagnosis they want to hear. It is the responsibility of professionals to help protect these parents from unscrupulous practitioners who will willingly diagnose the child as "learning disabled" or anything else the parents may wish to hear, and then offer special remediation programs. Such programs typically entail great expense and yield few if any positive results. When parents seek sanctions for these questionable programs, the most prudent approach may be to refer them to professionals whose judgments have been noted for their reliability or to organizations such as the AAMD or the Association for Retarded Citizens.

Searching for Help

Core Concept 13   Organizations such as the Association for Retarded Citizens can provide valuable information and services to parents.

Twenty-five years ago, a few parents of retarded people looked around and saw . . . nothing. They were suffering from the deep hurt that society has always handed out free to anybody who is 'different.' And they were different all right. They had the audacity to give birth to children who were not perfect. The citizenry was indifferent or the citizenry was offended and frightened. I imagine that many of these parents would have preferred to curl up and die rather than attempt to change a whole country. But that was the catch, they couldn't die either. If they died no one could be depended upon to care for these inconvenient retarded people. . . . So the Association for Retarded Citizens was born. (Isbell, 1979, p. 170)

Many parents are confused, and they find that professionals are often unable to give advice or to refer them to other resources beyond their own professional area of expertise. Physicians are able to provide basic medical information; the schools are a resource on educational matters. However, each is limited in the ability to provide information on other resources. One of the most comprehensive resources for information for families with a mentally retarded child is the Association for Retarded Citizens (ARC). This organization is comprised of anyone interested in promoting the welfare of persons with mental retardation, but the majority of the membership consists of families with retarded persons. This organization serves two very useful functions for parents. First, it makes them aware that they are far from being the only ones in the world with their seemingly unique problem. Within the group they will find other parents who have experienced the same frustration they are presently experiencing and who can share with them information about coping with these problems. Additionally, the more experienced parents and the professional staff can give advice regarding the various services available for their child. Parents with older retarded children can help the other parents anticipate future development.

If the community is so small that there is no local organization, the parents can contact the office of the state Association for Retarded Citizens to obtain both the necessary information and the location of the nearest local affiliate. Parents may write directly to the Association for Retarded Citizens (2501 Avenue J, Arlington, Texas 76011), from which a considerable amount of helpful literature is available.

There may be many other resources within the community to assist parents. For example, some communities have organized *pilot parent programs* to assist parents who have recently either given birth to a retarded child or learned of their child's disability. Pilot parents is a local group of parents helping other families with handicapped children.

On the national scene there are several federally funded advocacy programs for persons with handicaps. These include the Disability Rights Education and Defense Fund, which was established to advance the civil rights of disabled individuals through guiding and monitoring national public policy. The Developmental Disabilities and Bill of Rights Act of 1975 (Public Law 94–103) established in every state a *protection and advocacy system* for persons with a developmental disability. A state protection and advocacy system is authorized to pursue legal and administrative remedies to protect the rights of persons with developmental disabilities receiving education and treatment within that state. *Closer Look* (a magazine published by The National Information Center for the Handicapped) has provided special education and habilitation information to thousands of parents across the country. The information includes practical guides to finding services, parents' information packets that include a description of community resources, civil rights information, and access to reports that update parents on events concerning handicapped people. In 1986 *The Exceptional Parent*, a magazine for families, published a resource guide for parents (Directory of Community Resources, 1986). The directory includes information about recreation, religious organizations, resources for the disabled traveler, and architectural barriers.

Maintenance of Normal Family Functioning

Core Concept 14   Families with a child who is mentally retarded must be able to maintain as nearly normal functioning as possible.

There are many problems that may hinder maintaining a normal family unit. First, the parents may be so guilt-ridden for having the retarded child that they believe they must dedicate every moment of their lives to the child's welfare. These intense feelings of obligation may interfere with normal interactions of the parents with each other, with their normal children, and with their friends and relatives. Second, the additional financial burden of the retarded child may hinder normal expenditure for recreation and other activities and even for necessities. Third, the difficulties of caring for the retarded child may be such that the parents are either unwilling or unable to find someone to provide the necessary supervision while they engage in even minimal recreation or social activities.

These three problems are not uncommon. Parents may need assistance to dispel their feelings of guilt or at least minimize them. They must be helped to realize that the advent of a retarded child should not destroy normal family relations; few, if any, wish that to happen. At times, however, parents are so intensely engrossed with their retarded child that they become oblivious to the needs of other family members. The reality of the burdens of having a handicapped child make social and recreational enjoyment much more difficult to attain. Gayton (1975) suggested that the withdrawal tendencies of the parents tend to serve as a model for other family members and may convey to them that the handicapping condition is something to be ashamed of and hidden.

When the financial burdens created by the birth of the retarded child interfere with recreational and social activities, parents should be directed toward the many activities available at minimal or no cost. Care for the retarded child can be made available if various resources are tapped. Perhaps no one is available to care for the child in the manner parents would like, but people can be taught, and parents should make every effort to seek out individuals who are willing to learn. Parents may be willing to share babysitting responsibilities with other parents who have retarded children and who may be more in tune with the routine and needs of the retarded child. Respite care can provide temporary relief for families with a retarded child living at home. In this model the family can either leave their child with trained personnel in a community living setting for short periods of time, or have someone actually come to their home and provide care for the child. This allows the parents to leave the child for short periods of time knowing he or she is receiving good care. In a survey of 339 families, Upshur (1982) reported that the most common reason for day or evening care is the "need for relief time; the most common for overnight care is recreation or vacation" (p. 5).

The ability of the family to maintain some degree of normal socialization may be partly a function of the degree of acceptance by the extended family and by the neighbors within the community. Studies conducted in the 1960s found that the wife's side of the family tended to be more accepting and supportive (Barsch, 1968; N. W. Farber, 1968). The husband's mother tended to blame her daughter-in-law for the birth of the retarded child. Parents of retarded children appear to be able to maintain positive relationships with the neighbors, although some parents had to contend with misconceptions and suspicions regarding retarded children. It appears that successful integration with the extended family and with neighbors may well depend upon educating these other two groups, as well as the retarded child's immediate family, to accept the child. Whereas the advent of a retarded child into the family creates many additional burdens and problems, life within the family unit must continue in a manner that will provide optimal opportunity for everyone involved to develop and maintain sound mental health.

Bennett provided some advice to parents regarding a balanced approach to parenting a child with disabilities.

> Get the best expert advice you can and use it.
> Develop realistic and specific goals for your child for both the present and the future.
> Don't continually "second guess" yourself or your mate.
> Spend a reasonable amount of time and effort working with your child.
> Reach out to other parents. (1986, pp. 50–52)

Planning for the Future

Core Concept 15   One of the greatest concerns of parents of a retarded child is what the future will hold for their child when they are no longer able or available to provide care.

In the early years the retarded child usually lives at home and is entitled to attend public school until the maximal attendance age is reached. At this age the retarded individual may not function socially and intellectually as an adult, but the responsibility of the schools has ended. If vocational rehabilitation and employment services are available, then there may be some continuing assistance.

Parental concerns often center on where and how the child's needs ultimately will be met. The thought of forcing the child into an institution after spending a large number of years in the community and family setting may be difficult for parents to accept. Whereas normal siblings have frequently been called on to assume the responsibilities of their parents, it is fair neither to them nor to their families to have this responsibility unless they choose to accept it.

It may be in the best interests of the child if parents are able to make necessary arrangements for continued maintenance and other matters through carefully planned provisions, such as trusts with specific stipulations about care. This view of maintenance focuses on providing funds, but parents can at least have some assurance that adequate care will be provided for their child when they are no longer able to do so themselves. Parents who are interested in providing a trust for their child can usually locate, through reliable organizations, an attorney with this particular expertise. Plans can be made for the mildly retarded child to lead a reasonably productive and independent life. For the moderately retarded and those more seriously handicapped, specific provisions must be made.

NEEDS OF THE CHILD WITH MENTAL RETARDATION

Mentally retarded children are more similar to their non-retarded peers than they are different from them and therefore have all of the basic needs of their nonretarded age-mates.

Communication

Core Concept 16 Among the primary needs of the retarded child is the need for communication.

Like their parents, retarded children need clear, concise, understandable messages. They can sense when things are wrong and when they are presented with half-truths. They, more than anyone, must be able to deal with their limitations. Some need to know what their limitations are and how these limitations will affect their lives. They need to know how they can make the best of their lives and reach their full potential for a meaningful existence.

Professionals and parents have often been guilty of minimizing the feelings of children, but a child's personal feelings are as important and valid as an adult's. Parents and professionals frequently fail to include the retarded children in the decision-making process, yet the decisions affect them more than anyone else. Adults are sometimes prone to speak about the child in an uncomplimentary manner when he or she is present, as if the child can neither hear nor understand what is being said. The retarded child needs straightforward and congruent messages from others with respect to their feelings. Limited in understanding abstractions and less able to pick up cues, a retarded child is often confused by subtle insinuations, silent treatments, and other indirect cues. If a particular behavior is unacceptable to the parent or professional worker, the child needs to know it. The child needs to know why it is unacceptable and what can be done to remedy the problem. Shielding the child from the truth usually serves no useful purpose and may damage the child's ability to grow.

Acceptance

Core Concept 17	Like all people, individuals with mental retardation need to feel accepted.

Acceptance is one of the basic needs of all human beings. Retarded children are no different from anyone else in this respect. They need to be accepted as worthy individuals, both by others and from their own personal views.

The parents' severe loss of self-esteem, feelings of inadequacy, and depression can make loving the retarded child difficult. Physical stigmata or lack of normal responsiveness may also retard normal parental attachment to a child (Gayton, 1975). The effects on the child are insidious, and many retarded children desperately seek someone with whom they can identify. They need good models, and the professional can help to provide these models. With the mainstreaming of retarded children into classes and schools with nonretarded children, acceptance is even more crucial. By carefully educating a child's classmates and teachers about the child, fears of the unknown may be dispelled, leaving the way open for acceptance. The professional can and should be an individual who exudes a feeling of warmth and acceptance. By finding and capitalizing on the positive attributes of the child, the professional can assist the parents to realize the worth of the child and can help bring about acceptance.

Freedom to Grow and Develop

Core Concept 18 Every retarded child, no matter how severely handicapped, has the ability to grow and develop.

It is the responsibility of both parents and professional to provide the fertile environment and the proper atmosphere for the child's growth to full potential. The range and variety of potential experiences and activities may be limited, but unless these children are provided with a wide variety of experiences, their learning and adjustment may be greatly curtailed. Parents sometimes are easily embarrassed about and overly sensitive to what others may think when their child's behavior is observed in public. Parents must realize, however, that unless retarded children have the opportunity to visit the zoo, ride a bus, and eat in a restaurant, they will be deprived of important experiences that all children should have for maximum social development.

A second important variable that affects adjustment is a balance of control within the child's environment. The child who is unnecessarily completely dependent on the normal members of the family may develop a habit of helplessness and loss of self-identity. It is often far easier for a parent to dress a retarded child, for example, than it is to teach the process of dressing. The latter may be a long and painful experience. However, when the child has accomplished this, another level of independence has been achieved and self-concept has probably improved. The other extreme is equally insidious. A retarded child who completely controls and dominates the environment by overwhelming an overly patronizing family with unreasonable demands also fails to make an acceptable environmental adjustment. The child learns to interact, participate, and accept responsibilities successfully within the family; these learned experiences are usually transferred into the educational setting, peer group relationships, and other social contacts later in life.

NEEDS OF SIBLINGS

Core Concept 19 The effect of a retarded child on the normal siblings is receiving increasing attention by professionals.

As the sibling of a mentally retarded child, I felt cheated because my brother was not the same as other kids. I was waiting for the day he would wake up and be like me, a day that will never come. So many times he pleaded for the affection he desperately needed and so many times I turned my back and ignored his appeal. I did not understand. (Dubinsky, 1986, p. 54)

Literature in the field of mental retardation has focused a great deal of attention on the effects of a retarded child on parents, but the effects on the normal siblings have in the past been ignored or relegated to a secondary level of importance. Considerable attention recently has been focused on this important subject. Researchers have become increasingly aware that the birth of a retarded child may have direct consequences on the overall development of other children in the family. The literature has addressed itself to the following questions:

How does the retarded child affect the development and adjustment of normal siblings?
What are the attitudes of the normal siblings toward the retarded child?
What factors influence these attitudes?
What are the fears and concerns of the normal siblings? How can the negative effects be avoided or minimized?

To investigate the attitudes of normal siblings toward their handicapped brother or sister, Barsch (1968) provided a group of parents with a checklist of possible normal sibling reactions or attitudes. Although there were occasional indications of some resentment, the majority of the parents indicated that their normal children had favorable attitudes toward the handicapped child. It is quite possible, however, that these parents may have been insensitive to the real feelings of their normal children or that they could not accept negative feelings toward the retarded child either from themselves or from their other children.

As a child grows older and actual abilities become more apparent, there is an occasional readjustment of roles and expectations. Regardless of the siblings' birth order, the retarded child eventually becomes the youngest child socially. Normal siblings can be under pressure to assume more responsibility and act older than they actually are. In a study of severely retarded children and their normal siblings, Farber found that the latter's relationship with their mother was adversely affected by the handicapped child's high degree of dependency. Younger normal and retarded children tend to be treated on a more equal basis, but as they grow older, the normal siblings assume a superordinate position in the relationship. N. W. Farber (1968) found that siblings who, as young children, had limited interaction with their retarded brother or sister were less affected than those who had interacted freely. Schild (1976) suggested that one of the potential problems faced by normal siblings is the unrealistically high expectations for them by parents, who are trying to compensate for the retarded child's deficiencies.

Communication

Core Concept 20	Normal siblings need to be involved in the total family communication process.

The advent of a retarded child is a concern of the total family. As family members, the normal children in the family need to be involved in the total family communication process. Too frequently the decisions related to the retarded child are made without prior discussion or explanation to others in the family. The other children have many feelings about their retarded siblings; they also have feelings and concerns about themselves. They need to feel free to communicate these feelings to their parents.

Siblings want to know and understand the condition of their disabled brother or sister. They need to know how to act and react as a family member. They need their questions answered. If communication is opened up to include the siblings, the positive relationship with their retarded brother or sister is greatly enhanced. C. B. Lamb (1980) reviewed several books that may be used therapeutically to help children accept siblings with disabilities. These stories help a normal child understand the joys and frustrations of being the sibling of a disabled child. Sometimes parents relate to the normal children with good intentions but poor techniques. They do what they think is best for the family, but what they do may not have a positive outcome or be in the best interest of the family unit. However, if they can communicate what they are doing and why they are doing it, the unpleasantness of the situation may at least be understandable to the normal children.

Normal siblings must also deal with peer reaction such as teasing and ridicule. These may come at an age when the normal child lacks the maturity and understanding of the situation to resolve them effectively. Parents sometimes compound the frustration and confusion of the normal children by refusing to discuss with them the problems of mental retardation (Grossman, 1972). Many parents are so overwhelmed with the burden of dealing with their own problems and identities with respect to their retarded child that they are ill equipped to recognize the needs of their other children. Often they are unable to recognize or to help them in the many stresses and traumas created by the presence of the retarded child.

Schreiber and Feeley (1965), working with normal adolescent siblings of retarded children, developed a group process in which 10 siblings met bimonthly for 8 months for sessions lasting an hour and a half. During the sessions many concerns emerged:

1. How do you tell friends about your retarded brother or sister?
2. How do you deal with your parents when they have not discussed the problems of mental retardation and its implications for the family?

3. How do you deal with those who speak offensively about retarded children?
4. Are parental expectations of normal siblings fair to all involved?
5. What is the responsibility of the normal children to the retarded child in the event of parental death?
6. What do you do when parents have no affection toward the retarded child?
7. Does retardation in the family lessen the prospects of marriage, and is retardation hereditary?

Grossman (1972) conducted a similar group interaction program for adolescents. Some of the problems encountered in establishing the group were directly related to lack of parental cooperation. These adolescents were dependent on their parents for transportation, and lack of parental cooperation in this area precluded participation. It appeared that many of the apprehensive parents were fearful of their children revealing family secrets during the sessions. Many of the concerns expressed by this group were similar and in some instances identical to those raised in the Schreiber and Feeley (1965) study. Some of the concerns expressed by the participants in Grossman's group included the following:

1. Apprehension about being identified with the retarded child.
2. Lack of understanding about the retarded sibling's capabilities, such as how much the child knew and could understand.
3. When acting as parent substitutes, how should they discipline the retarded child?

Unlike many functional disturbances, the problem of mental retardation as a family concern can usually be traced to the particular time when the retardation was identified. Thus if professionals such as nurses, physicians, theologians, psychologists, and teachers will work toward providing the types of counseling and therapeutic services needed, chances for adjustment by both parents and normal siblings will be maximized.

Attention

Core Concept 21   Normal siblings are often neglected members of the family unit.

Normal siblings are neglected for a number of reasons. They are neglected because the parents are sometimes overwhelmed with the responsibilities of caring for the retarded child. They are neglected because the parents may be so filled with guilt that they think they must devote all their time to the handicapped child. Sometimes they are neglected because the parents are attempting to escape from the entire family, which is such a threat to their self-esteem. They may even be neglected because the parents operate under the assumption that they are unfit because they have produced a child whom they view as defective. Others are neglected because their parents are incompetent as parents and would not have given them adequate attention regardless of the situation. These children are often in desperate need of attention. If they are unable to secure the attention they need from their parents, they may secure it in socially unacceptable ways at home, at school, and in the community.

Acknowledgment of Feelings Without Guilt

Core Concept 22	Normal siblings must be able to acknowledge their feelings without guilt.

It is only natural that the normal siblings will develop some negative feelings. One of the most comprehensive studies on 83 normal siblings of retarded children was done by Grossman (1972); her research was conducted with four groups of university students. Two groups were students from a private university. These groups included normal brothers of retarded children as one group and normal sisters of retarded children as a second group. The other two groups were obtained from a community college and consisted of normal brothers and sisters of retarded children. Students participated in the study on a voluntary basis but received a small remuneration for their time spent on the project. It should be emphasized that not all eligible subjects contacted agreed to participate; that is, some normal siblings of retarded children declined. Some assumptions may be made: those agreeing to participate may have represented groups that had more positive attitudes toward mental retardation, and some of those with more negative attitudes may have eliminated themselves from the study.

Grossman found that the students from the private university frequently came from more affluent families that could be considered upper socioeconomic class. The parents usually had a high educational background and held positions of high occupational status. (Subjects from the community college, however, often came from lower middle socioeconomic families and had already obtained or were in the process of obtaining a higher level of educational preparation than their parents had done.) Because of the economic status of the families of the students from the private university, the retarded child presented no particular financial burdens on the family. There were no financial limitations for any services for the retarded children and none with respect to domestic help.

Grossman found that the parents of students from the private university tended to shield their normal children as much as possible from the inconveniences of a retarded sibling. The brothers in the group had less direct contact with the retarded child than did their sisters, who were more involved with and participated in child-rearing activities of both younger siblings and, to some extent, the retarded child. Brothers in the community college sample also tended to be uninvolved with the handicapped sibling. Many were involved with full-part-time jobs and were financially independent of their parents. Some were married and had their own families. Of the four groups, they appeared to be the least involved with the retarded sibling. Sisters from the community college, however, seemed to be the most involved of the four groups with their retarded siblings. Some had major roles in the child-rearing responsibilities, and some served as mother surrogates. Some believed they knew more about caring for the retarded child than did their parents and may indeed have possessed greater skills, having had preparation in special education classes as well as volunteer work with retarded children in the community.

With the 83 university subjects, Grossman attempted to determine if the impact of the retarded child had a negative or a positive overall effect on the normal siblings. Grossman found that 45% of the subjects benefited from the experience of having had a retarded child in the family. These individuals seemed to have a greater understanding and tolerance for people in general and for the handicapped in particular. They were more sensitive to prejudice and its consequences and had a greater appreciation for their own good health and intelligence. Grossman's findings support those of Kramm (1963), who found that 76% of 50 families with children with Down syndrome had benefited from having a retarded child.

Farber (1968) suggested that normal siblings who interact regularly with the retarded child and at times act as parent surrogates internalize welfare norms and tend to opt for the more altruistic vocational choices, emphasizing "devotion of mankind" and "devotion to worthwhile causes." Farber further stated that the effect of the retarded child on normal siblings may even influence marriage choices. Normal siblings who maintain close relationships to their retarded brother or sister may not consider as a marriage partner anyone who demonstrates little tolerance for the handicapped child.

Resentment. Resentment is a common and natural reaction on the part of a normal child with a retarded sibling. Although resentment is common, many parents and children who feel resentment do not realize that such feelings are to be expected. It is important that the parents and normal siblings be assisted in dealing with these feelings in an emotionally constructive manner.

Hunter, Schucman, and Friedlander (1972) suggested that a normal child in the family may develop feelings of anger toward the retarded siblings. Anger may be felt because of the lack of personal attention for the normal child and the apparent favoritism shown toward the child with a handicap. Resentment may develop because the handicap prevents the family from going on certain types of outings; because treatment, therapy, special schooling, and so on place financial constraints on the family; and because the normal child may have to assume certain unpleasant responsibilities such as baby-sitting. The normal child may even wish for the other child's death or, at least, that the retarded sibling would just go away (Gordon, 1975; Grossman, 1972).

Guilt, Fear, Shame, and Embarrassment. The normal sibling may have guilt feelings because of negative reactions toward the retarded child. Guilt feelings may even be present because the sibling was fortunate enough to be normal and the other child handicapped.

The normal child may also feel fear. When they are younger, normal siblings may be fearful that they, too, may become retarded. As they become older, they may be afraid that their own children may be handicapped. They may also be fearful that someday, when the parents are no longer able to provide care, they will have total responsibility for the handicapped sibling (Grossman, 1972). Grossman suggested that younger normal siblings tend to have fears and anxieties and may even fantasize. She cites an example of one child who, after the retarded child had been institutionalized, had fears that a "boogey man" would take her away. Parents, either by themselves or with professional help, must somehow deal with the many concerns and fears that normal siblings have. Younger children who do not have accurate information may develop fears and fantasies.

Normal siblings often have feelings of shame and embarrassment. They may be embarrassed to be seen in public with their sibling, embarrassed to tell their friends, embarrassed to bring their friends home, or embarrassed to have a date pick them up at their home. It is understandable why a teenager may be reluctant to be picked up at the house by a friend if a retarded sibling is ill mannered and exhibits unpredictable behavior.

Wentworth (1974) suggested that embarrassment is perhaps the second most prevalent emotional reaction that nonhandicapped siblings experience. She further suggested that the degree of embarrassment may be a function of the ages of both the handicapped and nonhandicapped child and the type of handicap. A younger child with a handicap presents an image of a helpless individual who needs to be mothered. It may be easier for the normal children and their peers to accept the child at this age. As retarded children become older and more difficult to control and their childhood cuteness begins to dissipate, they can be a much greater source of embarrassment. Older children, particularly adolescents, become more cognizant of and easily influenced by peer approval. Because teenagers can be cruel in their remarks, normal siblings may become increasingly embarrassed as tactless remarks are made about a brother or sister with a handicap.

In summary, the needs of normal siblings in the family are often overlooked. Careful guidance by parents and professional workers can lead to a healthy adjustment to the problems created by the presence of the retarded child.

Core Questions

1. Discuss the stages parents may progress through as they attempt to adjust to a child with mental retardation.
2. Discuss the eight common parental reactions to a retarded child addressed in this text.
3. In searching for a cause, parents often seek either theological or medical explanations. Compare and contrast these two sorts of answers.
4. Discuss some organizations that may benefit parents of retarded children who are seeking assistance.
5. What are three problems that may hinder normal family functioning?
6. Discuss three basic needs of children with mental retardation.
7. Discuss three basic needs of normal siblings.

ROUND TABLE DISCUSSION

In this chapter, you learned about stages that parents may progress through in dealing with a retarded child in the family. These stages include awareness of the problems, recognition of the problem, searching for a cause, searching for a cure, and acceptance of the child. Review the discussion of these stages from pages 383–385 of the text.

In your study group, organize a role-playing activity. Beginning with awareness and moving through acceptance, assign individuals to role-play the reactions and feelings of parents at each stage as they face the challenges of raising a retarded child.

REFERENCES

Barash, A., & Maury, E. (1985). Giving the news about a child's disability. *The Exceptional Parent, 15*(4), 32.

Barsch, R. H. (1968). *The parent of the handicapped child.* Springfield, IL: Thomas.

Begab, M. J. (1966). The mentally retarded and the family. In I. Philips (Ed.), *Prevention and treatment of mental retardation.* New York: Basic Books.

Bennett. C. (1986). Parenting a special child: How difficult is it? *Exceptional Parent, 16*(4), 50–52.

Blacher, J. (1984). Sequential stages of parental adjustment to the birth of a child with handicaps: Fact or artifact? *Mental Retardation, 22* (2), 55–68.

Chinn, P. C., Winn, J., & Walters, R. H. (1978). *Two-way talking with parents of special children: A process of positive communication.* St. Louis: Mosby.

Christiansen, J. (1969). *Theological implications of having a handicapped child.* Panel discussion, University of Utah, Salt Lake City.

Cleveland, M. (1980) Family adaptation to traumatic spinal cord injury: Response to crisis. *Family Therapy, 29*(4), 558–565.

Directory of community resources. (1986). *Exceptional Parent, 16*(1), 33–36.

Dubinsky, P. (1986). My special brother. *Exceptional Parent, 16*(3), 54.

Farber, B. (1959). Effects of a severely mentally retarded child on family integration (Monograph). *Society for Research in Child Development, 24*(2).

Farber, B. (1968). *Mental retardation: Its social context and social consequences.* Boston: Houghton Mifflin.

Farber, N. W. (1968). *The retarded child.* New York: Crown.

Featherstone, H. (1980). *A difference in the family: Living with a disabled child.* New York: Penguin.

Gallagher, J. J. (1956). Rejecting parents? *Exceptional Children, 22,* 273–276.

Gayton, W. F. (1975). Management problems for mentally retarded children and their families. *Pediatric Clinics of North America, 22*(3), 561–570.

Gordon, S. (1975). *Living fully.* New York: John Day.

Greer, B. G. (1975). On being the parent of a handicapped child. *Exceptional Children, 41,* 519.

Grossman, F. K. (1972). *Brothers and sisters of retarded children.* Syracuse, NY: Syracuse University.

Hardman, M. L., Drew, C. J., & Egan, M. W. (1987). *Human exceptionality: Society, school, and family* (2nd ed.). Newton, MA: Allyn & Bacon.

Hart, N. W. (1970). Frequently expressed feelings and reactions of parents toward their retarded children. In N. R. Bernstein (Ed.), *Diminished people.* Boston: Little, Brown.

Henley, C., & Spicknall, H. (1982). Solving school-related problems. *The Exceptional Parent, 12*(4), 21–26.

Hunter, M. H., Schucman, H., & Friedlander, G. (1972). *The retarded child from birth to five: A multidisciplinary program for the child and family.* New York: John Day.

Hutchinson, G. (1968). *Theological implications of having a handicapped child.* Panel discussion, East Texas State University.

Isbell, L. (1979). Yes! In T. Dougan, L. Isbell, & P. Vyas (Eds.), *We have been there.* Salt Lake City: Dougan, Isbell, & Vyas.

Kramm, F. R. (1963). *Families of mongoloid children* (Publication No. 401). Washington, DC: U.S. Children's Bureau.

Kravaceus, W. C., & Hayes, E. N. (1969). *If your child is handicapped.* Boston: Porter Sargent.

Lamb, C. B. (1980). Fostering acceptance of a disabled sibling through books. *The Exceptional Parent, 10*(1), 12–13.

Lamb, M. E. (1983). Fathers of exceptional children. In M. Seligman (Ed.), *The family with a handicapped child: Understanding and treatment.* New York: Grune and Stratton.

Mattson, A., & Agle, D. (1972). Group therapy with parents of hemophiliacs. *Journal of the American Academy of Child Psychiatry, 11,* 558–571.

Neal, C. (1968). *Theological implications of having a handicapped child.* Panel discussion, East Texas State University.

Payne, J. S., & Patton, J. R. (1981). *Mental retardation.* Columbus, OH: Merrill.

Rosen, L. (1955). Selected aspects in the development of the mother's understanding of her mentally retarded child. *American Journal of Mental Deficiency, 59,* 522.

Safford, P. L., & Arbitman, D. C. (1975). *Developmental intervention with young physically handicapped children.* Springfield, IL: Thomas.

Sawyer, H. W., & Sawyer, S. H. (1981). A teacher-parent communication training approach. *Exceptional Children, 47*(4), 305–306.

Schild, S. (1976). The family of the retarded child. In R. Koch & J. C. Dobson (Eds.), *The mentally retarded child and his family* (Rev. ed.). New York: Brunner/ Mazel.

Schreiber, M., & Feeley, M. (1965). Siblings of the retarded: A guided group experience. *Children, 12,* 221–225.

Seligman, M., & Seligman, D. A. (1980). The professional's dilemma: Learning to work with parents. *The Exceptional Parent, 10*(5), 511–513.

Upshur, C. C. (1982). Respite care for mentally retarded and other disabled populations: Program models and family needs. *Mental Retardation, 20* (1), 2–6.

Volpe, J. J., & Koenigsberger, R. (1981). Neurologic disorders. In G. B. Avery (Ed.), *Neonatology, pathophysiology, and management of the newborn* (2d ed.). Philadelphia: Lippincott.

Wentworth, E. H. (1974). *Listen to your heart: A message to parents of handicapped children.* Boston: Houghton Mifflin.

Wolfensberger, W., & Kurtz, R. A. (1969). Religious and pastoral counseling. In W. Wolfensberger and R. A. Kurtz (Eds.), *Management of the family of the mentally retarded* (331–332). Chicago: Follett.

Wolraich, M. L. (1982). Communication between physicians and parents of handicapped children. *Exceptional Children, 48*(4), 324–329.

Zuk, G. H. (1959). The religious factor and the role of guilt in parental acceptance of the retarded child. *American Journal of Mental Deficiency, 64,* 139–147.

13

Social and Ethical Issues

1. Social and ethical issues relating to mental retardation are complex but often become reduced to questions of individual versus societal rights.

2. Ethical questions emerging during the prenatal period usually focus on the prevention of mental retardation by minimizing the probability of such individuals being born.

3. Ethical issues emerging during the early years of life are particularly troubling to many, because they often involve questions regarding the life or death of a mentally retarded individual that has already been born.

4. Social and ethical issues during the school years often relate to questions regarding both society's responsibility and level of effort required to meet the retarded individual's educational and other treatment needs.

5. Social and ethical issues emerging during the adult years once again tend to pit the interests of society against the retarded individual's rights, and they often relate to questions of adult functions such as marriage and reproduction.

6. Research and professional ethics in mental retardation involve a wide variety of issues where individual rights must be balanced against both the need for scientific information and complex questions regarding appropriate treatment.

It has become increasingly obvious as we have proceeded through this volume that mental retardation is an extremely complex phenomenon. Although this has been explicitly stated in earlier chapters, the stark emphasis provided by the study of retardation presents a more dramatic commentary than written language can ever transmit. There are few if any simple answers; philosophies vary, and viewpoints and value systems often conflict. It seems only appropriate that one of the concluding chapters in this book examine what is perhaps the most fluid of all areas: social and ethical issues related to mental retardation.

Social issues and considerations are central to the mental retardation problem and have been throughout history. As noted in earlier chapters, attitudes toward and treatment of retarded individuals have always reflected the prevailing philosophies concerning human existence and worth. These philosophies are the basis of what we call ethics, the rules that guide the "determination of what is good or bad" (Tymchuk, 1976, p. 44).

Many of the issues discussed in this chapter have recurred in the philosophies and prevailing actions of societies throughout history. During certain periods they have represented routine practices that were unquestioned because they were accepted as being in harmony with the best interests of the human species and civilized society. Contemporary civilization has, however, publicly abhorred earlier attitudes and practices (such as euthanasia, or mercy killing) and has described their perpetrators as inhumane and barbaric. At the same time that these judgments have been voiced, many of the actions that have been so loudly denounced have been quietly continued. Only in the last 10 to 15 years have public statements and examinations of these practices been forthcoming, breaking what Duff and Campbell termed a "public and professional silence on a major social taboo" (1973, p. 894). Although these authors were specifically discussing the withholding of care from defective infants, others have described a variety of treatment conditions and practices that are equally dramatic (Blatt & Kaplan, 1966; Horan & Mall, 1977). As public awareness has been heightened, many have been shocked not only by the actions and conditions that exist but also by the realization that we are, in many ways, a hypocritical society (Lusthaus, 1985). It is now our task to progress from a stage of being shocked to one of seriously examining our fundamental values concerning what is right and important in this society and to determine the most effective means to put moral and ethical theory into practice. Additionally, we must balance these considerations with our ability and willingness to pay. This chapter attempts to initiate this process of examination.

BACKGROUND

Core Concept 1	Social and ethical issues relating to mental retardation are complex but often become reduced to questions of individual versus societal rights.

Examining social and ethical issues in relation to any topic requires some exploration of the philosophic foundations of society. Our daily activities seldom include any conscious consideration of philosophy, and in many quarters it has become fashionable to vocalize indifference to or even unfavorable attitudes about its place in contemporary civilization. Regardless of how we view philosophy, each of us operates on the basis of a set of guiding principles, either explicit or implicit, that forms a general code of ethics governing our behavior. Further, any reasonably consistent ethical code is derived from a philosophy concerning what life is about.

Tymchuk (1976) summarized two philosophic positions that he viewed as important in an examination of social and ethical issues related to mental retardation. These philosophies—utilitarianism and formalism—represent extreme polarities in viewpoints from which to consider the rights and worth of individuals in society. Utilitarianism holds that an individual has "only those rights granted by the larger society," whereas formalism maintains that it is the individual "with basic rights which can be neither abrogated nor curtailed by society and the individual's rights as superordinate to those of society" (Tymchuk, 1976, p. 45). Neither of these two extremes is workable in a complex society such as ours. Exclusive subscription to a pure form of utilitarianism leads to the group with the greatest power continuing in power and often expanding their position by substantially limiting the rights of those with less power. Pure formalism also presents a dilemma in that as the rights of some are strengthened and defended the rights of others must necessarily be reduced. We must determine where on the continuum between these two extremes we can operate comfortably. This is an enormously difficult question, but one that must be seriously addressed if we are to ensure human rights in a reasonable fashion without undesirable cost to society generally (Boggs, 1986).

One of the topics to be discussed in this chapter, euthanasia, has previously been mentioned. Euthanasia is defined in Webster's New Collegiate Dictionary as the act or practice of killing individuals that are hopelessly sick or injured for reasons of mercy. This topic, although not unknown to most people, was brought dramatically into the public eye by the case of Karen Ann Quinlan, a 22-year-old New Jersey woman whose life was being maintained by means of an artificial support system. For nearly a full year from the time of her admission to the hospital in April 1975, Karen remained in a coma-like state with her life being apparently sustained by a respirator and tubal feeding. At the time of the New Jersey Supreme Court decision in March 1976, which permitted disconnection of the respirator, it was the opinion of all individuals involved that there were no medical procedures available that would enable Karen to recover and that termination of artificial support would result in almost immediate death. This case entered the courts because of a disagreement between Karen's family and the attending medical personnel. After much agony and soul-searching, her parents had requested that the life-support system be terminated. The physicians involved refused to take this action. To make a complex case even more difficult, after cessation of life support, Karen continued to survive in a comatose state and, in fact, was moved to a nursing home. She died in June of 1985, more than 10 years after she was initially admitted to the hospital. Although that closed her story in one sense, the issues raised by this case will continue for a very long time.

The frequency with which treatment is withheld and patients are allowed to die is not well documented on a general basis, although some investigations have been conducted with specific populations (Duff & Campbell, 1973). However, the regular occurrence of decisions "not to resuscitate" is a commonly known fact among hospital personnel. The practice is sufficiently common that most hospitals use some type of "Code 90" sticker that indicates that the patient is to receive no intensive care or resuscitation (Fletcher, 1973).

The general topic of euthanasia is certainly one that warrants a great deal of attention, but more directly related to our present area of inquiry is a consideration of euthanasia in relation to mentally retarded individuals. As later discussions will indicate, attention to this issue (at least in terms of published material) has focused most heavily on the euthanasia of newborns who are or appear to be retarded at birth. This action usually involves a request on the part of the parents to withhold some sort of routine surgical or medical treatment that is needed for the infant to survive. If the physician agrees to the request, the newborn usually dies.

The practice of life management is far more widespread than most of us realize but is not typically open for public discussion. Robertson (1975, p. 214) characterized it as "now common practice for parents to request, and for physicians to agree, not to treat" infants who are defective at birth. Duff and Campbell (1973) investigated the background in 299 consecutive deaths that were recorded in a special-care nursery and found that 43 of them involved the withholding of treatment. This figure represents over 14% of the sample studied. Other cases have come to light since Duff and Campbell published their findings. Robertson characterized the withholding of treatment from handicapped infants as a procedure that "is rapidly gaining status as 'good medical practice' " (1975, p. 214).

One's initial reaction to the topic of euthanasia may be rather straightforward—that it is a barbaric practice and should not be permitted. Unfortunately, the situation is not quite that simple. It is an issue that is plagued with incredible complexities from many different perspectives, which are discussed more fully in later portions of this chapter.

One of the factors influencing the complexity of social and ethical problems has been indirectly mentioned previously in the discussion of formalist philosophy. Pure formalism presents a dilemma involving the curtailment of the rights of some individuals or segments of society as the rights of others are emphasized. This dilemma has been termed the "competing equities issue" (Boggs, 1977) and presents some perplexing problems to contemporary society, particularly in the area of handicapped citizens' rights. For example, the competing equities issue enters into the controversy surrounding the subject of euthanasia. Some would contend vigorously that it makes little sense to expend the extraordinary resources necessary to maintain life support for a terminally ill patient when such resources are so badly needed by others. Another part of this same contention is the sentiment that valuable resources such as expensive equipment and medical talent should be deployed in a manner that will generate the most benefit for society in general. This viewpoint, basic in utilitarian philosophy, would greatly diminish the resources available for certain segments of society, such as terminally ill, aged, and mentally retarded citizens.

The competing equities issue also comes into play with philosophical viewpoints that are not clearly in the utilitarian vein. For example, formalism is very much in evidence in the call for maximal effort to save the lives of infants who are severely handicapped at birth. This position is often based on the infants' right to life, which from the formalist viewpoint must not be abridged in any fashion. Competing equities are evident in the potential conflict between the rights of the infant and the rights of the parents. Some have argued that the psychological, social, and economic burdens imposed by a mentally retarded child are so extreme that parents should have the right to choose another alternative, particularly when extraordinary life support measures are involved. The rights of parents and the rights of handicapped infants present a potentially conflicting situation—one that is complex and without easy answers (Hardman & Drew, 1980).

The competing equities issue is by no means limited to the area of euthanasia; the principle is familiar to most of us in our daily lives. Further discussion in later sections shows how it is relevant to many social and ethical considerations in the field of mental retardation.

It is evident from this brief overview that a wide variety of social and ethical issues will be addressed in this chapter. They represent complexities and controversies that defy simple solution. It is not the purpose of this chapter to attempt to present answers or to promote one position on a given issue as more appropriate than another. In most cases the proponents on both sides are not only earnest in their viewpoints, but they are also armed with legitimate arguments to support their opinions.

THE LIFE CYCLE: ISSUES AND ETHICS

Although many of the topics to be discussed are not limited to a given age group, certain patterns are evident that relate to different states of the life cycle. The remaining portions of this chapter are therefore organized in the life cycle format represented by the rest of the book. Discussions focus on ethics and issues at the prenatal stage followed by those particularly relevant to the early postnatal years, then to the school years and finally to adulthood. Certain principles, such as competing equities, transcend life cycle stages and are examined as relevant throughout this chapter.

Prenatal Ethics and Issues

Core Concept 2   Ethical questions emerging during the prenatal period usually focus on the prevention of mental retardation by minimizing the probability of such individuals being born.

The prenatal period of the life cycle presents some uniquely difficult ethical questions. Since we are referring to the time before a child is born, we are addressing the task of prevention of mental retardation. The concept of preventing retardation historically has had a very favorable ring to it and continues to sound like an extremely laudable goal. Some have questioned the philosophical basis for this as a generic position (Hauerwas, 1986), and some of the means that may be involved in attaining this end have been controversial, to say the least. From some perspectives they strike at the very core of morality and therefore become prominent as social and ethical issues.

Genetic Screening and Counseling. Previous chapters have made note of certain disorders that are associated with inherited conditions or predispositions. Some of these represent conditions in which the probability of occurrence increases because of family origin (such as Tay-Sachs disease). Others become more probable because of the age or condition of the parent(s) (such as Down syndrome). Many professionals believe that genetic screening and counseling should be routine when such situations exist. Although this is quite logical when viewed from the perspective of preventing mental retardation, such suggestions have raised concern and objections on the part of some segments of the population. Some view genetic screening and counseling as an interference with individual rights and freedom to mate and reproduce by choice. These objections strike particularly sensitive chords when they relate to conditions associated with certain ethnic or family origins, such as sickle cell anemia and Tay-Sachs disease. It is understandable how such procedures could be viewed as discriminatory and aimed at controlling the reproduction of certain ethnic groups. However, such a perspective goes far beyond the purpose typically defined and associated with genetic screening and counseling.

Genetic screening has been defined as "a search in a population for persons possessing certain genotypes that (1) are already associated with disease, (2) may lead to disease in their descendants, or (3) produce other variations not known to be associated with disease" (National Academy of Sciences, 1975, p. 9). Since our current discussion focuses on the prenatal period, the second genotype is of immediate concern.

Genetic screening leads to genetic counseling for the parents or potential parents involved. Such counseling includes providing information about the condition in question, the frequency with which it occurs (if possible, translated into the probability of occurrence in the situation at hand), and what behavioral and physical characteristics might be expected if it does occur. All of these subjects should be dealt with, in addition to the various reproductive options. The genetic counselor must also be prepared to answer all questions openly and completely for the parent to become informed concerning the problem being faced (Harper, 1981; Milunsky, 1979).

The fundamental purpose of screening and counseling is to ensure that the parents or potential parents are thoroughly informed regarding the genetic disorder under consideration. It is not the counselor's task to make a decision for them. If counselors limit themselves to information provision and discussion, then the argument of discrimination and interference with individual rights is largely disarmed. Parents are better prepared to exercise their rights if they are fully aware of the potential outcomes and options, but as with most emotionally charged issues, this point of view does not prevent some from continuing to put forth arguments against genetic screening and counseling.

Prenatal Assessment. The prenatal development period presents other difficult ethical questions in addition to those already discussed. These include consideration of problems relating to assessment and resulting actions. The discussion in chapter 4 indicated that there are a variety of techniques currently available that permit prenatal assessment of fetal status (e.g., amniocentesis, chorion biopsy, fetoscopy, ultrasonography) (Cadkin, Ginsberg, Pergament, & Verlinski, 1984; Perone, Carpenter, & Robertson, 1984). In this area, as in genetic screening, significant advances in technological developments for prenatal fetal assessment can present certain dilemmas (Perone et al., 1984; Zaner, 1986).

In chapter 4 we took the position that evaluation should not be conducted unless it has a purpose. This position is in opposition to the practice of merely evaluating because it is the popular thing to do. In this earlier context we were most directly referring to assessment that, if one subscribes to the above assumption, must result in some action related to service delivery (such as educational programming). If we are to remain consistent, the same assumption must be considered in the case of prenatal assessment. However, as we will see, intervention in this context is controversial.

Abortion. Viewing the preceding assumption in relation to prenatal assessment, one is immediately faced with the types of action that might result. If prenatal assessment indicates either that the fetus is (or is likely to be) defective, one alternative that might be considered is abortion.

Perhaps no single topic has been, and remains, as controversial as abortion. Some factions have contended vigorously that the practice of abortion is murder. This notion is based on the view that a life exists, with human rights and qualities, from the time of conception or shortly thereafter. On the other side of the issue is a substantial segment of the population that maintains, with equal vigor, that abortion should be an option for any woman under any circumstances. This viewpoint is based on the generic proposition that a woman has the right to be in control of her body and that being forced to continue an unwanted pregnancy is a violation of that right.

The perspectives seem to be altered somewhat when the abortion issue is approached in relation to mental retardation. A portion of the population still voices a blanket opposition to abortion. However, this position is held far less strongly and is represented by fewer individuals when the question applies to a handicapped fetus. Some who would not favor abortion in a general sense, because of religious or personal philosophy, are ready to accept it in the context of handicapping conditions. In many cases this shift in perspective is not limited to mental handicaps but is generalized more broadly to any handicapping condition.

This shift in philosophy is not limited to the issue of abortion. As we proceed through this chapter on social and ethical issues, we will encounter this phenomenon in relation to other topics. Reconciliation of the apparent inconsistency in philosophic position has not, for the most part, been seriously undertaken by our society. In some ways the shifting situational ethics may be viewed as an indictment of society in general and specifically those who represent this type of an inconsistent philosophy. Such an indictment, however, would seem to serve little productive purpose. It is more important to realize that belief systems are fluid as they are operationalized.

Many people hold certain beliefs concerning practices such as abortion in the context of mental retardation that may be quite different from their posture relative to abortion in general. Abortion is one alternative that may be taken if prenatal assessment indicates that the developing fetus is defective. We believe that in all cases the belief system of the parents involved should prevail in the decision of whether to abort. This may present some conflict to the attending medical personnel if their personal value system is opposed to the practice of abortion. When such a situation does occur, the physician should inform parents of their right to seek the services of other medical personnel if they so desire.

The decision to abort a defective fetus is obviously in conflict with the position that abortion should not be permitted under any circumstances. This latter viewpoint is often based on the belief that the fetus has a right to life that cannot be abridged for any reason. Those who are more inclined to abort a defective fetus often argue that the quality of life for the handicapped individual is likely to be so diminished that no one would choose to live under such circumstances. This, of course, puts them in the position of deciding what the fetus would or would not choose if that action were possible (a point that the opposing faction is quick to emphasize). A further point of contention involves the effect of a handicapped child on the parents and siblings. In many cases the immediate and continuing financial, psychological, and social burdens are extreme and affect the family in an undesirable fashion. Those who favor abortion contend that parents should at least have the option to decide. Of course, the opposing view counters with the right of the unborn fetus to life regardless of the consequences for others.

The conflict characterized by the opposing value system is not reconcilable, because the disagreement is so fundamental. It is a situation in which we are faced with competing equities that probably cannot be resolved to the satisfaction of both sides. More importantly, it presents a very difficult dilemma for parents (Kessler, 1979; Wojcik, 1978).

Ethical Issues During the Early Years

Core Concept 3   Ethical issues emerging during the early years of life are particularly troubling to many, because they often involve questions regarding the life or death of a mentally retarded individual that has already been born.

Ethical issues related to mental retardation during the early years are as complex as those encountered at the prenatal stage. Some of these have been noted briefly in the introductory section of this chapter. In all cases the issues involve agonizing problem situations, without easy or simple solutions. As with previous portions of this volume, the period from birth to 5 years of age is considered in a discussion of the early years.

Each developmental period is critical, in one fashion or another, to a child's overall growth process. The first 2 months after birth, usually termed the neonatal period, is our first focus for discussion. Chapter 5 indicated that many authorities view the first half of the neonatal period as the most dangerous in the total life span. Many of the developmental processes that were underway prenatally remain uncompleted and are continuing at an extremely rapid rate, and the infant is now without the protective environment provided by the mother's womb. Until a more complete arsenal of defenses is developed, the baby is perhaps more vulnerable to hazardous influences than at any other time.

Life Management Issues. The first few hours after birth and the first month of extrauterine life also represent a prime setting for one of the most controversial ethical issues relating to the life of a handicapped infant. Chances may be greatest during this period for consideration about withholding treatment for infants who are diagnosed as defective. As indicated in the introductory sections of this chapter, this practice is often termed euthanasia, although there are some important distinctions between euthanasia and the decision "not to prolong life," as we shall see in later discussion.

Ethical Issues. It is not surprising that there are some important parallels between the ethical reasoning applied to abortion on one hand and to decisions about postnatal survival of an infant on the other. If one is to be philosophically consistent, the same arguments and postures that are presented in relation to abortion should also be used in connection with the practice of euthanasia. To some degree this is the case, although we have already witnessed considerable fluidity in ethical reasoning and will see more as we examine further issues.

The polarized viewpoints described previously for abortion are also encountered in the issues of postnatal survival. Ramsey (1973), for example, held that abortion should not be an option even when prenatal assessment indicates that the fetus is severely defective or diseased. It was his contention that whatever arguments are used to justify abortion may also be used to support infanticide, or the killing of infants. Ramsey's argument was not based on the position that we would commit a given act; he was essentially saying that there is no distinct moral difference between infanticide and abortion and that if we would not practice the former, then we should not practice the latter. Similar consistency is evident on the opposite side of the issue, which was perhaps best expressed by Joseph Fletcher (1973). He not only maintained that such abortion is appropriate but suggested that there is a moral obligation to abort a fetus that is diagnosed as defective, and futher contended that the same reasoning holds for the practice of euthanasia with defective infants.

As would be expected, there are a variety of philosophical positions that fall somewhere between these two extreme points of view. John Fletcher, for example, supported an approach that "accentuates parental freedom to participate in life-and-death decisions independently in both the prenatal and postnatal situations, accepts abortion of a seriously defective fetus, but disapproves euthanasia of defective newborns" (1975, p. 75). It was his viewpoint that there are "morally relevant differences between abortion and euthanasia" that must be considered (p. 76).

Fletcher discussed three points that he viewed as representing these differences. His first consideration involved the fact that an infant now has a separate physical existence from the mother, which was not the case on a prenatal basis. This situation places the infant in the position of being a patient with independent rights for care and support. The essence of Fletcher's point was that the newborn has an independent status and can and should be considered separately from the mother. On the other hand, the prenatal fetus does not have independent status, so, he maintains, the status of the fetus should not be considered separately. Fletcher's second point related closely to his first. Since the newborn is separate physically from the mother, he or she is now much more accessible than was the case prenatally. Fletcher argued that this places a greater obligation on the physician to heal and relieve suffering. Fletcher's third point rounds out what he saw as the morally relevant differences between abortion and euthanasia. In this context he noted a major difference in parental acceptance and loyalty to the unborn fetus when compared with the newborn: parental loyalty is much stronger to the newborn than to the unborn fetus.

The above points are presented to support John Fletcher's position, which accepts abortion but views euthanasia with disfavor. He noted two further points that argue against euthanasia that are frequently discussed and debated in the context of this complex issue. The first of these points is the obvious danger of euthanasia practiced by unprincipled individuals. His second point involved the inherent danger in changing societal attitudes toward the birth of infants from one of great caring to one of accepted selective euthanasia.

It should be pointed out that, throughout the discussion of John Fletcher's point of view, the term euthanasia has been used. This is because of the fact that he was very careful to use that term when examining the rationale for his position. For Fletcher and many others interested in this area, the term euthanasia has a very specific connotation.

In many situations with seriously defective infants, the decision is whether to prolong life rather than whether to perform actual euthanasia. These two concepts convey different meanings, which may have considerable importance from legal and moral standpoints. Euthanasia suggests mercy killing, or the beneficent termination of a life that may otherwise continue. According to G. P. Fletcher, on the other hand, failure to prolong life conveys the idea of not "artifically lengthening a life that would otherwise end" (1968, p. 119). These differences, although appearing subtle to some, clearly become a part of the controversy as we proceed to examine this issue.

Legal Issues. From a legal standpoint the distinction between euthanasia and not prolonging life is essentially the difference between acts and omissions. Euthanasia, as described above, involves the act of terminating a life that would continue if the act was not committed. Not to prolong life, on the other hand, involves omission in that the physician fails to act and permits death to occur. G. P. Fletcher (1968) noted that the act of terminating life is first-degree murder in the eyes of the law, regardless of motive. The legal view of omitting action depends on the relationship of the physician to the other person. If the individual is a patient who has a reasonable expectation that the physician will provide treatment, the physician's failure to do so is legally no different than acting to terminate a life. If the individual is not a patient, the physician is not legally bound to intercede in the same fashion. G. P. Fletcher also pointed out that "there is a significant gap between the law in theory and the law in practice" (1968, p. 120). He cited only one case in which a physician was brought to trial for a euthanasia act. In this case the physician was acquitted, even though he admitted performing the act and his nurse testified as a witness. With regard to acts of omission the gap between theory and practice seems even greater. Fletcher noted that no cases can be found in which a physician has been found either criminally or civilly liable for deciding not to prolong life.

The absence of case law pertaining to acts of omission seems particularly significant when viewed in the context of a defective newborn. Since there is usually an attending physician during and after birth, it seems that the establishment of the patient status on the part of the infant is automatic. As mentioned previously, if the physician omits lifesaving action for a patient who has a reasonable expectation of treatment, the law views this no differently from an act to terminate life. What appears clear is that, in practice, society has chosen to look the other way when decisions not to prolong life are made. Further, it appears that this is particularly true when the decision involves a defective newborn. Even John Fletcher modified his position on postnatal practice under such circumstances. He stated that "allowing the infant to die by withholding support while relieving pain is a decision, in my view, that can be ethically justified for reasons of mercy to the infant and relief of meaningless suffering of the parents and medical team" (1975, p. 77). He was careful to qualify this position, however, by using such terms as "cases of terribly damaged newborns for whom death is the desirable outcome when therapy either is not available or will only prolong the ordeal" (p. 77). Thus he remained more reluctant than some to permit postnatal management of life in this fashion, even in the cases involving handicapped infants. This is not the case with many physicians and ethicists dealing with this issue.

The preceding discussion clearly illustrates a discrepancy between the theoretical legal view and the practiced legal view of postnatal life management. This seems to raise the question of whether or not the theoretical legal view should be changed. If society has implicitly determined that selective euthanasia and decisions not to prolong life are within acceptable zones of behavior, then one might wonder why the formal statements of those acceptable zones (i.e., the laws) are not redefined. As might be expected, this issue has been raised.

The study by Duff and Campbell (1973) was of particular importance because it provided at least a limited public data base concerning the frequency with which treatment is withheld from handicapped infants. After examining their data and the ethical ramifications thereof, Duff and Campbell turned to the legal issues in their final statements. They took the rather strong position that if withholding treatment from severely handicapped infants is a "violation of the law, we believe the law should be changed" (1973, p. 894). Others have preceded this position with considerable debate concerning the legislation of voluntary euthanasia (Kamisar, 1958; Williams, 1958, 1966). It is evident that the topic of changing the law has received some attention from both sides. The logic in favor of changing the law is perhaps deceptively simple when presented, as it was, in relation to the acceptable zones of behavior given above. There are, however, some persuasive arguments against such change.

One of the arguments against changing the laws lies with the extreme difficulty of developing legal standards that can be effectively operationalized. One might expect that legislation removing criminal liability for decisions to withhold treatment would be very narrow in its definitions. Those that are most reluctant to speak to these issues use terms such as "terribly diseased," "tragically deformed," and "hideously damaged." However, even if legislation were developed with very strict and narrow criteria, application of legal standards by society and the development of case law has a way of continuously expanding the legal jurisdiction. Both G. P. Fletcher (1968) and Burt (1976) noted that there is great difficulty in distinguishing between the clear cases and those that are less clear. For example, Robertson (1975) suggested that treatment might be withheld from "profoundly retarded, nonambulatory hydrocephalics who are blind and deaf" (p. 267). To this Burt responded by asking, "What about those only blind? only deaf? and so on" (p. 439). This illustrates the difficulty of defining standards that can be effectively operationalized from a legal standpoint. Regardless of the care with which definitions are prepared, there will always be the "next hard case" that does not quite fit the description and requires professional judgment.

Burt also presented other persuasive points to argue against changing the laws. One of his points involved the change in attitude that frequently occurs when court arguments are made over issues that are specifically authorized by legislation. Experience has shown that litigation relating to acts specifically addressed by legislation often involves arguments presented in a fashion that might be characterized as cool, rational, and dispassionate. Burt clearly believed that the dispensing of life or death is an issue that we cannot afford to treat in a dispassionate manner. His concern was that explicit authority, such as that which might be found in legislation, would place life and death decisions for defective newborns in a context in which either choice might be made with equal ease. Burt believed that this should not be the case and that decisions should be reached reluctantly. It was his contention that the current state of affairs promotes that reluctance as a result of the mere existence of potential criminal liability.

The description of Burt's arguments might suggest that he was firmly opposed to the withholding of treatment. This is not the case. It should be emphasized that he was in opposition only to changing the law and thereby specifically authorizing such action. With the following statements, he placed this position squarely in the arena of social and ethical issues:

> I am not suggesting that existing values must change or that no self-respecting physician would ever or should ever withhold treatment from a newborn. Rather, I am suggesting that if we are evolving toward new values in this

matter, we must do so gradually, hesitantly, and looking backward to what
we have been, as often as we look forward to imagine what we will become.
(Burt, p. 446)

Burt's arguments warrant serious consideration whether one holds a similar position or not. One does not have to search very far into the past to discover topics and issues that have experienced an expansion of what is
authorizable. Some of the topics, such as abortion and euthanasia, are discussed, examined, and practiced in ways that would have been clearly beyond
the limits of possibility 30 years ago. In some cases technological advances
have occurred that seem to have subtly governed philosophical changes. In
other areas it is not altogether clear what influences have fostered such changes,
but we still find ethical considerations being examined that would previously
have been thought wildly impossible. Perhaps nowhere is there more reason
to give pause than in the issues of postnatal life management.

Life Management Decisions. As we look both backward and forward in
examining our values, several immediate questions arise in relation to life
management. Although there may be many other issues, one is promptly
faced with how life management decisions are made, who makes such decisions and under what circumstances, and for whom these decisions will
be made. Some examination of this last consideration has been previously
debated and presented. In most cases those who debate the issues of life
management are discussing infants who are extremely damaged or defective
at birth. However, terms such as "extremely" are adjectives that may be
broadly defined and are subject to differing interpretations.

The Johns Hopkins Case. In at least one case that received considerable
visibility, substantial debate occurred relative to the degree of handicap that
the infant represented. This involved a case that occurred at Johns Hopkins
Hospital with a 2-day-old, full-term male infant who had facial characteristics and other features giving to a clinical impression of Down syndrome.
No cardiac abnormalities were evident, but the infant began vomiting a
greenish substance shortly after birth. X-ray examination indicated the existence of an intestinal obstruction that was clinically labeled as duodenal
atresia (a congenital absence or closure of a portion of the duodenum).

It is important to momentarily discuss the duodenal atresia to place this
case in perspective. Diamond (1977) reviewed this specific case and examined the issues involved in medical intervention through surgical correction
of the intestinal obstruction. He stated that the problem could be corrected
with a survival rate of about 98% and that the mortality was higher for
newborn infants with acute appendicitis. Diamond thought that the ethics
and value structure which would require performance of this virtually risk-
free operation on a nonhandicapped infant do not place the same obligation
in the case of a handicapped infant.

In the Johns Hopkins case an intestinal obstruction could be surgically corrected with negligible risk. The infant reportedly had no additional complicating factors other than the clinical impression of Down syndrome. Is Down syndrome an example of an extremely handicapping condition? This may be a debatable question. Some would answer in an unqualified affirmative manner. Others might note the potential intellectual range of Down syndrome children and would disagree. The answer is not clear-cut, although one factor that may come into play occasionally is that Down syndrome is visually evident. The decision in the Johns Hopkins case was to withhold treatment. Following discussion with the parents, the surgical correction of the duodenal atresia was not performed, and all feeding and fluids were discontinued. Fifteen days later the infant died of starvation and dehydration.

There are many ethical issues raised by the Johns Hopkins case. One can certainly question if it is humane to permit an infant to starve to death over a 15-day period. This is a particularly difficult question, since the decision to not operate made it impossible for the infant to receive food and fluids in a normal manner. However, the question about the degree of handicap represented by Down syndrome is equally provocative in terms of our question regarding on whom life management decisions will focus. It is questionable whether Down syndrome necessarily can be described as an extreme, a terrible, or a tragic handicap. Some Down syndrome children may reach a level of intellectual functioning that would be classified as moderate or even mild mental retardation.

The possibility that mildly or moderately retarded infants are vulnerable to negative life management decisions raises serious concerns. This is particularly true in the context of earlier discussions about proposals to enact legislation authorizing selective life management. It was noted before that application of legal standards by society and the development of case law has a tendency to continuously expand legal jurisdiction. Even in the absence of legal authorization, use of advancing technology frequently seems to desensitize society to encroachment on value structure boundaries. These tendencies should be carefully considered as we heed Burt's plea to look both backward and forward as we evolve new values in the matter of life management. Will future life management decisions include the mildly handicapped? This may already be the case in visible handicaps such as Down syndrome. Will future life management include the parents' election of a particular sex? Perhaps only beautiful infants will receive favorable decisions. These suggestions are clearly repugnant and sound wildly impossible; however, many of the practices that society once thought were wildly impossible are now considered acceptable by some. It should be forcefully emphasized that this discussion is not presented to take a position on life management practices. Instead, it is meant to provoke the most serious examination possible of the social and ethical issues related to such treatment alternatives with mentally retarded individuals.

Decisions: Who and How. The earlier questions posed included those of how life management decisions are made and who makes such decisions and under what circumstances. In part these issues are related to the discussion just presented, but certain other points warrant at least brief attention in terms of these questions.

Both the "how" and "why" questions are not answered simply. Shaw (1977) presented a series of case vignettes from his pediatric surgery practice and from others' practices that exemplify the difficulties posed by life management decisions with handicapped newborns. His presentation included attention of both who and how, with an emphasis on what he terms "informed consent." He noted that patients, when they are adults and mentally competent, have the right to be fully informed about proposed medical treatment. It is generally agreed that such patients then have the legal right to accept or reject that treatment and, in fact, to reject any treatment. When the patient is a minor, however, or not judged to be mentally competent, the decision process is vastly altered. In the case of handicapped infants, parents have the right to informed consent but do not have sole decision-making prerogatives. It was Shaw's contention that the parents' decision is "subject to review when physicians or society disagree with that decision" (1977, p. 76). His statement concerning review by physicians and society specifically addressed situations when the parents' decision involves the rejection of treatment. It is clear from published reports that this is the case in terms of public decision making. It would be patently unacceptable for medical personnel to publicly reverse a parental decision to prolong life. Off the record, medical personnel do, however, report cases in which unilateral (but not public) decisions are made to withhold treatment in certain circumstances.

Consent. The act of consent is not as simple as is suggested by the term informed consent, which is a term that has achieved popular usage, although it is a misnomer. The American Association on Mental Deficiency (AAMD) viewed the problems of consent as sufficiently significant that a special task force was commissioned to examine the complexities of this topic. This effort resulted in publication of the AAMD *Consent Handbook* (Turnbull, 1977), which examined consent in a detailed manner and from both definition and application standpoints.

Although consent has specific meanings in a variety of contexts, the ramifications of consent often result in legal interpretations. This is certainly the case in context of the current discussion. The *Consent Handbook* defined consent principally as a legal concept. From this standpoint there are three elements of consent that must be considered: capacity, information, and voluntariness. For the most part these three elements must be present for consent to be effective. It is also important to realize that consent is seldom, if ever, permanent and may be withdrawn at almost any time.

Generally the act of withdrawing consent must also include the three elements of capacity, information, and voluntariness.

The elements of consent are particularly important in the context of our discussion of life management decisions with handicapped infants. The *Consent Handbook* defined the first element—capacity—in terms of three factors: the person's age, competence, and particular situation. An infant does not have the legal or logical capacity to consent specifically on at least two of these factors. A person under the age of majority (generally 18 years) is legally incompetent to make certain decisions. Likewise, it is clear that an infant does not have the developed mental competence to understand and give consent. Thus in terms of capacity the parents, legal guardians, or other persons acting on behalf of the parents have the authority to consent for an infant. The issues involved in decision making generally, for and by mentally retarded persons, are complex (Drane, 1985; Gaylin & Macklin, 1982).

The second element of consent—information—also must receive careful consideration. The *Consent Handbook* discussed this element in the following manner:

> The focus is on *"what" information is given and "how" it is given* since it must be effectively communicated (given and received) to be acted upon. The concern is with the *fullness* and *effectiveness* of the disclosure: *is it designed to be fully understood, and is it fully understood?* The burden of satisfying these two tests rests on the professional. (Turnbull, 1977, p. 8)

The last sentence of this quotation is particularly important in terms of life management decisions with handicapped newborns. Clearly the giving or withholding of consent rests primarily with the parents, but in a sense such decisions are the joint responsibility of parents and medical personnel. For the element of effective information to be present, it is the physician's responsibility to see that the information about the infant's condition is designed to be fully understood and is fully understood.

The third element of consent—voluntariness—also has great relevance in the context of our discussion of life management decisions with handicapped newborns. Although voluntariness may appear to be a simple concept, subtle influences in the process of giving or withholding consent make it far from simple. The *Consent Handbook* noted that the consenting individual must be "so situated as to be able to exercise free power of choice without the intervention of any element of force, fraud, deceit, duress, overreaching or other ulterior form of constraint or coercion" (Turnbull, 1977, p. 10). This places even further responsibility on a physician. The information provided must be complete and without explicit or implicit inclusion of personal judgment. This may be particularly difficult, since physicians, frequently perceived as power figures by the lay public, certainly are not without their own feelings or inclinations in such situations. It may also be the case that parents are highly vulnerable to persuasion immediately after the birth of a handicapped infant (Hardman & Drew, 1980).

Life management in terms of euthanasia or withholding treatment from handicapped infants may be one of the most complex social and ethical issues related to mental retardation. The preceding discussion has illustrated the individual agonies involved in these decisions and has also suggested that social value structures are under stress in such situations. Perhaps nowhere is the concept of competing equities so evident. The rights of the infant and the rights of the parents may be in direct conflict, depending on the values and attitudes of the parents. Such conflict is not a new observation for those who work with retarded children and their families. What may be new or unique is the stark realization that the decisions being made involve a degree of seriousness that is totally unfamiliar to most of us—the actual dispensing of life or death.

Other Issues. The neonatal period and the remaining portion of the early years also represent a high-risk time for other actions involving a mentally retarded infant. Some of these actions also come under consideration as we examine social and ethical issues. If a child is definitely identified as being mentally retarded during this period of time, it is quite likely that a visible clinical syndrome is evident (e.g., Down syndrome) or that the handicap is in the moderate to severe or profound range. More often that not a mildly retarded child without physical evidence of a problem is not diagnosed with any degree of certainty until formal schooling begins. Parents of this latter type of child may have some concerns about developmental delays, but these are often private concerns that frequently remain in the back of their minds and either are not discussed or are rationalized and denied. However, parents of children who are diagnosed as mentally retarded during their early years must address the issues of care and early education on a more immediate basis, which often raises ethical considerations that are emotionally laden and cause extraordinary stress.

Institutionalization Decisions. Both the type of care and where such care is going to be given frequently surface as considerations with children who are diagnosed as retarded during their early years. One issue that often arises is whether or not these children should be institutionalized. This is always an agonizing choice for parents and frequently is made doubly difficult by the type and amount of information on which they can base their decision. The discussion in chapter 4 indicated that prediction of a child's ultimate level of functioning is extremely difficult during the very early periods of life. Although predictive accuracy improves as the child grows older, assessment procedures that are useful during infancy are quite unreliable in terms of later functioning. Additionally, parents of very young retarded children are often interacting with medical personnel as their primary source of information. Historically physicians have had too little training to effectively meet this challenge, although significant efforts have recently been made in many medical schools to include such preparation. Assessments of retarded children by physicians have consequently been subject to considerable error, particularly when there is also a physical handicap or defect present (Drew & Hardman, 1977; Hardman & Drew, 1977). For example, research by Pearson and Menefee (1965) indicated that pediatricians consistently underestimated the level of intellectual functioning of such individuals, which resulted in a tendency to recommend institutionalization more frequently.

A variety of social and ethical issues are involved in this situation. One immediate consideration pertains to the inclination to recommend or at least favor institutionalization based on estimates of the degree of handicap by medical personnel. Although Pearson and Menefee included older individuals in their sample, their findings give rise to concern about the handicapped infant and the young handicapped child. The more generalized concern relates mostly to the apparent magnitude of consistent error in estimates by pediatricians. Their results indicated that approximately two thirds of the assessments were close to one full standard deviation away from administered standardized test scores. This, coupled with their report that pediatricians consistently misjudged and underestimated the level of functioning, heightens the concern even further. The data showing such misjudgments by physicians seem to suggest a rather uncertain basis for the decision to institutionalize.

A brief note to moderate the potential interpretation of this discussion seems in order before proceeding. First of all, it was mentioned previously that some recent efforts have been made to improve the preparation of physicians for working with handicapped individuals and their families. We have observed significant leadership by some medical personnel responsible for preparation programs, which are excellent and appear to be having a substantial impact. Some pediatricians involved in teaching hospitals have become extremely knowledgeable about education of handicapped individuals and have done a great deal to foster an interdisciplinary team effort with special education and psychology. The fact remains, however, that many medical personnel who are currently in practice were trained before the advent of this concern. Their level of knowledge and the nature of their approach to handicapped children remains unknown on an individual basis but may, as a group, reflect the type of findings reported by Pearson and Menefee.

Placement of a young retarded child in an institution once again raises the issue of consent and of the three elements that must be present for consent to be effective. As stated previously, effective consent must include capacity, information, and voluntariness. The parents must give consent with these three elements functionally present in order for institutionalization of the child to be legitimate. In the context of the previous discussion, the element of information raises particular concern. The parents may be interacting with medical or other professional personnel who are not properly equipped to provide a complete and appropriate data base for decision making. There has been little consequence in the past for professionals who have provided inadequate information or advice in terms of a child's placement. Turnbull and Turnbull (1975) noted that such immunity may disappear as parents and advocates for retarded individuals undertake litigation to alter decisions previously made on inadequate information or advice. They further suggested that malpractice might be an appropriate and emerging concept for professions other than medicine.

Institutional Conditions. No decision for treatment or placement of a retarded child should be undertaken casually or without full consideration of its ramifications. This seems to be particularly the case when the decision involves potential placement of a retarded child in a residential institution. Such a decision involves perhaps the most restrictive placement possible and represents a dramatic removal of the individual from the societal mainstream. Although this type of placement is appropriate in certain situations, the outcomes can be very detrimental when it is undertaken inappropriately.

Residential institutions historically have had a very poor image as treatment and habilitation agencies for retarded individuals. While some of this poor image may be undeserved or due to extenuating circumstances, conditions in institutions have often been undesirable, and in some cases they have been deplorable. Burt (1976) considered them "warehouses for human beings, if anything, an understated depiction of many, perhaps most, of these large-scale, geographically isolated institutions" (p. 441). Others have portrayed the conditions in institutions in equally dramatic and unfavorable terms (Blatt & Kaplan, 1966). A judiciary subcommittee of the United States Senate conducted five days of hearings during the summer of 1977 while considering legislation on the civil rights of institutionalized persons. The hearings resulted in over 1,100 pages of testimony and exhibits by individuals, either professionals or other interested parties, involved with mentally retarded people. These pages include extremely graphic descriptions, much of them most unfavorable, of institutional problems and conditions.

The desirability of institutional placement may thus be questioned on arguments of unacceptable conditions alone (although the restrictiveness of placement raises additional questions). The assignment of any human being to live in some of the subhuman conditions that have existed raises serious issues of societal values. Fortunately, as noted earlier, others have raised and continue to raise such questions in a number of public forums, and dramatic changes are underway. Some of these changes have been initiated by institutional personnel themselves, and others have emerged as a result of efforts by advocates for retarded citizens. In general there is a diminishing propensity to commit very young children to institutions. This represents a favorable move in view of the assessment difficulties that have previously been discussed. It also reduces the likelihood that institutionalization will occur because of inadequate information and increases the probability that other treatment alternatives will be given more serious consideration. Although favorable changes are underway, it is important for society to continue examination of its value structure relative to services for mentally retarded individuals. Was it by intent or by neglect that the deplorable institutional conditions were allowed to evolve? Do such conditions represent an implicit statement of society's philosophical position on the value of human life or a statement of belief that retarded individuals are somehow "less human"? Such questions are much like those posed earlier; they have no single or simple answers.

A final note is in order relative to institutional placement in general and to early placement in particular. The issue of competing equities once again presents itself, placing the handicapped child in a polar position opposite the parents and the rest of the family. On one hand there is the right of the retarded child to live and develop in the best environment possible; on the other hand there is the possibility of the child's negative impact on the family. What effect does the child's presence (and the presence of a handicap) have on the parents and any nonretarded siblings that may be a part of the family constellation? In many cases the impact is unknown at the outset, and reports have varied all the way from favorable results to essential destruction of the family unit. One factor is a constant in this consideration: the impact is not minimal.

Ethical Issues During the School Years

Core Concept 4   Social and ethical issues during the school years often relate to questions regarding both society's responsibility and level of effort required to meet the retarded individual's educational and other treatment needs.

In part, social and ethical issues that surface during the school years are similar to some that have been discussed in earlier parts of this chapter. Competing equities, consent, and placement issues are not limited to a particular age level. In fact, they are so fundamental that they can be observed in nearly all arenas of service delivery to handicapped individuals. However, the manner in which these issues emerge is affected considerably by the context of different phases of the life cycle.

Placement Issues. The placement of mentally retarded children in educational settings raises a variety of issues, including generic philosophical questions as well as those related to the manner in which implementation is undertaken. A certain amount of historical context is helpful in examining both philosophical and implementation questions. The major portion of this discussion, however, examines the current issues and those that might be anticipated in the future.

Earlier sections of this book have examined the educational programming for mentally retarded children and youth. From these discussions it is clear that one placement alternative involves what some have termed "pull-out programs." Such programs are characterized by removing a retarded child from the educational mainstream and essentially providing the complete educational experience in a situation isolated from the child's non-handicapped peers. Examples of this type of placement include self-contained special education classes, special schools, and residential institutions. Earlier sections have noted that such placements exist as alternatives but should be viewed as existing on a continuum with others that involve specialized programming for the child within the educational mainstream. This view is not one that has prevailed from a historical perspective.

Special classes and other pull-out programs for mentally retarded children have a long history. The first public school special classes in the United States were organized in 1896. Enrollment in such programs increased at a steady rate until recently. By 1922 there were over 23,000 children enrolled in special classes, and by 1958 the number had increased to over 196,000 (Mackie & Robbins, 1960). The increase in special classes for retarded children was based on the belief that such placement was more beneficial than maintaining them in regular classroom settings. As noted in earlier chapters, both the data and logic supporting this as the sole approach to educating handicapped children have been seriously questioned in recent years. Without recounting the details presented in chapter 9 we can briefly summarize current thinking by referring to Deno's cascade of services model (1970) and the basic principles of P.L. 94–142. These sources suggest that handicapped individuals should be treated and educated as much as possible with the mainstream of society. In the context of our present discussion this focuses on the formal educational process.

Much of the current thinking regarding the education of handicapped children has been expressed in P.L. 94–142, which is discussed in chapter 14. As suggested by this earlier discussion, P.L. 94–142 is an extremely complex piece of legislation that raises many questions and issues. One of these relates specifically to the placement of handicapped children in the least restrictive appropriate educational environment. This concept is very different from the logic that supported pull-out programs as the primary means for educating mentally retarded children. The least restrictive environment concept emphasizes a continuum of service alternatives and requires that education agencies develop procedures to assure that handicapped children are educated with non-handicapped children to the degree that it is appropriate. The least restrictive placement concept thus emphasizes that special classes, separate schooling, or other removal of handicapped children from the regular educational environment should be alternatives of choice only when the child's handicap is such that satisfactory education cannot be accomplished in regular classes, even with the use of supplementary aids and services. There are many issues that are raised by the least restriction principle. Many of these have been examined in earlier chapters on the school years and legal issues. Additionally, the least restriction principle has raised several questions and issues that warrant attention in the context of social and ethical domains.

Least Restriction Principle. One of the issues raised by the least restriction principle represents a somewhat fluid combination of competing equities and the formalism-utilitarianism philosophical conflict. As suggested earlier, the formalist philosophy presents a dilemma in its pure form because as the rights of some are emphasized, the environment of others is often affected. This dilemma is nearly definitional in the way it relates to competing equities. Education of mentally retarded children in least restrictive placements may create some of these exact problems. For example, least restrictive placement will mean that a rather substantial number of mildly retarded children will have their primary placement in regular classrooms. Even with the supplementary aids and ancillary services that may be available, they will require certain additional in-class attention that the teacher may not be accustomed to providing and perhaps may require certain skills that the teacher does not possess. This situation is described in a tentative fashion, but it is clear that many teachers face it with great anxiety.

In certain parts of the country, teacher expectations related to least restrictive placements have emerged in contract negotiations between school districts and teachers' bargaining organizations (that is, unions and professional associations). For example, in some areas teacher organizations have taken the stand that class size must be reduced by three non-handicapped children for each handicapped child that is placed in the regular classroom. This raises an immediate question of where those three non-handicapped children will be placed. If a regular class had three handicapped children enrolled, it would result in the displacement of nine non-handicapped children under this type of plan. Such an arrangement could easily result in a significant increase in the number of classrooms, and even schools, in a district. This instantly gives rise to the issue of cost and also the possibility of increased busing. When these matters are considered, the competing equities problem emerges very significantly. Taxpayers are already less than enthusiastic about the portion of their income that is being absorbed by public education. Parents of non-handicapped children will have some legitimate reasons for irritation as they are asked to pay more while their children are shifted from class to class (or are bused).

The difficulties just described represent only some of the instances in which we face the competing equities issue in the schooling of mentally retarded children. The dilemma is found squarely on the philosophical questions raised by formalism in our complex society. When we make more distinct the legitimate rights to an appropriate education for some, we may impinge on those same rights of others. The social value question at stake is at once simple and complex: who sacrifices? Is it a matter of requiring that all be equally disadvantaged or all equally advantaged? Or do we turn to a utilitarian philosophy in which an individual only has those rights granted by society at large (the privileged)? It may be possible for society to ensure an appropriate education for all handicapped children without significantly imposing a disadvantage on non-handicapped children. This cannot, however, be accomplished without a cost, and society must determine if it is willing to pay that cost. The least restriction principle places a strain on societal values in that this question cannot go unanswered. This is a tall order for a social structure that is not accustomed to addressing such difficult questions in an orderly manner.

Appropriate Education Issues. The language of P.L. 94–142 raises many questions that can be discussed in the context of social issues related to the school years. A complete examination of these matters far exceeds the scope of this chapter or of this volume. However, one particular piece of the language is strikingly provocative. The term "appropriate" was mentioned in the discussion of least restriction: least restrictive appropriate placement. This term is found in several parts of the legislation and is essentially intended to connote a qualitative description of the educational programming. The placement and educational program should be appropriate for the nature and degree of the handicap.

Legislation dealing with appropriate education may be problematic from at least two standpoints. The first relates to the term itself, which, like many such adjectives, is a general term that is subject to a wide variety of definitions. Although this is characteristic of legislative language, the range of implemental or operational outcomes is as varied as the number of individuals responsible for implementation. This brings us to the second problem with the term appropriate. Public Law 94–142 is a revolutionary piece of legislation. Some have suggested that it is so revolutionary that it may die of its own weight, because it may be too difficult to make the changes required on a mass basis. Consequently, professionals have been so engaged in responding to its major and obvious tenets that the term appropriate has been largely ignored. This presents a significant dilemma, because the appropriateness of the educational or treatment program was the essential raison d'etre for the legislation. In fact, an appropriate education is a fundamental assumption that underlies the public's support of public education in general. Some responses to the concepts of P.L. 94–142 have seemed to ignore appropriateness to such a significant degree that ethical questions appear to be raised. Drew (1978) described example situations, specifically related to least restrictive placement, that give rise to such concerns. One of these involves what he termed a "paper compliance" in which efforts are concentrated more on making a child's program look appropriate on paper than on ensuring the actual appropriateness of the program. Although such situations have existed in the past, it seems that efforts are intensifying with the advent of the federal legislation.

The type of activity represented by paper compliance certainly detracts from the effectiveness of educational programming, which was the fundamental purpose of the legislation. It also brings into question the professional ethics of those who undertake such plans. Initial reaction to this type of compliance may be much like that suggested in the context of life management—that it is unethical practice and should not be permitted. Whereas most of us would agree in principle, this problem, like those we have discussed previously, is plagued with complexities that make a simple solution difficult.

Although one cannot excuse paper compliance, it is not difficult to understand some of the reasons why such responses occur. First of all, the public schools are not generally well equipped to implement P.L. 94–142 on a widespread basis. Chapter 14 outlines in detail the major principles of the law. It is a massive piece of legislation, which, if interpreted and implemented literally (as intended), means immense changes in most school districts. In many cases these changes require personnel and skills that are not currently available. In fact, some of these resources might not be available by the time that compliance is required even if the schools did have the financial capability to buy them. Thus from the perspective of those who are charged with the responsibility of implementation, the task often seems overwhelming. Once again, while we many not excuse or condone paper compliance, it is not difficult to see how this response occurs.

Additional factors add to the complex issue of providing appropriate educational programming as defined in P.L. 94–142. It is a prescriptive piece of federal legislation that, from many educators' viewpoint, is being imposed on them by outsiders. Many who are required to comply with the legislation perceive at least two outside sources. First of all, many regular elementary and secondary educators view the law as being imposed on them by special education. This is not met with favorable reaction because one segment of the profession (and a smaller one at that) is dictating what is appropriate education to another, larger, segment of the profession. The outside imposition perspective also becomes evident because this is a federal law that dictates certain matters about how education will be conducted at the state and local levels. This raises an immediate question of whether or not such a definition of appropriate education is federal intervention in states' rights. It should be noted, however, that P.L. 94–142 is a grant-in-aid program. States may choose to participate or not. If they do not, they are not eligible for federal funding under this law.

These factors, as well as others, contribute in a variety of ways to the development of paper compliance plans and other procedures that are highly questionable in terms of fostering appropriate educational programming for handicapped children. Prior to their examination it may have been rather easy for us to declare such approaches unethical and contrary to the fundamental purpose of education, and discussion may not lessen this concern in regard to the ultimate benefit for retarded children. Such discussion does, however, highlight the complex nature of the situation. Appropriate education, least restrictive placement, competing equities, and states' rights are merely examples of how social value questions related to the school years are difficult and without simple solutions. Although in a different context, the philosophical and operational differences are no less complicated nor more easily resolved than those we confronted in discussing the early years.

Consent. The introductory comments to this section stated that consent is also a relevant issue for the school years. Parents must be actively involved in the decision process that results in changing the educational program for their child. In terms of our specific focus—the mentally retarded child—this process includes consent for assessment or diagnosis as well as any programming changes that might occur as a result of such assessment.

Consent in the context of the school years involves the same basic principles that were discussed previously with regard to life management decisions. Effective parental consent for all action, including assessment and programming, must have the three elements of capacity, information, and voluntariness. As before, consent is seldom if ever permanent and may be withdrawn at nearly any time. The educator who is attempting to obtain consent carries a heavy burden—just as the medical professional did in our previous discussion—in terms of ensuring that the three elements of consent are present.

One element of consent that is altered somewhat in the context of the school years is capacity. For the most part, capacity to consent for the mentally retarded child must continue to remain with the parents. From a strictly legal standpoint, the capacity to consent does not rest with a child because of age (under the age of majority) and lack of mental competence to fully understand the nature and consequences of consent. However, good practice would suggest that a blanket assumption of incapacity throughout the school years is inappropriate. Specifically, older retarded individuals (adolescents or young adults) who are functioning at a near normal level may be quite capable of participating in the consent process. Depending on the situation and the individual, such individuals may be able to give consent directly, or they may best give consent concurrently with a third party, such as their parents. The likelihood that a third party must participate in consent is raised if the information is complex or if the individual appears less able. As before, the process of obtaining effective consent is one that involves the exercise of considerable judgment. There are few set rules that one can follow to relieve the need for exercising solid professional judgment. The burden of obtaining effective consent rests heavily with the professional and may create a certain amount of discomfort, but this must obtain if the rights of retarded individuals are to be adequately protected.

Ethical Issues During Adulthood

Core Concept 5   Social and ethical issues emerging during the adult years once again tend to pit the interests of society against the retarded individual's rights, and they often relate to questions of adult functions such as marriage and reproduction.

Social and ethical issues that surface during adulthood ring familiar following the discussions of earlier sections in this chapter. Many of the generic principles, philosophical differences, and agonizing social questions remain relatively constant. As before, however, the manner in which these issues emerge is altered considerably by the context of the adult years. A comprehensive discussion of all social and ethical issues relevant to the mentally retarded adult is far beyond the scope of this chapter. Consequently, we focus on those we hope will promote the most serious questioning on the part of the reader.

The emergence of certain social and ethical issues during the adult years is not surprising. Questions related to marriage, reproduction, and sterilization, if they are to arise, most logically become considerations during this part of the life cycle. As with most of the issues discussed in this chapter, these topics have been subject to considerable controversy.

Sterilization Issues. Although the topics related to life management decisions are complex, issues concerning sterilization of retarded individuals are no less perplexing. Controversy surrounding sterilization has a very long history, and legal authority related to sterilization varies throughout the country. This section does not recount the history nor the legal basis, because those have previously been addressed. Our focus here is an analysis of the issues per se.

Arguments For and Against. One of the ways to approach the topic of sterilization is to examine how and why mentally retarded individuals receive different consideration than their nonretarded peers (Macklin & Gaylin, 1981). Both the historical controversy and the legal authority to sterilize mentally retarded individuals (see chapter 14) clearly indicate that different consideration is given. For example, although voluntary sterilization of nonretarded citizens is mostly viewed as an individual prerogative (as means of birth control), involuntary sterilization laws pertaining generally to nonretarded citizens are essentially unheard of. A variety of justifications have been advanced to support sterilization of mentally retarded people. Krishef (1972, p. 36) summarized these arguments as those that hold sterilization to be "(1) in the best interest of society and the state, (2) in the best interest of the retarded individuals, and (3) in the best interest of the unborn children."

As with other issues examined in this chapter, there are also those people who express strong opposition. Arguments against sterilization of mentally retarded individuals are varied and include (1) concern about the potential misuse of legal authority to sterilize, (2) some evidence that certain of the pro-sterilization arguments noted before do not consistently hold true, and (3) concern about the rights of the retarded individual and the manner in which the process is undertaken. Each of these areas presents serious societal and legal questions and issues that warrant examination (Sherlock & Sherlock, 1982).

The first pro-sterilization argument held that sterilization of mentally retarded individuals was in the best interest of society and the state. This is a particularly difficult premise, depending on how one views the support for it. This proposition may also exemplify, perhaps more clearly than any other issue, how the best interest of the state may come into conflict with rights of an individual. One very important basis for the "benefit to society and state" argument involves a reduction in the numbers of retarded individuals in the population. In a very real sense this is another approach to the prevention of mental retardation. Proponents of this position point to the fact that such a reduction would decrease the number of citizens that require extra services from society and thereby would lessen the cost burden for such care on the state and the taxpayers. This argument would seem to be based on a utilitarian philosophy since such savings, if they were to occur, could be redirected to those societal needs that might ultimately result in greater productive return to the general public.

One question that is immediately raised concerns the degree to which such a practice would actually result in reduced incidence of mental retardation. The answer is anything but obvious. If sterilization is viewed as preventing only the transmission of inferior or damaged genetic material, then the reduced incidence would appear quite minimal. Mental retardation that can be directly attributed to genetic causation represents a rather small proportion of the total mentally retarded population. Furthermore, those individuals whose mental retardation can be attributed to genetic causation are more likely to be functioning at lower levels, some in the severe to profound range. For a number of reasons one can make the case that such individuals are less likely to be engaged in procreation to begin with. The difficulty with this particular pro-sterilization argument becomes evident when one views the broad perspective of mental retardation. First of all, earlier sections of this volume have examined the nature versus nurture controversy in considerable detail relative to the development of intelligence (and mental retardation causation). It is clear from these earlier discussions that determination of environmental influences cannot be accomplished with great precision. It is also evident that the environment does have a significant impact on mental retardation causation, particularly in the milder range of handicap. Therefore sterilization is not solely focusing on the transmission of inferior genetic material.

The question remains: To what degree would a massive sterilization program reduce the incidence of mental retardation? Although the answer must remain somewhat speculative, there are some data available. Bass (1967) made reference to a Danish program that involves genetic counseling and voluntary sterilization of retarded people. This program, directly aimed at preventing reproduction by retarded individuals, had been in operation for 25 years at the time of Bass's research; results suggested that the incidence of mental retardation was reduced by "approximately 50% a generation" (1967, p. 45). Bass also cited the work of Reed and Reed (1965), who suggested a similar reduction in incidence might be expected if voluntary sterilization were to become widely accepted in the United States.

Although limited, this literature does suggest that a rather substantial reduction in the incidence might be expected if sterilization of mentally retarded individuals were conducted systematically. This might appear to lend support to the "best interest of society" argument. It is evident, however, that our complex and diverse society is not willing to accept such a practice in a single-minded fashion. The reasons for this are as many and varied as our culture itself.

One very strong influence is our apparent unwillingness to overrule the rights of individuals in favor of the rights of the larger society in any blanket fashion, and one of the individual rights that seems to loom large in this regard is the right of procreation. As early as 1921 the importance of this individual right was noted in legal interpretation of the federal Constitution. At this time the Michigan attorney general issued an opinion, based on the Constitution, that held that the right to have and retain the power of procreation was second only to the right to life itself (Price & Burt, 1976). It is generally accepted that such a fundamental individual right can be abrogated only on a voluntary basis by the individual involved. One must then ask the question regarding how compulsory sterilization laws came to exist in certain states. Obviously, in these situations the interests of state were deemed to supercede the rights of mentally retarded people.

Consent Issues. Even voluntary sterilization of mentally retarded individuals presents some complex questions both conceptually and with regard to implementation. The moment we move into a voluntary status with respect to sterilization we are once again faced with the question of consent. The concept of consent in the context of sterilization does, however, present some interesting implementation problems that we have not encountered in earlier discussions.

The element of capacity was discussed earlier with particular focus on the person's age and competence. As mentioned previously, a person under the age of majority is legally incompetent to make certain decisions. Since our main focus in this section is the adult years, age will not be a substantial consideration with regard to the capacity element. Competence does, however, become an issue. The basic question is whether or not a retarded adult has the mental competence to understand what sterilization is and what the implications are. This would not seem to be an answerable question in a general sense. It would seem most logical to consider each case individually, depending on the person's level of functioning, but some would disagree vigorously. A decision concerning sterilization has been described as being so "complicated and extraordinarily important" that many individuals who are of normal intelligence are perhaps not competent to fully comprehend its implications (Baron, 1976, p. 273). Whereas this may be true for only some nonretarded individuals, it does seriously raise the competence issue when a mentally retarded person is involved. Baron was emphatic, however, in his contention that the opinion of the retarded person being considered for sterilization should not be ignored. He stated that "although the consent of the candidate should not be considered alone to be sufficient basis for sterilization, it should certainly be considered important evidence along with such other evidence as is available, that sterilization is in fact in his best interest" (1976, p. 273).

The natural place to turn for assistance in obtaining consent would seem to be the parents (or legal guardians) of the retarded individual. This has been the case in our earlier discussions of other procedures requiring consent. It is assumed that they will consider such decisions with the best interests of their ward being the first and foremost concern. This may not, however, be a sound assumption with respect to sterilization. In fact, Murdock suggested that "parents or guardians often have interests that conflict with those of the retarded child. The parents of a retarded child may have understandable fears that the grandchild will also be retarded. Moreover, parents may perceive a danger of their retarded child proving to be an unfit parent, and might wish to avoid the risk of shouldering responsibilities of grandchildren" (1974, p. 917). If such a situation does exist it is clear that parental input in the consent process may not be motivated solely by consideration of the candidate's best interest.

Baron (1976) indicated that there has been a noticeable tendency for the courts to intervene and review parental decisions regarding consent for sterilization. The court's interest is that of ensuring that the retarded individual's best interests are protected and are the sole determining factor influencing the sterilization decision. This presents a difficult dilemma, one that makes the consent process extremely complicated. Court intervention itself is complicated. To assure objectivity the court must be presented with information and arguments on both sides. This requires that advocates for both sides be present in court and be equally informed and articulate regarding the manner in which they inform the court. It further requires that the arguments on both sides include all relevant information and that information that is presented be limited to the issues pertaining to the "best interests" of the retarded individual. This latter point eliminates the presentation of information or arguments relating to either the state's interests or those of the parents.

This brief discussion represents only the tip of the iceberg in terms of the complex issues related to consent for sterilization. Although we began our examination with a focus on the element of capacity, the elements of information and voluntariness quickly became intertwined in the considerations. This discussion highlights the manner in which issues can become extremely complicated as attempts are made to protect individual rights. It also raises other social questions that are not easily answered: Do the parents' rights and interests have no value? What about the interests of the state? The concept of competing equities becomes evident in situations in which the rights and interests of all parties are not in harmony. These are familiar questions, reminiscent of the extreme philosophical differences that were presented in the beginning of this chapter.

Marriage Issues. The issues pertaining to marriage of mentally retarded adults are closely related to sterilization, and the two are often considered together. Marriage issues are perhaps not as legally complicated (i.e., consent), since an irreversible medical procedure is not involved. Possibly the overriding issues or questions in this area rest with the mere existence of laws restricting marriage of retarded individuals. As indicated in other chapters, there are many states with laws that place some type of restriction on the right to marry for those classified as mentally retarded. One has to ask why these laws exist. Are these laws aimed at the protection of the individual or are they basically for the protection of society?

This question is presented by us in a spirit of issue examination. For some, the evidence is so compelling that objective examination of this issue is tantamount to ignoring the manner in which such laws were developed. Wolfensberger (1975) discussed restrictive marriage laws as a part of society's need to prevent procreation by mentally retarded individuals. Credence for the perception certainly arises from the observation that 56% of the states have both sterilization and restrictive marriage laws in common (Krishef, 1972). If not credence, certainly intrigue is added to this examination by the wording of early legislation cited by Wolfensberger. He referenced an 1895 bill passed by the Connecticut House of Representatives, which reads as follows:

> Every man who shall carnally know any female under the age of forty-five years who is epileptic, imbecile, feeble-minded, or a pauper, shall be imprisoned in the State prison not less than three years. Every man who is epileptic who shall carnally know any female under the age of forty-five years, and every female under the age of forty-five years who shall consent to be carnally known by any man who is epileptic, imbecile, or feeble-minded, shall be imprisoned in the State prison not less that three years. (1975, p. 40)

Wolfensberger also noted that a law to prohibit marriage of "feeble-minded and insane" was proposed at the national level in 1897 and received a great deal of support. One could interpret the above wording from either perspective (that is, individual or societal protection) since specific mention of the intent is absent. There is little question regarding intent, however, as Wolfensberger continued. The commentary historically seems to be captured by Wilmarth in 1902 whose focus was on the "abatement of this evil" and a search for ways to accomplish it (quoted in Wolfensberger, 1975, p. 40).

It does seem that society's interests were paramount, at least historically. One must raise the question of whether or not this is still the case. Some of these old laws remain on the books. What about current legislation? Are current laws and efforts merely more carefully disguised attempts to protect the best interests of society or are they really aimed at achieving some balance between the rights of individuals and the rights of our larger society? There are strong arguments on both sides.

The questions and issues discussed throughout this chapter are not pleasant topics. They represent areas that we may wish to avoid. They are, however, social and ethical questions of great importance, issues that test the strength of societal fabric. We cannot ignore what seems to be the fundamental question: Are mentally retarded individuals considered subhuman, or at least less deserving of the rights of the rest of humanity?

RESEARCH AND PROFESSIONAL ETHICS IN MENTAL RETARDATION

Core Concept 6 Research and professional ethics in mental retardation involve a wide variety of issues where individual rights must be balanced against both the need for scientific information and complex questions regarding appropriate treatment.

The field of mental retardation has a special link to ethics, as is evident from our foregoing discussion. People who are mentally retarded are in a high risk category with respect to ethical vulnerability. They are among those "who by virtue of some characteristic (such as age, institutionalization, physical illness, mental disability, or the like) need special consideration and protection" (Keith-Spiegel, 1976, p. 53). This places great responsibility on professionals working in the field as researchers and care providers.

To learn more about mental retardation it is necessary to conduct research on individuals within that population. This often raises concern because by investigating those with mental retardation, we are in some ways invading their privacy and subjecting them to risk, even though we might have the most honorable of intentions. In order to discover more effective methods of teaching, placing, medicating, and otherwise treating these individuals it is necessary to study them and learn about their characteristics. We cannot avoid conducting research with mentally retarded people in order to protect them. In fact some have held that it would be unethical *not* to conduct such research (e.g., Haywood, 1976).

Conducting research with mentally retarded individuals while simultaneously protecting their rights as individuals requires constant vigilance. A careful balance must be struck between the behavioral scientist's need to invade and the individual subject's rights to privacy. For the population we are discussing special care must be taken in areas of consent, privacy, and harm. Likewise, issues of deception (explicitly lying to subjects as well as omitting details about the study) remain controversial in mental retardation, as they do in all behavioral science (Baumrind, 1985; Fisher,1986; Trice, 1986). Certain medications and other treatments inherently pose some risk, and inappropriate applications may be harmful. All of these considerations make research on mental retardation challenging. Safeguards such as Institutional Review Boards (sometimes known as Human Subjects Committees) used by universities and other agencies to monitor research are vital for protecting subjects and maintaining a balance between the needs of scientists and subjects' rights. Likewise many professional associations and societies employ ethics committees and codes of ethics to guide their members (Drew & Turnbull, 1987; Turnbull, 1986).

Research is not the only area where professional ethics come into play in the field of mental retardation. Schools, treatment centers, and other care provision agencies must also be cautious to administer efficiently the most effective treatment possible while simultaneously remaining conscious of the rights of mentally retarded people. In some cases, treatment may be administered that carries with it a certain degree of risk, as in the case with some medications. Once again mentally retarded people are "at risk" and more vulnerable than humans in general. It is vitally important for professionals to be adequately trained and qualified to administer the treatment being employed. Occasionally (and, we hope, rarely), the best treatment is lacking because of personnel shortages, a lack of knowledge, or carelessness. As before, it is essential that agencies and professional associations remain vigilant to ensure the welfare of mentally retarded people (Drew & Turnbull, 1987; Turnbull, 1986).

Core Questions

1. How do the utilitarian and formalist philosophies relate to individual and societal rights in mental retardation?
2. How do genetic counseling and abortion relate to prevention of mental retardation?
3. Duff and Campbell (1973) have taken the position that if nontreatment of certain infants is in violation of the law, then the law should be changed. How does this position fit with formalist philosophy, and how does it fit with utilitarianist philosophy? What are your views, and why do you believe the way you do?
4. It appears that selective nontreatment of defective infants is a more common practice than the general public knows. Who should make these judgments, which are literally life and death decisions? On what basis(es) did you determine your response?
5. Special services for mentally retarded children often cost a great deal more than educational services for their nonretarded peers. To what degree do you think that parents of nonretarded children should be held responsible for the increased costs of educating mentally retarded children? On what basis do you believe as you do?
6. Sterilization of mentally retarded adults is often justified on the basis of the general welfare of society and the state. How might the best interests of the state and those of the retarded individual be in conflict? Whose interests should prevail and why?
7. How did early marriage laws related to mentally retarded people seem to place society's interests above those of the individual? Has this changed? Explain your reasoning in both cases.
8. How may scientific investigations aimed at improving the lot of those with mental retardation also be in conflict with their individual rights?
9. How does the interdisciplinary nature of the mental retardation field contribute to professional ethical difficulties?

ROUND TABLE DISCUSSION

Social and ethical issues related to mental retardation are complex and vary to some degree depending on the life cycle period being considered. However, in many ways these questions can be reduced to the fundamental questions of individual versus societal rights which are embodied in the utilitarianism and formalism philosophies. These perspectives are found in various forms throughout the study of mental retardation.

In your study group or on your own, examine mental retardation from the viewpoint of both individual and societal interests. Think in terms of prevention of mental retardation, abortion, withholding treatment, provision of service, sterilization, and research. Where do you stand philosophically? Does your position shift depending on age, topic, severity, or other basis(es)? Do you feel comfortable with your position(s)? Why?

REFERENCES

Baron, C. H. (1976). Voluntary sterilization of the mentally retarded. In Milunsky, A., & Annas, G. J. (Eds.), *Genetics and the law* (pp. 267–284). New York: Plenum.

Bass, M. S. (1967). Attitudes of parents of retarded children toward voluntary sterilization. *Eugenics Quarterly, 14,* 45–53.

Baumrind, D. (1985). Research using intentional deception: Ethical issues revisited. *American Psychologist, 40,* 165–174.

Blatt, B., & Kaplan, F. (1966). *Christmas in purgatory.* Boston: Allyn & Bacon.

Boggs, E. M. (1977). *Competing equities: An issue raised by, but going beyond, Section 504.* Memorandum to the Legislative and Social Issues Committee of the American Association on Mental Deficiency, January 1977.

Boggs, E. M. (1986). Ethics in the middle of life. In P. R. Dokecki & R. M. Zaner (Eds.). *Ethics of dealing with persons with severe handicaps: Toward a research agenda* (pp. 1–15). Baltimore: Brookes.

Burt, R. A. (1976). Authorizing death for anomalous newborns. In Milunsky, A., & Annas, G. J. (Eds.), *Genetics and the law* (pp. 435–450). New York: Plenum.

Cadkin, A. W., Ginsberg, N. A., Pergament, E., & Verlinski, Y. (1984). Chorionic villi sampling: A new technique for detection of genetic abnormalities in the first trimester. *Radiology, 151,* 159–162.

Deno, E. (1970). Special education as developmental capital. *Exceptional Children, 37,* 229–237.

Diamond, E. F. (1977). The deformed child's right to life. In Horan, D. J., & Mall, D. (Eds.), *Death, dying and euthanasia* (pp. 127–138). Washington, DC: University Publications of America.

Drane, J. F. (1985). The many faces of competency. *Hastings Center Report. 15* (2), 17–26.

Drew, C. J. (1978). *Least restrictive alternatives: A concept in search of definition.* Paper presented at the one-hundred second annual convention of the American Association on Mental Deficiency, Denver.

Drew, C. J., & Hardman, M. L. (1977). *The PMR multihandicapped: A review on retardation and physical handicaps.* Paper presented at the third annual Western Research Conference on Mental Retardation, Carmel, CA.

Drew, C. J., & Turnbull, H. R., III. (1987). Whose ethics—whose code: An analysis of problems in interdisciplinary intervention. *Mental Retardation, 25,* 113–117.

Duff, R., & Campbell, A. (1973). Moral and ethical dilemmas in the special-care nursery. *New England Journal of Medicine, 289,* 890–894.

Fisher, K. (1986). Ethics in research: Having respect for the subject. *The APA Monitor, 17*(4), 1, 34–35.

Fletcher, G.P. (1968). Legal aspects of the decision not to prolong life. *Journal of the American Medical Association, 203,* 119–122.

Fletcher, Joseph (1973). Ethics and euthanasia. In R. H. Williams (Ed.), *To live and to die: When, why, and how* (pp. 113–122). New York: Springer-Verlag.

Fletcher, John (1975). Abortion, euthanasia, and care of defective newborns. *New England Journal of Medicine, 292,* 75–78.

Gaylin, W., & Macklin, R. (Eds.). (1982). *Who speaks for the child: The problems of proxy consent.* New York: Plenum.

Hardman, M. L., & Drew, C. J. (1977). The physically handicapped retarded individual: A review. *Mental Retardation, 15*(5), 43–48.

Hardman, M. L., & Drew, C. J. (1980). Parent consent and the practice of withholding treatment from the severely defective newborn. *Mental Retardation, 18,* 165–169.

Harper. P. S. (1981). *Practical genetic counseling.* Baltimore: University Park.

Hauerwas, S. (1986). Suffering the retarded: Should we prevent retardation? In P. R. Dokecki & R. M. Zaner (Eds.) *Ethics of dealing with persons with severe handicaps: Toward a research agenda* (pp. 53–70). Baltimore: Brookes.

Haywood, H. C. (1976). The ethics of doing research . . . and of not doing it. *American Journal of Mental Deficiency, 81,* 311–317.

Horan, D. J., & Mall, D. (Eds.).(1977). *Death, dying, and euthanasia.* Washington, DC: University Publications of America.

Kamisar, Y. (1958). Some non-religious views against proposed "mercy- killing" legislation. *Minnesota Law Review, 42,* 969–1042.

Keith-Spiegel, P. (1976). Children's rights as participants in research. In G. P. Koocher (Ed.), *Children's rights and the mental health profession* (pp. 53–81). New York: Wiley.

Kessler, S. (1979). The psychological foundations of genetic counseling. In S. Kessler (Ed.), *Genetic counseling: Psychological dimensions* (pp. 17–34). New York: Academic Press.

Krishef, C. H. (1972). State laws on marriage and sterilization of the mentally retarded. *Mental Retardation, 10*(3), 36–38.

Lusthaus, E. W. (1985). Involuntary euthanasia and current attempts to define persons with mental retardation as less than human. *Mental Retardation, 23,* 148–154.

Mackie, R. P., & Robbins, P. B. (1960). Exceptional children in local public schools. *School Life, 43,* 14–16.

Macklin, R., & Gaylin, W. (Eds.). (1981). *Mental retardation and sterilization: A problem of competency and paternalism.* New York: Plenum.

Milunsky, A. (1979). *Genetic disorders and the fetus: Diagnosis, prevention, and treatment.* New York: Plenum.

Murdock, C.W. (1974). Sterilization of the retarded: A problem or a solution? *California Law Review, 62,* 917–943.

National Academy of Sciences. (1975). *Genetic screening: Programs, principles and research.* Washington, DC: Author.

Pearson, P. H., & Menefee, A. R. (1965). Medical and social management of the mentally retarded. *General Practitioner, 31,* 78–91.

Perone, N., Carpenter, R. J., & Robertson, J. A. (1984). Legal liability in the use of ultrasound by office-based obstetricians. *American Journal of Obstetrics and Gynecology, 150,* 801–804.

Price, M. E., & Burt, R. A. (1976). Non-consensual medical procedures and the right to privacy. In Kindred, M., Cohen, J., Penrod, D., & Shaffer, T. (Eds.), *The mentally retarded citizen and the law* (pp. 94–112). New York: Free Press.

Ramsey, P. (1973). Abortion. *Thomist, 37,* 174–226.

Reed, E. W., & Reed, S. C. (1965). *Mental retardation: A family study.* Philadelphia: Saunders.

Robertson, J. A. (1975). Involuntary euthanasia of defective newborns: A legal analysis. *Stanford Law Review, 27,* 213–269.

Shaw, A. (1977). Dilemmas of "informed consent" in children. In Horan, D.J., & Mall, D. (Eds.), *Death, dying and euthanasia* (pp. 75–90). Washington, DC: University Publications of America.

Sherlock, R. K., & Sherlock, R. D. (1982). Sterilizing the retarded: Constitutional, statutory and policy alternatives. *The North Carolina Law Review, 60,* 943–983.

Trice, A. D. (1986). Ethical variables? *American Psychologist, 41,* 482–483.

Turnbull, H. R., III (Ed.) (1977). *Consent handbook.* Washington, DC: American Association on Mental Deficiency.

Turnbull, H. R., III. (1986). Public policy and professional behavior. *Mental Retardation, 24,* 265–275.

Turnbull, H. R., III, & Turnbull, A. P. (1975). Deinstitutionalization and the law. *Mental Retardation, 13*(2), 14–20.

Tymchuk, A. J. (1976). A perspective on ethics in mental retardation. *Mental Retardation, 14*(6), 44–47.

Williams, G. L. (1958). "Mercy-killing" legislation: A rejoinder. *Minnesota Law Review, 43*(1), 1–12.

Williams, G. L. (1966). Euthanasia and abortion. *University of Colorado Law Review, 38,* 181–187.

Wojcik, J. (1978). *Muted consent: A casebook in modern medical ethics.* West Lafayette, IN: Purdue University.

Wolfensberger, W. (1975). *The origin and nature of our institutional models.* Syracuse, N.Y.: Human Policy.

Zaner, R. M. (1986). Soundings from uncertain places: Difficult pregnancies and imperiled infants. In P. R. Dokecki & R. M. Zaner (Eds.), *Ethics of dealing with persons with severe handicaps: Toward a research agenda* (pp. 71–92). Baltimore: Brookes.

Legal and Legislative Issues

Core Concepts

1. The influence of legal and legislative activities has had a profound effect on the delivery of services for all disabled persons.
2. The Constitution and the Bill of Rights do not directly specify whether education is a right or a privilege.
3. A number of court cases over the past thirty years have had a direct impact on all aspects of special education programs and service delivery models.
4. *Brown v. Board of Education of Topeka* (1954) was the first time that education was unequivocally determined to be a "right" that was to be available for all persons on equal terms.
5. Legislative actions have required that all children be provided a free and appropriate education in the least restrictive setting.
6. It is important that concerned individuals maintain a continuing interest in the legislative process at both the state and federal levels.
7. The impact of local, state and federal laws such as those concerning housing, marriage, voting rights, licenses, etc. have a profound effect on the ability of persons with intellectual handicaps to function in society.

A chapter on legal and legislative issues in a book such as this would have been almost unheard of in the not-so-distant past. In fact, many texts published within the past 10 years neglected this area; or, if a section was included, the orientation was geared toward historical aspects with no more than a passing reference to legislation. Today it is inconceivable that texts relating to the exceptional child would omit the dramatic changes that have occurred, particularly in the past few years. Although the seeds of change were planted many years ago, we in special education have only recently become involved in the legal and legislative arena.

The use of the law to influence social changes in the United States is not a recent event. Gilhool stated:

> In going to the courts, exceptional citizens have joined an old tradition in the United States. That tradition, the use of the courts to achieve social change, to achieve justice, dates back at least to 1905 when W. E. B. Dubois and his associates founded the National Association for the Advancement of Colored People (NAACP). (1976, p. 16)

The interaction between the legal system and special education advocate groups is producing profound changes that will undoubtedly influence our society for generations to come.

Core Concept 1   The influence of legal and legislative activities has had a profound effect on the delivery of services for all disabled persons.

One fact must be kept in mind by all concerned with the legal issues as they relate to the exceptional person. Even though our involvement in legal and legislative actions is of recent occurrence, nothing essentially new is being proposed. The change represents a belated recognition by society that exceptional persons have not been dealt with fairly and that "the right to be human, based upon principles of equality, is applicable to all individuals" (Drew, Hardman, & Bluhm, 1977, p. 101).

If a democratic society is to remain viable, there has to be a direct correspondence between the laws of that society and the equal application of those laws to all citizens. The fact that this has not always been the case is apparent to anyone with even a cursory understanding of history. However, it is not whether a nation, through its laws, has fairly applied those laws, but whether it has ensured the open access, both for the individual and the group, to the laws for redress of grievances. The historically recent legislative and legal activity is evidence that the rights of the exceptional person at long last are being recognized and responded to in a manner that has far-reaching implications for *all* persons.

However, those concerned with the well-being of all citizens know that in a changing world nothing is truly secure. This is particularly true of the most fragile of all societal priorities: human rights. Decisions that this group or that group is of little consequence or importance are still far too common. History should have taught us that such attitudes eventually undermine everyone's rights and freedoms. Recent events in the United States can only underscore this observation. The federal efforts to eliminate or at least weaken existing laws by repeal or budgetary cuts should be a clear warning to all that gains once made can be quickly lost or eroded without our continual involvement (Norman and Taymans, 1982). A long-delayed beginning has been made, but there must be a continued and vigilant involvement by all persons concerned with the human condition.

This chapter is not intended to provide an exhaustive account of the varied political, economic, and social issues that led to recent legislative and legal actions. The emphasis of this chapter is to examine some historical antecedents that have influenced recent legislation and court decisions, to provide a detailed review of current legislation, to discuss related legal aspects, and to identify some of the legal issues concerning education that will be of continuing concern.

HISTORICAL ANTECEDENTS

Core Concept 2   The Constitution and the Bill of Rights do not directly specify whether education is a right or a privilege.

All concerns about education come under the framework of promoting health, morals, comfort, and general welfare. The purposes of education have been many and varied; they have been influenced by many factors, such as the prevailing philosophies of the times, economics, and political vicissitudes. There has been a general agreement that the schools have the responsibility to prepare students to take their place in society. The New Hampshire Supreme Court in *Fogg v. Board of Education*, for example, made the following ruling:

> The primary purpose of the maintenance of the common school system is the promotion of the general intelligence of the people constituting the body politic and thereby increase the usefulness and efficacy of the citizens, upon which the government of society depends. Free schooling funded by the state is not so much a right granted to pupils as a duty imposed upon them for the public good. (1912, p. 174)

Such rulings laid the groundwork for later court decisions that further delineated the states' responsibility towards all citizens in regard to education. Public education functions as an arm of the state and provides for the education of future citizens. It is a given that such delegation of power places education squarely in the center of the political process and all of its related pressures and varied interest groups. This is evident in our history and in current laws that have been enacted by federal and state legislatures. Schools are both a social institution and a governmental agency and are, thereby, affected by society's awareness and acceptance of needs as expressed by changing political climates.

There has been a relatively long history of actions by the federal government that relate to the handicapped. LaVor (1976a) has provided a succinct accounting of federal legislation concerning exceptional persons (see chapter appendix). However, some events that have been direct antecedents to the current state of affairs need to be traced.

Core Concept 3   A number of court cases over the past thirty years have had a direct impact on all aspects of special education programs and service delivery models.

Since World War II, there has been a decided change in the legislative and legal involvement in special education in general and for the mentally retarded in particular. This involvement has included a variety of individuals and groups who may be characterized as "significant others" and has resulted from many factors, including (a) the impact of the barbaric practices toward minorities in Nazi Germany, (b) the multitude of maimed and crippled soldiers returning from World War II and the Korean and Vietnamese wars, (c) the advent of economic prosperity, (d) a national recognition that disability does not mean lack of worth to either the community or the individual, (e) the involvement of parent groups, and (f) the advances in medical and social sciences, which serendipitously stimulated interest in mental retardation. Additional impetus has been given by the highly visible accomplishments of individuals disabled in some way, such as Helen Keller and President Franklin D. Roosevelt. The visibility of mental retardation has been aided by the public admission of previously hidden handicaps; we know for example, about President John F. Kennedy's sister, Senator Hubert Humphrey's granddaughter, and Senator S. I. Hayakawa's son, all of whom are mentally retarded. All of these influences and others have interacted to bring about actions that are historically unprecedented.

LITIGATION

Public education provisions for the handicapped, including the mentally retarded, closely parallels the establishment of minority group rights in the United States. Let us begin with *Roberts v. the City of Boston* (1849), a case concerning the denial of admission of Sarah Roberts, a black woman, to a school for whites. The court ruled that Sarah was not being denied instruction by being refused admission to the school in question, but no consideration was given either to the possibility that her educational experiences were not equivalent to those offered in white schools or to the future educational consequences. This legal decision set a precedent for related exclusionary cases in the years to come.

School boards have the power to assign pupils to particular schools, unless it is shown to be so arbitrary as to negate the efficacy of the placement (*Williams v. Board of Education*, 1908). Most educational legal decisions involving the exceptional child have been exclusionary rather than facilitative. That is, they were concerned with the protection of the schools rather than the educational and social needs of the "undesirable" child. A philosophical change came about in this country in the early part of the twentieth century. Two cases are of particular importance: *Beattie v. State Board of Education, City of Antigo* (1950) and *State Board of Education v. In Re: Petty* (1950). Although neither of these cases involved persons with mental retardation, they are important as precedents for later decisions.

The first case, *Beattie v. State Board of Education, City of Antigo*, concerned a boy with cerebral palsy excluded from a public school class because of his condition, which, it was argued, caused a depressing effect on his classmates and his teachers. The public schools had recommended placement in a school for deaf and speech-defective children and refused his enrollment in the regular school program. The boy refused such placement and was supported in his decision by his parents. An appeal was made to the local school superintendent, who asked for a ruling from the State Superintendent of Public Instruction for Wisconsin. After no firm direction was given by the state school superintendent, the school refused to allow the boy to enroll in the public school. The critically important factor in this case was the action of the jury in the municipal court of Antigo, Wisconsin, where the issue was first deliberated outside of the public school arena. The jury ruled in favor of reinstating the boy in the public school. This decision signaled a change, it was one of the first times that the rights of a student were given precedence over the traditional view that "defective" children were to be segregated. Although this decision was overruled on appeal to the Wisconsin Supreme Court, an important dissenting opinion was written. It was based on two important, and later significant reasons: that the school board should yield to public opinion as represented by the municipal court jury, and that the boy's physical appearance and related behaviors (cerebral palsy) did not have a harmful effect or infringe on other children's right to an education.

The second case (*State Board of Education v. In Re: Petty*, 1950) occurred in Iowa. In this case an argument almost diametrically opposed to that of the Beattie case was heard. The school board sought permission from the parents to place their child in a school that would best meet his educational needs. The court decision directed the parents to place the boy, who was deaf, in the state school for the deaf. The parents refused and instead placed him in a rural school near where they lived. An appeal, heard by the Iowa Supreme Court, was based on the parents' contention that it had not been proved that the boy could not be educated in the public rural school. After expert testimony the Iowa Supreme Court unanimously ruled that the boy would have to be enrolled in the school for the deaf. This case is important in that it established, at least indirectly, a handicapped child's right to an appropriate education.

Core Concept 4   *Brown v. Board of Education of Topeka* (1954) was the first time that education was unequivocally determined to be a "right" that was to be available for all persons on equal terms.

A dramatic change of events occurring in 1954 was to have far-reaching effects on education. In *Brown v. Board of Education of Topeka* (1954), the issue was segregation and the concomitant "equal opportunity." The U.S. Supreme Court in reaching its decision stated:

> Today education is perhaps the most important function of state and local governments. Compulsory school attendance laws and the great expenditure for education both demonstrate our recognition of the importance of education to our democratic society. . . . In these days, it is doubtful that any child may reasonably be expected to succeed in life if he is denied the opportunity of an education. Such an opportunity, where the State has undertaken to provide it, is a right which must be made available to all on equal terms. . . . We conclude that in the field of public education the doctrine of "separate but equal" has no place. Separate educational facilities are inherently unequal. Therefore, we hold that the plaintiffs and others similarly situated for whom actions have been brought are, by reason of the segregation complained of, deprived on the equal protection of the laws guaranteed by the Fourteenth Amendment. (p. 492)

The effect of the Brown case has had a profound effect on special education. The importance rests primarily with the fact that the decision stated unequivocally that education is a "right" and must be "available to all on equal terms." This decision removes any argument that education is a privilege and in effect has opened the doors to all children for a free and appropriate education. Subsequent legislation, such as Public Laws 93—-380 and 94–142 which will be discussed in a later section, has provided support for the rights of the handicapped by protecting them against discrimination solely on the basis of the handicapping condition. This legislative activity has emphasized areas such as access to public facilities, procedural due process, least restrictive placement, free and appropriate education, and nondiscriminatory evaluation.

It should be recalled that education is a state, not federal, responsibility. Although the focus of this chapter is on federal legislation, committed professionals would be remiss if they did not become as equally aware of their state constitutions and statutes.

In recent years there has been a multitude of court cases involving special education, either directly or indirectly. These cases have focused on matters relating to architectural barriers, classification, commitment to institutions, criminal law, custody, education, employment, guardianship, intelligence testing, limitation of treatment, sterilization, voting, and zoning. The status of court cases in these areas has been reported at various times in journals such as *Mental Retardation and the Law* (President's Committee on Mental Retardation), *Exceptional Children* and *Education and the Handicapped Law Review.*

In 1967 in *Hobson v. Hansen*, Judge J. Skelly Wright ruled that placing children in different tracks based on performance on various tests during their early school years violated the equal protection clause of the Constitution. In reviewing this case Judge Wright found that there was a disproportionate number of blacks in special education and stated:

> The evidence shows that the method by which track assignments are made depends essentially on standardized aptitude tests which, although given on a system-wide basis, are completely inappropriate for use with a large segment of the student body. Because these tests are primarily standardized on and are relevant to a white middle class group of students, they produce inaccurate and misleading test scores when given to lower class and Negro children. As a result, rather than being classified according to ability to learn, these students are in reality being classified according to their socioeconomic and psychological factors which have nothing to do with innate ability. (p. 514)

On appeal in *Smuck v. Hobson* (1969), the Court of Appeals supported Judge Wright's ruling abolishing a tracking system in the District of Columbia public schools.

One of the first cases involving classes for the mentally retarded was heard in the Superior Court of Orange County, California *(Arreola v. Board of Education,* 1968). This case was brought to trial on behalf of 11 Mexican-American children and sought to prohibit special education classes for the educable mentally retarded unless the following three conditions were met: (*a*) that a hearing be held before placement (due process), (*b*) that the use of intelligence tests allow for cultural differences, and (*c*) that the curriculum be educationally sound and provisions for retesting be periodically scheduled.

Beginning in 1970 a number of other cases that directly involved classes for the mentally retarded were contested in the courts. In *Spangler v. Pasadena Board of Education* (1970), the United States District Court for the Southern District of California found that the Pasadena schools had a racial imbalance in both the faculties and student bodies, had used intelligence tests that were both inaccurate and unfair, and had increased segregation by a disproportionate number of black students being assigned to "slow" classes. A case filed in the Massachusetts Federal District Court in the same year *(Stewart v. Phillips,* 1971) also related to testing and minority students. In this case, for the first time, monetary damages were included in the grievance of the plaintiffs (poor and black). It was alleged that pupils had been irreparably harmed when, based on a single IQ score of a discriminatory test, they had been placed in classes for the mentally retarded.

Again in 1970, in *Diana v. State Board of Education*, the United States District Court for the Northern District of California concluded that there had been a denial of equal educational opportunity for nine Mexican-American children. The plaintiffs maintained that they were placed in classes for the educable mentally retarded on the basis of tests (Wechsler and Stanford-Binet intelligence tests) that were felt to be culturally biased. Since the children were from homes in which Spanish was spoken, it was argued that undue discrimination had occurred because the children were tested in English and tests had been standardized on Anglo-American children. Certain conditions were agreed upon for future direction in special education decisions: (a) if the home language was other than English, the child must be tested in both English and the home language; (b) testing was to be restricted to tests or test sections that did not include "unfair" verbal questions; (c) that children whose primary language was not English and who had already been placed in classes for the mentally retarded must be retested; (d) all school districts were required to provide both information about retesting and a plan to assist children to return to the regular program; (e) the IQ tests were to be revised and normed for Mexican-American children; and (f) if a significant difference existed between the percentage of Mexican-American pupils in classes for the retarded and in the school as a whole, a written explanation for this difference must be provided (Ross, deYoung & Cohen, 1971).

A related and essentially a follow-up case was *Covarrubias v. San Diego Unified School District* (1971). This case was filed on behalf of 17 minority students (5 Mexican-Americans and 12 blacks) who were enrolled in classes for the educable mentally retarded in the San Diego School District. The basis of the case also was denial to equal education because of cultural bias of the Wechsler and Stanford-Binet intelligence tests. In this case monetary damages were requested, however, as in *Stewart v. Phillips* (1970). The rationale for this request was that the school district had deprived the students of equal protection under the law. It was further requested that special education classes be discontinued until testing approaches could be altered to account for cultural influences.

During 1970 the Association of Black Psychologists requested that the San Francisco School Board impose a moratorium on both intelligence and ability testing of black children. The basis of their presentation was the issue of inappropriate norms and content validity of standardized tests used with black children. This issue was brought to the courts in *Larry P. v. Riles* (1972). In this case, a class action suit, the plaintiffs contended that the tests used were discriminatory when used to place and maintain minority children in classes for the mentally retarded. In the case, which was filed in behalf of 6 black elementary-aged children in San Francisco, the plaintiffs argued that the children were not mentally retarded but were victims of tests that failed to take into account their ethnic background. The lawyers requested that the public schools be required to do the following: (a) assess black children with tests that would take into account their cultural background; (b) prevent placement of black children in special classes on the basis of inappropriate tests; (c) direct the San Francisco public schools to reevaluate, by using nondiscriminatory tests, all black children presently enrolled in classes for the mentally retarded; *(d)* remove any indication of the plaintiffs ever having been in classes for the mentally retarded; *(e)* require the schools to ensure that the distribution of blacks in special education classes for the retarded is proportional to the number of black children in the total population; and *(f)* declare that the assignment of black children on the basis of discriminatory tests is a violation of the Fourteenth Amendment of the Constitution.

In 1972 a preliminary injunction was issued by the presiding judge that stated that black children could not be placed in educable mentally retarded classes on the basis of IQ tests as traditionally administered. The preliminary injunction was supportive of the six points made by the plaintiffs, as indicated above. In 1979 in *Larry P. v. Riles*, on appeal, the Chief Judge, U.S. District Court for the Northern District of California, ruled in favor of the plaintiffs. The court held that the defendants had violated both state and federal statutes by using tests that were racially and culturally biased and discriminatory against blacks, and that the defendants allowed a disproportion of black children in classes for the educable mentally retarded. The final impact on special education of this case is yet to be determined, but its implications for classification and assessment issues may prove to be very influential in the coming years (Prasse & Reschly, 1986).

In a case related to *Larry P. v. Riles*, IQ test items were not found to be discriminatory against black children. In *Parents in Action on Special Education (PASE) v. Hannon, et al.*, (1980) the judge in his concluding remarks stated that he differed with Judge Peckham (of the *Larry P. v. Riles* case) because of the orientation to the legal consequences of racial bias and testing and that the tests had not been analyzed. The court also found that only one Stanford-Binet test item and eight test items on the WISC and WISC—R were biased against black children and that these few test times did not make the tests unfair or have a significant effect on the child's score.

It should be noted that the approach used by the judge is based on a priori judgment. The only scientific way to ascertain cultural fairness of test items is to analyze responses across ethnic groups. The controversy regarding tests is therefore going to be a continuing one. For example, in *Brookhart v. Illinois State Board of Education* (1983) the test validation issue was again addressed. The court essentially avoided the issue by not stating whether tests for graduation should reflect a pupil's individual ability or whether the use of nonvalidated tests violated federal law.

Probably three of the more important cases about providing free, appropriate education for the handicapped have been *Pennsylvania Association for Retarded Children v. Commonwealth of Pennsylvania* (1972), *Mills v. Board of Education of the District of Columbia* (1972), and *Battle v. Commonwealth of Pennsylvania* (1980). In referring to the precedent set in *Brown v. Board of Education of Topeka* (1954), the courts in the first two cases ruled that when a state has assumed the responsibility to provide public education, it must make it available to all on equal terms. In the Pennsylvania Association for Retarded Children decision the court ruled that Pennsylvania had a constitutional duty to provide a free public education to all retarded children in the Commonwealth. Further, the court reasoned that because all mentally retarded children can benefit from educational and training programs, there was no rationale for exclusion of such children from the educational system. This case has caused a number of similar class action suits, which collectively led Congress to enact Public Law 93–380, The Education Amendment of 1974.

In *Mills v. Board of Education of the District of Columbia* (1972) the court ruled that the Board of Education has the obligation to provide specialized education that would be of benefit to the child. The court further held that to deny educational opportunity to handicapped children is a violation of due process of law. Therefore, it is illegal to suspend, expel, or reassign children without prior hearing or a periodic review.

The issue of extending the school year for some handicapped children was addressed in *Battle v. Commonwealth of Pennsylvania* (1980). It was argued that pupils who were either severely and profoundly impaired or severely emotionally disturbed often required a longer school year because of the regression that occurred during summer vacations. The court ruled that the school year could be extended based on the "free and appropriate education" provision of the Education for Handicapped Act when required on an Individualized Education Plan (IEP). In *Georgia Association of Retarded Citizens v. McDaniel* (1981) the issue of an extended school year was again heard. The Court ruled in favor of an extended school year, when justified. The case was appealed to the U.S. Supreme Court which refused to hear arguments, leaving the lower court's decision standing.

Other cases related to education that have been landmark court actions include: *Wyatt v. Stickney* (1972), *Jackson v. Indiana* (1972), *Souder v. Brennan* (1973), and *Wyatt v. Aderholt* (1974). In *Wyatt v. Stickney* (1972) it was established that the mentally ill had the right to treatment in the least restrictive environment. This includes the right to (a) an individualized treatment program, (b) an environment that is psychologically and physically humane, (c) a qualified and adequate staff, and (d) programs that are offered in the least restrictive way possible. The case that ensured due process relative to institutional commitment was *Jackson v. Indiana* (1972). The court ruled that to commit a person to an agency (such as a state institution or a mental hospital) until recovered could in effect be a life sentence without recourse to appeal; this would be a denial of both equal protection and due process. It was the court's decision that persons who were not competent to stand trial must either be released or be civilly committed. In a related case (*Souder v. Brennan*, 1973) it was ruled that persons in state institutions could not be subjected to involuntary servitude.

It was required that work records of patient-laborers in state institutions be kept and that their rights be explained to them.

Since the mid-1960s there has been a series of cases establishing the rights of the mentally ill and mentally retarded to treatment in state institutions. One such case, *Pennhurst State School v. Halderman* (1981), eventually reached the U.S. Supreme Court. In this case, the trial court judge had found that the mentally retarded had a constitutional right to appropriate treatment in the setting least restrictive of personal freedom. The judge ordered the state school for the mentally retarded to be closed, holding it was too restrictive a setting for minimally adequate treatment. On appeal, the Court of Appeals for the Third Circuit found that under the Developmentally Disabled Assistance and Bill of Rights Act of 1975 (P.L. 94–103) the substantive rights of the mentally retarded were enforceable and that Pennhurst State School had violated those rights. The U.S. Supreme Court (1981) reversed the Court of Appeals decision. In so doing the Supreme Court interpreted P.L. 94–103 to be a funding bill rather than an Act requiring enforcement of the provision in the Fourteenth Amendment. Further, the Court stated that they found nothing in the Act (P.L. 94–103) that required the States to provide funding for federally mandated programs such as appropriate treatment in the least restrictive environment for the mentally retarded.

The public schools have also been sued because of beliefs that proper services had not been provided. *Jose P. v. Ambach* (1979) was a class action suit which concerned the referral, evaluation, and placement of handicapped children in appropriate programs in New York City. The case was precipitated by the New York City Schools' delay in evaluating and placing children in appropriate programs due to lack of staff, organizational structure and programs. The result has been the ongoing restructuring of special education provisions and programs in the New York City Schools. This and related court cases have been reviewed by Fafard, Hanlon and Bryson (1986) and Wood, Johnson, and Jenkins (1986). Three recent cases to have been heard by the U.S. Supreme Court are: *Hendrick Hudson District Board of Education v. Rowley* (1982), *Irving Independent School District v. Tatro* (1984) and *Burlington School Committee of the Town of Burlington v. Department of Education of the Commonwealth of Massachusetts* (1985). While none of these cases concerned persons with mental retardation, they are all important because of the precedents set and their implications for future court cases.

In *Hendrick Hudson District Board of Education v. Rowley* (1982) the issue was whether a severely hearing-impaired child should be provided with a sign language interpreter in academic classes. It had been stipulated on her IEP that she be enrolled in the regular program, be provided a hearing aid, given speech therapy, and receive additional instruction from a tutor of the deaf. It was argued by the parents that she also needed a sign language interpreter. The school officials maintained that such an interpreter was not required because she was making satisfactory social and academic progress. The U.S. Supreme Court's decision was that a free and appropriate education was being provided by the personalized program that had been developed along with necessary supplementary services. Further, the Court reasoned that a law cannot and does not guarantee that schools maximize the potential of handicapped children, but only that they make public education available to all.

The case of *Irving Independent School District v. Tatro* (1984) concerned an 8-year-old girl with spina bifida. She needed a catheter replaced every three to four hours in order to be able to stay in school. The public schools contended that such a procedure was a medical service and was not required under P.L. 94–142. The U.S. Supreme Court agreed to hear the case and decided that replacement of the catheter could be provided by a school nurse or a trained lay person and was not a medical service per se. To do otherwise would deny the child access to an education in the least restrictive setting.

The U.S. Supreme Court heard *Burlington School Committee of the Town of Burlington v. Department of Education of the Commonwealth of Massachusetts* (1985), disputing whether the public schools were obligated to pay for private schooling for a pupil whose parent unilaterally placed the child in a private facility while the case was still under review. The Court ruled in favor of the parent, indicating that to do otherwise would be in violation of a *free* appropriate public education for the child and would lessen the parents' right to participate in developing an IEP. However, parents who unilaterally place their child in a separate program may be reimbursed for the expense only if the private educational program is subsequently approved through appeal (Goldberg, 1986).

The preceding review of important court cases is representative of a multitude of legal actions that have been litigated over the past several years. As noted earlier, there are many others that we have not examined here, because such a lengthy review would be beyond the scope of any single chapter.

FEDERAL LEGISLATION

As a direct result of the court cases reviewed in the preceding section, the United States Congress has enacted a number of laws that are having and will continue to have a tremendous impact on education. In this section we review major legislation passed by Congress, particularly two major public laws that are of particular importance to special education: Public Laws (P.L.) 93–380 and 94–142.

Legislation: 1965–1973

Our decision to review federal legislation acts beginning with 1965 is not to be interpreted as indicating that previous legislation is unimportant. Indeed, laws passed before 1965 have had significant effects on educational provisions for the handicapped and in establishing vocational rehabilitation programs. In regard to mental retardation, certainly P.L. 85–926 (1958) and P.L. 88–164 (1963) were indications of increased federal involvement in these areas. However, it was not until the early 1960s that legislation at the federal level was generated that had profound impact nationally. A review of past federal legislation by Congress is provided in the Appendix to this chapter.

Federal aid to education became a fact of life beginning in the mid-1960s with P.L. 89–10, the Elementary and Secondary Education Act (ESEA) of 1965. P.L. 89–10 represented, for the first time, a commitment by the federal government to improve public school education in the United States. This law included assistance to local public schools in terms of meeting the needs of children designated as "educationally deprived." A companion bill enacted in 1965, P.L. 89–313, amended a section (Title I) of P.L. 89–10 and provided for support of children in state-operated (or state-supported) schools serving the handicapped, but which had not been included for funding purposes under the original act.

ESEA was amended again in 1967 (P.L. 89–750). A section (Title VI) of the act made funds available to states in order to expand programs and better meet the needs of handicapped children. Also under this act, a National Advisory Committee on Handicapped Children was instituted to advise the Commissioner of Education. It was during this period that Congress established the Bureau of Education for the Handicapped (BEH) to be the office responsible for administering all educational programs for the handicapped.

In 1967 ESEA was again amended (P.L. 90–247) to provide more programs for the handicapped. It was recognized that, despite passage of ESEA, a number of handicapped students were still being excluded. Therefore, P.L. 90–247 amendments specifically designated funds for the handicapped (Title III) and for assisting state education agencies to expand their programs for the handicapped. In P.L. 90–576, the Vocational Education Amendment of 1968, the Congress required that at least 10% of each state's vocational education funds coming from the federal government be allocated for the handicapped.

Experimental preschools and early education programs for the handicapped were highlighted in 1968 with the passage of P.L. 90–538, the Handicapped Children Early Education Assistance Act. Also in 1969, P.L. 91–60 was passed, this established a National Center on Educational Media and Materials for the Handicapped.

A direct precursor to P.L. 93–380 and P.L. 94–142 was P.L. 91–230 (1970), specifically the amendment creating the Education of the Handicapped Act (EHA) (1971). Part B of EHA provided grants to states (and to trust territories) to assist their initiation, expansion, and improvement of programs for the education of handicapped children.

P.L. 91–517 (1970), the Developmental Disabilities Services and Facilities Construction Act, was oriented toward the broader area of developmental problems and away from traditional special education categories. This act was for the purpose of assisting the states to provide necessary community services and to construct facilities to carry out state plans. In addition, P.L. 93–112, Rehabilitation Amendments of 1973, extended and recodified the Vocational Rehabilitation Act first passed in 1943 (P.L. 78–113). In the 1973 amendment (P.L. 93–112), Congress included a section that prohibits discrimination on the basis of mental or physical disability (Section 504). This law affects every federally assisted program or activity in the United States. Major features of this law included the following:

1. Requiring state rehabilitation agencies to give priority to individuals with the most severe handicaps and to expand and improve services to these individuals
2. Instituting written rehabilitation programs for each client
3. Authorizing states to develop a Consolidated Rehabilitation Developmental Disabilities Plan
4. Studying the role of sheltered workshops for rehabilitation and employment of the handicapped
5. Studying the coordination of programs for the handicapped
6. Forbidding discrimination against qualified handicapped persons in federally assisted programs
7. Establishing a federal Interagency Committee on Handicapped Employees
8. Providing a client assistance program
9. Developing an interagency board to assure compliance with the Architectural Barriers Act of 1968

The final regulations were in effect June 3, 1977; by July 5, 1977 all institutions receiving financial assistance from the Department of Health, Education and Welfare (HEW) were required to return an Assurance of Compliance with regard to this law. During the balance of 1977 all agencies submitted data that ensured that (a) existing facilities would be accessible to the handicapped, (b) agencies that receive funds from HEW and that employ 15 or more persons do not discriminate on the basis of handicap, and (c) any structural changes required in existing facilities would be identified and a plan developed to ensure completion of such changes. During

1978 it was required that all agencies receiving HEW funds were to evaluate themselves as to their accommodation, both with programs and with accessibility, of handicapped individuals and organizations. Also, all public schools were required to provide a free, appropriate education for all qualified handicapped children by September 1, 1978. By June 2, 1980, all structural changes in existing facilities to accommodate handicapped persons needed to be completed.

Legislation: 1974–1986

This section will review the public laws that have, and will continue to have, a significant impact on education and our society in the coming years. It will be obvious that the laws have historical references stemming from identified needs generated in developing programs, legislation, and court decisions.

P.L. 93–380, Education Amendments of 1974. Public Law 93–380 extended and amended the Elementary and Secondary Education Act of 1965 and its subsequent amendments, the Education of the Handicapped Act, and a number of other education statutes emanating from Congress. This public law encompassed some rather significant implications for the handicapped, including provisions for significantly increased funding designed to assist states in meeting the "right to education" requirements imposed by courts and legislatures. Also, this legislation required states to develop plans for implementing educational opportunities for all handicapped children, including the institution of procedural safeguards to prevent discrimination in identification, the evaluation and placement of the handicapped, and the retention of the handicapped in regular classrooms whenever possible. Additionally, P.L. 93–380 included sections on aid to state-supported schools; this provision allowed handicapped children in an appropriate program to be counted as one and a half children for computation purposes and permitted up to 20% of formula monies for adult education to be used for educational programs for institutionalized persons.

P.L. 93–383, Housing and Community Development Act of 1974. In P.L. 93–383 the 93rd Congress revised all major housing legislation that had previously been passed in congressional sessions. Several aspects of this law had an impact on the handicapped; the law included provisions that assured that the handicapped, along with the elderly, received financial assistance from the Department of Housing and Urban Development (HUD) in leasing adequate housing. It also authorized HUD to make government loans for housing the elderly and the handicapped. As a part of this governmental involvement, HUD was authorized to award grants for special demonstration projects for the purpose of designing housing for persons with special needs.

P.L. 93–156, Rehabilitation Act Amendments of 1974. This legislation authorized the president to call a White House conference to investigate problems of handicapped citizens and to propose administrative and legislative recommendations for handling these problems. This law also included several amendments to the Rehabilitation Amendment of 1973 (P.L. 93–112), such as providing a broader definition of "handicapped." The definitional emphasis was changed away from a focus on handicaps related to employment or vocational objectives and toward a focus on limitations of functioning level in one or more of an individual's main life activities. Also, vocational rehabilitation clients must be provided the opportunity to be involved in decisions affecting their programs, and the requirements for written rehabilitation plans were refined in providing services for each client.

P.L. 93–647, Social Service Amendments of 1974. Public Law 93–647 involved a complete revision of federal and state social services program agreements. The following goals were set forth relative to the handicapped: (a) economic self-support to prevent, reduce, or eliminate dependency; (b) self-sufficiency to reduce and prevent dependency; (c) prevention of abuse, neglect or exploitation of both children and adults unable to protect themselves; (d) provision of community-based, home-based, or other less intensive and more natural care of individuals to prevent inappropriate institutional care; and (e) referral, admission, and other services to institutionalized persons when other types of care are not feasible or appropriate.

The law also specified requirements for the states to submit plans to the Department of Health, Education and Welfare that include: (a) fair hearing restrictions of client information, (b) identification of responsible state agencies, and (c) other factors that would ensure proper care of persons being served by vocational rehabilitation programs. A lack of state compliance might result in termination of funding or withholding of a percentage of federal funds.

P.L. 94–103, The Developmentally Disabled Assistance and Bill of Rights Act of 1974. This act significantly amended P.L. 91–517 (1970) by (a) broadening the term "developmental disabilities," (b) extending formula grant supports to states and grants to university-affiliated centers, and (c) requiring grant recipients to take affirmative action in employing and advancing qualified handicapped persons. The act also specified actions to be taken in protecting the rights of persons with developmental disabilities.

P.L. 94–142, Education for All Handicapped Children Act of 1975. The enactment of this law represents a culmination of legal and legislative activities by both parents and professionals. In many ways it is a continuation of what Dimond (1973) termed "the quiet revolution," which essentially had its beginnings in the civil rights movement of the 1950s.

Core Concept 5   Legislative actions have required that all children be provided a free and appropriate education in the least re-
strictive setting.

As is apparent in the preceding sections of this chapter, P.L. 94–142 does
not represent a totally new concept relative to requirements or the involvement of the federal government in determining education rights. In fact,
this legislation includes much of what had been included in P.L. 93–380,
the Education Amendment of 1974, and Section 504 of P.L. 93–112, the
Rehabilitation Amendment of 1973. This law builds on previous actions
and underscores the statement of the National Advisory Committee on the
Education of the Handicapped: "In law and as national policy, education is
today recognized as the handicapped person's right" (1976, p. 143).

P.L. 94–142 was signed into law by President Ford (albeit reluctantly)
on November 28, 1975, after it received overwhelming congressional support
(Senate vote 87 to 7; House vote 404 to 7). President Ford's reservations
were not with the objectives of the Act, but with the cost of implementation
and with the additional federal encroachment on state and local domains.
The Education for All Handicapped Children Act has four major purposes.

1. Full Education Opportunities. The goal is to provide all handicapped
children with a free and appropriate education. Priorities are given to children not being served and to children who are severely handicapped.

2. Procedural Safeguards. The act specifies policies and procedures for
safeguarding the due process rights of parents and children. Similarly, educational agencies are protected by the same procedural safeguards. These
safeguards include the following:

a. The right to be fully informed and included in all decisions
   concerning identification, evaluation, educational planning and
   programming, and program evaluation
b. The assurance that placement decisions will not be based on biased or
   discriminatory data
c. The assurance that educational placement will be in the least
   restrictive setting, that is, with non-handicapped children whenever
   and wherever possible
d. The right to have access to and control over all educational records
   with assurance of the confidentiality of such information
e. The right to appeal decisions made by the schools regarding any facet
   of the child's educational program
f. The right to obtain an independent evaluation of the child

g. The child's right to be represented by surrogate parents for those children who are wards of the state or whose parents or guardians are unknown or not available

h. The right to an impartial hearing regarding program disputes between the parents or child and the school

3. Appropriate Education. To ensure that each eligible handicapped child receives an appropriate education, the law requires that an Individualized Education Program (IEP) be developed. The criteria of eligibility apply to children who meet the statutory definition and who are in need of special education or related services. The definition in Section 4 of the Act includes children who are mentally retarded, hard of hearing, deaf, orthopedically impaired, other health impaired, speech impaired, visually impaired, severely emotionally disturbed or children with specific learning disabilities who are in need of special education and related services. However, not all children who are disabled need or require special education, since some can successfully attend school without additional assistance. An IEP would not be required for these children. The following definition of the IEP is from Section 4 of the Act:

> A written statement for each handicapped child developed in any meeting by a representative of the local educational agency or any intermediate educational unit who shall be qualified to provide, or supervise the provision of, specially designed instruction to meet the unique needs of handicapped children, the teacher, the parents or guardians of such child and, whenever appropriate, such child, which shall include (A) a statement of the present levels of educational performance of such child, (B) a statement of annual goals, including short-term instructional objectives, (C) a statement of the specific educational services to be provided to such child, and the extent to which such child will be able to participate in regular education programs, (D) the projected date for initiation and anticipated duration of such services, and appropriate objective criteria and evaluation procedures and schedules for determining, on at least an annual basis, whether instructional objectives were being achieved. (P.L. 94–142, *Federal Register*, Nov. 29, 1975, p. 4)

This description is obviously one of the most critical components of P.L. 94–142. It is a plan of action and a statement of goals for the child, developed by the school in conjunction with the parents of the child. It is not a contract, although school districts are legally responsible for ensuring that special educational services are provided. The IEP is not a day-by-day instructional map, but a plan that delineates needed special educational services that are appropriate for the child.

4. State Assistance. To implement P.L. 94–142 the federal government will provide supplementary monies, guidelines, and technical assistance to state and local educational agencies. The purpose of this assistance is to ensure that an equal educational opportunity is provided for all handicapped children needing services. The subsidy under P.L. 94–142 is based on the *excess cost* of educating children in special education and providing related services.

During the 1977–1978 school year, all states in compliance with the law received assistance based on the number of children (ages 3 through 21 years) receiving services. Additional allocations were possible for service provisions for the preschool handicapped. A ceiling on the number of handicapped children (ages 5 though 17 years) was set at a 12% level for each state. Federal financial assistance to the states is based on a payment formula that specifies a gradually increasing percentage. The formula was derived on the national average expenditure per child multiplied by the number of handicapped children in each state who receive special education and related services that are publicly augmented.

P.L. 95–602, the Rehabilitation Comprehensive Services and Developmental Disabilities Act Amendments of 1978. This Act changed the criteria to be used in defining a developmental disability. No longer would a categorical disability (e.g., mental retardation) suffice. Henceforth, severity and chronicity were to be used along with three or functional limitations (e.g., capacity for independent living, economic self-sufficiency, learning, mobility, self-care, self-direction, and receptive and expressive language) in defining disability. In addition, the law required that states select what priorities would be emphasized in providing services (e.g., case management, child development, etc.). Grant funds were to be tied to the service delivery pattern chosen by each state.

P.L. 97–35, Omnibus Budget Reconciliation Act of 1981. This Act reduced federal funding for domestic programs and emphasized defense spending. The effect was to hold special education (and other related areas) funding levels constant from 1981–1984. The Act also discontinued financial support for many services needed by persons who were mentally retarded. For example, home services, respite care, habilitation services, etc., were no longer to be paid for out of federal funds. For those states requesting waivers the requirement was that they had to show that such care was less expensive than what could be provided in an institution.

P.L. 99–457, Education of the Handicapped Amendments of 1986. This legislation extended the provisions contained in the 1975 Education of the Handicapped Act (P.L. 94–142). In addition, these amendments allowed for full service programs for both infants and toddlers (birth through two years of age) and for preschool handicapped children (three to five years of age).

For persons interested in more information than can be provided here regarding the laws and their impact on federal funding for those with mental retardation, we recommend the works of Braddock (1986a, 1986b).

LEGISLATIVE INVOLVEMENT

Core Concept 6   It is important that concerned individuals maintain a continuing interest in the legislative process at both the state and federal levels.

We strongly believe that persons involved in and concerned about special education should be knowledgeable about legal and legislative activities. However, knowledge without active commitment and demonstrated activity in the legal and legislative process is an acceptance of the status quo. The court battles and the legislative actions that have been reviewed in this chapter attest to the power that committed individuals can have in influencing the direction of laws, both for obtaining the rights of the handicapped and for providing better education for all. A debt of gratitude is owed by all handicapped children, their parents and special educators to those persons and organizations who have led the way thus far in ensuring that the Constitution is a viable document and in demonstrating that the "system" can be made to be responsive.

For some it is a comfortable position to "cop-out," claiming that the political arena is far too big (or dirty, or self-serving, or unresponsive) to become involved in or to influence. The material previously reviewed effectively counters such a position. Others may be comfortable, noting that gains have been made in behalf of the handicapped and feeling that there is no reason to become personally active. For these people, this review points out that even though the battle for the rights of the handicapped (and indeed for all persons) has been engaged, the war is far from over. A third group may take the comfortable position of leaving such political activity to their colleagues who are carrying the banner of human rights. A cursory understanding of history (e.g., Nazi Germany) should be ample demonstration that a lack of commitment to civil rights by all persons can be disastrous. In the United States, for example, it was not until 1954 *(Brown v. Board of Education)* that education was established as a right. A fourth group may protest that such laws as have been enacted are too expensive to implement and that further action may financially be impossible. Such a position has merit in a world of competing equities. However, this argument must be envisioned not only in a recognition of priorities, but also in the evidence that there is a significant return in earning power generated by employment of the mentally retarded (Conley, 1976). We must ask what kind of society we will have if there is no emphasis placed on the rights of all citizens. In the opinion of the authors and our colleagues, priority must always be given to the human condition.

The Legislative Process

This section is oriented toward providing a description of the legislative process and identifying various publications that the interested person can refer to for continual updating of the status of court decisions and congressional bills that are in committee or possibly will be forthcoming.

A discourse on all of the ramifications involved in the legislative process would be far too lengthy and probably not very effective in communicating the essence of the process. Therefore, we will attempt to provide a description of the basic structure of the process, from initiating legislation through the final approval of a proposed bill. Although the illustration is at the federal level, the same process is typically applicable to local and state governments. The process can be a lengthy, time-consuming activity, but in many respects this can be healthy by ensuring that the various viewpoints about proposed legislation are heard, considered, responded to and thoughtfully evaluated.

Initiating Legislation. New legislation can be introduced by the President (or governor or mayor, as the case may be) or by Congress. The initial idea, however, can originate either from within the governmental structure or from the community. Indeed, all new or revised legislation begins with a perceived need.

If the initial idea is considered to be of sufficient importance, a legislator or the President may begin the process of determining (through legislative staff, executive staff, or appointed task force) its viability. This involves developing considerable documentation to establish a need, a purpose, a delineation of implications relative to extant laws, and the constitutionality of the idea.

During, and as a part of, this translation of an idea into a proposal, there would be continuing contact and dialogue with "significant others" for their reactions, concerns, and possible support. These significant others would be both inside and outside government. Assuming that all the details are worked out, that the federal (or state) agency that would be administratively responsible is identified (e.g., Department of Health and Human Services), and that sufficient legislative and community support is generated to ensure its initial acceptance, the proposal can be introduced in either the House or the Senate via the committee having initial responsibility for reviewing proposed bills.

Legislative Procedures. After being referred to the responsible committee (in the House or Senate or both) the proposed legislation is again studied and researched, and hearings are held involving persons from both inside and outside the governmental structure. Legislative subcommittees may be established to look at various aspects of the proposed bill to ensure a thorough examination of all of its facets. It should be apparent that at any stage of this truncated description, the process can be discontinued because of lack of viability or continued support.

Assuming again that all of the hurdles are successfully negotiated through continued support, compromise, or revision of difficulty parts, the next step is the introduction of the bill into the House or Senate. The bill is identified in the House by a number signifying its sequential place in the number of bills being introduced in that session (for example, H.R. 128 would indicate it would be the 128th bill to be considered by the House during that session). The Senate would identify the proposed bill by a similar designation (for example, S.B. 72).

At the appropriate time the bill reaches the floor of the House and the Senate (not necessarily at the same time) and again is considered in detail. Amendments can be offered and can be accepted or rejected. If a bill is passed by one legislative body it must then be forwarded to the other. However, if different versions are passed, the bill must be sent to joint conference committee of both houses to obtain a compromise agreement. The bill can then be returned to committee (House, Senate or both), where it can languish or die, or it can be returned with modifications for reconsideration by both houses of the Congress.

If the proposed act is passed by the Congress, it is given a designation such as Public Law 94–142. This indicates that this is the 142nd law passed by the 94th Congress. Then the President can accept it by signing the bill into law, return it for further consideration by the Congress, or veto the proposed Act. A President's veto can be overridden by two-thirds vote of both houses, whereupon the bill becomes law.

Although this rather simplistic account of the legislative process delineates the major events leading to the enactment of a bill into law, it is recognized that considerable flavor has been lost. A much more animated version of the process is referred to in LaVor's (1976b) delightful chapter entitled "Martin Hatches an Egg: A Fairy Tale Describing the Way Laws Are Made."

Suggested References

An attempt to provide a complete listing of pending legislative and court proceedings is not feasible given their tenuous and ever-changing nature. The following sources, although not all-inclusive, are geared to a continued updating of legislative and legal events.

1. *Mental Retardation and the Law: A Report on Status of Current Court Cases.* This publication is issued quarterly under the aegis of the U.S. Department of Education, President's Committee on Mental Retardation, Washington, DC 20201.

2. *Programs for the Handicapped.* This publication is now oriented toward providing a cross-section review of governmental activities that relate to the handicapped. Office of Handicapped Individuals, 338 D., Hubert H. Humphrey Building, 200 Independence Ave., S.W., Washington, DC 20201.

3. *American Association on Mental Deficiency.* This association has a broad range of professional interests, including legislation, that are oriented toward the mentally retarded. Their address is 1719 Kalorama Rd., N.W., Washington, DC 20009.

4. *Council for Exceptional Children.* This Council is involved in all areas of exceptionality. As such, it has been extremely influential in legal and legislative activities at the local, state, and federal levels. Policy Implementation, Governmental Relations Unit, Council for Exceptional Children, 1920 Association Drive, Reston, VA 22091.

5. *The National Association for Retarded Citizens.* This organization is involved in a wide variety of activities related to retarded citizens. The membership is composed of both parents and professionals. Their address is 2709 Avenue E, East, Box 6190, Arlington, TX 76011.

6. *Federal Government.* Copies of all federal laws may be obtained by writing to the House of Representatives or the Senate, Document Room, U.S. Capitol, Washington, DC 20510. Be sure to include the public law desired in your request. Also, copies of all public laws can be found in any Law School library.

7. *National Center for Law and the Handicapped.* For information concerning legal rights of the handicapped, the Center can be contacted at 1235 North Eddy Street, South Bend, IN 46617.

8. *Mental Health Law Project.* Their address is 1220 19th Street, N.W., Suite 300, Washington, DC 20036.

9. *American Bar Association.* For specific information on retardation and the law write to Mental Disability Legal Resource Center, 1800 M Street, N.W., Washington, DC 20036.

10. *The National Organization on Legal Problems of Education.* Southwest Plaza, Suite 223, 3601 S.W. 29th St., Topeka, KS 66614.

Related Legal Issues

Core Concept 7   The impact of local, state, and federal laws such as those concerning housing, marriage, voting rights, licenses, etc. have a profound effect on the ability of persons with intellectual handicaps to function in society.

Housing. As a result of legislation and legal decrees, such as those reviewed previously, there is an increasing need for independent living arrangements for the mentally retarded as well as for the handicapped in general. The concept of *normalization*, in particular, has stressed both physical and social integration of the retarded, of which housing is one important dimension (Wolfensberger, 1972). The mainstreaming concept implies the least restrictive placement in an educational sense, but the concept has much more far-reaching implications that affect society in general. It has been demonstrated over the years that the retarded person can be successfully integrated into the community (Baller, 1936; Baller, Charles & Miller, 1967; Charles, 1953; Edgerton, 1967, Edgerton & Bercovici, 1976; Miller, 1965). This is not to say that problems do not exist, but it does indicate that they are not insurmountable if appropriate supplementary services are available. Despite such evidence, there appears to be a continued reluctance by communities to incorporate mentally retarded individuals into their midst. Examples include nationwide problems in establishing half-way houses, hostels, and other arrangements in residential neighborhoods. Trippi, Michael, Colao, and Alvarez (1978) conducted a study to investigate attitudes of landlords toward prospective mentally retarded tenants. The results of this study indicated that of 100 persons advertising rentals, 52 stated the apartment was not available after finding the prospective tenant was mentally retarded; 47 attempted to discourage the prospective retarded renter by downgrading the apartment in some way; only one person responded in such a way as to indicate an intent in renting to a retarded person. In conclusion, the authors stated, "It appears that programs designed to replace public misconceptions and negative attitudes with more accurate information and positive experiences must be placed high on the list of priorities for helping the handicapped" (Trippi, Michael, Colao, & Alvarez, 1978, p. 443).

Marriage. As a result of the eugenics movement at the turn of the century, a fear has been manifested in the United States concerning the marriage of mentally retarded persons (Blanton, 1975). The reaction has been excessive response by many states in enacting laws prohibiting marriage of mentally retarded persons. Krishef (1972) reported that in a state-by-state survey 24% of the states prohibited marriage of retarded persons, 37% had no law, 6% permitted such marriages, no information was available for 29% of the states, and no reply was reported for 4% of the states.

Floor, Baxter, Rosen and Zisfein (1975) found that marriage between formerly institutionalized retarded persons can be successful but that there were some difficulties primarily stemming from lack of preparation (a condition not unknown to the nonretarded population). Their survey found that " . . . about 50% of the couples studied can sustain a marriage for several years with a reasonable degree of competence, and that children do not, at least in the first few years, serve as an overwhelming burden" (Floor, Baxter, Rosen & Zisfein, 1975, p. 37). By comparing married with single persons (all of whom had been institutionalized) the authors found that the single individuals demonstrated a greater number of personal and social problems than did those who had married. Related articles tend to show that retarded individuals, although not without problems, can and do respond adequately to marriage, particularly if they are well adjusted (Bowden, Spitz, & Winters, 1971; Katz, 1968; Mattinson, 1970; Peck & Stephens, 1965). However, Whitcraft and Jones (1974) in their survey found that of 652 respondents (parents, professionals, and others) 53% believed that retarded individuals could not carry out a successful marriage and 59% believed that retarded persons could not be successful in rearing children.

Sterilization. Coupled with the problems of marriage and the influence of the eugenics movement in the early 1900s is the issue of sterilization of the mentally retarded. Krishef (1972) reported that at the time of his survey, 24 states permitted sterilization and only two states prohibited sterilization of retarded persons. The other states had no extant law (two did not reply to the survey). Of those states having laws in effect, all required consent in some form (parent, guardian, the retarded person, court, agency, or a combination of these). However, by 1983, as reported in the *Congressional Record*, there were 15 states having statutes authorizing compulsory sterilization of mentally ill or mentally retarded individuals.

Voting. Several articles have addressed the topic of the voting rights of the retarded (Cleland, Swartz, McGaven & Bell, 1973; Gerard, 1974; Osborne, 1975). The general trend of the research indicates that with adequate preparation and instruction, the retarded can and do responsibly carry out this citizenship right. However, Kokaska (1972) found that most retarded adults do not exercise their voting rights.

A survey of the 50 states and the District of Columbia by Olley and Fremouw (1974) found that 20 states have laws that permit the retarded to vote unless they have, by legal action, been judged to be legally incompetent. Twenty-two states have not provided regulations for exercising the voting privilege by retarded persons. Four states did not respond to the survey, and the other five states have informal procedures with certain restrictions.

Licenses. Two licenses are of particular importance for the mentally retarded: driver's licenses and licenses that are required for certain jobs. In our society the inability to drive is a particularly incapacitating problem, both for mobility and for employment requiring a driver's license. Under the Department of Transportation there are several divisions that are oriented at least partially toward assisting the handicapped. The trend toward road signs that pictorially provide information about road conditions and warnings are of particular benefit to nonliterate persons. For example, the Office of Driver and Pedestrian Education and Licensing (Department of Transportation) have developed audio techniques to assist functional illiterate groups. The mentally retarded are not prevented from obtaining driver's licenses because of retardation. The criterion is the ability of the person to perform competently. Adequate training and subsequent performance is the key for the retarded, as it is for everyone.

Contracts. Although there may be initial concern by some banks, loan companies, or other loaning agencies about a retarded person's loan application, mental retardation is not the most important criterion. As with anyone else, the important factor is the ability of the person to knowledgeably enter into a contract and to fulfill the obligation contained in the agreement. The danger is one of not understanding the contractual agreement, but this is not much different, if at all, from the problems encountered by naive persons. Education concerning the pitfalls of the purchasing of a car, television, or other expensive item is again the key. The emphasis in the past few years on consumer rights serves to highlight the fact that all of us are naive at times and need assistance regarding contractual agreements.

Crime and Delinquency. In the late nineteenth and early twentieth century it was generally concluded that crime and related antisocial behaviors were highly correlated with low intelligence. Many of our statutory laws developed during this period. Those individuals judged to be mentally retarded were more often victims of the law than citizens with rights. One of the reasons for this was the application of the law in a rigid, inflexible manner, without any differentiation between retarded persons and the rest of the population.

It goes without saying, perhaps, that this is a very complex area involving judgments on competence to stand trial, the relationship between intelligence and criminal behavior, the retarded person's understanding of right and wrong, and a host of other related factors. In a review of research in this area, Menolascino (1974) found no clear-cut relationship between mental retardation and crime. There appears to be a stronger relationship between environment and the incidence of criminal behavior than between retardation and crime (Allen, 1970; Morris, 1948). Related articles in this area that should be reviewed for additional insight include Allen (1966, 1968a, 1968b, 1970); Biklen (1977); Brown and Courtless (1968, 1971); Marsh, Friel and Eissler (1975); and the President's Committee on Mental Retardation (1977).

Education. Legal and legislative issues have been discussed both in this chapter and elsewhere in the book. Therefore, this subsection does not attempt to summarize, but addresses that aspect of law relating to due process, particularly the concept of administrative hearings. Under P.L. 94–142 there is an administrative process oriented toward attempting to provide due process steps to assist children, parents, and school representatives in resolving educational concerns without initially resorting to civil court involvement. The concepts employed in the process have been referred to as "impartial hearings."

The procedural aspects of this approach include any placement, evaluation, program changes, education plan development, or exclusion from a program. The child, parents (or surrogate parents), or school can request an impartial hearing if the problem cannot be resolved between the school and the parents. The initial step is the appointment of an impartial hearing officer to hear both sides of the issue with full disclosure of the facts as perceived by both sides. The decision of this officer is considered to be binding on all parties. However, appeal procedures to the state board of education are an option of either the parents or the school. After review by a panel (usually composed of trained impartial hearing officers) appointed by the state, a recommendation is provided to sustain, modify, or reject the officer's decision. The panel's recommendation is to the appropriate state body (usually a State Board of Education), which is then responsible for making a final administrative decision that is legally binding. Of course, the parents or the school have recourse to civil court if they desire to pursue a decision more favorable to themselves.

The material reviewed in this chapter reflects a new era for special education, with many far-reaching implications for our society. The involvement of the legal profession and legislative bodies with education is an example of a cross-disciplinary interaction that has been used to end discrimination toward the handicapped. It is a well-recorded fact that the treatment of mentally retarded persons has been exclusionary and has denied them their rights as citizens. However, the passing of laws and various court actions are but one part of the problem's solution. It is one thing to authorize monies to implement the laws, but it is quite another to appropriate the necessary funds to implement what the laws require. In the same vein, only half the necessary effort has been expended in the passing of laws; the other half must be made by the field of education, particularly special education, in generating the necessary administrative procedures to effectively comply with the law and to deliver effective programs to the handicapped.

The enactment of legislation will not, however, accomplish the task alone. There is an additional influence that must become operative for the laws to be effective and actually end discrimination against the handicapped. That influence is the crucial attitudinal changes required of everyone in meeting the spirit of the law. This may, in the long run, be the most difficult task of all, but certainly not an impossible one. The attitudinal difficulties are many and varied and are the least controllable variable relative to the spirit of the law. There are several concepts that may need to be rethought by educational professionals. Perhaps the most important one is a definition of education. Since many children who were previously excluded now have a *right* to education, public schools are being faced with additional responsibilities. If education is defined in only an academic sense, which is certainly a basic concept, then many handicapped children are not going to "fit" in a restricted educational definition. However, if education is defined as bringing people to a higher level of functioning than they previously had attained, then the entire range from severely/profoundly retarded through gifted children can be conceptually, administratively and functionally included. A second concept related to attitudinal difficulties is the need for all people to learn to look beyond the label and see the *person* behind the demonstrated disability.

The nondiscriminatory aspects of the laws should assist us in accepting and understanding the handicapped. Exclusionary practices have tended to separate "different" persons and make them an unknown, and hence an "anxiety-fear" phenomenon has developed in many cases. This phenomenon is demonstrated both concretely and abstractly in many reactions of non-retarded persons to a retarded person. An example of concrete expression involves concern about the criminal tendencies, suspected sexual proclivities, and other subjectively implied deviations about this population. These commonly held misconceptions have great attitudinal impact on housing and social interchanges. We hope that the inclusion of the handicapped into the mainstream of our society will assist in negating this anxiety-fear phenomenon. Perhaps by providing early contact, we can promote a gradual understanding of the handicapped as people who have the same needs for love, respect, care, and nurturing as everyone else.

There are additional concerns of major importance in implementing the law. It is the opinion of many that time lines for compliance are too restrictive. On the one hand it is argued that, after many decades of demonstrated curtailment of citizenship rights for the handicapped, we must move with haste. This point is well taken and certainly backed by evidence. However, as Drew (1978) has pointed out in discussing the "least restrictive placement" dimensions of the law, we may be attempting to implement without full understanding. That is, accepting the concept without fully exploring the complexities of least restrictive placement may actually detract from implementation and have unfavorable long-range implications. Drew identified three major problem areas that influence the full realization of the concept: (a) its impact on the total educational community, because many regular educators see it as something new being imposed on them, (b) the enthusiastic reaction by others, particularly special educators, that the time is appropriate and everything must be done to implement least restrictive placement, and (c) a "paper compliance," in which many school districts embrace the concept in theory but actually change little from a program standpoint. It can be argued that we cannot wait until everything is in place before proceeding with full implementation of and compliance with the law. There is little debate about the truth of these arguments. At the same time, without major concern for the long-term ramifications, we may be doing more harm than good. This is to be construed not as a negative position but as a concern that we do not promise more than can be delivered. There is a serious possibility that in our use of concepts

> we commit serious errors in being so apparently casual concerning these matters (casual as if we understand; many are not casual in their exuberance). I believe that we must be thoughtful, thoughtful concerning meaning, thoughtful concerning implications, and *preeminently* thoughtful about our outcomes in regard to these concepts. This is the only way, in my opinion, that we can be fully effective in understanding the context in which we operate and hopefully, in the implementation of the *law*. (Drew, 1978, p. 2)

The concern here is that, without such thoughtfulness, we may be the recipients of a backlash that can be counter-productive to what is right, needed, past due, and backed by the law. Without proper concern and caution, and by promising too much, handicapped children can be unfortunate victims of our conceptual mistakes.

Core Questions

1. What were some of the factors that have influenced a change in attitude toward those with mental retardation since World War II?
2. What was the importance of *Beattie v. State Board of Education* (1950) and *State Board of Education v. In Re: Petty* (1950) in relation to persons with mental retardation?
3. What is the importance of *Brown v. Board of Education of Topeka* (1954) for providing programs for disabled persons?
4. Review the litigation reported in the chapter from 1970 to the present. Identify and briefly discuss the primary rulings in these cases and the implications for special education.
5. What did Dimond (1973) mean by the "quiet revolution?"
6. Identify and briefly describe the four major purposes of the Education for All Handicapped Act.
7. Briefly discuss the processes involved in initiating new legislation.
8. What are some of the major problems facing special education in the years to come?

ROUND TABLE DISCUSSION

The relationship between legislatures and the courts should be well understood by professionals in the field of special education. In your discussion group identify what you feel is an important need relative to providing a better program, improved social conditions, or modification of existing laws for persons who are mentally retarded. Next discuss the ways you, as a group, could go about seeking sponsorship for the idea. For example, how would your group go about deciding what information to gather; whose assistance and what resources would be important; what form a proposal should take; what would be the process used to identify likely sponsors of the proposal.

REFERENCES

Allen, R. (1966). Toward an exceptional offenders court. *Mental Retardation, 4,* 3–7.

Allen, R. (1968a). Legal norms and practices affecting the mentally deficient. *American Journal of Orthopsychiatry, 38,* 635–642.

Allen, R. (1968b). The mentally retarded offender: Unrecognized in court and untreated in prison. *Federal Probation, 32,* 22–27.

Allen, R. (1970). The law and the mentally retarded. In F. T. Menolascino (Ed.), *Psychiatric approaches to mental retardation* (pp. 585–611). New York: Basic.

Arreola v. Board of Education, 160–577, Superior Court, Orange County, Calif., 1968.

Baller, W. R. (1936). A study of the present social status of a group of adults who when they were in elementary schools were classified as mentally deficient. *Genetic Psychology Monographs, 18,* 165–244.

Baller, W. R., Charles, D. C., & Miller, E. L. (1967). Mid-life attainment of the mentally retarded: A longitudinal study. *Genetic Psychology Monographs, 75,* 235–329.

Battle v. Commonwealth of Pennsylvania, 629 F.2d 269 3rd Cir. (1980).

Beattie v. State Board of Education, City of Antigo, 169 Wisc. 231, 172 N.W. 153 (1950).

Biklen, D. (1977). Myths, mistreatment and pitfalls: Mental retardation and criminal justice. *Mental Retardation, 15,* 51–57.

Blanton R. (1975). Historical perspectives on classification of mental retardation. In N. Hobbs (Ed.), *Issues in the classification of children,* Vol. 1 (pp. 164–193). San Francisco: Jossey-Bass.

Bowden, J., Spitz, H., & Winters, J. Jr. (1971). Follow-up of one retarded couple's marriage. *Mental Retardation, 9,* 42–43.

Braddock, D. (1986a). From Roosevelt to Reagan: Federal spending analysis for mental retardation and developmental disabilities. *American Journal of Mental Deficiency, 90,* 479–489.

Braddock D. (1986b). Federal assistance for mental retardation and developmental disabilities. *Mental Retardation, 24,* 209–218.

Brookhart v. Illinois State Board of Education, 697 F.2d 184 7th Cir. (1983).

Brown v. Board of Education of Topeka, 347 U.S. 483, 74 Sup. Ct. 686 (1954).

Brown, B., & Courtless, T. (1968). The mentally retarded in penal and correctional institutions. *American Journal of Psychiatry, 124,* 1164–1170.

Brown, B., & Courtless, T. (1971). *The mentally retarded offender.* Rockville, MD: National Institute of Mental Health, Center for Studies on Crime and Delinquency.

Burlington School Committee of the Town of Burlington v. Department of Education of the Commonwealth of Massachusetts, 53 LW 4509 (1985).

Charles, D. C. (1953). Ability and accomplishment of persons earlier judged mentally deficient. *Genetic Psychology Monographs, 47,* 3–71.

Cleland, C., Swartz, J., McGaven, M., & Bell, K. (1973). Voting behavior of institutionalized mentally retarded. *Mental Retardation, 11,* 31–35.

Congressional Record, Vol. 25, No. 129, September 26, 1981.

Conley, R. (1976). Mental retardation: An economist's approach. *Mental Retardation, 14,* 20–24.

Covarrubias v. San Diego Unified School District, 7–394, Tex. Rptr., 1971.

Diana v. State Board of Education, C–70, 37 RFP, N.D. Cal., 1970, 1973.

Dimond, P. (1973). The constitutional right to education: The quiet revolution. *The Hastings Law Journal, 24,* 1087–1127.

Drew, C. J. (1978). *Least restrictive alternative: A concept in search of definition.* Paper presented at the one-hundred-second annual convention, American Association on Mental Deficiency, Denver, CO.

Drew, C. J., Hardman, M. L., & Bluhm, H. P. (1977). *Mental Retardation: Social and educational perspectives.* St. Louis: Mosby.

Edgerton, R. B. (1967). *The cloak of competence: Stigma in the lives of the mentally retarded.* Berkeley, CA: University of California.

Edgerton, R. B. & Bercovoci, S. M. (1976). The cloak of competence: Years later. *American Journal of Mental Deficiency, 80,* 485–497.

Fafard, M. B., Hanlon, R. E., & Bryson, E. A. (1986). Jose P. v. Ambach: Progress toward compliance. *Exceptional Children, 52,* 313–322.

Floor, L., Baxter, D., Rosen, M., & Zisfein, L. (1975). A survey of marriages among previously institutionalized retardates. *Mental Retardation, 13,* 33–37.

Fogg v. Board of Education, 82 Atl. 173, 1912.

Georgia Association for Retarded Citizens v. McDaniel, 511 F. Supp. 1263 (N.D. GA, 1981).

Gerard, E. P. (1974). Exercise of voting rights by the retarded. *Mental Retardation, 12,* 45–47.

Gilhool, T. K. (1976). Education: An inalienable right. In J. F. Weintraub, A. Abeson, J. Ballard, & M. L. Lavor (Eds.), *Public policy and the education of exceptional children* (pp.14–21). Reston, VA: Council for Exceptional Children.

Goldberg, S. S. (1986). Reimbursing parents for unilateral placements in private special education schools. *Exceptional Children, 52,* 390–394.

Hendrick Hudson District Board of Education v. Rowley, 73 L.Ed. 2d 690 (1982).

Hobson v. Hansen, 269 Fl Supp. 401 (D.D.C. 1967).

Irving Independent School District v. Tatro, 82 L.Ed. 2d,644 (1984).

Jackson v. Indiana, 406 U.S. 715, 1972.

Jose P. v. Ambach 3EHLR 551: 245, 27 (E.D.N.Y. 1979)

Katz, E. (1968). *The retarded adult in the community.* Springfield, IL: Thomas.

Kokaska, C. J. (1972). Voter participation of the EMR: A review of the literature. *Mental Retardation, 10,* 6–8.

Krishef, C. H. (1972). State laws on marriage and sterilization of the mentally retarded. *Mental Retardation, 10,* 36–38.

Larry P. v. Riles, C–71–2270 US.C, 343 F. Supp. 1306 (N.D. Cal. 1972).

Larry P. v. Riles, 343 F. Supp. 1306, 502 F. 2d 963 (N.D. Cal. 1979).

LaVor, M. L. (1976a). Federal legislation for exceptional persons. In J. F. Weintraub, A. Abeson, J. Ballard, & M. L. LaVor (Eds.) *Public policy and the education of exceptional children* (pp. 96–111). Reston, VA: The Council for Exceptional Children.

LaVor, M. L. (1976b). Martin hatches an egg: A fairy tale describing the way laws are made. In F. J. Weintraub, A. Abeson, J. Ballard, & M. L. LaVor. (Eds.) *Public policy and the education of exceptional children* (pp. 324–329). Reston, VA: Council for Exceptional Children.

Marsh, R. L., Friel, C. M., & Eissler, V. (1975). The adult MR in the criminal justice system. *Mental Retardation, 13*, 21–25.

Mattinson, J. (1970). *Marriage and mental handicaps.* Pittsburgh: University of Pittsburgh.

Menolascino, F. J. (1974). The mentally retarded offender. *Mental Retardation, 12*, 7–11.

Miller, E. L. (1965). Ability and social adjustment at mid-life of persons earlier judged mentally deficient. *Genetic Psychology Monographs, 72*, 139–198.

Mills v. Board of Education of the District of Columbia, 348 F. Supp. 866 (D.D.C. 1972).

Morris, J. V. (1948). Delinquent defectives: A group study. *American Journal of Mental Deficiency, 52*, 345–369.

National Advisory Committee on the Education of the Handicapped. (1976). *The unfinished revolution: Education of the handicapped.* Washington DC: U.S. Government Printing Office.

Norman, M., & Taymans, J. (1982). Looking back: A calendar of political events—Campaign '80 to May '82. *Counterpoint*, May/June, p. 11.

Ollcy, G., & Fremouw, W. (1974). The voting rights of the mentally retarded: A survey of state laws. *Mental Retardation, 12*, 14–16.

Osborne, A. G., Jr. (1975). Voting practices of the mentally retarded. *Mental Retardation, 12*, 15–17.

Parents in Action on Special Education (PASE) v. Hannon, et al., C.A. No. 74 C 3586 (1980).

Peck, J. R. & Stephens, W. B. (1965). Marriage of young adult male retardates. *American Journal of Mental Deficiency, 69*, 818–827.

Pennhurst State School v. Halderman, Civil action nos. 79–1404. 79–1489. 79–1414. 79–1415, 79–1489, U. S. Third Circuit Court of Appeals (1981).

Pennsylvania Association for Retarded Children v. Commonwealth of Pennsylvania, 343 F. Supp. 279 (E.D. Pa. 1972).

Prasse, D. P., & Reschly, D. J. (1986). Larry P.: A case of segregation, testing, or program efficacy? *Exceptional Children, 52*, 333–346.

President's Committee on Mental Retardation. (1977). *Mental retardation: Past and present.* Washington DC: U.S. Government Printing Office.

Roberts v. City of Boston, 59 Mass. (5 Cushing) 198 (1849).

Ross, S. L., Jr., DeYoung, H. G., & Cohen, J. S. (1971). Confrontation: Special education placement and the law. *Exceptional Children, 38*, 5–11.

Smuck v. Hobson, 408 F. 2d. 1975 (1969).

Souder v. Brennan, 367 F. Supp. 808 (D.D.C. 1973).

Spangler v. Pasadena Board of Education, 311 F. Supp. 501 (C.D. Cal. 1970).

State Board of Education v. in Re: Petty, 241 Iowa 506, 41, N.W. Reporter, 672 (1950).

Stewart v. Phillips, 70–1199–F. (D. Mass. 1971).

Trippi, J., Michael, R., Colao, A., & Alvarez, A. (1978). Housing discrimination toward mentally retarded persons. *Exceptional Children, 44,* 430–433.

Whitcraft, C. J., & Jones, J. P. (1974). A survey of attitudes about sterilization of retardates. *Mental Retardation, 12,* 30–33.

Williams v. Board of Education, 79 Kan. 202, 99 Pac. 216 L. R. A. (N.S.) 584 (1908).

Wolfensberger, W. (1972). *The principle of normalization in human services.* Toronto, Canada: National Institute of Mental Retardation.

Wood, F. H., Johnson, J. L., & Jenkins, J. R. (1986). The Lora Case: Nonbiased referral, assessment and placement procedures. *Exceptional Children, 52,* 323–331.

Wyatt v. Aderholt, 368 F. Supp. 1382, 1383 (M.D. Ala. 1974).

Wyatt v. Stickney, 344 F. Supp. 387, 344 F. Supp. 373(M.D. Ala. 1972).

APPENDIX: MAJOR FEDERAL LEGISLATION FOR EDUCATION OF THE HANDICAPPED: 1827–1986

The following list of major legislation affecting the handicapped is adapted from LaVor (1976a, pp. 103–111). It was thought that this material would be of particular importance in associating titles with public law numbers and as a historical overview of congressional actions.

Public Law	Title	Enacted
19–8	An Act to provide for the location of the two townships of land reserved for a seminary of learning in the territory of Florida, and to complete the location of the grant to the Deaf and Dumb Asylum of Kentucky	1/29/1827
29–11	An Act to extend the time for selling the lands granted to the Kentucky asylum for teaching the deaf and dumb	2/18/1847
33–4	An Act to establish in the District of Columbia a government hospital for the insane	3/3/1855
34–5	An Act to establish the Columbian Institution for the Deaf and Dumb	2/16/1857
34–46	An Act to incorporate the Columbian Institution for the Instruction of the Deaf and Dumb and the Blind	2/16/1857
34–59	An Act to amend the "Act to incorporate the Columbian Institution of the Deaf and the Dumb and the Blind"	5/29/1858
35–154	An Act making appropriations for sundry civil expenses of the government (first appropriations bill)	6/12/1858
38–52	An Act to authorize the Columbian Institution for the Deaf and Dumb and Blind to confer degrees	4/8/1864
38–210	An Act making appropriations for sundry civil expenses of the government for the year ending June 30, 1865, and for other purposes	7/2/1864
38–50	An Act to amend an Act entitled, "An Act to incorporate the Columbian Institution for the Instruction of the Deaf and the Dumb and the Blind"	2/23/1865

Public Law	Title	Enacted
39–167	An Act making appropriations for sundry civil expenses of the government for the year ending June 30, 1868, and for other purposes	3/2/1867
39–169	An Act to amend existing laws relating to Internal Revenue and for other purposes	3/2/1867
45–186	An Act to promote the education of the blind	3/3/1879
55–HR4304	An Act regulating postage on letters written by the blind	7/7/1898
58–171	An Act to promote the circulation of reading matter among the blind	5/27/1904
59–288	An Act to modify the requirements of the Act entitled "An Act to promote the education of the blind," approved 3/31/1879	6/25/1906
62–336	An Act making appropriations for the services of the Post Office Department of the fiscal year ending June 30, 1913, and for other purposes	8/24/1912
65–178	Vocational Rehabilitation Act (for discharged military personnel)	6/27/1918
66–24	An Act providing additional aid for the American Printing House for the Blind	8/4/1919
66–236	An Act to provide for promotion of vocational rehabilitation of persons disabled in industry or otherwise and their return to civil employment	6/2/1920
66–384	An Act providing additional hospital facilities for patients of the Bureau of War Risk Insurance and of the Federal Board for Vocational Education, Division of Rehabilitation, and for other purposes	3/4/1921
67–47	An Act to establish a Veterans' Bureau and to improve the facilities and services of such bureau and further to amend and modify the War Risk Insurance Act	8/9/1921
67–370	An Act amending Subdivision 5 of Section 302 of the War Risk Insurance Act	12/18/1922
68–197	An Act to authorize an appropriation to enable the Director of the United States Veterans Bureau to provide additional hospital facilities	6/5/1924
68–200	An Act to amend sections 1, 3, and 6 of an Act entitled, "An Act to provide for the promotion of vocational rehabilitation of persons disabled in industry or otherwise and their return to civil employment"	6/5/1924
68–218	An Act to incorporate the United States Blind Veterans of the World War	6/7/1924
68–242	World War Veterans' Act of 1924	6/7/1924
69–584	An Act to amend the Act providing additional aid for the American Printing House for the Blind	2/8/1927
69–655	An Act to amend paragraph (1) of section 22 of the Interstate Commerce Act by providing for the carrying of a blind person, with a guide, for one fare	2/26/1927
71–317	An Act to amend an Act entitled, "An Act to provide for the promotion of vocational rehabilitation of persons disabled in industry or otherwise and their return to civil employment"	6/9/1930
71–787	An Act to provide books for the adult blind	3/3/1931
72–222	To amend an Act entitled, "An Act to provide for the promotion of vocational rehabilitation of persons disabled in industry or otherwise and their re-	6/30/1932

Public Law	Title	Enacted
	turn to civil employment," approved June 2, 1920, as amended	
72–439	To amend section 1 of the Act entitled, "An Act to provide books for the adult blind," approved 3/3/31	3/4/1933
73–214	To amend the Act entitled, "An Act to promote the circulation of reading matter among the blind," approved April 27, 1904, and Acts supplemental thereto	5/9/1934
74–139	To authorize an increase in the appropriation for books for the adult blind	6/14/1935
74–271	Social Security Act	8/14/1935
74–732	To authorize the operation of stands in federal buildings by blind persons, to enlarge the economic opportunities of the blind, and for other purposes	6/20/1936
75–37	To provide special rates of postage on matter for the blind	4/15/1937
75–47	To authorize an increase in the annual appropriation for books for the adult blind	4/23/1937
75–184	To amend the Interstate Commerce Act (Seeing Eye dogs)	7/5/1937
75–339	To amend the Act approved August 4, 1919, as amended, providing additional aid for the American Printing House for the Blind	8/23/1937
75–412	United States Housing Act of 1937	9/1/1937
75–523	To amend the Acts for promoting the circulation of reading matter among the blind	5/16/1938
75–739	To create a Committee on Purchases of Blind-made products and other purposes—Wagner-O'Day Act of 1938	6/25/1938
76–118	To amend the Act entitled, "An Act to provide books for the adult blind," approved 3/3/31	6/7/1939
76–379	Social Security Act Amendments of 1939	8/10/1939
76–562	To amend the Act entitled, "An Act to provide books for the adult blind," approved 3/3/31	6/6/1940
77–270	To further amend the Acts for promoting the circulation of reading matter among the blind	10/14/1941
77–330	To permit Seeing Eye dogs to enter government buildings when accompanied by their blind masters, and for other purposes	12/10/1941
77–726	To amend section 1 of the Act entitled, "An Act to provide books for the adult blind," approved 3/3/31, as amended	10/1/1942
78–16	To amend Title 1 of Public Law Number 2, 73rd Congress, March 30, 1933, and the Veterans Regulation to provide for rehabilitation of disabled veterans, and for other purposes	3/24/1943
78–113	Vocational Rehabilitation Act Amendments of 1943	7/6/1943
78–235	To provide revenue, and for other purposes, or "The Revenue Act of 1943"	2/25/1944
78–338	To amend the Act entitled, "An Act to provide books for the adult blind"	6/13/1944
78–346	Servicemen's Readjustment Act	6/22/1944
79–661	To amend the Act entitled, "An Act to provide books for the adult blind"	8/8/1946
79–719	Social Security Act Amendments of 1946	8/10/1946
80–471	Revenue Act of 1948	4/2/1948

Public Law	Title	Enacted
80–617	To amend the Civil Service Act to remove certain discrimination with respect to the appointment of persons having any physical handicap to positions in the classified civil service	6/10/1948
80 642	To maintain status quo in respect of certain employment taxes and Social Security benefits pending action by Congress on extended Social Security coverage	6/14/1948
81–162	Authorizing an appropriation for the work on the President's Committee on National Employ the Physically Handicapped Week	7/11/1949
81–290	To permit the sending of braille writers to or from the blind at the same rates as provided for their transportation for repair purposes	9/7/1949
81–734	Social Security Act Amendments of 1950	8/28/1950
82–308	To restore to seventy pounds and one hundred inches in girth and length combined the maximum weight and size limitations for appliances or parts thereof, for the blind, sent through the mails	4/9/1952
82–354	To amend the Act approved 8/4/1919 as amended, providing additional aid for the American Printing House for the Blind	5/22/1952
82–446	To amend the Act entitled, "An Act to provide books for the adult blind"	7/3/1952
82–590	Social Security Act Amendments of 1952	7/18/1952
83–420	To change the Columbian Institution of Gallaudet College, define its corporate powers, and provide for its organization and administration and other purposes	6/18/1954
83–531	To authorize cooperative research in education	7/26/1954
83–565	Vocational Rehabilitation Amendments of 1954	8/3/1954
83–761	Social Security Amendments of 1954	9/1/1954
84–825	To amend the Interstate Commerce Act in order to authorize common carriers and such attendants at the usual fare charged for one person	7/27/1956
84–880	Social Security Amendments of 1956	8/1/1956
84–922	To amend the Act to promote the education of the blind, approved March 3, 1879, as amended, so as to authorize wider distribution of books and other special instructional material for the blind, to increase the appropriations authorized for this purpose, and for other purposes	8/2/1956
85–308	To amend an Act entitled, "An Act to provide books for the adult blind"	9/7/1957
85–840	Social Security Amendments of 1958	8/28/1958
85–864	National Defense Education Act of 1958	9/2/1958
85–905	To provide in the Department of Health, Education and Welfare a loan service of captioned films for the deaf	9/2/1958
85–926	To encourage expansion of teaching in the education of mentally retarded children through grants to institutions of higher learning and to state educational agencies	9/6/1958
86–372	Housing Act of 1959	9/23/1959
86–778	Social Security Amendments of 1960	9/13/1960

Public Law	Title	Enacted
87–276	To make available to children who are handicapped by deafness the specially trained teachers of the deaf needed to develop their abilities and to make available to individuals suffering speech and hearing impairments the specially trained speech pathologists and audiologists needed to help them overcome their handicaps	9/22/1961
87–294	To amend the Act to promote the education of the blind, approved March 3, 1879, as amended, so as to authorize wider distribution of books and other special instruction materials for the blind, and to increase the appropriations authorized for this purpose, and to otherwise improve such Act	9/22/1961
87–543	Public Welfare Amendments of 1962	7/25/1962
87–614	To authorize the employment without compensation from the Government of readers for blind Government employees, and for other purposes	8/29/1962
87–715	To provide for the production and distribution of educational and training films for use by deaf persons, and for other purposes	9/28/1962
87–765	To establish in the Library of Congress a library of musical scores and other instructional materials to further educational, vocational, and cultural opportunities in the field of music for blind persons	10/9/1962
87–838	To amend the Public Health Service Act to provide for the establishment of an Institute of Child Health and Human Development	10/17/1962
88–156	Social Security Act Amendments of 1963	10/24/1963
88–164	Mental Retardation Facilities and Community Mental Health	10/31/1963
88–242	To authorize the President to issue annually a proclamation designating the first week in March of each year as "Save Your Vision Week"	12/30/1963
88–443	Hospital and Medical Facilities Amendments of 1964	8/18/1964
88–628	To authorize the President to proclaim October 15 of each year as "White Cane Safety Day"	10/6/1964
88–641	Social Security Amendments of 1964	10/13/1964
88–650	Social Security Amendments of 1964	10/13/1964
89–10	Elementary and Secondary Education Act of 1965 as amended	4/11/1965
89–36	National Technical Institute for the Deaf Act	6/8/1965
89–97	Social Security Amendments of 1965	7/30/1965
89–105	Mental Retardation Facilities and Community Mental Health Centers Construction Act of 1965	8/4/1965
89–109	Community Health Service Extension Amendments of 1965	8/5/1965
89–239	Heart Disease, Cancer and Stroke Amendments of 1965	10/6/1965
89–258	Captioned Films for the Deaf Act	10/19/1965
89–313	Federal Assistance to State Operated and Supported Schools for the Handicapped	11/1/1965
89–333	Vocational Rehabilitation Act Amendments of 1966	11/8/1965
89–522	An act to provide books for the adult blind	6/30/1966
89–511	Library Services and Construction Act Amendments of 1966	7/19/1966
89–601	Fair Labor Standards Amendments of 1966	9/23/1966
89–614	Military Medical Benefits Amendments of 1966	9/30/1966

Public Law	Title	Enacted
89–694	Model Secondary School for the Deaf Act	10/15/1966
89–749	Comprehensive Health Planning and Public Health Services Amendments of 1966, "Partnership for Health"	11/3/1966
89–750	Elementary and Secondary Education act Amendments 1966	11/3/1966
89–752	Higher Education Act Amendments of 1966	11/3/1966
90–31	Mental Health Amendments of 1967	6/24/1967
90–35	To amend Title V of the Higher Education Act and to redesignate as the Educational Professions Development Act	6/29/1967
90–99	Vocational Rehabilitation Amendments of 1967	10/3/1967
90–154	To amend the Library Services and Construction Act	11/24/1967
90–170	Mental Retardation Amendments of 1967	12/4/1967
90–174	Partnership for Health Amendments of 1967	12/5/1967
90–206	Postal Revenue and Federal Act of 1967	12/16/1967
90–247	Elementary and Secondary Education Amendments of 1967	1/2/1968
90–248	Social Security Amendments of 1967	1/2/1968
90–391	Vocational Rehabilitation Amendments of 1968	7/7/1968
90–415	To increase size of the Board of Directors of Gallaudet College	7/23/1968
90–458	To establish a register of blind persons in the District of Columbia, to provide for the mandatory reporting of information concerning such persons and for other purposes	8/3/1968
90–480	Elimination of Architectural Barriers to Physically Handicapped	8/12/1968
90–489	Establishment of National Eye Institute	8/16/1968
90–538	Handicapped Children's Early Education Assistance Act	9/30/1968
90–574	Health Services and Facilities Amendments of 1968	10/15/1968
90–575	Higher Education Amendments of 1968	10/16/1968
90–576	Vocational Education Amendments of 1968	10/16/1968
91–17	To authorize the President to issue a proclamation designating the first week in June of 1969 as "Helen Keller Memorial Week"	5/28/1969
91–61	To provide for a National Center on Educational Media and Materials for the Handicapped and for other purposes	8/20/1969
91–69	Older Americans Act Amendments of 1969	9/17/1969
91–172	Tax Reform Act of 1969	12/30/1969
91–205	To ensure that certain federally constructed facilities be constructed so as to be accessible to the physically handicapped	3/5/1970
91–209	To extend the Migrant Health Act for three years, and provide increased authorization thereof	3/12/1970
91–230	To extend program for assistance for elementary and secondary education	4/13/1970
91–375	Postal Reorganization Act	8/12/1970
91–442	To broaden National Employ the Handicapped Week to apply to all handicapped workers	10/8/1970
91–453	To provide long-term financing for expanded urban mass transportation programs	10/15/1970
91–490	To revise certain criteria for handling mentally retarded persons in the Forest Haven Institution in the District of Columbia	10/22/1970

Public Law	Title	Enacted
91–517	Developmental Disabilities Services and Facilities Construction Amendments of 1970	10/30/1970
91–572	To improve family planning services and population research activities of the federal government	12/24/1970
91–587	To authorize Gallaudet College to maintain and operate the Kendell School as a demonstration elementary school for the deaf	12/24/1970
91–596	Occupational Safety and Health Act of 1970	1/29/1970
91–609	Housing and Urban Development Act of 1970	12/31/1970
91–610	To extend for one year the authorization for various programs under the Vocational Rehabilitation Act	12/31/1970
91–695	To provide assistance in developing and administering lead-based paint elimination programs	1/13/1971
92–28	Wagner-O'Day Amendments	6/23/1971
92–58	Military Medical Benefits Amendments	7/29/1971
92–178	Revenue Act of 1971	12/10/1971
92–223	Intermediate Care Amendments of 1971	12/28/1971
92–316	Free or reduced-rate transportation for the blind	6/22/1972
92–318	Education Amendments of 1972	6/23/1972
92–336	Social Security Benefit Increase	7/1/1972
92–345	Maternal and Child Health Amendments	7/10/1972
92–424	Economic Opportunity Amendments of 1972	9/19/1972
92–515	Rights of the blind and other physically handicapped in the District of Columbia	10/21/1972
92–563	National Advisory Commission on Multiple Sclerosis Act	10/25/1972
92–595	Small Business Investment Act Amendments of 1972	10/27/1972
92–603	Social Security Amendments of 1972	10/30/1972
93–29	Older Americans Comprehensive Services Amendments of 1973	5/3/1973
93–42	National Autistic Children's Week	6/15/1973
93–45	Health Programs Extension Act of 1973	6/18/1973
93–53	Maternal and Child Health Amendments	7/1/1973
93–66	Renegotiation Act Amendments	7/9/1973
93–76	Committee for Purchase of Products and Services of the Blind and Other Handicapped	7/30/1973
93–87	Federal Aid Highway Act of 1973	8/13/1973
93–112	Rehabilitation Amendments of 1973	9/26/1973
93–113	Domestic Volunteer Services Act of 1973	10/1/1973
93–146	Amtrak Improvement Act of 1973	11/3/1973
93–151	Lead-based Paint Poisoning Prevention Amendments	11/9/1973
93–233	Social Security Amendments of 1973	3/28/1974
93–269	General Education Amendments	4/18/1974
93–326	National School Lunch and Child Nutrition Act of 1974	6/30/1974
93–335	Extend Food Stamp Eligibility to Supplemental Security Income Recipients	7/8/1974
93–348	National Research Act	7/12/1974
93–358	Wagner-O'Day Act Amendments	7/25/1974
93–368	Foreign Equipment Import Duty (Social Security rider)	8/7/1974
93–380	Education Amendments of 1974	8/21/1974
93–383	Housing and Community Development Act of 1974	8/22/1974
93–415	Juvenile Delinquency and Prevention Act of 1974	10/26/1974
93–484	Import Duty on Horses (Social Security rider)	10/26/1974
93–503	National Mass Transportation Assistance Act of 1974	11/26/1974
93–516	Rehabilitation Act Amendments of 1974	12/7/1974

Public Law	Title	Enacted
93–561	March of Dimes Month	12/30/1974
93–640	National Arthritis Act of 1974	1/4/1975
93–641	National Health Planning and Resources Development Act of 1974	1/4/1975
93 643	Federal-Aid Highway Amendments of 1974	1/4/1975
93–644	Community Services Act of 1974	1/4/1975
93–647	Social Services Amendments of 1974	1/4/1975
94–44	To extend Supplemental Security Income to continue food stamp elegibility for recipients	6/28/1975
94–103	The Developmentally Disabled Assistance and Bill of Rights Act of 1974	10/4/1975
94–142	Education of All Handicapped Children Act	11/28/1975
94–482	The Educational Amendments of 1976	10/12/1976
95–561	The Educational Amendments of 1978	11/1/1978
95–602	The Rehabilitation, Comprehensive Services and Developmental Amendments of 1978	11/6/1978
96–88	An Act to create a federal Department of Education	10/17/1979
97–35	The Omnibus Budget Reconciliation Act of 1981	8/13/1981
98–199	Education of the Handicapped Act Amendments of 1983	12/2/1983
99–457	Education of the Handicapped Amendments of 1986	10/8/1986

LEGAL CASE CITATION INDEX

Italics indicate that an item is cited in the references.

AUTHOR INDEX

SUBJECT INDEX